4 vols.

35 —

MS.

# THE LETTERS AND PRIVATE PAPERS OF WILLIAM MAKEPEACE THACKERAY

## VOLUME I

LONDON : HUMPHREY MILFORD
OXFORD UNIVERSITY PRESS

MR. AND MRS. RICHMOND THACKERAY AND THEIR SON WILLIAM IN 1814
*From a water-color sketch by George Chinnery*

THE LETTERS AND PRIVATE PAPERS OF

# William Makepeace
# THACKERAY

Collected and edited by

*Gordon N. Ray*

In four volumes

*Volume I: 1817–1840*

HARVARD UNIVERSITY PRESS

Cambridge, Massachusetts

1945

PRINTED AT THE HARVARD UNIVERSITY PRINTING OFFICE

CAMBRIDGE, MASSACHUSETTS, U.S.A.

*For*

HESTER THACKERAY FULLER

*"constant to the dead"*

# CONTENTS OF VOLUME I

# ILLUSTRATIONS IN VOLUME I

*(The name of the owner of each illustration taken from the original is noted in parenthesis.)*

# LIST OF LETTERS

| No. | Date | Addressee | Owner* or Depositary |
|---|---|---|---|
| | | **1817** | |
| 1. | 3 July | Mrs. Richmond Thackeray | Mrs. Fuller |
| 2. | 25 November | Mrs. Ritchie | Mrs. Fuller |
| | | **1818** | |
| 3. | 10 March | Mrs. Ritchie | Mrs. Fuller |
| 4. | 24 April | Mrs. Carmichael-Smyth | Mrs. Fuller |
| 5. | 11 June | Mrs. Carmichael-Smyth | Mrs. Fuller |
| | | **1820** | |
| 6. | 24 August | Mrs. Carmichael-Smyth | Mrs. Fuller |
| | | **1823** | |
| 7. | 20 January | Mrs. Carmichael-Smyth | Mrs. Fuller |
| | | **1827** | |
| 8. | 20 June | Mrs. Carmichael-Smyth | Mrs. Fuller |
| | | **1828** | |
| 9. | 4–8 February | Mrs. Carmichael-Smyth | Mrs. Fuller |
| 10. | 12–21 February | Mrs. Carmichael-Smyth | Mrs. Fuller |
| | | **1829** | |
| 11. | 29 January | John Frederick Boyes | Mr. Parrish |
| 12. | 23 February | Mrs. Carmichael-Smyth | Mrs. Fuller |
| 13. | 28 February– 5 March | Mrs. Carmichael-Smyth | Mrs. Fuller |
| 14. | 6–14 March | Mrs. Carmichael-Smyth | Mrs. Fuller |
| 15. | 14–22 March | Mrs. Carmichael-Smyth | Mrs. Fuller |
| 16. | 22–29 March | Mrs. Carmichael-Smyth | Mrs. Fuller |
| 17. | 29 March– 8 April | Mrs. Carmichael-Smyth | Mrs. Fuller |

* If no owner's name is given, the original has not been traced. If the owner's name is enclosed in brackets, the text has been taken from some source other than the original.

| No. | Date | Addressee | Owner or Depositary |
|---|---|---|---|
| 18. | 13–19 April | Mrs. Carmichael-Smyth | Mrs. Fuller |
| 19. | 20–26 April | Mrs. Carmichael-Smyth | Mrs. Fuller |
| 20. | 3 May | Mrs. Carmichael-Smyth | Mrs. Fuller |
| 21. | 4–10 May | Mrs. Carmichael-Smyth | Mrs. Fuller |
| 22. | 11–17 May | Mrs. Carmichael-Smyth | Mrs. Fuller |
| 23. | 25 May | Mrs. Carmichael-Smyth | Mrs. Fuller |
| 24. | 25–29 May | Mrs. Carmichael-Smyth | Mrs. Fuller |
| 25. | 3 June | Mrs. Carmichael-Smyth | Mrs. Fuller |
| 26. | 18–? July | Mrs. Carmichael-Smyth | Mrs. Fuller |
| 27. | 6 August | Mrs. Carmichael-Smyth | Mrs. Fuller |
| 28. | 20–28 August | Mrs. Carmichael-Smyth | Mrs. Fuller |
| 29. | 21 August | Mrs. Carmichael-Smyth | Mrs. Fuller |
| 30. | 2–4 September | Mrs. Carmichael-Smyth | Mrs. Fuller |
| 31. | 10–13 September | Mrs. Carmichael-Smyth | Mrs. Fuller |
| 32. | 1 November | Mrs. Carmichael-Smyth | Mrs. Fuller |
| 33. | 22 November | Mrs. Carmichael-Smyth | Mrs. Fuller |

### 1830

| No. | Date | Addressee | Owner or Depositary |
|---|---|---|---|
| 34. | 16 July | Mrs. Carmichael-Smyth | Mrs. Fuller |
| 35. | 31 July | Mrs. Carmichael-Smyth | Mrs. Fuller |
| 36. | ?–12 August | Mrs. Carmichael-Smyth | Mrs. Fuller |
| 37. | 15 August | Mrs. Carmichael-Smyth | Mrs. Fuller |
| 38. | 6–7 September | Mrs. Carmichael-Smyth | Mrs. Fuller |
| 39. | 28 September | Mrs. Carmichael-Smyth | Mrs. Fuller |
| 40. | 20 October | Mrs. Carmichael-Smyth | Mrs. Fuller |
| 41. | 29 October | Miss Wilkie | Huntington Library |
| 42. | 17 November | Mrs. Carmichael-Smyth | Mrs. Fuller |
| 43. | 3 December | Mrs. Carmichael-Smyth | Mrs. Fuller |
| 44. | 31 December | Mrs. Carmichael-Smyth | Mrs. Fuller |

### 1831

| No. | Date | Addressee | Owner or Depositary |
|---|---|---|---|
| 45. | 18 January | Mrs. Carmichael-Smyth | Mrs. Fuller |
| 46. | 25 January | Mrs. Carmichael-Smyth | Mrs. Fuller |
| 47. | ?–25 February | Mrs. Carmichael-Smyth | [          ] |
| 48. | June | Robert Langslow | [          ] |
| 49. | 18 July | Edward Fitzgerald | Mrs. Fuller |
| 50. | 26? August | Frau von Goethe | [Goethe-Schiller Archives] |
| 51. | 8–9 September | Edward Fitzgerald | Berg Collection |
| 52. | 29 September | Edward Fitzgerald | Berg Collection |

| No. | Date | Addressee | Owner or Depositary |
|---|---|---|---|
| 53. | 2 October | Edward Fitzgerald | Berg Collection |
| 54. | 5–9 October | William Makepeace Thackeray | Mrs. Fuller |
| 55. | 16–23 November | Edward Fitzgerald | Mrs. Fuller |
| 56. | 8–10 December | Major Carmichael-Smyth | Mrs. Fuller |
| 57. | 15–16 December | Mrs. Carmichael-Smyth | Mrs. Sherburne Prescott |
| 58. | ? | James Fraser | Berg Collection |

## 1832

| No. | Date | Addressee | Owner or Depositary |
|---|---|---|---|
| 59. | 14–16 January | Mrs. Carmichael-Smyth | Mrs. Fuller |
| 60. | 25 January | Frau von Goethe | [          ] |
| 61. | 27 January | John Allen | Fitzwilliam Museum |
| 62. | 2 April–23 November | [Diary] | Mrs. Fuller |
| 63. | April ? | Edward Fitzgerald | Berg Collection |
| 64. | 20–21 April | Edward Fitzgerald | Berg Collection |
| 65. | 23 May | Mrs. Carmichael-Smyth | Mrs. Fuller |
| 66. | 25 June | Mrs. Carmichael-Smyth | Mrs. Fuller |
| 67. | 5–7 July | Edward Fitzgerald | Berg Collection |
| 68. | 8 August | Mrs. Carmichael-Smyth | Mrs. Fuller |
| 69. | 27–31 October | Edward Fitzgerald | Berg Collection |
| 70. | 22 November | Edward Fitzgerald | Berg Collection |
| 71. | ? November | George Cruikshank | Huntington Library |
| 72. | 29 November | James Carmichael-Smyth | Widener Collection |

## 1833

| No. | Date | Addressee | Owner or Depositary |
|---|---|---|---|
| 73. | 2 May | Mrs. Carmichael-Smyth | Mrs. Fuller |
| 74. | 6 July | Mrs. Carmichael-Smyth | Mrs. Fuller |
| 75. | 6 September | Mrs. Carmichael-Smyth | Mrs. Fuller |
| 76. | 22–30 October | Mrs. Carmichael-Smyth | Mrs. Fuller |
| 77. | 12 November | Mrs. Carmichael-Smyth | Mrs. Fuller |
| 78. | 23 December | Mrs. Carmichael-Smyth | Mrs. Fuller |

## 1834

| No. | Date | Addressee | Owner or Depositary |
|---|---|---|---|
| 79. | 5 October | Mrs. Carmichael-Smyth | Mrs. Fuller |
| 80. | 8 October | Edward Fitzgerald | Mr. Adrian Van Sinderen |
| 81. | 1–2 November | [Diary] | Mrs. Fuller |

| No. | Date | Addressee | Owner or Depositary |
|---|---|---|---|
| | | **1838** | |
| 114. | 19 February | Edward Fitzgerald | Berg Collection |
| 115. | 3 March | Mrs. Thackeray | Mrs. Fuller |
| 116. | 5 March | James Fraser | [        ] |
| 117. | 5 March | Mrs. Thackeray | Mrs. Fuller |
| 118. | 11–14 March | Mrs. Thackeray | Mrs. Fuller |
| 119. | 15–17 March | Mrs. Thackeray | Mrs. Fuller |
| 120. | 20–25 March | Mrs. Thackeray | Mrs. Fuller |
| 121. | April | James Fraser | Berg Collection |
| 122. | 23 May | George Wright | Mr. Carlebach |
| 123. | 12 July | Mrs. Shawe | Huntington Library |
| 124. | July | George Wright | [        ] |
| 125. | 23 July | Mrs. Shawe | Mrs. Fuller |
| 126. | 4 September | George Wright | Berg Collection |
| 127. | 4 September | ? George Wright | Houghton Library |
| 128. | 4 September | George Cruikshank | Berg Collection |
| 129. | 29 November | William Makepeace Thackeray | Mrs. Fuller |
| 130. | 29 November | ? Thomas Barnes | [        ] |
| 131. | 29 December | ? Bryan Waller Procter | Widener Collection |
| | | **1839** | |
| 132. | January | Mrs. Procter | [Major Smith] |
| 133. | ? March | John Mitchell Kemble | Dr. Metzdorf |
| 134. | March | Mrs. Carmichael-Smyth | Mrs. Fuller |
| 135. | ? May | George Cruikshank | Berg Collection |
| 136. | 15 May | Mrs. Carmichael-Smyth | Mrs. Fuller |
| 137. | 16? May | Mrs. Carmichael-Smyth | Mrs. Fuller |
| 138. | June | Henry Cole | [        ] |
| 139. | June | Henry Cole | Berg Collection |
| 140. | 21? June | Henry Cole | Berg Collection |
| 141. | 1 July | James Fraser | [        ] |
| 142. | 3 July | Mrs. Carmichael-Smyth | Mrs. Fuller |
| 143. | 15 July | George Wright | Berg Collection |
| 144. | 19 November | Mrs. Carmichael-Smyth | Mrs. Fuller |
| 145. | 1–2 December | Mrs. Carmichael-Smyth | Mrs. Fuller |
| 146. | 16–20 December | Mrs. Carmichael-Smyth | Mrs. Fuller |
| 147. | 23–31 December | Mrs. Carmichael-Smyth | Mrs. Fuller |

| No. | Date | Addressee | Owner or Depositary |
|-----|------|-----------|---------------------|
| | | 1840 | |
| 148. | January ? | John Mitchell Kemble | Berg Collection |
| 149. | 14 January | James Fraser | [          ] |
| 150. | 15 January | ? | Huntington Library |
| 151. | 18 January | Mrs. Carmichael-Smyth | Mrs. Fuller |
| 152. | 24 January | Mrs. Shawe | Mrs. Fuller |
| 153. | February | James Robinson Planché | Huntington Library |
| 154. | 11–15 February | Mrs. Carmichael-Smyth | Mrs. Fuller |
| 155. | 16 February | Mrs. Procter | [Major Smith] |
| 156. | 3 March | Mrs. Carmichael-Smyth | Mrs. Fuller (in part) |
| 157. | 11 March | Mrs. Carmichael-Smyth | Mrs. Fuller |
| 158. | 20 March | Jane Shawe | Mrs. Fuller |
| 159. | March | Mrs. Carmichael-Smyth | Mrs. Fuller |
| 160. | April | Mrs. Carmichael-Smyth | Mrs. Fuller |
| 161. | 30 April | Mrs. Carmichael-Smyth | Mrs. Fuller |
| 162. | May | Mrs. Carmichael-Smyth | Mrs. Fuller |
| 163. | 22 May | Mrs. Procter | [Major Smith] |
| 164. | 1 June | Mrs. Carmichael-Smyth | Mrs. Fuller |
| 165. | 28–29 June ? | Mrs. Carmichael-Smyth | Mrs. Fuller |
| 166. | 29 June | Alexander Blackwood | [          ] |
| 167. | 2 July | Richard Monckton Milnes | [          ] |
| 168. | 5 July | Richard Monckton Milnes | [          ] |
| 169. | 6?–18 July | Mrs. Carmichael-Smyth | Mrs. Fuller |
| 170. | 7 July | Mrs. Procter | [Major Smith] |
| 171. | 12 July | James Wilson | [Mr. Cohen] |
| 172. | 12 July | John Forster | [          ] |
| 173. | July | Bryan Waller Procter | [Major Smith] |
| 174. | 18 July | Henry Fothergill Chorley | [          ] |
| 175. | 30 July | Mrs. Carmichael-Smyth | Mrs. Fuller |
| 176. | 4 August | Mrs. Carmichael-Smyth | Mrs. Fuller |
| 177. | 20–21 August | Mrs. Carmichael-Smyth | Mrs. Fuller |
| 178. | ? August–1 September | Mrs. Carmichael-Smyth | Mrs. Fuller |
| 179. | 8 September | Chapman and Hall | Berg Collection |
| 180. | 10 September | Mrs. Ritchie | Mr. Carlebach |
| 181. | 10 September | Mrs. Shawe | Mrs. Fuller |
| 182. | 10 September | Mrs. Carmichael-Smyth | Mrs. Fuller |
| 183. | 17 September | Mrs. Carmichael-Smyth | Mrs. Fuller |

| No. | Date | Addressee | Owner or Depositary |
|---|---|---|---|
| 184. | 19–20 September | Mrs. Carmichael-Smyth | Mrs. Fuller |
| 185. | 21–23 September | Mrs. Carmichael-Smyth | Mrs. Fuller |
| 186. | 30 September | Mrs. Carmichael-Smyth | Mrs. Fuller |
| 187. | 4–5 October | Mrs. Carmichael-Smyth | Mrs. Fuller |
| 188. | 11 October | Mrs. Shawe | Mrs. Fuller |
| 189. | 11 October | Mrs. Carmichael-Smyth | Mrs. Fuller |
| 190. | 3 December | James Fraser | Huntington Library |
| 191. | 1840 | George Cruikshank | Berg Collection |
| 192. | 1840 | George Cruikshank | Mr. Parrish |

### 1841

| No. | Date | Addressee | Owner or Depositary |
|---|---|---|---|
| 193. | 10 January | Edward Fitzgerald | Mrs. Fuller |
| 194. | 21 January | Mrs. Procter | [Major Smith] |
| 195. | January ? | Edward Fitzgerald | Berg Collection |
| 196. | 27 February–6 March | Mrs. Carmichael-Smyth | Mrs. Fuller |
| 197. | 19 March | Mrs. Procter | [Major Smith] |
| 198. | 5 April | Mrs. Procter | [Major Smith] |
| 199. | 6 April | Edward Fitzgerald | Berg Collection |
| 200. | April | Mrs. Carmichael-Smyth | Mrs. Fuller |
| 201. | 25 April | Major Carmichael-Smyth | Mrs. Fuller |
| 202. | 28 May–5 June | Mrs. Procter | [Major Smith] |
| 203. | 10 July | Richard Monckton Milnes | [            ] |
| 204. | 24 July | James Fraser | Berg Collection |
| 205. | 27 July–11 August | [Diary] | Mrs. Fuller |
| 206. | 19 August | Mrs. Ritchie | Mr. Carlebach |
| 207. | 13 September–October | Edward Fitzgerald | Mrs. Fuller |
| 208. | 15 October | Mrs. Ritchie | Mr. Carlebach |

### 1842

| No. | Date | Addressee | Owner or Depositary |
|---|---|---|---|
| 209. | 7 January | William Harrison Ainsworth | Huntington Library |
| 210. | 6 February | George William Nickisson | Mr. Lilly |
| 211. | 10 February | Mrs. Spencer | [Mrs. Fuller] |
| 212. | 25 February | Chapman and Hall | Mrs. T. F. Madigan |

| No. | Date | Addressee | Owner or Depositary |
|-----|------|-----------|---------------------|
| 249. | 3 May | Mrs. Carmichael-Smyth | Mrs. Fuller |
| 250. | 3? May | Mrs. Thackeray | Mrs. Fuller |
| 251. | 5 May | George Potemkin Perry | Huntington Library |
| 252. | 15 May | Chapman and Hall | Mr. Eric |
| 253. | 20 May | Mrs. Carmichael-Smyth | Mrs. Fuller |
| 254. | 25 May | John Forster | Huntington Library |
| 255. | 26 May | Rev. William Brookfield | [          ] |
| 256. | 29 May | ? | Huntington Library |
| 257. | 10 August | Mrs. Carmichael-Smyth | Mrs. Fuller |
| 258. | 12 August | To Whom It May Concern | [          ] |
| 259. | 17 August | Mrs. Carmichael-Smyth | Mrs. Fuller |
| 260. | 30 August | Amédée Pichot | Mr. Carlebach |
| 261. | 26 September | Mrs. Carmichael-Smyth | Mrs. Fuller |
| 262. | 27 September | William Harrison Ainsworth | Berg Collection |
| 263. | 13 October | Mrs. Ritchie | Mrs. Fuller |
| 264. | 10 November | Chapman and Hall | Miss Benjamin |
| 265. | 18 November | ? Rev. William Brookfield | Berg Collection |
| 266. | 24 November | Mrs. Carmichael-Smyth | Mrs. Fuller |
| 267. | 12 December | William Jerdan | Huntington Library |
| 268. | ? December | William Harrison Ainsworth | [          ] |
| 269. | ? December | Daniel Maclise | Mr. Castles |
| 270. | 17–18 December | Thackeray's family | Mrs. Fuller |
| 271. | 21 December | Richard Bedingfield | [          ] |
| 272. | December | John Allen | Berg Collection |
| 273. | 25 December | Peter Purcell | [          ] |

## 1844

| No. | Date | Addressee | Owner or Depositary |
|-----|------|-----------|---------------------|
| 274. | 1 January–9 December | [Diary] | Mrs. Fuller |
| 275. | 28 January | Henry Wikoff | Mrs. Fuller |
| 276. | 2 February | M. Giraldon | Mrs. Fuller |
| 277. | 4 February | William Harrison Ainsworth | Mr. Eric |
| 278. | 6 February | George William Nickisson | Mr. Parrish |
| 279. | 23 February | Chapman and Hall | Berg Collection |
| 280. | 26 February | Bradbury and Evans | [Mrs. Fuller] |
| 281. | 11 March | Mrs. Thackeray | Mrs. Fuller |
| 282. | 13 April | Henry Colburn | [          ] |
| 283. | 13 May | Richard Bedingfield | Berg Collection |
| 284. | 15 May | Henry Colburn | [          ] |
| 285. | 1 June | Mrs. Carmichael-Smyth | Mrs. Fuller |

| No. | Date | Addressee | Owner or Depositary |
|-----|------|-----------|---------------------|
| 286. | 11 June | Mrs. Carmichael-Smyth and Anne Thackeray | Mrs. Fuller |
| 287. | 12 June | Charlotte Ritchie | Mr. Carlebach |
| 288. | 16 July | Chapman and Hall | Lehigh University Library |
| 289. | 19 July | Chapman and Hall | Mr. Carlebach |
| 290. | 5 August | Mrs. Carmichael-Smyth | Mrs. Fuller |
| 291. | 20 August | George William Nickisson | Drexel Institute |
| 292. | 21–22 August | Mrs. Carmichael-Smyth | Mrs. Fuller |
| 293. | 31 August | Chapman and Hall | Berg Collection |
| 294. | 31 August | Mrs. Carmichael-Smyth | Mrs. Fuller |
| 295. | 17 September | Mrs. Carmichael-Smyth | Mrs. Fuller |
| 296. | 17 September | Mrs. Thackeray | Mrs. Fuller |
| 297. | 17 September | Mrs. Carmichael-Smyth | Mrs. Fuller |
| 298. | 23–28 October | Charlotte Ritchie | Mr. Carlebach |

## 1845

| No. | Date | Addressee | Owner or Depositary |
|-----|------|-----------|---------------------|
| 299. | 10 January | Chapman and Hall | Berg Collection |
| 300. | 6 February | Mrs. Carmichael-Smyth | Mrs. Fuller |
| 301. | March ? | Henry Vizetelly | [            ] |
| 302. | 28 March | Mrs. Carmichael-Smyth | Mrs. Fuller |
| 303. | 6 April | Thomas Longman | [British Museum] |
| 304. | 21 April | George William Nickisson | Berg Collection |
| 305. | 1 June | Richard Bedingfield | [            ] |
| 306. | 9–11 June | Charlotte Ritchie | Mr. Carlebach |
| 307. | June | Mrs. Carmichael-Smyth | Mr. Carlebach |
| 308. | 30 June | William Harrison Ainsworth | Berg Collection |
| 309. | July ? | Chapman and Hall | Morgan Library |
| 310. | 7 July | Mrs. Carmichael-Smyth | Mrs. Fuller |
| 311. | 9 July | Edward Chapman | Mr. Carlebach |
| 312. | 16 July | Professor Macvey Napier | [British Museum] |
| 313. | 21 July | ? | [            ] |
| 314. | 26 July | Mrs. Carmichael-Smyth | Mrs. Fuller |
| 315. | 2 August | Mrs. Carmichael-Smyth | Mrs. Fuller |
| 316. | August | William Frederick Pollock | Mr. Carlebach |
| 317. | August | Charlotte Ritchie | Mr. Carlebach |
| 318. | 9 August | Mrs. Thackeray | [            ] |
| 319. | August | Anne Thackeray | Mrs. Fuller |
| 320. | 25 August | Mrs. Carmichael-Smyth | Mrs. Fuller |
| 321. | 7 September | Mrs. Carmichael-Smyth | Mrs. Fuller |
| 322. | September | Professor Macvey Napier | [British Museum] |
| 323. | 16 October | Professor Macvey Napier | [British Museum] |

| No. | Date | Addressee | Owner or Depositary |
|---|---|---|---|
| 324. | 18 October | Mrs. Carmichael-Smyth | Mrs. Fuller |
| 325. | 28 November | Mrs. Carmichael-Smyth | Mrs. Fuller |
| 326. | 7 December | William Makepeace Thackeray | Mr. Hill |
| 327. | December ? | Edward Chapman | Berg Collection |
| 328. | 22 December | Edward Chapman | Morgan Library |
| 329. | 27 December | Mrs. Procter ? | Morgan Library |
| 330. | 30 December | Mrs. Carmichael-Smyth | Mrs. Fuller |
| 331. | 30 December | Anne Thackeray | Mrs. Fuller |
| 332. | ? December | George Pryme | Berg Collection |
| 333. | 1845 ? | William Harrison Ainsworth | Mr. Eric |

### 1846

| No. | Date | Addressee | Owner or Depositary |
|---|---|---|---|
| 334. | January ? | Major Carmichael-Smyth | Mrs. Fuller |
| 335. | 2 January ? | Mrs. Procter | [Major Smith] |
| 336. | 6 February | William Charles Macready | Huntington Library |
| 337. | February ? | Edward Fitzgerald | Berg Collection |
| 338. | 16 February | Mrs. Carmichael-Smyth | Mrs. Fuller |
| 339. | 6 March | Mrs. Carmichael-Smyth | Mrs. Fuller |
| 340. | March | Mrs. Carmichael-Smyth | Mrs. Fuller |
| 341. | 24 April | Mrs. Procter | [Major Smith] |
| 342. | 26 April | Mrs. Procter | [Major Smith] |
| 343. | 30 April | Edward Marlborough FitzGerald | Mrs. Fuller |
| 344. | June | William Charles Macready ? | Widener Collection |
| 345. | 2 July | Mrs. Carmichael-Smyth | Mrs. Fuller |
| 346. | July | Jane Shawe | Mrs. Fuller |
| 347. | 18 July | John Forster | Huntington Library |
| 348. | 18 July | Mrs. Carmichael-Smyth | Mrs. Fuller |
| 349. | 25 July ? | Mrs. Carlyle | [          ] |
| 350. | 6 August | Mrs. Carmichael-Smyth | Mrs. Fuller |
| 351. | 11–18 August | [Diary] | Mrs. Fuller |
| 352. | 13 September | Henry Vizetelly | [          ] |
| 353. | 21 September | Horace Smith | [          ] |
| 354. | September ? | Mrs. Carmichael-Smyth | [Mrs. Fuller] |
| 355. | 1–3 October | Sir James Emerson Tennent | Berg Collection |
| 356. | 3 October | George William Nickisson | [          ] |
| 357. | 25 November ? | Mrs. Procter | [Major Smith] |
| 358. | 4 December | Mrs. Carmichael-Smyth | Mrs. Fuller |
| 359. | 12 December | Mrs. Pryme | Berg Collection |
| 360. | 22 December | John Forster | [          ] |
| 361. | 23 December | Mrs. Carmichael-Smyth | Mrs. Fuller |

| No. | Date | Addressee | Owner or Depositary |
|---|---|---|---|
| 362. | 1846 | Edward Chapman | Morgan Library |
| 363. | 1846 | Frederick J. Goldsmith | [          ] |
| 364. | 1846 ? | Mrs. Procter | [Major Smith] |
| 365. | 1846 ? | Mrs. Procter | [Major Smith] |

### 1847

| No. | Date | Addressee | Owner or Depositary |
|---|---|---|---|
| 366. | 2 January | William Edmondstoune Aytoun | [          ] |
| 367. | 5 January | Mrs. Caroline Norton | Mr. Wells |
| 368. | January | Mrs. Procter | [Major Smith] |
| 369. | January | William Makepeace Thackeray | Berg Collection |
| 370. | 11 January | William Edmondstoune Aytoun | [          ] |
| 371. | 11 January | George Hodder | Berg Collection |
| 372. | 15 January | Mrs. Procter | [Major Smith] |
| 373. | 15 January | Mrs. Brookfield | Morgan Library |
| 374. | 27 January | Albany Fonblanque | Huntington Library |
| 375. | 3 February | Rev. William Brookfield | [Dr. Rosenbach] |
| 376. | 18 February | Rev. John Allen | Library of Trinity College, Cambridge |
| 377. | 18 February | William Makepeace Thackeray | [          ] |
| 378. | 22 February | Rev. John Allen | Library of Trinity College, Cambridge |
| 379. | 22 February | Henry Reeve | Mr. Carlebach |
| 380. | 23 February | Henry Reeve | Berg Collection |
| 381. | 24 February | Mark Lemon | Berg Collection |
| 382. | 25 February | Rev. Alexander John Scott | Berg Collection |
| 383. | 1 March | George William Nickisson | [Charterhouse School] |
| 384. | 13 March | Henry Bradbury | Berg Collection |
| 385. | 16 March | Bess Hamerton | Mrs. Fuller |
| 386. | 16 March | Mrs. Carmichael-Smyth | Mrs. Fuller |
| 387. | 6 April | Mrs. Carmichael-Smyth | Mrs. Fuller |
| 388. | 15 April | Mrs. Carmichael-Smyth | Mrs. Fuller |
| 389. | 20 April | Rev. Alexander John Scott | Berg Collection |
| 390. | 29 May | Edward Chapman | Mr. Scheuer |
| 391. | 29 May | Mrs. Carmichael-Smyth | Mrs. Fuller |
| 392. | 1 June | William Harrison Ainsworth | Goodspeed's Book Store |
| 393. | 3 June | John Murray | [          ] |
| 394. | 9 June | William Makepeace Thackeray | Mrs. Fuller |
| 395. | 9 June | John Forster | [Comte de Suzannet] |

| No. | Date | Addressee | Owner or Depositary |
|-----|------|-----------|---------------------|
| 396. | 9 June | William Makepeace Thackeray | Mrs. Fuller |
| 397. | 9 June | John Forster | [          ] |
| 398. | 10 June | Tom Taylor | [          ] |
| 399. | 11 June | Charles Dickens | [Comte de Suzannet] |
| 400. | 11 June | Charles Dickens | [          ] |
| 401. | 11 June | John Forster | [          ] |
| 402. | 12 June | Charles Dickens | [          ] |
| 403. | 12 June | Tom Taylor | [          ] |
| 404. | 15 June | Mrs. Macready | [          ] |
| 405. | 15 ? June | Rev. William Brookfield | Morgan Library |
| 406. | 21 June | Arthur Shawe | Mrs. Fuller |
| 407. | June ? | Rev. William Brookfield | Morgan Library |
| 408. | June ? | Leigh Hunt | Berg Collection |
| 409. | 2 July | Mrs. Carmichael-Smyth | Mrs. Fuller |
| 410. | July | Charles Wentworth Dilke | Boston Public Library |
| 411. | 23 July | Abraham Hayward | Dr. Metzdorf |
| 412. | August ? | Rev. William Brookfield | Morgan Library |
| 413. | 27 ? August | Mrs. Procter | [Major Smith] |
| 414. | 5 September | Abraham Hayward | Berg Collection |
| 415. | September | Miss Ker | Berg Collection |
| 416. | 21 October | Mrs. Carmichael-Smyth | Mrs. Fuller |
| 417. | 23 October | William Smith Williams | Berg Collection |
| 418. | 25 October | James Justinian Morier | Mr. Carlebach |
| 419. | October ? | Edward Chapman | Morgan Library |
| 420. | 2 November | Mrs. Carmichael-Smyth | Mrs. Fuller |
| 421. | November | Rev. William Brookfield | Morgan Library |
| 422. | 15 November | Arthur Shawe | Mrs. Fuller |
| 423. | 23 November | Richard Bedingfield | [          ] |
| 424. | December ? | Mrs. Brookfield | [          ] |
| 425. | 28 December | Edward Chapman | Mr. Sessler |
| 426. | 28 December | Major Compton | Berg Collection |
| 427. | 29 December | Abraham Hayward | Berg Collection |
| 428. | 1847 ? | Richard Bedingfield | [          ] |
| 429. | 1847 ? | Richard Bedingfield | [          ] |
| 430. | 1847 ? | Richard Bedingfield | [          ] |
| 431. | 1847 ? | Mrs. Carmichael-Smyth | Mrs. Fuller |
| 432. | 1847 ? | Mrs. FitzGerald | Morgan Library |
| 433. | 1847 | Leigh Hunt | University of Iowa Libraries |
| 434. | 1847 ? | Mrs. Procter | [Major Smith] |

| No. | Date | Addressee | Owner or Depositary |
|---|---|---|---|
| | | **1848** | |
| 435. | 3 January | Leigh Hunt | Berg Collection |
| 436. | 7 January | Mrs. Carmichael-Smyth | Mrs. Fuller |
| 437. | 9 January | William Makepeace Thackeray | [            ] |
| 438. | 11 January | Mrs. James | Colonel Drake |
| 439. | 18 January | Mrs. Edward Marlborough Fitzgerald | Morgan Library |
| 440. | January | William Smith Williams | [            ] |
| 441. | January ? | Mrs. Procter | [Major Smith] |
| 442. | January | Francis Fladgate | Widener Collection |
| 443. | 26 January | Miss Wedderburn | Berg Collection |
| 444. | 28 January | Mark Lemon | Berg Collection |
| 445. | 31 January | Mrs. Edward Marlborough Fitzgerald | Morgan Library |
| 446. | February | Leigh Hunt | Berg Collection |
| 447. | 4 February | Graham Willmore | Huntington Library |
| 448. | 4 February | Mrs. Carmichael-Smyth | Mrs. Fuller |
| 449. | 5 February | Mrs. Ritchie | Huntington Library |
| 450. | February | Mrs. Irvine | [            ] |
| 451. | 18 February | Mark Lemon | Drexel Institute |
| 452. | 6 March | George Henry Lewes | Berg Collection |
| 453. | 7 March | Andrew Doyle ? | Historical Society of Pennsylvania |
| 454. | 8 March | Frederick Goldsmith | Miss Benjamin |
| 455. | 10 March | Mrs. Carmichael-Smyth | Mrs. Fuller |
| 456. | 10 March | Abraham Hayward | Mr. Carlebach |
| 457. | 10–15 March | [Diary] | Mrs. Fuller |
| 458. | March-May | Edward Fitzgerald | Berg Collection |
| 459. | 30 March | Charles Rowland Dicken | Berg Collection |
| 460. | 30 March | Dr. Carpenter | [            ] |
| 461. | 30 March | William Makepeace Thackeray | Berg Collection |
| 462. | 2 April | Lady Molesworth | [            ] |
| 463. | 14 April | John Forster | [Clifton College] |
| 464. | 14 April | Mrs. Carmichael-Smyth | Mrs. Fuller |
| 465. | 29 April | Richard Doyle | Dr. Eliot |
| 466. | 1 May | Duke of Devonshire | [            ] |
| 467. | 2 May | Mr. and Mrs. Henry Cole? | Mrs. Haight |
| 468. | 11 May | John Leycester Adolphus | [            ] |
| 469. | 15–16 May | Mrs. Carmichael-Smyth | Mrs. Fuller |
| 470. | 5 June | Mrs. Carmichael-Smyth | Mrs. Fuller |

| No. | Date | Addressee | Owner or Depositary |
|---|---|---|---|
| 471. | 6 June | Miss Smith | [            ] |
| 472. | June | Mrs. Procter | [Major Smith] |
| 473. | June | Mrs. Procter | [Major Smith] |
| 474. | June ? | Mrs. Procter | [Major Smith] |
| 475. | June ? | ? | Huntington Library |
| 476. | June ? | Henry Vizetelly | [            ] |
| 477. | June | Mrs. Brookfield | Mrs. Fuller |
| 478. | June | Mrs. Brookfield | Morgan Library |
| 479. | 22 ? June | Mrs. Brookfield | Mrs. Fuller |
| 480. | 29 June | Mrs. Carmichael-Smyth | Mrs. Fuller |
| 481. | 29 June | Mrs. Procter | [Major Smith] |
| 482. | 30 June | Mrs. Procter | [Major Smith] |
| 483. | 30 June | Mrs. Brookfield | Morgan Library |
| 484. | 1 July | William Makepeace Thackeray | Morgan Library |
| 485. | July ? | William Joyce | Dr. Rosenbach |
| 486. | 10 July | Mrs. Brookfield | Morgan Library |
| 487. | July | Mrs. Procter | [Major Smith] |
| 488. | July | Frederick J. Goldsmith | [            ] |
| 489. | July | Mr. and Mrs. Sartoris | Berg Collection |
| 490. | 18 July | Edward Chapman | Huntington Library |
| 491. | 18 July | William Henry Ashurst | [            ] |
| 492. | 18 July | Mrs. Carmichael-Smyth | Mrs. Fuller |
| 493. | 21 July | William Charles Macready | Widener Collection |
| 494. | 25 July | Mrs. Procter | [Major Smith] |
| 495. | 26–28 July | Mrs. Brookfield | Morgan Library |
| 496. | 26–29 July | Mrs. Carmichael-Smyth | Mrs. Fuller |
| 497. | July ? | Mrs. Brookfield | Berg Collection |
| 498. | 1–5 August | Mrs. Brookfield | Morgan Library |
| 499. | 4 August | Mrs. Carmichael-Smyth | Mrs. Fuller |
| 500. | 20 August | Lady Blessington | Huntington Library |
| 501. | 21 August | Rev. William Brookfield | Morgan Library |
| 502. | 31 August | Mrs. Brookfield | Morgan Library |
| 503. | 3 September | Robert Bell | [            ] |
| 504. | 5 September | Mrs. Brookfield | Morgan Library |
| 505. | September | Lady Blessington | Huntington Library |
| 506. | September | Lady Blessington | Huntington Library |
| 507. | 13 September | Mrs. Procter | [Major Smith] |
| 508. | 19 September | Jane Shawe | Mrs. Fuller |
| 509. | 25 ? September | Lady Blessington | Huntington Library |
| 510. | 1 October | Lady Blessington | Huntington Library |
| 511. | 4 October | Joseph Cundall | Huntington Library |

| No. | Date | Addressee | Owner or Depositary |
|-----|------|-----------|---------------------|
| 552. | 1848 | Mrs. Brookfield | Morgan Library |
| 553. | 1848 ? | Rev. William Brookfield | Morgan Library |
| 554. | 1848 ? | Rev. William Brookfield | Morgan Library |
| 555. | 1848 ? | Rev. William Brookfield | Morgan Library |
| 556. | 1848 ? | Mrs. Crewe | [          ] |
| 557. | 1848 ? | Rev. William Harness | Berg Collection |
| 558. | 1848 ? | George Henry Lewes | University of Iowa Libraries |
| 559. | 1848 | Antonio Panizzi | [Mr. Blatner] |
| 560. | 1848 ? | Marguerite Power | Berg Collection |
| 561. | 1848 ? | Mrs. Procter | [Major Smith] |

### 1849

| No. | Date | Addressee | Owner or Depositary |
|-----|------|-----------|---------------------|
| 562. | 3 January ? | Mrs. Brookfield | [Dr. Rosenbach] |
| 563. | 1–2 February | Mrs. Brookfield | Morgan Library |
| 564. | 2 February | Mrs. Ritchie | Colonel Drake |
| 565. | 4 February ? | W. Raymond Sams | Huntington Library |
| 566. | 4–5 February | Mrs. Brookfield | Morgan Library |
| 567. | February | Mrs. Brookfield | Morgan Library |
| 568. | 14 February | Mrs. James | Morgan Library |
| 569. | 12–13 March | Mrs. Brookfield | Morgan Library |
| 570. | 14 March | Dr. Frederic Thackeray | Fitzwilliam Museum |
| 571. | 9 April | Rev. William and Mrs. Brookfield | Morgan Library |
| 572. | 18 April | Mrs. Elliot | [          ] |
| 573. | 18 April | Mrs. Parr | Harvard College Library |
| 574. | 20 April | Mrs. James | Berg Collection |
| 575. | 20 April | John Bell | Huntington Library |
| 576. | 23 April | William Makepeace Thackeray | [          ] |
| 577. | April | Rev. William Brookfield | Morgan Library |
| 578. | April | Rev. William Brookfield | Morgan Library |
| 579. | April | Adelaide Procter | Berg Collection |
| 580. | 27 April | Mrs. Brookfield | Morgan Library |
| 581. | 27 April | Mrs. James | Berg Collection |
| 582. | 28 April | William Makepeace Thackeray | [          ] |
| 583. | May ? | Mrs. Bayne | Berg Collection |
| 584. | May | Henry Vizetelly | [          ] |
| 585. | 3 May | Frederick Mullett Evans | [          ] |
| 586. | 4 May | Mrs. Brookfield | Morgan Library |
| 587. | May | Rev. William Brookfield | Morgan Library |
| 588. | 6 May | Lady Blessington | Huntington Library |

| No. | Date | Addressee | Owner or Depositary |
|---|---|---|---|
| 589. | May, 1849 | William Makepeace Thackeray | Morgan Library |
| 590. | 9 May | Mark Lemon | Mr. Goodyear |
| 591. | 11 May | Dr. John Brown | [          ] |
| 592. | 16 May | Rev. William and Mrs. Brookfield | Morgan Library |
| 593. | 17–19 May | Mrs. Brookfield | Morgan Library |
| 594. | 26 May | Lady Castlereagh | [          ] |
| 595. | 27 May | Arthur Shawe | Mrs. Fuller |
| 596. | May ? | Dr. Quin | Berg Collection |
| 597. | 1 June | Mrs. Yorke | [          ] |
| 598. | 8 June | Mrs. Brookfield | Morgan Library |
| 599. | 8–9 June | Mrs. Procter | [Major Smith] |
| 600. | 14 June | Mrs. Procter | [Major Smith] |
| 601. | June ? | Mrs. Brookfield | Morgan Library |
| 602. | 29 June | James Hannay | Wellesley College Library |
| 603. | 29 June | A. J. Paget | Huntington Library |
| 604. | 29 June | Mrs. Elliot and Kate Perry | Huntington Library |
| 605. | 30 June | Mrs. Brookfield | Morgan Library |
| 606. | 1 July | Mrs. Brookfield | Morgan Library |
| 607. | July | Rev. William Brookfield | [Dr. Rosenbach] |
| 608. | 7 July | Mrs. Brookfield | Morgan Library |
| 609. | July | Mrs. Brookfield | Mrs. Fuller (in part) |
| 610. | 12 July | Rev. William Brookfield | Morgan Library |
| 611. | 13 July | Mrs. Brookfield | [Dr. Rosenbach in part] |
| 612. | 15–16 July | Mrs. Brookfield | [Dr. Rosenbach in part]; Morgan Library (in part) |
| 613. | 18 July | Mrs. Carmichael-Smyth | Mrs. Fuller |
| 614. | 24 July | Mrs. Brookfield | Morgan Library |
| 615. | July | Lady Eddisbury | Huntington Library |
| 616. | 5 ? August | Adelaide Procter | [Major Smith] |
| 617. | August ? | Mr. and Mrs. Procter | [Major Smith] |
| 618. | 18 August | Lady Eddisbury | Huntington Library |
| 619. | 29 August | Lord Holland | Mr. Castles |
| 620. | 29 August | Charlotte Ritchie | Huntington Library |
| 621. | 30 August | Mrs. Carmichael-Smyth | Mrs. Fuller |
| 622. | 1 September | William Makepeace Thackeray | [          ] |
| 623. | 2–3 September | Mrs. Brookfield | Morgan Library |
| 624. | 4 ? September | William Makepeace Thackeray | [          ] |
| 625. | 4–6 September | Mrs. Brookfield | Morgan Library |
| 626. | 9 September | Mrs. Brookfield | Mr. Carlebach |
| 627. | 13 September | Mrs. Brookfield | Morgan Library |

| No. | Date | Addressee | Owner or Depositary |
|---|---|---|---|
| 628. | 18 September | Mrs. Procter | [Major Smith] |
| 629. | September | Sir Frederick Pollock | Berg Collection |
| 630. | 29 September | Sir Frederick Pollock | Berg Collection |
| 631. | October | Mrs. Brookfield | Morgan Library |
| 632. | October | Mrs. Carlyle | Berg Collection |
| 633. | October | Rev. William and Mrs. Brookfield | Morgan Library |
| 634. | October | Mrs. Procter | [Major Smith] |
| 635. | October | Mrs. Procter | [Major Smith] |
| 636. | 15 October | Mrs. Carmichael-Smyth | Mrs. Fuller |
| 637. | 17 October | Mrs. Gibson | Morgan Library |
| 638. | 17 October | Mrs. Procter | [Major Smith] |
| 639. | 23 October | Mrs. Brookfield | Morgan Library |
| 640. | 23 October | Anne and Harriet Thackeray | Mrs. Fuller |
| 641. | 23 October | Mrs. Brookfield | Morgan Library |
| 642. | 25 October | Mrs. Brookfield | Morgan Library |
| 643. | 26 October | Mrs. Procter | Huntington Library |
| 644. | October | Anne Thackeray | Mrs. Fuller |
| 645. | October | Anne and Harriet Thackeray | Mrs. Fuller |
| 646. | October | Mary Agnes Elton | Huntington Library |
| 647. | 31 October | Rev. William and Mrs. Brookfield | Morgan Library |
| 648. | 5 November | Maria Hamerton | Mrs. Fuller |
| 649. | 7 November | Eyre Crowe | [          ] |
| 650. | 19 November | Mrs. Ritchie | Mr. Carlebach |
| 651. | 21 November | David Bogus | Berg Collection |
| 652. | 29 November | ? | [Mr. Beyer] |
| 653. | December | Joseph Cundall | Berg Collection |
| 654. | December | Edward Chapman | Mr. Carlebach |
| 655. | December | Edward Chapman | Berg Collection |
| 656. | December | Edward Chapman | Mr. Carlebach |
| 657. | December | Mrs. Brookfield | Morgan Library |
| 658. | 25 December | Mrs. Brookfield | Morgan Library |
| 659. | 31 December | Mrs. Montgomery | Retz and Storm |
| 660. | 31 December | Charlotte Low | [          ] |
| 661. | 1849 ? | William Edmondstoune Aytoun | Mr. Carlebach |
| 662. | 1849 | Mrs. Brookfield | Morgan Library |
| 663. | 1849 | Mrs. Brookfield | Morgan Library |
| 664. | 1849 | Mrs. Brookfield | Morgan Library |
| 665. | 1849 | Mrs. Brookfield | Morgan Library |
| 666. | 1849 ? | Mrs. Brookfield | Morgan Library |

| No. | Date | Addressee | Owner or Depositary |
|-----|------|-----------|---------------------|
| 667. | 1849 ? | Rev. William Brookfield | Morgan Library |
| 668. | 1849 ? | Rev. William Brookfield | Morgan Library |
| 669. | 1849 ? | Lady Eddisbury | Huntington Library |
| 670. | 1849 ? | Lady Eddisbury | Huntington Library |
| 671. | 1849 ? | Mrs. Fanshawe | Mr. Weitz |
| 672. | 1849 ? | Mrs. Fanshawe | Mr. Weitz |
| 673. | 1849 | Richard Monckton Milnes | [          ] |
| 674. | 1849 ? | Mrs. Montgomery | Berg Collection |

### 1850

| No. | Date | Addressee | Owner or Depositary |
|-----|------|-----------|---------------------|
| 675. | 3 January | Mrs. Procter | [Major Smith] |
| 676. | 3 January | Lady Castlereagh | Berg Collection |
| 677. | 5 January | James Spedding | Mr. Ball |
| 678. | 8 January | John Douglas Cook | [          ] |
| 679. | 25 January | Abraham Hayward | Mr. Carlebach |
| 680. | 1 February | Abraham Hayward | Mr. Carlebach |
| 681. | 4 February | Mrs. Brookfield | Morgan Library |
| 682. | 26 February | William Makepeace Thackeray | Berg Collection |
| 683. | 26 February | Magdalene Brookfield | Berg Collection |
| 684. | 26 February | Rev. William Brookfield | Berg Collection |
| 685. | 27 February | Mrs. Fanshawe | Mrs. Fuller |
| 686. | 28 February | Mrs. Brookfield | Morgan Library |
| 687. | 1–2 March | Mrs. Brookfield | Morgan Library |
| 688. | 5 March | Mrs. Brookfield and Mrs. Fanshawe | Morgan Library |
| 689. | 10 March | Antonio Panizzi | Huntington Library |
| 690. | 18–20 March | Mrs. Brookfield | Morgan Library |
| 691. | 27 March | Mrs. Brookfield | Morgan Library |
| 692. | 28 March | Mrs. Sartoris | [          ] |
| 693. | 29 March | Mrs. Brookfield | Morgan Library |
| 694. | March ? | Mrs. Fanshawe | Mr. Carlebach |
| 695. | 3 April | John Forster | Berg Collection |
| 696. | April ? | Rev. William Brookfield | Morgan Library |
| 697. | 26–30 April | Mrs. Brookfield | Morgan Library |
| 698. | 13 May | Benjamin Lumley | Huntington Library |
| 699. | 15 May | Mrs. Bayne | Mr. Wells |
| 700. | May | Mrs. Fanshawe | Mr. Pforzheimer |
| 701. | 22 ? May | Anne Thackeray | Mrs. Fuller |
| 702. | 26 May | Anne and Harriet Thackeray | Mrs. Fuller |
| 703. | 30 May | John Forster | Huntington Library |

| No. | Date | Addressee | Owner or Depositary |
|---|---|---|---|
| 704. | 3–5 June | Anne and Harriet Thackeray | Mrs. Fuller |
| 705. | 11 June | Richard Monckton Milnes | [      ] |
| 706. | June | ? | Berg Collection |
| 707. | 15 June | Rev. Robert Montgomery | Huntington Library |
| 708. | 21 June | Mrs. Strutt | Retz and Storm |
| 709. | 6 July | Mrs. Brookfield | Morgan Library |
| 710. | 13 July | Mrs. Brookfield | Charles Scribner's Sons |
| 711. | 22 July | Mrs. Brookfield | Morgan Library |
| 712. | 26 July | Mrs. Brookfield | Morgan Library |
| 713. | 3 August | Rev. Robert Montgomery | Huntington Library |
| 714. | 22 August | Edward Chapman | Huntington Library |
| 715. | 22 August | William Makepeace Thackeray | Morgan Library |
| 716. | 24 ? August | Mrs. Brookfield | Morgan Library |
| 717. | 15 September | Anne and Harriet Thackeray | Mrs. Fuller |
| 718. | 1 October | Mrs. Gore | Mrs. Martin |
| 719. | 3 October | Henry Taylor | [      ] |
| 720. | 3 October | Mrs. Brookfield | Morgan Library |
| 721. | 8 October | Mrs. Brookfield | Morgan Library |
| 722. | October | Lady Eddisbury | Huntington Library |
| 723. | October–3 November | Mrs. Sartoris | [      ] |
| 724. | 4 November | Dr. Elliotson | Berg Collection |
| 725. | November | Mrs. James | Berg Collection |
| 726. | November | Mrs. Fanshawe | Mrs. Fuller |
| 727. | 26–28 November | Mrs. Carmichael-Smyth | Mrs. Fuller |
| 728. | 27 November | Mrs. Brookfield | Morgan Library |
| 729. | 29–30 November | William Allingham | [      ] |
| 730. | 18 December | Lady Pollock | [      ] |
| 731. | 22 December | ? | Mr. Hill |
| 732. | 23 December | Mrs. Brookfield | Morgan Library |
| 733. | 24 December | Anne Thackeray | Mrs. Fuller |
| 734. | 26 December | Mrs. Brookfield | Morgan Library |
| 735. | 29 December | Robert Smith Surtees | Mr. Parrish |
| 736. | December ? | George Morland Crawford | [      ] |
| 737. | 1850 | Edward Chapman | Berg Collection |
| 738. | 1850 ? | Mrs. Brookfield | [      ] |
| 739. | 1850 | Mrs. Gore | Huntington Library |

| No. | Date | Addressee | Owner or Depositary |
|---|---|---|---|
| 776. | 23 May | Abraham Hayward | [          ] |
| 777. | 26 May ? | Secretary of the Royal Literary Fund | Drexel Institute |
| 778. | 27 May ? | Mrs. Butler | Haverford College Library |
| 779. | 27 ? May | Mrs. Procter | [Major Smith] |
| 780. | 29 May ? | Mrs. Procter | [Major Smith] |
| 781. | 31 May | Thomas Washbourne Gibbs | [British Museum] |
| 782. | 5 June | Mrs. Bayne | Berg Collection |
| 783. | 11 June | Mrs. Bayne | Mr. Wells |
| 784. | 19 June | Charles Lamb Kenney | Mr. Parrish |
| 785. | 2 July | Mr. Moffatt | Berg Collection |
| 786. | 3 ? July | William Makepeace Thackeray | [          ] |
| 787. | 4 July | Lord Stanley of Alderley | [          ] |
| 788. | 6 July | Mrs. Jameson | [          ] |
| 789. | 7 July | Mr. Hawkins | Berg Collection |
| 790. | 13–15 July | Mrs. Brookfield | Morgan Library |
| 791. | 15 July | Mrs. Carmichael-Smyth | Mrs. Fuller |
| 792. | 17–21 July | Mrs. Brookfield | Morgan Library |
| 793. | July | Mrs. Carmichael-Smyth | Mrs. Fuller |
| 794. | 23 August | Frederick Gale | Mr. Carlebach |
| 795. | 12 September | Thomas Washbourne Gibbs | [British Museum] |
| 796. | 21 September | Dr. John Brown | Berg Collection |
| 797. | 24 September | Anne Thackeray | Mrs. Fuller |
| 798. | 9 October | ? | Mr. Carlebach |
| 799. | 9 October | Dr. John Brown | [          ] |
| 800. | October | Lady Stanley of Alderley | Huntington Library |
| 801. | 25 October | Williams and Norgate | Berg Collection |
| 802. | 28 ? October | Lady Stanley of Alderley | Huntington Library |
| 803. | 29 October | Anne Thackeray | Mrs. Fuller |
| 804. | 10 November | Mrs. Carmichael-Smyth | Mrs. Fuller |
| 805. | 10 November | Mrs. Procter | [Major Smith] |
| 806. | 17–18 ? November | Mrs. Carmichael-Smyth | Mrs. Fuller |
| 807. | 6 December | Lady Stanley of Alderley | Huntington Library |
| 808. | 9 December | Anne and Harriet Thackeray | [          ] |
| 809. | 10 ? December | Mrs. Elliot and Kate Perry | Morgan Library |
| 810. | 10 ? December | Anne Thackeray | Mrs. Fuller |
| 811. | December | Harriet Thackeray | Mrs. Fuller |
| 812. | 22 ? December | Andrew Coventry Dick | [          ] |
| 813. | 28 December | Lady Stanley of Alderley | Huntington Library |
| 814. | December | Mrs. Elliot | Morgan Library |

| No. | Date | Addressee | Owner or Depositary |
|---|---|---|---|
| | | **1852** | |
| 815. | 5 January | Mrs. Brown | [          ] |
| 816. | 7 January | Anne Thackeray | Mrs. Fuller |
| 817. | 9 January | Russell Sturgis | Berg Collection |
| 818. | 10 January | ? | Mr. Bromback |
| 819. | 31 January | Mrs. Bayne | Mr. Wells |
| 820. | 2 February | Lady Elizabeth Thackeray | Mr. Wells |
| 821. | 5 February | Mary Holmes | Berg Collection |
| 822. | 7 February | Richard Doyle | Berg Collection |
| 823. | 15 February | Richard Pryme | Berg Collection |
| 824. | February | Mary Holmes | Berg Collection |
| 825. | 25 February | Mary Holmes | Bemis Estate |
| 826. | 26 February | Mrs. Carmichael-Smyth | Mrs. Fuller |
| 827. | February ? | Eyre Crowe | [          ] |
| 828. | 1 March | Mary Holmes | Berg Collection |
| 829. | 5 March | Mary Holmes | Berg Collection |
| 830. | 10 March | Albert Smith | Mr. Parrish |
| 831. | 13 March | Lady Pollock | Colonel Drake |
| 832. | 15 March | Mrs. Carmichael-Smyth | Mrs. Fuller |
| 833. | 16 March | Richard Lee | Berg Collection |
| 834. | 22 March | Mary Holmes | Berg Collection |
| 835. | April | Mrs. Gore | Berg Collection |
| 836. | 9 April | Mary Holmes | Berg Collection |
| 837. | April | William Makepeace Thackeray | [          ] |
| 838. | 14 April | Dr. John Brown | [          ] |
| 839. | 16 April | Mrs. Brown | [          ] |
| 840. | 16–17 April | Harriet Thackeray | Mrs. Fuller |
| 841. | 17 April | Mrs. Elliot and Kate Perry | Huntington Library |
| 842. | 17–19 April | Mrs. Carmichael-Smyth | Mrs. Fuller |
| 843. | 22 April | Anne and Harriet Thackeray | Mrs. Fuller |
| 844. | 23 April | Rev. Grantham Yorke | Dr. Eliot |
| 845. | 25 April | Dr. John Brown | Berg Collection |
| 846. | 26 April | Anne and Harriet Thackeray | Mrs. Fuller |
| 847. | April ? | Mary Holmes | Berg Collection |
| 848. | 21 May | Willard L. Felt | [          ] |
| 849. | 24 May | Dr. John Brown | [          ] |
| 850. | 29 May | Rev. William Brookfield | [          ] |
| 851. | 18–20 June | Anne and Harriet Thackeray | [          ] |
| 852. | 21 June | Mrs. Elliot and Kate Perry | Berg Collection |
| 853. | 30 June | Anne and Harriet Thackeray | [          ] |

| No. | Date | Addressee | Owner or Depositary |
|---|---|---|---|
| 854. | 5–6 July | Mrs. Carmichael-Smyth | Mrs. Fuller |
| 855. | 14 July | Anne Thackeray | Mrs. Fuller |
| 856. | 6 August | Anne and Harriet Thackeray | Mrs. Fuller |
| 857. | 6 August | Miss Martin | Mr. Hill |
| 858. | 6 August | William Allingham | [          ] |
| 859. | 7 August | Lady Stanley of Alderley | Huntington Library |
| 860. | 10 August | Mary Holmes | Berg Collection |
| 861. | 16 August | Thackeray's family | [          ] |
| 862. | 16 August | Lady Stanley of Alderley | Huntington Library |
| 863. | 20 August | Lady Holland | Mr. Papantonio |
| 864. | 28 August | Anne and Harriet Thackeray | Mrs. Fuller |
| 865. | September ? | Mrs. Gore | Berg Collection |
| 866. | September ? | Mrs. Gore | Berg Collection |
| 867. | 10 September | Harriet Thackeray | Mrs. Fuller (in part) |
| 868. | 15 September | Richard Lee | Berg Collection |
| 869. | September | Eyre Crowe | Berg Collection |
| 870. | 19 September | Mrs. Fanshawe | Berg Collection |
| 871. | 21 September | Anne Thackeray | Mrs. Fuller |
| 872. | 21 September | Rev. Alexander Scott | Berg Collection |
| 873. | September | Lady Elizabeth Thackeray | Mr. Wells |
| 874. | 26 September– 20 January, 1853 | William Makepeace Thackeray | Mrs. Fuller |
| 875. | 29 September | Lady Stanley of Alderley | Huntington Library |
| 876. | 30 September | Lady Stanley of Alderley | Huntington Library |
| 877. | October ? | Samuel Laurence | Berg Collection |
| 878. | October ? | Samuel Laurence | Berg Collection |
| 879. | 6 October | Dr. John Brown | [          ] |
| 880. | 14 October | Willard L. Felt | Berg Collection |
| 881. | October | Anne Thackeray | Mrs. Fuller |
| 882. | 14–18 October | Anne and Harriet Thackeray | Mrs. Fuller |
| 883. | 27 October | Edward Fitzgerald | Berg Collection |
| 884. | 27 October | Lady Pollock | Berg Collection |
| 885. | 27 ? October | Miss Trulock | Mr. Carlebach |
| 886. | 29 October | Mary Holmes | Berg Collection |
| 887. | 29 October | Richard Monckton Milnes | [          ] |
| 888. | 29 October | Mrs. Procter | [Major Smith] |
| 889. | 29 October | Lady Elizabeth Thackeray | Mr. Wells |
| 890. | 29–30 October | Anne and Harriet Thackeray | Mrs. Fuller |
| 891. | 2–11 November | Anne and Harriet Thackeray | Mrs. Fuller |

| No. | Date | Addressee | Owner or Depositary |
|---|---|---|---|
| 892. | 11–12 November | Mrs. Carmichael-Smyth | Mrs. Fuller |
| 892a. | 13 November | William Hickling Prescott | Mr. Carlebach |
| 893. | 12 November | William Hickling Prescott | Berg Collection |
| 894. | 15 November | William Makepeace Thackeray | Mrs. Fuller |
| 895. | November | Colonel Lawrence | Mr. Parrish |
| 896. | 23 November | Anne and Harriet Thackeray | Mrs. Fuller |
| 897. | 23 November | Mrs. Brookfield | Morgan Library |
| 898. | 23 November ? | Mrs. Bancroft | Massachusetts Historical Society |
| 899. | 25 November | William Makepeace Thackeray | Mrs. Fuller |
| 900. | 25 November | ? | Mr. Carlebach |
| 901. | 26 ? November | William Henry Appleton | Massachusetts Historical Society |
| 902. | 26–27 November | Anne and Harriet Thackeray | Mrs. Fuller |
| 903. | 27 November | Brothers Harper | [        ] |
| 904. | 27 November | George Palmer Putnam | [        ] |
| 905. | 28 November–1 December | Mrs. Elliot and Kate Perry | Berg Collection |
| 906. | 29 November | ? | Mrs. Madigan |
| 907. | 29 November | ? | Morgan Library |
| 908. | 30 November | William Makepeace Thackeray | [        ] |
| 909. | 2 December | ? | Historical Society of Pennsylvania |
| 910. | 5 December | William Makepiece Thackeray | [        ] |
| 911. | 7 December | Anne and Harriet Thackeray | Mrs. Fuller |
| 912. | 19 December | Edward Livingston Wells | Mrs. Madigan |
| 913. | December ? | Libby Strong | [        ] |
| 914. | 20 December | Mrs. Carmichael-Smyth | Mrs. Fuller |
| 915. | 20 December | William Dickinson | Berg Collection |
| 916. | 21 December | Mrs. Baxter and Sally Baxter | [        ] |
| 917. | 22 December | Sally Baxter | Mr. Carlebach |
| 918. | 22 December | Mrs. Procter | [Major Smith] |
| 919. | 23 December | Abbott Lawrence | Harvard College Library |
| 920. | 24 December | Henry Corry Rowley Becher | Mrs. Plummer |
| 921. | 24 December | Frederick Pratt Barlow | Mr. Eric |
| 922. | 24 December | Mrs. Baxter | Mr. Beyer |
| 923. | 30 December | Mrs. Baxter | [        ] |
| 924. | 30 December | Mrs. Baxter | Mr. Carlebach |
| 925. | 30 December | William Makepeace Thackeray | [        ] |
| 926. | December | James T. Fields | Mr. Carlebach |
| 927. | 1852 | Mr. Leslie | [        ] |

| No. | Date | Addressee | Owner or Depositary |
|-----|------|-----------|---------------------|

## 1853

| No. | Date | Addressee | Owner or Depositary |
|-----|------|-----------|---------------------|
| 928. | 1 January | George Edward Rice | Colonel Drake |
| 929. | 1 ? January | Lucy Baxter | Berg Collection |
| 930. | 2 January | Mrs. Baxter | Berg Collection |
| 931. | 2 ? January | James Russell Lowell | Goodspeed's Book Shop |
| 932. | 2 January | Rev. Theodore Parker | Mr. Wolf |
| 933. | 4 January | Mrs. Carmichael-Smyth | Mrs. Fuller |
| 934. | 15 January | John Reuben Thompson | Carnegie Bookshop |
| 935. | 17 January | Harriet Thackeray | Berg Collection |
| 936. | 20 January | Mrs. Baxter | Mrs. Haight |
| 937. | 21 January | Lady Stanley of Alderley | Huntington Library |
| 938. | 21–23 January | Mrs. Brookfield | [Dr. Rosenbach] |
| 939. | 23 January | Professor Henry Hope Reed | [Mrs. Gibson] |
| 940. | 23 January | Clement Cornell Biddle | [         ] |
| 941. | 26 January | Mrs. Carmichael-Smyth | Mrs. Fuller |
| 942. | 1–4 February | Anne Thackeray | Mrs. Fuller |
| 943. | 2 February | Morton McMichael | [         ] |
| 944. | February | Morton McMichael | [         ] |
| 945. | 7–14 February | Kate Perry | [Dr. Rosenbach] |
| 946. | 9 February | Edward Everett | Massachusetts Historical Society |
| 947. | 11 February | John Pendleton Kennedy | Peabody Institute |
| 948. | 13 February | Mrs. Carmichael-Smyth | Mrs. Fuller |
| 949. | 14 February | William Bradford Reed | [         ] |
| 950. | 16 February | Mrs. Baxter | Berg Collection |
| 951. | 16 February | Morton McMichael | [         ] |
| 952. | 19 February | Lucy Baxter | Berg Collection |
| 953. | 22 February | ? | Massachusetts Historical Society |
| 954. | 24 February | Mrs. Baxter | [         ] |
| 955. | 25 February | Mrs. Baxter | Berg Collection |
| 956. | 26 February | Lucy Baxter | Berg Collection |
| 957. | 26 February | Mrs. Carmichael-Smyth | Mrs. Fuller |
| 958. | 1 March | Mrs. Synge | Mr. Carlebach |
| 959. | 3 March | Mrs. Baxter | [Mr. Barrett] |
| 960. | 3 March | Mrs. Elliot and Kate Perry | [Dr. Rosenbach] |
| 961. | 3 March | Anne Thackeray | Mrs. Fuller |
| 962. | 4 March | Albany Fonblanque | [         ] |
| 963. | 8 March | William Makepiece Thackeray | Mrs. Fuller |
| 964. | 11 March | Lucy Baxter | [         ] |
| 965. | 11 March | Harriet Thackeray | Huntington Library |
| 966. | 12 March | Mrs. Baxter | [         ] |

| No. | Date | Addressee | Owner or Depositary |
|---|---|---|---|
| 967. | 14–19 March | Anne and Harriet Thackeray | [         ] |
| 968. | 19 March | James T. Fields | [         ] |
| 969. | 23 March | ? | [         ] |
| 970. | 25 March | Dr. John Brown | [         ] |
| 971. | 25–28 March | Mrs. Carmichael-Smyth | Mrs. Fuller |
| 972. | 2 April ? | John Reuben Thompson | Berg Collection |
| 973. | 2 April | James T. Fields | Massachusetts Historical Society |
| 974. | 4 April | Mrs. Procter | [Major Smith] |
| 975. | 5 April | Mrs. Bayne | [         ] |
| 976. | 5 April | Alice Jane Trulock | [         ] |
| 977. | 15 April | Lucy Baxter | Berg Collection |
| 978. | 20 April | George Baxter | Berg Collection |
| 979. | 20 April | James T. Fields | [         ] |
| 980. | 20 April | George B. Jones | [         ] |
| 981. | 3 May | Mrs. Baxter | Mrs. George A. Martin |
| 982. | 10 May | Mrs. Baxter | Berg Collection |
| 983. | 10 May | Mr. Chambers | [Dr. Radin] |
| 984. | 15–17 May | Mrs. Elliot and Kate Perry | Morgan Library |
| 985. | 18–19 May | The Baxters | Berg Collection |
| 986. | 25 May | Mrs. Baxter | Miss Maude Frank |
| 987. | June | Mrs. Procter | [Major Smith] |
| 988. | 3 June | Mrs. Baxter | Berg Collection |
| 989. | 9 June | Anne Thackeray | Mrs. Fuller |
| 990. | 17 June | Nassau William Senior | Berg Collection |
| 991. | 21 June | Sir Edward Bulwer-Lytton | [         ] |
| 992. | 25–30 June | The Baxters | Mr. Carlebach |
| 993. | 4–5 July | Sarah Baxter | [         ] |
| 994. | 5 July | Mrs. Scott | Berg Collection |
| 995. | 18 July | Mrs. Carmichael-Smyth | Mrs. Fuller |
| 996. | 18 July | Libby Strong | Berg Collection |
| 997. | 18 July | Mr. and Mrs. Synge | Mr. Carlebach |
| 998. | 21 July | William Bradford Reed | [         ] |
| 999. | 21 July | Oliver Strong | Historical Society of Pennsylvania |
| 1000. | 26 July–7 August | Sarah Baxter | [         ] |
| 1001. | 1 September | Bradbury and Evans | [         ] |
| 1002. | 1 September | Dr. and Mrs. Brown | Berg Collection |
| 1003. | 1 September | Mrs. Carmichael-Smyth | Mrs. Fuller |
| 1004. | 6 September | Lady Molesworth | Mr. Carlebach |
| 1005. | September | Bryan Waller Procter | [Major Smith] |
| 1006. | 23 September | Mrs. Procter | [Major Smith] |

| No. | Date | Addressee | Owner or Depositary |
|---|---|---|---|
| 1007. | 23 September | Mrs. Carmichael-Smyth | Mrs. Fuller |
| 1008. | 27 September | Mrs. Baxter | Berg Collection |
| 1009. | October | Lord Holland | Mr. Emerson |
| 1010. | 13 October | Eyre Crowe | Morgan Library |
| 1011. | 17–18 October–3 November | Libby Strong and Lucy Baxter | Huntington Library |
| 1012. | 3 November | Mrs. Baxter | [          ] |
| 1013. | 3 November | Sarah Baxter | [          ] |
| 1014. | 18 November | George Bancroft | [Massachusetts Historical Society] |
| 1015. | 18 November | George Ticknor | Berg Collection |
| 1016. | 18 November | George Baxter | Berg Collection |
| 1017. | 22 November | John Thaddeus Delane | [          ] |
| 1018. | 22 November | Anne Thackeray | Mrs. Fuller |
| 1019. | 24 November | ? | Mrs. Madigan |
| 1020. | 30 November | Mrs. Carmichael-Smyth | Mrs. Fuller |
| 1021. | 30 November | Mrs. Carmichael-Smyth | Mrs. Fuller |
| 1022. | 30 November | Mrs. Carmichael-Smyth | Mrs. Fuller |
| 1023. | 5 December | Mrs. Carmichael-Smyth | Mrs. Fuller |
| 1024. | 17 December | Mrs. Baxter and Sarah Baxter | Berg Collection |
| 1025. | 31 December | Mrs. Carmichael-Smyth | Mrs. Fuller |
| 1026. | 1853 | Mr. Compton | Berg Collection |
| 1027. | 1853 ? | Robert Smith Surtees | [          ] |
| 1028. | 1863 ? | William Webb Follett Synge | Mr. Carlebach |

### 1854

| No. | Date | Addressee | Owner or Depositary |
|---|---|---|---|
| 1029. | 25–28 January | Mrs. Carmichael-Smyth | Mrs. Fuller |
| 1030. | January–4 February | Mrs. Procter | [Major Smith] |
| 1031. | 28 January | Lady Olliffe | Mr. Carlebach |
| 1032. | 6 February | Charlotte Ritchie | Mr. Carlebach |
| 1033. | 7 February | Mrs. Sartoris | [          ] |
| 1034. | 7 February | Mrs. Carmichael-Smyth | Mrs. Fuller |
| 1035. | 18 February | Lord Holland | Berg Collection |
| 1036. | 25 February | Percival Leigh | Morgan Library |
| 1037. | 7–8 March | Mrs. Carmichael-Smyth | Mrs. Fuller |
| 1038. | 8 March | Percival Leigh | Morgan Library |
| 1039. | 17–28 March | Mrs. Baxter | Berg Collection |
| 1040. | 26 March | George Godwin | [          ] |

| No. | Date | Addressee | Owner or Depositary |
|-----|------|-----------|---------------------|
| 1041. | 1 April | Mrs. Carmichael-Smyth | Mrs. Fuller |
| 1042. | April | Jane Ritchie | Mr. Carlebach |
| 1043. | 12 April | Percival Leigh | Berg Collection |
| 1044. | 10 May | Mrs. Carmichael-Smyth | Mrs. Fuller |
| 1045. | 11 May | Mrs. Carmichael-Smyth | Mrs. Fuller |
| 1046. | May | George Hodder | [          ] |
| 1047. | May | ? | Mrs. Madigan |
| 1048. | 18 May | Lucy Baxter | [          ] |
| 1049. | 18 May | Robert Herbert Story | Retz and Storm |
| 1050. | 23 May | Mrs. Bayne | Mr. Wells |
| 1051. | 28 May | Mrs. Cunningham | Mr. Pforzheimer |
| 1052. | 5 June | Mrs. Procter | [Major Smith] |
| 1053. | 5 June | Richard Doyle | Berg Collection |
| 1054. | 8 June | Lady Morgan | Huntington Library |
| 1055. | June | Lady Stanley of Alderley | Huntington Library |
| 1056. | 12? June | Mrs. Carmichael-Smyth | Mrs. Fuller |
| 1057. | 14 June | Mrs. Procter | [Major Smith] |
| 1058. | 16 June | Dean Milman | [          ] |
| 1059. | 21 June | Mrs. James | Berg Collection |
| 1060. | 24 June | Percival Leigh | Widener Collection |
| 1061. | 18 July | Elizabeth Strong | Huntington Library |
| 1062. | 15 August | Mrs. Procter | [Major Smith] |
| 1063. | 18 August | Mr. Ballard | Berg Collection |
| 1064. | 18 August | Willard S. Felt | Mr. Carlebach |
| 1065. | 19 August | ? | Berg Collection |
| 1066. | 19 August | ? | Berg Collection |
| 1067. | 20 August | Richard Doyle | [          ] |
| 1068. | 28 August | Anne Thackeray | Mrs. Fuller |
| 1069. | August ? | Bradbury and Evans | Berg Collection |
| 1070. | 6 ? September | Mrs. Procter | [Major Smith] |
| 1071. | September | Anne and Harriet Thackeray | Mrs. Fuller |
| 1072. | 14 September | Algernon West | Mr. Metzdorf |
| 1073. | 16 September | Paul Émile Daurand Forgues | [          ] |
| 1074. | 29 September | Anne and Harriet Thackeray | Mrs. Fuller |
| 1075. | 17 October | Mrs. Procter | [Major Smith] |
| 1076. | 24–25 October | Mrs. Procter | [Major Smith] |
| 1077. | 7–8 November | Mrs. Carmichael-Smyth | Mrs. Fuller |
| 1078. | 8 November | John Forster | Mr. Arents |
| 1079. | 8 November | William Bradford Reed | [          ] |

| No. | Date | Addressee | Owner or Depositary |
|---|---|---|---|
| 1080. | 20 November | Lady Olliffe | Mr. Carlebach |
| 1081. | 2 December | James Hain Friswell | Mr. Carlebach |
| 1082. | 4 December | Lady Stanley of Alderley | Huntington Library |
| 1083. | 10 December | William Makepeace Thackeray | Mr. Carlebach |
| 1084. | 11 December | Selina Shakespear | [          ] |
| 1085. | 30 December | John Blackwood | Mr. Wells |
| 1086. | 31 December | Dr. and Mrs. Brown | [          ] |
| 1087. | 1854 | Morton McMichael | [          ] |
| 1088. | 1854 ? | Amédée Pichot | Berg Collection |
| 1089. | 1854 ? | ? | Huntington Library |

### 1855

| No. | Date | Addressee | Owner or Depositary |
|---|---|---|---|
| 1090. | January | A.A. | Mr. Wells |
| 1091. | 1 February | David Roberts | Dr. Rosenbach |
| 1092. | 1 February | Rev. Whitwell Elwin | Mr. Haight |
| 1093. | 2 February | Mrs. Carmichael-Smyth | Mrs. Fuller (in part) |
| 1094. | 3 February | ? | Miss Benjamin |
| 1095. | 4 February | George Smith | [          ] |
| 1096. | 5 February | Percival Leigh | Mr. Carlebach |
| 1097. | 7 February | Rev. John Allen | Trinity College, Cambridge |
| 1098. | 7 February | Robert Herbert Story | Mr. Carlebach |
| 1099. | 10 February | The minister of the English church at Le Havre | Berg Collection |
| 1100. | 16 February | Mrs. Blackburn | Huntington Library |
| 1101. | 21 February | Edward Sartoris | [          ] |
| 1102. | 21 February | William Bevan | [          ] |
| 1103. | 26 February | Lady Stanley of Alderley | Huntington Library |
| 1104. | March | William Bevan | Retz and Storm |
| 1105. | 6–7 March | Mrs. Carmichael-Smyth | Mrs. Fuller |
| 1106. | 17 March | ? | Huntington Library |
| 1107. | March ? | Mrs. Procter | [Major Smith] |
| 1108. | 23 March | William Makepeace Thackeray | [          ] |
| 1109. | 24 March | Frederick Mullett | [          ] |
| 1110. | 26 March | William Makepeace Thackeray | Berg Collection |
| 1111. | 26 March | Edward Sterling | Mr. Carlebach |
| 1112. | 30 March | ? | Berg Collection |
| 1113. | 11 April | ? | [Library, Charterhouse School] |
| 1114. | 17 April | Joseph Yorke | Mr. Lilly |
| 1115. | 22 April | Mrs. Carmichael-Smyth | Mrs. Fuller |
| 1116. | 26 April | Mrs. Goldsmid | Mrs. Madigan |
| 1117. | 26 April | Mr. Toulin | Mr. Wells |

| No. | Date | Addressee | Owner or Depositary |
|---|---|---|---|
| 1118. | 28 April, 1855 | George Henry Lewes | [                    ] |
| 1119. | 2 May | S. N. Rowland | [                    ] |
| 1120. | 4 May | Mrs. Bray | [                    ] |
| 1121. | 9 May | John Forster | Mr. Carlebach |
| 1122. | 19 May | George Hodder | Mr. Castles |
| 1122a. | 19 May | Richard Lee | Berg Collection |
| 1123. | 25 May | William Ritchie | Mr. Carlebach |
| 1124. | 28 May | Lady Elizabeth Thackeray | Mr. Wells |
| 1125. | 3 June | John Forster | Berg Collection |
| 1126. | 11 June | Lady Pollock | [                    ] |
| 1127. | 11 June | Lady Stanley of Alderley | Huntington Library |
| 1128. | 13 June | William Howard Russell | [                    ] |
| 1129. | 15 June | Samuel Morley | Fitzwilliam Museum |
| 1130. | June ? | George B. Jones | Boston Public Library |
| 1131. | June ? | George B. Jones | Goodspeed's Book Shop |
| 1132. | 2 July | Kate Perry | [                    ] |
| 1133. | 11 July | Percival Leigh | Gimbel Brothers |
| 1134. | 19 ? July | Albany Fonblanque | [                    ] |
| 1135. | 27 July | James Buchanan | Historical Society of Pennsylvania |
| 1136. | 1 August | Tom Taylor | [Miss Taylor] |
| 1137. | 3 August | Mrs. Baxter | Berg Collection |
| 1138. | August ? | William Wetmore Story | Berg Collection |
| 1139. | 6 September | Rev. Whitwell Elwin | Berg Collection |
| 1140. | 6 September | George Hodder | [                    ] |
| 1141. | 6 September | Charles Gavan Duffy | [                    ] |
| 1142. | 12 September | Rev. Whitwell Elwin | Berg Collection |
| 1143. | 14 September | Willard Felt | [Mr. Barrett] |
| 1144. | 22 September | George Smith | [                    ] |
| 1145. | 29 September | Edmund Yates | [                    ] |
| 1146. | 2 October | Mrs. Fanshawe | Morgan Library |
| 1147. | 5 October | The Baxters | Berg Collection |
| 1148. | 5 October | Mrs. Procter | [Major Smith] |
| 1149. | October | Charles Neate | Huntington Library |
| 1150. | 9 October | William Allingham | [                    ] |
| 1151. | 11 October | Mrs. James | Berg Collection |
| 1152. | 11 October | Lady Stanley of Alderley | Huntington Library |
| 1153. | 11 October | Lady Elizabeth Thackeray | Mr. Wells |
| 1154. | 11 October | Mrs. Procter | [Major Smith] |
| 1155. | 13 October | Mrs. Carmichael-Smyth | Mrs. Fuller |
| 1156. | 13 October | William Webb Follett Synge | Mr. Carlebach |

| No. | Date | Addressee | Owner or Depositary |
|---|---|---|---|
| 1157. | 13 October | Mrs. Elliot and Kate Perry | [          ] |
| 1158. | 22–23 October | Anne and Harriet Thackeray | Mrs. Fuller |
| 1159. | 30 October | James T. Fields | [          ] |
| 1160. | 30–31 October | Thackeray's family | Mrs. Fuller |
| 1161. | 31 October | John Forster | Berg Collection |
| 1162. | 1 November | James T. Fields | Miss Benjamin |
| 1163. | 1 ? November | The Baxters | [          ] |
| 1164. | November | Bayard Taylor | [          ] |
| 1165. | 6 November | Anne and Harriet Thackeray | Mrs. Fuller |
| 1166. | 9 November | James T. Fields | Mrs. Madigan |
| 1167. | 13–14 November | Thackeray's family | Mrs. Fuller |
| 1168. | 14 November | Frank Fladgate | Mr. Carlebach |
| 1169. | 14 November | Mrs. Elliot and Kate Perry | Morgan Library |
| 1170. | 16 ?–20 November | Mrs. Carmichael-Smyth | Mrs. Fuller |
| 1171. | 20 November | William Charles Macready | Retz and Storm |
| 1172. | 22 November | William Wetmore Story | Berg Collection |
| 1173. | 24 November | R. B. Campbell | Mr. Browning |
| 1174. | 25–28 November | Anne and Harriet Thackeray | Mrs. Fuller |
| 1175. | 27 November | William Wetmore Story | Berg Collection |
| 1176. | 27–28 November | Mrs. Elliot and Kate Perry | [          ] |
| 1177. | 3 December | Dr. William Prescott Dexter | [Mr. Schuman] |
| 1178. | 3 December | Frederick Swartout Cozzens | New York Public Library |
| 1179. | 3–4 December | Anne and Harriet Thackeray | Mrs. Fuller |
| 1180. | 9–11 December | Anne and Harriet Thackeray | Mrs. Fuller |
| 1181. | 11 December | Charles Bradenbaugh | [Library, Charterhouse School] |
| 1182. | 11 December | Mrs. Baxter and Sarah Baxter | Berg Collection |
| 1183. | 14–18 December | Mrs. Procter | [Major Smith] |
| 1184. | 15 December | James T. Fields | Berg Collection |
| 1185. | 15 December | Mrs. Baxter | [          ] |
| 1186. | 18 December | Anne Thackeray | Mrs. Fuller |

| No. | Date | Addressee | Owner or Depositary |
|---|---|---|---|
| 1187. | 19 December | Mrs. Baxter | Miss Frank |
| 1188. | 19 December | Mrs. Baxter | Miss Frank |
| 1189. | 21 December | Charles Bradenbaugh | [        ] |
| 1190. | 29 December–1 January, 1856 | Mrs. Carmichael-Smyth | Huntington Library |
| 1191. | 1855 | George William Curtis | [        ] |
| 1192. | 28 December–1 January, 1856 | Mrs. Elliot | [        ] |

### 1856

| No. | Date | Addressee | Owner or Depositary |
|---|---|---|---|
| 1193. | 5 January | Charles H. Brainard | Berg Collection |
| 1194. | 5 January | Henry Corry Rowley Becher | [John and Alexander Becher] |
| 1195. | January ? | Morton McMichael | [        ] |
| 1196. | 6 January | James T. Fields | [        ] |
| 1197. | 6–13 January | Anne and Harriet Thackeray | Mrs. Fuller |
| 1198. | 7 January | ? | Haverford College Library |
| 1199. | 11 January | Mrs. Baxter | Berg Collection |
| 1200. | 15 January | Mrs. Carmichael-Smyth | Mrs. Fuller |
| 1201. | 16 January | James T. Fields | Harvard College Library |
| 1202. | 16 January | William Bradford Reed | [        ] |
| 1203. | 17–27 January | Mrs. Elliot and Kate Perry | Berg Collection |
| 1204. | 21 January | James T. Fields | Dr. Rosenbach |
| 1205. | 21 January | George William Curtis | Goodspeed's Book Store |
| 1206. | 28 January–23 March | Rev. Whitwell Elwin | Huntington Library |
| 1207. | 31 January | Secretary, Georgia Historical Society | [Mr. Barrett] |
| 1208. | 2–7 February | Anne and Harriet Thackeray | Mrs. Fuller |
| 1209. | 6–7 February | Mrs. Elliot and Kate Perry | Mr. Carlebach |
| 1210. | 9 February | Judge King | [Mr. Parrish] |
| 1211. | ?–16 February | Eyre Crowe | Huntington Library |
| 1212. | 14–16 February | Kate Perry | [Dr. Rosenbach] |
| 1213. | 15 February | Anne and Harriet Thackeray | [        ] |
| 1214. | 17 February | Mrs. Baxter | Mr. Carlebach |

| No. | Date | Addressee | Owner or Depositary |
|---|---|---|---|
| 1215. | 22–24 February | Anne and Harriet Thackeray | Mrs. Fuller |
| 1216. | 23 February | Mr. Knowles | Mr. Castles |
| 1217. | 29 February–4 March | Anne and Harriet Thackeray | Mrs. Fuller |
| 1218. | 7–10 March | Anne and Harriet Thackeray | Mrs. Fuller |
| 1219. | 10 March | Mrs. Elliot | Berg Collection |
| 1220. | 15 March | Mrs. Procter | [Major Smith] |
| 1221. | 17 March | Anne and Harriet Thackeray | Mrs. Fuller |
| 1222. | 22–23 March | Rev. Whitwell Elwin | Huntington Library |
| 1223. | 24–26 March | Mrs. Elliot | Mr. Hogan |
| 1224. | 26 March | John Crerar | Berg Collection |
| 1225. | 26 March | Anne and Harriet Thackeray | Mrs. Fuller |
| 1225a. | 26 March | Louis J. Cist | R. B. Adam Collection |
| 1226. | 26 March | William Duer Robinson | Berg Collection |
| 1227. | 8 April | Mrs. Carmichael-Smyth | Mrs. Fuller |
| 1228. | 9 April | Fullerton and Raymond | Morgan Library |
| 1229. | 10 April | John Crerar | Berg Collection |
| 1230. | 24 April | William Bradford Reed | [          ] |
| 1231. | 26 April | George Curtis and Mrs. Shaw | Mr. Parrish |
| 1232. | April | Judge Daly | [          ] |
| 1233. | 7 May | Mrs. Baxter | Mr. Wells |
| 1234. | 7–9 May | William Duer Robinson | Berg Collection |
| 1235. | 16 May | Baron Tauchnitz | [          ] |
| 1236. | 19 June | Mrs. Baxter | Mr. Carlebach |
| 1237. | 23 June | Rev. Alexander John Scott | Berg Collection |
| 1238. | 4 July | Mrs. Procter | [Major Smith] |
| 1239. | 12–13 July | Mrs. Hampton | [          ] |
| 1240. | 28 July | William Wetmore Story | Berg Collection |
| 1241. | 29 July | William Leighton Leitch | Huntington Library |
| 1242. | 10 September | Mrs. Elliot and Kate Perry | Berg Collection |
| 1243. | 15 September | George Smith | [          ] |
| 1244. | 14 October | William Macready | Berg Collection |
| 1245. | 15 October | Mr. McDowell | Morgan Library |
| 1246. | 15 October | John Jones Merriman | Mr. Carlebach |
| 1247. | 16 October | William Webb Follett Synge | Mr. Carlebach |
| 1248. | 17 October | Mr. Bowie | Berg Collection |
| 1249. | 19 October | Dr. John Brown | [          ] |
| 1250. | 24 October | ? | Morgan Library |
| 1251. | 29 October | Eyre Crowe | Berg Collection |

| No. | Date | Addressee | Owner or Depositary |
|---|---|---|---|
| 1252. | 30 October | Anne Thackeray | Mrs. Fuller |
| 1253. | 2 November | Mrs. Baxter | Berg Collection |
| 1254. | 7 November | Anne and Harriet Thackeray | Mrs. Fuller |
| 1255. | 7 ? November | Mrs. Fanshawe | Mr. Carlebach |
| 1256. | 8–11 November | Anne and Harriet Thackeray | Mrs. Fuller |
| 1257. | 11 November | Mrs. Fanshawe | Berg Collection |
| 1258. | 12 November | Miss Sinclair | Library, University of California in Los Angeles |
| 1259. | 18–21 November | Anne and Harriet Thackeray | Mrs. Fuller |
| 1260. | 19 November | S.P. | Huntington Library |
| 1261. | 24 November | William Ritchie | Mr. Carlebach |
| 1262. | 25 November | Anne and Harriet Thackeray | Mrs. Fuller |
| 1263. | 26 November | Mrs. Procter | [Major Smith] |
| 1264. | 27 November | Dr. and Mrs. Brown | [            ] |
| 1265. | 27 November | Mrs. Fanshawe | Mayfair Bookshop |
| 1266. | 1 ? December | John Allen | Huntington Library |
| 1267. | 3 December | Anne and Harriet Thackeray | Mrs. Fuller |
| 1268. | 4 December | Anne and Harriet Thackeray | Mrs. Fuller |
| 1269. | 5 December | Charlotte and Jane Ritchie | Mr. Carlebach |
| 1270. | 5 December | Anne and Harriet Thackeray | Mrs. Fuller |
| 1271. | 5 December | ? | Mr. Hill |
| 1272. | 5 December | Sir Henry Davison | Widener Collection |
| 1273. | 6 December | Lady Stanley of Alderley | Huntington Library |
| 1274. | December | Mrs. Merivale | Berg Collection |
| 1275. | December | William Webb Follett Synge | Mr. Carlebach |
| 1276. | 10–12 December | Mrs. Hampton | [            ] |
| 1277. | 12 December | Mrs. Dunlop | [            ] |
| 1278. | 19 December | Major Carmichael-Smyth | Mrs. Fuller |
| 1279. | 27 December | Mr. Carter | [            ] |
| 1280. | 1856 ? | Anthony Coningham Sterling | [            ] |

1857

| No. | Date | Addressee | Owner or Depositary |
|---|---|---|---|
| 1281. | 1 January | Major and Mrs. Carmichael-Smyth | Mr. Carlebach |
| 1282. | 6–8 January | Mrs. Carmichael-Smyth | Mrs. Fuller |
| 1283. | 9–12 January | Mrs. Carmichael-Smyth | Mrs. Fuller |
| 1284. | 11 January | William Harrison Ainsworth | Berg Collection |

| No. | Date | Addressee | Owner or Depositary |
|---|---|---|---|
| 1285. | 13 January | ? | Berg Collection |
| 1286. | 13 January | William Harrison Ainsworth | [          ] |
| 1287. | 17 January | ? | Huntington Library |
| 1288. | 23 January | Mrs. Carmichael-Smyth | Mrs. Fuller |
| 1289. | 30 January | ? | Mr. Carlebach |
| 1290. | 8 February | Rev. Whitwell Elwin | Huntington Library |
| 1291. | 8 February– 5 April | Frederick Cozzens | Mr. Carlebach |
| 1292. | 13 February | Anne and Harriet Thackeray | [          ] |
| 1293. | 17 February | Anne and Harriet Thackeray | [          ] |
| 1294. | 22 February | Anne and Harriet Thackeray | Mrs. Fuller |
| 1295. | February | Anne and Harriet Thackeray | Mrs. Fuller |
| 1296. | 26 February | A. Edmonston | Berg Collection |
| 1297. | 26 February | John Everett Millais | Mr. Wells |
| 1298. | 3 March | John Everett Millais | [          ] |
| 1299. | 3 March | Anne and Harriet Thackeray | Mrs. Fuller |
| 1300. | March | Mrs. Fanshawe | Berg Collection |
| 1301. | 8 March | Anne and Harriet Thackeray | Mrs. Fuller |
| 1302. | 17 March | Lady Louisa de Rothschild | [          ] |
| 1303. | 17 March | Anne Thackeray | Mrs. Fuller |
| 1304. | 18 March | Lady James Hay | Berg Collection |
| 1305. | 20 March | ? | Widener Collection |
| 1306. | 24 March | Anne and Harriet Thackeray | Mrs. Fuller |
| 1307. | 26 March | J. D. Milne | Mr. Pforzheimer |
| 1308. | 26 March | Anne and Harriet Thackeray | Mrs. Fuller |
| 1309. | 30 March | Robert Carruthers | Dr. Rosenbach |
| 1310. | 30 March | Lady Jane Ogilvy | [          ] |
| 1311. | 30 March | William Webb Follett Synge | Mr. Carlebach |
| 1312. | 2 April | Lady Murray | Huntington Library |
| 1313. | 2 April | Anne and Harriet Thackeray | Mrs. Fuller |
| 1314. | 7 April | Thornton Hunt | Wellesley College Library |
| 1315. | 7 April | Lady James Hay | Berg Collection |
| 1316. | 14 April | George Frederick Pardon | Mrs. Madigan |
| 1317. | 2 May | James Reynolds Young | [          ] |
| 1318. | 14 May | William Bradford Reed | Mr. Carlebach |
| 1319. | 21 May | George Frederick Pardon | Berg Collection |
| 1320. | 29 May | Bayard Taylor | [          ] |
| 1321. | 31 May | William Alexander Mackinnon | Mr. Carlebach |
| 1322. | June | Bayard Taylor | Berg Collection |
| 1323. | 22 June | Dr. John Brown | [          ] |
| 1324. | 11 July | Anne and Harriet Thackeray | [          ] |

| No. | Date | Addressee | Owner or Depositary |
|---|---|---|---|
| 1325. | July | Lady Molesworth | Huntington Library |
| 1326. | 16 July | William Hepworth Dixon | Huntington Library |
| 1327. | 23 July | Lady Holland | Mrs. Madigan |
| 1328. | 3 August | Thomas Buchanan Read | Historical Society of Pennsylvania |
| 1329. | 16 August | Colonel Sykes | Berg Collection |
| 1330. | September ? | Mrs. Synge | Mr. Carlebach |
| 1331. | 13 September | William Macready | Mr. Metzdorf |
| 1332. | 25 September | Joseph Parkes | Mrs. Haight |
| 1333. | 26 October ? | Lady Olliffe | Mr. Carlebach |
| 1334. | 31 October | A. I. Hopkins | Berg Collection |
| 1335. | 31 October– 27 November | The Baxters | Berg Collection |
| 1336. | 3 December | Bradbury and Evans | Huntington Library |
| 1337. | 4 December | William Makepeace Thackeray | Widener Collection |
| 1338. | 7 December | Charles Dickens | Widener Collection |
| 1339. | 11 December | S. Low and Sons | Berg Collection |
| 1340. | 24 December | Friends of Lady Blessington | Widener Collection |
| 1341. | 25 December | Mrs. Carmichael-Smyth | Mrs. Fuller |
| 1342. | 25 December–2 January, 1858 | Dr. John Brown | [          ] |
| 1343. | 1857 | William Howard Russell | Berg Collection |

### 1858

| No. | Date | Addressee | Owner or Depositary |
|---|---|---|---|
| 1344. | 23 January– 25 February | William Duer Robinson | Berg Collection |
| 1345. | 19 February | William Charles Macready | Huntington Library |
| 1346. | 22 February | William Charles Macready | Huntington Library |
| 1347. | 25 February | John Reuben Thompson | Mr. Carlebach |
| 1348. | 3 March | Dr. John Brown | [          ] |
| 1349. | 11 March | Lady Stanley of Alderley | Huntington Library |
| 1350. | 21 March | William Makepeace Thackeray | [          ] |
| 1351. | 2 April | Mrs. Carmichael-Smyth | Mrs. Fuller |
| 1352. | 3 April | Thomas Fraser | [Mr. Blatner] |
| 1353. | 9 April | Mrs. Carmichael-Smyth | Berg Collection |

| No. | Date | Addressee | Owner or Depositary |
|-----|------|-----------|---------------------|
| 1354. | 10–23 April | Mrs. Baxter | Mr. Carlebach |
| 1355. | May | James Wilson | Comte de Suzannet |
| 1356. | 24 May | Lady Stanley of Alderley | Berg Collection |
| 1357. | May | Mrs. Carmichael-Smyth | Mrs. Fuller |
| 1358. | 4 June | Adelaide Procter | [Major Smith] |
| 1359. | 13 June | Edmund Yates | Mrs. Fuller |
| 1360. | 15 June | William Makepeace Thackeray | [          ] |
| 1361. | 17 June | William Makepeace Thackeray | [          ] |
| 1362. | 19 June | Committee of the Garrick Club | [          ] |
| 1363. | 19 June | Committee of the Garrick Club | [          ] |
| 1364. | 19 June | Edmund Yates | [          ] |
| 1365. | 23 June | Committee of the Garrick Club | [          ] |
| 1366. | 26 June | William Makepeace Thackeray and Edmund Yates | [          ] |
| 1367. | 28 June | Mrs. Becher | Berg Collection |
| 1368. | 1 July | Committee of the Garrick Club | [          ] |
| 1369. | 6 July | Edmund Yates | [Comte de Suzannet] |
| 1370. | 10 July | Chairman of the General Meeting of the Garrick Club | Mrs. Fuller |
| 1371. | 10 July | General Meeting of the Garrick Club | [          ] |
| 1372. | 10 July | N. Clayton | Mr. Wilson |
| 1373. | 17 July | Edmund Yates | [          ] |
| 1374. | 25 July | Bradbury and Evans | Mr. Carlebach |
| 1375. | 27 July | William Makepeace Thackeray | Mrs. Fuller |
| 1376. | 18 August | ? | Berg Collection |
| 1377. | 25 August | The Baxters | Mr. Carlebach |
| 1378. | 20–23 September | Lady Stanley of Alderley | Huntington Library |
| 1379. | 18 October | Patrick Kennedy | Morgan Library |
| 1380. | 4–10 November | Dr. John Brown | [          ] |
| 1381. | 24 November | William Makepeace Thackeray | [          ] |
| 1382. | 26 November | Charles Dickens | [          ] |
| 1383. | 28 November | Committee of the Garrick Club | [Mrs. Fuller] |
| 1384. | 4 December | Anne and Harriet Thackeray | Mrs. Fuller |
| 1385. | December ? | Lady Morgan | Berg Collection |
| 1386. | 27 December | Captain Atkinson | Berg Collection |
| 1387. | 27 December | Robert Chambers | [          ] |
| 1388. | 1858 ? | Madame Le Vert | [          ] |

| No. | Date | Addressee | Owner or Depositary |
|---|---|---|---|
| | | **1859** | |
| 1389. | 22 January | Sir Henry Knight Storks | [ |
| 1390. | 26 January | Dr. John Brown | [      ] |
| 1391. | February | Mrs. Carmichael-Smyth | Mrs. Fuller |
| 1392. | 2 March | Mr. Leeming | Berg Collection |
| 1393. | March | Frederic Chapman | Berg Collection |
| 1394. | 12 March | Charles Kingsley | Berg Collection |
| 1395. | 29 March | William Duer Robinson | Mrs. Fuller |
| 1396. | 2 April | William Bradford Reed | [      ] |
| 1397. | 2 April | ? | Mr. Sessler |
| 1398. | 3–4 April | Dr. John Brown | [      ] |
| 1399. | 20 April | William Hepworth Dixon | Huntington Library |
| 1400. | 6 May | Francis St. John Thackeray | [      ] |
| 1401. | 14 May | ? | Mr. Carlebach |
| 1402. | 15 May | Mrs. Theresa Hatch | Mr. Carlebach |
| 1403. | 27 ? May | Mrs. Dick | Berg Collection |
| 1404. | 28 May | Mrs. Blackwood | [      ] |
| 1405. | 28 May | Miss Cole | Huntington Library |
| 1406. | 1859 | Charles Lever | Widener Collection |
| 1407. | 27 June | Charles Lever | Widener Collection |
| 1408. | 28 June | John Elliot Jr. | Huntington Library |
| 1409. | 24 July | Lady Molesworth | Mr. Carlebach |
| 1410. | 3 August | Thomas Carlyle | Berg Collection |
| 1411. | 3 ? August | Rev. William Brookfield | Morgan Library |
| 1412. | 23 August | Anne and Harriet Thackeray | Mrs. Fuller |
| 1413. | 7 September | George Smith | [      ] |
| 1414. | 10 September | Mrs. Procter | [Major Smith] |
| 1415. | ? September–16 October | Alfred Tennyson | [      ] |
| 1416. | 29 September | George Smith | [      ] |
| 1417. | 1 October | Mrs. Carmichael-Smyth | Mrs. Fuller |
| 1418. | 4 October | George Smith | [      ] |
| 1419. | 19 October | John Hollingshead | [      ] |
| 1420. | 20 October | William Makepeace Thackeray | [      ] |
| 1421. | 28 October | Anthony Trollope | [      ] |
| 1422. | 1 November | A Friend and Contributor | [      ] |
| 1423. | 1859 | George Smith | [      ] |
| 1424. | 9 November | Rev. Whitwell Elwin | Mr. Browning |
| 1425. | 10 November | ? | Berg Collection |
| 1426. | 16 November | Henry Wadsworth Longfellow | [      ] |

| No. | Date | Addressee | Owner or Depositary |
|---|---|---|---|
| 1427. | 18 November | Mr. Cupples | Berg Collection |
| 1428. | 19 November | Robert Browning | [        ] |
| 1429. | 28 November | ? | Berg Collection |
| 1430. | 6 December | Thomas Hood | Huntington Library |
| 1431. | 15 December | A. Anderson | Mr. Pforzheimer |
| 1432. | 15 December | Mrs. Tennyson | Berg Collection |
| 1433. | 16 December | Mrs. Irvine | Huntington Library |
| 1434. | 27 December | William Makepeace Thackeray | [        ] |
| 1435. | 1859 | Samuel Lucas | Widener Collection |

1860

| No. | Date | Addressee | Owner or Depositary |
|---|---|---|---|
| 1436. | 4 January | William Allingham | [        ] |
| 1437. | 17 January | William Makepeace Thackeray | [        ] |
| 1438. | 23 January | George Smith | [Mrs. Fuller] |
| 1439. | 26 January | Kate Perry and Mrs. Crawfurd? | [        ] |
| 1440. | 26 January | Rev. Samuel Reynolds Hole | Huntington Library |
| 1441. | 7 February | Rev. Alexander MacEwen | Berg Collection |
| 1442. | 20 February | William Makepeace Thackeray | [        ] |
| 1443. | February ? | Henry Thompson | [        ] |
| 1444. | March | George Smith | [        ] |
| 1445. | 6 March | C. W. Jones | Mrs. Pearson |
| 1446. | March | Sir Edwin Landseer | Mr. Carlebach |
| 1447. | 8 March | George Smith | [        ] |
| 1448. | 10–19 March | John Frederick Boyes | Morgan Library |
| 1449. | 13 March | Sir Edwin Landseer | Berg Collection |
| 1450. | 15 March | Henry Thomas Buckle | Huntington Library |
| 1451. | 18 March | William Makepeace Thackeray | [        ] |
| 1452. | March | Adelaide Procter | [        ] |
| 1453. | 31 March | William Makepeace Thackeray | Mrs. Fuller |
| 1454. | 13 April | William Makepeace Thackeray | [        ] |
| 1455. | April | George Smith | [        ] |
| 1456. | 29 April | Thornton Hunt | University of Rochester Library |
| 1457. | 4 May | Sir Henry Davison | [        ] |
| 1458. | 18 May | Bishop of St. Davids | [Mr. Thirlwall] |
| 1459. | 24 May | William Makepeace Thackeray | [        ] |
| 1460. | 26 May | William Makepeace Thackeray | [        ] |
| 1461. | 2 June | Ernest Jones | Huntington Library |
| 1462. | June ? | George Smith | [        ] |
| 1463. | 8 July | Samuel Allibone | Huntington Library |
| 1464. | 10 July | Henry C. Penwell | Mr. Carlebach |

| No. | Date | Addressee | Owner or Depositary |
|---|---|---|---|
| 1465. | 11 July | William Duer Robinson | [          ] |
| 1466. | 18 July | Robert Dale Owen | Huntington Library |
| 1467. | 28 July | Rev. Whitwell Elwin | [          ] |
| 1468. | July | Adelaide Procter | [          ] |
| 1469. | 27 August | Mrs. Gore | Berg Collection |
| 1470. | 27 August | William Smith Williams | Widener Collection |
| 1471. | August | Robert Bell | Mr. Carlebach |
| 1472. | August ? | William Smith Williams | Huntington Library |
| 1473. | 1 September | Lord ? | Huntington Library |
| 1474. | 27 September | Lady Elizabeth Thackeray | Mr. Wells |
| 1475. | September | Lord ? | Wake Forest College Library |
| 1476. | 28 September | William Duer Robinson | Berg Collection |
| 1477. | September ? | George Augustus Sala | [          ] |
| 1478. | 3 November | ? | University of Texas Library |
| 1479. | 8 November | Lady Elizabeth Thackeray | Mr. Wells |
| 1480. | 15 November | William Makepeace Thackeray | Mr. Parrish |
| 1481. | 17 November | Anthony Trollope | Mr. Parrish |
| 1482. | 5 December | Thomas Colley Grattan | Mr. Carlebach |
| 1483. | 14 December | John Skelton | [          ] |
| 1484. | 19 December | William Makepeace Thackeray | Mrs. Fuller |
| 1485. | 21 December | William Makepeace Thackeray | Mrs. Fuller |
| 1486. | 25 December | The Baxters | [          ] |
| 1487. | 1860 | George Smith | Library of the Drexel Institute |

### 1861

| No. | Date | Addressee | Owner or Depositary |
|---|---|---|---|
| 1488. | 1 January | George Smith | [          ] |
| 1489. | January | Dr. John Brown | [          ] |
| 1490. | January ? | George Smith | Harvard College Library |
| 1491. | 13 January | William Makepeace Thackeray | Mrs. Fuller |
| 1492. | 21 January | Frederick Walker | [          ] |
| 1493. | January | Frederick Locker | [          ] |
| 1494. | 11 February | Frederick Locker | [          ] |
| 1495. | 11 February | Frederick Walker | [          ] |
| 1496. | February | William Duer Robinson | [          ] |
| 1497. | 1 April | The Misses Jones | Berg Collection |
| 1498. | 2 April | Mrs. Browning | Berg Collection |
| 1499. | 18 April | William Makepeace Thackeray | [          ] |
| 1500. | 21 April | William Makepeace Thackeray | Mrs. Fuller |
| 1501. | 25 April | Mrs. Baxter | Miss Frank |
| 1502. | 2 May | William Webb Follett Synge | Mr. Carlebach |

| No. | Date | Addressee | Owner or Depositary |
|---|---|---|---|
| 1503. | 21 May | William Makepeace Thackeray | Mrs. Fuller |
| 1504. | 24 May | Mrs. Baxter | Berg Collection |
| 1505. | 24–31 May | Rev. Whitwell Elwin | [          ] |
| 1506. | May ? | Frederick Walker | [          ] |
| 1507. | 13 June | Miss Campbell | Berg Collection |
| 1508. | June | Rev. Whitwell Elwin | Berg Collection |
| 1509. | 1 July | Dr. John Brown | [          ] |
| 1510. | 31 July | Thomas Fraser | Retz and Storm |
| 1511. | 6 August | ? | Berg Collection |
| 1512. | August ? | Frederick Walker | [          ] |
| 1513. | 3 September | George Smith | [          ] |
| 1514. | 1 October | John Frederick Boyes | Berg Collection |
| 1515. | 3 October | Miss Thackeray | Berg Collection |
| 1516. | 14 October | The Misses Jones | Berg Collection |
| 1517. | 17 October | Francis D. Finlay | Mrs. Fuller |
| 1518. | 20 October | Miss Gassiot | Berg Collection |
| 1519. | 21 October | Lady Olliffe | Berg Collection |
| 1520. | October ? | Frank Fladgate | Widener Collection |
| 1521. | 2 November | Frank Fladgate | Widener Collection |
| 1522. | 19 November | Mr. Holl | Mr. Emerson |
| 1523. | 30 November | Lady Olliffe | Mr. Carlebach |
| 1524. | 13 December | George Virtue | [          ] |
| 1525. | 24 December | Mr. and Mrs. Martin | [          ] |
| 1526. | 1861 | John Skelton | [          ] |
| 1527. | 1861 | Adelaide Procter | Berg Collection |
| 1528. | 1861 | ? | Mr. Carlebach |

### 1862

| No. | Date | Addressee | Owner or Depositary |
|---|---|---|---|
| 1529. | January ? | Frederick Walker | [          ] |
| 1530. | February ? | Frederick Walker | [          ] |
| 1531. | 1 March ? | George Augustus Sala | [          ] |
| 1532. | 4 March | George Smith | [          ] |
| 1533. | 6 March | George Smith | [          ] |
| 1534. | March | Joseph Swain | Mrs. Haight |
| 1535. | 18 March | Contributors and Correspondents, *The Cornhill Magazine* | [          ] |
| 1536. | April | Frederick Mullett Evans | [Mr. Scheide] |
| 1537. | 21 April | Anne and Harriet Thackeray | Mrs. Fuller |
| 1538. | April ? | Stephen Spring Rice | [          ] |
| 1539. | 1 May | ? | Retz and Storm |

| No. | Date | Addressee | Owner or Depositary |
|---|---|---|---|
| 1540. | May | William Webb Follett Synge | [          ] |
| 1541. | 6?–9 May | Mr. and Mrs. Baxter | Berg Collection |
| 1542. | May | Frederick Clay | Berg Collection |
| 1543. | May | George Smith | [          ] |
| 1544. | 31 May | Sir William Wellesley Knighton | Berg Collection |
| 1545. | 15 June | Frederick Walker | [          ] |
| 1546. | 30 June | Mr. Durham | Harvard College Library |
| 1547. | 1 July | George Smith | [          ] |
| 1548. | 5 July | Mrs. Carmichael-Smyth | [          ] |
| 1549. | 20 July | Mrs. Carmichael-Smyth | [          ] |
| 1550. | August | Albany Fonblanque | [Mr. Parrish] |
| 1551. | August | Mrs. Procter | [          ] |
| 1552. | 22 September | Dr. Elliotson | Mr. Carlebach |
| 1553. | 3 November | Mrs. William Ritchie | Mr. Carlebach |
| 1554. | 17 November | George Cruikshank | Berg Collection |
| 1555. | November ? | ? | Berg Collection |
| 1556. | 25 December | The Baxters | [          ] |

1863

| No. | Date | Addressee | Owner or Depositary |
|---|---|---|---|
| 1557. | 12 January | Dr. Elliotson | Berg Collection |
| 1558. | 21 January | Sir Frederick Pollock ? | Colonel Drake |
| 1559. | 4 February | ? | Fitzwilliam Museum |
| 1560. | 9 March | Rev. Whitwell Elwin | Berg Collection |
| 1561. | 17 March | Lord Granville | [          ] |
| 1562. | 18 March | Mrs. William Ritchie | Berg Collection |
| 1563. | 24 March | Mrs. Martin | [          ] |
| 1564. | March | Thomas James Thackeray ? | Berg Collection |
| 1565. | 1 May | Lady Londonderry | Berg Collection |
| 1566. | May | Mrs. James | Berg Collection |
| 1567. | 13 June | Charles Heath | Huntington Library |
| 1568. | 21 June | ? | Mr. Parrish |
| 1569. | 20 July | Sir William and Lady Knighton | Berg Collection |
| 1570. | August | Mrs. Procter | [Major Smith] |
| 1571. | 4 September | Mrs. Caspar Wistar | Berg Collection |
| 1572. | September | Mr. Alexander | Morgan Library |
| 1573. | 23 September | Dr. John Brown | [          ] |
| 1574. | September ? | George Smith | [          ] |
| 1575. | September ? | Albany Fonblanque | [          ] |
| 1576. | 16 November | Mrs. Benzon | Berg Collection |

| No. | Date | Addressee | Owner or Depositary |
|---|---|---|---|
| 1577. | 17 December | George Smith | [          ] |
| 1578. | 20 ? December | Mrs. John Leslie | [Mr. Shane Leslie] |
| 1579. | 1863 | William Bradford Reed | [          ] |
| 1580. | 1863 | Henry Thompson | [          ] |

### 1864

| | | | |
|---|---|---|---|
| 1581. | 30 April–1 May | Mrs. Baxter | [Miss Frank] |
| 1582. | 24 October | Mrs. Baxter | [Miss Frank] |

### LETTERS OF UNCERTAIN DATE

| No. | Date | Addressee | Owner or Depositary |
|---|---|---|---|
| 1583. | [1855–1862] | Lady Airlie | Berg Collection |
| 1584. | [1854–1862] | Mrs. Arabin | [          ] |
| 1585. | [1854–1862] | Mrs. Bacon | Berg Collection |
| 1586. | [1837–1845] | Rev. Richard Harris Barham | Berg Collection |
| 1587. | [1854–1862] | Mrs. Bayne | Mr. Wells |
| 1588. | [1846–1853] | Mr. Blunt | Mr. Carlebach |
| 1589. | [1846–1853] | Mrs. R. Boyle | Berg Collection |
| 1590. | [1847–1858] | Bradbury and Evans | New York Public Library |
| 1591. | [1848–1851] | Mrs. Brookfield | Morgan Library |
| 1592. | [1848–1851] | Mrs. Brookfield | Morgan Library |
| 1593. | [1848–1851] | Mrs. Brookfield | Morgan Library |
| 1594. | [1848–1851] | Mrs. Brookfield | Mr. Pforzheimer |
| 1595. | [1848–1851] | Rev. William and Mrs. Brookfield | Morgan Library |
| 1596. | [1842–1851] | Rev. William Brookfield | Morgan Library |
| 1597. | [1846–1851] | Rev. William Brookfield | Morgan Library |
| 1598. | [1846–1851] | Rev. William Brookfield | Morgan Library |
| 1599. | [1846–1851] | Rev. William Brookfield | Morgan Library |
| 1600. | [1852–1863] | Rev. William Brookfield | Morgan Library |
| 1601. | [1843–1846] | Mrs. Carmichael-Smyth | Huntington Library |
| 1602. | [1840–1863] | Edward Chapman | Morgan Library |
| 1603. | [1846–1853] | Edward Chapman ? | [          ] |
| 1604. | [1846–1853] | Chapman and Hall | [Mr. Sessler] |
| 1605. | [1846–1863] | Edward Chapman | [Mr. Sessler] |
| 1606. | [1846–1849] | Chapman and Hall | Mr. Weitz |
| 1607. | [1860–1862] | Mr. Chester | Berg Collection |
| 1608. | [1860–1862] | Mrs. Archer Clive | Berg Collection |
| 1609. | [1854–1863] | Mrs. Cole | [          ] |

| No. | Date | Addressee | Owner or Depositary |
|-----|------|-----------|---------------------|
| 1610. | [1848–1863] | Henry Cole | Berg Collection |
| 1611. | [1854–1862] | Henry Cole | Berg Collection |
| 1612. | [1860–1862] | Henry Cole | Berg Collection |
| 1613. | [1860–1862] 14 February | Henry Cole | Berg Collection |
| 1614. | [1837–1840] | John Payne Collier | Folger Shakespeare Library |
| 1615. | [1854–1862] | Dudley Costello | Berg Collection |
| 1616. | 19 November | George Cruikshank | Mr. Pforzheimer |
| 1617. | [1849–1863] | Mrs. Cunningham | Mr. Pforzheimer |
| 1618. | [1857–1863] 2 October | Charles Anderson Dana | Mrs. Madigan |
| 1619. | [1846–1856] | Henry Davison | [            ] |
| 1620. | [1837–1863] | Secretary of the Deanery Club | [            ] |
| 1621. | [1836–1858] | Charles Dickens | Mr. Elkins |
| 1622. | [1848–1863] | Richard Doyle | Berg Collection |
| 1623. | [1846–1863] | D. | Mr. Carlebach |
| 1624. | [1848–1851] | Mrs. Elliot | [            ] |
| 1625. | [1846–1853] | Dr. Elliotson | [            ] |
| 1626. | [1855–1863] 5 April | Rev. Whitwell Elwin | Huntington Library |
| 1627. | [1846–1851] | Frederick Mullett Evans | [            ] |
| 1628. | [1847–1851] | Frederick Mullett Evans | [            ] |
| 1629. | [1847–1851] May | Frederick Mullett Evans | Mrs. Tieken |
| 1630. | [1849–1851] | Mrs. and Miss Fanshawe | Mr. Weitz |
| 1631. | [1849–1851] | Mrs. Fanshawe | Mr. Weitz |
| 1632. | [1852–1857] | Mrs. Fanshawe | Mr. Weitz |
| 1633. | [1854–1862] | Mr. Faulkner | [            ] |
| 1634. | [1848–1851] | Mrs. John FitzGerald | Morgan Library |
| 1635. | [1846–1853] | John Forster | [            ] |
| 1636. | [1846–1856] | John Forster | Mr. Wells |
| 1637. | [1838–1840] 1 July | James Fraser | [            ] |
| 1638. | [1841–1846] | Thomas Fraser | Huntington Library |
| 1639. | [1860–1862] | Mrs. Hall | Huntington Library |
| 1640. | [1846–1856] | Mrs. Hawes | Mr. Pforzheimer |
| 1641. | [1856–1862] | Lady Hawes | Mr. Parrish |
| 1642. | [1846–1859] | Leigh Hunt | [            ] |
| 1643. | [1848–1863] | Mrs. Irvine | [            ] |
| 1644. | [1837–1843] | William Jerdan | Mr. Pforzheimer |

| No. | Date | Addressee | Owner or Depositary |
|---|---|---|---|
| 1645. | [1848–1850] | John Kenyon | Berg Collection |
| 1646. | [1862–1863] | Sir William Knighton | [ ] |
| 1647. | [1843–1863] | John Leech | Berg Collection |
| 1648. | [1854–1862] | William Leighton Leitch | Berg Collection |
| 1649. | [1862–1863] | Mrs. MacCullagh | Mr. Carlebach |
| 1650. | [1841–1852] | Mrs. Macready | Berg Collection |
| 1651. | [1846–1853] | Lord Mahon ? | [ ] |
| 1652. | [1856–1858] | Mrs. Martin | Berg Collection |
| 1653. | [1860–1862] | Mrs. Martin | Bodleian Library |
| 1654. | [1846–1851] | Richard Monckton Milnes ? | Widener Collection |
| 1655. | [1846–1853] | Sir William and Lady Molesworth | Huntington Library |
| 1656. | [1846–1851] | Mrs. Montgomery | Berg Collection |
| 1657. | [1848–1851] | Mrs. Montgomery | Mr. Pforzheimer |
| 1658. | [1848–1863] | Alfred Montgomery | Mr. Carlebach |
| 1659. | [1846–1855] | Lady Morley | Gimbel Brothers |
| 1660. | [1846–1851] | Lady Morgan ? | Huntington Library |
| 1661. | [1841–1846] | George William Nickisson | Mr. Carlebach |
| 1662. | [1848–1853] | Mrs. Olliffe | Fitzwilliam Museum |
| 1663. | [1853–1863] | Lady Olliffe | Mr. Carlebach |
| 1664. | [1853–1863] | Lady Olliffe | [ ] |
| 1665. | [1844–1850] | Joseph Parkes | New York Public Library |
| 1666. | [1856–1863] | Kate Perry | [ ] |
| 1667. | [1848–1854] 1 May | Sir Jonathan Frederick Pollock | [ ] |
| 1668. | [1857–1862] 27 April | Mr. Prideaux | Mr. Pforzheimer |
| 1669. | [1848–1852] 28 May | Mrs. Prinsep | Huntington Library |
| 1670. | [1841–1843] | Mrs. Procter | [Major Smith] |
| 1671. | [1844–1863] | Mrs. Procter | Berg Collection |
| 1672. | [1848–1863] 30 March | Bryan Waller Procter | [Major Smith] |
| 1673. | [1846–1853] | R. | Berg Collection |
| 1674. | [1854–1862] | A. Radcliffe | Mrs. Madigan |
| 1675. | [1849–1854] | Charlotte Ritchie | New York Public Library |
| 1676. | [1847–1851] 29 June | Samuel Rogers | [ ] |
| 1677. | [1846–1853] | Lady Rachel Russell | Huntington Library |
| 1678. | [1848–1863] | Laura Smith | [ ] |

| No. | Date | Addressee | Owner or Depositary |
|---|---|---|---|
| 1679. | [1854–1861] | James Spedding | Mr. Ball |
| 1680. | [1837–1843] | Clarkson Stanfield | [Mrs. Walton] |
| 1681. | [1848–1863] | Mrs. Sturgis | [          ] |
| 1682. | [1860–1863] | William Makepeace Thackeray Synge | [          ] |
| 1683. | [1853–1863] | William Webb Follett Synge | Mrs. Madigan |
| 1684. | [1853–1863] | William Webb Follett Synge | Mr. Carlebach |
| 1685. | [1853–1863] | William Webb Follett Synge | Mr. Carlebach |
| 1686. | [1860–1863] | William Webb Follett Synge | Mr. Carlebach |
| 1687. | [1841–1863] | Alfred Tennyson | [          ] |
| 1688. | [1848–1851] | Anne Thackeray | Mrs. Fuller |
| 1689. | [1854–1862] | Anne Thackeray | Mrs. Fuller |
| 1690. | [1849–1856] | Anne and Harriet Thackeray | Mrs. Fuller |
| 1691. | [1854–1860] | General Thackeray | Mr. Wells |
| 1692. | [1846–1863] | Mr. Tornow | Berg Collection |
| 1693. | [1861–1862] | Anthony Trollope | New York Public Library |
| 1694. | [1849–1863] | Horatio Waddington ? | Mr. Carlebach |
| 1695. | [1854–1862] | Mr. Waller | [          ] |
| 1696. | [1848–1852] | Mrs. Eliot Warburton | Huntington Library |
| 1697. | [1853–1863] | Samuel Ward | Boston Public Library |
| 1698. | [1857–1862] | Samuel Warren | Berg Collection |
| 1699. | [1848–1852] 10 October | Williams and Norgate | Berg Collection |
| 1700. | [1841–1846] | William Yardley | [          ] |
| 1701. | [1837–1840] | ? | Huntington Library |
| 1702. | [1841–1843] | ? | Berg Collection |
| 1703. | [1842–1851] | ? | Berg Collection |
| 1704. | [1846–1853] | ? | Berg Collection |
| 1705. | [1846–1853] | ? | Berg Collection |
| 1706. | [1847–1851] 4 January | ? | Mr. Carlebach |
| 1707. | [1848–1863] | ? | Berg Collection |
| 1708. | [1850–1853] | ? | Berg Collection |
| 1709. | [1854–1861] 2 June | ? | Retz and Storm |
| 1710. | [1856–1862] | ? | Berg Collection |
| 1711. | [1857–1863] | ? | Berg Collection |
| 1712. | [1860–1862] | ? | [          ] |

# A CHRONOLOGY OF THACKERAY'S LIFE

| | | |
|---|---|---|
| 1811 | July 18 | Born in Calcutta |
| 1812 | Jan. 3 | Baptized at St. John's Church, Calcutta |
| 1815 | Sept. 13 | Death of his father, Richmond Thackeray |
| 1817 | June 15 | Arrives in England from India |
| | Nov. | At the Arthurs' school in Southampton |
| | | Mrs. Richmond Thackeray marries Captain Henry Carmichael-Smyth |
| 1819 | | At the Turners' school in Chiswick |
| | | Captain and Mrs. Carmichael-Smyth return to England |
| 1822 | Jan. | Enters Charterhouse School in London |
| | Aug. 7 | Major Carmichael-Smyth becomes Governor of Addiscombe |
| 1824 | April 6 | Major Carmichael-Smyth resigns the governorship of Addiscombe |
| 1825 | | Becomes a day boy at Charterhouse School, boarding with Mrs. Boyes |
| | | The Carmichael-Smyths move to Larkbeare, near Ottery St. Mary's, in Devon |
| 1828 | April 16 | Leaves Charterhouse School |
| | May-June | Ill at Larkbeare |
| 1829 | Feb. | Matriculates at Trinity College, Cambridge |
| | July-Sept. | Vacations in Paris |
| 1830 | April | Surreptitious visit to FitzGerald in Paris |
| | June | Leaves Cambridge after losing £1,500 at play |
| 1831 | July to March | In Germany, chiefly at Weimar |
| | June 3 | Admitted to the Middle Temple |
| 1832 | June-July | In Devon and Cornwall electioneering for Charles Buller |
| | July 31–Nov. 25 | In France, chiefly at Paris |
| 1833 | Jan. | In London at 5 Essex Court, engaged in bill-discounting |
| | May | Becomes part owner of *The National Standard* |
| | June-Aug. | Paris correspondent of *The National Standard* |
| | Oct.-Nov. | Studies art in Paris |
| | | Loses the bulk of his fortune in the failure of an Indian bank |

| | | |
|---|---|---|
| 1834 | Feb. 1 | Issues the last number of *The National Standard* |
| | Sept. | Settles in Paris to study art |
| 1835 | | Major and Mrs. Carmichael-Smyth move from Larkbeare to 18 Albion Street, London |
| | | Meets Isabella Shawe |
| 1836 | April | Publication of *Flore et Zéphyr* |
| | Aug. 20 | Marries Isabella Shawe at the British Embassy in Paris |
| | Sept. 19 | First article as Paris correspondent of *The Constitutional* published |
| 1837 | March | Settles in London at 18 Albion Street |
| | June 9 | Birth of Anne Isabella Thackeray (later Lady Ritchie) |
| | July 1 | Issues last number of *The Constitutional* |
| | Nov. | First installment of *The Yellowplush Correspondence* appears in *Fraser's Magazine* |
| 1838 | | Moves his household to 13 Great Coram Street |
| | May | First installment of *Catherine* appears in *Fraser's Magazine* |
| | July 9 | Birth of Jane Thackeray |
| 1839 | March 14 | Death of Jane Thackeray |
| 1840 | May 27 | Birth of Harriet Marian Thackeray (later Mrs. Leslie Stephen) |
| | June | First installment of *A Shabby Genteel Story* appears in *Fraser's Magazine* |
| | July | Publication of *The Paris Sketch Book* |
| | Aug. 1?–16 | Travelling in Belgium alone |
| | Aug. 20–Sept. 6 | With his family in Margate |
| | Sept. 13? | His wife's insanity is revealed when she attempts to drown herself *en route* from London to Cork |
| | Sept. 15–Oct. 9 | With his family in Cork, living near Mrs. Shawe |
| | Oct.–Nov. | Takes his family to Paris by way of Clifton and London |
| | Nov. | Places his wife in Esquirol's *Maison de Santé* |
| 1841 | Jan. | Publication of *The Second Funeral of Napoleon* |
| | April 5 | Removes his wife from Esquirol's *Maison de Santé* |
| | May | Entrusts his wife to a nurse |
| | June 25–July 20 | Visits John Bowes in South Durham and Milnes in Yorkshire |
| | Aug.–Oct. | With his wife at a sanatorium near Boppard on the Rhine |
| | Sept. | First installment of *The Great Hoggarty Diamond* appears in *Fraser's Magazine* |

| 1842 | Jan.? | Meets Mrs. Brookfield |
| | Feb. 9 | Places his wife with Dr. Puzin at Chaillot |
| | May | Living at 13 Great Coram Street with Colonel and Mrs. Carmichael |
| | June 18 | First identified contribution to *Punch* |
| | July 4–Nov. 1 | In Ireland |
| 1843 | April | Gives up 13 Great Coram Street |
| | May | Publication of *The Irish Sketch Book* |
| | Aug. 4–30 | Visits the Low Countries with Stevens |
| | Dec. | Takes rooms at 27 Jermyn Street |
| 1844 | Jan. | First installment of *Barry Lyndon* appears in *Fraser's Magazine* |
| | Aug. 22 | Leaves from Southampton on a tour of the Mediterranean |
| | Nov. 26 | Arrives in Rome from Egypt |
| | Dec. | Final installment of *Barry Lyndon* appears in *Fraser's Magazine* |
| 1845 | Feb. | Returns to London from Rome |
| | April | Moves from 27 Jermyn Street to 88 St. James's Street |
| | May | Early chapters of *Vanity Fair* in Colburn's hands |
| | June | Mrs. Carmichael-Smyth and his children visit him in London |
| | Oct. | His wife is brought to England and placed in the care of Mrs. Bakewell in Camberwell |
| 1846 | Jan. | Publication of *Notes of a Journey from Cornhill to Grand Cairo* |
| | March 7 | First installment of *The Book of Snobs* appears in *Punch* |
| | June | Moves to 13 Young Street, Kensington |
| | Sept. | His children come to live with him in London |
| | Dec. | Publication of *Mrs. Perkins's Ball* |
| 1847 | Jan. | First number of *Vanity Fair* appears |
| | Feb. 2 | Brookfield protests against the warmth of his affection for Mrs. Brookfield |
| | Feb. 7 | Final installment of *The Book of Snobs* appears in *Punch* |
| | June | "False as Hell" quarrel with Forster |
| | Dec. | Publication of *Our Street* |
| 1848 | April | The Brookfields settle at 15 Portman Street, where Harry Hallam comes to live with them later in the year |
| | June 29 | *Vanity Fair* finished |
| | July 26–Aug. 19 | Travelling on the continent alone |
| | Aug. 3 | Begins *Pendennis* |

| | | |
|---|---|---|
| | Oct. | Major and Mrs. Carmichael-Smyth visit him in London |
| | Oct. 25?–30 | With Mrs. Brookfield at Clevedon Court |
| | Nov. | First number of *Pendennis* appears |
| | Dec. | Publication of *Dr. Birch and his Young Friends* |
| 1849 | Jan. 3 | Henry Hallam, Sr. remonstrates against his intimacy with Mrs. Brookfield |
| | Jan. 31–Feb. 14 | In Paris |
| | April–Nov. | Major and Mrs. Carmichael-Smyth visit England and Wales |
| | July 20?–23 | With Mrs. Brookfield at Ryde on the Isle of Wight |
| | Aug. 30–Sept. 13 | In Paris |
| | Sept. 17–Nov. | Serious illness followed by slow convalescence (*Pendennis* not published between October and December) |
| | Dec. | Publication of *Rebecca and Rowena* |
| 1850 | Jan. 3–8 | "Dignity of Literature" controversy |
| | Feb. 26 | Birth of Magdalene Brookfield |
| | Mar. 5–23 | In Paris |
| | March | Mrs. Carmichael-Smyth visits London |
| | July 4–11 | At Dieppe |
| | Aug. 4?–20 | With Mrs. Brookfield at Southampton |
| | Aug. 24–Sept. 19? | Travelling alone on the continent |
| | Oct. 4–11 | At the Grange |
| | Nov. 26 | *Pendennis* finished |
| | Dec. | Reading for *The English Humourists* |
| | Dec. | Publication of *The Kickleburys on the Rhine* |
| 1851 | Jan. 8–Feb. 7 | With his daughters in Paris |
| | Mar. | The Brookfields move to 64 Cadogan Place |
| | May 22–July 3 | Lectures on *The English Humourists* in London |
| | July 10–Aug. 22? | Travelling on the continent with his daughters |
| | Aug. | Begins *Esmond* |
| | Sept. 23? | Breaks with the Brookfields |
| | Sept. 24–Oct. 9 | Travelling in the country alone |
| | Oct. 29 | Sees the Brookfields at the Grange |
| | Nov. 5 | The Brookfields leave for Madeira |
| | Nov. 14–Dec. 2 | Lectures in Cambridge and Oxford |
| | Dec. 8–24? | Lectures in Scotland |
| | Dec. | Resigns from *Punch* (to which, however, he contributes a few more papers in 1853 and 1854) |
| 1852 | Jan. | Lectures in London |
| | April | Lectures in Scotland |
| | May | The Brookfields return to England |
| | May 28 | *Esmond* finished |
| | June 14–Aug. 5 | Travelling alone on the continent |

|      |                    |                                                                                 |
|------|--------------------|---------------------------------------------------------------------------------|
|      | Sept. 28–Oct. 15   | Lectures at Manchester and Liverpool                                            |
|      | Oct.               | Publication of *Esmond*                                                         |
|      | Oct. 30–Nov. 12    | Sails from Liverpool to Boston on the *Canada*                                  |
|      | Nov. 16–Dec. 20    | Lectures in New York and meets the Baxters                                      |
|      | Dec. 20 to }       | Lectures in Boston and Providence                                               |
| 1853 | Jan. 13 }          |                                                                                 |
|      | Jan. 15–28         | Lectures in Philadelphia                                                        |
|      | Jan. 31            | First delivers "Charity and Humour" in New York                                 |
|      | Feb. 7–26          | Lectures in Baltimore and Washington                                            |
|      | Feb. 28–April 1    | Lectures in the South (chiefly at Richmond, Charleston, and Savannah)           |
|      | March 18           | Birth of Arthur Montagu Brookfield                                              |
|      | April 2–20         | In New York                                                                     |
|      | April 20–May 2     | Sails from New York to Liverpool on the *Europa*                               |
|      | May 2–July 6       | In London and Paris                                                             |
|      | July 6–Aug. 30     | Travelling in Germany and Switzerland with his daughters                        |
|      | July 9             | Begins *The Newcomes*                                                           |
|      | Aug. 31–Nov. 27    | In London and Paris                                                             |
|      | Oct.               | First number of *The Newcomes* appears                                         |
|      | Nov. 27–Dec. 3     | Travels to Rome with his daughters                                              |
|      | Dec. 3 to }        | Ill at Rome (and henceforth never really well)                                  |
| 1854 | Feb. 8 }           |                                                                                 |
|      | Jan.               | Begins *The Rose and the Ring*                                                  |
|      | Feb. 9–March 30    | In Naples                                                                       |
|      | March 1–16         | His daughters sick with scarletina                                              |
|      | March 30–April 21  | Travels to London by way of Paris                                               |
|      | May 18             | Moves to 36 Onslow Square, Brompton                                             |
|      | June 26–Sept. 10   | At the Château Brecquerecque, Boulogne, with his daughters and the Carmichael-Smyths (apart from several short trips) |
|      | Nov. 1             | *The Rose and the Ring* finished                                               |
|      | Nov. 12–29         | In Paris                                                                        |
|      | Dec.               | Publication of *The Rose and the Ring*                                         |
| 1855 | Jan.               | His *Punch* friends offended by his article on Leech in *The Quarterly Review* |
|      | Jan.               | In Paris with his daughters                                                     |
|      | June 16–July 27    | At Paris and travelling in Germany                                              |
|      | June 28            | *The Newcomes* finished                                                        |
|      | Aug.–Oct.          | Writes *The Four Georges*                                                       |
|      | Oct. 13–25         | Sails from Liverpool to Boston on the *Africa*                                 |
|      | Oct. 28–Dec. 4     | Lectures on *The Four Georges* in New York                                     |
|      | Dec. 6–25          | Lectures in Boston and Providence                                               |
|      | Dec. 12            | Marriage of Sally Baxter to Frank Hampton                                       |
|      | Dec. 26–28         | Lectures in Albany and Buffalo                                                  |

| | | |
|---|---|---|
| 1856 | Jan. 2–7 | Lectures in Philadelphia |
| | Jan. 8–27 | Lectures in Baltimore and Richmond |
| | Jan. 29–Feb. 19? | Lectures in Charleston, Augusta, and Savannah |
| | Feb. 22–March 18 | Lectures in Macon, Mobile, and New Orleans |
| | March 26–31? | Lectures in St. Louis and Cincinnati |
| | April 4–25 | In New York and Philadelphia |
| | April 25–May 8 | Sails from New York to Liverpool on the *Baltic* |
| | July | Lectures privately in London |
| | July 29 | Begins *The Virginians* (which he shortly abandons, not returning to it until May, 1857) |
| | Aug. 14–Sept. 4 | Travelling on the continent with his daughters |
| | Sept. 5–Oct. 6 | In Paris |
| | Oct. 21–28 | In Paris |
| | Nov. 4–Dec. 20 | Lectures in Scotland and the north of England |
| 1857 | Jan.–Feb. | Lectures in London and southern England |
| | Feb.–March | Lectures in the north of England and Scotland |
| | April–May | Lectures in southern and central England |
| | July 8–21 | Defeated in a parliamentary election for the City of Oxford |
| | Sept. | In Hamburg |
| | Nov. | First number of *The Virginians* appears |
| 1858 | June 12 | Edmund Yates publishes an offensive article on him in *Town Talk*, precipitating the "Garrick Club Affair" |
| | July 10 | Yates is expelled from the Garrick Club |
| | July 13–Aug. 17 | Travelling on the continent |
| | Sept. | In Paris |
| | Nov. | In Paris |
| | Dec. 5 | Yates brings suit against the Garrick Club |
| | Dec. and Jan. } | In Paris |
| 1859. | | |
| | Feb. 19 | Agrees to write serials for *The Cornhill Magazine* |
| | March | Yates abandons his suit against the Garrick Club |
| | Aug.? | Accepts editorship of *The Cornhill Magazine* |
| | Sept. 7 | *The Virginians* finished |
| | Sept.–Oct. 16 | Travelling on the continent with his daughters |
| 1860 | Jan. | Initial number of *The Cornhill Magazine* appears, including his first *Roundabout Paper* and the opening installment of *Lovel the Widower* |
| | Jan. | In Paris |
| | March 8 | Buys 2 Palace Green, Kensington |
| | Sept. | Travelling on the continent with his daughters |
| 1861 | Jan. | First installment of *Philip* appears in *The Cornhill Magazine* |
| | Sept. | In Paris |
| | Sept. 9 | Death of Major Carmichael-Smyth |

| | | |
|---|---|---|
| 1862 | March 6 | Resigns editorship of *The Cornhill Magazine* |
| | March 31 | Moves to 2 Palace Green, Kensington |
| | April | In Paris |
| | July 3 | *Philip* finished |
| | Sept. | In Paris |
| 1863 | April 6?–16 | Visits Yorkshire with his daughters |
| | April 25 | Attack in *The Athenæum* on Anne Thackeray's *Story of Elizabeth*, which leads to his trouble with the National Shakespeare Committee |
| | May | Begins *Denis Duval* |
| | Aug. 17–27 | In Belgium and France |
| | Nov. | His last *Roundabout Paper* appears in *The Cornhill Magazine* |
| | Dec. 24 | Death |
| | Dec. 29 | Burial in Kensal Green Cemetery |

# CUE-TITLES AND SYMBOLS

| | |
|---|---|
| *American Family* | Lucy W. Baxter ed., *Thackeray's Letters to an American Family*, New York, 1904. |
| *Biographical Intro-ductions* | Lady Ritchie's Biographical Introductions to *The Works of William Makepeace Thackeray*, London, 1898–1899. |
| *Centenary Biograph-ical Introductions* | Lady Ritchie's Biographical Introductions to *The Works of William Makepeace Thackeray*, London, 1910–1911. |
| *Centenary Works* | The "Centenary" edition of *The Works of William Makepeace Thackeray*, London, 1910–1911, 26 volumes. |
| *Chapters* | Lady Ritchie, *Chapters from Some Unwritten Memoirs*, London, 1894. |
| *Collection of Letters* | Mrs. Brookfield ed., *A Collection of Letters of Thackeray*, New York, 1887. |
| *Dr. Brown* | John Brown and D. W. Forrest ed., *Letters of Dr. John Brown*, London, 1907. |
| *Genealogy* | A Thackeray genealogy, in Volume IV of the present work. |
| *Goodyear Catalogue* | Catalogue of the sale of Mr. A. C. Goodyear's collection of autograph letters at the Anderson Galleries, February 1–2, 1927. |
| *Howe Proofs* | Proofs of a (never published) catalogue of the Thackeray collection formed by the late W. T. H. Howe. |
| *Lambert Catalogue* | Catalogue of the sale of Major William H. Lambert's collection of Thackerayana at the Metropolitan Art Association, February 25–27, 1914. |
| *Memoranda* | Memoranda concerning certain persons who figure in Thackeray's correspondence, pages lxxxi–clxxiii of the present volume. |
| *Memorials* | Mrs. Richard Pryme and Mrs. William Bayne, *Memorials of the Thackeray Family*, London, 1879, privately printed. |
| *Mrs. Brookfield* | Charles and Frances Brookfield, *Mrs. Brookfield and her Circle*, New York, 1905, 2 volumes numbered as one. |

| | |
|---|---|
| *Ritchies in India* | Gerald Ritchie, *The Ritchies in India*, London, 1920. |
| *Thackeray and his Daughter* | Hester Thackeray Ritchie (later Mrs. Fuller) ed., *Thackeray and his Daughter*, New York, 1924. |
| *Thackeray in the United States* | General James Grant Wilson, *Thackeray in the United States*, London, 1904, 2 volumes. |
| *Works* | The "Biographical" edition of *The Works of William Makepeace Thackeray*, London, 1898–1899, 13 volumes. |
| ⟨ ⟩ | Conjectural restoration by the editor where the text is irrecoverably mutilated. |
| ⟨. . .⟩ | A gap in the text caused by irrecoverable mutilation, the extent of which is indicated in the notes. |
| . . . | A gap in the text where the letter comes from a printed source. |
| * * * | The beginning or end of a fragment in letters which have survived only in part. |
| [ ] | Matter supplied by the editor. |
| † † | Matter overscored but recovered. |
| { } | Matter lined out. |

### NOTE

Because of the mechanical difficulties involved, cross references in this edition have had to be to letters by number rather than to page and volume. *These references must be understood to include the footnotes attached to the letter in question.*

# INTRODUCTION

These volumes, published eighty years after Thackeray's death, form the first collected edition of his correspondence. Such apparent neglect of an important part of the production of a writer who throughout this period has enjoyed the devotion of the general reader as well as the good word of the critics cannot be attributed to a want of interest in his letters, which have long had their niche among the classics of epistolary literature. It derives instead from Thackeray's injunction to his older daughter that no life be written of him, a prohibition that she inevitably extended to his letters as the indispensable foundation of intimate biography. Though Lady Ritchie, as we shall see, was at last constrained by the flood of uninformed and misleading print about her father to relax the restriction he had placed upon her, only a small part of his correspondence was printed while she lived. Her children, Mrs. Richard Fuller and Mr. W. T. D. Ritchie, have come to feel that Thackeray now belongs to literature rather than to his family; and wishing to dispel the cloud of mystery that has made him seem the most enigmatic personality among the great Victorians, they have sought by authorizing this comprehensive collection of his letters to "pour on misty doubt resistless day."

## THE EARLIER HISTORY OF THACKERAY'S LETTERS

The first considerable group of Thackeray's letters to achieve publication was a selection from those that he wrote to Mrs. Brookfield. Sorely in need of money for her children as well as for herself, Mrs. Brookfield sold the privilege of printing a part of Thackeray's correspondence with her to Charles Scribner's Sons of New York in 1887. *A Collection of Letters of Thackeray* accordingly appeared in *Scribner's Magazine* between April and October, 1887, and was published in book form during the same year. Though the publishers announce in their preface that they "have enjoyed the privilege of advice and assistance from Mr. James

Russell Lowell," an examination of the manuscript of their volume, which is still in Scribner's files, reveals that it was entirely prepared by Mrs. Brookfield. Her work affords little opportunity for praise. She was of course fully justified in excising any portions of Thackeray's letters that might offend living persons, but one is at a loss to understand why hardly a letter in her manuscript is accurately transcribed or correctly dated. Happily no degree of editorial incompetence could obscure the excellence of her material, and *A Collection of Letters of Thackeray*, which had great success on both sides of the Atlantic,[1] gave Thackeray a secure place among the great English letter writers. Sometime afterwards Mrs. Brookfield sold the letters included in her book, together with a number of others, to Augustine Daly, from whom they passed in 1900 to their permanent home in the Pierpont Morgan Library.

Encouraged, perhaps, by the success of Mrs. Brookfield's venture and convinced of the need for an authentic account of her father's life, Lady Ritchie in 1898 and 1899 prepared a series of Biographical Introductions for a new edition of Thackeray's *Works*. These essays, which were revised and enlarged for the *Centenary Works* of 1910 and 1911, have been the starting point for all subsequent lives of Thackeray. They contain a great many of his letters, chosen chiefly from his correspondence with his family and with Mrs. Procter, but Lady Ritchie rarely prints these letters in full, for it was her practice to weave them, fragment by fragment, into her narrative.

The year 1904 added two further collections of Thackeray's letters to the printed record. General James Grant Wilson's two-volume *Thackeray in the United States*, which had grown out of a

---

[1] The book was printed in England by Smith, Elder and Company, then holders of the Thackeray copyrights, which had been made specifically to include unpublished letters. For the lively controversy between George Smith and Charles Brookfield which followed its English publication, see *The Standard* of November 30, 1887. In the American edition Lady Ritchie permitted Mrs. Brookfield to include in the preface a note from her which begins: "I am very glad to hear that you have made a satisfactory arrangement for publishing your selections from my Father's letters. I am of course unable myself by his expressed wish to do anything of the sort." But even this note, with its unmistakable implied rebuke, was omitted from the English edition.

pair of essays printed in *The Century Magazine* for December, 1901, and January, 1902, included more than a hundred letters dealing with Thackeray's American tours. And Lucy Baxter's *Thackeray's Letters to an American Family*, first printed in *The Century Magazine* between November, 1903, and March, 1904, and published as a book in October of the latter year, brought to light nearly the whole of Thackeray's correspondence with the Baxter family.

The next event is by all odds the most sensational in our brief chronicle. We have seen that the published letters from Thackeray to Mrs. Brookfield were acquired by J. Pierpont Morgan. But Mrs. Brookfield retained in her possession a number of more intimate, unpublished letters. Though she had desired her son Charles to burn these after her death, he instead sold them to a London agent. Their next purchaser was Major William H. Lambert of Philadelphia, to whom they came "still tied in a little package with a bit of faded ribbon." [2] Meantime, a complementary packet of Thackeray's letters had also gone astray. Though part of Thackeray's correspondence with Mrs. Elliot and Kate Perry was given to the Elliot family, most of it was kept by Miss Perry, who lived on till she was almost ninety.

The last time I saw her [writes Lady Ritchie, evidently about 1900] she said to me that she had some letters of my father's which she valued above most of her possessions. She said if I really wished it she would give them to me. But she looked so regretful that I said: 'Why of course not, much the best is to burn them yourself, for I have my own letters, and these were for you.' She said that was what she felt and she had left instructions for Mary to burn them. Mary was her faithful maid to whom she left everything. Mary unfortunately died suddenly and some lodging-house keepers came in for the last two years, who managed the house, looked after Miss Perry, and at her death announced that she had signed a will revoking any previous legacies to friends and leaving pictures and everything she had to them, and that she had specially given them the letters. I wrote to Mr. Reginald Smith to try and buy them back from this man. Sir Gerald, a nephew, thought of going to law, but the expense and difficulty was so great that he preferred to let the money

[2] See the letters of Frederick S. Dickson and W. Gordon McCabe to *The New York Sun* of February 3, 1914.

and furniture go. Miss Perry had been wanting at times, and then again she was herself at others, so that it was a most difficult case.[3]

These letters, too, found their way into Major Lambert's hands. Though he does not appear to have felt any compulsion to burn his treasures, he did maintain a discreet silence about them, and in 1914 when the whole story of the Brookfield Affair was revealed for the first time in the generous excerpts from Thackeray's letters printed in the auction catalogue for Major Lambert's collection, the literary world was taken altogether by surprise. The press observed a decent decorum for the most part, but there were exceptions to this praiseworthy restraint, which go far to explain Thackeray's motives for wishing to remain without a biographer. In *The New York Times's* Sunday supplement of February 8, for example, a lavishly illustrated page devoted to quotations from the *Lambert Catalogue* is headed: "SECRET OF THACKERAY'S HOPELESS LOVE NOW REVEALED: His Lifelong Passion for Mrs. Brookfield Hitherto Supposed to Be Only His Friend, Discovered Through His Heretofore Unpublished Letters — How It Embittered His Relationship with Her Husband." Major Lambert's Brookfield and Elliot-Perry letters were bought by Mr. A. C. Goodyear, and at the sale of Mr. Goodyear's collection in 1927 they passed to Dr. A. S. W. Rosenbach, who still owns them.

The last volume to claim our attention appeared in 1924 under the editorship of Mrs. Fuller (then Miss Ritchie). Entitled *Letters of Anne Thackeray Ritchie* in England and *Thackeray and his Daughter* in the United States, it includes a number of Thackeray's letters as well as a selection from his daughter's correspondence. The section of the book devoted to Thackeray was first published in *Harper's Magazine* between December, 1923, and March, 1924.

It will be understood that I have described only the principal collections of Thackeray's correspondence. Smaller groups of his letters have appeared in a variety of books, brochures, magazines, and newspapers, which it would be tedious to enumerate. Indeed, the haphazard manner in which his correspondence has found its

---

[3] Quoted from the *Lambert Catalogue*, p. 51, where Lady Ritchie's letter is mistakenly assigned to 1890.

way into print has given Thackeray's readers ample ground for complaint. Enough was published to show how good the whole must be, but much of what had appeared was not easily accessible, and a still larger part remained unpublished. Confronted by this confused and discouraging picture, an occasional Thackerayan may have taken comfort from the prescient words of George Saintsbury:

Time lifts a great many (though not perhaps all) the restraints upon publication . . . and it will probably be possible some day for posterity to possess, not only a collected body of the now scattered Thackeray letters, but a considerably larger one than has ever appeared even in extracts and catalogues. It will be an addition to our Epistolary Library which can bear comparison with any previous occupant of those shelves: and one of the books which deserve, in a very peculiar sense, the hackneyed praise of being 'as good as a novel.' For it will be almost the equivalent of an additional novel of its author's own — a *William Makepeace Thackeray* in the familiar novel-form of title, and in the old Richardsonian form of contents — but oh! how different from anything of Richardson's. . . .[4]

### THE PRESENT EDITION

Aware that an opportunity such as rarely offers itself to a literary scholar awaited the editor of Thackeray's letters, it was with great eagerness that I accepted this trust from Mrs. Fuller during a visit to England in the summer of 1939. Since I had shortly to return to the United States, we agreed that I should visit England again in the spring of the following year to collect my materials. The impracticability of our plan became evident on September 3, the date on which I chanced to sail for New York from a blacked-out Naples, and my work from beginning to end has been done in the United States. I trust that this fact will serve to excuse certain of the more patent deficiencies in text and commentary that the trained eye will detect in these volumes. Apart from Thackeray's correspondence with his family and a few other letters from scattered sources, no English holdings are here represented, and I have depended in my notes exclusively on the resources of American libraries.

[4] *A Letter Book* (London, 1922), pp. 66–67.

This edition has notwithstanding attained to a degree of inclusiveness that I hardly anticipated. Upon first assembling my manuscript, indeed, I bethought myself with some uneasiness that it could be accurately described in lines (slightly altered) of Wordsworth, drawn from an ominous context:

> I've measured it from side to side:
> 'Tis three feet long and one foot wide.

I have been able to print some 1,600 of Thackeray's letters, more than 100 letters to and about him (some of great biographical interest), and nineteen of his diaries and account books. Three-fifths of his letters are altogether unpublished, while less than a fourth have previously appeared in their entirety. Of his six principal correspondences, those with his family, with Edward Fitz-Gerald, with Mrs. Procter, and with the Baxters are printed as completely as their survival permits; that with the Brookfields appears with only a few omissions; and a substantial part of that with Mrs. Elliot and Kate Perry is also included.[5] Thus the very great majority of Thackeray's important letters are printed, and printed for the first time, in these volumes. But it would be idle to assert that this edition is in any sense definitive. My search of auction records has given me knowledge of several hundred letters the originals of which I have not traced, and English collections remain largely unexplored.

There is a massive body of precedent today to control the editing of literary correspondence. Yet each large body of material presents its peculiar problems, and I offer no apology for the following summary of editorial principles.

*Text.* The letters in this edition have been transcribed for the most part from photostats which have since been placed on permanent deposit in the Harvard College Library, though I have not

---

[5] The missing letters to Mrs. Brookfield, Mrs. Elliot, and Kate Perry belong for the most part to Dr. Rosenbach. But I have been able to print a number of the letters to Mrs. Brookfield in his possession from transcripts made by Mrs. Fuller some years ago, and the remaining letters to Mrs. Brookfield as well as all of those to Mrs. Elliot and Kate Perry are represented by sizable excerpts from the *Lambert* and *Goodyear Catalogues*, in Appendix XXVI.

hesitated to use what printed sources are available for those letters of which the originals could not be traced. Where I had photostats, I have printed a literal text. Thackeray, the most informal of letter writers, was a past master at shaping his sentences in the precise contour of his thoughts by oddities of punctuation and orthography and by whimsical distortions of words not unlike Swift's "little language" in the *Journal to Stella*. Not to reproduce these peculiarities faithfully would be to falsify the tone and blur the meaning of his letters. I have consulted the reader's convenience, however, in some minor normalizations: all new paragraphs have been indented, though Thackeray often indicates paragraphing merely by a wide break between sentences; all postscripts are printed below the body of the letter, no matter where they appear in the original; all symbols for *and* are transcribed by &; and most dashes and colons under superior letters are printed as dots.

*Dating.* Thackeray rarely dated his letters in full; he often failed to give any indication of date whatsoever; and the dates he did supply were not always accurate. Consequently the task of arranging his correspondence in chronological order was a difficult one, resembling nothing so much as putting together a huge jigsaw puzzle of which half the pieces are missing. Postmarks were helpful in many instances, and internal evidence provided a precise date in many more. But a number of short notes remained that could not be placed within a year, and these have been arranged by correspondents under the heading "Letters of Uncertain Date."

*Headnotes.* Taken together, the list of letters and headnotes supply the address (if any); the postmarks (if any), only the first and last being noted where there are more than two; the place and extent of first previous publication and of subsequent publications in which additional matter was included; the source of the text here printed; and the location of the original. Where letters were published in book form shortly after they appeared in magazines, I have judged it more convenient to give my references to the book. To the statement "hitherto unpublished," wherever it occurs, I must add the qualifying phrase, "to the best of my knowledge." If no source is indicated for the text, as is true of the great majority of letters, it has been transcribed from a photostat now on deposit in the Harvard College Library.

*Memoranda and Footnotes*. The commentary in these volumes is considerably more extensive than is usual in editions of nineteenth century correspondence. I cannot hope to give satisfaction to those who find all annotation distracting, who are prompted by any display of minute information to cry *in tenui labor!*, or who resent editorial reminders of facts with which they happen already to be acquainted. But I believe that my scheme of annotation will seem sufficiently warranted to readers who are mindful of the place this edition occupies in the development of Thackeray scholarship.

For reasons that have been stated, Thackeray had no Boswell, no Lockhart, no Forster — no contemporary who essayed a comprehensive narrative of his life. Even Lady Ritchie, who most nearly supplied this deficiency in her Biographical Introductions and in that minor classic, *Chapters from Some Unwritten Memoirs*, deals with only one aspect of her father's career. Later biographers, among whom Lewis Melville and Mr. Malcolm Elwin may be particularly mentioned, based their books on a fraction of Thackeray's correspondence and had consequently to limit themselves to partial portraits.

There being no standard biography to which I could refer the reader, I have judged it part of my task to provide a commentary that would supplement as well as explain Thackeray's letters. In the *Memoranda* to this edition I have endeavored to give succinct accounts of the principal persons who figured in Thackeray's life, and in the notes I have tried to bring together the significant primary source material about him scattered through hundreds of Victorian memoirs, magazines, and newspapers. The re-creation of any personality, after all, is made possible by the accumulation of many kinds of *petits faits vrais*, and to see Thackeray in the round, we must know what his contemporaries wrote about him, as well as what he wrote about himself.

The letters themselves, dealing as they do with the activities of an astonishingly varied and busy life, required a good deal of glossing. I soon abandoned hope of identifying everyone who appears in them. The poet may have his Melchizedek and Ucalegon, but the editor's peace of mind is disturbed by a hundred shadowy worthies who grew up and perished, as the summer fly. If the abundance of genealogical information arouses the impatience of the democratic reader, I can only plead that in Victorian times a man's birth was often the most important thing about him. Was it not Mr. Sparsit's supreme distinction to have been a Powler? Most of the books I have used are specifically mentioned in the notes, but I must here record a general indebtedness to the following reference works: Frederic Boase's *Modern English Biography*; the various editions of Burke's *Peerage* and *Landed Gentry*; G. E. C.'s *Complete Peerage*, both in the first edition and, insofar as it has progressed, in the revision of the Hon. Vicary Gibbs; *The Dictionary of American Biography*; *The Dictionary of National Biography*; Pierre Larousse's *Grand dictionnaire universel du XIXᵉ siècle* and the *Larousse du XXᵉ siècle*; Henry Richards Luard's *Graduati Cantabrigienses*; and W. D. Parish's *List of Carthusians*.

Carlyle, who was an experienced but not a remarkably scrupulous scholar, even by Victorian standards, described editing as "literary navvy work," and there are hours when the modern editor, of whom so much more diligence is expected, must confess to intense weariness of the flesh. But to have the job done is in the end reward enough, and I plan after the war to supplement this edition with a volume of Thackeray's unpublished letters in English collections. Before I say farewell to Thackeray, I hope also to write his biography, attempting a somewhat more ambitious treatment than was possible before the publication of his correspondence.

### ACKNOWLEDGMENTS

I come finally to the pleasant duty of thanking the persons whose generosity has made this edition possible. Though limitations of space restrict me for the most part to a roll-call, I assure those to whom I am indebted that my acknowledgments are only in appearance perfunctory. I question if any editor has had more reason to be grateful for the kindness with which he has been received or the readiness with which he has been assisted.

My primary obligation is to Mrs. Fuller, who (with Mr. Ritchie) authorized the preparation of these volumes and permitted me to include in them all of Thackeray's letters to his family, the essential nucleus of any comprehensive collection of his correspondence. She has also given me more than a hundred transcripts of her grandfather's letters — including nearly all of those to Mrs. Procter — of which the originals are not accessible, and she has supplied me with a rich store of illustrations from which to choose. My notes embody many valuable details of family history that she has communicated to me, and I have been cheered throughout my work by her interest and encouragement.

If this edition owes its very existence to Mrs. Fuller, its breadth of scope may in large measure be attributed to the concentration of a substantial portion of Thackeray's extant correspondence in four American collections. The most extensive of these accumulations is that in the Berg Collection of the New York Public Library, which includes the Thackeray holdings formerly belonging to Mr. Owen D. Young and to the late W. T. H. Howe. The Henry E. Huntington Library and Art Gallery has fewer letters but possesses a wealth of Thackeray drawings. In the Pierpont Morgan Library are the great majority of Thackeray's letters to Mrs. Brookfield. Mr. Herbert Carlebach, faithful to an enthusiasm conceived while a student of Professor Charles Townsend Copeland at Harvard, has assembled an admirably selected Thackeray collection that is rich in manuscript material. My profound thanks are due to the authorities of the New York Public Library, the Huntington Library, and the Morgan Library, and to Mr. Carlebach and Mr. Young (who allowed me to have photostats made of many of his letters before they passed from his possession), and I wish particularly to express my gratitude to Dr. John Gordan for many services during his term as Curator of the Berg Collection.

For the use of original letters and for certain of my illustrations I have also to thank:

(1) The following collectors: Mr. George Arents, Mr. E.

Arthur Ball, Mr. Oliver Barrett, Messrs. John and Alexander Becher, Mr. William D. Blatner, Mr. Charles Bromback, Mr. Edward Browning, Mr. John W. Castles, Mr. A. H. Clough, Mr. J. A. Waley Cohen, Dr. Ellsworth Eliot, Mr. William M. Elkins, Mr. R. D. H. Emerson, the late Howard Eric, Miss Maude Frank, Mrs. Emma B. Gibson, Mr. A. C. Goodyear, Mrs. Sherman Haight, Mr. Frank Hogan, Miss Elizabeth Hudson, Mr. Josiah K. Lilly, Jr., Mrs. George A. Martin, Dr. Robert Metzdorf, Mr. Morris Parrish, Mrs. Edward Pearson, Mr. Harry T. Peters, (Mrs.) Alice E. F. Plummer, Mrs. Sherburne Prescott, Dr. Herman T. Radin, Mr. John Hinsdale Scheide, Mr. Jacob H. Scheuer, Mr. Schuman, the Comte de Suzannet, Mrs. Theodore Tieken, Mr. Adrian Van Sinderen, Mr. Stanley Wilson, Mr. Ralph Wolf, and Mr. Craig Wylie.

(2) The authorities of the following institutions: the Bodleian Library, the Boston Public Library, Charterhouse School, the Drexel Institute, the Fitzwilliam Museum, the Folger Shakespeare Library, the Garrick Club, the Harvard College Library, the Haverford College Library, the Historical Society of Pennsylvania, the University of Iowa Libraries, the Lehigh University Library, the Massachusetts Historical Society, the Peabody Institute, the University of Rochester Library, the University of Texas Library, the Library of Trinity College, Cambridge, the Library of the University of California at Los Angeles, the Wake Forest College Library, and the Wellesley College Library.

(3) The following dealers in rare books and manuscripts: Miss Mary Benjamin, Mr. Bernard J. Beyer, Mr. Halpern of the Carnegie Bookshop, Colonel James F. Drake, Gimbel Brothers, Goodspeed's Book Store, Mr. Walter Hill, Mrs. Thomas F. Madigan, the Mayfair Bookshop, Mr. Michael Papantonio, Mr. Arthur Pforzheimer, Messrs. Retz and Storm, Dr. A. S. W. Rosenbach, Charles Scribner's Sons, Mr. J. Leonard Sessler, Mr. Leo Weitz, and Mr. Gabriel Wells.

(4) To this list should be added the names of Mrs. Livingston, who placed at my disposal the Thackeray letters and sketches in the Harry Elkins Widener Memorial Collection of the Harvard

College Library, and of Mr. Clarence S. Brigham, who supplied me with a photostat of a valuable letter from the Frank B. Bemis Estate.

Of the many friends who have helped me, there are some whose services I cannot pass by without specific mention. Dr. Robert W. Rogers undertook the laborious task of checking my transcripts of Thackeray's letters against the photostats from which they were made. I have profited by discussing the editing of Victorian documents with Professor Gordon S. Haight of Yale, who has come to my relief in certain perplexities of annotation. Dr. Robert Metzdorf of the University of Rochester, one of the most zealous of American Thackerayans, entrusted to me his large collection of auction catalogue clippings concerning Thackeray's letters. Professor William A. Jackson of Harvard has been a sage guide to the strange world of rare books. Miss Queenie Bilbo provided me with proofs of a (never published) catalogue, largely compiled by her, of the Howe Thackeray collection. Mrs. Edgar F. Wells served me for the better part of a year as an accurate and conscientious secretary. Dr. Dumas Malone and Mr. David Pottinger of the Harvard University Press have been the most agreeable and accommodating of publishers. Professor James B. Munn of Harvard has taken a lively interest in this edition from its inception, on more than one occasion giving me timely and tangible support, and latterly I have had the experienced and skilful aid of Professor George W. Sherburn of Harvard in obtaining publication subsidies for these volumes.

I have also to thank for assistance of various kinds Professor Fernand Baldensperger and Professor Douglas Bush of Harvard; Dr. Charles Macfie Campbell, Director of the Boston Psychopathic Hospital; Dr. Stanley Cobb, Psychiatrist in Chief, Massachusetts General Hospital; Mr. Willard Connely, Director of the American University Union; Dean William Clyde De Vane of Yale; Mr. Geoffrey Gomme; Miss Granniss of the Grolier Club; Professor Will T. Hale of Indiana University; Mr. Harzof; Dr. John Johnson, Printer to the University of Oxford; Dr. Chester M. Jones, Clinical Professor of Medicine at the Harvard Medical

School; Professor Percy W. Long, Secretary of the Modern Language Association of America; Professor John Livingston Lowes of Harvard; Professor Howard Foster Lowry of Princeton; Mr. William McCarthy of the Harvard College Library; Sir Humphrey Milford; Professor John Robert Moore of Indiana University; Mr. David Randall; Mr. Henry R. Robins; Dr. William Ruff; Professor Ralph L. Rusk of Columbia; the Savannah Unit of the Georgia Writers' Project; Professor and Mrs. Donald Smalley of Indiana University; Mr. J. L. Stokes, Librarian of Charterhouse School; Mr. Arthur Swann; Mr. James J. Talman, Librarian of the University of Western Ontario; Mr. Halsted Billings Van der Poel; Professor Karl Viëtor of Harvard; Mr. Orlando F. Weber, Jr.; Mr. C. C. Williamson, Director of the Columbia University Libraries; and Mr. Denys A. Winstanley, Vice-Master of Trinity College, Cambridge.

One of the solaces of an American scholar's labor is the cheerful and expert attention with which he meets in his country's great libraries. I have made much use of the American Antiquarian Society Library, the Grolier Club Library, the Henry E. Huntington Library, the Morgan Library, and the New York Public Library, but my principal obligation is to the staff of the Harvard College Library, and to Dr. Keyes D. Metcalf and Mr. Robert H. Haynes, Librarian and Assistant Librarian.

Since the editing of a large correspondence necessitates disbursements that cannot be sustained on a Harvard instructor's salary, I must make grateful acknowledgment of financial assistance from several sources. Dexter Travelling Scholarships from Harvard enabled me to devote the summers of 1939 and 1940 to collecting Thackeray's letters. Grants from the Joseph H. Clark Bequest of Harvard University, from the American Philosophical Society, and from various book funds of the Harvard College Library paid a large part of my editorial expenses. The Guggenheim Fellowship which I have held during the last seventeen months has permitted me to devote the whole of this period to my work, the completion of which would otherwise have been indefinitely postponed. It is appropriate that I should also record here my appreciation of the sympathetic and operative understanding which Mr. Henry Allen Moe, Secretary-General of the Guggenheim Foundation, has brought to bear on the financial problems of this edition.

Publication of these volumes has been made possible by subsidies from the American Council of Learned Societies (pursuant to the recommendation of the Research Committee of the Modern Language Association of America) and the Guggenheim Foundation, and by the generous gift of Mr. Roy E. Larsen, President of Time, Inc., and an Overseer of Harvard.

Words will hardly serve to repay my last debt of gratitude. It was to my friend and colleague Howard Mumford Jones that I turned first for advice after undertaking this edition. During the whole of its preparation his aid and comfort have been invaluable to me. And now, when circumstances prevent me from seeing my work through the press, he has himself assumed this infinitely onerous task.

G. N. R.

Cambridge, Massachusetts,
November, 1942.

In Dr. Ray's absence all references, citations and quotations have been checked against the originals wherever possible, the exceptions arising in the case of material inaccessible because of the war. The texts of the letters and diaries have also been verified in those instances wherein verification had not been made before Dr. Ray left for the Navy.

My own thanks are due to the patient and kindly staff of the Harvard College Library as also to that of the Houghton Library. The care and skill of three research assistants have also gone into the edition; and I acknowledge a special debt of gratitude to Miss Keith Glenn, Bessie Z. Jones, and Miss Cynthia Gano for their accurate and sympathetic help. Mistakes and errors there are bound to be; but Dr. Ray left us so superb a manuscript that these have been, we trust, reduced to a minimum.

HOWARD MUMFORD JONES

February 15, 1945

# MEMORANDA

## Concerning Certain Persons Who Figure in Thackeray's Correspondence

### ARCHDEACON ALLEN

"Anyone who knew [John Allen] and has studied 'Vanity Fair,'" writes the Archdeacon's son-in-law and biographer, "will recognize his portrait, *mutatis mutandis,* in the simple-minded, chivalrous Major Dobbin." [1] This judgment is confirmed by Lady Ritchie, who goes on to point out the resemblance between Allen — a tall, dark, gaunt, rather homely man, who was careless about his dress — and Thackeray's portraits of Dobbin in later life. [2] Even without such signposts one would unfailingly be reminded of Dobbin by what Thackeray says of Allen in his letters, and as one studies the Archdeacon's life, all doubt concerning his kinship with Amelia's faithful lover disappears. The key to Allen's character, as to Dobbin's, was a contempt for the selfish maxims of Vanity Fair, an unremitting effort to guide his life by Christian precept rather than by worldly prudence. Realizing this, one understands why there were few men whom Thackeray respected and admired more than this impractical, guileless divine, whose determined innocence was the delight and despair of his friends.

John Allen (1810–1886) was the youngest son of the Rev. David Bird Allen, a country rector who later became Rural Dean and Prebendary of Brecon. Fourteen years in his father's sternly pious household imbued him with a settled faith and strict principles that remained unshaken even by the harsh ordeal of life at Westminster School, where he was enrolled from 1824 to 1828. He matriculated at Trinity College, Cambridge, in the autumn of 1828. It was his intention to prepare himself for the church, and during

---

[1] R. M. Grier, *John Allen* (London, 1889), p. 29. This biography is the chief source for my brief notice of Allen. I have not seen Anna O. Allen's *John Allen and his Friends.*   [2] *Biographical Introductions,* I, xxx.

his first year he applied himself closely to his books. Afterwards, however, he relaxed the rigor of his studies and made many friends, among them Thackeray, FitzGerald, and James Spedding. His manuscript diary of 1830 and 1831 [3] brings the Allen of these days vividly to life. His existence is revealed as a constant battle between the flesh and the spirit, though the reader is never in much anxiety as to the ultimate triumph of the latter. Pride, Gluttony, and Indolence were his chief enemies among the deadly sins, and many are the accesses of remorse recorded in his diary after a spurt of conviviality or a failure to rise at his accustomed hour. He neglects no opportunity to enumerate the blessings that have been showered on him, and he never omits to inquire, why has such favor been shown to one so vile? There is about this diary, which would be a most repellent document if marked by the slightest taint of hyprocrisy, a kind of quaint charm. One sees how Allen's college friends must have been attracted by his earnestness, his naïveté, his affectionate nature, and even by his habit of exclaiming, when anything surprised him, "It is very admonitory!"

After receiving his B. A. degree at Cambridge in January, 1832, Allen was for a short time second master of a school in Pimlico, a post which he secured through Thackeray. Later in the year he became mathematical lecturer at King's College, London, and in 1833 he was made chaplain and divinity lecturer at the same institution. His particular patron was John Lonsdale, Principal of King's College and later (1843) Bishop of Lichfield. In 1834 he made a most fortunate marriage to a Miss Higgins, his engagement with whom extended back to the Long Vacation of 1831. Though Mrs. Allen loved and revered her husband, she was a thoroughly practical woman who saw that he stood urgently in need of unobtrusive guidance. Ten children were born to the pair, seven during their years in London. They lived successively at Milman Place, Great Coram Street, and St. John's Wood. While in the second of these localities their neighbors directly across the street were Thackeray and his wife, with whom they were for some

---

[3] The passages concerning Thackeray are printed in Appendix I below.

time on intimate terms. In 1839 the newly created Committee of Council on Education made Allen one of the three original inspectors of schools. A story of this date illustrates the Johnsonian playfulness that relieved the general seriousness of his character:

> Then, as always, there was a certain pathos, almost plaintiveness of tone, in John Allen's voice. He was resigning his mathematical lectureship on being appointed as Inspector of Schools, and was saying "Good-bye" to his pupils. "Well, gentlemen, I am sorry to say we shall no longer meet here; but I trust we shall all meet in another place ——————" We all looked solemn, almost like St. Paul's hearers. And then he added, after a pause, "I mean, gentlemen, in the Divinity Lecture Room." General sense of relief and satisfaction.[4]

In 1846 Allen was made Vicar of Prees in Shropshire by the Bishop of Lichfield, and during the following year the Archdeaconry of Salop was added to this preferment. Thackeray henceforth saw little of him, for the remainder of his life was passed in the country. Allen found Prees in a sad state of spiritual disrepair, to which his predecessor, whose pleasant custom it had been to give out in church the meeting of the hounds, had contributed not a little. A parishioner described the village, in which there were eleven public houses to serve 2,000 inhabitants, as "one of the wickedest places on earth."[5] Allen set about the task of reformation with his usual vigor, and despite his peculiarities he soon had everyone's respect. He was able to set the poorest members of his flock at ease, and it is related that a peasant said of him after his death: "'Eh, dear, he was wonderful good company.'"[6] To encourage the temperance movement he became an abstainer himself for a time.

> His object in taking the pledge [writes his son-in-law] was to encourage a poor drunkard in the village of Prees to do the same. "If you, sir," said the man, "will take it, I will take it also." The appeal was irresistible. A fortnight afterwards the poor fellow who made it was drunk again; and the Archdeacon, two years later, was persuaded by some medical man to go back to the use of wine. . . . To those who knew him and his manner of life . . . there must be something intensely comic in the remark of an old woman to Mrs. Allen during the brief

[4] Quoted by Grier, *John Allen*, pp. 68–69.
[5] The same, p. 144.
[6] The same, p. 290.

period of his teetotalism, "Eh, dear, mum, what a comfort it must be to you, when the Archdeacon's out of a night, to know that he's taken the pledge!" [7]

Allen worked hard over his sermons, which were effective if characteristically eccentric. "There are, I take it," his son-in-law remarks, "few preachers who would say in a sermon, 'If at the dinner-table I help myself to the best part of a dish I am carving, I am a child of Satan.'" [8] Allen was abundantly happy at home with his wife, his children, and his books; he was an industrious and successful vicar and archdeacon; but when he sought a larger audience for his views, he was less fortunate. His simplicity of mind together with his firm convictions in matters of right and wrong led him to protest in letters to *The Times* if men in public life did anything of which he did not approve. As may well be supposed, his interference was usually most unwelcome, and he found himself involved in many verbal battles from which he emerged by no means victorious. In 1883 ill-health and old age at last led Allen to exchange his vicarage for the Mastership of St. John's Hospital in Lichfield. He resigned his archdeaconry in 1886, a few months before his death.


## LORD AND LADY ASHBURTON

William Bingham Baring (1799–1864), second Baron Ashburton, belonged to a rich and powerful family of merchant princes. His father, the first Baron, for eighteen years head of the great firm of Baring Brothers, had as a young man conducted the financial negotiations for the sale of the Louisiana territory to the United States and in 1842 crowned his distinguished political career by securing the adoption of the "Ashburton Treaty," which set the boundaries between Canada and the United States. The second Baron was by no means so successful as his father in parlia-

[7] The same, p. 248.
[8] The same, p. 299.

ment, though he faithfully sat for his family's boroughs from 1826 to 1848. Naturally shy and self-effacing, he preferred to devote his considerable talents to learning rather than to active political life, and when in 1848 he inherited the Ashburton estates, which in 1883 totalled 36,772 acres with an annual rent-roll of £46,685,[9] he gave up his public duties for study and society.

He and his wife, the former Lady Harriet Mary Montagu [10] (1805-1857), oldest daughter of the sixth Earl of Sandwich, whom he married in 1823, had served a long social apprenticeship among the varied celebrities that the first Lord Ashburton was accustomed to assemble at Bath House, Piccadilly, and the Grange, Alresford, Hampshire. In the decade of life that remained to her after her husband's accession to his title, Lady Ashburton gained a remarkable ascendancy over the Victorian world. When she died, Charles Greville described her as "the most conspicuous woman in the society of the present day," [11] and so altogether dissimilar a witness as Carlyle added that "She was the greatest lady of rank I ever saw, with the soul of a princess and captainess had there been any career possible to her but that fashionable one." [12]

No doubt Lady Ashburton's remarkable success as a hostess would have been impossible but for the advantages that her own birth and her husband's money gave her, yet she could hardly have failed to make her mark in any walk of life. Of commanding presence, though not pretty, she was a wonderfully witty, energetic, and intelligent woman of great strength of character. Her superb situation allowed her to give free rein to her native imperiousness and to lay down her own social laws. Admission to her home came through talent rather than position, and she included among her

[9] John Bateman, *The Great Landowners of Great Britain and Ireland* (London, 1883), p. 16.

[10] For Lady Ashburton and her place in Victorian society, see James Anthony Froude's *Thomas Carlyle. A History of his Life in London* (New York, 1884); Lord Houghton's *Monographs* (London, 1873); and Sir Henry Taylor's *Autobiography* (London, 1885).

[11] *The Greville Memoirs*, 8 vols., ed. Lytton Strachey and Roger Fulford (London, 1938), VII, 286.

[12] Froude, *Carlyle*, II, 159.

closest friends Charles Buller, Carlyle, Lord Houghton, John
Stuart Mill, James Spedding, Sir Henry Taylor and George
Venables. Conversation she cultivated as a fine art, and in her
drawing room was heard the best talk in London, talk that was
free from conventional insipidity, witty, and vigorous even to the
point of brutality. Despite the distinction of her guests, she rarely
found a conversational rival, and she deserved the Princess Lieven's
compliment, *"Qu'il vaudrait bien s'abonner pour entendre causer
cette femme."* [13]

Thackeray was introduced to Lady Ashburton by Charles Buller
during the middle forties, but it was not until 1848 that he was
admitted to her inner circle. And even then, we learn from Lord
Houghton, his docility by no means matched that of most of her
other admirers.

Having been most kindly received, he took umbrage at some hard
rallying, perhaps rather of others than of himself, and not only declined
her invitations, but spoke of her with discourtesy and personal dislike.
After some months, when the angry feeling on his part had had time to
die out, he received from her a card of invitation to dinner. He returned
it, with an admirable drawing on the back, representing himself kneeling
at her feet with his hair all aflame from the hot coals she was energeti-
cally pouring on his head out of an ornamental brazier. This act of
contrition was followed by a complete reconciliation, and much friendship on her part towards him and his family. [14]

Thackeray wrote many other letters and notes to Lady Ashburton,
more than a few of which are illustrated, but though the correspondence is still extant, it has not proved possible to print any part
of it in this edition. The intimacy of his friendship with the Ashburtons is sufficiently attested, however, by his references to them
in other letters, and by his dedication of *Esmond* to Lord Ashburton, "for the sake of the great kindness and friendship which I
owe to you and yours." [15]

[13] Lord Houghton, *Monographs*, p. 231.
[14] The same, p. 233.
[15] *Works*, VII, 3.

## THE BAXTERS

Thackeray made many friends in the United States, but none that meant more to him than the family of George Baxter of New York. Baxter was a warehouse owner who had offices at 104 Wall Street and lived at 286 Second Avenue, between Twentieth and Twenty-first Streets.[16] He and his wife had four children: Sally (1833-1861), Lucy (b. 1836), Wyllys, and George. Libby Strong, Lucy's particular chum and the daughter of Mrs. Baxter's brother, was so frequently in the house as to be regarded as a third daughter.

The Baxters, who were fond of reading novels in their family circle, eagerly discussed each of Thackeray's books as it appeared, and they looked forward with relish to hearing him lecture in New York. It was quite by chance, however, that they made his acquaintance. Among Sally's suitors was a young Englishman named Henry Bingham Mildmay, who had met Thackeray in London. When he called on Thackeray at the Clarendon Hotel, late in November, 1852, he insisted on taking Mr. Baxter with him, despite the latter's protestations of unworthiness. Lucy Baxter continues the story:

The entire simplicity and frankness of my father's accost, added to the warm expressions of interest from our English friend, seemed to attract Mr. Thackeray, and from the first visit to the "Brown House," as he later always called it, he evidently felt at home among us. No doubt he was very homesick when he first reached America, everything was so new and strange, and he had left, almost for the first time, the mother and daughters, so fondly loved, as his letters testify. He came to us whenever he could, with perfect freedom and informality. He begged to dine with us before the lectures, which even at first bored him greatly, and in the end became a real burden. The monotony of saying the same things over and over again, and the constraint of being obliged to be ready at a given time, whether he felt in a talking mood or not, were very trying to him. He became greatly attached to my mother, whose quiet sympathy soothed him, and his place at her right hand, with the claret-pitcher ready for him, was an established arrangement before a lecture. He would sometimes stop in the midst of the desultory conver-

---

[16] *Trow's New-York City Directory, 1853-1854.*

sation then in progress, and roll out in a deep voice, with an exaggerated accent, the opening sentences of the lecture next to be delivered, making us all laugh at his comic distaste for the performance.[17]

. Thackeray's favorites among his new friends were Mrs. Baxter, Lucy, and Sally. Mrs. Baxter was a pretty, tender, sympathetic woman, whom Thackeray likened to Lady Castlewood. He talked and wrote to her almost as to his own mother, for her ready affection, her humor, and her fondness for gossip made her an excellent correspondent. Lucy was a simple, fresh, unaffected girl of sixteen, who kept his own daughters always present in Thackeray's mind. To her he wrote a series of playful, confidential letters, dealing, it is true, with nothing very weighty, yet very pleasant and human.

But from the first it was Sally in whom Thackeray was most interested. Indeed, without the incentive of seeing her, he would perhaps not have made the frequent visits to the Brown House during which he grew fond of Mrs. Baxter and of Lucy. She was a clever, thoughtful, rather melancholy girl, whose occasional perversities of mood only added to her charm. He thought her astonishingly like Beatrix Esmond and fell in love with her almost at once. But his feeling for her was quite dissimilar to the passion he had lavished on Mrs. Brookfield. If he still liked to deal in the small change of love, his *éducation sentimentale* was over. He was forty-one and looked ten years older; Sally was not yet twenty. His affection for her was a rigidly controlled thing, which he was careful to mask by posing as an elderly, paternal person. There can be no doubt, moreover, that he cultivated this last love in the hope that it might sever permanently the cords that bound him to Mrs. Brookfield. "Il y a un moment dans les séparations," writes Flaubert, "où la personne aimée n'est déjà plus avec nous." This moment appears to have come for Thackeray during the first weeks of his association with Sally Baxter.

When Thackeray wrote *The Newcomes*, his recollections of Miss Baxter and the letters he continued to receive from her after he returned to England played a large part in the creation of Ethel Newcome, the most attractive of his heroines. He had only to

[17] *American Family*, pp. 3–4.

transfer his memories from New York to London, for Sally was one of the great beauties of her day in the former city, and had, when he first met her, just begun to take her place in its social life. "An American ball-room amused him greatly," writes Lucy Baxter. "The bright, gay talk, the lively girls full of enjoyment, which they did not fear to show, made a contrast to the more conventional entertainments of London. . . . In his picture of Ethel Newcome, as she holds a little court about her at one of the great London balls, Thackeray reproduces some impressions made by [my sister]. Some of Ethel's impatience for the disillusions of society, its spiteful comment and harsh criticism, might well be reflections from discussions with my sister in the Brown House library, where Mr. Thackeray passed many an hour talking of matters grave and gay." [18]

Though the Baxters met Thackeray in Boston in October, 1855, when he landed on his second trip to America, he was much less in their home than during his earlier visit. The Brown House was given over to preparations for Sally's marriage to a young Charleston gentleman named Frank Hampton, and Thackeray missed the tranquil domestic quiet to which he had earlier become accustomed. Nor was he able to contemplate Sally's marriage without a twinge of jealousy, unreasonable as he knew this to be. He took advantage of his ill-health and lecturing engagements to excuse himself from being present at her wedding on December 12. Not until two months later when he visited Charleston, where Lucy was staying with the Hamptons, had he entirely adapted himself to Sally's new circumstances.

Thackeray did not again see the Baxters after leaving New York in 1856, and apart from his letters there is little record of the later history of the family. We catch a glimpse of Sally, "a lovely lady, with pathetic dark eyes and a look of ill health," in the memoirs of Julia Ward Howe, who met her in Havana in the early months of 1859. She was accompanied by her husband and her little son, born in 1856, and during their talks about Thackeray, she told Mrs. Howe "that she recognized bits of her own conversation in some

[18] The same, pp. 6–7.

of the sayings of Ethel Newcome." [19]  After they returned from Cuba, the Hamptons lived at Columbia, South Carolina, in the house of Wade Hampton, Frank's older brother. There a daughter Lucy (later Mrs. John Haskell) was born to them. The story of Mrs. Hampton's death in 1861 and of how it affected Thackeray is briefly related by Henry Adams:

The last time Henry Adams saw Thackeray, before his sudden death at Christmas in 1863, was in entering the house of Sir Henry Holland for an evening reception. Thackeray was pulling on his coat downstairs, laughing because, in his usual blind way, he had stumbled into the wrong house and had not found it out till he shook hands with old Sir Henry, whom he knew very well, but who was not the host he expected. Then his tone changed as he spoke of his — and Adam's — friend, Mrs. Frank Hampton, of South Carolina, whom he had loved as Sally Baxter and painted as Ethel Newcome. Though he had never quite forgiven her marriage, his warmth of feeling revived when he heard that she had died of consumption at Columbia while her parents and sister were refused permission to pass through the lines to see her. In speaking of it, Thackeray's voice trembled and his eyes filled with tears. [20]

After Thackeray died, his daughters carried on the friendship that he had begun with the Baxters. Mrs. Leslie Stephen (Harriet Thackeray) and her husband stayed at the Brown House when they visited the United States in 1868, and in 1892 Lucy Baxter visited Mrs. Richmond Ritchie (Anne Thackeray) at Wimbledon. The Baxters have long been familiar to many of Thackeray's readers through the handsome little volume called *Thackeray's Letters to an American Family* which Lucy Baxter published in 1904.

## JOHN BOWES BOWES

Among the friends Thackeray made at Cambridge was John Bowes Bowes [21] (1811–1885), who matriculated at Trinity College

[19] Julia Ward Howe, *Reminiscences, 1819–1899* (Boston and New York, 1899), pp. 234–235.
[20] *The Education of Henry Adams* (Boston and New York, 1918), p. 131.
[21] See *Modern English Biography*, by Frederic Boase, 6 vols. (Truro, 1892–1921), I, 358–359; G. E. C., *The Complete Peerage*, ed. Vicary Gibbs

in 1828 and took his B. A. degree in 1832. Bowes was the natural son, by Mary Milner of Staindrop in Derby, of John Bowes, tenth Earl of Strathmore and Kinghorne in the peerage of Scotland and first Baron Bowes of Streatlam Castle in the peerage of the United Kingdom. As he lay *in extremis* on July 2, 1820, the Earl of Strathmore took it into his head to marry Miss Milner, hoping thereby to legitimatize their son according to Scotch law, so that the boy might succeed to his titles as well as his property. The ceremony was duly performed, and Lord Strathmore died the following day. In the *cause célèbre* that ensued, Bowes's claim to his father's honors was disallowed on the ground that his parents had no Scotch domicile. The Scotch peerage and lands passed to his uncle, the Barony became extinct, and Bowes had to content himself with his father's legacy of 43,200 acres in the North Riding of Yorkshire and in Durham, the annual rent-roll of which (in 1883) was £21,071.[22]

After he left Cambridge, Bowes, who perhaps found his position in English society ambiguous, chose to live chiefly in France, and Thackeray next saw him in Paris during the autumn of 1832. His principal interests at this period were horse-racing and the theatre. He was one of the earliest members of the Jockey Club and had such success with his stable that he was known as "the luckiest man on the turf." He won the Derby four times, and he is supposed to have gained £25,000 by his first triumph in 1835 with Mundig. But Bowes also took some part in English politics, for he represented South Durham in parliament from 1832 to 1847. In June and July, 1841, when Bowes was standing for reëlection, Thackeray passed three weeks at Streatlam Castle, a visit made eventful by his conversations with his host about family history.

"I have in my trip to the country," Thackeray wrote to James Fraser a few days later, "found materials (rather a character) for a story, that I'm sure must be amusing." The character was Andrew Robinson Stoney, who had played a sensational rôle in the

and others, 9 vols. (London, 1910–1936), *passim*; and an obituary notice in *The Illustrated Sporting & Dramatic News*, XXIV (1885), 107.
[22] John Bateman, *Great Landowners of Great Britain and Ireland*, p. 51.

annals of the Strathmores.[23] John Lyon, ninth Earl of Strathmore and Bowes's grandfather, had in 1767 married the great
heiress Mary Eleanor, daughter of George Bowes of Streatlam
Castle and Gibside Park, at the same time replacing the name of
Lyon by that of Bowes. He died on March 7, 1776, and his widow
married Stoney (afterwards Stoney-Bowes), an Irish adventurer
who had fought a duel on her account, on January 17, 1777.
Stoney-Bowes made her miserably unhappy, and after some years
she contrived to obtain a separation from him. On November 10,
1786, however, Stoney-Bowes gained access to her on pretense of a
warrant from Lord Mansfield and carried her off to his house in
county Durham. "The town was ringing about . . . Countess
Strathmore," wrote Horace Walpole on December 1, "and the
enormous barbarities of her husband, who beat her for six days
and nights

> Round Stainmore's wintry wild,

for which the myrmidons of the King's Bench have knocked his
brains out — almost." [24] But though the constables rescued Lady
Strathmore from her husband, she did not escape his persecution
entirely until she divorced him in 1789. He was detained within
the Rules of the King's Bench Prison from this time until his death
in 1810. Lady Strathmore died in 1800 and was buried in Westminster Abbey, "attired," it is related, "in a superb bridal dress."
Readers of *The Memoirs of Barry Lyndon* will recognize how
closely the later chapters of that novel follow the history of Stoney-
Bowes and his lady.

After 1853 Bowes's passion for horse-racing subsided, though
he still maintained a stable. He was Sheriff of South Durham in
1854, and he appears to have passed most of his later life in England as a great country magnate. The exploitation of large deposits
of coal discovered at Gibside Park greatly increased his income,

[23] The fullest contemporary account of Stoney's history appears to be Jesse
Foote's *Lives of Andrew Robinson Bowes and the Countess of Strathmore*
(London, 1810?).

[24] *The Letters of Horace Walpole*, ed. Mrs. Paget Toynbee, 16 vols. (Oxford, 1903–1905), XIII, 423–424.

and he was a partner in the ship-building firm of Bowes and Palmer of Newcastle-on-Tyne. In 1872 he married Josephine Benoîte, Countess of Montalbo, and after her death two years later he erected the "Josephine and John Bowes museum and park" at Barnard Castle, Durham, at a cost of £80,000. He married again in 1877, a few years before his death, his second choice being Alphonsina Marie de St. Amand, Comtesse de Courten.


## CHARLOTTE BRONTË

Charlotte Brontë and Thackeray became famous almost simultaneously, for *Jane Eyre* appeared in October, 1847, not long after the appearance of the tenth number of *Vanity Fair*. Miss Brontë's novel was sent to Thackeray, who afterwards recollected "how with my own work pressing upon me, I could not, having taken the volumes up, lay them down until they were read through!" [25] Miss Brontë, for her part, was ecstatic over *Vanity Fair*. In its author she discovered "an intellectual boa-constrictor," "a Titan, so strong that he can afford to perform with calm the most herculean feats," and "the legitimate high priest of Truth." [26] And without any personal acquaintance with her idol, she dedicated the second edition of *Jane Eyre* to him in the most glowing terms, thus inadvertently giving rise to one of the notorious canards of Victorian literary history.[27]

When she at last met Thackeray in December, 1849, she was puzzled to find that he was not after all "terribly in earnest against the falsehood and follies of the world." Indeed, she failed altogether to comprehend either his ambivalent outlook on London society, which, though he might satirize, he could not do without, or his thoroughly practical view of literature, induced by a dozen years of writing for his living. Thackeray, who despaired of pre-

[25] *Works*, XII, 189. See below, No. 417.
[26] Thomas James Wise and Alexander Symington, *The Brontës*, 4 vols. (Oxford, 1932), II, 160, 201, and 244.
[27] See below, No. 440.

senting his ideas in a light that would win her sympathy, took refuge in persiflage.

Charlotte Brontë's heroics roused Thackeray's antagonism [writes George Smith]. He declined to pose on a pedestal for her admiration, and with characteristic contrariety of nature he seemed to be tempted to say the very things that set Charlotte Brontë's teeth, so to speak, on edge, and affronted all her ideals. He insisted on discussing his books very much as a clerk in a bank would discuss the ledgers he had to keep for a salary. But all this was, on Thackeray's part, an affectation: an affectation into which he was provoked by what he considered Charlotte Brontë's high falutin'. Miss Brontë wanted to persuade him that he was a great man with a 'mission'; and Thackeray, with many wicked jests, declined to recognise the 'mission.' [28]

Whenever they met in the future, the misunderstanding of their first encounter reasserted itself, and they were always slightly uncomfortable in each other's company. Miss Brontë became noticeably less extravagant in her praise of Thackeray, whom she regarded henceforth "as 'twere with a defeated joy." She deplored his "criminal carelessness of great faculties," and concluded that he was an "indolent intellectual Hercules." [29]

It is unfortunate that the correspondence has not been preserved in which Miss Brontë took Thackeray to task for his shortcomings, and he in turn defended himself as best he might. Her exhortations may perhaps have borne fruit in the more careful workmanship and nobler tone of *Esmond*, the first two volumes of which were sent to her in manuscript for criticism. But Miss Brontë's uncompromising idealism and Thackeray's easy worldliness were after all irreconcilable, and the most enduring memorial of their association lies in the high comedy of their various meetings, recorded with a nice sense of dramatic contrast by Lady Ritchie and George Smith.[30]

[28] *George Smith A Memoir* (London, 1902), p. 100.
[29] Wise and Symington, *The Brontës*, III, 233.
[30] See below, No. 652; No. 705; No. 783.
It should be mentioned that Thackeray was not pleased at the freedom with which Charlotte Brontë's biographer used his name. Sir Frederick Pollock (*Personal Remembrances*, 2 vols., London, 1887, II, 57) relates that when he dined with Thackeray on April 23, 1857, "He spoke in some disgust of Mrs. Gaskell's recent *Life of Miss Brontë*, not without personal reason."

## THE BROOKFIELDS

Thackeray's friendship with William Henry Brookfield [31] (1809–1874) began in the autumn of 1829 when both were undergraduates at Cambridge. Brookfield was a lively, handsome young man to whom the university offered a welcome escape from a gloomy boyhood in the home of a dissenting solicitor. He soon made a place for himself in Cambridge. An admirable mimic, he was particularly esteemed for his comic songs, and his inexhaustible vein of rather labored verbal wit exactly suited the taste of his contemporaries. These facile talents and his gentlemanly manners brought him into the best undergraduate society, though he was without the customary passports of money and aristocratic connections.[32] Nor did his luck desert him when he left Cambridge in 1834. He was engaged as private tutor to the future Lord Lyttleton, and spent the next six months, while looking about for a profession, in one after another of the great country homes of England. He decided at last for the church, not from any sense of dedication, but because it seemed to afford the most convenient avenue to preferment. As a clergyman the very qualities that would have made his fortune as a lawyer or an actor (his real vocation, had it been open to a Victorian gentleman) aroused suspicion and distrust, and his first curacy at Maltby in Lincolnshire, comfortably described by Lord Lyttleton, who did not have to live there, as "a most dreary little place," [33] was only a prelude to the series of chastening experiences that life held in store for him. He was grateful for his translation in 1836 to a curacy in the thriving town of Southampton.

[31] The chief source of information about the Brookfields is *Mrs. Brookfield and her Circle*, a clever but disingenuous tribute to his mother compiled by Charles Brookfield with the aid of his wife Frances. The memoir by Lord Lyttleton prefixed to *Sermons by the late William Brookfield*, ed. Mrs. Brookfield (London, 1875), may also be consulted with profit.

[32] "I have heard my father say," writes Lady Ritchie (*Biographical Introductions*, II, xxx), "that in his early days at Cambridge it was considered a distinction by the young men to be seen out walking with Mr. Brookfield."

[33] *Sermons by the late William Brookfield*, p. xiii.

When he met Jane Octavia Elton (1821–1896) a year later, he was twenty-seven and she sixteen. The youngest daughter of the scholar and country gentleman Charles Elton, later (1842) sixth Baronet of that name, she had passed her uneventful girlhood in the provincial society of Bristol. When she came to know Brookfield, she already gave promise of a beauty and intelligence that served to excuse her not extravagant vanity. In comparison with the other men of her acquaintance she found him infinitely gifted and attractive, and she firmly believed that he was destined to a brilliant career, a conviction that she would hardly have entertained had her knowledge of the world been wider. Brookfield, for his part, was equally taken with this lovely, fresh, and unsophisticated girl. The two became engaged in 1838, and their marriage took place three years later, after Brookfield had been appointed Curate of St. James's, Piccadilly, and of the District Church of St. Luke's, Berwick Street.

When they settled in London in 1842, the success — so long deferred — which Brookfield had promised himself seemed within his grasp, and his wife hoped to ease his way to advancement by her gifts as a hostess. But they had calculated without the realities of their situation. Their income was small, and Mrs. Brookfield, brought up in a family that gave no thought to money, was not a thrifty housewife. Though she admired her husband as he appeared in his clerical robes before the fashionable congregation of St. James's, she could not interest herself in his real work, the care of the poor in the parish of St. Luke's.[34] Her health, which was always delicate, broke down most inopportunely in 1844, and she was an invalid during the next four years. As she came to realize that her confined circumstances were likely to prove permanent, she looked about her with disenchanted eyes. Comparing her husband with the distinguished men that she met in London society, she perceived that he was after all a rather ordinary person. Brookfield, meanwhile, had his own grievances. He resented his wife's domestic shortcomings; he was hurt by her withdrawal of

[34] See "The Curate's Walk" (*Works*, VI, 545–552), in which Brookfield figures as the Rev. Frank Whitestock.

the adoring affection to which he had become accustomed during their engagement and the early days of their marriage; and he was oppressed by a tormenting sense of failure both as a man and as a husband. It was the Brookfields' final cross that though they both wanted children, they had none. When Brookfield's appointment as Inspector of Elementary Church Schools enabled them to take a residence at 15 Portman Street in April, 1848, his household still presented a serene front to the world, but both he and his wife were inwardly living lives of quiet desperation.

Thackeray witnessed the whole course of the Brookfields' slow estrangement. Though he met his friend's wife early in 1842, it was not until 1845, when he had given up all hope that his own wife might recover her sanity, that Mrs. Brookfield began to play an important part in his life. From 1845 to 1848 he was on terms of the closest intimacy with Brookfield, but deeply as he admired Mrs. Brookfield, he found little favor in her eyes. She was accustomed to admiration, and there was nothing as yet to center her attention on Thackeray's burly person. During these years he remained to her "William's friend," and with this humiliating rôle he was perforce content.

Not until the summer of 1848 did any change occur in their relationship. The celebrity that Thackeray gained through *Vanity Fair* had by this time made his homage very flattering to Mrs. Brookfield. She looked forward to the hours they passed together, enlivened by sprightly gossip about common acquaintances, as cheerful interludes in her monotonous existence. To Thackeray these conversations meant much more, for they gave his life a new emotional focus. When he left London, he continued them by letter, thus initiating the correspondence that for the next three years brings us perhaps closer to him than we come at any other time during his life. And in October he was admitted to a further degree of friendship. He visited Mrs. Brookfield at Clevedon Court, her father's country home near Bristol, and there she told him for the first time of her husband's unkindness and her own unhappiness. Thackeray had sensed these things long before, but hitherto Mrs. Brookfield had allowed his understanding of them to remain tacit. Her confidences showed him that he might look to her for affection and sympathy, if nothing more, and henceforth he addressed her in his letters no longer as madame or friend but as my dear lady or my sister.

Thackeray's patent love for Mrs. Brookfield and the friendly intimacy that she accorded him aroused protest, but not in the quarter where it might have been expected. Brookfield remained apathetic. He was too fond of Thackeray to deprive him of the solace that he found in Mrs. Brookfield's companionship, and his "pride of possession" was flattered by this tribute from one of London's most eminent men. Not that Brookfield should be likened to

> Heroic, stoic Cato the sententious,
> Who lent his lady to his friend Horentius.

He and his wife were still lovers — that at least remained to them of their early passion —, and Brookfield knew that in this respect he had nothing to fear from Thackeray, to whom, indeed, Mrs. Brookfield seems never to have permitted so much as an embrace or a kiss. The protest came from Mrs. Brookfield's uncle, Henry Hallam the historian (whose interest, though he may not himself have realized it, was rather more than avuncular), and was weighted by a substantial allowance that he made to his niece. Thackeray defended himself in a letter of January 3, 1849, to Mrs. Brookfield:

thank God I have never concealed the affection I have for you — your husband knows it as well as you or I do, and I think I have such a claim to the love of both of you as no relationship, however close, ought to question or supersede.

As the months passed, Thackeray's position as the privileged *ami de la maison* became firmly established, nor was it at all modified by the birth of the Brookfields' first child, Magdalene, on February 26, 1850. Mrs. Brookfield walked the precarious tightrope on which she found herself with great adroitness. It is impossible, indeed, to overlook a rather repellent element of calculation in her character; she is not likely to become a heroine of literary history. Both she and Thackeray, whose own balance grew gradually more assured, felt that theirs was a permanent relationship about which they might build their lives.

The first hint that Brookfield did not intend to hold to his part of the tacit agreement on which his wife and Thackeray relied was his withdrawal to Southampton on the plea of illness in April, 1851, just before Thackeray scored his great success as a lecturer. Brookfield no longer trusted his friend. One does not know precisely why. Perhaps whispering tongues had poisoned truth. Perhaps he could not endure that his wife and Thackeray should continue to enjoy a happiness from which he felt excluded. In any event, when Thackeray returned from abroad in the latter part of August, he found that Brookfield's treatment of his wife had for some time past been outrageous. He held his peace for a month, but on September 23 (it would appear) his patience reached its breaking point. In Thackeray's presence Brookfield overwhelmed his wife with the grievances he had accumulated in ten years of marriage, and Thackeray, losing his self-control, rebuked him in terms that he realized himself were unforgivable. Brookfield was thus afforded an opportunity of insisting on a separation between his wife and his friend. Seeing that they must part and wishing to strengthen Mrs. Brookfield's purpose, Thackeray gave his tongue free rein. "I stabbed the husband express," he wrote later, "to put her up as high as I could and to make zusamenkunft impossible." Thackeray never again gave Brookfield his confidence. When Lord and Lady Ashburton brought the two men together five weeks later, their reconciliation was purely formal. Thackeray said in effect, "Let us be friends, but at a distance." To his mind Brookfield's action, coming three years after he and Mrs. Brookfield had been allowed to make their friendship the emotional center of their lives, was nothing less than treason. Towards Mrs. Brookfield his feelings were mixed. He believed that in giving him up, she was doing her duty, but the natural man in him was unsatisfied. What a small return he had received for years of devotion! His vanity was grievously hurt; he wondered if after all he had not been a fool; he was not sure that she had ever really loved him.

Henceforth Thackeray saw and wrote to his former friends only rarely, though he held indirect communication with Mrs. Brookfield through Mrs. Elliot and Kate Perry.[35] The Brookfields continued to frequent London society assiduously, and for many years Brookfield was a fashionable morning preacher at Berkeley Chapel, Mayfair, with a reputation for pulpit eloquence not unlike that of the Rev. Charles Honeyman in *The Newcomes*. In 1864 he gave up his Inspectorship of Schools and became Rector of Somerby-with-Hainby, near Grantham, but he and his wife continued to spend most of each year in London. Mrs. Brookfield's interests centered in her children, Magdalene, Arthur (b. 1853), and Charles (b. 1857), though in later life she wrote a number of mediocre novels, beginning with *Only George* (1864).

## DR. JOHN BROWN

On May 10, 1849, Thackeray was agreeably surprised by the arrival of a silver statuette of Mr. Punch, sent him — so he learned from its inscription — by eighty Edinburgh admirers. The moving spirit behind this testimonial, the first that Thackeray had received,

---

[35] Since Charles Brookfield set out to picture his parents' union as a "perpetual fountain of domestic sweets," he omitted all mention of their break with Thackeray from *Mrs. Brookfield and her Circle*. His brother Arthur is sufficiently candid to admit that there was a quarrel, though he adheres otherwise to Charles's thesis. "Obeying an unfortunate impulse," he writes (*Annals of a Chequered Life*, London, 1930, pp. 13–14), "[Thackeray] took upon himself to push into the private domestic affairs of one of his friends, and lecture a most devoted husband on the way he should treat an equally devoted wife. That the mutual devotion of these two persons truly existed will be apparent to anyone who has read the letters they exchanged — which have since been published [in *Mrs. Brookfield and her Circle*] — at the very time when Thackeray seems to have thought that his advice was called for. Nothing but narrowness of means ever really interfered with their happiness, and they both faced that inconvenience with a great deal of philosophy and courage." Charles Brookfield prints no letters exchanged by his parents between July 22, 1851, and August 18, 1855.

was Dr. John Brown (1810–1882), a Scottish physician who devoted his leisure to letters. Thackeray did not meet his benefactor
until December, 1851, when he made his first trip to Edinburgh.
He and Brown took to each other at once, and it was not long before
Thackeray was a favorite as well with Mrs. Brown (d. 1864) and
with the children, John ("Jock") and Helen. Subsequent visits to
Edinburgh, where Brown's residence at 23 Rutland Street became
a second home to Thackeray, cemented the friendship between the
two men, and a long series of letters, in which Thackeray expresses
himself more freely than to any other man except FitzGerald, is
the lasting record of their association. Brown amply deserved
Thackeray's confidence, both by the high esteem in which he held
his friend, his hero after Sir Walter Scott, and by his loyal labor
from first to last for his friend's books. An even better guarantee
that Thackeray's trust was not misplaced was the perfect integrity
of Brown's life and character.[36]

Brown was the son of Dr. John Brown of Biggar in Lanark-
shire, a distinguished biblical scholar, and was educated at home
by his father until the family moved to Edinburgh in 1822. After
four years at school, he entered Edinburgh University in 1826 and
was indentured shortly afterwards to James Syme, then just beginning his notable career as a surgeon. He received his M. D.
degree in 1833 and settled down to life-long practice in Edinburgh.
His history henceforth has few landmarks, save for his marriage
in 1840 to Catherine Scott M'Kay and the chronicle of his writings.
He had always been fond of literature, and it was natural that, once
established in his profession, he should turn to authorship. His
first contributions were to *The Scotsman,* but in 1846 and 1847 he
also began to write for Hugh Miller's *Witness* and *The North
British Review.* Though he was soon a favorite with periodical
readers, it was not until 1858 that the first series of his collected

[36] The chief sources of information concerning Dr. Brown, apart from
the many autobiographical passages in his *Horæ Subsecivæ* (Edinburgh, vol. I,
1858; vol. II, 1861; vol. III, 1882) are John Taylor Brown's *Dr. John
Brown* (London, 1903), E. T. McLaren's *Dr. John Brown and his Sister
Isabella* (Edinburgh, 1890), Alexander Peddie's *Recollections of Dr. John
Brown* (Edinburgh, 1894), and *Letters of Dr. John Brown.*

papers was published under the disarming title *Horæ Subsecivæ*. A second series, which contains the famous story "Rab and his Friends," appeared in 1861, and a third, including "Thackeray's Death," was added in 1882. Brown's essays and narratives deal with a variety of topics, with medicine, with art and with literature, with great figures of the past and with friends of the present, with children and with dogs, but all are given a common stamp by the impress of his personality. Like Thackeray and Thackeray's eighteenth century favorites, Brown was primarily a humorist, a writer in whose work the humorous ego plays over the affairs of life.

In this kind of writing, the quality of the author's personality is all important. Of Brown it may happily be said that his books and the records of his life unite to testify that he was a singularly sweet and charming man — a man of strong character and forceful opinions, yet mild and retiring, impatient of all ostentation and acutely uncomfortable on ceremonial occasions. Though an able and conscientious physician, whose profession was the main concern of his life, he was admired by men rather as a rare personality than as a doctor. Women readily admitted him to fatherly or brotherly intimacy, and he had an excellent way with children. His peculiar charm perhaps derived in part from the union in his mind of a lively sense of humor and a pronounced but gentle melancholy, a combination to which the grave, sad face of his portraits, a face that is yet deeply lined about the mouth by frequent laughter, bears witness. In his bitter-sweet outlook, as in many other things, he was very like Thackeray, a fact that goes far to explain the close sympathy between the two men. Each saw in the other what he might himself have been: Brown was a Thackeray of modest talent playing out his destiny in the retirement of a provincial city, Thackeray a Brown whose genius had given him a splendid rôle in the great world.

## THE BULLERS

Thackeray owed his introduction to the Bullers [37] to his Anglo-Indian connection. Charles Buller senior (1774–1848), a younger son of John Buller of Morval, near Looe in Cornwall, went out to Calcutta as a young man in the revenue department of the East India Company. In 1805 he married Barbara Isabella (d. 1849), daughter of General William Kirkpatrick, and he and his wife became very friendly with Thackeray's parents. The Bullers returned to England with their two sons, Charles (1806–1848) and Arthur William (1808–1869), shortly before 1812, and a third boy, Reginald, was born to them in 1818. Charles was sent to Harrow for a time, but in 1821 he was removed from school, and in the following year he and Arthur were placed under the tuition of Carlyle. Both brothers went to Trinity College, Cambridge, Charles from 1824 to 1828 and Arthur from 1826 to 1830, and both studied at Lincoln's Inn and were in 1831 and 1834 called to the bar. Meanwhile, Charles had in 1830 and 1831 begun his political career as M. P. for his family's pocket borough of West Looe.

In 1832 Thackeray began a friendly association with the Bullers which was interrupted henceforth only when he or they were out of London. During that year he was a frequent visitor at their residence in the city and spent several weeks in Cornwall and Devon helping Charles in his successful campaign for the parliamentary seat of Liskeard. A glimpse of Mrs. Buller shortly before this time is afforded in a letter of John Sterling's. She is described as "a renowned beauty and queen of Calcutta, [who] has still many striking and delicate traces of what she was. Her conversation is more brilliant and pleasant than that of any one I know." [38] Her

---

[37] The details of the Bullers' family history will be found in Burke's *Landed Gentry*. A lively picture of the older generation is provided in *Letters and Memorials of Jane Welsh Carlyle*, 3 vols., ed. Thomas Carlyle and James Anthony Froude (New York, 1883), I, 113–136. The most recent account of Charles Buller is E. M. Wrong's *Charles Buller and Responsible Government* (Oxford, 1926).

[38] Thomas Carlyle, *The Life of John Sterling*, Part I, chapter 7.

husband, according to Carlyle, "was considerably deaf, a real sorrow to one so fond of listening to people of sense; for the rest, like his wife, a person of perfect probity, politeness, truthfulness, and of a more solid type than she; he read (idly, when he must), rode for exercise, was, above all, fond of chess, in which game he rarely found his superior." [39]

But it was with Arthur and Charles that Thackeray was most intimate. Arthur, who was accounted in youth "one of the handsomest men in England," [40] went on the Western Circuit for several years after being called to the bar. He was Queen's Advocate in Ceylon from 1840 to 1848, and he married Anne Henrietta Maria Templer (d. 1907) during his third year in that colony. He returned to England to be knighted in 1848 and departed not long after for Calcutta, where he served as judge until 1858. He passed the final decade of his life in London as M. P. for Devonport and Liskeard.

Charles was the family's great man, and he might, except for his untimely death, have attained to the front rank of Victorian statesmen. He was very like Thackeray in appearance, for he was six feet three inches in height and his nose had been broken in childhood. He had been President of the Union at Cambridge, and he was not long in parliament, where he represented Liskeard from 1832 until his death, before he had made a brilliant reputation as a speaker. When Lord Durham crossed the ocean as Governor-General of Canada in 1838, Buller accompanied him as Secretary, and the celebrated *Durham Report* appears to have been in part his work. A Philosophical Radical in early years, he wrote leaders in 1836 for *The Constitutional*, the militantly liberal journal for which Thackeray worked in the months after his marriage. But as the radical party disintegrated, his views came to approximate those of the Whigs, and in 1846 Lord John Russell, the new Whig Prime Minister, appointed him Judge-Advocate-General. When

---

[39] *Letters and Memorials of Jane Welsh Carlyle*, I, 114.

[40] Carlyle, *Life of Sterling*, Part I, chapter 7. The accuracy of this judgment is witnessed by Thackeray's water-color portrait of Arthur Buller in the Shawe albums of the Huntington Library.

he died he had just been made President of the Poor Law Commission, and the highest prizes appeared to be within his grasp.

Testimony is united as to Buller's great charm and wit. Indeed, the very qualities that most recommended him to Thackeray and that made him popular in Early Victorian society were the heaviest checks on his political career.

He was seduced [writes Greville] by his keen perception of the ridiculous and an irresistible propensity to banter into an everlasting mockery of everything and everybody, which not only often became tiresome and provoking, but gave an appearance of levity to his character that largely deducted from the estimation in which he would otherwise have been held. It was impossible to be sure when he was in earnest and when he was in jest, when he really meant what he said, and when he was only jeering, gibing, and making game. It is incredible what damage this pernicious habit did him; for it created a notion that though he was very witty and entertaining, he had no settled principles and convictions, and that he 'made a mockery of life.' [41]

No one relished Buller's mental agility more than Lady Harriet Ashburton, his closest friend and, according to some contemporaries, the *grande passion* of his life.[42] "They had both the same spirits and cleverness in conversation," Greville remarks, "and the same quickness and drollery in repartee. . . . their talk was like that in the polite conversation between Never Out and Miss Notable." [43]


## MRS. BUTLER

It may be surmised that Thackeray did not go far afield for his model when he drew old Miss Crawley in *Vanity Fair*. Living with him in 1847 was his maternal grandmother, Harriet Butler (c. 1770–1847), a selfish and imperious old lady to the worldly follies of whose youth had succeeded beads and prayer-books as

[41] *Greville Memoirs*, ed. Strachey and Fulford, VI, 137.

[42] Though Buller never married, he was not without other ties. See *Memoranda* below, Theresa Reviss.

[43] *Greville Memoirs*, ed. Strachey and Fulford, VII, 287.

appropriate toys of age. Mrs. Butler tired of her husband, John Harman Becher, not long after the birth of Thackeray's mother in 1792, and eloped with another Calcutta gentleman, Colonel E. W. Butler of the Bengal Artillery, whom she married after Becher's death in 1800.[44] She reappears in the Thackeray chronicle twenty-seven years later, a widow with a substantial income who has become reconciled with her daughter's family, but her intimacy with Thackeray did not begin until after he had lost his fortune. Then she came very generously to his assistance, and he spent the winter of 1834–1835 with her in Paris, putting up as best he could with the cantankerousness that she felt justified in displaying as the capitalist of the family. She was a member of his household again in 1840 and 1841, when he described her as "a hale handsome old lady of seventy, the very best-dressed and neatest old lady in Paris." [45] As the years passed, Thackeray conceived a real affection for his grandmother, and he was glad to welcome her once again to his home in 1847. Lady Ritchie remembered her at this time as "an old lady wrapped in Indian shawls . . . [who] rarely spoke, and was almost always in her room," adding that "she put on her spectacles and read 'Vanity Fair' in the intervals of her books of devotion." [46] Mrs. Butler died in Paris on November 1 of the same year.

## THOMAS CARLYLE

Thackeray first met Carlyle during 1837, shortly after removing to London. He reviewed *The French Revolution* in *The Times* during August of that year and soon afterwards formed a firm friendship and alliance with its author. Like many young writers of the day he was an enthusiastic convert to Carlyle's crusade against cant and humbug, whatever reservations he might make about certain of his master's other ideas and manner of ex-

[44] I am indebted to Mrs. Fuller for this information.
[45] *Works*, IV, 696.
[46] *Biographical Introductions*, I, xxvii-xxviii.

pression. On one occasion, indeed, he was able to be of assistance
to Carlyle in exposing a notorious instance of *blague*, the kind of
humbug peculiar to the French. In the first edition of his *French
Revolution* Carlyle, accepting the traditional French version of
the incident, recorded that when the *Vengeur* sank during an action
against the English fleet in June, 1794, her whole crew, preferring
death to surrender, had shouted *Vive la République* from the
upper deck as the *Vengeur* went to the bottom.[47] But not long
after his history appeared, Carlyle discovered that this glorious
story was a mere fabrication, designed by Barrère to bolster the
morale of the National Assembly, and he accordingly communicated a true account of the episode to *Fraser's Magazine*.[48] When
a translation of his article appeared in the *Revue Britannique*, together with an intemperate reply by one Labédollière, great indignation was felt in France, and Carlyle was taken to task by various
angry Frenchmen, among them Jules Baget of the *Journal du
peuple*, who in a set of hysterical verses hailed him as the "*Détrac-
teur orgueilleux de notre vieille gloire.*" Thackeray entered the
fray with a sarcastic riposte in *Fraser's Magazine* of March, 1840,[49]
in which Messrs. Labédollière and Baget are made to look decidedly silly, and there the quarrel seems to have ended.

Thackeray and Carlyle continued on good terms until January,

[47] Book V, chapter vi. Carlyle was enabled, by a thrifty rhetorical device, to
preserve nearly the whole of his original account of the *Vengeur's* sinking in
later editions.

[48] "Epistles to the Literati. No. XI. Thomas Carlyle, Esq. to Oliver Yorke,
Esq., On the Sinking of the Vengeur," *Fraser's Magazine*, CXV (1839),
76–84.

[49] "Epistles to the Literati. No. XIV. On French Criticism of the English,
and Notably in the Affair of the Vengeur. By Nelson Tattersall Lee Scupper,
Esq., Late Ensign in her Majesty's Horse-Marines, to ——— Labédollière,
Esq.," pp. 332–345. That this article, which has not previously been assigned
to Thackeray, was his work is shown by the following fragment of a letter to
James Fraser, quoted from an auction catalogue clipping: "The only dun I
have in the world is growing obstreperous. Can you give me two sheets of
the Magazine for next month? They will pay him and leave me eleven
shillings over. I have got the Revue Britannique and have settled with
Carlyle to write an article on the Vengeur, half of it is done; it will run to 13
pages probably for I have plenty of matter."

1846, when they fell out over Carlyle's cruel comparison of Thackeray's trip to the Mediterranean as the guest of the Peninsular and Oriental Steam Navigation Company with "the practice of a blind fiddler going to and fro on a penny ferry-boat in Scotland and playing tunes to the passengers for halfpence." [50]  During the next four or five years Thackeray regarded his erstwhile friend without great sympathy.  We find Kate Perry, for example, reporting the following conversation at a dinner given by the Misses Berry on January 22, 1850:

Carlyle was discussed, and Miss Berry asking what his conversation was like, Kinglake said Ezekiel which we all thought a happy illustration of the denouncing style with which he cries out woe & desolation to all existing ordinances, men, & habits of the world.  Thackeray said he was a bully — attack him with persiflage & he was silenced, in fact Carlyle is no longer the Prophet he used to be considered — I remember his palmy days when his words were manna to the Israelites.[51]

Throughout the whole of this period, however, Thackeray was friendly with Mrs. Carlyle, who was very kind to his daughters, and a reconciliation was gradually effected between him and her husband.  Carlyle attested his renewed good will by attending Thackeray's first series of lectures in 1851.

Most of Carlyle's pungent comments on Thackeray find a place in the notes to this edition, but three more general estimates may appropriately be quoted here.  On September 9, 1853, he wrote to Emerson:

Thackeray has very rarely come athwart me since his return [from America]: he is a big fellow, soul and body; of many gifts and qualities (particularly in the Hogarth line, with a bit of Sterne superadded), of enormous *appetite* withal, and very uncertain and chaotic in all points except his *outer breeding*, which is fixed enough, and *perfect* according to the modern English style.  I rather dread explosions in his history.  A *big*, fierce, weeping, hungry man; not a strong one.[52]

[50] See below, No. 337.

[51] From Miss Perry's manuscript diary for 1850, owned by Mr. Orlando F. Weber, Jr.

[52] *The Correspondence of Thomas Carlyle and Ralph Waldo Emerson*, 2 vols., ed. Charles Eliot Norton (Boston, 1883), II, 229–230.

George Venables tells of an encounter between Carlyle and Thackeray which shows evidence of having taken place during their estrangement — when Thackeray had recourse to persiflage. Carlyle, he writes,

had never insisted on the faultless excellence which involves some negative qualifications. He had naturally but little sympathy with Thackeray's instinctive dislike of greatness, as it is exemplified in his antipathy to Marlborough and to Swift. I think it was after a conversation between them on the character of Swift that I heard Carlyle say, 'I wish I could persuade Thackeray that the test of greatness in a man is not whether he (Thackeray) would like to meet him at a tea-party.' He liked Thackeray himself, and I think he never spoke of him with the contempt which, before he became comparatively intimate with Dickens, he expressed for 'the infinitely small Schnüspel, the distinguished novelist.' " [53]

And to Charles Gavan Duffy in 1880 Carlyle reiterated his conviction of Thackeray's superiority to Dickens:

Thackeray had far more literary ability [than Dickens], but one could not fail to perceive that he had no convictions, after all, except that a man ought to be a gentleman, and ought not to be a snob. This was about the sum of the belief that was in him. The chief skill he possessed was making wonderful likenesses with pen and ink, struck off without premeditation, and which it was found he could not afterwards improve. Jane had some of these in letters from him, where the illustrations were produced, apparently as spontaneously as the letter.[54]

Though I have been able to print only four of Thackeray's letters to the Carlyles in this edition, there must be many more in existence. A characteristic self-caricature, incidentally, is included in his note to them of 23? May, 1851.

## COLONEL AND MRS. CARMICHAEL

Pendennis, it will be recalled, was an only child, but his mother's household included Miss Laura Bell, who was brought up with

[53] "Carlyle's Life in London," *Fortnightly Review*, XLII (1884), 605.
[54] *Conversations with Carlyle* (New York, 1892), p. 77.

him as his sister. Thackeray's Laura was Mary ("Polly") Graham (1815–1871), the daughter of Captain Allan Graham of the Bengal Artillery and Harriet Becher, Mrs. Carmichael-Smyth's older sister. Left an orphan in 1826, she came to live with the Carmichael-Smyths, with whom she remained till her marriage fifteen years later. She was a girl of considerable talent who wrote poetry, sang, and composed, but the praise that these accomplishments commanded in the provincial society frequented by the Carmichael-Smyths gave her an inordinate sense of personal worth that was a source of much bitterness to her in later life. In her younger days, however, she was simple and unassuming, and she and Thackeray were on very affectionate terms. " 'William had the sweetest possible temper,' " she told Richard Bedingfield. "She also said that the want of money, when he was a young fellow, did not seem to weigh on his mind; for in Paris he would come to her and say, 'Polly, can you lend me a franc? I want some cigars.' " [55] And in 1841 it was her timely loan of £500 that gave Thackeray a much needed period of recuperation after the breakup of his marriage.

During the same year Major Carmichael-Smyth's younger brother Charles Montauban Carmichael-Smyth (1790–1870), later (1842) Carmichael,[56] returned to Europe from India. He had entered the Bengal Army as a cornet in 1806 after four years at Charterhouse School, and his career was crowned by a lieutenant-colonelcy in 1838 and a C. B. awarded the following year for bravery displayed during the first Afghan War. His heroism in battle and a serious illness that he suffered in 1840 having made him an interesting figure in Miss Graham's eyes, he wooed and won her by post from India. The two were married in Italy on March 4, 1841, and during the next few years three children were born to them: Charles Henry Edward, called "Chéri" (1842–1895); Rose Gordon; and Florence Graham (d. 1873).

Though the Carmichaels' marriage was successful at first, the

[55] "Recollections of Thackeray," *Cassell's Magazine*, II (1870), 30.
[56] For an account of Colonel Carmichael's character and career, see Alexander F. Baillie's *The Oriental Club and Hanover Square* (London, 1901), pp. 69–76.

difference in their ages and backgrounds proved an insuperable barrier to permanent harmony. Mrs. Carmichael tired of her adoring, stupid, fogeyfied husband and surrounded herself with a court of admirers. We may be sure that she was not altogether displeased when financial necessity forced Lieutenant-Colonel Carmichael to go out to India six or seven years after they were married, leaving her in Paris. He returned to Europe in 1851 and was made a colonel in 1852. In 1853 he and his wife moved to a small residence in Brompton to which they gave the imposing title of Hyndford House,[57] and there they lived in increasing unhappiness till after Thackeray's death.[58]

Thackeray remained friendly with Mrs. Carmichael until the early months of 1843 when she and her husband made their home with him at 13 Great Coram Street. But once they were constantly together, she could not conceal her overweening vanity and her jealous awareness that Mrs. Carmichael-Smyth's maternal love was by no means equally divided between her and Thackeray, and a lasting estrangement followed Thackeray's decision against the Carmichaels in a dispute which they had asked him to decide. When a reconciliation of sorts was effected in 1849, Thackeray was astonished at the change that had occurred in Mrs. Carmichael's character. Laura Bell had become Blanche Amory. "Becky," he wrote, "is a trifle to her." After she and her husband moved to Brompton, her conduct become so erratic that Thackeray had for his children's sake to break off all association with her. He went on seeing Colonel Carmichael, however, and it was from this old Indian officer (who continued to wear long mustachios many years after the fashion had been abandoned) that he derived the conception of Colonel Newcome's appearance upon which Doyle based his drawings.

[57] Colonel Carmichael's nephew, Sir James Robert Carmichael, was an unsuccessful claimant to the dormant Earldom of Hyndford in the peerage of Scotland.
[58] There is a rather awful picture of the Carmichaels' domestic life in Henriette Corkran's *Celebrities and I* (London, 1902), pp. 150–154.

## MAJOR AND MRS. CARMICHAEL-SMYTH

Anne Becher (1792–1864) was the second daughter of John Harman Becher, a Writer in the service of the East India Company, and his wife Harriet. As has already been related,[59] Anne's mother eloped with Colonel Butler not long after her birth, and when her father died in 1800, the child was sent to Fareham in Hampshire, where lived her grandmother and aunt. Old Mrs. Becher was a stern and decorous lady, who ruled her household with tyrannical authority. But her severely Evangelical piety did not make her insensible of the advantages of wealth and position, and when her granddaughter grew up to be a very beautiful young lady, Mrs. Becher determined that she should make a brilliant marriage.[60]

Anne, as it turned out, had her own views on this subject. At an Assembly Ball in Bath during 1807 she met Henry Carmichael-Smyth [61] (1780–1861), a younger son of a good Scottish family, who was an ensign of the Bengal Engineers. He told her of the ten years of active service that he had seen in India; of his part in the capture of Allyghur, the battle of Delhi, the siege of Agra, the battle of Laswarree, the battle and siege of Deeg, and the first siege of Bhurtpore; and she learned from others that he had been several times mentioned in despatches for exemplary valor. Weighed against these achievements, the fact that he had neither money nor prospects seemed to her of little importance. The two young people were soon very much in love, and despite the prohibitions of Mrs. Becher, who altogether refused to countenance their engagement, they continued to meet after Anne returned from Bath to Fareham.

Their secret trysting place [writes Mrs. Fuller] was a terrace at the end of the Bechers' garden, past which flowed the broad tidal river

[59] See above, Mrs. Butler.

[60] The stories of Anne Becher's early life which follow were told by her to Lady Ritchie, and by Lady Ritchie to Mrs. Fuller.

[61] His military career is outlined in Colonel H. M. Vibart's *Addiscombe: Its Heroes and Men of Note* (London, 1894), pp. 59–62.

which skirts the town. Here Anne was accustomed to wait for the boat that brought her lover. But their meetings were discovered, and Anne was ordered to her room, where she was kept under lock and key until she should give her word of honour that she would not again see Ensign Carmichael-Smyth. With this order she refused to comply, and she was supported in her confinement by the letters which the Ensign managed to smuggle to her by a maid, and to which she replied by the same agent.

Then suddenly the letters ceased, and one day old Mrs. Becher hobbled into her granddaughter's room and told her to muster all her courage to bear a great blow; the Ensign had died of a sudden fever and on his death-bed had sent her messages of his undying love. Anne pined and mourned in silence. After a time a family council decided that the broken-hearted young woman should be sent out to India as soon as possible to stay with her Becher relations.

So it happened that Anne Becher departed for India in 1808, "dressed for the six months' voyage in a long riding habit of dark green cloth and a high hat swathed in veils." She had great success in Calcutta society, and from among the many suitors for her hand she two years later chose Richmond Thackeray [62] (1781-1815), whom she married on October 13, 1810. Thackeray joined with great business abilities the interest of a powerful Anglo-Indian connection, and his rise in the East India Company's Civil Service had been rapid. He was at Eton from 1791 to 1796 and came out to Bengal in 1798. After the usual apprenticeship he was appointed Collector of the frontier district of Birbhum from 1803 to 1807, and in 1808 he was promoted to the secretaryship of the Board of Revenue in Calcutta. He was an amateur of books and *objets d'art* who enjoyed an excellent position in Bengal society, and if — like most bachelor Anglo-Indians of his time — he had kept a native mistress,[63] he still met all the requirements of the splendid marriage that Mrs. Becher had desired for her granddaughter.

[62] The authoritative account of Richmond Thackeray's life in Bengal is to be found in Sir William Wilson Hunter's *The Thackerays in India* (London, 1897), pp. 141-172.

[63] The daughter of this woman was left an annuity by Richmond Thackeray. She married a certain Blechynden, and their daughter (who was quite black!), visited Thackeray in London during 1848. See below, No. 458.

The Richmond Thackerays' short life together seems to have been uniformly happy. Their only son, to whose letters this edition is devoted, was born on July 18, 1811, and five months later Richmond Thackeray received the coveted post of collector of the district lying around Calcutta. He and his wife went to live in the collector's house at Alipur — which had been "the country lodge of Sir Philip Francis in the last century: the 'villa inter paludes' where he held his weekly symposiums" —, [64] and there a dramatic episode took place.

Returning from his club in Calcutta one day [writes Mrs. Fuller], Richmond Thackeray said to his wife: 'I have just made the acquaintance of a most delightful and interesting Engineer officer; he only arrived yesterday morning, knows no one, and I have invited him to dine with us to-night so that we can introduce him to our friends.'

The hour of the dinner party arrived, the guests assembled, and the last to come was the stranger. The servant announced in a loud voice, 'Captain Carmichael-Smyth,' and in walked Anne's long-lost lover!

What that dinner was like no words can describe. After what seemed an eternity, Anne and Captain Carmichael-Smyth had a moment to themselves, and in a low trembling voice she exclaimed: 'I was told you had died of a sudden fever.' And with bitter reproach he replied, 'I was informed by your grandmother that you no longer cared for me and had broken our engagement. As a proof, all my letters to you were returned unopened. And when in despair I wrote again and again begging for an interview, you never gave me an answer or a sign.'

After a while the situation become so impossible that Richmond Thackeray had to be told; he listened gravely, said little, but was never the same to Anne again.

Richmond Thackeray died on September 13, 1815, and a year and a half later his widow sent her son home to England to be educated. During the following winter she married Captain Carmichael-Smyth, in whose company she herself returned to England in 1819. Her husband received his majority in 1821. The history of the Carmichael-Smyths is henceforth bound up so closely with Thackeray's that it need not be traced here. More to the point is Lady Ritchie's account of the little corner of the Parisian English colony in which the Major and Mrs. Carmichael-Smyth lived be-

[64] Hunter, *Thackerays in India*, p. 169.

tween 1838 and 1861, a milieu that was also very much a part of the lives of Thackeray and his children:

My grandmother had a little society of her own at Paris, in the midst of which she seemed to reign from dignity and kindness of heart; her friends, it must be confessed, have not as yet become historic, but she herself was well worthy of a record. Grandmothers in books and memoirs are mostly alike, stately, old-fashioned, kindly, and critical. Mine was no exception to the general rule. She had been one of the most beautiful women of her time; she was very tall, with a queenly head and carriage; she always moved in a dignified way. She had an odd taste in dress, I remember, and used to walk out in a red merino cloak trimmed with ermine, which gave her the air of a retired empress wearing out her robes. She was a woman of strong feeling, somewhat imperious, with a passionate love for little children, and with extraordinary sympathy and enthusiasm for any one in trouble or in disgrace. How benevolently she used to look round the room at her many *protégés*, with her beautiful gray eyes! Her friends as a rule were shorter than she was and brisker, less serious and emotional. They adopted her views upon politics, religion and homœopathy, or at all events did not venture to contradict them. But they certainly could not reach her heights, and her almost romantic passion of feeling. . . .

I don't think we ever came home from one of our walks that we did not find our grandfather sitting watching for our grandmother's return. We used to ask him if he didn't find it very dull doing nothing in the twilight, but he used to tell us it was his thinking-time. My sister and I thought thinking dreadfully dull, and only longed for candles and *Chambers's Miscellany*. A good deal of thinking went on in our peaceful home, we should have liked more doing. One day was just like another; my grandmother and my grandfather sat on either side of the hearth in their two accustomed places; there was a French cook in a white cap, who brought in the trays and the lamp at the appointed hour; there was Chambers on the book-shelf, *Pickwick*, and one or two of my father's early books, and *The Listener*, by Caroline Fry, which used to be my last desperate resource when I had just finished all the others. We lived in a sunny little flat on a fourth floor, with windows east and west and a wide horizon from each, and the sound of the cries from the street below, and the confusing roll of the wheels when the windows were open in summer. In winter time we dined at five by lamplight at the round table in my grandfather's study. After dinner we used to go into the pretty blue drawing-room, where the peat fire would be burning brightly in the open grate, and the evening papers would come in with the tea. I can see it all still, hear it, smell the peat, and taste the odd herbaceous tea and the French bread and butter. On the band of the *Constitutional* newspaper was printed 'M. le Major Michel Eschmid.' It was not my grandfather's name or anything like it, but he would gravely say that when English people lived in France they must expect to have their names gallicised, and his paper certainly found him out evening after evening. While my grandmother with much emphasis read the news (she was a fervent republican, and so was my grandfather), my sister and I would sit unconscious of politics and happy over our story-books, until the fatal inevitable moment when a ring was heard at the bell and evening callers were announced. Then we reluctantly shut up our books, for we were told to get our needlework when the company came in, and we had to find chairs and hand tea-cups, and answer inquiries, and presently go to bed.

The ladies would come in in their bonnets, with their news and their comments upon the public events, which, by the way, seemed to go off like fireworks in those days expressly for our edification. Ours was a talkative, economical, and active little society, — *Cranford en Voyage* is the impression which remains to me of those early surroundings. If the ladies were one and all cordially attached to my grandmother, to my grandfather they were still more devoted. A Major is a Major. He used to sign their pension papers, administer globules for their colds, give point and support to their political opinions. I can see him still sitting in his arm-chair by the fire with a little semicircle round about the hearth. Ours was anything but a meek and disappointed community. We may have had our reverses, — and very important reverses they all seem to have been, — but we had all had spirit enough to leave our native shores and settle in Paris, not without a certain implied disapproval of the other people who went on living in England regardless of expense. My father did not escape this criticism. Why, they used to say, did he remain in that nasty smoky climate, so bad for health and spirits? Why didn't he settle in Paris and write works upon the French? [65]

Since by far the longest and most important of all Thackeray's correspondences is addressed to his mother, the reader will find ample material with which to form his conception of the personalities of Major and Mrs. Carmichael-Smyth. It may not be superfluous to mention, however, that Major Carmichael-Smyth was the principal model for Colonel Newcome, and that Mrs. Carmichael-Smyth is very faithfully portrayed as Helen Pendennis.

[65] *Chapters*, pp. 15–16 and 18–21.

## THE CROWES

Apart from his own family and the Ritchies, there was no household which Thackeray knew so long and so intimately as that of Eyre Evans Crowe [66] (1799–1868). Crowe was an Irishman who as a young man had left Trinity College, Dublin, without a degree and come to London to make his fortune by literature. During the eighteen-twenties he wrote a series of unsuccessful novels and a *History of France* (1830) for Dr. Lardner's *Cabinet Encyclopædia*. Meanwhile, he had married Margaret, daughter of Captain Archer of Newtown Mount Kennedy in the county of Wicklow, in 1823, and the needs of his growing family forced him not long after 1830 to accept the post of Paris correspondent of *The Morning Chronicle*. When Thackeray in the autumn of 1834 first visited the Crowes at their home at the corner of the Grande Rue des Batignolles and the Rue des Dames on the outskirts of Paris, they already had five children, Eyre (b. 1824), Joseph (1825–1896), Eugenie Marie, Edward (b. 1829), and Amy Marianne (1831–1865). George, their last child, was born in 1841.

Later in 1834 the Crowes moved into central Paris, establishing themselves on the sixth floor of an apartment building at 5 Rue du 29 Juillet. There Mrs. Crowe held a reception every Saturday evening, and Thackeray fell into the habit of coming on that day to the apartment about an hour before dinner, whereupon the children would surround him and beg for a drawing. *"The Count's" Adventures*, the principal series sketched for their amusement and certainly among the most spirited and comic of Thackeray's caricatures, is reproduced for the first time in Appendix V below. After dinner the party was usually increased by the painters William Darley and John Brine (the "Count" of Thackeray's drawings), by Jack Sheehan, by Captain and Mrs. Hankey, and by a variety of Frenchmen and Germans. Mrs. Crowe played Irish jigs and Scotch reels on the piano, and choruses were sung by all present,

[66] This brief notice is based chiefly on Sir Joseph Crowe's *Reminiscences of Thirty-Five Years of my Life* (London, 1895).

"the supreme enjoyment being a song from Thackeray." [67]  When Thackeray married, his wife made another at these gatherings, and not long after the Thackerays removed to London in 1837, the Carmichael-Smyths supplied their place in the Crowe circle. Nor did Thackeray omit to visit the Crowes at St. Germain, where they lived between 1838 and 1842, and at St. Cloud, where they spent the winter of 1842–1843, when he was in Paris during those years.

Crowe became a leader writer on *The Morning Chronicle* in the autumn of 1843, and by 1844 his entire family was settled at 5 Devonshire Place, Hampstead, which was their home during the next seven years. There Thackeray was a frequent caller, and it was largely through Crowe's influence that he became the principal book reviewer of *The Morning Chronicle* between 1844 and 1846.[68]  Crowe left *The Morning Chronicle* late in 1845 to write leaders for *The Daily News*, the first issue of which appeared on January 1, 1846. He replaced John Forster as editor of that journal during the following October, and he was able, through his friendship with Lord Palmerston and Lord John Russell, to make *The Daily News* for some years the authoritative mouthpiece of the government. Yet when the Whig ministry was on the point of resigning in November, 1851, Crowe was made to retire from the paper, and he and his family sank without warning from comfort to indigence. Crowe returned to France, where he supported himself by contributing to *The Examiner* and by historical writing. Mrs. Crowe, who some time before had been severely injured in a carriage accident, was discovered to be suffering from cancer. She died after a long and painful illness on October 22, 1853. Among the children, provision had been made only for Eugenie, who had married Robert Wynne, a Welsh squire, in 1850. But three of the others found a good Samaritan in Thackeray.

At the time of his family's disaster, Joseph Crowe was a trained

[67] The same, p. 11.

[68] I have found it possible through clues in Thackeray's letters to discover more than thirty of his contributions to *The Morning Chronicle* that have not previously been identified. These are listed in Appendix XII.

journalist, for during the past eight years he had been a reporter for *The Morning Chronicle* and *The Daily News*. He found it difficult, nonetheless, to secure work, and during the next two years he devoted his abundant leisure to research with Giovanni Battista Cavalcaselle, an old friend as impecunious as he, which led to the writing of *The Early Flemish Painters* (1856), the first of the pioneer histories of painting that were to make their names famous. In November, 1853, Thackeray persuaded Charles Mackay to appoint Crowe Crimean correspondent of *The Illustrated London News*. Henceforth Crowe's career was a distinguished one. He reported the Indian mutiny and the Austrian-Italian war for *The Times*, being present at the battle of Solferino. He became Consul-General for Saxony in 1860 through Lord John Russell's interest. In 1872 he was appointed Consul-General for Westphalia and the Rhenish Provinces, in 1880 Commercial Attaché for the embassies at Berlin and Vienna, and in 1882 Commercial Attaché for the whole of Europe. He was made a K. C. M. G. in 1890.

When Thackeray arrived in Paris in April, 1854, he found that Amy Crowe, who had attended her mother faithfully in her last illness, had been for some months without a suitable home. He accordingly took her into his own family, and for the next eight years she lived with him as a third daughter. In 1862 she married Edward Talbot Thackeray, whom she accompanied to India. After her death in childbirth three years later, her two children, Margaret and Anne, were entrusted to Thackeray's daughters, who took care of them for many years.[69]

But of all the Crowes' children Thackeray was perhaps fondest of Eyre. In 1851 he too was at a loose end, for though he was trained as a painter, he had no customers, and no money for further study. Thackeray employed Crowe as his amanuensis while he

[69] "Our babies are the children of Amy Crowe," Anne Thackeray writes to Mrs. Baxter in a letter of March 3, 1866, owned by Miss Maude Frank. "She died dear love when her littlest baby was born & then [her husband] brought them back to us from India & they are upstairs now. The poor Father had to go back quite alone two months ago, but the children are very bright & sweet & think poor darlings that there are only 'aunts' in the world to love little children."

was writing *Esmond* in the winter of 1851–1852 and the following autumn took him to the United States as his secretary. When they returned to England, Thackeray was active in securing commissions for his friend, who afterwards became an inspector at the South Kensington Museum and an A. R. A. During his later life he wrote two little books embodying his recollections of Thackeray.[70] Henry James, who first met Crowe during his visit to America, relates that he encountered him many years after in London, lagging superfluous on the stage, "the most touchingly resigned of the children of disappointment."

Not only by association was he a Thackerayan figure, but much as if the master's hand had stamped him with the outline and the value, with life and sweetness and patience — shown, as after the long futility, seated in a quiet wait, very long too, for the end. That was sad, one couldn't but feel; yet it was in the oddest way impossible to take him for a failure. He might have been one of fortune's, strictly; but what was that when he was one of Thackeray's own successes? — in the minor line, but with such a grace and such a truth, those of some dim second cousin to Colonel Newcome.[71]

## CHARLES DICKENS

Faithful to the persuasion that "animosities are mortal, but the humanities live forever," biographers of Dickens and Thackeray have generally minimized the clash between the two novelists in what is known as the Garrick Club Affair. The vogue of this interpretation was established by Forster, who refers to the episode in his *Life of Charles Dickens* (1872–1874) as an "estrangement . . . hardly now worth mention even in a note."[72] Far from supporting Forster's view, Thackeray's letters, by providing a consecutive history of his relations with Dickens, suggest that the quarrel over Edmund Yates brought into the open a hostility that had long been

[70] *With Thackeray in America* (New York, 1893) and *Thackeray's Haunts and Homes* (London, 1897).

[71] *A Small Boy and Others* (New York, 1913), pp. 90–91.

[72] Ed. J. W. T. Ley (London, 1928), p. 697, note.

latent. They afford ground for believing that Thackeray's line of conduct was rather more consistent than has been supposed, and they reveal the reason for Dickens's willingness to join in the fray.

Thackeray first met Dickens in April, 1836, when he made an unsuccessful application to illustrate *Pickwick Papers*. For the next ten years the two were on friendly but not intimate terms. Thackeray, who hugely enjoyed Dickens's early novels, freely offered him the homage to which he was accustomed, and Dickens, if he had no particular taste for Thackeray's work, recognized his talent and wished him well.

The success of *Vanity Fair* in 1847 and 1848 materially altered their respective positions. Dickens's preëminence among Victorian novelists had hitherto been unquestioned save by an occasional admirer of Bulwer-Lytton; during the remaining years of Thackeray's life he had a formidable rival for public esteem. *Dombey and Son* appeared concurrently with *Vanity Fair*, *David Copperfield* with *Pendennis*, *Bleak House* with *Esmond*, *Hard Times* with *The Newcomes*, *The Tale of Two Cities* with *The Virginians*, and *Great Expectations* with *Philip*. Friction was inevitable in this prolonged competition. Though both Thackeray and Dickens sought to avoid contention, each had injudicious partisans among his friends who were determined that their idol should be supreme. So Thackeray had reason to feel that he was badly treated by Forster in *The Examiner*, and Dickens might justly have complained of the opinion of his books expressed by Thackeray's friends connected with *The Scotsman* and *The North British Review*. It would be idle to maintain, moreover, that there was close personal sympathy between the two men. Their backgrounds, their casts of mind, and their interests were disparate and in some respects conflicting. Thackeray could not rid himself of the conviction that there was a taint of vulgarity in Dickens, nor could Dickens entirely absolve Thackeray from the charges of insincerity and cynical levity.

They managed, nevertheless, to remain on passably good terms until 1858. On June 12 of that year Edmund Yates published his offensive article about Thackeray in *Town Talk*. When Thackeray demanded an apology in a letter of the utmost severity, Yates turned to Dickens for counsel. Had Dickens been altogether himself, we may presume that he would have abstained from becoming involved in a dispute to which his participation could alone give importance. Unhappily he was passing through a period of mental and emotional agitation, during which he attached little weight to considerations of prudence or decorum.

Three weeks earlier he had separated from his wife, to whom he had been married for twenty-one years and who had borne him ten children. Rumor associated the separation with an intimacy which he had formed with a young actress named Ellen Ternan. In this difficult situation Yates earned Dickens's gratitude by performing certain confidential services, the nature of which is not known, and Thackeray, though innocent of any malice, inadvertently incurred the suspicion of spreading precisely the rumor that Dickens wished to suppress.[73] Even Dickens's immense popularity did not protect him from general censure when he announced that he had left his wife, nor was his own conscience untroubled. Knowing that his conduct was open to criticism, he could not bear to have it criticised, and for the time being he judged his friends almost entirely by their willingness to approve the step that he had taken. Yates was with him, Thackeray appeared to be against him, and by siding with the former in their controversy, he saw an opportunity of hitting back at those who had attacked his domestic arrangements.

Dickens helped Yates to write the letter to Thackeray of June 15 that made private settlement of their quarrel impossible, and directed Yates's campaign against Thackeray until March, 1859, when the affair was terminated by the publication of *Mr. Thackeray, Mr. Yates, and the Garrick Club*.[74] During 1858 and the

[73] See below, No. 1381 and No. 1356.

[74] Yates had Dickens's assistance in writing this pamphlet (*Letters*, ed. Walter Dexter, London, 3 vols., 1938, III, 94). There is nothing to show, as has often been hinted, that Dickens's defence of Yates was part of a carefully dissimulated cabal against Thackeray. The charge, indeed, is specifically denied by Yates (probably at Dickens's instance) on pp. 14–15 of *Mr. Thackeray, Mr. Yates, and the Garrick Club* (privately printed, 1859) and by

following years all intercourse ceased between Thackeray and Dickens, except for an occasional perfunctory handshake when they happened to meet in public. Dickens's hostility inevitably entailed a coolness on the part of Forster, and what hurt Thackeray most about the quarrel was his belief that these two old friends were trying to set other old friends against him.[75]

Fortunately our narrative does not end on this discord. Shortly before Thackeray's death he and Dickens made up their difference.[75a] Dickens was present at his funeral and wrote a moving memorial article for Thackeray's own magazine.[76]

## RICHARD DOYLE

Richard ("Dicky") Doyle [77] (1824–1883) was brought up by a governess and tutor in the devoutly Catholic home of his father John Doyle (1797–1868). The older Doyle was the well known political cartoonist "HB," who in some 900 lithographs executed

---

Dickens himself, writing to Peter Cunningham on February 11, 1859 (*Letters,* ed. Dexter, III, 93). Nor is it possible to credit the assertion of John Cordy Jeaffreson (*A Book of Recollections,* 2 vols., London, 1894, I, 269) that Thackeray said of his quarrel with Yates, "*I am hitting the man behind him.*" Both Dickens and Thackeray had quick tempers and were capable of sustained anger, but neither would stoop to a calculated intrigue.

[75] See below, No. 1424 and No. 1504.

[75a] "There were no lookers on what passed between Thackeray & Dickens but myself," writes Sir Theodore Martin in an unpublished letter of October 12, 1906 (*Howe Proofs,* pp. 381–382). "I was standing in the Athenæum Hall chatting with Thackeray — Dickens came out of the Reading Room, passed us quite close, & taking no notice of either of us. 'There's Dickens!' Thackeray exclaimed, & went so quickly after Dickens, that he caught him at the foot of the stairs. He held out his hand to Dickens, saying a few words, and then Dickens took his hand. A few words, & Thackeray came back to me, and told me what had passed between them. The speaking was chiefly Thackeray's — to the [purpose that] 'the estrangement must not go on, that they should shake hands, and be the friends they had used to be.' "

[76] "In Memoriam," *Cornhill Magazine,* February, 1864.

[77] For information concerning Doyle, see Graham Everitt's *English Caricaturists* (London, 1893), pp. 381–394, and an anonymous article entitled "Richard Doyle, Painter and Humorist" in *The Month,* L (1884), 305–319.

between 1829 and 1851 made the features of most of the notable parliamentarians of his time familiar to the English public, and it was from him that Richard received his instruction in drawing. The boy soon developed an individual style, which gained him an appointment as *Punch's* second cartoonist when he was only nineteen. During the next seven years he was one of the magazine's ablest workers. His contributions included many influential political cartoons and a famous survey of London life in 1849 called "Ye Manners and Customs of ye English."

Yet in 1850 Doyle was courageous enough to throw away his assured future at the dictates of his conscience. After the restoration of the Catholic hierarchy in England, a step popularly known as the "Papal Aggression," *Punch* became violent against the Roman church. Doyle protested, but to no avail, against these attacks on his faith. His last cartoon appeared in *Punch* for November 16, in which was also published a tirade by Douglas Jerrold called "A Short Way with the Pope's Puppets." Doyle refused to continue his association with a magazine in which the Pope was advised "to feed his flock on the wafers of the Vatican," and on November 27 he resigned.[78]

No one regretted Doyle's withdrawal from *Punch* more than Thackeray. He had met the cartoonist often at the Procters' and elsewhere in the London world, and the two men had long been good friends. Thackeray wrote a discerning appreciation of Doyle's illustrations to Edward Taylor's *The Fairy Ring* in 1845,[79] and when in 1849 he was prevented by illness from illustrating *Rebecca and Rowena*, the plates were supplied by Doyle. It was with real pleasure, therefore, that Thackeray in 1853 offered the task of executing the plates for *The Newcomes* to Doyle, who had been hard put to find work since he left *Punch*. These illustrations, which occupied Doyle until 1855, were received with great enthusiasm by Thackeray's readers, though not in every instance by Thackeray himself.

[78] See *The Month*, L, 310–311.
[79] "Christmas Books — No. 2," *The Morning Chronicle*, December 26, 1845. This article has not previously been identified as Thackeray's.

After the conclusion of *The Newcomes* Thackeray and Doyle appear to have seen little of each other, though a series of "Bird's-eye Views of English Society" from Doyle's hand was published in *The Cornhill Magazine* during Thackeray's editorship. Doyle's later life was chiefly devoted to marine painting.

## MRS. ELLIOT AND KATE PERRY

Among the eight children of James Perry (d. 1821), editor of *The Morning Chronicle* from 1789 to 1819, were two inseparable sisters, Jane and Kate. It was not long after Jane married Thomas Frederick Elliot (1808–1880) that Kate joined the new household at 37 Chesham Place, Belgrave Square. Elliot, who was the sixth son of Hugo Elliot, Governor of Madras, and the nephew of Gilbert Elliot, first Earl of Minto, had entered the Colonial Office in 1825. In 1840 he received his first important post, the chairmanship of a board of advice and management over colonial land and emigration, and in 1847 he was appointed Assistant Under-Secretary of State for the Colonies, a position he held until his retirement in 1868. He was made a K. C. M. G. in 1869. Until his wife's death at least, he had a place in society much more than commensurate with his not overly prominent official status, and for this he had his lively sister-in-law chiefly to thank. Landseer had proposed to her when she was twenty,[80] but she refused him and all other suitors because of her uncertain health. Growing stronger as she grew older and having no household cares, she devoted her energies to society, in which she acquired a host of friends and acquaintances.

Miss Perry first met Thackeray at Brighton in 1846, where she was staying with an older brother.

Mr. Thackeray and I [she writes] went through no gradations of growth in our friendship, it was more like Jack's bean stalk in a pantomime, which rushed up sky high without culture; and, thank God, so remained till his most sad and sudden end. . . . he brought his morn-

[80] *Mrs. Brookfield*, p. 469.

ing work to read to me in the evening; he had just commenced "Vanity Fair," and was living at the old Ship Inn, where he wrote most of the first volume. He often then said to me, "I wonder whether this will take, the publishers accept it, and the world read it?" I remember answering him, "That I had no reliance upon my own critical powers in literature, but that I had written yesterday to my sister, Mrs. F. Elliot, and said, 'I have made a great friendship with one of the principal contributors of *Punch*, Mr. Thackeray, he is now writing a novel, but cannot hit upon a name for it. I may be wrong, but it seems to me the cleverest thing I ever read. The first day he dined with us I was fearfully alarmed at him, the next we walked in Chichester Park, he told me all about his little girls, and great friendship with the Brookfields, I told him about you and Chesham Place.'" When he heard this and my opinion of his novel, he burst out laughing, and said "Ah! M^lle. (as he always called me) it is *not* small beer; but I do not know whether it will be palatable to the London folks." He told me some time afterwards that after ransacking his brain for a name for his novel, it came upon him unawares, in the middle of the night, as if a voice had whispered, "Vanity Fair." (He said,) "I jumped out of bed and ran three times round my room, uttering as I went, 'Vanity Fair, Vanity Fair, Vanity Fair.'" [81]

When Thackeray returned to London, he was duly introduced to the Elliots, and he soon ranked them and Miss Perry among his closest friends.

During the next twelve years Chesham Place was one of Thackeray's favorite houses of call. Grander society was open to him in many other homes, but he became accustomed to the Elliots' circle, which had the recommendation of including the Brookfields, and passed many evenings there among old friends that he would otherwise have devoted to the great world.

How plainly it all rises before one! [writes Lady Ritchie] Kate Perry floating into the room, with her graceful ways and wonderful wreaths of crisp waving, auburn hair; and the good-looking master of the house, with quick, brilliant alertness, and the kind mistress with deep-set grey eyes. It was a kind, amusing house, full of welcome and interest

[81] *Reminiscences of a London Drawing Room*, pp. 2–3. This privately printed brochure seems to have appeared in 1883, for that date is written inside the front cover in Miss Perry's presentation copy to Kinglake in the Widener Collection of the Harvard College Library.

and discussion, with a certain amount of criticism and habit of the world to make its sympathy amusing. Lord Lansdowne used to go there, and Mr. Kinglake and Sir Henry Taylor. The great clan of Elliot used to be seen there, and most of the persons who, in those days, were writing and reading and making speeches; and Lady Theresa Lewis herself, and the charming Kent House coterie, and Mr. Spedding, and Mr. Venables, and Lord Houghton, and all the philosophers.[82]

Before his quarrel with Brookfield in September, 1851, Thackeray wrote only an occasional note to the two sisters. But after he was cut off from direct communication with Mrs. Brookfield, he made them his confidantes and addressed to them one of the most intimate and revealing of his longer correspondences. They had followed the whole progress of his love for her, and he could be sure that they would tell her all that he said or wrote. One can surmise what admirable comforters they must have been from certain stanzas in "The Pen and the Album," which Thackeray set down in Miss Perry's autograph-book during 1852:

> Go back, my pretty little gilded tome,
> To a fair mistress and a pleasant home,
> Where soft hearts greet us whensoe'er we come!
>
> Dear friendly eyes, with constant kindness lit,
> However rude my verse, or poor my wit,
> Or sad or gay my mood, you welcome it.
>
> Kind lady! till my last of lines is penn'd,
> My master's love, grief, laughter, at an end,
> ‘Whene'er I write your name, may I write friend!
>
> Not all are so that were so in past years;
> Voices, familiar once, no more he hears;
> Names, often writ, are blotted out in tears.
>
> So be it: — joys will end and tears will dry —
> Album! my master bids me wish good-bye,
> He'll send you to your mistress presently.
>
> And thus with thankful heart he closes you:
> Blessing the happy hour when a friend he knew
> So gentle, and so generous, and so true.[83]

[82] *Blackstick Papers* (London, 1908), p. 142.
[83] *Works*, XIII, 70–71.

Mrs. Elliot died on January 4, 1859, but Thackeray continued to see Miss Perry frequently until his own death nearly five years later. Miss Perry survived till almost the end of the century.

## THE REV. WHITWELL ELWIN

Elwin (1816–1900) was the younger son of an old Norfolk family. He received his education in small schools near his home and at Caius College, Cambridge, where he matriculated in 1834. He married Frances Elwin (d. 1898), a distant relative, a year before he was given his B. A. degree in 1839, and shortly afterward took holy orders. Having held curacies in Bath from 1839 to 1843 and in Hemington near Bristol from 1843 to 1849, he in the latter year became the incumbent of his family's living of Booton in Norfolk, where he remained rector until his death. Elwin early determined to live out his life as a country parson, refusing all offers of preferment, however advantageous, that would attract him away from his congenial *Kleinleben,* and to this resolve he faithfully adhered.

After leaving the university, he continued to devote his leisure to study and writing. His first contribution to *The Quarterly Review* was accepted in 1843, and it was not long before he was the most trusted aide of John Gibson Lockhart, the editor of that venerable publication. When Lockhart's failing health forced his retirement to Italy in 1853, Elwin succeeded to his post. Though he continued scrupulously to fulfil his duties at Booton, he came up to London every quarter to get out the *Review,* and his circle of acquaintance was immensely widened. Among the new friends he made was Thackeray, whom he persuaded to write an article on Leech for the *Quarterly* of January, 1855.

This friendship, which is recorded in a series of whimsical and affectionate letters, was one of the pleasantest episodes of Thackeray's later life. Elwin endeared himself to Thackeray by his unquestioning hero-worship and by his delightful simplicity.

Though he knew most of the great men of the age, he never faltered in his conviction that Thackeray towered head and shoulders above the rest of mankind. Thackeray would not have been human if he had been displeased by the homage of this learned and amiable divine. Yet he was accustomed to flattery, and it was chiefly Elwin's fresh and piquant eccentricity of character that won his regard.

This quality in Elwin led Thackeray to call him Dr. Primrose, and, indeed, his annals are filled with incidents that Goldsmith might appropriately have recited of the Vicar of Wakefield.[84] As a young man in Bath, for example, Elwin was accustomed to read poetry to his wife as they drove slowly along the country lanes in their pony carriage. One day when he was lost in a recitation from Wordsworth, his pony suddenly made for its stable at top speed, and turning a sharp corner emptied Elwin, his wife, and their volume of Wordsworth into the road. Nor did he fare better travelling by public conveyance. "I walk to a coach which passes at three miles' distance," he writes in 1844, "and which being generally full, the coachman accomodates me, as a favour, with a seat on the top of the luggage. In this conspicuous situation I have become a known character to all the idle little boys on the road, who hoot at me as we pass."

His permanent settlement at Booton found him still struggling with petty adversities. He was eager to live in the new rectory that he had commissioned, but he could not persuade the builders' men to make proper haste in their work. At last in exasperation, suspecting the workmen of using his unfinished house as a shop in which they did work for other customers, he moved in with walls still unpapered and unpainted, a state in which they remained, to the ever-renewed astonishment of his visitors, for nearly fifty years. His landscape gardeners proved equally dilatory, and for several years the field that surrounded his house was cut into an

[84] There is prefixed to Elwin's *Some XVIII Century Men of Letters*, 2 vols. (London, 1902) a long memoir, apparently by his son Warwick, which is the chief source of information regarding his life. The anecdotes which follow are related on pp. 29, 58–60, 66–67, and 255 of this biography.

almost impassable quagmire by carts. It was typical of Elwin that, apart from preliminary gusts of irritation, he adapted himself to these inconveniences with the utmost complacency.

A similar disregard for ostentation marked Elwin's quarterly "Sacrament Sunday." "The clerk used to bring the requisites for the Celebration in a wicker basket," Elwin's son relates, "which was pushed under the altar, where it was plainly visible below the big white cloth that replaced the musty covering of other times. With the sacred vessels were placed on the altar an ordinary loaf of bread and a black bottle of wine, covered over with a napkin. As the main part of the congregation retired, the rector removed this covering, took a corkscrew and opened the bottle, and prepared the elements in sight of the communicants." When Elwin in later years succumbed to the attractions of aristocratic society and took pleasure in visiting great estates, the simplicity of his luggage matched that of his sacramental services. He was conspicuous among guests who never travelled without squadrons of trunks by his habit of bringing with him only "a tiny hand-portmanteau and small carpet-bag," which he insisted on carrying himself and reso-lutely refused to let out of his sight while in transit. The affection-ate amusement of his hosts on these occasions is illustrated by a remark of Lord Bath's to Elwin, as they opened an old cupboard to consult some manuscripts that were covered with dust: "You had better let me go first, for I have another coat to put on, and you know you haven't."

In 1860 Elwin resolved to give up the editorship of *The Quar-terly Review*, his decision being motivated chiefly by a desire to devote his time to John Murray's edition of Pope, for which he had become responsible on the death of John Wilson Croker in 1857. This was his chief employment for more than a decade. He pub-lished four volumes in 1870 and another in 1872, but old age, ill health, and private sorrows, reinforced by the adverse criticism with which his work had been received in some quarters, led him in 1878 to abandon the edition to Professor Courthope. The principal interest of his declining years was the reconstruction of his parish church at Booton, but his continued devotion to literature is witnessed by a fragmentary biography of Thackeray, published after his death.[85]


## JAMES THOMAS FIELDS

Fields [86] (1817–1881) was born and brought up in Portsmouth, New Hampshire, where without much help from formal schooling he managed to acquire a good general education by solitary reading. He came to Boston at the age of fourteen to take a position as a clerk in a bookstore. Within seven years he was a junior partner in the firm of Ticknor, Reed, and Fields, which he later controlled. Under his guidance the concern became the most discriminating and one of the most successful of American publishing houses, for Fields was thoroughly acquainted with the commercial aspects of his trade, and he had a remarkable gift for making the authors that wrote for him his friends.

It was in 1852, during the visit to England which followed the death of his first wife, that Fields met Thackeray. Seeking to persuade the novelist to bring his lectures to America, he did not go directly to Thackeray, but first approached his friends at the Garrick Club. They gave him little encouragement.

Next morning [Fields writes], after this talk at the Garrick, the elderly damsel of all work announced to me, as I was taking breakfast at my lodgings, that Mr. *Sackville* had called to see me, and was then waiting below. Very soon I heard a heavy tread on the stairs, and then entered a tall, white-haired stranger, who held out his hand, bowed profoundly, and with a most comical expression announced himself as Mr. Sackville. Recognizing at once the face from published portraits, I knew that my visitor was none other than Thackeray himself, who, having heard the servant give the wrong name, determined to assume it on this occasion.

[85] "The Boyhood of Thackeray," *Monthly Review*, XV (June, 1904), pp. 161–184; "Thackeray at Cambridge," *Monthly Review*, XVI (Sept., 1904), pp. 151–172; and "Thackeray in Search of a Profession," *Monthly Review*, XVII (Oct., 1904), pp. 88–105.

[86] The chief source of information about Fields is his wife's *James T. Fields* (Boston, 1881).

For years afterwards, when he would drop in unexpectedly, both at home and abroad, he delighted to call himself Mr. Sackville, until a certain Milesian waiter at the Tremont House addressed him as Mr. Thack*uary*, when he adopted that name in preference to the other.[87]

Such was the auspicious beginning of Thackeray's association with Fields, auspicious because it set the tone which prevailed throughout their friendship. Effete readers have been surprised, not to say distressed, at the jolly, even boisterous Thackeray who appears in Fields's *Yesterdays with Authors* (1872), a book from which I shall often have occasion to quote. Yet Fields has given a picture of an important side of Thackeray's character, if a side that he did not care in later years to display to every comer. It is a testimony to Fields's fund of joviality and humor that Thackeray should have judged masculine fun and unaffected good sense to be the common ground on which they could most easily meet. Not many of those who knew him could write, as Fields does, that "In the midst of the most serious topic under discussion he was fond of asking permission to sing a comic song, or he would beg to be allowed to enliven the occasion by the instant introduction of a brief double-shuffle." [88]

During both of Thackeray's American visits Fields joined forces with the Mercantile Library Association of New York to relieve him of the tiresome business details incidental to lecturing. Fields was his constant companion when he was in Boston, and on his second tour he found another friend in the former Annie Adams (1834–1915), herself a writer, whom Fields had married in 1854. Thackeray later had the opportunity of entertaining both Fields and his wife during more than one of their visits to Europe.

In 1861 Fields succeeded Lowell as editor of *The Atlantic Monthly*, a position that he filled with distinction until his retirement from business in 1870. His last years were devoted to writing and to popular lecture tours.

[87] *Yesterdays with Authors* (Boston and New York, 1900), p. 14.
[88] The same, p. 22.

## EDWARD FITZGERALD

Had the correspondence between Thackeray and Edward Fitz-
Gerald (1809–1883) been preserved in its entirety, it would be
as extensive and at least as interesting as any group of Thackeray's
letters except those to his mother. Unfortunately Thackeray kept
little of what FitzGerald wrote to him, and FitzGerald burnt most
of Thackeray's early letters because he was "really ashamed of
their kindness." Yet enough of their correspondence remains to
make any account of their friendship superfluous. For nearly two
decades after they first met at Cambridge in the autumn of 1829
they were on the most intimate terms. When *Vanity Fair* was published, FitzGerald, a shy and sensitive man who regarded his own
life as a "total failure & mess," was awed by his friend's success
and crept back into his shell, but his affection for Thackeray did not
waver. And when Anne Thackeray asked her father in the last
year of his life which of his friends he had cared for most, he replied: "There was 'Old Fitz,' and I was very fond of Brookfield
once." After a pause, he added: "We shall be very good friends
again in hell together."

## JOHN FORSTER

Thackeray appears first to have met Forster (1812–1876) at the
Procters', nearly a decade after he came up to London from Newcastle in 1828. As Dickens's trusted adviser and chief critic of *The
Examiner*, he was already a power in the literary world, and he
gave many a good dinner to the leading authors of the day in his
comfortable chambers at 58 Lincoln's Inn Fields. He was not
unwilling to strike up an alliance with a promising young magazine
writer, however, and Thackeray was long indebted to him for
generous praise in conversation and in print. Forster's irascibility,
his sternly authoritative manner, and his total want of the smooth
veneer of good breeding prized by Victorian gentlemen did not

prevent Thackeray from discovering beneath this forbidding exterior a loyal, sensitive, and considerate friend.

For years the two men remained good companions, yet even during this period they occasionally disagreed. Thackeray admired his friend's learning, talent, and hard-headed practicality in business matters, but he did not feel that these qualities warranted Forster's habitual assumption, however well-intentioned, of dictatorial authority over the affairs of others. In the combination of Forster's ponderous person and magisterial airs he found a subject that cried out for caricature, and kind friends were not slow to inform Forster of his handiwork. Moreover, though he made no complaint, Thackeray can hardly have been pleased by Forster's appointment in 1842 as editor of *The Foreign Quarterly Review*, for he wanted the post himself.

While *Vanity Fair* was appearing, Thackeray's relations with Forster underwent a decisive change. The *modus vivendi* which the two had maintained when Thackeray was a struggling journalist collapsed when he became a great man. Forster was too ingenuous to hide the stirrings of jealousy to which the unexpected triumph of his early comrade of the press gave rise. He honestly believed that Thackerayan realism reflected a false and misleading view of life, which it was his duty to combat, and he inveighed against the decline in public taste that was revealed by the current tendency to place Thackeray above or on a par with Dickens. Inevitably his reviews in *The Examiner* reflected his convictions. Where Thackeray was accustomed to generous praise, he was now dismayed to meet with harsh and, so he felt, unjust criticism.

The first serious quarrel between the two old friends occurred in June, 1847, when Tom Taylor told Thackeray that Forster had abused the early installments of "*Punch's* Prize Novelists" (later called *Novels by Eminent Hands*) to him, and had said that their author was "false as hell." [89] This fracas was patched up, but others followed. A letter to Thackeray written (but possibly not sent) by Forster about October, 1854, summarizes the stormy his-

[89] The letters exchanged on this subject are printed below, Nos. 394–403.

tory of their association during the years that followed *Vanity Fair*: [90]

I am sorry that in that note of yours you should reopen things long past. I avoided them in my note, though I could *not* avoid protesting against what I felt to be an injustice done by you to me, quite unprovoked and still unretracted.

I dare say I may have done you injustice in former times; I am only sure that I never meant to do it. But you are not entitled to reproduce the old Pendennis charge. [91] I publicly rejected the interpretation you placed upon it, derogatory to your personal honour, and I saw you and discussed the matter with you openly and fairly as a public one, and rejoiced when it closed with friendly notes on both sides. You ought not to have reopened that, I think.

Into our dispute relating to the Lectures [92] I would not enter for the same reason. It is too late to apportion the provocation or the wrong on either side. You volunteered your hand to me, I took it, and I believed all that was over too. You came to see me when I was ill. [93] It was the last time I saw you before you sailed to America, and there was nothing in the shake of your hand at parting to tell me that it had been levelling, under a very thin disguise, and in the permanent form of a book, an imputation against me amounting to neither more or less than "treachery." [94]

You tell me now you thought me an unfair critic — but not for unfair motives. Yet the charge you brought against me was that for the motive of currying favor with one friend I did not hesitate to commit injustice to another. And this, in the same breath in which you acquit me of unfair motive, you continue to think "not unfair" on your part.

You continue also to think me, it seems, an unfair critic. I am Steele's man, you say. Of course you cannot perceive, and would not on any account say, that Mr. Macaulay is Addison's man. [95] He is to indulge his literary partisanship and to be highly complimented on ac-

---

[90] My text of Forster's letter is taken from a transcript made by the Comte de Suzannet from the draft in his possession. I have not traced the notes exchanged before Forster's letter was written.

[91] Forster alludes to the "Dignity of Literature" controversy, for which see below, No. 678.

[92] See below, No. 779.

[93] See below, No. 849.

[94] See below, No. 779.

[95] Forster's notice of Macaulay's *The Life and Writings of Addison* (1852) in *The Quarterly Review* of March, 1855 (pp. 509–568) is largely a defence of Steele.

count of it, for is he not a great man and a privy councillor? If you charge me with my leanings, shall I altogether acquit you of yours?

I am Goldsmith's man, too, though with no kindness. I will venture to say that no man has discriminated to the same degree as myself his weaknesses and faults. But I did not require to know that my writings have seldom had your good word, whatever you may have thought of them, — or that, at a time when such a word from you would have brought inexpressible satisfaction and pride to me, you have preferred to name me in the lump with that highly discriminating and impartial biographer, Mr. Prior.[96]

Coming down to quite the other day, too, you told me I am also Stanfield's man — and if I deserve to be so called for seeing that kindness was done to an old friend with more than usual emphasis, at a time when he was suffering great distress from an injustice which that kindness might help to relieve — of course I must undergo the name and any reproach there may be in it.

I would rather not [have] had to speak in a way to bring up old grievances. I wished to forget them all. But I could not forget that I should not have a claim to the renewed friendship and cordiality I sought if I did not assure you of the groundlessness of an imputation which, if wholly founded, would have made me really unworthy of what I sought. I had long had the desire to do this — and when I took the determination to write, on hearing that you had expressed a wish to meet me —, it was with no intention of writing a word that could awaken an angry feeling.

If I know myself, and the changes (I will dare to say in all respects for the better) which time has wrought in me, I believe that if, without forfeiting of self-respect on either side, and with the sense that there was really nothing to intercept an honest regard for each other, we could meet and shake hands, it would be for the advantage and happiness of us both. In that spirit, and recognizing that I had contributed my full share to past differences, I wrote to you the other day, and now write again. If you can renew the old intercourse on those terms — if you think a sincere resolve to forget as far as possible whatever has been painful in the past, likely to prove any reasonable security for a future better understanding — I earnestly offer such a guarantee from myself and most strongly solicit it from you. But if, notwithstanding this

[96] In the printed text of *The English Humourists* there is no mention either of Forster's *Life and Adventures of Oliver Goldsmith* (1848) or of Sir James Prior's *Life of Oliver Goldsmith* (1837), though quotations from both are Goldsmith's biographers before he gave his manuscript to his publishers. given in Hannay's notes. It is possible that Thackeray excised a passage about

assurance, you think us still likely to "like each other better away," I shall respect, though regret your determination.

Yours, my dear T.

Always sincerely

J. F.

Forster effected a reconciliation with Thackeray not long after this letter was written. The uneasy friendship that ensued lasted until the Garrick Club Affair of 1858, in which (as in everything) Forster sided with Dickens. Thackeray and Forster never made up this final estrangement, which was intensified by a reproachful allusion to himself that Forster detected in *The Roundabout Papers*.[97]

## MATTHEW JAMES HIGGINS

Thackeray, we know, was tall and proportionately burly. Yet in the years after 1847 he was often to be seen riding in Rotten Row with a man beside whom he appeared almost dwarfish. This was Matthew James Higgins (1810–1868), six feet eight inches in height but of graceful carriage and handsome countenance, who was called by his friends the "gentle giant." Many anecdotes of Higgins's gigantic stature are related by his biographer. We learn, for example, that "A gentleman of the same name, whose height was about 6 feet 4 inches, used to complain that the overshadowing presence of his namesake caused him to be distinguished amongst his countrymen at Rome as 'little Higgins.' "[98] And it is further recounted that when Higgins and Thackeray went together one day to see a show giant, "At the door, Thackeray pointed to his companion and whispered to the door-keeper, 'We are in the profession;' and so obtained free admission. 'But,' as Thackeray used to end the story, 'we were not mean, but paid our shillings as we came out.' "[99]

[97] See below, No. 1505.

[98] Sir William Stirling-Maxwell's memoir, prefixed to Higgins's *Essays on Social Subjects* (London, 1875), p. x.

[99] The same, p. lxvii.

Thackeray and Higgins became interested in each other's contributions when both were writing for *The New Monthly Magazine* in 1845, and each asked the editor to be introduced to the other. Thackeray discovered that his new friend was the only son of an Irish gentleman of extensive property. He had been educated at Eton and Oxford, and not being under the necessity of earning his living, he subsequently travelled in Italy, Spain, and the West Indies, where he had a large estate. When his first publication, "Jacob Omnium, The Merchant Prince," appeared in *The New Monthly Magazine* in 1845, he had settled in London at 1 Lowndes Square. From this story of an unscrupulous promoter, who bears a close resemblance to John Brough in *The Great Hogarty Diamond*, Higgins took the *nom de plume* over which many of his later contributions to *The Times*, *The Morning Chronicle*, *The Pall Mall Gazette*, and *The Cornhill Magazine* were written. Thackeray has given it a sort of permanence in one of his best ballads, "Jacob Homnium's Hoss," which tells of Higgins's revenge for a scandalous job put upon him and includes the tribute:

> His name is Jacob Homnium, Exquire;
> And if *I*'d committed crimes,
> Good Lord! I wouldn't ave that mann
> Attack me in the *Times*!

Higgins's controversial writings were, indeed, well calculated to arouse the admiration of such a master of literary polemics as Thackeray. He employed his pen chiefly in disinterested efforts to expose abuses, yet such was his hard sense and knowledge of the world that he invariably escaped seeming merely Quixotic. Many of his protests had practical effect, and the rest paved the way for later reforms. But if Higgins was quarrelsome in print, he was suave and genial in society. A polished gentleman and an accomplished conversationalist, he knew how to talk of literature, art, sport, and personalities in the West End, as he did of business and politics in the City and on Fleet Street. His acquaintance with the London world was nearly as extensive as Thackeray's, and the two had many common associates, among them Leech, Landseer, and the whole of the Elliots' circle.

Higgins was Thackeray's loyal friend for nearly twenty years, though occasional disagreements interrupted their intimacy. In 1850, when Thackeray was particularly hard pressed by work, Higgins made the generous proposal that he provide whatever money might be necessary to permit his friend to "lie fallow" for a year.[100] Though Thackeray declined this offer, he did not forget it or Higgins's many other services to him, and *Philip*, his last complete novel, is dedicated to Higgins "in grateful remembrance of old friendship and kindness." None of Thackeray's letters to Higgins, which must be as interesting as those to Brown or to Elwin, appears in this collection, but it is recorded that "many amusing notes and sketches" by Thackeray enriched his friend's scrapbook. Higgins's biographer describes only one of these, "in which an advertisement of a horse for sale cut from the day's morning paper headed the sheet, and the MS. consisted of this couplet:

> I read in the 'Times' of this wonderful bay cob,
> Now pray, if you love me, go see him, dear Jacob!
> W. M. T." [101]

## MARY HOLMES

In the early weeks of 1852 Thackeray received a letter from Miss Mary Holmes, whom he had known in Devon but had not seen for twenty years. She was now a Catholic convert living at Skipton in the West Riding of Yorkshire, only a few miles from Charlotte Brontë in Haworth, and she begged his help in getting a hearing for a little book on music that she had published and in finding a position as a governess. Thackeray's sympathies were stirred by the reappearance at a lonely time in his life of this half-remembered figure of his boyhood, struggling to the best of her feeble strength in a society where the odds were heavy against a

---

[100] See below, No. 691.
[101] Stirling-Maxwell, p. xxv.

solitary woman, and there followed one of the most candid and revealing of his shorter correspondences. For a few weeks he made Miss Holmes his confidante, writing to her of his youth and its re-creation in *Pendennis*, of Mrs. Brookfield (in a letter which Miss Holmes destroyed at his request), of Charlotte Brontë, and of Newman.

Encouraged by her newly found friend, who gave her money and appointed her music mistress to his daughters, Miss Holmes came to London in March to try her fortune. She stayed at Thackeray's home in Young Street for a few days, until she had secured lodgings, but the charm that he found in her letters proved to be absent from her person. She had red hair and a red nose and sought anxiously to make a Catholic of him. After she left his house, she wrote as indefatigably as ever, but Thackeray's letters became infrequent, shorter, and less confidential. He welcomed the opportunity afforded by his departure to America in October to put a period to the correspondence.

Miss Holmes, who appears to have spent much of her time writing to authors, had one other friend among the great Victorians. The solace of her difficult life was her correspondence with Cardinal Newman, which extended over many years. Thackeray was often its theme, and on December 27, 1863, Newman wrote her the following letter:

My best Christmas greetings to you, & to M^r & M^rs Leigh —
But I do not write to say what you will believe I feel, though I do not say it, but to express the piercing sorrow that I feel at Thackeray's death.
You know I never saw him, but you have interested me in him — & one saw in his books the workings of his mind — and he has died with such awful suddenness.
A new work of his had been advertised — & I had looked forward with pleasure to reading it — and now the drama of his life is closed, and he himself is the greatest instance of the text, of which he was so full, Vanitas vanitatum, omnia vanitas. I wonder whether he has known his own decay — for a decay I think there has been. I thought his last novel betrayed lassitude and exhaustion of mind — and he has lain by apparently for a year. His last fugitive pieces in the Cornhill have been almost sermons — One should be very glad to know that he had presentiments of what was to come.

What a world this is — how wretched they are, who take it for their portion. Poor Thackeray — it seems but the other day since we became Catholics — now all his renown has been since that, he has made his name, has been made much of, has been feted, and has gone out, all since 1846 or 1847, all since I went to Propaganda and came back a Philippine [102]

Ever yours aft<sup>ly</sup>

John H Newman

of the Oratory.[103]

## LORD HOUGHTON

Richard Monckton Milnes (1809–1885), whose acquaintance Thackeray made at Cambridge, was the son of Robert Pemberton Milnes of Fryston Hall in Yorkshire, a country gentleman who had a short but distinguished career as a statesman during the later Napoleonic period. Milnes matriculated at Trinity College in 1827, took his M. A. degree in 1831, and spent the next few years abroad. In 1835 he settled in London, where he devoted his best energies to society and to literature, publishing several volumes of poems and that minor classic, *The Life, Letters, and Literary Remains of John Keats* (1848). Though he represented Pontefract in parliament between 1837 and 1863, he had little success as a politician. In 1851 he married the Hon. Annabel Crewe, daughter of the second Baron Crewe, and seven years later he succeeded to his father's estates.[104] He was created Baron Houghton of Great Houghton in 1863.

Most readers will hardly require to be reminded of the salient points of Lord Houghton's character. He was a man of great wit,

[102] That is, since Newman set out to convert his Catholic opponents and returned himself converted.

[103] This letter has been partially printed in *Letters and Correspondence of John Henry Newman*, ed. Anne Mozley, 2 vols. (London, 1891), II, 478–479. My text is taken from the original in the Berg Collection of the New York Public Library.

[104] They totalled 7,599 acres, for the most part in Yorkshire, which were worth £11,787 annually in 1883 (Bateman, *Great Landowners*, p. 228).

amiability, and social talents, who in later years was recognized as England's premier host. He knew everybody, and his agile mind and broad sympathies led him to bring together the most oddly and piquantly assorted guests at his breakfasts in London and his house-parties at Fryston. Carlyle consoled him for his failure to attain political preferment by the assurance that the only post fit for him was that of "perpetual president of the Heaven and Hell Amalgamation Society," and on another occasion he remarked that "if Christ was again on earth Milnes would ask him to breakfast, and the Clubs would all be talking of the good things that Christ had said." [105] That Lord Houghton's cosmopolitan outlook and freedom from vulgar prejudices may have had their less edifying aspects is suggested by the fact that he possessed the largest and choicest library of erotic literature in London.

Thackeray does not appear to have seen much of Milnes until 1840, but Milnes treated him with great kindness during the tragic months that followed his discovery of his wife's insanity, and the two men were firm friends henceforth. This edition contains only six of Thackeray's letters to Milnes, but a much larger number must still be extant.

The correspondence between them [writes Lord Houghton's biographer] speaks of long years of close and affectionate intimacy, not altogether without occasional breaks, due to the temperaments of both men, but never seriously affected by these rare differences. 'Dear Milnes,' writes Thackeray at a very early stage in their acquaintance, when the great novelist was living in Paris, 'the young Chevalier is arrived, and to be heard of at the Bedford Hotel in Covent Garden, or at the Garrick Club, King Street. He accepts breakfasts — and dinners still more willingly.' There is no signature to this note, but, instead of signature, there is, on the opposite page, a sketch from the masterly pen of Michael Angelo Titmarsh, in which Thackeray depicts himself in the costume of the period — bell-shaped hat, high collar, velvet stock, and closely-buttoned frock-coat, on the breast of which glitters an immense star. Many of his letters to Milnes are decorated by similar sketches. As for the dinners and breakfasts which Thackeray was 'willing to accept,' they were not to be counted. When, after his marriage, Milnes was enabled

[105] Thomas Wemyss Reid, *The Life, Letters, and Friendships of Richard Monckton Milnes, First Lord Houghton*, 2 vols. (London, 1890), I, 187.

to keep a record of the guests at his table, there was hardly any name which figured more frequently in it than that of the author of 'Vanity Fair.' [106]

After Thackeray's death Lord Houghton, like Dickens and Trollope, wrote a memorial tribute for the magazine of which his friend had been the first editor.[107]

## THE KEMBLES

Among the friends of Thackeray's young manhood were the brilliant but erratic children of Charles Kemble (1775–1854), for nearly fifty years one of the most popular and versatile of English actors, and his wife, the former Marie Thérèse Decamp (1774–1838), who was herself an actress of some ability. Thackeray's intimacy with the family began in 1829 when he met the older son John Mitchell Kemble (1807–1857) at Trinity College, Cambridge, where the latter matriculated in 1826 and took his B.A. degree in 1830. After Thackeray returned from Weimar in 1831, John and his brother Henry were his constant companions for the better part of a year. Five years followed during which Thackeray saw little of John, who in this period established his reputation as a pioneer student of English philology by his edition of *The Anglo-Saxon Poems of Beowulf* (1833) and his lectures at Cambridge on Old English. But when Thackeray brought his wife to England in 1837, he renewed his intimacy with his friend, who had himself married Natalie, daughter of Professor Wendt of Göttingen, and was editing *The British and Foreign Review*, a post he held between 1835 and 1844. Though Kemble became Examiner of Stage Plays in 1840 and held that office until his death, he passed most of the latter part of his life outside of England in linguistic and archeological investigations.

Thackeray first saw Fanny Kemble (1809–1893), John's famous sister, as Juliet in her début at Covent Garden on October 5, 1829,

[106] The same, I, 425–426.
[107] "Historical Contrast," *Cornhill Magazine*, February, 1864, p. 133.

and long afterwards he told her, speaking of this time, "all of us
. . . were in love with you, and had your portrait by Lawrence in
our rooms." [108] Until she departed for her American tour in 1832,
Thackeray was her devoted admirer, but he could not bring himself
to like her when she returned to England as Mrs. Pierce Butler
after her unhappy marital experience, and there was no real intimacy between them (despite the evidence of Mrs. Kemble's various
volumes of reminiscence) in later life.

Of all the Kembles Thackeray liked best the younger daughter
Adelaide (1814?-1879), with whom he was on terms of close
friendship for more than twenty-five years. She was one of the
most accomplished of English sopranos, and her professional career, though short, was of extraordinary brilliance. She made her
début at Covent Garden in *Norma* on November 2, 1841, and
retired from the stage on December 23 of the following year.
Soon afterwards she married Edward John Sartoris (1817-1879)
of Warnford Park, Hampshire, an idle man-about-town, whose
estates in 1883 were worth £4,988 annually.[109] Her husband, on
whom she lavished an almost doting affection, appears to have neglected her. The Sartorises had two children and in later years
lived much in Italy.

## JOHN LEECH

"I am sure," writes Lady Ritchie, "there was no one among all
his friends whose society my father enjoyed more than he did that
of John Leech, whom he first remembered, so he has often told us
with a smile, a small boy at the Charterhouse, in a little blue
buttoned-up suit, set up upon a form and made to sing 'Home,
sweet home,' to the others crowding about." [110] Leech (1817-
1864) was at Charterhouse from 1825 to 1832, and his first three

[108] Frances Ann Kemble, *Records of Later Life* (New York, 1882), p. 627.
[109] Bateman, *Great Landowners*, p. 396.
[110] *Chapters*, p. 93. The principal sources of information about Leech are
William Powell Frith's *John Leech* (London, 1891); Everitt's *English*

years at the school thus coincided with Thackeray's last. To please his father he next became a student at St. Bartholomew's Hospital, where his companions included Percival Leigh, Albert Smith, and Gilbert à Beckett. Further apprenticeship to a private physician followed, but before his medical education was completed, his father found himself forced to discontinue his allowance. Leech had consequently to support himself by drawing, a pursuit in which, being entirely self-taught, he for some years met with little success. It is recorded, indeed, that during 1838 he more than once saw the inside of a spunging house. His engagement as *Punch's* first cartoonist in 1842 was the turning point in his fortunes. During the next twenty-two years he made more than 3,000 sketches for the magazine, most of which are collected in his *Pictures of Life and Character from the Collection of Mr. Punch* (1854–1863). He also found time to illustrate many books, most notably Surtees's sporting novels. In 1862 he struck out in a new line with an exhibition of "sketches in oil," *Punch* drawings enlarged and transferred to canvas, from which he realized £5,000.[111]

Leech was a tall, slim, handsome man of gentlemanly manner and kind but melancholy nature. After his marriage in 1843 to Ann Eaton, from whom he drew his pretty young ladies in *Punch*, he passed most of his time at home over his drawing-table or with his two children, Ada and John George Warrington Leech. Though he mingled little in society, he was fond of hunting, being a cautious but persistent rider. His colleagues of the press liked him well and delighted in his rendition of gloomy songs, his particular favorite being Procter's "King Death." Yet he had few intimates, for he was impatient of all vulgarity, not easily approachable, and subject in later years — when his susceptibility to street noises became a phobia — to recurring fits of nervous depression.

Though only a single note in this collection testifies to their

---

*Caricaturists*, pp. 277–335; and Dr. John Brown's *Horæ Subsecivæ*, *Third Series*, "John Leech and Other Papers" (Edinburgh, 1882), pp. 1–79.

[111] Thackeray's review of this exhibition appeared in *The Times* of June 2, 1862. "Leech was hugely delighted —," writes Dr. Brown (p. 37), "rejoiced in it like a child, and said, 'That's like putting £1000 in my pocket.'"

intimacy,[112] Thackeray was one of Leech's closest friends. They appear to have renewed their Charterhouse acquaintance about 1843, when Thackeray first began to attend the dinners that the *Punch* staff held every Saturday (later every Wednesday) evening on the second floor of Bradbury and Evans's offices at 11 Bouverie Street. In his frequent clashes with Douglas Jerrold, the other dominant personality at these dinners, Thackeray found himself supported by Leech, as well as by Doyle and Percival Leigh. A sense of this alliance perhaps explains the disproportionate resentment expressed by the other *Punch* writers at a harmless sentence in Thackeray's classic essay on Leech, in which his praise of his friend is inadvertently made to depend upon a depreciation of the work of *Punch's* other contributors.[113] The intimacy of Thackeray and Leech extended to their families as well, and there was much intercourse between the two households.[114] But perhaps the best testimony to their closeness of sympathy is the community of mind displayed in their work. Leech's drawings occupy the same position in the history of English caricature as do Thackeray's novels in the history of English fiction. Each artist dealt in a new kind of social realism, presenting a view of middle and upper class life at once more faithful and more refined than that of their predecessors. "Whilst we live we must laugh, and have folks to make us laugh," Thackeray writes in describing Leech's achievement. "We cannot afford to lose Satyr with his pipe and dances and gambols. But we have washed, combed, clothed, and taught the rogue good manners." [115]

Leech died a little less than a year after Thackeray and was buried in Kensal Green Cemetery at one tomb's remove from his friend.

[112] Thackeray's letters to Leech must none the less have been numerous, and it is possible that many of them have been preserved.

[113] See below, No. 1092.

[114] See *Chapters*, pp. 93–102.

[115] *Works*, XIII, 484.

## CHARLES LEVER

"Poor Thackeray!" wrote Lever to John Blackwood on January 2, 1864, "I cannot say how I was shocked at his death. He wrote his 'Irish Sketch-Book,' which is dedicated to me, in my old house at Templeogue, and it is with a heavy heart I think of all our long evenings together, — mingling our plans for the future with many a jest and many a story." [116] But if, as we see, Thackeray's association with Lever began and ended auspiciously, it was interrupted by an estrangement of more than a decade. When the two men became friends in Dublin during the summer and autumn of 1842, Lever was already famous and Thackeray was as yet little known. By accepting the dedication of *The Irish Sketch Book*, which brought down on his head the abuse of Irishmen of all parties infuriated by Thackeray's candid observations about their country, and by reviewing this volume favorably in *The Dublin University Magazine* of June, 1843, Lever felt that he had placed Thackeray considerably in his debt. He had some reason to think that he had been treated shabbily, therefore, when he read his friend's notice of *Tom Burke of Ours* in *Fraser's Magazine* for February, 1844.[117] Thackeray was not conscious of having written anything offensive in this essay, and today his strictures seem singularly discerning and judicious. Yet Lever, in the first flush of his popularity, could hardly be expected to relish impartial dissection of his faults where he anticipated warm praise. He broke off with Thackeray, complaining that his friend had acted "most basely and cruelly."

In August, 1847, the breach between the two novelists was widened by the appearance of "Phil Fogarty," Thackeray's devastating parody of Lever, in "Punch's Prize Novelists." Lever retaliated in November of the following year with a savage but ineffectual (because unrecognizable) portrait of Thackeray as

---

[116] Edmund Downey, *Charles Lever: His Life in his Letters*, 2 vols. (Edinburgh and London, 1906), II, 2.

[117] See *Works*, XIII, 400–406.

Elias Howle, the Cockney traveller and wit of *Roland Cashel.*[118] As Thackeray did not fail to note, the curious name of Howle was chosen to indicate that Lever was replying to "Phil Fogarty," a song which concludes:

> And so let us give his old sowl
> A howl
> For 'twas he made the noggin to rowl.[119]

It was not until eight years later that Thackeray and Lever were reconciled. Their original rôles were then reversed, for Thackeray had long been famous and Lever was almost forgotten. It devolved upon the former, therefore, to take the first step.

Thackeray dined yesterday at Dilke's [Lever wrote on May 22, 1856] & hearing, I was in town — said he was most anxious to meet me: he spoke, as I heard, very handsomely of me — &c[.] I am glad of it — as grudges between men in the same walk are always to be deprecated, & the world not unnaturally thinks unfavorably of both — [120]

Henceforth the two novelists were on good terms and saw each other frequently during Lever's visits to London. Thackeray helped Lever to arrange for the publication of his later books and secured many contributions to *The Cornhill Magazine* from him.

## LOUIS MARVY

Though Thackeray lived for several years in France and knew many Frenchmen, he appears to have had only one intimate French friend. This was Louis Marvy [121] (1815–1850), an etcher who was born at Versailles and studied art under Jules Dupré. Marvy's original work in landscape, which was unimportant, may be studied in his series of twenty etchings called *Un Été en voyage* (1844).

[118] See below, No. 522.

[119] *Works*, VI, 491.

[120] Franklin P. Rolfe, "Letters of Charles Lever to His Wife and Daughter," *The Huntington Library Bulletin*, Number 10 (October, 1936), p. 157.

[121] There is a brief paragraph on Marvy's life in the *Nouvelle biographie générale*, XXXIV (1861), 114.

His real talent was for the reproduction of paintings, which he did with notable effectiveness by a process of *vernis mou*. But if his prints from the modern French school were influential in gaining popular recognition for such artists as Corot and Diaz, they brought him no reputation, nor did he ever make from them more than a livelihood.

Thackeray first met Marvy in February, 1841, not long after Mrs. Thackeray was placed in Esquirol's *Maison de Santé* in Paris. He was trying to adjust himself to the cataclysmic change that his wife's insanity had brought about in his life, and he preferred for the most part to be alone. During these difficult months he found that Marvy's *atelier,* no doubt because it carried him back to those happy years — now irrecoverably over — he had passed on Coram Street, was almost the only place at which he cared to call. He describes his friend's household in "Shrove Tuesday in Paris," which he wrote for the *Britannia* of July 5, 1841:

I have just been to visit a man who has sinned most cruelly against one of the severest laws of French Society. He is only five-and-twenty, has not a shilling in the world but what he earns, and has actually committed the most unheard-of crime of *marrying*. . . .

He is an engraver and artist by trade; and if he gains a hundred-and-fifty pounds a-year by his labour, it is all that he does. Out of this he has to support a wife, a child, and a *bonne* to cook for him; and to lay by money, if he can, for a rainy day. He works twelve hours at least every day of his life. He can't go into society of evenings, but must toil over his steel-plates all night; he is forced to breakfast off a lump of bread and cheese and a glass of water, in his *atelier*; very often he cannot find time to dine with his family, but his little wife brings him his soup, and a morsel of beef, of which he snatches a bit as he best may, but can never hope for anything like decent comfort. Fancy how his worthy parents must be *désolés,* at this dreadful position of their son. *Régardez donc Louis,* say his friends, *et puis faites la bêtise de vous marier!*

Well, this monster, who has so outraged all the laws of decency, who does not even smoke his pipe at the café, and play his *partie* at dominoes, as every honest reputable man should, is somehow or the other, and in the teeth of all reason, the most outrageously absurdly happy man I ever saw. His wife works almost as hard at her needle as he does at his engraving. They live in a garret in the Rue Cadet, and have got a little child, forsooth (as if the pair of them were not enough!), a little rogue that is always trotting from her mother's room to her father's, and is disturbing one or the other with her nonsensical prattle. Their lodging is like a cage of canary-birds; there is nothing but singing in it from morning to night. You hear Louis beginning in a bass voice, Tra-la-la-la, Tra-la-la-la, and as sure as fate from Madame Louis's room, comes Tra-la-la-la, Tra-la-la-la, in a treble. Little Louise, who is only two years old, must sing too, the absurd little wretch! — and half-a-dozen times in the day, Madame Louis peeps into the *atelier*, and looks over her husband's work, and calls him *lolo*, or *mon bon*, or *mon gros*, or some such coarse name, and once, in my presence, although I was a perfect stranger, actually kissed the man.[122]

Not long after February, 1848, Marvy appeared in London as a political exile. Mindful of the "many happy hours" that he had passed in the "constant cheerfulness and sunshine" of his friend's *atelier*,[123] Thackeray considered how he could be of use to the refugee. By undertaking to write the accompanying text himself, he persuaded the publisher Bogue to bring out a volume of *Sketches after English Landscape Painters* made by Marvy's special process. And he insisted that Marvy should pass the winter of 1848–1849 at Young Street. "He was a very charming and gentle person, in delicate health," Lady Ritchie recalls. "He lived quietly in our house, chiefly absorbed by his work."[124] Marvy was permitted to return to France later in 1849, but he died on November 15 of the following year. His family was left entirely without resources, and for many years Mme. Marvy was one of Thackeray's pensioners.

## SAVILLE MORTON

Though Saville Morton was the intimate friend of Tennyson, Thackeray, and FitzGerald, little information is available about any part of his career except his death.[125] It is known that he

[122] *Works*, XIII, 570–571.
[123] From Thackeray's preface to *Sketches after English Landscape Painters*, a volume without pagination.
[124] *Records of Tennyson, Ruskin and Browning* (London, 1893), p. 159.
[125] It should be noted, however, that there is in existence a collection of

matriculated at Trinity College, Cambridge, in 1830, and took his B.A. degree in 1834. "Mr. Morton was a man of great literary acquirements; educated as an architect"; *The Annual Register* of 1852 relates further, "but being in youth possessed of a good fortune, he had devoted himself to the fine arts, and was a proficient in painting, music, and had also studied medicine. He had visited several capitals as correspondent of English journals." [126] Thackeray knew Morton best in the late eighteen-thirties and early eighteen-forties, before he was forced into journalism by the loss of his money; during these years he was, indeed, Thackeray's most intimate friend after FitzGerald. When Morton established himself in Paris as correspondent of *The Daily News*, Thackeray saw him only rarely.

By the testimony of nearly everyone who knew him, Morton had great personal charm. "A very intelligent person, full of general information —," is FitzGerald's word-portrait, "undecided and of a nervous temperament — has infinite taste for the fine arts — very tender in feeling and sentiment — very uncertain in spirits — not a good manager of time or purse." [127] But FitzGerald omits from his sketch the capital trait in Morton's character, that he was a confirmed rake. There are revealing glimpses in Thackeray's letters of his incessant pursuit of women, and Henry Sutherland Edwards [128] recalls that Morton's current mistress, the notorious adventuress Lola Montes, involved him not long before his death in a duel with Roger de Beauvoir.

We are thus not unprepared for the lurid scene that rang down the curtain on Morton's life.[129] Among his friends in Paris were

---

fragmentary letters from Morton to FitzGerald, which might prove unexpectedly enlightening. I learn from Mr. Winstanley that these, like the rest of the FitzGerald papers owned by Trinity College, Cambridge, have been removed from the Trinity College Library, and will not be accessible till the end of the war.

[126] II, 402.

[127] Thomas Wright, *The Life of Edward FitzGerald*, 2 vols. (London, 1904), II, 225.

[128] *Personal Recollections* (London, 1900), pp. 31–32.

[129] What follows is based on *The Annual Register* (1852), II, 402–407, and Edwards's *Personal Recollections*, pp. 32–36.

Elliott Bower, correspondent of *The Morning Post*, and his wife. Mrs. Bower had known Morton well before her marriage, and when she discovered that her husband had taken a mistress, she turned to her friend for consolation. Many months later, on September 2, 1852, she was delivered of her fifth child, and though her convalescence at first was satisfactory, she soon developed puerperal fever. In her delirium she insisted that Morton be always near her, and for a week he hardly left her room. During this period she treated her husband with the utmost scorn, feeding her anger with a letter from his mistress which she refused to relinquish, and exclaiming to him on one occasion, *"Vade retro, Sathanes!"* According to the *Acte d'Accusation* later issued against Bower,

On the 1st of October the relatives of Mrs. Bower and the mother of her husband were assembled in the dining-room. She caused Bower to be sent for, and he went to her chamber. After having reproached him with the acts of violence which he had exercised on her person, she cried, in the delirium of madness and of fever, at the same time showing him the child she held in her arms, 'This child is not yours — it is Morton's!' and, as Bower protested against this revelation, her fury became greater, and she added, 'that on the 2nd of December, 1851, in the absence of her husband, she had sent for Morton; that he had passed the night with her; and that she became a mother on the 2nd of September.' 'If I believed that,' cried Bower, 'I would kill the child!' These words carried to a height the furious madness of Mrs. Bower, and she said, addressing her sister, who was present, 'Queen of England, drive away this man!' [130]

Bower thereupon returned to the dining-room, where Morton was seated. He caught up a carving knife that lay on the table and ran at his erstwhile friend. Morton endeavored to escape, but Bower reached him at the head of the staircase and stabbed him to death. Though Bower thought it necessary to flee to England, he was acquitted when he came back to Paris to stand trial a few weeks later. Mrs. Bower had perfectly recovered in the interval, and she was observed in the deepest mourning — for Morton.

[130] *Annual Register* (1852), II, 403-404.

## THE PROCTERS

Anne Skepper (1799–1888) was the only child of a York lawyer who died not long after her birth. Her mother, being left without provision, accepted a position as governess of the curiously assorted children by two marriages of the widowed Basil Montagu, a London barrister who as the editor of Bacon saw much literary society, and in due time she became the third Mrs. Montagu. Anne grew up in the Montagu household, which Carlyle describes as "a most singular social and spiritual ménagerie," and throve on the difficulties of her position. She developed into "a brisk, witty, prettyish, sufficiently clear-eyed and sharp-tongued young lady," decidedly the "flower of the collection" among the eccentric Montagus.[131]

In 1824 she married Bryan Waller Procter [132] (1787–1874) and escaped to a home of her own. Procter was both a poet and an attorney. The friend of most of the famous literary men of his time, he had himself, as "Barry Cornwall," a modest niche in the romantic pantheon, yet his business abilities were such that from 1832 to 1861 he held a lucrative appointment as Commissioner of Lunacy. He, his wife, and the seven children that were born to them were enabled by this useful if prosaic employment to lead a quiet and prosperous existence in London. They lived from 1832 to 1843 at 5 Grove End Road, St. John's Wood; from 1843 to 1853 at 13 Upper Harley Street; and after 1853 at 32 Weymouth Street.

Procter was an amiable, unpretentious, self-effacing man, with a habit of dozing off after dinner, who was quite content to follow his wife's lead in social matters. Mrs. Procter's tremendous energy and genius for gossip made her a hostess of distinction, and her drawing room was for more than half a century an institution of literary London. Everyone who knew her testifies to her strong good sense and to the brilliance of her wit, the acid

[131] Carlyle, *Reminiscences*, ed. Froude (New York, 1881), pp. 176–181.
[132] The best account of Procter, in which there is some incidental mention of his wife, is Professor Richard Willard Armour's *Barry Cornwall* (Boston, 1935).

flavor of which led Kinglake to call her "our Lady of Bitterness," [133] and it was perhaps inevitable that her admirers should have been chiefly men. The Lake Poets, Lamb, and Hazlitt were the friends of her youth; Browning, Henry James, and Lowell (then Ambassador to England) were her regular visitors in old age; and in mid-Victorian days she included among her intimates Carlyle, Dickens, Milnes, Forster, Kinglake, Dicky Doyle, Henry Reeve, and Eliot Warburton.

Thackeray first met the Procters shortly after he brought his wife to England in 1837, and he remained their friend until his death. Except for his immediate family and Mrs. Brookfield, he wrote more letters to Mrs. Procter than to any other correspondent. She had known him during his brief period of domestic happiness, and when his marriage collapsed, it was from her, after his mother, that he derived most comfort. She was among the first to recognize his true literary stature, and she labored unceasingly to bring her influential friends to a sense of his real worth. And as Thackeray must have realized, she alone among the women that he chose as his confidantes was in any sense his intellectual equal. Though *Vanity Fair* is dedicated to Procter, it is actually to Mrs. Procter that Thackeray is offering his tribute.

Of the Procters' children we hear in Thackeray's letters only of Adelaide Ann (1825–1864), who began writing poetry at an early age and published two volumes of *Legends and Lyrics* in 1858. Particularly after her conversion to Catholicism about 1851 she was a difficult person with whom to get along, and Thackeray appears to have regarded her rather with respect and admiration than with affection.


## WILLIAM BRADFORD REED

No American city gave Thackeray a warmer welcome than Philadelphia, and of the many friends that he made during his visits there in 1853 and 1856, the closest was perhaps the lawyer,

[133] *Eothen* (London, 1898), p. xxi.

politician, and author William Bradford Reed [134] (1806–1876). Reed was the grandson of the Revolutionary soldier and statesman Joseph Reed (1741–1785), whose biography he wrote, as he did that of Esther de Berdt, the loyalist's daughter whom Joseph Reed married. Reed's father was for many years Recorder of Philadelphia, and that city was Reed's home during nearly the whole of his life. He was a precocious boy, who graduated from the University of Pennsylvania at the age of sixteen. After building up a lucrative law practice and serving two terms in the state legislature, he became in 1838 the youngest Attorney-General in Pennsylvania history. His leisure, meantime, had been devoted to study and writing, and he had gained some recognition as an authority on the American Revolution. When Thackeray first met him, he was District Attorney of Philadelphia, a post he held from 1850 to 1856, and part-time Professor of American History at the University of Pennsylvania.

Thackeray found a congenial companion in this brilliant and scholarly man of affairs, and he was equally attracted to his brother Henry Hope Reed, a lifelong student of English literature who also taught at the University of Pennsylvania. He made the Reed home his house of call in Philadelphia, as the Baxter residence was in New York.

He seemed to take a fancy to me and mine [Reed writes in *Haud Immemor* [135]]; and I certainly loved him. He used to come to my house, not the abode of wealth or luxury, almost every day, and often more than once a day. He talked with my little children, and told them odd fairy tales; and I now see him (this was on his second visit) one day in Walnut Street, walking slowly along with my little girl by the hand; the tall, grey-headed, spectacled man, with an effort accomodating himself to the toddling child by his side; and then he would bring her home; and one day, when we were to have a great dinner given to him at the Club, and my wife was ill, and my household disarranged, and

[134] The most accurate account of Reed's life is that in *The Dictionary of American Biography*, but Manton Marble's brief memoir prefixed to *Memories of Familiar Books* (New York, 1876), a collection of the literary papers of Reed's last years, may also be consulted with profit.

[135] His memorial essay on Thackeray, privately printed in 1864. The passage quoted is on pp. 3–4.

the bell rang, and I said to him: 'I must go and carve the boiled mutton for the children, and take for granted you do not care to come'; and he got up, and, with a cheery voice, said: 'I love boiled mutton, and children too, and I will dine with them,' and we did; and he was happy, and the children were happy, and our appetite for the club dinner was damaged. Such was Thackeray in my home.

Not long after Thackeray left Philadelphia in 1853, the British Consul to that city died, and Reed wrote suggesting that he apply for the post. This was the beginning of a correspondence that continued until a few months before Thackeray's death and is among the most interesting of his later years. There intervened between his two visits to the United States the death of Reed's brother Henry aboard the ill-fated *Arctic*, shortly after he had visited Thackeray in London, and the letter of sympathy that Thackeray wrote Reed on this occasion served materially to strengthen their friendship.

Reed's services to Buchanan, the successful candidate in the presidential election of 1856, gained him an appointment as American Minister to China in 1857. When he passed through London in April, 1859, on his way home to the United States, Thackeray had a welcome opportunity to repay the hospitality which Reed had dispensed with such liberality in Philadelphia. It seemed an auspicious hour for Reed, who had been notably successful in China, but actually his distinguished career was over. He was destined to devote the rest of his life to the futile advocacy of a lost cause. His Quixotic crusade against what he called "that sentimental disease of 'Abolitionism,' " [136] persistently maintained throughout the Civil War and even after, cost him both his law practice and his friends. In 1870 he moved from Philadelphia to New York, where until his death he supported himself and his daughter, almost the only companion of his last years, by journalism.

[136] *Haud Immemor*, p. 26.

## THERESA REVISS

Speculation as to whether Becky Sharp was drawn from life began with the publication of the first number of *Vanity Fair* in 1847 and still continues today.[137] The conclusion to which one is forced after examining the evidence available is that Becky had no single original but shaped herself in Thackeray's mind from his observation of many women and his reading of many books. Thackeray's intimacy with the Bullers, however, gave him ample opportunity to study a girl — she was only fifteen in 1847 [138] — with whom he seems to have identified Becky when he began his novel,[139] though Becky's later adventures are rather in the nature of prophecy than of history. This precocious young lady was Miss Theresa Reviss, Mrs. Buller's adopted daughter and, it would appear, the child of Charles Buller.[140] Mrs. Carlyle sketches her early career in a letter of January 7, 1851, to John Welsh. In an unguarded moment she had invited Miss Reviss to visit her tiny house in Cheyne Row, and on January 1 her guest had arrived with a lady's-maid and an immense amount of luggage.

Have you been reading Thackeray's 'Pendennis'? [writes Mrs. Carlyle.] If so, you have made acquaintance with Blanche Amory; and

[137] It has been surmised, for example, that Becky was drawn from the authoress of *Jane Eyre* (before anything was known of Charlotte Brontë), the governess in the household of the Duc and Duchesse de Praslin, and the novelist Lady Morgan. The last hypothesis is supported in Professor A. Lionel Stevenson's "*Vanity Fair* and Lady Morgan," *Publications of the Modern Language Association*, XLVIII (1933), 547–551. Other critics have sought her origins in literature. For a discussion of Thackeray's possible indebtedness to Valérie Marneffe of Balzac's *La Cousine Bette* in portraying Becky, see my unpublished Harvard doctoral dissertation, *Thackeray and France*, pp. 319–323.

[138] *Letters and Memorials of Jane Welsh Carlyle*, ed. Carlyle and Froude, I, 398.

[139] William Gerald Elliot (*In My Anecdotage*, London, 1925, pp. 27–28) relates that his mother, who had known Miss Reviss in Calcutta, met Thackeray in Paris at the Ritchies on her return to Europe and found him eager for news of that young lady. After she had satisfied his curiosity, she inquired if he had Miss Reviss in mind when he drew Becky. He nodded his head in affirmation, but said nothing.          [140] See above, "The Bullers."

when I tell you that my young lady of last week is the original of that portrait, you will give me joy that she, lady's maid, and infinite baggage, are all gone! Not that the poor little [Theresa Reviss] is quite such a little devil as Thackeray, who has detested her from a child, has here represented; but the looks, the manners, the wiles, the *larmes,* 'and all that sort of thing,' are a perfect likeness. The blame, however, is chiefly on those who placed her in a position so false that it required extraordinary virtue not to become false along with it. She was the only legitimate child of a beautiful young 'improper female,' [141] who was for a number of years [Charles Buller]'s mistress (she had had a husband, a swindler). His mother took the freak of patronising this mistress, saw the child, and behold it was very pretty and clever. Poor Mrs. [Buller] had tired of parties, of politics, of most things in heaven and earth; 'a sudden thought struck her,' she would adopt this child; give herself the excitement of making a scandal and braving public opinion, and of educating a flesh and blood girl into the heroine of the three-volume novel, which she had for years been trying to write, but wanted perseverance to elaborate. The child was made the idol of the whole house; her showy education was fitting her more for her own mother's profession than for any honest one; and when she was seventeen, and the novel was just rising into the interest of love affairs, a rich young man having been refused, or rather jilted by her, Mrs. [Buller] died, her husband and son being already dead; and poor [Theresa] was left without any earthly stay and with only 250L. a year to support her in the extravagantly luxurious habits she had been brought up in.

She has a splendid voice, and wished to get trained for the opera. Mrs. [Buller]'s fine lady friends screamed at the idea, but offered her nothing instead, not even their countenance. Her two male guardians, to wash their hands of her, resolved to send her to India, and to India she had to go, vowing that if their object was to marry her off, she would disappoint them, and return 'to prosecute the artist life.' She produced the most extraordinary *furore* at Calcutta; [142] had offers every week; refused them point-blank; terrified Sir ———— by her extravagance; tormented Lady ———— by her caprices; 'fell into consumption' for the nonce; was ordered by the doctors back to England! and, to the dismay of her two cowardly guardians, arrived here six months ago

[141] "A girl in the Baker Street bazaar," according to Elliot (*In My Anecdotage,* p. 28).

[142] "In India she apparently was a regular little devil," writes Elliot (*In My Anecdotage,* p. 28). "She appeared one night at a big fancy-dress ball attired as his Satanic Majesty with a long tail. All the old gentlemen present went wild about her."

*with her health perfectly restored!* But her Indian reputation had preceded her, and the fine ladies who turned their backs on her in her extreme need now invite a girl who has refused Sudar Judges by the dozen. She has been going about from one house to another, while no home could be found for her. The guardians had a brilliant idea — 'would we take her?' 'Not for her weight in gold,' I said; but I asked her to spend a day with me, that I might see what she was grown to, and whether I could do anything in placing her with some proper person. . . .

She has saved us all further speculation about her, however, by engaging herself to someone (from ——shire) who came home in the ship with her, and seems a most devoted lover.[143] She told me she 'had been hesitating some time betwixt accepting him, or going on the stage, or drowning herself.' I told her her decision was good, as marrying did not preclude either 'going on the stage' at a subsequent period, or 'drowning herself'; whereas had she decided on the drowning, there could have been no more of it.

I have my own notion that she will throw him over yet; meanwhile it was a blessed calm after the fly rolled her away from here on Saturday. 'Oh, my dear!' Mr. Carlyle said, 'we cannot be sufficiently thankful!' [144]

As Mrs. Carlyle had foreseen, Miss Reviss refused to belie the promise of her early years by lapsing into tepid domesticity with a devoted country gentleman. Her subsequent history, indeed, affords a remarkable instance of life imitating art; one would be hard put to conceive a more appropriate alternative career for Becky or for Blanche than that described in the following narrative:

The Lord Chancellor of the day, [Mr. E. M. Underdown, K. C., told William Gerald Elliot,] who was rather a merry dog, once took her out in his yacht for a trip. In mid-ocean she suddenly wrung her hands,

[143] Apparently Captain Neald. See below, No. 793.

[144] *Letters and Memorials,* ed. Carlyle and Froude, I, 399–401. Lady Ritchie (*Biographical Introductions,* I, xxx) affords us another glimpse of Miss Reviss, probably at about this time: "I may as well also state here, that one morning a hansom drove up to the door, and out of it emerged a most charming, dazzling little lady dressed in black, who greeted my father with great affection and brilliancy, and who, departing presently, gave him a large bunch of fresh violets. This was the only time I ever saw the fascinating little person who was by many supposed to be the original of Becky; my father only laughed when people asked him, but he never quite owned to it. He always said that he never consciously *copied* anybody. It was, of course, impossible that suggestions should not come to him."

said that she was compromised, and asked to be put ashore at once. The Lord Chancellor settled her in a charming Italian villa with costly furniture and *objets d'art*. Here she married one Count Gateschi, a Knight of the Holy Roman Empire, who had been a courier, and later, when the Lord Chancellor died, Mr. Underdown was commissioned by his family to go out and interview her with the purpose of trying to get back the villa and the *objets d'art* which the legal luminary had given her. Mr. U. told me that she was most charming and gave everything up at once. Then she disappeared, but Mr. U. believed that she turned up again a good deal later in London as the Countess de la Torre, who was, I remember, being constantly had up by the police for not feeding her cats. She must have died somewhere in the '80s.[145]


## THE RITCHIES

Among Thackeray's many relations none except his immediate family had so secure a place in his affections as the Ritchies.[146] John Ritchie (d. 1849) was a Scotsman who passed his youth at Baltimore, Maryland, in the employ of a concern owned by his family. In 1815, not long after he came to London to establish a branch of this firm, he met and married Charlotte Thackeray (1786–1854), a sister of Thackeray's father. The couple settled in a house on Southampton Row, the lower floor of which was Mr. Ritchie's place of business and the upper the living quarters of himself and his wife. There five children were born to them: William (1817–1862), Charlotte (1820?–1878), Jane (1822?–1865), John (1824?–1847), and Emily (1828?–1842). Thackeray may almost be said to have grown up in this household, for until the Carmichael-Smyths returned from India, it was a second home to him, and he was a frequent visitor there while at Charterhouse. Sir Richmond Shakespear, another Anglo-Indian boy often at Southampton Row, tells that Thackeray used to amuse his cousins by drawing caricatures and by acting in their little plays. "I re-

[145] *In My Anecdotage*, pp. 28–29.
[146] This notice of the Ritchies is based on the following books: *Memorials*, pp. 415–481; *The Ritchies in India*; and *Some Family Letters of W. M. Thackeray*, ed. Mrs. Warre-Cornish (Boston and New York, 1911).

member him in a wig," he relates, "capitally got up as Dr. Pangloss." [147]

The Ritchies moved to Paris in 1830, where they resided until 1839. During much of this period Thackeray was himself in Paris, and he was often to be seen at their apartment and in their summer house at "les Thermes." He met with William, a tall, handsome, clever lad who was the hope of the family, only occasionally, for, as befitted an older son, William was sent to Eton from 1829 to 1835 and to Trinity College, Cambridge, from 1835 to 1839. Upon his graduation the Ritchies removed again to London, taking a house on Albany Street to provide him with a home while he studied for the bar. In November, 1841, not long after William became a barrister, Mr. Ritchie lost most of his considerable fortune through the failure of a bank in which he was a director. When William ascertained that less than £400 a year remained with which to provide for the entire family, he determined not to pursue the slow advancement offered by the London bar, but to go out to Calcutta, where he could earn his living from the first. His family retired to Paris, at that time the usual resort of middle-class English households in straitened circumstances.

Before William left England on September 1, 1842, he became engaged to Miss Augusta Trimmer (1817?–1888), who agreed to join him in Calcutta when he was able to support her. It is a measure of his rapid success that he married her in Calcutta on December 4, 1845. Within a few years his practice brought him £5,000 annually, and when he was made Advocate General in 1855, he earned thrice this sum every year. He closed his career as Legal Member of Council, a post to which he was appointed in November, 1861, and was generally regarded as one of the most distinguished Anglo-Indian civilians of his time.

[147] *Ritchies in India*, p. 12. This appears to have been the performance that separated Thackeray for a few years from the Turners, his mother's relatives. Richard Bedingfield (*Cassell's Magazine*, II, 12) writes that Thackeray borrowed a barrister's wig from Dr. Turner "(who was at the Bar before he went into the Church), wishing to enact a part in private theatricals, and lost the wig! In consequence of this mishap, boy-like, he did not venture to show his face at Chiswick for a considerable time."

William Ritchie and his wife made only two short visits to England, in 1855 and 1859, but they sent their children home to be brought up by the older Ritchies, in accordance with time-honored custom. At the Ritchies' Parisian apartment, the little Indian children often saw Thackeray [148] and his daughters, the older of whom writes:

I loved my great-aunt Ritchie, as who did not love that laughing, loving, romantic, handsome, humorous, indolent old lady? Shy, expansive in turn, she was big and sweet-looking, with a great look of my father. Though she was old when I knew her, she would still go off into peals of the most delightful laughter, just as if she were a girl.[149]

Mrs. Ritchie was perhaps Thackeray's favorite in the family, but he was also very fond of Charlotte and Jane. The former suffered a severe attack of smallpox when she was eighteen which destroyed her good looks and for a time rendered her nearly blind. When she recovered, she devoted herself to religion, being particularly attracted, like Mrs. Carmichael-Smyth, to the French Protestant Church of Paris and its Pastor, Adolphe Monod. Jane, on the other hand, was pretty, fond of music and society, and of a very lively temperament.

After Mr. Ritchie died, his wife and daughters established

[148] Blanche Ritchie (later Mrs. Warre-Cornish), the second child to be sent home, tells several stories of Thackeray's visits during these years, among them the following: "There is a straight-backed armchair of the Louis Philippe period in my possession, with cushioned arms on which I used to perch beside my grandmother. . . . In that 'Grandmother's chair' now sat Mr. Thackeray, very fresh, very wise-looking behind his spectacles, very attractive with his thick curling hair and rosy cheeks. . . . He was exceedingly sad and silent. He was wondrously droll. Above all, he was kind, so that the child perched beside him questioned him: —

'Is you good?' (from the perch).
'Not so good as I should like to be' (from Mr. Thackeray).
'Is you clever?'
'Well, I've written a book or two. Perhaps I am rather clever.'
'Is you pretty?'
'Oh, no, no, no! *No! No! No!*' (I recall Mr. Thackeray bursting out laughing.)
'I think you's good, and you's clever, and you's pretty.' " (*Some Family Letters of W. M. Thackeray*, pp. 4–5.)

[149] *Ritchies in India*, p. 172.

themselves in a large apartment on the third floor of 36 Rue Godot
de Mauroi. There they lived a happy life with William Ritchie's
children, the number of whom had reached six by 1859, and with
two faithful servants, Félicie, the maid, and Annette, the cook.

Charlotte cheered up at times [writes Lady Ritchie, who frequently
stayed at the apartment], and we were often merry over the reception
days, when quite a number used to drop in. There would be rubbers of
whist; hating cards, Charlotte was a skilful player and generally devoted herself [to them]. Then there was music, or even a dance got up.
How well I remember it! Dear Aunt Ritchie looking sweet and pretty
in velvet dress — the funny English — the polite French — the solemn
whist — the compliments passing — and Félicie, then a young, slim
and pretty girl, doing the refreshment part so well. Then the evenings
when we were alone, the green-shaded lamp, Janie playing, my Aunt
softly humming the tune, — Char. reading or working, and Félicie
bringing in the large cups of tea and longing for a chat.[150]

Their mother's death in 1854 caused little change in the habits of
Jane and Charlotte, who still had their brother's children to bring
up. After William Ritchie died, however, they were left alone in
their apartment, for his wife took her children to live in England,[151]
and three years later Jane passed away. During the rest of her life
Charlotte busied herself indefatigably with visits to hospitals,
prisons, and sickbeds; she made her rooms a haven for governesses
and their charges, for old maids, and for widows; and she became
the indispensable helper of the Minister of the English chapel on
the Rue d'Aguesseau. Though the children she had brought up
and befriended often came to see her — one of the most faithful
visitors being Lady Ritchie, who dedicated to her aunt a volume
appropriately entitled *Spinsters and Toilers* —, for the most part
her only companion was Félicie. Even the Siege of Paris in the
winter of 1870–1871 failed to interrupt her charitable labors, and
when she died, the Parisian poor figured largely among the
mourners at her grave.

[150] The same, p. 163.
[151] See Mrs. Warre-Cornish's recollections of Thackeray's last years in
*Some Family Letters of W. M. Thackeray*, pp. 55–77.

## THE SHAWES

Though most of our knowledge of the Shawes comes from Thackeray's letters, some information can be added from other sources. Five children were born to Colonel Matthew Shawe, C. B., who is said to have been Military Secretary to the Marquess of Wellesley in India,[152] and to his wife, the former Isabella Creagh of Doneraile, County Cork: Isabella (1818–1893), Jane, Arthur, Henry, and one other son. After her husband's death Mrs. Shawe brought her family to Paris, where it was possible for them to live decently on the small army pension that was their only source of income. Thackeray, happening to dine one evening at their boarding house on the invitation of a friend, fell in love with Isabella, whom he married after a year of stormy courtship on August 20, 1836.

Mrs. Shawe's determined efforts to prevent Thackeray from marrying her daughter, the story of which is touched upon in his letters and told more fully in *Philip*,[153] were symptoms of a mental condition that is better understood today than it was in Thackeray's time. And though they are certainly set down in malice, Thackeray appears to have told no more than the truth about her vicious yet serenely self-righteous character in his portraits of the mother-in-law in "Denis Haggarty's Wife," of "The Campaigner" in *The Newcomes*, and of Mrs. General Baynes in *Philip*. With such a mother, it is not surprising that only two of the Shawe children were entirely normal. Henry was a dipsomaniac, Jane pitifully neurotic, and Isabella, as we know, lost her mind not long after the birth of her third daughter in the summer of 1840.[154]

That Thackeray's four years of happy marriage were the central

[152] L. E. Steele, *Athenæum*, November 8, 1890, pp. 628–629.

[153] "Philip is unfortunately going into poverty and struggle," Thackeray writes in a fragment of a letter to George Smith of July 9, 1861 (the original of which I have not traced), "but this can't be helped; and as he will, *entre nous*, take pretty much the career of W. M. T. in the first years of his ruin and absurdly imprudent marriage, at least the portrait will be faithful" (*Biographical Introductions*, XI, xliii).

[154] See Appendix VII.

experience of his life is shown by the frequency with which he returns to them in his later work, drawing Isabella over and over again, as Mrs. Samuel Titmarsh in *The Great Hoggarty Diamond*, as Amelia (in whom there is also something of Mrs. Brookfield), as Rosie Mackenzie in *The Newcomes*, and as Charlotte Baynes in *Philip*. Not till several years after she became insane did Thackeray at last give up hope of her recovery, but late in 1845 he placed her permanently with Mrs. Bakewell, an old and trusted acquaintance who lived in Camberwell, and henceforth he felt justified in living his own life. A decade later, during his second American visit, he spoke to William Bradford Reed of "a friend"

whose wife had been deranged for many years, hopelessly so; and never shall I forget [writes Reed] the look, and manner, and voice with which he said to me, 'It is an awful thing for her to continue so to live. It is an awful thing for her so to die. But has it never occurred to you, how awful a thing the recovery of lost reason must be, without the consciousness of the lapse of time? She finds the lover of her youth a grey-haired old man, and her infants young men and women. Is it not sad to think of this?' [155]

Mrs. Thackeray, whose placidity of mind came to equal that of Mr. Dick in *David Copperfield*, lived on for thirty years after Thackeray's death.

I can remember my grandmother in her old age [relates Mrs. Fuller]. Although in good health, she lacked coherence and her mind was clouded. The extreme smallness of her person, and the erectness of her carriage were the most noticeable things about her. She had a round face, fair complexion, and bright little grey eyes.

I do not think that she knew that my mother was her daughter or that I was her grandchild. She used to play me Irish jigs and every other sort of gay dance music, and I would like to watch her beautiful white hands skimming over the keys of the piano. She always wore the engagement ring which her husband had given her, and about this ring, in which a diamond was set between two opals, there is an ominous story. Thackeray, delighted with his purchase, showed it with beaming pride to a friend, who exclaimed in dismay, 'But, William, see what you have done, this is a mourning ring, not an engagement ring.' And sure enough, the setting of the opals was black enamel.

[155] *Haud Immemor*, p. 6.

## GEORGE SMITH

There was no more distinguished or successful Victorian publisher than George Smith [156] (1824–1901). A tall, well-built,
vigorous man, who kept in athletic trim by riding, he was as much
at home in society as in business. In the "Dr. John" of *Villette*
Charlotte Brontë has left a faithful portrait of this shrewd, energetic, kindly gentleman, who combined a flair for literature with a
close understanding of practical affairs. Though never a part of
the inner circle of Thackeray's intimates, a position that would in
any event not have sorted well with his reverential awe of the
novelist, he was one of the most esteemed friends of Thackeray's
later life and the recipient of many of his letters.

Smith was the oldest son of the founder of Smith and Elder
(later Smith, Elder, and Company), a firm of East India agents,
bankers, and publishers established in 1816. He was brought up
at 65 Cornhill, where the business offices of the concern remained
until 1868. Discovering that he was not profiting from school,
Smith's parents put him to work at Smith, Elder, and Company,
and by 1843 the publishing department of the firm was under his
direction. He assumed charge of the entire business on his father's
death in 1846. From the first he had rare luck in discovering new
authors. In 1843 he brought out the first volume of Ruskin's
*Modern Painters,* and in 1847 he published *Jane Eyre.* Through
Miss Brontë he in December, 1849, met Thackeray,[157] with whom,
more than any other author, Smith and his firm are associated.

This meeting was the first step towards the fulfillment of a
long-cherished ambition.

[156] The chief sources of information about Smith are *George Smith A
Memoir,* which reprints Sir Sidney Lee's article on Smith in *The Dictionary
of National Biography* and four autobiographical papers that Smith contributed
to *The Cornhill Magazine;* and Dr. Leonard Huxley's *The House of Smith,
Elder* (London, 1923), which incorporates the autobiographical fragments
that Smith did not use in his *Cornhill* essays. Both of these volumes are privately printed.

[157] See below, No. 652.

I have a vivid recollection [Smith writes] of the first time I ever heard of Thackeray or his writings some fifty years ago. It was the custom of publishers and of large dealers in 'remainders' (a term for unsold stock bought at a very reduced price from the original publisher) to have what were called 'coffee-house sales.' A publisher would invite the booksellers to dinner at an early hour — three or four o'clock in the afternoon — and after dinner he, or an auctioneer acting on his behalf, offered his books one after another from a printed list at a lower price than that at which they were usually sold to the trade. Orders were taken in the room, and each bookseller — even if he were not a buyer — entered the price of the work on his catalogue with the names of the larger purchasers, as a guide to the sources whence he might afterwards supply his demands.

Shortly after my appearance at Cornhill, and while I was still very young, I was sent to represent the firm at Messrs. Tegg & Son's coffee-house sale, with instructions to mark my catalogue. This I did conscientiously, until Mr. Thackeray's 'Paris Sketch-Book' was handed round. When the copy reached me I opened it, and my eyes fell on the sketch of Mr. Deuceace.[158] I commenced to read and I was fascinated! I forgot the scene around me. I read on till the end of the sale, and then awoke to the fact that my catalogue was unmarked. I asked Mr. Tegg if I might have a copy of the book for the price at which it had been offered to the trade. Its original retail price had been a guinea: the price at which it was offered was 1s. 9d. My joy at the possession of this treasure was chastened by the thought of how I should face my father with my unmarked catalogue; but I persuaded a good-natured confrère to lend me his list, and I copied his prices on to mine before I went to bed that night. I still preserve the book which first introduced me to the writings of Thackeray, whose name I had never heard till it fell from the lips of the auctioneer in that coffee-house sale. I fondly — though perhaps not quite accurately — believe I then resolved if ever I became a publisher I would publish the works of that writer.[159]

Smith's opportunity came late in 1850 when Thackeray offered him *The Kickleburys on the Rhine*, for which Chapman and Hall had failed to make a fair bid. In 1852 he published *Esmond* and in 1854 *The Rose and the Ring*.

[158] Since Deuceace does not figure in *The Paris Sketch Book*, it is likely that the books offered at Tegg's sale were the remaining copies of Cunningham's edition of Titmarsh's *Comic Tales and Sketches*, published in 1841, the first volume of which contains *The Yellowplush Papers*.

[159] Huxley, *House of Smith, Elder*, pp. 66–67.

Not until 1859, however, did Smith succeed in securing Thackeray's exclusive services. When he conceived the plan of *The Cornhill Magazine* in that year, he persuaded Thackeray to become first his principal contributor and then his editor. The unparalleled success of their venture cemented the friendship of the two men, which continued unaltered even after Thackeray resigned the *Cornhill's* editorship in March, 1862. During these years Thackeray, who was always careless about money, came to use his publisher as his banker.

His mode of suggesting to me that a cheque would be convenient was characteristic [Smith relates]. He would walk into my room in Pall Mall with both his trouser pockets turned inside out, a silent and expressive proof of their emptiness. I used to take out my cheque-book and look at him enquiringly. He mentioned the sum required and the transaction was completed.[160]

After Thackeray's death, Smith was long the trusted adviser of his daughters. He bought their father's copyrights from them for what was considered at the time a very generous sum, and most of the standard editions of Thackeray's *Works* have consequently appeared under the imprint of Smith, Elder, and Company. This investment proved most fortunate, and Smith was not less happy in his other enterprises. His large fortune enabled him in 1882 to crown his career by undertaking the publication of *The Dictionary of National Biography*, one of the supreme achievements of English scholarship, which he did not live to see completed.


## THE STANLEYS OF ALDERLEY

*Vanity Fair* gained Thackeray an enviable position in English society and opened many doors that had hitherto been closed to him. Among his new associates he found few more congenial than the ranking Whig aristocrats, but though he knew the Hollands, the Palmerstons, and the Russells well, he formed his closest alli-

[160] The same, p. 72.

ance with a less prominent family, the Stanleys of Alderley. His friendship with Lady Stanley, then Lady Eddisbury, began early in 1849. The letters that she received from her mother-in-law, the former Maria Josepha Holroyd (1771-1863), daughter of Lord Sheffield and friend of Gibbon, afford a lively illustration of the prejudices Thackeray had to combat in securing his *entrée* to the London world, though it should be remembered that the older Lady Stanley had been living for many years in a remote corner of Cheshire and that her opinions, if trenchant, were somewhat antiquated. In any event, we find her writing on March 9, 1849:

I *have* read Vanity Fair & how anybody can like to associate with the author astonishes me — tho' I daresay his conversation may not be like his book exactly but I should so dislike the man who could give such a work to the publick. Where do you meet with him? [161]

So it was at first, but by March 13 of the following year Lady Stanley had resigned herself to ineffectual protest:

How can you tolerate Thackeray for shewing you all up in the manner he does — mothers & daughters, & to call one of the latter Blanche! Really he should be banished from the society he has so wonderfully found his way into only to hold it up to ridicule.[162]

Edward Stanley (1802-1869), the oldest son of this formidable matron, was descended through his father from one of the most ancient families in the peerage, a fifteenth century ancestor being a younger brother of the first Earl of Derby. He ranked high among the minor Whig politicians of his day,[163] and though indolent,

---

[161] *The Ladies of Alderley*, ed. Nancy Mitford (London, 1938), p. 236. This volume is the chief source of the accounts of Lord and Lady Stanley which follow.

[162] The same, p. 280.

[163] Stanley was a Whig M. P. from 1831 to 1841 and again in 1847 and 1848. In 1833 and 1834 he was Under-Secretary for the Colonies and in the latter year for Home Affairs as well. Between 1835 and 1841 he served as Patronage Secretary to the Treasury and principal Whig whip. When the Whigs returned to office in 1846, the best post that could be found for him was that of Under-Secretary for Foreign Affairs, with Palmerston as his chief. From 1852 to 1855 he was Vice-President of the Board of Trade, and from 1855 to 1858 he at last attained cabinet rank as President of the Board of

selfish, and not undeserving of the sneer, reported by Greville, that he was "the man they call Sir Benjamin Backbite," [164] he managed to be at the same time a witty and agreeable *grand seigneur*. In 1826, not long after he left Oxford, he married Henrietta Maria Dillon-Lee (1808–1896), oldest daughter of the thirteenth Viscount Dillon, who gave him twelve children during the next three decades. He was created Baron Eddisbury in 1848 and succeeded his father as second Baron Stanley on October 23, 1850. Even more welcome than his hereditary title were the family estates, consisting (in 1883) of 10,971 acres in Cheshire and Anglesea worth £16,320 annually,[165] for he had hitherto experienced great difficulty in subsisting on the £3,000 or £4,000 a year allotted to him while his father lived. And he was glad to move his family from the cramped quarters of Winnington Hall in Cheshire to his ancestral seat of Alderley Park, a few miles away.

Thackeray's real friend among the Stanleys, however, was her Ladyship. This remarkable woman was everywhere recognized to be an admirable hostess, but she was also much more. An ardent liberal, she was devoted throughout her mature life to the cause of women's education. She took more interest in her husband's career than he did himself — indeed, in the eighteen thirties when Stanley was Whig whipper-in, Lord Palmerston described him as "joint-whip with Mrs. Stanley" —, and she had many famous literary intimates, among them Carlyle, Maurice, and Jowett. But perhaps the neglect she had to endure from her husband was a surer avenue to Thackeray's sympathies than all her talents. While Lord Stanley took his pleasure, he was accustomed, particularly before 1850, to leave her at home to care for their large family on a quite inadequate allowance. Her love for her husband was such that she did not find this humiliation unendurable, yet her letters are not without plaintive and even rebellious asides. In 1849, for example, we find her writing to her husband, while he was staying with the

Trade. He concluded his career as Postmaster-General, an office he held between 1860 and 1866.

[164] *Greville Memoirs*, ed. Strachey and Fulford, III, 62.

[165] Bateman, *Great Landowners*, p. 420.

Ashburtons at the Grange: "you have got your smart lot. I hate them all so much." [166] Lady Stanley was a beautiful woman when Thackeray first met her, and so she remained nine years later when Motley described her as "a tall, fair, agreeable dame, with blonde hair and handsome features, apparently thirty-five, yet one of those wonderful grandmothers of which England can boast so many, and who make one almost a convert to the 'delicious women of sixty.' " [167]

Of the Stanleys' children, all of whom Thackeray came to know well during his visits to Alderley and to their London residence on Grosvenor Crescent, only Henrietta Blanche (1829–1921) need be mentioned. As the chief beauty of the family, she received her share of the whimsical homage that Thackeray was accustomed in later years to offer to handsome young ladies of his acquaintance. In September, 1851, she made a splendid marriage to the seventh Earl of Airlie, head of the old and wealthy Scottish family of Ogilvy, and became mistress of Cortachy Castle near Forfar, but Thackeray continued to see her frequently in London society.

## ANTHONY TROLLOPE

In the summer of 1859 Anthony Trollope determined to remove from Ireland, where he had made his home since 1853, and to settle at Waltham Cross near London. As the author of nine novels, several of which had been moderately successful, he was by no means unknown to Victorian readers. Yet he had not attained great popularity, and he was singularly ill-acquainted with literary London. Luckily he took it upon himself on October 23 to offer Thackeray certain short stories for *The Cornhill Magazine*. His letter was a turning point in his life. He was engaged to write *Framley Parsonage*, which by Thackeray's courtesy was given the place of honor in *The Cornhill Magazine* previously reserved for

[166] *Ladies of Alderley*, p. 266.
[167] *The Correspondence of John Lothrop Motley*, 2 vols., ed. George William Curtis (New York, 1889), I, 240.

the editor's *Lovel the Widower,* and it was this serial that in public estimation raised him to the front rank of Victorian novelists. What was even more important, he was introduced to Thackeray's circle of literary friends, many of whom — among them Robert Bell, Millais, and Sir Charles Taylor — became his intimates in later years.[168]

Trollope's initial encounter with Thackeray was by no means happy.

We lightened our labours in the service of the *Cornhill* by monthly dinners [George Smith relates]. The principal contributors used to assemble at my table in Gloucester Square every month while we were in London; and these 'Cornhill dinners' were very delightful and interesting. Thackeray always attended, though he was often in an indifferent state of health. At one of these dinners Trollope was to meet Thackeray for the first time and was equally looking forward to an introduction to him. Just before dinner I took him up to Thackeray with all the suitable empressement. Thackeray curtly said, 'How do?' and, to my wonder and Trollope's anger, turned on his heel! He was suffering at the time from a malady which at that particular moment caused him a sudden spasm of pain; though we, of course, could not know this. I well remember the expression on Trollope's face at that moment, and no one who knew Trollope will doubt that he *could* look furious on an adequate — and sometimes on an inadequate — occasion! He came to me the next morning in a very wrathful mood, and said that had it not been that he was in my house for the first time, he would have walked out of it. He vowed he would never speak to Thackeray again, etc., etc. I did my best to soothe him; and, though rather violent and irritable, he had a fine nature with a substratum of great kindliness, and I believe he left my room in a happier frame of mind than when he entered it. He and Thackeray became afterwards close friends.[169]

Trollope had long looked up to Thackeray as his master in fiction, regarding *Esmond* as the finest of all novels, and his affection for the man soon came to match his admiration for the writer. When Thackeray died, he wrote a memorial article for *The Cornhill Magazine,* and in 1879 he contributed the volume on Thack-

[168] See Trollope's *An Autobiography* (Stratford-upon-Avon, 1929), pp. 98–110.

[169] Huxley, *House of Smith, Elder,* p. 104.

eray to the *English Men of Letters* series. This proved to be a
meager and disappointing work, chiefly because the reticence of
Thackeray's family gave Trollope little biographical material with
which to deal, but also because his determination not to be led astray
by his affection for his subject made him something less than generous. Yet he could not altogether conceal his idolatry, for he
wrote that Thackeray was "one of the most soft-hearted of human
beings, sweet as Charity itself, who went about the world dropping
pearls, doing good, and never wilfully inflicting a wound." [170]

[170] *Thackeray* (London, 1879), p. 61.

LETTERS, 1817–1840

# TO MRS. RICHMOND THACKERAY [1]
## 3 JULY 1817

*Address:* To M^rs R. Thackeray. | Mess^rs Palmer & Co — | Calcutta — *Post-marks:* 3 JY 1817, 13^th 1818 Febr. Published in part, *Memorials*, pp. 326–327; facsimile of first page in Lady Ritchie's "The Boyhood of Thackeray," *St. Nicholas*, XVII (1889), 104.

My dear Mama

I hope you are quite well: I have given my dear Grandmama [2] a kiss. my Aunt Ritchie [3] is very good to me I like Chiswick [4] there

[1] See *Memoranda*, Mrs. Carmichael-Smyth. The events of Thackeray's life before he was sent from India to England are entered in the *Chronology* above. This is his earliest surviving letter, and it may well be the first that he wrote. It was dispatched to his mother shortly after he arrived off Weymouth aboard the *Prince Regent* on June 15, 1817 (see below, No. 880, 14 October 1852). The trip made an abiding impression on Thackeray's mind. He recalled in later years "a ghaut, or river-stair, at Calcutta; and a day when, down those steps, to a boat which was in waiting, came two children, whose mothers remained on the shore" (*Works*, XII, 339). His companion was his cousin Richmond Shakespear, and the two boys were in the charge of a native attendant. In a familiar passage in *The Four Georges* (*Works*, VII, 663) Thackeray relates that during the voyage their ship put in at St. Helena, "where my black servant took me a long walk over rocks and hills until we reached a garden, where we saw a man walking. 'That is he,' said the black man: 'that is Bonaparte! He eats three sheep every day, and all the little children he can lay hands on!' " Thackeray remarks elsewhere in this paragraph that when he first saw England, "she was in mourning for the young Princess Charlotte," a statement that his biographers have interpreted too strictly. He meant merely to indicate the general period of his arrival, for the Princess did not die until November 6, 1817.

[2] Thackeray was entrusted to the care of his mother's family, the Bechers, and his father's relatives, the Ritchies. His great-grandmother, Mrs. Becher, was eighty-one when he first met her. She is described in *Roundabout Papers* (*Works*, XII, 377) as "A most lovely and picturesque old lady, with a long tortoiseshell cane, with a little puff, or *tour*, of snow-white (or was it powdered?) hair under her cap, with the prettiest little black-velvet slippers and high heels you ever saw." Lady Ritchie gives a further account of her in *St. Nicholas*, XVII, 102.          [3] See *Memoranda*, Mrs. John Ritchie.

[4] Dr. and Mrs. Turner, Thackeray's great-uncle and great-aunt, kept a school for boys at Chiswick, the site of Miss Pinkerton's academy for young ladies in *Vanity Fair*.

are so many good Boys to play with. S$^t$ James's Park is a very fine place S$^t$ Pauls Church too I like very much it is a finer place than I expected I hope Captain Smyth [5] is well. give my love to him and tell him he must bring you home to your affectionate little Son

William Thackeray

William got so tired of his pen he cou'd not write longer with it,[6] so he hopes you will be able to read his pencil.

Our kind love to all.

Shou'd you be acquainted with Col! Lamb you may have the pleasure of informing him his four sons are in high health, & that the eldest, won one of the orders of merit on the Speech day, & spoke very well. the little one lives half the day with us, & calls, G-Mama & Aunt Becher,[7] *win* you give me a penny, win you. Tell Harriet [8] I had a letter from Warwick ten days ago they were all well. I had a letter from her of the date of mine.

William drew me your house in Calcutta not omitting his monkey looking out of the window & Black Betty at the top drying her Towells. & told us of the number you collected on his Birth day in that large Room he pointed to us!

[5] See *Memoranda*, Major Henry Carmichael-Smyth. The sketch above is presumably of him.

[6] Thackeray's tracing in ink extends only through *I like very much*.

[7] Anne Becher, Thackeray's great-aunt, lived with her mother in Fareham, Hampshire, the Fareport of *Denis Duval*. We learn from Lady Ritchie (*Biographical Introductions*, VIII, xiii) that she was the original of Miss Martha Honeyman in *The Newcomes*. Lady Ritchie's memories of a childhood visit with Miss Becher in Fareham are recorded in *St. Nicholas*, XVII, 102–103.

[8] Harriet Graham, wife of Captain Allan Graham of the Bengal Artillery, who was the oldest sister of Thackeray's mother.

RICHMOND THACKERAY IN 1810

*From a miniature*

MRS. RICHMOND THACKERAY ABOUT 1810

*From a painting*

Your Aunt Turner the D$^r$, Sons, & Daughters, join with your G Mother & me in kind love to you & wishes for your happiness & believe me

your truly aff$^{te}$ Aunt —

A: M: Becher —

My d$^r$ Sister Anne

I have seen my dear little nephew & am delighted with him I hope often to see him & report [to] you of him. accept kind wishes from Your Bro' Teddy [9]


2.

TO MRS. RITCHIE

25 NOVEMBER 1817

*Address:* M$^{rs}$ Ritchie | Chatham Place. | London — *Postmark:* 28 NO 1817. Hitherto unpublished.

Southampton.

November 25$^{th}$ 1817

My dear Aunt

It gives me great pleasure to write to you. M$^{rs}$ Arthur [10] took some of the young Gentlemen and me to the Play and I was much entertained with it. Give my love to my Uncle,[11] and I remain my dear Aunt

Your affectionate Nephew

W. Thackeray.

[9] The signature is by no means clear, but it cannot be *Charles*, as Lady Ritchie (*Biographical Introductions*, VIII, xv) suggests.

[10] "We Indian children," Thackeray writes (*Works*, XII, 339) of the establishment kept by Mr. and Mrs. Arthur at Southampton, "were consigned to a school of which our deluded parents had heard a favourable report, but which was governed by a horrible little tyrant, who made our young lives so miserable that I remember kneeling by my little bed of a night, and saying, 'Pray God, I may dream of my mother!' " And he exclaims elsewhere: "what a dreadful place that private school was: cold, chilblains, bad dinners, not enough victuals, and caning awful!" (*Works*, XII, 289).

[11] See *Memoranda*, John Ritchie.

Dear Madam —

I am happy to inform you Master Thackeray is in excellent health and has been so ever since he came to school. I have already provided him with worsted stockings, shoes, and a suit of warm cloth⟨es;⟩ he has suffered a little with chilblains but they are now quite gone, and with a little attention I hope he will have no more.

The vacation commences on the 17th of Decbr The Master Shakespears 12 are quite well, and will with three of their school-fellows, spend their holidays with me — Mr Arthur unites with me in respects to Mr Ritchie, and I remain Dear Madam

Your obliged & humble Servant<br>R Arthur —

3.        TO MRS. RITCHIE<br>10 MARCH 1818

*Address:* To Mrs Ritchie | 8 Chatham Place | London. *Postmark:* 10 MR 1818. Hitherto unpublished.

Southampton. March

My dear Aunt,

I feel great pleasure in writing to you and have seen Mrs English who was so kind as to bring me some very nice Oranges and promised the next time she came to Southampton to call and see me again. Mama wrote to me about five weeks ago and I have since

12 George Trant Shakespear (1809–1844), *Genealogy* (83), and Richmond Campbell Shakespear (1812–1861), *Genealogy* (84), Thackeray's cousins. The former was at Charterhouse in 1823 and afterwards became an officer in the Indian Artillery. Writing a year before George Shakespear committed suicide, William Ritchie described him as "a fat, shy, eccentric, but most witty, entertaining old fellow" (*Ritchies in India*, p. 96). Richmond Shakespear entered Charterhouse in 1823 and was enrolled in the East India Company's Military Seminary at Addiscombe from 1827 to June, 1828, when he became a Second Lieutenant in the Bengal Artillery. Apart from one short visit to England, he passed the rest of his life in the East. In 1840 he negotiated the liberation of some 400 Russian prisoners detained at Khiva and escorted them safely to Orenburg, a feat for which he was knighted the following year. In

written her a very long letter [1] and sent it to Aunt Becher to send
to her. My new clothes came home last week. they look very well
indeed and I am much pleased with them. It seems a long time
since I saw you: and I remain dear Aunt

Your dutiful Nephew<br>
W Thackeray.

Dear Madam

Master Thackeray has for some time been very anxious to write
to you, consequently I have allowed him to send you these few
lines I am happy to say he is in good health. and with respects to
M^r Ritchie I remain dear Madam

Your obliged<br>
R Arthur —

4.          TO MRS. CARMICHAEL-SMYTH [2]
24 APRIL 1818

*Address:* Miss Becher | Fareham | Hants. Published by Lady Ritchie, *St.
Nicholas*, XVII, 103.

Southampton. April 24^{th}, 1818.

My dear Mama,

I received your kind letter which M^{rs} Arthur was so good as to
read to me. as I am not able to read your letters yet but hope I
soon shall. I have been twice with George and Richmond to dine

1842 he took an important part in revenging the massacre at Kabul and
rescued a number of British fugitives. He married Sophia Thomson, *Genealogy* (85), in 1844 and had nine children. In later years he was British
representative successively at the courts of Gwalior, Jodpur, Baroda, and
Indur. See *Memorials*, pp. 313–316; Colonel H. M. Vibart's *Addiscombe*,
pp. 441–444; and *Works*, XII, 339–340.

[1] This letter has not been preserved.

[2] Thackeray's mother had recently married Captain Henry Carmichael-
Smyth, who is the *Papa* mentioned below.

with Mͬ Shakespeare ³ he was very kind and gave me a great many pretty books to read and promised I should go every time George and Richmond went. I wrote a long letter to you in February and sent it to Aunt Becher to send to you. I have learned Geography a long time an⟨d⟩ have began latin and ciphering which I like very much. Pray give my love to Papa and I remain dear Mama

Your dutiful Son

W. Thackeray.

5.             TO MRS. CARMICHAEL-SMYTH
                    11 JUNE 1818 ⁴

*Address:* Mͬˢ Carmichael Smyth | Agra. Published in facsimile by Lady Ritchie, *St. Nicholas*, XVII, 105–106.

My dearest of all dear Mamas

I have much pleasure in writing to you again from Fareham to tell how happy I am. I went to Roche Court to see Mͬ & Mͬˢ Thresher. I saw a birds nest with young ones in it in a beautiful Honeysuckle bush, and a Robbins in another place. This has been Neptune day with me I call it so becase I go into the water & am like Neptune Your old acquaintances are very kind to me & give me a great many Cakes, & great many Kisses but I do not let Charles Becher ⁵ kiss me I only take those from the Ladies. I dont have many from Grandmama. Miss English gives her very kind love to you, and begs you will soon come home Pray give my kindest love to Pappa. Aunt Becher bought me a Caliduscope, it is a very nice one.

I have spent a very pleasant day at Catesfield, Miss O'Bryen

³ No doubt an uncle of Thackeray's cousins. Their father, John Talbot Shakespear (d. 1825), *Genealogy* (51), appears to have been in India at this time (*Memorials*, p. 309).

⁴ This note may confidently be dated 1818, for it is unlikely that Thackeray's relatives would send him a second year to a school that he had good reasons for detesting.

⁵ Thackeray's uncle.

gave me a very pretty jest Book. I should like you to have such another pretty house as Mrs O'Bryens, there is such a beautiful Garden. I am grown a great Boy I am three feet 11 inches and a quarter high I have got a nice boat. I learn some poems which you was very fond of such as the Ode on Music &c.[6] I shall go on Monday to Chiswick to see my Aunt Turner & heare the Boys speak. I intend to be one of those heroes in time. I am very glad I am not to go to M^rs Arthurs. I have lost my Cough and am quite well, strong, saucy, & hearty; & can eat Granmamas Goosberry pyes famously after which I drink yours & my Papa's Good health & a speedy return.

believe me my dear Mama
Your dutiful Son
W Thackeray

Fareham.  June 11^th
Hants.

6.            TO MRS. CARMICHAEL-SMYTH
            24 AUGUST 1820 [1]

Thackeray's letter is hitherto unpublished. Part of Mrs. Carmichael-Smyth's note was published by Lady Ritchie, *St. Nicholas*, XVII, 108.

Chiswick August 24^th 1820.

My dearest Mother

I have just recieved your letter; but I am sorry to say I did not get on very well last week, but I am getting on a good deal better this. I am very sorry to inform you that Valpy is very ill; and Miss

[6] No doubt Collins's "The Passions. An Ode to Music," which in a later letter (see below, No. 14) Thackeray writes of having parodied.

[1] Thackeray's mother and step-father appear to have returned to England in 1819. Mrs. Carmichael-Smyth describes her first meeting with her son in a letter to India: "He was not at Chatham when we arrived, but Mr. Langslow brought him from Chiswick the next morning, for Mrs. Turner would not part with him till we came, that I might see him in full bloom; and truly he is so, dear soul. He had a perfect recollection of me; he could not speak, but kissed me and looked at me again and again. I could almost have said, 'Lord,

Hellen said he was past recovery; but M^r Turner [2] told me this morning that he was a great deal better, but in much danger; he is more rational than he was, but the weak state he is in and his soreness cause him a great deal of pain, but we still entertain some hopes of his recovery. D^r Turner has given us a holliday So M^rs Turner thought it most proper for me to write now we have had the holiday Papa asked for. M^r Papendick has put me Indian Ink.[3] My love to all at home and accept the same from

Your affectionate & dutiful son

W M Thackeray

---

Poor Billy Boy you [4] see almost lost his wits & I am obliged to send him a *lecture* to spur him on; you never saw such a fellow for spending money, a guinea is gone without anything to show for it but *presents* to his particular friends so I have not given him Pollys [5] present or yours, he cant rest till its gone; you would laugh to hear what a Grammarian he is, we were talking about odd characters, some one here mentioned I forget who; Billy said "Undoubtedly he is a Noun Substantive, Why my dear? because Mama he stands by himself — "

---

now lettest thou thy servant depart in peace, for mine eyes have seen thy salvation.' He is the living image of his father, and God in heaven send he may resemble him in all but his too short life. He is tall, stout, and sturdy, his eyes are become darker, but there is still the same dear expression." (Lady Ritchie, *St. Nicholas*, XVII, 107)

[2] Thackeray had been for some time at Dr. Turner's school in Chiswick. "I don't think there could be a better school for young boys," Mrs. Carmichael-Smyth remarks in a letter that must have been written before the death of George III on January 29, 1820. "My William is now sixth in the school, though out of the twenty-six there are only four that are not older than himself. He promises to fag hard till midsummer, that he may obtain a medal, and after that I think of placing him at the Charterhouse. He tells me he has seen the Prince Regent's yacht in Southampton Waters, and the bed on which his Royal Highness breathes his *royal snore*." (*Centenary Biographical Introductions*, XII, xxi)

[3] Possibly meaning: "Mr. Papendick has put me into [i.e., promoted me to] Indian Ink." The text is, however, correctly transcribed.

[4] Mrs. Carmichael-Smyth is writing to her sister Mrs. Graham.

[5] Mrs. Graham's daughter Mary. See *Memoranda*, Mrs. Charles Carmichael.

7.                TO MRS. CARMICHAEL-SMYTH
                         20 JANUARY 1823

*Address:* M^rs H C Smyth | Addiscombe | near Croydon | Surry. *Postmark:*
JA 22 1823. Extracts published in *Memorials*, pp. 327–328; the whole
letter in facsimile by Lady Ritchie, *St. Nicholas*, XVII, 110–111.

                              Charter House.[1] Jan: 20 1822 [2]
My dear Mother
    I am now going to begin bothering you that letter I wrote to
Butler [3] was only a bit of a preface I dare say you are surprised to
see me use a whole sheet of paper but I have laid in a stock for the

    [1] Charterhouse School in London was at the height of its reputation when
Thackeray entered it at the beginning of the Long Quarter in January, 1822.
Indeed, the Duke of Wellington describes it in a letter of 1820 as "the best
school of them all." His praise can hardly have been occasioned by the teaching which Charterhouse provided. Dr. John Russell (1787–1863), Headmaster from 1811 to 1832, had introduced the Madras or Bell system of
instruction, in which masters were replaced in the lower forms by picked boys
or *præpositi* whose duty it was to teach and keep order. "I have heard Thackeray, at a Founder's Day dinner, tell the story," writes a later Headmaster, the
Rev. Gerald S. Davies (*Charterhouse in London*, London, 1921, p. 265),
"how once Russell entered a classroom where chaos appeared to be ruling, and
there being no sign of a 'præpositus' — 'Where is your præpositus?' cried
Russell. 'Please, sir, here he is,' and they fished out, from under the desk, the
very small boy who had been set to rule over them. They had placed him
there to be out of the way." Thackeray's memories of his years at Charterhouse find a place in many of his books, most notably in *Dr. Birch and his
Young Friends* and *The Newcomes*. A less pleasant picture of Charterhouse
life in Thackeray's time is given by his schoolfellows, Liddell (Henry L.
Thompson, *Henry George Liddell*, London, 1899, pp. 3–11), the Rev.
Thomas Mozley (*Reminiscences of Oriel College and the Oxford Movement*,
2 vols., London, 1882, I, 63–64 and 157–175), and Martin Tupper (*My
Life as an Author*, London, 1886, pp. 14–24). Davies's authoritative "Thackeray as Carthusian" (*The Greyfriar*, II, 1892, pp. 61–67) includes among
much other valuable information an accurate account of Thackeray's fight with
Venables in 1822, during which the bridge of his nose was broken. There
appears to be no foundation for the lurid variant of this narrative communicated by John Ward to *Notes and Queries*, Eleventh Series, III (1911), 162.
    [2] A mistake for 1823, as the postmark shows.
    [3] Possibly a relative by marriage of Mrs. Butler, Thackeray's grandmother.

quarter pens ink and all — I hope you will write to me soon at least oftener than you did last quarter & tell me all about Addiscombe [4] & the *Gentlemen Cadets* and tell me if Papa has got a *cock hat* that will fit him. My hands are so cold that I can hardly write. I have made a vow not [to] spend that five shilling piece you gave me till I get into the 8th form which I mean to ask for tomorrow.[5] The holidays begin on the 23rd of April [6] but it wants 13 weeks to them it will be your time to ask me out in three weeks two more Saturdays must pass and then it will be the time for me to go out. Is Butler gone to Addiscombe with you? We have got a new master his name is Dickin — Dickins or Dickinson [7] Give my love to Papa and

I remain

Yours truly

W M Thackeray

Write again as quick as you can

[4] Major Carmichael-Smyth was *pro tem.* Resident Superintendent of the East India Company's Military Seminary at Addiscombe from August 7, 1822, till April 6, 1824 (Vibart, *Addiscombe*, pp. 57 and 61).

[5] The *Charterhouse Blue Book* for May, 1823, places Thackeray in the seventh form; in May of the previous year he had been in the tenth form. During Dr. Russell's headmastership at Charterhouse the highest form was not the sixth, as is customary in English public schools, but the first.

[6] Though no description of this holiday has been preserved, we have in "Tunbridge Toys" (*Works*, XII, 223–228) Thackeray's recollections of the May to August term at Charterhouse in 1823 and of the ensuing Long Vacation, which he passed with Major and Mrs. Carmichael-Smyth at Tunbridge Wells.

[7] Charles Rowland Dicken (1801–1873), who remained a Charterhouse master for several decades and spent his last years as Rector of Balsham, Cambridgeshire. "Some Few Thackerayana" (*National Review*, XIII, 1889, pp. 794–803) by D. D., a later-day master at Charterhouse, is based chiefly on Dicken's recollections. Readers of this article may find the following key of service: Crook Hall is Brook Hall; Dr. Crushall is Dr. Russell; Dr. Double-first, later Dean of Flatlands, is Dr. Augustus Page Saunders (1801–1878), Headmaster from 1832 to 1853, afterwards Dean of Peterborough; Bishop Meadowbloom is Charles James Blomfield, Bishop of London; the Rev. Charles Oldfield is Dicken; and Dr. Senior is Dr. Edward Elder (1812–1858), Thackeray's schoolfellow between 1826 and 1828 and Headmaster from 1853 to 1858.

THACKERAY IN 1822

*From a bust by Delvile*

DRAWINGS BY THACKERAY IN HIS EUCLID

8.          TO MRS. CARMICHAEL-SMYTH
                    20 JUNE 1827

*Address:* M^rs H. C. Smyth | Larkbeare House | Ottery S^t Mary | Devon.
*Postmark:* JU 20 1827. Hitherto unpublished.

My dear Mother —

Now my fortnight has expired and you see with what consummate regularity I sit down to write to you. I got the paper yesterday tho' with your notice in it. I have sent you a couple of John Bulls.¹ I think John Bull is rather amusing just now quite to your heart's content, "The Revolution has begun" (this is a very bad passage to take out of it tho' for I do not think that the Revolution would be to your hear⟨t's⟩ content). We have had very fine weather for the last fortnight, strawberries have just come in I bought a bottle yeserday for the first time. I suppose your strawberries are flourishing just now ² — Charley ³ has not got out of the twelfth form yet, but Russell says he will put him up when he comes to examine the form, for he never puts any boy up unless he has an examination of the form the boy is in — He spent five shillings in fishing tackle & his money was gone a fortnight ago. He seems very happy. I generally go into the green about a quarter before seven & find him there, sweating or else walking about & playing with the sleeve of his gown. Some dons so * — his breeches are rather long for him, He told me a few days back he had got "Quentin Durward" out of the Library: but had not read much of it — I spent a day at George Elliott's & called on him yesterday he offered me a

¹ A rabid Tory paper, the principal writer of which was Theodore Hook. Thackeray is teasing his mother, for both she and her husband were ardent liberals.

² From 1825 to 1835 Major and Mrs. Carmichael-Smyth lived in a country house called Larkbeare, near Ottery St. Mary, in Devon. Thackeray's life there is reflected in *Pendennis*, in which Larkbeare becomes Fairoaks; Ottery St. Mary, Clavering St. Mary; and the nearby city of Exeter, Chatteris.

³ Charles Smyth, no doubt a distant relative of Thackeray's step-father. He was born in India, entered Charterhouse in 1827, and later became a Captain in the army.                              * See sketch at top of next page.

ticket for the house of Commons, but I did not feel very well so I refused it — I went to Matthews [4] on Saturday night — I was very much amused indeed. he performed the Trip to Paris — his french man was the most com-

plete I ever saw. that French r or rather rrrr he has got completely — but I cannot draw the French men [as] Matthews can make them I have been to Parkinson's & got the ugly bar put into my mouth. It is very uncomfortable indeed — Suppose a the bar & B the teeth and all the front

teeth are tide to this bar & by that means forced out I cannot eat meat at all so I in general have eggs for my dinner, & bread and milk for my supper & breakfast. I am getting rather thin upon it tho' I assure you. Tell Mary [5] that I expect to hear from her in a few days. this is my day for a letter & I am disappointed — Shall I give Charley any tip I think half a crown would be acceptable to

him & it would be no loss to me I know you think I hope Helen says her lessons very well this is the shape of Mary's cross — I got a letter from Sir James [6] the other [day], he thought

[4] Charles Mathews (1776–1835), the celebrated comedian.

[5] After the death of her mother, Mary Graham came to live with the Carmichael-Smyths.

[6] Major-General Sir James Carmichael-Smyth (1780–1838), Major Carmichael-Smyth's older brother.

my holidays were beginning & invited me down —, & I am in a terrible fright for I dont know whether I answered it or not! What shall I do. He will think it very impolite my not answering him and very odd my sending a second letter — Good bye my dear Mother

Believe me your affectionate Son

W. M. Thackeray.

Tell Grandmamma [7] that book has just been sold.

9.                TO MRS. CARMICHAEL-SMYTH
                      4–8 FEBRUARY 1828

*Address:* M^rs Carm! : Smyth. | Larkbeare House | Ottery S^t Mary's | Devon. *Postmark:* FE 9 1828. Extracts published in *Biographical Introductions,* II, xiv.

Feb^r 4. Thank you for your very long letter, Dear Mother  I must confess it is more than I deserve.  I have just penned a letter to M^rs Brown, I have followed your text as closely as possible and I hope her Religious and Gracious mightiness will deem it worthy of a perusal and of her humble admirer and faithful servant, William Makepeace Thackeray —  The first Wrangler this year was of course a "Trinity Man" [1] — I got a note from Wentworth Huyshe [2] t'other day he is quite well.  D^r Russell is most vehemently vociferous at present

"So have I seen on Africs arid shore
  A hungry lion give a mighty roar.
  That mighty roar echoed along the Shore

---

[7] Mrs. Butler, Mrs. Carmichael-Smyth's mother. See *Memoranda.*

[1] Charles Perry (1807–1891) of Trinity College, Cambridge, was Senior Wrangler in 1828.

[2] The only son (b. 1812) of the Rev. Francis Huyshe, Rector of Clyst-Hydon in Devon. He died at Madeira in November, 1829, the month in which he was to have matriculated at Trinity College, after a brilliant career (1825–1829) at Harrow.

And another Lion (thats I) thinks the first (thats Russe⟨ll⟩)
'a Bore' " —³

Dont say I'm not well read now — I hope that the habit of making
puns is discontinued — I got a letter from Malta to day, from a
friend of mine called Stoddart ⁴ — I was at Chiswick yesterday

³ From the fourth scene of *Bombastes Furioso* (1810), a burlesque tragic
opera by William Barnes Rhodes (1772–1826):

> "BOMBASTES:
> So have I heard on Afric's burning shore,
> A hungry lion give a grievous roar;
> The grievous roar echo'd along the shore.
> ARTAXOMINOUS:
> So have I heard on Afric's burning shore
> Another lion give a grievous roar,
> And the first lion thought the last a bore."

The following program for a private performance of Rhodes's burlesque at
about this time is taken from the original in Thackeray's hand in the Morgan
Library:

> "THIS EVENING
> will be performed the tragedy of
> BOMBASTES FURIOSO

| | |
|---|---|
| Arta⟨xom⟩inous . . . | Mʳ Young |
| Bom⟨bas⟩tes | Ewbank |
| Fusbos | Thackeray |
| Distaffina | Miss Carne. |

> Courtiers, Soldiers, Fifers Drums
> Trumpets, Bottles, Glasses &c —
> With entirely new scenery, Dresses & Decorations —"

⁴ Thackeray and William Wellwood Stoddart (1809–1856) lived for several years at the same boarding house, though Stoddart attended Merchant
Taylors' School (1819–1929) rather than Charterhouse. In "A Memorial of
Thackeray's School-Days" (*Cornhill Magazine*, XI, 1865, p. 127) John
Frederick Boyes writes that "Stoddart . . . was, perhaps, Thackeray's greatest
favourite of all [among his early companions], . . . one of the most noble-
hearted men I ever knew, and one of the faithfulest friends: as such he was
cherished to the last by Thackeray. He brought from home anecdotes of the
men in whom we were interested — of Scott, Coleridge, Wordsworth, Lamb,
and Hazlitt, with all of whom his father, Sir John Stoddart, was closely intimate. How well I remember his bringing in the first series of Hood's *Whims
and Oddities* [1826], then a new book, and how we all crowded round him!
He was well read and quiet, and had an infinite relish for Thackeray's
humour." In 1828 Stoddart entered St. John's College, Oxford, with which
he was connected in one capacity or another for the rest of his life.

Very gracious they were. Played two games at Chess with M$^{rs}$ T [5] and 2 rubbers at whist with the young ladies! Delightful — Did Papa dance at the "Hawktry" Invitation Ball? —

Febr$^y$ 5. I have just come out of school and feel rather cozy. "Rude Boreas" has done blustering for to day at least — The Carthusian [6] does not come on at all, they seem to have dropped all idea of it — The novelty of the thing has gone off; perhaps it[s] as well for it strikes me that we should make but poor work of it — I have just heard of my Crony Carne; [7] he was upset on his road from Bodmin to Exeter! and to crown all on getting into a chaise, his box was lashed behind and the bottom came out, he had the consolation of losing thirteen pounds and all his clothes; so he [has] just gone "back agin hame" and I suppose will take some time in refitting. Doctor Russell is going to give up his establishment at Blackheath, and live at Charter-House, his old house is going to be pulled down, and a new one built for him; so M$^r$ Batten's story of his leaving, is not true. I meditate a walk to Miss Watsons tomorrow, as it is a half holiday — I seriously believe I have had, and have now got some remains of THE GOUT. I shall not make much of a diary if I write so much every day, but I always feel as if I were at home when I am writing, and although it may give you very little amusement, it certainly is very amusing to me (that is to say, when I once begin)      I went the other day to see a very beautiful Panorama of the battle of Navarino [8] — I don't know whether I told you of it before. Ill try and copy a couple of Rus-

[5] Mrs. Turner.

[6] George Venables refers to *The Carthusian* when he writes that Thackeray "took part in a scheme, which came to nothing, for a school magazine, and he wrote verses for it, of which I only remember that they were good of their kind" (Anthony Trollope, *Thackeray*, p. 5).

[7] Joseph Carne (1809–1836), son of Joseph Carne the geologist. Carne entered Charterhouse in 1824 and matriculated at Trinity College, Cambridge, in 1827. He did not take a degree. Boyes (*Cornhill Magazine*, XI, 127) describes him as "a good English verse writer, rather in Praed's manner. He could recite Walter Scott, Southey, and Pope's *Homer* without limit; could give and take well in a contest of wit, and was a capital speaker."

[8] Squadrons of the Russian, French, and British navies had destroyed the Egyptian fleet in the battle of Navarino on October 20, 1827. War between Egypt's ally Turkey and Russia broke out the following year.

sians, one a chaplain and the other an officer in the navy, they
are from Stoddart at Malta — I will try —
They are not very faithful copies — The
Chaplain is rather an odd looking fellow, I
calculate. The complexion is a copper kettle
breathed on. Charley has just demanded five
shillings of me, which I have given him —
He has oo      The little boys are making a great row; with pop-
ping off crackers in the fire.

Feb. 7. What a shame it was in me writing no journal yesterday
was not it? I did not go to Miss Watsons, but partook of a dinner
at Captain Langslow's. His mutton was very good and his wine
was very bad to my taste — I had the little Doctor to my feet
yesterday evening      he has consoled me by telling me it is not
the gout. I felt mightily relieved I assure [you] at the welcome
intelligence. We have had a miserable, drizzling rainy day here,
and I dare say it has not been much better with you. Russell is
strong and fierce as a young lion. Miss Roebuck called about your
silk, and I was out I will send it ⟨to you⟩ by our trusty Gyp⁹ "Joseph
Belcher." I have only read ⟨one⟩ novel since I came back, and I
dare say shall ⟨not⟩ read another. I have not yet drawn out a plan
for my studies, when I get home, but certain germs thereof are
budding in my mind. Which I hope by assiduous application will
flourish, yea and bring forth fruits — My friend Wells is going
abroad in a fortnight to learn military "tictacs," he is going into the
army, he is rather old for it "I guess" — Little Dick Bedingfield ¹⁰
is a very clever little chap. I bought him two little books, one containing the history of Robin Hood the other that far famed and
redoubtable narrative yclept The Forty Thieves. I must get some

⁹ The Cambridge name for a college servant.
¹⁰ Richard Bedingfield, the grandson of Dr. and Mrs. Turner and Thackeray's friend for many years. He recorded his cousin's opinions on a variety
of topics in "Recollections of Thackeray" (Cassell's Magazine, II, 12–14,
28–30, 72–75, 108–110, 134–136, and 230–232) and in "Personal Recollections of Thackeray" (Cassell's Magazine, II, 296–299). In later letters we
shall meet with Thackeray's criticisms of Bedingfield's indifferent fiction, The
Miser's Son (1843), The Peer and the Blacksmith (1844), and The Blind
Lover (1845). The second of these novels is dedicated to Thackeray.

sketches of Charterhouse, before I take my final adieu of it. The new buildings are very handsome, they would not make a very good sketch tho' — Poor Charley was degraded for his holiday's task. They are so eternally veering and changing at this blessed place that one does not know what is right or what is wrong, for I had flattered myself I could construe a dozen lines of Ovid without making many mistakes in it — He repeated it very well, as the Master told him. I dont think the paper is much improved by crossing,[11] so when I have filled another sheet I will write Believe me till my next Your aff! Son —

W. M. Thackeray.

Thursday Night near eleven o'clock.

Feb. 8. There is nothing for me to say on this day my dear Mother. I have no new matter to indite — No change in the Ministry    No news from Turkey, that I know of. We have a very nice fellow coming here to supper, this evening. Captain Marshall by name — I hope he will spin us a long yarn this evening. I am going tomorrow to the Langslows,[12] I dont know whether I shall go there on Sunday. I had an hour's chat with Robert Frith [13] this afternoon — He leaves Charterhouse early in March and about May goes to Utrecht with his father, to learn Dutch, before he enters the counting-house at Rotterdam — This I daresay you

[11] Before the introduction of the penny post in 1840, letter writers often made their stationery do double service by turning each page, as they came to the bottom, and writing across the lines already penned. Thackeray's last two letters from Charterhouse and most of those he wrote from Cambridge are "crossed" in this fashion.

[12] Robert Langslow (d. 1853), *Genealogy* (63), who was married to the former Sarah Jane Henrietta Thackeray (1797–1847), *Genealogy* (62), shared with Francis Thackeray the duty of administering Thackeray's fortune. Admitted to the bar in 1823, he served as Attorney-General of Malta from 1832 to 1838 and as Judge of Colombo in Ceylon from 1840 to 1843. He was suspended from the latter post on December 11, 1843, and removed in July, 1844, under circumstances described below, No. 306, 9 June 1845. The Captain Langslow mentioned earlier in this letter was probably his brother.

[13] Robert William Frith, who had entered Charterhouse in 1824 at the age of thirteen.

knew     I was very much amused at seeing Warren acting King
among the Under-fellows, he seems to be quite an oracle with them.
Good night my dearest Mother, I shall soon send my next when
the paper is quite full I mean  Love to Papa and Mary from

your affectionate son.

W. M. Thackeray

Pray send me Grandmamma's direction     I must write to her

## 10.          TO MRS. CARMICHAEL-SMYTH
### 12–21 FEBRUARY 1828

*Address:* Mʳˢ Carm! Smyth. | Larkbeare House | near Ottery Sᵗ Marys | Devon.
*Postmark:* FE 21 1828. Published in part, *Memorials*, pp. 334–335; additions in *Biographical Introductions*, II, xv–xvi.

Tuesday. Feb. 12. 1827.[14]

Snow! Snow! Snow! we have had lots of it here, my dearest
Mother and I don't know whether it is to be succeeded by frost or
not; of all horrors in this blessed town, snow is most horrible, in its
consequences I mean; for when a thaw shall have moistened the
snow flakes, and the genial influence of spring shall have put to
flight Mʳ John Frost — I am getting quite into the Georgic Style,
dont you think so?  The fruits of half an hours lazy labor at those
delectable compositions — There is a ventriloquist coming to Charter-House tomorrow. I was going to be so generous as to treat
Charley, but I find he has got a ticket of his own. A Mʳ Lee
⟨. . .⟩gg!,[15] is it not an elegant name? Has Papa shot any cocks and
snipes. He did not, I suppose make up his fifty brace of partridges
— There is nothing in London to do now, not a new sight of any
kind, that I can hear of. Mʳˢ Boyes [16] and I have agreed this term

---

[14] A mistake for 1828, as the postmark shows.
[15] Two letters have here been torn away.
[16] From 1825 to 1828 Thackeray was a dayboy at Charterhouse, living in a
boarding house kept by Mr. and Mrs. Benjamin Boyes at 7 Charterhouse
Square. The "Memorial of Thackeray's School-Days" written by their son,
John Frederick Boyes (1811–1879), a student at nearby Merchant Taylors'

very well we have not had a single tiff. But whistling will bring wind, so I must have care on my health, or her mighty self will launch her Thunders on my luckless head, I reckon — I think I have begun to day's letter in a proper manner, close at the top of

---

School, provides a discerning account of Thackeray in his last years at Charterhouse: "He was then a rosy-faced boy with dark curling hair, and a quick, intelligent eye, ever twinkling with humour, and *good* humour. He was stout and broad-set, and gave no promise of the stature, which he afterwards reached. It was during a short but severe illness, just before he left school, that he grew rapidly, leaving his sick-bed certainly a good many inches taller than he was when he entered it. . . .

For the usual schoolboy sports and games Thackeray had no taste or passion whatever. . . . [Yet] for a non-playing boy he was wonderfully social, full of vivacity and enjoyment of life. His happy *insouciance* was constant. Never was any lad at once so jovial, so healthy, and so sedentary. . . . We were now and then, indeed, out together in small fishing parties, but it was for the talking, and the change, and the green fields, and the tea abroad instead of at home — cakes, &c. accompanying (for he was always rather gustative, never greedy) — that Thackeray liked these expeditions. . . .

He was eminently good-tempered to all, especially the younger boys, and nothing of a tyrant or bully. Instead of a blow or a threat, I can just hear him saying to one of them, 'Hooky' (a sobriquet of a son of the late Bishop Carr, of Bombay), 'go up and fetch me a volume of *Ivanhoe* out of my drawer, that's a good fellow; in the same drawer you will, perhaps, find a penny, which you may take for yourself.' The penny was, indeed, rather problematical, but still realized sufficiently often to produce excitement in the mind of the youth thus addressed, and to make the service a willing one. When disappointed, it was more than probable that the victim would call Thackeray a 'great snob' for misleading him, a title for which the only vengeance would be a humorous and benignant smile. . . .

He was an omnivorous reader, that is, of good English books; a trashy volume he would have thrown down in five minutes. His taste selected good books, and so his style was in a continual course of formation on good models. Memoirs, moralists like Addison and Goldsmith, and fiction and poetry from the best hands, were his favourites; but in those days he never worked in earnest at anything serious in the way of composition, or put his power to the stretch in any way.

We took in the Magazines — *Blackwood*, the *New Monthly*, the *London*, and the *Literary Gazette* — then in nearly their first glory, and full of excellent articles. . . . The constantly fresh monthly or weekly supply of short articles seemed to bring home the fact of literary production, and made it appear, in some degree, within reach. This was the real commencement of Thackeray's connection with the Magazines, which he used to read with the greatest eagerness, little interfered with by any school responsibilities." (*Cornhill Magazine*, XI, 118–119 and 126–127)

the paper, but I never intend to cross, unless I can help it — I have
not read any novel this term, except one [17] by the Author of Granby.
not so good as Granby — I have read a curious book on the Inquisi-
tion, with plates delineating faithfully the various methods of
torture! Delectable! Is the Capitano [18] in town yet? I have heard
or seen nothing of him — I really think I am become terribly industrious, though I cant get D[r] Russell to think so, or at least to say
so — When I come home, I mean to get up at five o'clock every
morning and to get four hours "sweat" before breakfast, then there
will be only two short hours more, and the day will be my own!
But I have filled this side of the paper, and have talked a great deal
of nonsense, and given you no news. So good night my dear
Mother and goodnight Papa and Mary —

Feb. 13. I have not been out of the house all day. I have got a
headache, but do not like to stay out of school for the Doctor would
tell me that it was a disgraceful shuffle, and a lie and all that sort of
thing: so I think it better to bear the pain — I have been to see a
ventriloquist at Charter-House to day. Such nonsense! I came
away before it was over. I did not see Charles there. I hope he was
there, for it would have entertained him and varied the monotony
of Charter-House Life — I feel ever[y] day, as if one link were
taken from my chain, I have a consolation in thinking there are not
many links more — I have not procured any Valentines for expor-
tation, indeed I dont know that I shall. I have been working all
the evening, and must be up by seven to work again tomorrow
morning — So good night dear Mother.

Feb 14. Valentines day; but I have had no valentines — Doctor
R has been fierce to day, yea and full of anger. We are going to
have a debate tomorrow night on the Expediency of a standing
army — We have not yet settled the sides which we shall take in
this important question. There has been a small row at Charter
House to day — The scrubs or unders were endeavouring to de-

[17] *Herbert Lacy* (1828), by Thomas Henry Lister (1800–1842), whose
*Granby* was published in 1826.
[18] Probably Captain Robert Forrest, who figures pleasantly as "Captain
Bob" in the *Roundabout Papers* (*Works*, XII, 224).

stroy the authority of a superior or upper. The under was the
stronger of the two but he was not allowed to make any resistance.
We have had more snow but I think it is thawing now — My head
ache went away after going to bed last night. and I felt much refreshed in mind and body this morning — Carne has come back,
after his overturn, and various other misfortunes — I have got the
most horrible pen, it will not go as I direct it — I have been to
supper with M^r and M^rs Boyes. I was the only under. How come
on all the Gardens and puppies and pigs and orchards? &c &c. I
shall fill up my paper too soon if I go on at this rate, so I must e'en
leave you and say good night and I hope you have had plenty of
Valentines — W. M. T. 10 O'clock.

Monday — Nothing written on Friday, Saturday, or Sunday —
Friday I was so hard at work. Saturday I went to Southampton
Row,[19] and they dined at two. Sunday ditto — I went to the
Adelphi on Saturday night, and fell in love with M^rs Yates.[20] I
have thought of nothing but M^rs Yates, since then — M^rs Yates.
M^rs Yates. M^rs Yates! She is so pretty, and so fascinating and so
ladylike and so — I need not go on with her good qualities — I am
glad I did not write before now for I should not have got your nice
long leter — Alfred Huyshe [21] never called on me, but I suppose
he had plenty to do without it — M^rs Dick [22] called on M^rs Ritchie
in the Christmas holy days; she said she had been taken ill the first
day she got to town, and was laid up for a month so that accounts
for my not seeing or hearing of her — I have got four hours of delightful Doctor Russell to day before me, is it not felicitous? Every
day he begins at me. Thackeray Thackeray! you are an idle
profligate shuffling boy, (because) your friends are going to take

[19] Where lived Mr. and Mrs. John Ritchie.

[20] Mrs. Elizabeth Yates (1799–1860), the mother of Edmund Yates, was
appearing at the Adelphi in a new burletta by James Robinson Planché (1796–
1880) called *Paris and London: Or, A Trip across the Herring Pond* (*The
Theatrical Observer*, February 14).

[21] A cousin of Wentworth Huyshe, later a Lieutenant in the Bengal Horse
Artillery.

[22] Thackeray's cousin, the former Emily Thackeray (b. 1804?), *Genealogy*
(77), who in 1821 had married William Flemming Dick, *Genealogy* (78).

you away in May &c &c — I have not stopped out of school once
this term — These five weeks have passed away very quick methinks! There goes the big bell and I must have done for the
present; but we will have a little more chat before night. I hope to
send this off this evening — Good bye till school is all over for
the day —

Feb 19. I am glad I did not send off my letter yesterday, for I
have had a letter from Ewbank [23] — His father has got three
vacan⟨cies⟩ and limits his number to eight — His terms are £150
per an⟨num and⟩ his direction Rev^d W Ewbank. Worksop Notts —
Ewbank had ⟨only just re⟩turned to Cambridge, he had a fall from
his horse which delayed him — I have just heard of a poor lad who
had got a commission in his fathers regiment and was expecting his
arrival from India every day — His father and mother, went up
the country previous to their departure, were seized with cholera
and both died on the same day! Doctor Russell is treating me
every day with such manifest unkindness and injustice, that I really
can scarcely bear it: It is so hard when you endeavour to work
hard, to find your attempts nipped in the bud — if I ever get a
respectable place in my form, he is sure to bring me down again; [24]
to day there was such a flagrant instance of it, that it was the general talk of the school — I wish I could take leave of him tomorrow — He will have this to satisfy himself with, that he has thrown
every possible object in my way to prevent my exerting myself [25]

[23] William Withers Ewbank (1807–1854), who entered Charterhouse in
1825, is described by Boyes (*Cornhill Magazine*, XI, 127) as "one of the oldest, and, in the school sense, one of the best Charterhouse men, . . . a medal-
list, when Charterhouse was one of our largest public schools. . . . He was a
true scholar, and more than that, a man of worth, genius, and taste, by no
means limited to Æschylus and Tacitus, but equally well up in Shakespeare
and Milton; his classical and English scholarship twined gracefully together:
he was one of Thackeray's ripeners." Ewbank matriculated at Christ's College, Cambridge, where he took his B. A. degree in 1830 and his M. A.
degree in 1843. From 1841 until his death he was Perpetual Curate of St.
George, Everton, in Liverpool.

[24] The *Charterhouse Blue Books* of May, 1827, and May, 1828, show
Thackeray well down in the first form: forty-fourth in 1827, thirty-second
in 1828.

[25] Chapter 2 of *Pendennis* and "Thorns in the Cushion" in the *Roundabout*

— I wish I might cut Lady-Day — I wonder what sort of a "Vale"
he will expect from me! On every possible occasion he shouts out
reproaches against me for leaving his precious school forsooth! He
has lost a hundred boys within two years, and is of course very
angry about [it] [26] — There are but 370 in the school, I wish there
were only 369. I am glad to hear Miss Graham sang the Butterfly [27]
with so much eclat. The snow seems determined to make a vigorous
stand against all attempts of sun and thaw — M^r Churton's [28] arch

---

*Papers* bear witness to the lasting impression made on Thackeray by Dr.
Russell's pillorying. Thomas Mozley (*Reminiscences*, I, 63–64) remarks that
"Russell was rough with Thackeray, not more so perhaps than with many
others, but when he saw Thackeray's spirit and humour rising with him, that
made matters worse. Hence a life-long resentment much to be lamented."

[26] In May, 1826, there were 462 boys at Charterhouse, in May, 1828, 367.

[27] "I'd be a butterfly born in a bower," a vastly popular song by Thomas
Haynes Bayly (1797–1839), which had been introduced at Drury Lane on
October 9, 1827, in *The Wealthy Widow*, a comedy by John Poole (1786–
1872).

[28] According to Martin Tupper (*My Life as an Author*, p. 15) the Rev. Edward Churton (1800–1874) was "the single really excellent teacher and
good clergyman" at Charterhouse. Mozley (*Reminiscences*, I, 63) recalls that
Churton assisted Russell with the written exercises of the upper school. "We
were summoned one after another to an anteroom, where we found Churton
already prepared with neatly-written criticisms and corrections. He did not
say much, but he said it gently and in a way to reach the understanding and
remain there. It was the only teaching addressed to oneself individually that I
had at that school, and I felt it invaluable.

Nor was I alone in this. Thackeray had the benefit of this personal instruction, and he acknowledged the debt. Meeting him one day in the Strand, I
told him I had just had a talk with Churton. He exclaimed, 'O tell me where
he is, that I may fall down and kiss his toe. I do love that man.' I told him I
was afraid he would not be able to do that, for it was at the exhibition of the
Royal Academy I had just met Churton." Another school-fellow, Alfred
Gatty (*Notes and Queries*, Seventh Series, V, 1888, p. 204), tells of an encounter between Thackeray and his old master after Churton had become
Archdeacon of Cleveland. "He had met Thackeray . . . on Founder's Day
[at Charterhouse], and they walked together homewards after dinner. When
they were parting at the steps of an hotel, near Lincoln's Inn Fields, Churton
asked his companion if he would 'go in, and have anything.' Thackeray
replied, 'If you will give me a cigar, I will smoke it on my way home.' Of
course this was provided, and the good archdeacon told me it was the only
cigar he had ever paid for, and he kept the record in the hotel bill in remembrance of Thackeray." A few years earlier Thackeray had drawn Churton's

was blocked up with snow, M꞉ Penny [29] came in and told the Doctor, "They have Bunged up M꞉ Churton's" Is not that elegant for a Charter-House Master? My Pen is split and I find it no easy task to write with it so Good night dear mother —

21. I did not write a journal yesterday, for just as I was going to begin I was told my hot-water was carried up, for my foots. I have had a little chat with Master Charles this evening — A Boy in this house has made me a present of a gold eye-glass, it is very ugly. I think I will give it to Miss Turner. Saw a pretty Panorama yesterday in Leicester Square painted by Burford, Rio Janeiro. My paper is out & so Good bye my dear Mother.[30]

---

portrait in *Dr. Birch and his Young Friends:* "The real master of the school is Prince; an Oxford man too: shy, haughty, and learned; crammed with Greek and a quantity of useless learning; uncommonly kind to the small boys; pitiless with the fools and the braggarts; respected of all for his honesty, his learning, his bravery (for he hit out once in a boat-row in a way which astonished the boys and the bargemen), and for a latent power about him, which all saw and confessed somehow." (*Works*, IX, 73–74)

[29] The Rev. Edmund Henry Penny (1797–1879), a master of mediocre abilities, kept the house where Thackeray lived from 1822 to 1824, before he became a dayboy (Rev. G. S. Davies in *The Greyfriar*, II, 64–65).

[30] After Thackeray returned to Larkbeare in May, he had a serious illness, which made it necessary for him to defer his matriculation at Cambridge until February, 1829. A fragment from a letter of June 25, 1828, to James Hine, in which he describes his recovery, is quoted in Sotheby's catalogue of June 15, 1937: "I hope you will make allowance for the inconsistency of this my letter, by the heat of the weather, and weight of my wig which since my late lamentable illness — As pants the hart for cooling streams — See Hymn Book — I have been compelled to assume." Thackeray later told Bedingfield (*Cassell's Magazine*, II, 296) that "he was quite a short fellow, being but five feet six at fifteen; but that he had an illness of some months' duration, and rose up at his full altitude of six feet three."

11.      TO JOHN FREDERICK BOYES
              29 JANUARY 1829

*Address:* John Frederick Boyes Esq<sup>re</sup> | 7. Charterhouse Square. | London.
*Postmark:* JA 29 1829. Hitherto unpublished.

My dear Freddy —

Thank you for nothing — or rather for a compilation of the most egregious nonsense w<sup>h</sup> ever issued even from your pen. I am deeply hurt that I have not recieved answers to my last six letters — — And I had a great mind not to have answered that last piece of absurdity of yours — But my feelings have got the better of me; & here I am that is to say here is your answer — The most remarkable incident w<sup>h</sup> has happened to me since I last wrote to you was a trip I took to Oxford to see Stoddart — I was with him for a week & then got introduced to all the Merchant Taylor men. Dunlap scil: & Guillemard, & Wood & Browne,[1] & sundry others not at present recollectable — I had some tolerably good fun — Stoddart seemed to be decidedly the gayest man — He gave a brace of wine & supper parties. I did not go to a regular spread at a single other mans rooms the whole time There is Stoddart's party; one man singing, another drinking another smoking, a third talking obscenity, a fourth listening to him & so on [2] — Tho I suppose when you went

---

[1] Arthur Dunlap (1809–1895), James Guillemard (1808–1858), Richard Wood (1811–1880), and Robert William Browne (1808–1895), fellow-students of Stoddart at St. John's College, all of whom had been trained at Merchant Taylors' School.

[2] In the *Book of Snobs* Thackeray describes the wine-parties of his college days: "We then used to consider it not the least vulgar for a parcel of lads who had been whipped three months previous, and were not allowed more than three glasses of port at home, to sit down to pineapples and ices at each other's rooms, and fuddle themselves with champagne and claret.

One looks back to what was called a 'wine-party' with a sort of wonder. Thirty lads round a table covered with bad sweetmeats, drinking bad wines, telling bad stories, singing bad songs over and over again. Milk punch — smoking — ghastly headache — frightful spectacle of dessert-table next morning, and smell of tobacco — your guardian, the clergyman, dropping in in the midst of all this — expecting to find you deep in Algebra, and discovering the gyp administering soda-water." (*Works*, VI, 355)

to Lincoln [3] you saw something of the kind — I have had a couple of Letters from Carne in the grand stile giving me a mathematical, critical, philological account of Cambridge; he introduces too some

of his good things in each letter. Thus — "I had a good cap a man stole it in Hall and left a most scurvy one instead. Luckily I percieved him departing & saw my cap on his head (This is so characteristic of the man) I went up & said Sir you have got my cap I believe Have I said he I'm sure I knew it not" I wonder how you could mistake them said I holding up his miserable Golgatha to the light; — Why I change my cap almost every day — And generally for the better I presume was the answer — " It will make him conceited I fear this Cambridge life; however he is an excellent fellow at bottom, & I think worth a dozen of Young — [4] Ewbank is mighty distant — Told Carne he did not consider me in the light of a correspondent I have commissioned Joey to tell him

[3] Boyes had been elected a scholar of Lincoln College, Oxford, but resigned to take the Andrew Exhibition of St. John's College.

[4] James Reynolds Young (1807–1884), whom Boyes (*Cornhill Magazine*, XI, 128) characterizes as "of ready wit, kind, good-natured and light-hearted," had been at Charterhouse with Thackeray from 1823 to 1827. We learn from John Cordy Jeaffreson (*A Book of Recollections*, I, 253–254) that Thackeray was a very frequent visitor during these years to St. Helen's Place, Bishopsgate, where Young lived with his parents. Young entered Caius College, Cambridge, in 1827 and received his B. A. degree in 1832. From 1847 until his death he was Rector of Whitnash in Warwickshire.

that for his corerspondence I have neither the time nor the inclination" — He has been afflicted with α'φροδι'τη to speak learnedly;
the spasms to speak commonly. I liked your Merchant Taylor men
much; Dunlap particularly Guillemard I think a very gentlemanly
man & so Browne — though of the latter I saw little — I must
w⟨rite⟩ you a good night my dear Fred & subscribe myself

Your sincere Friend<br>
W. M. Thackeray.

Write *directly*; tell Hine [5] I forget his London Direction he
must write & tell it me. Tell him I want to hear about the Theatres
&c & if he dont write I shall cut him — He came to Oxen while I
was there likewise on a wissit to Bully — Stoddart wears shoes just
low enough to give his corns room to grow — comme ça

 My drawing has blotted

12.          TO MRS. CARMICHAEL-SMYTH
                23 FEBRUARY 1829

*Address:* Mrs Carmichael Smyth | at Mrs Butlers | Sidmouth | Devon —.
*Postmark:* FE 23 1829. Extract published in *Biographical Introductions*,
II, xix.

Slaughters Coffee House.[6] Monday 5 o'c

We have arrived, my dear Mother, at the Coffee house with the
murderous name, & have ordered a roast sirloin of beef for dinner!
After wh I believe we proceed to the Adelphi — [7] I saw Mrs Boyes,

[5] James Hine (b. 1808) had been at Merchant Taylors' School from 1819
to 1826. He received his B. A. and M. A. degrees from Corpus Christi
College, Cambridge, in 1832 and 1835.

[6] In St. Martin's Lane, a favorite haunt of artists since Hogarth's time.

[7] "ADELPHI THEATRE. THIS EVENING will be presented the new
burletta, in three acts, founded on Mr. Mathews' celebrated 'Trip to America,'
called MONSIEUR MALLET; or, My Daughter's Letter. . . . After which
a new nautical burletta, called THE RED ROVER; or, The Mutiny of the

D.̣ Russell, & M.ʳ Ritchie to day, my Aunt was not at home. Russell was very gracious, and M.ʳˢ B very happy to see Thackeray, M.ʳ B not at home, but I shall breakfast there tomorrow. Jim ⁸ is not at Charter-House. Warren and Charles we both saw — I have just got a letter from M.ʳ Thackeray ⁹ with one enclosed to his brother of Cambridge, the Physician — ¹⁰ M.ʳˢ Ritchie will give me one for the Provost of ⟨King's.⟩ ¹¹ Father has just sent my "respectful compliments" ⟨to⟩ M.ʳ UL.¹² quite gratuitous on his part. We had that sage Senator Colonel Wood in the Coach with us this morning, he is very like M.ʳ Cartwright. My Uncle Frank ¹³ has lodgings in

---

Dolphin. To conclude with FREAKS AND FOLLIES." (*Times*, February 23)

⁸ James Robert Carmichael-Smyth (1817–1883), later (1838) second Baronet, oldest son of Major-General Sir James Carmichael-Smyth, entered Charterhouse in 1829. In 1841 he dropped the surname Smyth by royal license.

⁹ Thomas Thackeray (1767–1852), *Genealogy* (27), was trained as a surgeon by his father and sent out to India in the East India Company's medical service. He married in 1795 and returned to England after the death of his wife in 1800. The rest of his life was passed in Bath, where he married again and built up a good practice. See *Memorials*, pp. 80–84.

¹⁰ Dr. Frederic Thackeray (1774–1852), *Genealogy* (34), was educated at Rugby and established himself as a consulting surgeon in Cambridge. He was given an M.D. degree by Emmanuel College in 1820. See *Memorials*, pp. 123–130.

¹¹ Dr. George Thackeray (1777–1850), *Genealogy* (14), was educated at Eton and King's College. After some years as an Eton master, he was elected in 1814 Provost of King's College and held this remunerative post until his death. In 1816 he married Mary Ann Cottin, *Genealogy* (15), who died fifteen months later, leaving a baby daughter, Mary Ann Thackeray (d. 1879), *Genealogy* (19). His wife had been attended in her last illness by her sister Elizabeth Cottin (d. 1866), who remained with her brother-in-law to care for his child and preside over his household. After her father's death Mary Ann Thackeray and her aunt lived in considerable state in London, where Thackeray was a frequent visitor to their home at 27 Portman Square. See *Memorials*, pp. 235–243.

¹² William Whewell (1794–1866), Thackeray's tutor, was a fellow of Trinity College from 1817 until 1841, when he was elected Master. He achieved a wide reputation through his *History of the Inductive Sciences* (1837) and *The Philosophy of the Inductive Sciences* (1840). There are some traits of his character in Thackeray's portrait of Crump of St. Boniface in *The Book of Snobs* (*Works*, VI, 350–351).

¹³ Francis Thackeray (1793–1842), *Genealogy* (59), was educated at

Grosvenor Place near the Park, I shall meet him in Southampton Row tomorrow. Father dines at Colonel Arabian's. I have ordered a buckish Coat of blue-black with a velwet collar. Jimmy was very anxious for me to finish his puzzles where accident or carelessness may have rendered them imperfect — Father is going to o q p the next two pages so believe me, my dearest Mother, Your aff⸆ Son.

W. M. Thackeray

M⸆ Thackeray begins his letter to me, "My dear Cousin" —

---

I had the pleasure dearest on reaching Forests office this morning to get yours of Saturday, and lose no time in dispatching some of the *sine qua non*, that you may be at liberty to act according to circumstances — Sh⸆ you find it necessary to go, I would certainly greatly prefer that you sh⸆ post it, and take either John or Martha [14] with you, whichever you please, and take our own Carriage — I will write again tomorrow — Bill has been writing while I was penning a letter to M⸆ Whewell, I have taken our places on the Cambridge Coach for Wednesday — we start at 1/2 after seven — our dinner is on table so I must fold up my letter with only adding my kind love to Mother and Mary and w⸆ the assurance that I am always my dearest's most aff⸆ Husband

H. C. S.

P.S. Recollect you must write your name on the back of the order when you endorse —

---

Pembroke College, Cambridge, where he received his B. A. and M. A. degrees in 1814 and 1817. After his marriage to Anne Shakespear (d. 1850), *Genealogy* (60), on May 15, 1829, he resided at 20 Cadogan Place, where Thackeray was often to be found. At this time he was the incumbent of Belgrave Chapel in Halkin Street, and when he later retired to the country, his substantial private income made it possible for him to accept the curacy of Broxbourne in Hertfordshire. Francis Thackeray was a man of learning, known in his own day for *A History of William Pitt* (1827) which Macaulay reviewed. He helped to administer Thackeray's inheritance and is the "saintly Francis" apostrophised in *The Book of Snobs* (*Works*, VI, 342). See *Memorials*, pp. 494–496.

[14] The Goldsworthys, family servants of the Carmichael-Smyths. John remained with Thackeray until his death in 1845. His portrait serves as the initial letter for chapter 3 of *Pendennis*.

13.                TO MRS. CARMICHAEL-SMYTH
                   28 FEBRUARY–5 MARCH 1829

*Address:* M<sup>rs</sup> Carmichael Smyth | Larkbeare House | near Ottery S<sup>t</sup> Mary's |
Devon. *Postmarks:* CAMBRIDGE MA 5 1829, 6 MR 1829. Published in
part, *Memorials*, pp. 335–337; additions in *Biographical Introductions*, II, xx.

> Trinity. College. Cambridge —
> Saturday 28 February. 1829.

I am now about to begin my first journal, my dearest Mother,
which will I hope be always sent, with the regularity with which
it is now my full purpose to give to it. After Father left me I went
in rather low spirits to my rooms, & found myself just too late for
lecture. I was employed all the morning in nailing and hammering and such like delectable occupations, about one o'clock I went
to Hine's of Corpus, & with him strayed about among the groves
or rather fields w<sup>h</sup> skirt the Colleges of Kings Trinity &c & — afterwards I walked with Young up to Chesterton, & ran half the way
home again (Chesterton is two miles from Trinity)  You may
wonder what could have inspired my legs with such unusual activity — There was a boat race, at w<sup>h</sup> it is the duty of all the Under-
Graduates to attend, & shout for their various Colleges. Next I
did devour a vast dinner in Hall, next I went to Chapel in my
new surplice, & my new cap, & got an old greasy wretched thing in
its stead, and finally had Carne & Hine to tea with me who are now
gone, & have left me to write these few lines to my dearest Mother,
to remind her of her affectionate Son. W M T.

Sunday — I have not much to journalize to day except that I
went to tea at Old M<sup>rs</sup> Thackeray's (D<sup>r</sup> T's mother)[15] where I
passed the evening & saw the Vice-Provost of Kings [16] who invited

---

[15] Mrs. Thomas Thackeray (1737–1830), *Genealogy* (4), mother of Dr.
Frederic Thackeray.

[16] Martin Thackeray (1783–1864), *Genealogy* (37), had been educated at
Eton and at King's College, of which he was successively Fellow and Vice
Provost. He inherited a considerable fortune upon the death of his aunt, Miss
Theodosia Thackeray (1742–1830), *Genealogy* (9), and shortly before his

me to come and see him often & soon. I was at Chapel morning & evening & at St Mary's (The University Church) in the afternoon, so that my day has been tolerably well occupied with these employments, & a few calls w[h] I had to make in the morning — I am tired & sleepy for I passed (to tell you the truth a stupid evening at M[rs] Thackerays — The old lady talked of nothing but fevers and deaths, though she said she loved the name of Thackeray. My boxes have not yet arrived — Good night. dearest Mother —

Monday. This day I was introduced to my private tutor,[17] his name is Fawcett [18] he looks a decided reading character I read with him for about an hour & a quarter and am to go to him every evening from six to seven with Classics and Mathematics alternately. I read Algebra with him this evening and liked his method much   My books arrived at length   I disappointed poor Carne in this wise. My Gyp told me there was a vast parcel for me, and I met some men near my rooms with a hamper of wine & an old cloak   These I of course concluded to be for me, so I went over & asked Carne to come and taste my liquor and see whether it had hurt by travelling, on arriving however at my quarters I found what rejoiced my mind rather than my palate my books. The parcel cost me 2··19··11. —

---

marriage in 1834 to Augusta Yenn (d. 1869), *Genealogy* (38), he left Cambridge and purchased a house at 86 Gloucester Place, Portman Square, in London, where he and his wife passed the rest of their lives. He was a Whig and a member of the Reform Club. His niece, Mrs. Bayne, anything but a devil's advocate, admits that he was not a handsome man, and observes: "If he had a fault it lay in strong prejudices on some social and religious subjects . . . He was guided by 'a few strong instincts, and a few plain rules,' and was apt to be intolerant of those who were not." His intimacy with Thackeray extended over several decades. See *Memorials*, pp. 134–144.

[17] Whewell gave little attention to his tutees, and they had consequently to depend for guidance upon private tutors, graduates with distinguished records who were allowed to support themselves by tutoring until fellowships became available for them in their colleges.

[18] Henry Edward Fawcett of Trinity College, twenty-seventh wrangler and twelfth classic in 1828.

To morrow I hope to be elected ⟨to⟩ the Union — ¹⁹ I have some thoughts of wri⟨ting⟩ at a Co⟨lleg⟩e Prize an English Essay "On the influence of the Homeric Poems on the Religion the Politics, the Literature & Society of Greece — But it will require much reading, wʰ I fear I have not time to bestow on it. I rejoice with you on the downfall of the Peel.²⁰ Bong swawr as they say dear Mother.

Tuesday — I walked 10 miles today to Zuy and back. I was elected a Member of the Union; and had three men to tea with me after the debate they have just left me & it is past twelve o'clock. The report goes that "the Duke" has resigned ²¹ — I must say good night — We had a debate on the Catholic Question — adjourned to next week

Wednesday. Mʳ George Thackeray of Kings (a Fellow) ²² called on me to day he seems to be a very nice man — I went to call on Mʳ Thackeray the Vice-Provost, whom I much like — I went to a wine party at Carne's tonight, but was obligated to go away for an hour & a half to my Tutor (his time is an hour) by this I saved about seven glasses of wine, — I shall write a few lines tomorrow on this letter & send it off to morrow night, & so continue it for the future. I have not had much walking to day but plenty of reading — There were no public lectures because it was Ash Wednesday. Tomorrow however they begin again — I have given up all idea of the essay I shall not have time —

---

¹⁹ The famous undergraduate debating society.

²⁰ Robert Peel, Home Secretary in the Duke of Wellington's cabinet, had been elected M. P. for Oxford as an opponent of Catholic Emancipation. In February, 1829, when the fear of civil war led him to advocate concessions to the Catholics, he was severely criticised as a turncoat. He resigned his seat, stood for reëlection at Oxford, and was defeated. But his "downfall" was only temporary; he was immediately returned for another borough. Thackeray's earliest publication had been a squib against two supporters of Catholic Emancipation (reprinted by John Camden Hotten, *Thackeray: the Humourist and the Man of Letters*, New York, 1864, p. 190).

²¹ The Duke of Wellington, who had come to believe like Peel that Catholics should be admitted to political office, was also the target of popular abuse.

²² The fifth son (1806–1875), *Genealogy* (46), of Thomas Thackeray of Bath, who did not, however, become a fellow of King's College until later in the year.

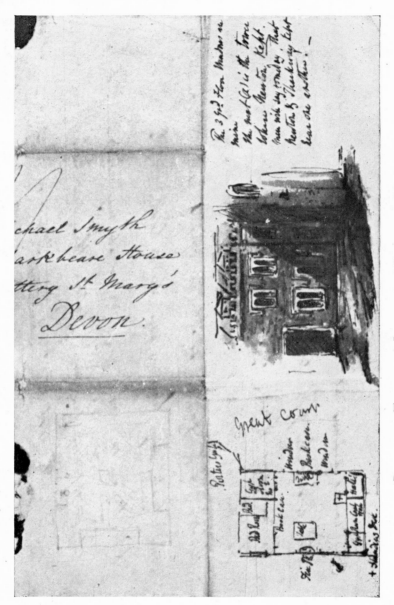

DRAWINGS IN THACKERAY'S LETTER OF 28 FEBRUARY–5 MARCH 1829

I find that sleeping from 12 until seven o'clock is quite enough for me. When it is lighter, I shall go to my tutor from 6 to seven in the morning & not at 6 in the evening as I do now. Goodnight Dear Mother — I have dismissed my reading lamp & returned it to the Brazier seeing that it emitteth no light. Your affectionate Son

W. M. Thackeray

Thank you for y$^r$ letter    I have obeyed your injunction & sent you a drawing of my rooms — I will pursue my journal to-night — & this day week you shall again hear from your aff$^{te}$ Son

William M. Thackeray

Thursday Night.

[See illustration facing page 34.]

The 3 gr$^d$ Floor Windows are mine
The mark (a) is the tower where Newton *kept*. Men will say someday, that Newton & Thackeray kept near one another! — [23]

14.     TO MRS. CARMICHAEL-SMYTH
6–14 MARCH 1829

*Address:* M$^{rs}$ Carmichael Smyth. | Larkbeare House | Ottery S$^t$ Mary's | Devon. *Postmark:* CAMBRIDGE MA 15 1829, 16 MR 1829. Published in part, *Biographical Introductions*, II, xxiii–xxiv.

Trinity Coll: — Friday March 5.[24] 1829.

I did not keep the promise conveyed in the journal w$^h$ I dispatched yesterday of continuing it on that day, but I will make up

[23] "A day, many days, might be spent exploring all to be seen round the Great Court of Trinity. Before we hasten on from the Great Gate, let us cast a reverent eye on E staircase near-by. Among the many famous men who once had rooms on this staircase (first to the right) are Sir Isaac Newton, Lord Macaulay and Thackeray." (Frank Rutter, *Guide to Cambridge*, Cambridge, 1937, p. 46)
[24] A mistake for Friday, March 6.

for my fault by writing a long & copious account of my proceedings to day. Yesterday nothing happened worth noticing, to day on the contrary mother has been marked with several wondrous occurrences! I had a letter from the Wine-Merchant, I walked to the observatory — I cut I am sorry to say my private tutor, but quite unintentionally for I was proceeding (about 9 o'clock) on a walk towards Trumpington with Carne — We had gone about half a mile onward when we heard the sound of sweet music, some fair maid was singing The light, The light guitar [25] So Carne & I walked slowly & silently under the window, & when she had arrived at the chorus we joined in. The door flew open, I know not what issued from it, for I ran with all the velocity my long legs are capable of towards Cambridge, while Carne ran the other way. I have been to his rooms, & find him safely returned. I have filled a paper so no more to night from y$^r$ affectionate Son.

William M. Thackeray.

Sunday. I have missed a day! but I trust you will forgive me the offence when I relate the circumstances which led to the omission      I had taken a desperate ride with Carne (after lectures) to Lord Herveys place at Wimpole [26] about 9 miles from here, in Wimpole Park we galloped for about half an hour and finally lost our way, that is to say found that we had fifteen miles to ride home instead of nine, at a quarter to three we were seven miles from Cambridge, and at ten minutes past three we were trotting very quietly down Trumpington Street! — All w$^h$ things made me very tired, however I worked resolutely with my private tutor, and after returning from him read resolutely on by myself till about nine o'clock when unluckily I fell asleep till ten, & then woke with such a splitting headache that I retired to bed, directly I was comfortably settled in baide the headache left me, it was all owing to

[25] A song by John Barnett (1802–1890) that attained great popularity; Silas Wegg quotes a stanza, with characteristic additions, in *Our Mutual Friend*, Book I, chapter 15.
[26] Wimpole Hall, seat of the third Earl of Hardwicke, nine miles southwest of Cambridge.

this cruelly unpleasant position of my head over the back of the sofa — This morning I felt vastly better for my ride, & went to Chapel in a most perfect state of bodily contentment only my joints were rather stiff with my yesterday's exertion — Poor Carne is quite done up with his exertion, & looks most miserably "seedy" We saw an ugly house, a delightful park, and some good pictures, & besides this I have had enough exercise to keep me going for a week — My Wine arrived yesterday — The Sauterne is pekooliarly good, the men come and drink it and then caution me not to ⟨serve⟩ it at wine parties — The wine parties are miser⟨ably⟩ stupid things in my opinion. I was at one on Thursday and at another to day — I shall keep clear of them. Tomorrow I intend to commence a steady, and systematic course of reading. I shall always "sport my oak" [27] while I am engaged in my studies — I fear I shall find it difficult to send a Journal a week, I ought to send two, I have taken these two pages already so I must say no more till tomorrow and see how my reading agrees with me. Good night dear Mother. W. M. T. I see Bolingbrokes works to be sold cheap, I shall buy them tomorrow.

Monday — I must be more concise for the future my dear Mother, otherwise I shall fill all my paper before I arrive at my week's end — To day M.^r Pryme called on me, he married D.^r Thackerays sister [28] I was quiet & steady all day —

Tuesday — I returned M.^r Pryme's call, & saw him like another Cincinnatus in his garden — He introduced me to his wife, who has

[27] That is, close the oaken outer door to his rooms, indicating thereby that he is not to be disturbed.

[28] George Pryme (1781–1868), *Genealogy* (42), took his B. A. degree at Trinity College in 1803 and returned to Cambridge as a barrister in 1808. In 1813 he married Jane Townley Thackeray (1788–1871), *Genealogy* (41). After he had represented Cambridge in parliament for three terms, his health forced him to retire from politics. He served as Professor of Political Economy at Cambridge from 1828 to 1864, having lectured on the subject since 1816. In 1847 he and his wife went to live on their estate of Wistow in Huntingdonshire. See *Memorials*, pp. 162–221. Thackeray was a good friend of the Prymes and of their daughter, Mrs. Bayne. It is to the coöperative work of mother and daughter, *Memorials of the Thackeray Family*, that we owe the only detailed accounts available of the careers of many of Thackeray's kin.

a very strong resemblance to the Thackeray family and is a pretty woman. M$^r$ P is a barrister, & Professor of Something in this University, he is also very scientific & wondrously ugly. M$^{rs}$ Pryme requests the pleasure of my company at an evening party on Thursday — I went to the Union where the Catholic Question was again agitated — The Tories lost by a very small majority — There was some excellent speaking; particularly on the Whig Side — A M$^r$ Cookesley [29] spoke in the most extraordinary manner — The Hero of the Union retired with diminished head before Cookesley — His name is Sunderland [30] and he is certainly a most delightful speaker — but is too fond of treating us with draughts of Tom Paine — I will work him next term for it — God bless you Dearest mother —

Wednesday. To day I have been quiet reading almost all day — And have no news except that taking a moonlight walk, I fell over head and ears in a ditch opposite Addingbrokes Hospital. I might have been drowned with the greatest facility! For I had my cap & gown on — I ran home as quick as I could changed all my clothes, &c &c and am now going to bed. So good night — Dear MA.

Thursday. I have been reading hard to day, and have just been to M$^{rs}$ Pryme's small tea party — it was terribly dull at first, but I managed to pick up some information with respect to Hiero-

[29] Henry Parker Cookesley, who matriculated at Trinity College in 1827 and took his B. A. degree in 1831.

[30] Thomas Sunderland (1806–1867) was admitted to Trinity College in 1825. Lord Houghton described him many years later as "the greatest speaker, I think, I ever heard, a man with the highest oratorical gift . . . who only lives in the memory of his own generation, and for this reason, that he was only known at the Union at Cambridge" (Reid, *Life of Lord Houghton*, I, 75). When Sunderland left Cambridge in 1830, he dropped completely out of sight. Only after his death was his eclipse explained. He had become insane while travelling on the continent, and though his malady soon ceased to be violent, there was henceforth a hint of derangement in everything that he said or wrote. Alfred Tennyson, alone of his fellow-students, seems to have doubted his ability. But Sunderland was not discomposed when he learned that Tennyson had drawn an unfavorable portrait of him in the little poem called "A Character." "Oh, really," he remarked, "and *which* Tennyson did you say wrote it? The slovenly one?" (Thomas R. Lounsbury, *The Life and Times of Tennyson*, New Haven, 1915, p. 157)

glyphics from the Marchese Spineto whose work if you recollect was reviewed in Blackwood.[31] M.[r] Thackeray the Vice-Provost of Kings was there, & was very kind to me, he asked me to wine with him on Saturday. He is a much more intelligent man than his brother and has as kind a heart I think. His rooms in Kings are the finest in the University — I took Carne to D.[r] Thackerays to day as he was not well & wanted advice. No more from y.[r] affectionate Son W. M. T. I walked about 20 miles —

Friday — To day I read all the morning till 3 o'clock for this is my private tutors examination day — After Hall I went to wine at Hine's. and sat with him till one o'clock in the morning — not drinking wine, but tea and talking metaphysics and morality — I must Chapelize to morrow So Good night Dear Mother.

Saturday. Something told me I sh.[d] hear from you to day. And it is the case — 8 shirts & 3 letters, & two fronts! — I know where the Yellow Paper came from as ⟨wrapp⟩ed the Soda box — Sly fellow a'nt I?

Saturday continued. I was thinking of making this a double letter, but I will continue my Journal in another sheet. I have been very idle to day, I worked so hard yesterday that I suppose I wanted relaxation. Carne & I were concocting all the morning a Parody on Collins' Ode On the Passions.[32] by the various passions we intended to represent the members of the Union — it is however no go — There is a most disgraceful Magazine just come out here,[33] w.[h] fool that I was I bought, together with the Oxford Literary Gazette, another periodical w.[h] appeared on the same day. they are both of them disgraceful to the Parent University — Thank you for your washing book — Carne has got a pretty washerwoman      I gave her a kiss this morning! — She said she was

---

[31] In "Marquis Spineto on Hieroglyphics" (*Blackwood's Magazine*, September, 1828, 313–326), an account of a series of lectures delivered at the Royal Institution in Albemarle Street, Spineto is described as an Italian nobleman, exiled from his own country for his political views, who is giving instruction at Cambridge in foreign languages.

[32] "The Passions. An Ode to Music."

[33] *The Cambridge Magazine. The Oxford Literary Gazette*, which endured for four numbers, was first published on March 11.

never so insulted in her life! — I will begin a larger sheet of Paper
and obviate the necessity of copying in my next — I have not been
on the water yet. Men only laugh when I tell them I can't row —
I must Learn however. I am going to a "Supper Party" at Carnes
to night — Those are the gayest things in the University I believe
(at least among us Pensionnaires [34] — The weather is miserably
cold! I must go call on M_r J^os Thackeray,[35] another son of M_r Bath
Thackeray & a fellow of Kings to boot. So good *day*      I will say
good night in the evening on another sheet of paper

Y_r affectionate Son — W. M. T.

I must mend my gloves to go out.


15.          TO MRS. CARMICHAEL-SMYTH
                 14–22 MARCH 1829

*Address:* M^rs Carmichael Smyth | Larkbeare. | Ottery S_t Mary's | Devon.
*Postmark:* CAMBRIDGE MA 22 1829. Published in part, *Memorials,* pp.
341–343.

Saturday Night.                              Trin. Coll. Cam.

I have just returned from Carnes supper, it was desperately
stupid and has consequently made me desperately sleepy w^h will I
trust make my excuse for saying Good Night to my dear Mother,
And courting the sweets of repose on my downy couch. I have had
to make certain little purchases w^h I find indispensable; viz. 2 Salt-
Spoons 3/6. 6 Egg Spoons 10/ w^h are things much wanted here
for the men eat eggs wondrously. The Sauterne is greatly admired — Five men came in here uninvited on purpose to drink
thereof this afternoon, so I just pretended to go & speak to a man
in the court, & left them in the lurch — w^h was I confess rather inhospitable in me. But they were boring me at the time — Miss

[34] Thackeray, like most students, was entered as a pensioner at Trinity
College. Below him were the poorer students or sizars, above him the noble-
men and fellow-commoners. See *Works,* VI, 348.
[35] Joseph Thackeray (1805–1880), *Genealogy* (45), a Fellow of King's
College from 1827 to 1846.

Shute's [36] friend William Barnes [37] is here I know him not he seems to be a gentlemanly man only rather like a man-milliner in face very like William Shakespear — Good Night dear Mother. Ever y$^r$ affte Son. W M T. I called on the 2 young M$^r$ Thackerays, [38] of Kings to day; the elder (the fellow) asked me to wine with him on Monday — I bought a set of foils & tackle to day — I have been fencing almost every day since I came here.

Sunday. I have no news for to day, but I have strong resolutions for to morrow. I purpose to begin a more regular course of reading than I have hitherto done, for though I have read this week, I have not done so with the regularity essential to my well-doing — I shall therefore begin tomorrow & read from half past 8 o'clock till half past one, & then again with my private tutor on alternate days from 4/30 to 5/30 or from 5 to 6 — The former is the most convenient hour of the two, for that is the time when the Wine-Parties commence I can therefore always plead an engagement on those days. Next week however I think I shall go to him, from six to seven in the morning, for I shall reap more benefit from his instruction in that early hour, than in after dinner. The ale here is a most fascinating beverage! & the plum pudding on Sundays most amiable! The meat is bad — The beef peculiarly so — I am told Pork is good it has never yet fallen in my way — The worst part however of our meat is that it is cold. Men eat enormously, & I am not much behind hand. We have a delightful organ in our Chapel w$^h$ you would like I think to hear. This however is only on Saints' days, & the eve of S$^{ts}$' Days — I sh$^d$ like much to come down to Cheltenham next month, but it would be almost a pity; For my rooms must be papered & painted, & I shall have plenty of time

[36] By his second wife, the former Anne Ricketts, Samuel Shute of Fernhill on the Isle of Wight had four daughters: Isabella; Emily; Matilda; and Anne, who married Dennis Hollingworth (Burke, *Landed Gentry*, 1847). Mrs. Shute was an intimate friend of Mrs. Carmichael-Smyth, and Thackeray must frequently have visited the Shutes' home at Cowes during his summers in Devon.

[37] William Maule Barnes (1811–1848), who matriculated at Trinity College in November, 1829.

[38] Joseph and George Thackeray.

then to read up the G<u>k</u> Play — &c. The vacation however is three weeks long — so that there w<u>d</u> be plenty of time: & perhaps you would like to see how pert priggish & dogmatical, six weeks at Cambridge will have made me. Farewell till tomorrow night dear Mother, when I will tell you the result of resolutions.

XXXX   his Mark.

I wrote a long letter to Stoddart today  I will write to Wentworth some time this w<u>k</u>

Monday.  I have just been wining with M<u>r</u> Joseph Thackeray of King's  he seemeth a gentlemanly man — I read all the morning & walked till hall — There is I hear to be but a poor debate at the Union tomorrow, I don't think I shall patronize it, although Carne is going to speak.  There was a petition going about Cambridge, against Catholic Emancipation, to w<u>h</u> many undergraduates had subscribed, but presently comes an Edict from the Vice-Chancellor, that no such petition is to be permitted! — Good night dear MA.

Tuesday.  I have followed up my reading to day rather vigorously tho' I find it a hard hard matter: it goeth very much against the grain — My letter is a most neat ⟨one⟩ covered with ink and blots, but in a journal of this nature (a daily hebdomadal!) these things will happen.  I went to the Union very late & missed Carne's speech.  The question was Whether the constitutional Assembly of France advanced the interests and merited the thanks of the French nation" — or something to that purpose.  I voted that it did Though in truth I know little about it — The next question is Whether Buonaparte up to 1808 advanced the interests, &c as above.  I think I shall give them a little jaw on the question.  The next is the E I Companys Charter.³⁹ *but* I will bore you no longer with this but wish you good night until tomorrow" — Your affectionate Son.  W M. Thackeray.

Wednesday.  I went to our library to day, & got out five stout quartos, but just as I was bearing them off, the library Keeper told

---

³⁹ At this time there was much argument in parliament and elsewhere as to whether the East India Company's charter should be renewed after its approaching expiration. See *The Annual Register* for 1830.

me they must be all returned by this day week! Which will give me rather hard work if I intend reading them. They allow you to keep 6 books out a whole quarter of a year, but they must be returned by quarter day w^h is next Wednesday. it is a most splendid room. I have read to day. Good night Dear Ma.

Thursday. I have not had any lectures to day. They (the lecturers) generally miss one a week — and instead of going to my private tutor I fell asleep. I am going to him from 8 till nine now every other day — For the Mathematical lectures w^h I think will be to my advantage. For I am occasionally sleepy after my dinner! — I have had 3 men drinking tea with me — it is now past eleven so good night Dear Mother. Men wished me to go to Ely tomorrow, but I think it w^d be rather a loss of time & money. I sold my Great-Coat to Carne for half its prime cost 1··16··0 —

Friday. I have just been drinking 3 cups of tea at D^r Thackerays, & another at a Freshman's of our College, of the name of Badger! [40] He and I are going to read Gk. Play together — from 11 until 12 every day; I am getting more into the way now of reading — I go to Fawcett every other morning from 8 to nine. to Fisher [41] (the Mathem lecturer) from nine to ten, & to Hare the classical one from ten to eleven. Then with Badger from eleven to twelve. twelve to half past one Euclid or Algebra and an hour in the evening at some one or other of the above or perhaps at some of the collateral reading connected with the Thucydides or Æschylus This is my plan w^h I trust to be able to keep — When therefore I say nothing, you may know I have kept it — I conversed with the Upholsterer to day, who says my rooms may be painted and papered for £13 — He is much the cheapest man in Cambridge — I have got a broad recess in my rooms 7 ft 6 inches high, & 6 feet broad w^h he is going to fit with a book-case, and cupboard; painted rosewood for £5. — he is to take my chest of drawers & book case at their original price w^h is 3··16··0. — A man, I know, gave £8 for

[40] Albert Badger, who was thirty-two years old when he matriculated at Trinity College in 1828.

[41] John Hutton Fisher and Julius Charles Hare, Assistant-Tutors at Trinity College from 1824 to 1832 and 1822 to 1832 respectively.

the same thing only smaller than mine is to be. I took a walk to
day to a place about 3 miles from Cam. yclept Colton. A very
pretty church, & village — I shall have no room for tomorrow
unless I take good heed. So good night Dear Mother.

Sunday. No journal yesterday, when I came home I had a pain
in my heel from having run a nail (or part of one of those tormenting nails with w^h the shoes are adorned) into my heel. It was rather
sore, & so I got some hot water for my toes, & went to baid        I
went to the Vice-Provost's of King's to wine yesterday — He
treated me with some such Hock! O such hock! never did I drink
such hock! However there was only half a bottle of it between
three — He had asked seven men to meet me, not one of them
came  the only man there was named Fawsett; [42] He was a schoolfellow of mine, & a sensible good natured fellow, only he thinks
[it] incumbent on him to talk elegant when he goes among [43]
Dons; in w^h he fails miserably — He told us among other things
that "The salubrity of the Cambridge air induced many valetudi-
narians to resort to it" — M^r Thackeray told me that he thought
every young man sh^d go abroad after he had taken his degree. I
was talking to day with a man whom I have made acquaintance
with whose name is King [44] — he was a wrangler, & he says that with
5 hours reading a day (not including 2 hours for lectures) I may
do anything at Cambridge — That was the time w^h he read, but he
never looked at a book in the Vacations. I do not find any harm
from Carne's idleness, rather good, for I am always rebuking him,
& consider I ought to act up to the principles I profess. We shall
have a good debate tomorrow — I have not spoken about your
letter, your long, kind letter, but I will do that more fully on another sheet of paper — So good bye for the present Dearest Mother
Tell Father I answered five questions out of the 12 (four of them
were probs in Euclid, & the other a long Algebraical one) & they

[42] Walter Barham Fawssett of Corpus Christi College, who had entered
Charterhouse in 1822.

[43] There is a large ink spot on the manuscript here, near which Thackeray
has written, "Ugly blot! —"

[44] George King, a fellow of Corpus Christi College, who had been sixteenth
wrangler in 1827.

were done most correctly. We have glorious plum-pudding in hall to day, and it has just struck — Good bye Father & Mother till evening — Remember me to George, I will send him my speech on the character of Napoleon. & some very entertaining Algebraic Formulæ with w^h (& treatises on the Gk. Article) [I] think to amuse him.

Whewell strongly recommends me not to go down next Easter. he says that it would be very much to my disadvantage.

16.          TO MRS. CARMICHAEL-SMYTH
             22–29 MARCH 1829

*Address:* M^rs Carmichael Smyth. | Larkbeare House | Ottery S^t Mary's | Devon. *Postmark:* CAMBRIDGE MA 29 1829. Published in part, *Biographical Introductions*, II, xxiv-xxv.

Trin: Coll: Cam: Sunday night. March 22. 1829.

I have just got rid of a man who has been pestering me like the old man of the sea did Sinbad, he came to my rooms to tea half tipsy, & afterwds insisted on my giving him some wine, however I steadily resisted and he has at length gone to his home wineless — It is now past twelve & my contest with this man has made me rather sleepy — So I must say good night MA & PA

Monday. I have made a fool of myself! — I have rendered myself a public character, I have exposed myself — how? I spouted at the Union. I do not know what evil star reigns to day or what malignant dæmon could prompt me to such an act of folly — but however up I got, & blustered & blundered, & retracted, & stuttered upon the character of Napoleon. Carne had just been speaking before me and went on in a fluent & easy manner but it was all flam — as for me I got up & stuck in the mud at the first footstep then in endeavoring to extract myself from my dilemma, I went deeper and deeper still, till at last with one desperate sentence to wit that "Napoleon as a Captain, a Lawgiver, and a King merited & recieved the esteem & gratitude & affection of the French Nation." I rushed out of the quagmire into w^h I had so foolishly plunged myself & sat down like Lucifer [45] never to rise again with open mouth in that august assembly — So much for the Union — I read from 8 o'clock till 1 this morning, & considerably more in the evening — So tho' I have been foolish to day I have not been idle — Tomorrow I must I fear cut one of the lectures, for going to the Union quite put out of my head that there was a preparation requisite before I c^d attend at lecture; I mean reading over the lecture before hand. I sh^d look rather foolish if I did not. I must read 2 books of Euclid for my examination on Friday — So till to-morrow Fare-thee well — W.

Tuesday — I have just returned from a long, metaphysical theological oratorical discussion with Hine of Corpus. he gave me some dinner at his rooms after w^h we wended to the rooms of a man named Wells [46] of Corpus at whose rooms we wined & staid till eight from w^h time until eleven I have been engaged in the conversation above mentioned — Hine is a fellow of very considerable talents and information w^h however do not shine in "company," owing to his excessive modesty I presume — In company he talks slang in private he talks sense & very good strong sense too. I read to day from 8 till two excepting about ten minutes for break-fast at ten. D^r Thackeray & his lady did me the honor of a visit, after w^h I walked till half after three, & then proceeded to the dis-cussion of a roast fowl & villainous rancid greasy sausages; to the latter however I did not pay much attention, to the fowl I was exceptionally polite. Wells is the brother of that Wells whom you may recollect at Boyes's — he is rather a Simeonite [47] men say. He is however a gentlemanly fellow for all that M^rs T asked me to a party at her house this evening at w^h I am glad I did not attend, for if I am to take M^rs Pryme's party as a specimen it must have been very very stupid. Notwithstanding my recent failure, I think I shall pluck up courage to jaw at the Union next Tuesday about the

[45] "How art thou fallen from heaven, O, Lucifer, son of the morning!" (Isaiah, 14, 12).

[46] Charles Rush Wells, who took his B. A. degree in 1830.

[47] Disciples of Charles Simeon (1759–1836), Fellow of King's College and an influential leader of the Evangelical party in the Church of England, were known as "Simeonites" or "Sims."

renewal of I: Company's Charter, & endeavour to retrieve myself. The Judges are here now; they (I believe) stay at Wordsworths (our Masters) while here,[48] the court was thronged with little boys & girls to behold the mighty men as they passed to the Judgement. Up this morning at eleven o'clock. I cut lecture to day (not my private tutor's tho' I was so seedy after last night's discomfiture that I received but little advantage therefrom. I must write no more till to morrow. So Good night D̲r̲ Father & Mother — I am going to walk at 6/30 tomorrow morn.

Thursday — No journal for Tuesday! for shame M̲r̲ Bill what can have caused such neglect? A most desperate fit of hard reading which brought on a most desperate fit of sleeping, which deprived me of all consciousness except for my bed — My good works to day have however made up for my evil ones of yesterday. I went and affixed my signature to a petition of the Undergraduates of this college against Catholic Emancipation — Lord Landsdowne [49] said in the House of Lords the other night that he knew that *all* the Under Graduates of Trinity amounting to 250 were ready to sign a petition in favor of Catholics — This petition was only got up last night and there are now more than 150 signatures to it, w̲h̲ will I think make the noble Marquis look rather foolish — I have had lots of blackguard boys a⟨round my⟩ windows these two last days to view the judges ⟨in their⟩ robes of scarlet. I called yesterday on M̲rs̲ Pryme, & took a long walk (that is of an hour & half) before eight o'clock in the morning — To day I purchased a Gibbon for 2··10··0. it is not yet paid for. I find a Mitford History of Greece [50] to be an absolutely necessary article thou it is desperately dear 5 guineas     however there is a shop here where I can get it

[48] It had been the custom since 1608 for the Judges of Assize to stay at Trinity College during the sittings in Cambridge (W. W. Rouse Ball, *Notes on the History of Trinity College, Cambridge*, 1899, pp. 77–78). They stayed in 1829 with Christopher Wordsworth (1774–1846), the youngest brother of the poet, who was master of Trinity from 1820 to 1841.

[49] Henry Petty FitzMaurice (1780–1863), third Marquess of Lansdowne. Thackeray afterwards came to know this great landed proprietor, called the "Nestor of the Whigs," who was one of the most distinguished statesmen of his time.

[50] *The History of Greece* (1784–1810) by William Mitford (1744–1827);

very handsomely bound for £5. But I thought it w$^d$ be better to write on the subject. To me forming a library it is a positive requisite — & so is a Hume & Smollett w$^h$ I can buy uncut in 13 vols $^{8°}$ for £3··3··0 but I must say Good night till tomorrow Y$^r$ affte Son. —

Friday. I read all the morning till 1/2 past one at Mathew Mattocks, after w$^h$ I proceeded to Granchester about 2 miles & a half with Carne. Went to Moody's [51] to drink tea, & accompanied him to hear M$^r$ Pemberton's [52] delineation of the character of Shylock. I could have done it as well myself. From Pemberton's I went to Hines at Corpus where I feasted on oysters & am now come home sleepy to bed, so good night — Y$^r$ affectionate Son —

Saturday — Now M$^r$ Bill, why did you not write a longer letter yesterday? because I was sleepy Father; & how do you intend atoning for your fault? By writing a great deal to day Mother! Then begin Sir & tell us the news— . . . I followed my usual course of reading this morning, until one o'clock when I went to call on Mazzinghi [53] to see if he w$^d$ go to the boat-race with me; I found him — in bed! — I aroused however the Young Swiss boy & we hied to the boat-race away — It is rather a fine sight that boat race particularly on a day when Nature conspireth with ale to render the race pleasant to the see-ers thereof. There are generally a thousand gownsmen on the banks who hie down to the place whence the boats start; & accompany them on their return, (w$^h$ by

---

David Hume's *History of England* (1754–1761), continued by Tobias Smollett.

[51] George Moody of St. John's College, who took his B. A. degree in 1830.

[52] Charles Reece Pemberton (1790–1840) had made his London début on March 2 as Virginius in the tragedy of that name by Sheridan Knowles. He played Shylock at Covent Garden on March 9. His performance in Cambridge appears to have been a reading.

[53] Thomas John Mazzinghi (1811–1893) had been at Charterhouse with Thackeray in 1826 and 1827. He matriculated at Trinity College in 1828, took his B. A. and M. A. degrees in 1832 and 1835, and became a barrister. Thackeray's letters afford occasional glimpses of his chequered subsequent career. In 1889 he was librarian of the William Salt Library at Stafford (*Letters & Literary Remains of Edward FitzGerald*, ed. T. Wright, 7 vols., London, 1902–03, I, 15, note).

the way requires no small exertion of the legs). I ran but it was very hot! methought — but I did not stop for a' that. Carne goes down on Wednesday with an ægrotat [54] and I shall immediately go into his rooms, & let the painter & paperers wreak their vengeance on my walls. I have chosen a genteel drab coloured paper; & am going to have my mantlepiece painted marble. The Judges have departed; The trumpeters who were wont to make music under my window, are silent  The criminals are waiting their sentences — Whether any will be hanged I know not nor have, I like some men I know, made a breakfast party on purpose to see them sus: per: col:[55] — There are no less than three Magazines in Cambridge — One in present existence w^h I think I mentioned The Cambridge Magazine: Another to be called the C. Gazette. & the 3^d to be called the Chimaera! [56] — But I must go no farther tonight  So Bong swar, dear Pa & Ma —

Sunday. O the delights of a College life! here am I just come home in order to enjoy a quiet evening; and I find my fire out, & my prospects in a consequent state of utter destitution — I had purposed to have washed my vest but it must pass undone — Thank you for your long long letter dear Mother! The questions given me to day were not all expected to be done; There was not time for them; there were five props of Euclid among them to write out w^h I did; & one question in Algebra; I did half of them you see — The weather has changed and has given me a cold w^h I wished much to get rid of to night but it is I fear in vain. I wish I had not said a word about Whewell's advice — For to tell truth I did expect you w^d have overruled any objections I might offer — I am glad I am not in Jim's case, that is to say Fancying my Mother does not care for me, for I am sure I sh^d get no such long letters

[54] A certificate testifying that a student is ill.

[55] Many years later this phrase gave Thackeray a pleasant beginning to his last novel. See *Works*, XII, 443.

[56] A prospectus for *The Chimæra* was issued when the first number of *The Cambridge Magazine* was published, but it was noted in *The Snob* of May 14 (p. 32) that *The Chimæra* "has taken cold, and is expected not to be able to leave her bed till October." During the summer Thackeray began an essay on Shelley for this magazine, but neither essay nor *Chimæra* ever appeared.

every week (or send them perhaps). How much sherry has Sir W. Pole [57] ⟨do you thi⟩nk? I envy the Miss Steads their vaccinating dispositions — ⟨Our⟩ petition is done up! Wordsworth has stopped it — It will however answer the purpose, for The B$^p$ of Bath & Wells [58] who was to present & will or ought to say that he had a petition signed by 160 undergr⟨aduates⟩ of Trin. w$^h$ was forbidden by the Master — I am going to give a Wine-party on Wednesday, & pay off all my debts — I shall ask about 13 men — I think — (Reading men always have the largest wine-parties). The provost of Kings, I know not — He is a cousin of the V. Provosts so a very distant connection of mine — He sees very little society, & has the reputation of being rather close-fisted — I perfectly agree with you that any rooms sh$^d$ be painted oak. I shall have them more than oak, I shall have them oaker!!! Beautiful! —

Here are some algebraic questions — Resolve x & y to the power of $^n$ Given x & y to find n. Given a & b to find s. Find the n$^{th}$ term of a+b &cc all w$^h$ things puzzle me — I breakfasted with Badger this morning — I eat (fancy) 1. Pigeon-Pie — 2. Ditto. 3. Muffins: · 4 Eggs. 5 Fowl: 6 Muffins: 7$^{th}$ Roll: 8$^{th}$ Radishes 9$^{th}$ Sausage — 10$^{th}$ radishes w$^h$ being involved in my stomach ought to occasion an evolution. Lord Winchilsea [59] is quite a young man. He succeeded to the title lately & unexpectedly — I wish he had legged "The Duke" — at the Battle of Battersea. But I must say Good bye Dearest Father & Mother — Y$^r$ aff$^{te}$ Son — W. M. Thackeray

All the bills are gone into Whewell — already — So it will be no use sending them down. I have them all safe. I have £2··7··0 in hand. Shall I get money from Whewell? when I want it?

[57] Sir William Templer Pole (1782–1847), seventh Baronet, a wealthy Devon land-owner whose country seat was situated near Axminster, a few miles from Ottery St. Mary.
[58] George Henry Law (1761–1845), Bishop of Bath and Wells from 1824 to 1845.
[59] George William Finch-Hatton (1791–1858) became tenth Earl of Winchilsea in 1826, when his cousin, the ninth Earl, died unmarried. In a public letter of March 14, 1829, Lord Winchilsea questioned the good faith of the Duke of Wellington in his *volte-face* regarding Catholic Emancipation. In the duel which ensued on March 21, Winchilsea stood Wellington's fire and discharged his own pistol into the air. (*Annual Register*, 1829)

17.　　　　TO MRS. CARMICHAEL-SMYTH
29 MARCH–8 APRIL 1829

*Address:* M^rs Carmichael Smyth | Larkbeare House | Ottery S^t Mary's |
Devon. *Postmark:* CAMBRIDGE AP 8 1829. Published in part, *Memorials*,
pp. 343–344; additions in *Biographical Introductions*, II, xxxii.

Sunday Night. I have just sent off my letter, & have no ⟨news⟩
but I like to have something on hand, some link between me and
home. I bought Sadler's & Wetherall's speeches [60] yesterday very
nicely printed for two-pence apiece. I paid out a shilling in tracts
of that kind I think. I got 6 little books & 3 or 4 papers — We are
to have a meeting on Tuesday in the Town-Hall; they say there
will be glorious fun. I shall strive to squeeze in my slim person —
I fell asleep to day over the life of Cardinal Wolsey.[61] When I
come home I will bring with me The Revolt of Islam by Percy
Bysshe Shelley,[62] it is in my opinion a most beautiful poem — Tho'
the story is absurd, & the republican sentiments in it conveyed if
possible more absurd — I think I have written enough for to night
— so I'll goo to baid — I have left off drinking ale almost — Dont

I sport a neat cypher. ⨯⨯⨯⨯ No — it is not well done.

Monday — I had taken my coat & waistcoat off to go to baid and
forgotten the Journal when some sudden thoughts of home brought
it again to my recollection so I came back just to save myself &
shew that I did not quite forget & that I am y^r aff^te Son —

Tuesday. I was rather brief in my epistle of yesterday, so I
must work double tides for to day. I have just come from the

Union where the subject discussed was the ⟨E.I.C.⟩ Charter —

[60] The speeches against the Catholic Emancipation Bill of Michael Thomas
Sadler (1780–1835) and Sir Charles Wetherell (1770–1846) are reported at
length in *The Annual Register* (1829), I, 43–50 and 54–57.
[61] Probably the *Life of Cardinal Wolsey* by George Cavendish, his gentleman usher, which Samuel Singer edited from the original manuscript in 1825.
There was a second edition in 1827.
[62] Shelley's vogue at Cambridge during 1829 and 1830 has been described
by Professor Lounsbury (*Tennyson*, pp. 150–161).

Which is of course to be annulled — I did not favor them with my sentiments — I have got into a scrape — returning from the U: we beheld a fire engine, upon wʰ heads some night-capped and some not popped out from the windows. One of the heads inquired what was the matter? There's fire, said I at the back of your own house! — The head popped back, & I learnt it was Mʳ Gunning [63] — I shall call tomorrow & apologize for my beayvier.

Carne made an absurd speech to night, he has rather wriggled himself into favour at the Union; & is now abusing it — He goes down tomorrow. with I think I told you Dʳ Thackerays advice, & proposes taking a walking tour in Derby-Shire — I have forgotten to present your respects to Badger, he & I are regular at the Greek Play — He came to me however to day rather indisposed, & so we read nothing but instead looked over a splendid folio of prints taken from the statues in the Museum of Florence, wʰ I have got out of the Trinity Library to try & copy the hands & feet — I have read one of the Sᵗ Bernard Tales [64] — it is good, but nothing equal to Salathiel     I begin to get into the knack of the wine-parties: yesterday I was at one, & drank a glass & a half of wine — To day I was at another and drank just the same quantity — To morrow the 1ˢᵗ April! I pay off my scores, & ask men to wine on my own account — I have asked nine — All the men who have asked me to theirs — I got a supper out of the man, who wanted to drink my wine in vain; I went into his rooms little thinking of anything of the sort; & there found 4 men playing whist and a veal-pie & Salad for 4 — I thought it was a pity they should over eat themselves so I made a fifth — in spite of the remonstrances of the host & the 3 men (who were of course my particular friends) — I manouvered better than mine host did in the case of the wine — There has been an Anticatholic meeting in the townhall to day — Grand

[63] Henry Gunning (1768–1854), esquire bedell of Cambridge University since 1789 and senior esquire bedell since 1827, remembered for his *Reminiscences of . . . Cambridge, from the Year 1780* (1854).

[64] *Tales of the Great Saint Bernard* (1828) and *Salathiel; a Story of the Past, the Present, and the Future* (1828) by the Rev. George Croly (1780–1860).

row — No Undergrads. admitted — I have written a good long
Journal, which I  'Carne
hope you will take  Wells Corpus Christi
in good part and so  Hine Do
I shall say, Good  'Fawssett Do —
Night.  Hailstone Trin.[65]
You asked for the  Heyworth Do — [66]
names of my friends  Badger Do.
Eyes right! There  'Mazzinghi Do.
they are, all for  'Young Caius
you Those marked '  'Moody S.t John's —
are Charter-House  'Baker Caius — [67]

Men. The others except Hine are College acquaintances —

Thursday — No journal yesterday — My wine party made me
so very sleepy that I could not think of anything except going to
bed; w.h I did right early — The men were very sober, there were
scarcely five bottles of wine drunk — The repast cost 27 shillings
w.h I have *not* paid for — I have not read a syllable to day — I have
been so busy superintending the operations in my rooms    I
write from Carnes, where I take up my quarters — he is gone
down. I find a card on my table for a supper party; how glad am I
that I did not come home till half past 10 from Hines! I go there
almost every night or he comes to me — I find it impossible to read
steadily at night — I read a novel at his rooms to night by Maturin,
a good thing rather entitled "Woman" [68] — I shall be very smelly
in my new rooms or rather in my newly-papered rooms — I have
some idea of asking Stoddart down here but I shall not allow him
to meddle with my reading, if I do so — Day to day have I meditated coming to Wordsworth, & day to day have I put it off. To-

[65] John Hailstone, who matriculated at Trinity College in 1828 and took
his B. A. and M. A. degrees in 1832 and 1835.
[66] James Heyworth, who matriculated at Trinity College in 1828 and took
his B. A. and M. A. degrees in 1833 and 1838.
[67] Henry Baker, admitted to Caius College in 1828 and later a surgeon in
the Royal Navy.
[68] *Women, or Pour et Contre* (1818) by Charles Robert Maturin (1780–
1824).

morrow however it shall be. Till when Believe me Dear Mother
& Father y͏ͬ aff͏ᵗᵉ ⟨Son.⟩

Saturday — I was nearly forgetting Journal to day but when I
go to say my prayers it generally recurs to me — I have read to
day as usual: went down to the boat-race; & afterwards in the evening took a long walk up the Ely Road. I have been tucking in to
Pigeon Pye & Salad at a Man's rooms — w͏ʰ I fear have made me
rather sleepy — I am going to wine at George Thackeray's tomorrow. He will be elected fellow in a week or two. I do not
know whether I sh͏ᵈ ask him in return, Whether his dignity would
allow him to come — I shd much like to take to riding for 20
guineas I could ride 70 times w͏ʰ is as much as I should do when I
keep a horse — w͏ʰ w͏ᵈ cost me 3 times the sum. — I have no news
Good night. Dear Father & Mother.

Saturday — I have been to a party at George Thackeray's at
Kings, w͏ʰ was very little to my taste. The men who were by the
way all King's men talked of nothing but horses &c; One man had
been or was going to buy a bit of leather, meaning a saddle at such
a place, another had been seeing his horses coat *cut* & his tail
docked — And various other witticisms of the same Kind — I have
been reading a great part of to day in our Magnificent Library w͏ʰ
I had no business to do — About one o'clock Young came to me, &
sculled me up to Granchester, he got aground there, & seemed to
have little hope of getting afloat again, so as my weight was only
an incumbrance, I got out and left him — and walked back — For
aught I know he may yet be there — Nine eight-oars & six-oars,
four oars, wherrys, Annies without number have gone to Ely to day
where dinner was to be prepared (I was told) for a hundred & fifty
men — This will rejoice Mr. Landlord of the Lamb at Ely — This
will likewise send most of the men home drunk — a catastrophe
w͏ʰ in such merry makings is perfectly natural. It is just eleven
o'clock & the man who keeps above me has not yet returned; he
has been abs⟨ent⟩ 15 hours he had to row 17 miles there & back; I
think I must put on my night cap, & seek soft slumber in my downy
baid So Good night dear Father & Mother — Y͏ͬ affte Son —

Sunday. I have not sent this letter off tonight, as I recieved no letter from you, and I expect one certainly tomorrow. I thought it would be as well to keep it a day. My private Tutor says that as I have not had the benefit of him the whole term, he will give me a fortnight's lecture in the Vacation, w^h I think is handsome of him — I wrote to Stoddart to day to ask him down here he will not at all interfere with my reading, for he will seldom be up before I have had a five hours spell on't — And then another hour with my private tutor — I hear to day with great grief & consternation, that there has been 105 in majority in the Lords for the Catholics — I have had the pleasure of being fined five shillings for keeping a book from the Union too long a time — I am so sleepy that I can hardly read what I am writing So Goodnight Dear FA & MA — How is Jim Smyth?

Sunday night — 1829.

Monday — No letter to day! What cause can have hindered the arrival of such letter? We have been into an examination in Algebra with the College-Tutor to day — I succeeded very tolerably — I have no news to day so Good night — Dear MA, PA —

Tuesday — The letter has at length arrived and a very long one it is. I will comply with the injunction concerning the accounts & send them with my next letter or perhaps by themselves I walked to day about 12 miles to Impington and Girton & some other places whose names I forget I performed it in 3 hours & a quarter w^h was very fair walking in my opinion — We had another examination from the Tutor to day w^h lasted 2 hours & a half. The subjects were much more difficult and posed all the men — I have unluckily left my examination paper in the lecture room w^h as it is the last day of lecture this term and as it was likewise adorned with a sweet

little cherub some what like may strike the lecturer with admiration — Good night Dear Mother.

Wednesday — I have spent to day (being the first day of term) quite idly — taken a tremendous walk, got tremendously wet, eat a tremendous lot of bread [&] cheese & no dinner in consequence and am come home from teaing with Hine with the benefit of two men to drink tea with me — Fawssett & Moody — Good bye dear

Father & Mother — an't I a charming correspondent? (I should not have delayed this letter, but for writing my accounts w^h I shall now send on the back of Whewell's Bill — W^h amounts to £157! I am told that even this is moderate

18.          TO MRS. CARMICHAEL-SMYTH
                    13–19 APRIL 1829

*Address:* M^rs Carmichael Smyth. | Larkbeare House | Ottery S^t Marys | Devon. *Postmarks:* CAMBRIDGE AP 19 1829, 20 AP 1829. Published in part, *Memorials,* pp. 338–340.

Monday, April 13. I resume my journal with an account of a dinner-party of ten given in these rooms though not by me. I had six one day but that was quite a minor affair — Soup, Smelts, Sole, Boiled Turkey, Saddle-Mutton, wild ducks, cream Jellies &c composed the feast — It was given by Hailstone who is a very hard reading man; I read this morning from half past seven till one at Classics, & afterwd^s read some of Hume's Essays with w^h I am very much pleased not for the language but for the argument. We are going to establish an Essay Club — There are as yet but four of us, Brome,[69] Moody, Young and myself, all Carthusians. We want no more Charter-House men. If we get ten, we shall scarcely have to write three essays a year so that it will take up but little of our time — I proposed that the Man who read his essay sh^d choose his own subject for his next trial, & so give him plenty of time, & his own favourite subjects — This will I think be the only way of getting much worth listening to — I am always up now by seven w^h very few men indeed can boast of here — But I find it very expensive seeing that my brown loaf diminishes with much greater rapidity, than it was wont when I kept later hours — When I get into my own rooms however, I shall strive to arise at six — They have been washed to day & the smell is quite out, for the last coating is put on with spirits the smell of w^h is much less lasting than

[69] John Brome entered Charterhouse in 1823 and matriculated at Trinity College in 1827.

oil — Tomorrow my carpet will be put down, & my book-Case introduced to its future abode, & on Wednesday I myself shall make a triumphal entry — I did not walk to day for more than an hour as it has been raining hard — Carne is wandering on foot in Wales — Young expects his father, governour, or πα-ποι (all three terms are here used). You mistake about the Library, it is not for my use. I may have five books out of it, by applying to a fellow of the College, & as Whewell is the only one I know, it is a bore both for him & for me to receive & to give many tickets of admission — Besides the books are so outrageously old that there is hardly a book w^h w^d be of use to me in the library — Mitford's Greece ɪ must have, I know where there is a copy quite new & very handsomely bound for five guineas. The original price in boards is [£]6. This is the best & the cheapest copy in Cambridge — for I have hunted at all the Shope — But I will say no more on this important subject for I have filled a very closely written sheet — Good night Dear Mother & Father     I am composing a deep & metaphysical letter for Wentworth.[70]     Your affectionate Son

William. M. Thackeray.

Tuesday — Another day of rain, & of reading though the evening has been thoroughly idle, since seven o'clock I have been talking — I have no news as I say every day. There has been a Proclamation by the Vice-Chancellor threatening expulsion to all who insult the proctors in such a manner again — These things are not ordered so at Oxford. It is a matter of course that the Proctor sh^d be hissed or clapped at his exit from office. The King has signed the bill! [71] I am glad of it, for a refusal would have only I think created disturbance, and have done no good — Breakfasted at Young's this morning with the Essay men. Beef steaks, & no dinner in consequence. Young has got a way of being learned on every subject w^h very much strikes men at first sight. He talked this morning about things of w^h he had not the slightest Knowledge save what he had got from some sixpenny pamphlet; and talked so

---

[70] Wentworth Huyshe.
[71] George IV signed the Catholic Emancipation bill on April 13.

fluently withal that men were astonished — I have not this happy
faculty — I went to a wine-party at my private Tutor's the other
day; Such fun!  If you can fancy Dominy Simpson [72] giving a wine
Party      He had had two dozen of wine in for the purpose, & I
think it was the most execrable stuff that ever forced itself down a
man's gullet.  I departed early as there was an animated debate
commenced on the Catholic question.  Did you tell Mʳ Huyshe [73]
of our abortive petition? — Good night, Good night, Good
night! —

Wednesday — I have been drinking tea at Dʳ Thackerays —
reading Aeschylus & Mathematics & Zillah,[74] playing two games at
chess; having been in doors almost all day from the rain — A violent blast of wind took it into its head to sweep my chimney this
morning, and ration the soot most liberally over my eatables and
drinkables — There has been a shocking earthquake in Spain as
you will see by the papers — Dʳ Thackeray has a young son [75] an
Etonian of course.  I have asked the little fellow to come & see me.
I am just beginning to find out the beauties of the Greek Play, with
wʰ I am of course delighted — I pursue a plan of reading only the
Greek without uttering a word of English, & thus having the language in itself wʰ I find adds to my pleasure in a very extraordinary
manner, & will if I pursue it, lead me, I hope, to *think* in Greek,
and of course will give me more fluency — My private tutor & I
get on very well, he is very well meaning and patient to a miracle
Just the thing for a beginner, I fear he wont do next year — But I
must say Good night till tomorrow  Yʳ affectionate Son.

Thursday — This day last year (as I just called to mind) did I
leave Charter-House.  and now I am sitting at Cambridge writing a

[72] Dominie Sampson in *Guy Mannering*.
[73] The Rev. Francis Huyshe (b. 1768), Rector of Clyst-Hydon and owner
of Sand in Devon, the father of Wentworth and Harriet Huyshe.  He became
Prebendary of Clutton in Exeter in 1831, when his brother John succeeded
him as Rector of Clyst-Hydon.  His wife was the closest of Mrs. Carmichael-
Smyth's Devon friends.
[74] *Zillah: a Tale of the Holy City* (1828), by Horace Smith (1779–1849).
[75] Frederic Thackeray, *Genealogy* (47).  The Thackeray connection at
Eton was very strong, though Dr. Thackeray had himself been educated at
Rugby.

letter home with a mind perfectly contented with the change the
year has wrought in my situation. I have just had two men here
who from 8 to 12 have been talking over Old Charterhouse doings,
telling for the hundredth time old Charter-House stories wʰ possessed but little interest at their first broaching, & a great deal less
at this their hundredth repetition    I have not that gratitude and
affection for that respectable seminary near Smithfield — which I
am told good scholars always have for the place of their education;
I can not think that school to be a good one, when as a child, I was
lulled into indolence & when I grew older & could think for myself
was abus⟨ed⟩ into sulkiness and bullied into despair — But this
must be a very ungrateful theme to you, I can readily fancy that
the outpouring of my but[t] of indignation will be but a bitter dose
for you, I will not therefore proceed in my Philippic — To day has
been with me an idle day rather — But a little idleness doth one
good. I had my hair cut yesterday and the comfort I feel in losing
some pounds of superfluous hair (or delapillated manhood, as
Griffin The Tonsor hath it.) is extraordinary — It can certainly
rain at Cambridge — I dined out at a man's rooms to day but retired at seven o'clock as I thought I saw movements predicating a
rubber at whist. wʰ is my aversion — I have been going about in
my walks lately drawing
churches here is one but
I forget whether Coton
or Granchester — What
I drew it for I cannot
say, only I think to see
whether I had lost the
acquirement or not. This

country is of course ugly in the extreme but there are a number of
quaint old buildings, and pretty bits scattered about. I think I shall
take solitary walks and see how I get on in this way of drawing —
I called yesterday at one o'clock on a man to walk & found him in
bed! — Men are here very fond of going to bed late, & getting up
late —. The former of these I like not, nor I hope the latter.
Good night —

An excellent question — if a story have (x) interest at 1ˢᵗ time of repetition what will it have at the hundredth time of telling —

Friday — I have been drinking tea with Wells of Corpus — I met there a man whose name is I know not what, but whose dwelling place is Sidmouth he has been talking about the Kennaways,[76] he says Sir John & Young John are delightful men both of them, and Maria exceedingly handsome! I did not fancy there could be found a person of such good judgement — [77] very hot in "Injah" is here cutting a swell — Only think! I believe I saw Miss Huyshe [78] to day! At least some one very like her, I passed her by not having seen her very clearly, but the men I was with told me she turned round and looked at me very hard — I gave chase, and enquired at the eagle and the Bull, but there were no ladies at either house. I still cannot help thinking it must be she — Tomorrow I will go to the Hoop and look for her. I know somebody who will say, "As you say Harry it was very odd that he should cut you" — I believe I shall delay going into my rooms til Monday for the smell of the paint is not yet out of them. They look however very stilish and I think have as great conveniences & comforts as any rooms in College — My bed maker is honest, The one belonging to these rooms is *not* as I have had reason to know with regard to my tea; wʰ was left open one unlucky day, when she pounced upon about half a pound of it: however it has taught me to keep a sharper look out for the future — To day it has been rather finer than usual, to night the moon is most bee--u--tifill. I would not recommend you to send Zillah. it is a silly thing in four volumes. I cannot read Mathematics of an evening that's pos: — I in

[76] Sir John Kennaway (d. 1836) was a Devon man who received his commission as a captain in the Bengal army in 1780 and saw action in the Carnatic during the invasion of Hyder Ali. He was created a Baronet in 1791 for his services as envoy to the court of the Nizam of Hyderabad. After his return to England he acquired the estate of Escot, Ottery St. Mary, and it was from him that the Carmichael-Smyths rented Larkbeare (*Memorials*, p. 330). His son, John Kennaway (1797–1873), succeeded him as second Baronet. Maria (d. 1876) was his second daughter. In 1883 the Kennaway properties in Devon were worth £5,038 annually (Bateman, *Great Landowners*, p. 249).

[77] Word undecipherable.

[78] Miss Harriet Huyshe.

general have a man or go to a man and have a chat for an hour or two. Young's governour arrived to day; I must ask him to breakfast I suppose. Tho he is no favorite of mine, for he is not a *gentleman*. This cross paper looks very gloomy. I think I will darken it no more for the present.

Good night — Goodnight —

Εἰρηγοποίομ Θαχεραίομ — [79]

Saturday — Here I am back in my old quarters — w$^h$ look so grand that I can scarcely take my eyes off them. To night I shall sleep in a bed, where I shall not be able to beat the devil's tattoo against the foot-board; an accomplishment w$^h$ I practised a great deal in Carne's rooms — On Monday I am going to begin a course of ferocious reading and shall put myself on a diet — I had a conversation with my private Tutor this morning, and he told me that in May we sh$^d$ have a weeks examination of eight hours a day — It has rather put me on my mettle. But when I look at the men about me I shall think myself very lucky if I have as many below me as above me — I cannot however do more than my best — Which I am determined to do. It will, I think, be certainly disadvantageous to me to keep a nonens [80] either for honor or for profit — For I think that I can by next year come up with most of the men (certainly not with all) — Were I to keep nonens the stimulus would be withdrawn, and with it I fear the exertion, for I then should keep terms with men inferior to me w$^h$ could never be to my advantage. I met D$^r$ Thackeray today, who told me he went for an hour every day to the savings-bank to see the poor people recieve their money — I should think his practice could not much incommode him! I asked Youngs Governor [81] to tea tonight, but he went I believe back to town he told me [he] had seen the Steeles who he

---

[79] I.e., "Peace-maker Thackeray."

[80] "*Non ens*, a Freshman in Embryo! one who has not been matriculated, . . . consequently is not considered as having any being!" (Quoted from *Gradus ad Cantabrigiam*, 1803, in *The New English Dictionary*)

[81] Described by John Venn, *Biographical History of Gonville and Caius College*, 4 vols. (Cambridge, 1897–1912, II, p. 205) merely as "William Young gent."

said were old friends of y.$^{rs}$ — I saw that girl again to day, it was not Miss Huyshe tho not unlike her. I have enjoyed a glass of Port-Wine Negus tonight greatly to the satisfaction of my inward man, it hath however caused an agreeable drowsiness w.$^h$ summons me to my repose — Good folks adieu  And if you'll blow a kiss to me I'll blow a kiss to you.[82]

Sunday — M.$^r$ Young is going to tea with me to night — he did not return to town as he had determined. so I must make the best of my time. Thank you for y.$^r$ letter, my dear Father — I have a plan to propose — w.$^d$ it not be better for me to have some of my money down here at Mortlocks? [83] it would save me a good deal in postage stamps. We had a grand feast to day in hall: After dinner an immense silver cup twice as big as a ———————— ("chamber" we call it here) was brought round filled with Audit Ale — good it was but not so good as what we had at D.$^r$ Thackeray's in bottle. Besides the idea of some thirty mouths at the cup before my own I sat by chance at the bottom of the table) was not over pleasant. — I have bought a chart of General History w.$^h$ I will bring down with me — It gives an excellent idea of the history of the world from the flood though not perhaps a very particular one. But M.$^r$ Young is just coming so I will shut up my letter though I have not got to the bottom of the page. I have been so busy that I have not had time to finish my letter to Wentworth Huyshe — I have been telling all the men what a star is about to shine over Cambridge next October    Yea — in the shape of a man from Harrow. Can such things come from Harrow? men say. Good bye.

Good-bye. till the next new sheet.    XXXX

[82] From the last stanza of "The Baby's Début" (James and Horace Smith, *Rejected Addresses*, London, 1812):

> And now, good gentlefolks, I go
> To join mama, and see the show;
>    So, bidding you adieu,
> I curtsey, like a pretty miss,
> And if you'll blow to me a kiss,
>    I'll blow a kiss to you.

[83] The Cambridge banker.

19.     TO MRS. CARMICHAEL-SMYTH
20–26 APRIL 1829

*Address:* M^{rs} Carmichael Smyth. | Larkbeare House | Ottery S^{t} Mary's | Devon. *Postmark:* CAMBRIDGE AP 26 1829, 27 AP 1829. Hitherto unpublished.

Monday. April 20.

Past twelve o'clock, moonlight night. I have been sitting up making an epitome of Grecian theatrical History to this witching hour of night; I have been able to take no long walks lately as I have been kept in all day almost by the rain — To day was the grand New-market day,[84] I sh^{d} like to have gone, but a horse is a guinea, w^{h} is I think a leetle too much for such a jaunt. I have had a walk & a run for my life to night from some angry old cove whom I aroused from his slumber, by thundering at his windows

There is no danger of being pulled up now as there is an interregnum for us — the last proctors have resigned, no others will accept the office. The snobs [85] are going about in large parties having drunk much, & in consequence swearing singing and hiccuping after the most approved fashion — Gownsmen are not I fear so very slow in imitating them — How comes it that I have recieved no newspaper? I find it very useful. — But I shall not rise at my accustomed hour if I do not seek my bed w^{h} I will do and say goo' night till it be morrow.

Tuesday — An excursion to Chesterton, a dinner then & a purchase of pike for a supper tomorrow form the recreations of this day. A ferocious set to at the Algebra all the morning, & a hard working at the Greek Play & the History therewith connected all the evening have been my labours — After these I sallied out at

[84] The Craven Meeting took place at Newmarket, the famous horseracing town thirteen miles north-east of Cambridge, on April 20 (*Times*, April 21).

[85] Thackeray here refers to the townsmen of Cambridge as opposed to the gownsmen of the University, but in the following months he came gradually to equate snobbishness with vulgarity. A decisive change in his point of view is implied by the classic definition he offered seventeen years later: "*He who meanly admires mean things is a Snob*" (*Works*, VI, 311).

about a quarter to ten for a walk, & walked till eleven — I am
therefore rather fatigay as they say — What with sailing, & walking, beefsteaks & Algebra, Greek Play & bottled
Ale "My limbs are weary, and my eyes are dull,
My head is heavy, and my stomach full  Now on
my bed my weary limbs I'll lay, and drown in
sleep the memory of the day" — Exit gaping
I cant draw

Wednesday. Hard work at the Algebra and Greek Play, & a
Glorious supper off pike are my adventures to day.  I have read
more this vacation and more to my profit than during the whole
term, but I have found myself so sleepy at night that I have not
written a quarter so much as usual.  The picture came to day very
nicely framed.  I wish it had been drawn by another hand than Miss
Shutes.  It looks very well, but w^d have looked better had it been
more decided in its light and shade.  I have not drawn for so long a
time that I have quite got out of the way thereof.  (I hope you admire my new mode of making "f's", [86] it is the newest and most
approved Cambridge fashion)  To day I have ordered myself a
cloak of water-proof cloth — It will cost me five guineas and a
half!  The taylor however says it will last out three of the 4··10··
ones — The cloth is the very finest & closest w^h is made, and in
rendering it water-tight it is shrunk considerably.  I have got one of
those awkward (how do you spell?) pens w^h cramp one's fingers so
I will throw it down for to night — Ever Dear Father & Mother
Y^r affectionate Son.

Thursday — More rain and more Algebra the night fine so I
have been taking a long walk & came in to rooms about eleven
without cap & gown ie "a la snob" — This is a subject of severe
censure here, w^h I quite forgot, but as it is Vacation I suppose nothing will be said — God save the King!  His majesty's birth day
ushered in little pigs for hall dinner [87] salad likewise w^h is a great
bl(blessing I was going to say) but I mean Joke!  I had a head

[86] Thackeray's new "f"s are modelled after the printed rather than the
written letter.
[87] The King is Visitor to Trinity College.

ach or two when I first came up     I did not live temperately enough, but I am now as well & cool as possible — Algebra is a great cooler of the head. I am going to have my window-curtains

dyed and hung on a brass rood come ça

Friday. Algebra Algebra nothing but Algebra and a few props from Euclid by way of recreation. I am going on like a little bean, like a brick, & like a house on fire (all these are Cambridge terms) We dined at one o'clock to day to make room for some second & third year men trying for scholarships — My new cloak came home to day, & it has been luckily raining all day, so that I have had an opportunity of trying it's efficacy — It has got a collar somehow so  that thing above it is the hat. The head completely enveloped in the capacious fur. The new Proctors were elected yesterday — To me it matters not whether there are or or not Proctors seeing that I am so steady & sober that I am quite a pattern, the imitation of all the youths in the University — I have been wining with Wells of Corpus, & met that Sidmouth man again whose name is Bacon [88] I find. Wells is Evangelical rather & is not ashamed of it, w^h most of the followers of Simeon in this University are. It has certainly this good effect, that you never hear an exceptional word from the lips of these men — Their more liberal & less scrupulous compeers are not very sparing of them. There is a man who was at Charter-House who swears in such an impertinent disgusting way, that three men (myself included) have cut him. I am at the end of my page. Addio —

Saturday. To day I have taken a whole holiday and not looked into a book of Algebra. I read, till two last night & was not up, till ten this morning — and nothing w^d satisfy me but drawing w^h I did till one when we dined — At four I went to the Fitzwilliam [89] &

[88] Probably John Bacon (1809–1891) of Corpus Christi College.
[89] The Fitzwilliam Museum, which houses the collection of engravings,

staid till six — Looking over Sir Robert Stranges [90] prints w$^h$ are I think superior even to his great pupils Morghen's. I saw a very fine portfolio of Rembrandts etchings — Professor Smyth [91] let me in very kindly, without my at all asking him — Dining at one I went into hall at eight & supped off pigeon pie then two other men carried me off to the Bull, where they gave me some milk punch & have sent me home in a great state of comfort to baid — They were for another bowl but to this I would not consent. I have got (as I believe I said) quite a reputation for Sobriety — I do not think that I ever had a pleasanter holiday — Next October I hope I shall be able to go to the Fitzwilliam oftener — I have had a good walk to night — and shall I think seek sweet slumber with the greatest imaginary alacrity. When I come home for the long vacation I intend to go by the wagon some part of the way — I have a great fancy for that sort of vehicle just at present. I believe however I have told you of this my plan before — There has been an American horse here to day w$^h$ trotted ten miles in less than half an hour. Good night Dear Father & Mother — Your affectionate Son.

Sunday — I have unwittingly delayed writing till it is almost too late I have taken a long walk of three hours to day, heard a splendid anthem in Chapel, wined with Badger, who is about as good a fellow as I ever knew. First he was thirteen years in a public-office, then he left that & because he did not wish to be idle took pupils, & paid his Father & Mother for his board by the money thus earned. Now he is come up expecting a living — I think it is hardly fair rebuking me for making plans of reform — I think I have read as much during this last month as most men in the University have.

Badger and I have made an agreement to walk every morning

---

paintings, drawings, etc. bequeathed to the University in 1816 by Viscount Fitzwilliam.

[90] The eminent engravers Sir Robert Strange (1721–1792) and Raffaello Sanzio Morghen (1758–1833).

[91] William Smyth (1765–1849), Regius Professor of Modern History from 1807 to 1849.

from six — Wells accompanies us. But I have no more time, &
must conclude this very laconic letter by writing adieu — Your
Affectionate Son —

William M. Thackeray.

20.          TO MRS. CARMICHAEL-SMYTH<br>3 MAY 1829

*Address:* Mʳˢ Carmichael Smyth. | Larkbear House | Ottery Sᵗ Mary's | Devon.
*Postmarks:* CAMBRIDGE MY 3 1829, 4 MY 1829. Hitherto unpublished.

Sunday. May 3. 1829.

I had no paper in my rooms on Monday, and forgot to order
any on Tuesday till it was too late to get out of college — So I
thought that instead of a journal I would this week write a letter —
I have just been drinking tea at Dʳ Thackeray's where I met his
Mother [92] & Aunt, The Vice-Provost of King's & Mʳ Gunning —
They were all declaiming against the degeneracy of the present age
or rather of the present youth — I p⟨ut⟩ in what I could for our
defence, but of course did not say much but listened in silence to
the abuse showered down upon our luckless generation. Mʳ Gunning was rich in good stories     He told us that his sister was once
travelling to town with an Oxonian who was a most complete exquisite — When they got to the Inn where they were to dine —
This Gentleman addressed the waiter — "Fellow — Do you sell
appetite at this Inn" (wʰ I thought was not ill said that is excepting
the first word) — Then when the Oxonian & the fair Miss Gunning had entered the Inn he said not a word but let her help herself
to what she wanted; at last he broke the silence with a monosyllable
uttered with ineffable languor & complacency "Wine" said he —
She was quite as short & said "No" and that was all that passed
during the journey — When I come to consider, this is a silly story
and has taken up a great deal of paper. The Vice-Provost told me
my Uncle Frank is going to be married within a month. Miss

---

[92] The former Lydia Whish, who had married Thomas Thackeray (1736–
1806), *Genealogy* (3), a Cambridge surgeon.

Shakespear [93] is the happy fair — I dont envy Miss Shakespear.[94]
She brings him four hundred a year — & he has known her a long
time. I recollect her fainting one evening at M^rs Langslow's, before you came home, & he then paid her great attentions, & trod
most heavily on my toes in his anxiety —

Who do you think walked in to my rooms yesterday at half past
two of the clock? The Rev^d Francis Huyshe! (I was almost
asleep — Having had no sleep all night from a cursed alarum clock
w^h I bought to wake me in the mornings that I might be ready for
my private Tutor by six o'clock, but w^h kept me awake with a vengeance) — Much was I astonished and greatly was I rejoiced — I
walked about with him for an hour, & he told me a grand secret
about a "grand access" to our grand house. I was not to tell that he
has been here but only to mention the "grand access" — But as y^r
letter of the morning shewed me that you w^d rather know of his
having seen me, than fan⟨cy⟩ me endowed with the power of divin-
ing that there was ⟨to be⟩ a "grand access." I thought I would dis-
obey him for once. He says he came straight to my rooms, from the
picture [95] w^h he saw at the back of my letter — His friend M^r
Hole [96] kept above me. We walked and saw the new St. Johns
buildings near w^h there is a tall iron gate — That is a gate w^h men
get over late at night     Said M^r Huyshe — Did you ever do such
a thing Sir? He went to call on Peacock — the
Tutor. Wentworth is entered on his side — The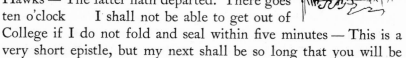
stair-case where Peacock kept was once called the
Menagerie, for in it dwelt Peacock, Hare, &
Hawks — The latter hath departed. There goes
ten o'clock     I shall not be able to get out of
College if I do not fold and seal within five minutes — This is a
very short epistle, but my next shall be so long that you will be

[93] See above, No. 12.

[94] There is a semicircle above this sentence, within which Thackeray has
written "in a whisper."

[95] See above, No. 13.

[96] Robert Hole of Georgeham, Devon, who matriculated at Trinity College
in 1819; George Peacock (1791–1858), Fellow of Trinity College from 1814
to 1839; Samuel Hawks, who became a Fellow of Trinity College in 1820.

nearly a fortnight reading it. Good night Dear Father & Mother. Your affectionate son

W. M. Thackeray.

I have read very hard all this week.

21.        TO MRS. CARMICHAEL-SMYTH
4–10 MAY 1829

*Address:* M^rs Carmichael Smyth. | Larkbeare House. | Ottery S^t Mary's | Devon. *Postmark:* CAMBRIDGE MY 10 1829, 11 MY 1829. Extract published, *Biographical Introductions*, II, xxv.

Monday —

Yesterdays letter was a very scurvy epistle, methinks, & if I send such another methinks I shall come in for a jobation, but perhaps a very long one this time may make my peace. I begin to get very sick of the Algebra and am going therefore to vary it with a little Euclid — My private Tutor intends an examination at the end of the week. M^r Pryme is going to lecture on Political Economy, I shall put my name down he lectureth from twelve till one, an hour w^h I can very well spare as I have generally read five hours by that time and taken a walk, a breakfast, & the benefit of Chapel. into the bargain, so you see I am an early riser — The Porter has promised to call me every morning at a quarter past five — This morning he kept his promise, & I was up by half past 5. Read half an hour for my private Tutor went to Chapel &c &c One of the lectures (the Classical) I have cut rather, as I recieve no benefit from it except that of hearing Greek construed ill & passages w^h require no explanation explained to the n^th The attendance is not at all necessary. The Mathematical Tutor (Fisher) is a clever fellow, but goes on at such a galloping rate there is no keeping up with him. I am now certain of taking but a mediocre place in the Examination. This is a great deal owing to my Private Tutor, he w^d not begin the Algebra over again with me as I begged him the consequence is I do not feel my ground — But next year I think I shall shew them a different game, Good night. Good night.

Tuesday. The faithless Porter forgot his office, & I woke not till six, & was therefore a quarter of an hour behind hand for my private Tutor. I forgot to say that I was at the Union last night when the officers were elected for the terms, the debates begin as usual to night — Subject Forty-Shilling Freeholders.[97] I did not go & fancied that the debate was to morrow instead of to day. w^h made me make the mistake above. Next Tuesday I think I shall tip them a little eloquence. Shelley is the subject for debate so by the time you get this letter this day week I shall be whetting my tusks for action — I wont speak unless I feel perfectly confident of making a respectable figure. The warm weather hath arrived, one may almost see the leaves growing, we have very nice walks here, & avenues &c. There is one long walk with a distant prospect of Coton Church at the end of it — Porson [98] called the "fellowship-walk" because it was a dull walk, with a church at the end on't. This time next year I shall sit for a scholarship, more for the pleasure of the thing than the profit, for there will not be much chance of getting one the first time of trying. Second & third year men only are allowed to try; & if there is anything like equality between a 2^nd year man, & a 3^rd year man, the latter has the scholarship — for the 2^nd year man may have another trial, whereas this is the ultima spes of the Senior Soph. I have got one of those horrid pens with w^h it is imposs. to write like a Christian. So Good night — Father & Mother & M     Doesn't the Charter-House Examination begin on Thursday?

Wednesday. I have been to New Market! & have been galloping about for the last eight hours. Carne came to me this morning, and begged me to go said he knew of two good horses to be had for 15 shillings, so having got Whewells permission, off we set — I find myself terribly stiff but a great deal better for my ride — I am

[97] The passage of the Catholic Emancipation bill made it necessary to raise the qualification for an elector in Ireland from two to ten pounds. The forty shilling freeholders thus disfranchised would otherwise have returned to parliament only those candidates favored by the Catholic clergy.

[98] Richard Porson (1759–1808), the celebrated Greek scholar, who lost his fellowship at Trinity College in 1791 because of his unwillingness to take holy orders.

not sorry that I have seen this place but shall not be again tempted ⟨I saw⟩ young Sir Mark Wood [99] there, he is as report goes making away with his father's money as ⟨fast as⟩ he well can manage — He had a beautiful horse there w$^h$ won a gold cup, it's cognomen was John de Burt. His face looked very bright after his good fortune & he seemed to take no little credit to himself for what his horse had done for him. The betting stand was a very curious sight, a couple of hundred men & horses gathered together, the men screaming out fifty to twenty, 6 to 4, &cc. the horses I suppose about as fine a body as any in the kingdom looking all the while as if they understood the whole thing. My steed before I knew where I was had carried me into the middle of the betting ring before I knew where I was, nor when once in could I easily get out again    They seemed to bet with all indiscriminately, otherwise I could not have supposed that such a set of ruffians horsedealers &c would have mixed in the ring. Carne was greatly taken with 25 Guinea horse, a very pretty one if dear too, but could not of course be worth so much. We lost our way about four miles returning w$^h$ with the remaining 13 miles made our ride seventeen miles  This we accomplished in an hour and a half, nor were the beasts at all tired when we got back — I am rather tired now so I will say good night & goo to baid.

Thursday. My limbs are in a very uncomfortable state this morning after yesterdays jolting; though they have not prevented me from smoking one cigar, & reading two books of Euclid, both of w$^h$ occupations have rendered me not a little sleepy. I went to Pryme's lecture to day, and was very much pleased, his delivery is very bad but his matter excellent as it ought to be, for his course is dear, 3 guineas the first, two the second, & gratis the third. I have bought Mill [100] & Malthus — The latter a bargain. We began Trigonometry to day. The thing is very different here to what it is

---

[99] Sir Mark Wood (1794–1837), who had become second Baronet on the death of his father, February 6, 1829.

[100] *Elements of Political Economy* (1821) by James Mill (1773–1836) and *Principles of Political Economy* (1820) by Thomas Robert Malthus (1766–1834).

in Hatton. That detestable Algebra there is no end of it. But I will go & sleep over my sorrows so Good night Dear Father & Mother.
Your affectionate Son.

Friday — Another book of Euclid to night, but there are six Richmonds in the field, that is six books of Euclid — two more. I must get up two-more-o by three o'clock. Pryme's lecture again very good     The attendants however are but three. The weather is very hot now — My only walk is up & down our avenues. In them I walk before breakfast, & dinner, & before tea, & after tea, they are my delights verily my comforts. I had a strong tug at the Triggynomatree this morning, & afternoon. I suppose Charles [101] is on his way no — at home — by this time — I saw something the other day, about a M<sup>r</sup> Smith in the paper who had a sister in Scotland, & a nephew at Charter-House — He was assaulted by his landlord & got 20 pound damages who can this be? Ask Charles — is it his Uncle Will? I must be up very early tomorrow for Euclid — so good night my dear Mother & Father. Y⟨our a⟩ffectionate Son.

Saturday. I have just drunk ⟨tea w⟩ith Professor Pryme. I met there Colonel & M<sup>rs</sup> Turner [102] & 2 daugh⟨ters,⟩ who are in some sort cousins of mine and whom I met at Captain Travers's at Cork. One of the ladies is very pretty, George Thackeray of Kings talked to her all the evening. The Dons parties are most desperately stupid. I at first was kicking my heels, & picking my lip without a soul to speak to, at length I got near M<sup>rs</sup> Turner. & talked to her (according to the fashion always at Cambridge) the whole night, till ten o'clock when I retired having been promised supper by a man — who jilted myself & 2 other men in the most cruel manner — And I had been fasting at Pryme's on purpose — So are human expectations frustrated — The nights are now unmercifully hot. My bed room window is & has been open day & night for the last month. It is luckily a sash window, & I open it at the top. My curtains are come home and look most glorious. Few men can I

[101] Charles Smyth.
[102] Colonel Turner was presumably the son of Dr. Turner of Chiswick.

think boast of such stilish rooms. I am at the end of my ⟨paper⟩ except a piece for Sunday. So good night Dear Father & Mother. Sunday. Woe is me, I am too late for Chapel. I must unburden my sorrows — & conclude my Sunday's Budget in another Sheet of Paper. Lo my idea about the assault case was correct, & Massa Charles was the nephew at Charter-House! How grand all the family of Carmichael will look in the Dining Room. The place would not have been worthy of them had it not been for the Grand Entrance, & Portiky. I think Mary has just reason to be offended. We men of Trinity are dignified fellows — The blue gown is so respected in the University, that we presume upon it. Don't we Mary? She should send me a letter of reproof. We had a beautiful sermon at S.<sup>t</sup> Mary's to day [103] about the undesigned coincidences w.<sup>h</sup> occur in the books of Moses, & thereby strengthen their authenticity. I have promised to give the Porter sixpence a week, if he will call me so I hope he will be more regular now. Pretty Miss Turner is at D.<sup>r</sup> Thackerays to night. I am free of the house — shall I go? — No. I must forego pretty Miss Turner — I'll een go out & take a walk, & then sit me down & read Grecian History. I will put -up my letter for to night Dearest Father & Mother. Your affectionate Son

W. M. Thackeray.

My debts are all paid — The book-bills are sad things.

Will you send a good impression of my arms on my next letter. My Uncle Frank wants them, I believe. I will send them & a letter to him.

---

[103] One of a series of sermons by John James Blunt (1794–1855), later (1839) Lady Margaret Professor of Divinity. The substance of Blunt's arguments is contained in *The Veracity of the Five Books of Moses argued from the Undesigned Coincidences to be found in them, when compared in their several parts* (1830).

22.            TO MRS. CARMICHAEL-SMYTH
                    11-17 MAY 1829

*Address:* M$^{rs}$ Carmichael Smyth | Larkbeare House | Ottery S$^{t}$ Marys. | Devon.
*Postmark:* CAMBRIDGE MY 17 1829. Published in part, *Memorials*, pp.
344-345; additions in *Biographical Introductions*, II, xxvi.

Monday.

I did not fulfill my promise of writing again yesterday, for I
went out for a walk, & returned to find my fire out, & to submit to
the horrid necessity of going to bed in the dark — The weather is
now most glorious in the middle of the day it is too hot to walk, but
early in the morning & late in the evening the walking is very
pleasant. The Porter was Faithful to his trust, such conversions
can six-pence a week cause in the breast of man! My eyes are so
heavy that I fear I must conclude this very laconic notice, ever y$^{r}$
aff$^{te}$ Son. W. M. Thackeray.

Tuesday. I have just returned from a long debate at the Union
at w$^{h}$ I had intended to have offered my opinions, the meeting is
however adjourned to next Tuesday when perhaps I may be more
prepared. Shelley appears to me to have been of very strong &
perhaps good feelings, perverted by the absurd creed w$^{h}$ he was
pleased to uphold; a man of high powers w$^{h}$ his conceit led him to
overrate, & his religion prompted him to misuse — But I am talking to uninitiated ears, I think I said I sh$^{d}$ bring home Shellys
Revolt of Islam with me, but I have rather altered my opinion, for
it is an odd kind of book containing poetry w$^{h}$ w$^{d}$ induce one to read
it through, & sentiments w$^{h}$ might strongly incline one to throw it
in the fire. It is this lat[t]er risk I w$^{d}$ guard against — Of the 4
men who spoke at the Union in favour of Shelley one is a Deist,
another is — he knows not what, & the 3$^{d}$ a Socinian; next Tuesday
we are to have a downright Atheist who in spite of his superiority
to vulgar prejudices is a great Ass. A pretty medley! Carne is
nearly as good a speaker as any there; he is very high in popular
favour. A "Poem of Mine" hath appeared in a weekly Periodical

THACKERAY IN 1829

*From a sketch by James Spedding*

here published & called "The Snob" [104] I will bring it home with
me. In a month I trust to be at home. I fear I shall lose this week,
a kind of fatality hath attended me I was late for Chapel again —
nevertheless I was up at five o'clock and ready — Good night and
joy be wi' you a'.[105]

Wednesday. My communications of to night will not be very
lively for I have been mystifying myself over Algebra $w^h$ is really
enough almost to put me in despair — To day I have been shewing
our Trinity Life to a man by the name of Lamb [106] who was at
Chiswick with me — He seems a good natured soul enough, but
such a gaby I never in my life set eyes on. I took him to our Library, & shewed him some busts of Caesar, Socrates, Demosthenes
&c & told him they were all Trinity men, he stopped before Caesars
bust and said, "he might have been at the University, but that he
thought he could not be a Trinity-Man". Then I told him there
were some fine manuscripts in the library, are they printed or
written?" quoth he. This was enough for me — so I hasted from
him as quickly as possible for fear of laughing in his face. He will
get sadly bullied I think. Had I before known his simplicity and
ignorance, I would have played him no tricks, as it was he went by
my orders into a "little house" to sign his name before entering the
library! He hath geraniums in his window, he possesseth two
flutes, a three & six penny fiddle on $w^h$ he makes the most horrid
noise, a painting-box $w^h$ he never useth & to crown all a pair of
curling irons, $w^h$ he is wont to deck his hair withal! I have en-
deavoured to rub him down a little, but as for my success I cannot
boast much. I saw to day the engravings of Canova's works in $w^h$ I
was very very much disappointed; they looked so mean & meagre,
& stiff, & studied to my most ill judging eye; that I cannot conceive
how any man by such works could have risen to such fame. Have

[104] Dissatisfaction with *The Cambridge Magazine* had led to the founding
of *The Snob*, the editor of which "thought he would try whether the genius
of the town did not equal that of the University." Thackeray's "Timbuctoo"
appeared on April 30 in the fourth number.

[105] From the "Gude Nicht" of Carolina, Baroness Nairne (1766–1845).

[106] Richard Martindale Lamb, who matriculated at St. Catherine's Hall in
1829.

you seen the "United Service Journal or Naval & Military Magazine" [107] it seemeth a good one. I fell in love to day with a pretty young 'oman of the name of Ladd. Some how or other I found that I had bought a pair of bronze candlesticks from her — She hath certainly a most enticing countenance — I will go dream of her — Goodnight. Goodnight with rosy dreams & slumbers light" — [108]

Thursday. I am sitting coatless & waistcoatless, having as nearly as possible forgotten my devoirs — My private Tutor for a wonder was not up when I went to him at six this morning — Poor Badger has gone down, his sister is dead. I cut lecture this morning & breakfasted with two Charter-House masters, Penny & Dicken — who are Charter-house masters all over. Young had a very pleasant wine-party at w^h for a short time I attended      Timbuctoo recieved much Laud — I could not help finding out that I was very fond of this same praise — The men Knew not the Author, but praised the Poem, how eagerly did I suck it in! — "All is vanity — " I think after the long vacation we shall set up a respectable periodical [109] here      I shall have four months to write for it — If you want a cheap & a correct history of Greece buy the Useful Knowledge Society's History it costs 4/6·· & contains about as much as 3 octavos. The weather is terribly hot — I find the great efficacy of soda water — men came in yesterday, & made sad havoc among my soda powders. Ewbank is going to read with a private tutor during the long vacation  he wanted me to go, & I think it would be a good plan but it will cost a hundred pounds! — So the plan must be laid aside. Good night Dear Father & Mother y^r aff^te Son.

Saturday. I wrote nothing last night, for I was so sleepy at half past nine that my thoughts would not have much conduced to your edification, & strongly inclined me to goo to baid. I saw the V. P of Kings to day, who recommends me to keep nonens. He says he will ask Peacock (one of our Tutors) what plan he would recommend. Keeping nonens will detain me another year at College.

[107] *The United Service Journal and Naval and Military Magazine*, which continued publication under various names until 1911, was founded in 1829.
[108] From the "Envoy" to Scott's *Marmion* (1808):
        To all, to each, a fair good-night,
        And pleasing dreams, and slumbers light!
[109] Probably *The Chimæra*. See above, No. 16.

I am going out to breakfast tomorrow with an old Charter-house man called Webster — [110] I had an invite to supper last night, but did not see it till past ten o'clock when the inexorable janitor would not permit my egress. This subjected me to the pleasure of receiving a drunken man in my rooms, whom I persuaded my name was Jenkins, & dismissed. I have been talking religion with Wells this evening, & reading Mathematics all the morning — if I get a fifth class in the examination I shall be lucky. The weather here is & hath been most divine early in the mornings & late in the evenings. "The Snob" goeth on & prospereth — Here is a specimen of my wit in the shape of an advertisement therein inserted Sidney Sussex College "Wanted a few freshmen apply at the Butteries where the smallest contributions will be gratefuly received" — [111] I have put Genevieve [112] into it with a little alteration — The clock hath struck eleven So Good night till it be tomorrow.[113]

Sunday. I have just left three drunken men, whom I had much ado to pacify     I dont know the reason, but I now (although I have only drunk two glasses of wine this day, & that a[t] 4 o'clock) feel half drunk myself. I am sure if I were in a madhouse I should be made mad. I have had a bad cold w$^h$ however hath departed — My bed room is very airy, as it has got a large sash window w$^h$ has been open at the top for this last month, & it is more airy than my keeping room. On Wednesday the tenth of June you may look out for my return to the maternal abodes. Will you ask Charles Kennaway [114] if he will give me lessons? I suppose he will not consider it. Next Wednesday fortnight Mother! My form then shall darken the Grand Access. I have time for a very short letter — Doctor Thackeray detained me a long time — he is a very nice

[110] Thomas Webster, who entered Charterhouse in 1823 and matriculated at Trinity College in 1828.

[111] *The Snob*, May 14. Sidney Sussex was the smallest of Cambridge colleges.

[112] "To Genevieve" (*The Snob*, May 14).

[113] From *Romeo and Juliet* (II, ii, 184–185):
    Good-night, good-night! Parting is such sweet sorrow,
    That I shall say good-night till it be morrow.

[114] The Rev. Charles Edward Kennaway (1800–1875), second son of Sir John Kennaway. He had taken his M. A. degree at St. John's College in 1825 and was a Fellow there in 1829.

good humoured man but most intolerably prosy — His brother the Vice Provost was with us. He always asks me very intelligent questions when I see him about my sight — Now can you see that tree, Now can you see that Kings College Chapel seven such questions have I answered him to da[y]. The weather has become cool & pleasant. Tell Mary she must be quite well before I come down. I suppose that swell Charles will have cut Larkbeare for town, before I arrive at my country seat.

Do you recollect a boy by the name of Burton [115] with whom I used to cronyize at Tunbridge Wells? He is here a gay fellow-commoner, cutting me of course, he had a supper for 30 last night, & the young heroes kept it up till five this morning. I was at S! Marys & had a good sermon from Blunt on the undesigned coincidences in Scripture. he was very ingenious almost too much so. We had I know that my Redeemer liveth [116] at Chapel. The organ was beautiful, but Mary can sing it better.

I shall travel down outside [117] this time both for economy & pleasure. What a glorious figure I should have cut with my bed in my keeping room! — I shall have no more coats this term, but shall get a thing for boiling water by spirit — A man who has used it all this term told me it has only cost him three shillings. My Uncle Frank is I hear married — I shall certainly not wish to congratulate him. But I must close my budget or it will not have time to go to the Post — Good night Dearest Father & Mother.

Your affectionate Son.

William M. Thackeray.

[115] Henry Stuart Burton (1808–1867), who matriculated at Trinity College in 1828.

[116] The opening "Air" of Part III of Handel's *Messiah*.

[117] In "Cockney Travels" (*Centenary Works*, XXVI, 94) Thackeray glances back regretfully at the days of his youth, when coaches were still the principal means of transportation: "I recollect going home for the holidays by the True Blue Coach, six inside — Bell and Crown at Holborn — and we were three and twenty hours nearly going to Bath! We left London at three, we refreshed ourselves at every stage on the way: and what a supper we had at Reading, and what a snug coffee-breakfast (the first of two) at an early hour some thirty miles on! In those days there was something *like* travelling."

23.          TO MRS. CARMICHAEL-SMYTH
25 MAY 1829

*Address:* M⸍ˢ Carmichael Smyth. | Larkbeare House | Ottery S⸍ᵗ Mary's |
Devon. *Postmark:* CAMBRIDGE MY 25 1829. Extract published, by
Charles Plumptre Johnson, *Early Writings of William Makepeace Thackeray*
(London, 1888), p. 7; additions in *Biographical Introductions,* II, xxx.

My dear Mother.

I have written no journal this week, for it would have only been
the diary of an Invalid on monday night, Myself & the Editor of
the Snob [118] (who, by the way) doth not much delight me) sat
down to write the Snob for the next Thursday — [119] We began at
nine, & concluded at two but I was so afflicted with laughter during
our attempts, that I came away quite ill & went to bed immediately.
The next day I was very ill, & on Wednesday took calomel, w⸍ʰ was
followed up by Salts on Thursday. Friday I was tolerably well,
but yesterday had as sweet a headache as ever it was mans lot to
Know. To day I am much better & tomorrow I trust to be myself
again. This week however has been completely lost to me, for I
found it quite impossible to read. To day I am
pretty well, but most desperately down in the
mouth. For the loss of this week will lose me
two classes in Examination. I made a mistake it
is not, alas, till June 10ᵗʰ I come home, so that
the grand access will be I trust finished, is it after
the model of a triumphal arch? I cannot draw
to night, in fact I believe the Genius of the

[118] Apparently William Garrow Lettsom (1804–1887), who contributed to
*The Snob* and in 1847 refused the dedication of Thackeray's *Book of Snobs*
(Crowe, *Thackeray's Haunts and Homes,* p. 54). Lettsom was enrolled at
Jesus College, Cambridge, in 1829 and 1830 but did not take a degree. He
afterwards held diplomatic appointments at Munich, Washington, Mexico,
and Uruguay, retiring on a pension in 1869. He was a F.R.A.S. and the
author with R. P. Greg of a *Manual of the Mineralogy of Great Britain and
Ireland* (1858).
[119] This number is almost entirely devoted to "The Blood-Stained Murderer," a burlesque tragedy patterned on Rhodes's *Bombastes Furioso.*

Pencil has deserted me. You do not mean that I should bring home my cap & gown? I should hear no end of it. Of all the Snobbish things a man can do this is the Snobbishest I sent for D.ʳ Thackeray this morning, but he was from home, & almost immediately afterwards my head-ache left me, so I went in person & counter-manded my order. Carne made I am told an excellent speech on Shelley last Tuesday, & Young tumbled out of a boat into the water. he is sadly unlucky. The other day he sprained his thumb in fighting some Snobs who wanted him to give them money. He ran for it, & fought as was the wont of the ancient Parthians flying.

If you wish me to be at home before I can as I leave this on Saturday, but I wanted to look about me a little, & behold some of my London friends — Won't Charley & I cross on the road in case I pursue my proposed plan of not leaving town 'till Tuesday? — my unfortunate head will not allow me to write much So with the promise of Journal next week, wʰ shall astound you from its magni-tude, I will write myself Dear Father & Mother

Your affectionate Son.

W. M. Thackeray.

I long to see Mary's new ink —

24.        TO MRS. CARMICHAEL-SMYTH
25–29 MAY 1829

*Address:* M.ʳˢ Carmichael Smyth. | Larkbeare House | Ottery S.ᵗ Marys | Devon. *Postmark:* CAMBRIDGE MY 29 1829, 30 MY 1829. Extract published in *Biographical Introductions,* II, xxx.

Monday, I am so sleepy to night that I can hardly keep my eyes open so I will only "not forget" journal

Tuesday. There was but a poor debate at the Union wʰ did not last more than half an hour. I have just put seven spoons-full of tea into my pot to make myself a very strong cup in a very short time — My patent water-boiler boils water in 3 minutes, so that in six minutes I shall have finished my tea, I have been pulling away at the Greek Play & Trigonometry to day, and am as sleepy as I was yesternight — Oh how I long for the end of the fortnight! — I don't know what my poor head will do stooping eight hours a day for five successive days besides reading — If I could put as much learning into my head as there will be blood, I should do pretty well — My private Tutor is a most desperate good-hearted bore; he in his endeavours to make me *au fait* in the Trigonometry hath made that obscure, w<sup>h</sup> I before thought that I pretty well understood. I wanted to steer clear of him this week altogether but could not persuade him to let me. Young is gone home to read all night. I have been trying in vain to dissuade him from it, he tried it before as I think I said & was asleep all day. Mess<sup>rs</sup> Taylor and Carlisle have left Cambridge    A great number of gownsmen had formed themselves into a club to — thrash them tomorrow, but their birds have flown. This is like one of the spirited acts of the Undergraduates of this University — Good night Dear Mother & Father

Your affectionate Son. W M T.

Thursday. I wrote nothing yesterday, for my head would not allow me seeing that I had had leeches applied to it, for the purpose of banishing that troublesome head ache which had there taken up its quarters (of course its "head" quarters)  The application of the leeches have made me quite myself again to day. It was by D<sup>r</sup> Thackeray's advice that they were put on — he will take no fee — What do you think me a Cannibal? quoth he, on my offer. He strictly enjoined me to come to him whenever I again felt myself unwell    The loss of these 10 days has been a most serious loss to me indeed; for I was beginning to comprehend the Algebra but it hath now passed away from my brain — Mary's new ink is most superb, (it has not made he⟨r⟩ hand very ⟨clear⟩ for I conned her letter with great difficulty). I had a bo⟨iled⟩ fowl, & some mutton Broth for dinner to day, as I was to be on a diet in company with another man. We left the bones of the fowl (w<sup>h</sup> by the way did not weigh two ounces I mean the fowl not the bones) & not a drop of the broth. I have got a stand made which raises my desk 3 inches from the table w<sup>h</sup> I find a great convenience    I am writing on it now, and find that I need not stoop at all for the purpose — I am going to breakfast tomorrow morning at eleven at Mazzinghis — but I shall run no danger. I must have a wine-party on Saturday, I fear — I never drink wine now & shall be in no danger at Mazzinghi's — I like practising forbearance  Good night. Good night.

I see I have begun on the wrong page.

Friday — I send off my journal according to orders, & am happy to say that I am perfectly recovered from "my late indisposition". I have been a long walk to day, that is to say about four miles, I went to the Cricket ground to see the Match between the Snobs & the University, & coming away turned to the left instead of to the right by w<u>h</u> I gained my walk & great advantage to myself, and those respectable members my legs. But, Mother mine, you must not be ill when I come home, or I shall be very much displeased for fear therefore of my displeasure I recommend you immediately to get well. I have been working the Algebra to day, but have lost all my chance even of mediocrity. The Waverley Novels have come out in their new form [120] I have got or rather have ordered Waverley, w<u>h</u> I think I shall reserve for reading on the coach next Saturday week. I have not seen D<u>r</u> Thackeray to day, but will I think shew myself to him tomorrow perfectly recovered.

God bless you, dearest Mother, I hope Sunday's letter will bring a better account of you. If Colonel Forrest [121] asks me to go down to Charlton for a day or two I should much like it, for on Tuesday there is Eaton Montem,[122] & on Wednesday the boat race

[120] The edition in forty-eight volumes published between 1829 and 1833 by Cadell.

[121] Lieutenant-Colonel William Forrest of the Bengal Army, who in 1816 had married Georgiana Carmichael-Smyth, Major Carmichael-Smyth's younger sister.

[122] ". . . this celebrated ceremony," writes Disraeli (*Coningsby*, Book I, chapter 11), "of which the origin is lost in obscurity, and which now occurs triennially, is the tenure by which Eton College holds some of its domains. It consists in the waving of a flag by one of the scholars, on a mount near the village of Salt Hill, which, without doubt, derives its name from the circumstance that on this day every visitor to Eton, and every traveller in its vicinity, from the monarch to the peasant, are stopped on the road by youthful brigands in picturesque costume, and summoned to contribute 'salt,' in the shape of

between the 2 Universities at Henley: both of w$^h$ I should be glad to see, that w$^d$ delay me 2 days from home though — Good bye.

Your affectionate Son. W. M. Thackeray.

25.      TO MRS. CARMICHAEL-SMYTH<br>3 JUNE 1829

*Address*: M$^{rs}$ Carmichael Smyth. | Larkbeare House | Ottery S$^t$ Mary's | Devon. *Postmark:* CAMBRIDGE JU 3 1829. Hitherto unpublished.

Wednesday.

You need be under no anxiety for me, Dear Mother, for I am perfectly well, when I wrote home I had quite recovered myself and was as well as possible, now I am better still!

We have had no end of examination this week, eight hours a day with one's mind on a continual stretch it is very, very hard work    I cannot possibly be anything but low, had I not lost this fortnight I might have held a better place — but it must pass — next year my name will I trust stand a hundred places higher than it does this. We have viva voce Examinations w$^h$ I much dreaded I passed these however "with great credit" They do not tell much in your place in the List, but, I flatter myself, they show what sort of scholar a man is. I have just been to Hall supping of Lobster &c, there are glorious suppers in Hall during the Examination week, & it is the fashion to go for we dine at 2 so that one may sup at nine (if there is no tea taken) with great propriety. We have 2 days more examination — It is more fatiguing work than walking 20 miles — I sleep very soundly indeed every night — I did not wake this morning till nine o'clock, & was not in Examination till 1/2 past, 1/2 an hour after my time; one of the fellows came up & rebuked me & put my name down in the black book. I know not what punishment hangeth over me for mine offence. We had an English Verse Translation from Virgil to do to day, w$^h$ will I hope

coin of the realm, to the purse collecting for the Captain of Eton, the senior scholar on the Foundation, who is about to repair to King's College, Cambridge."

tell in my favour for I think mine poor tho' they were, were better than what others I saw. — I will bring Mary down some flesh coloured Paper. I have bought Murray's Life of Napoleon [123] w<sup>h</sup> I will bring home — it is a very nice little book indeed — I have also bought Waverley in Scotts new Edition — It is a very beautifully "got up" work.

I have been to a jolly supper lately at Young's. They kept it up till two o'clock singing songs & drinking punch, I say *They* mind, for *I* am noted for my temperance this is the 3<sup>d</sup> time I have praised myself in this mine epistle. What is the origin of this self-congratulatory mood of mine I am at a loss to say.

I shan't be able to get out of gates if I do not close my communication — So till we meet Good bye Dearest Father & Mother

Your affectionate Son<br>
W. M. Thackeray.

26.      TO MRS. CARMICHAEL-SMYTH
18–? JULY 1829

*Address:* M<sup>rs</sup> Carmichael Smyth. | Larkbeare House. | Ottery S<sup>t</sup> Mary's | Devon. *Postmark:* AU 1 1829. Hitherto unpublished.

July 18<sup>th</sup>

I forgot, Dear Mother, when I last wrote [124] that this eventful day was so near, otherwise I should not have assigned so long a time as ten days for my next letter. This therefore will come to you as a surprise and a surprizing mark of my goodness. We have changed our quarters in the Rue de Rivoli, & have taken up our abode at chez Madame La Baronne de Vaude Rue Louis le Grand close to the Boulevards, The situation is noisy but cheerful, of an

---

[123] The first of two volumes entitled *The Life of Napoleon Bonaparte* was published in the "Family Library" of John Murray in 1829. This anonymous narrative, which breaks off at the Peace of Amiens, is described by a reviewer in *The Spectator* (April 18, 1829) as an abridgment of Scott's *Life of Napoleon Buonaparte* (1827).

[124] This letter has not been preserved.

evening particularly so, when the Snobs male & female who look all like Lords & Ladies appear in their gay costume either walking or sitting round little tables drinking eau sucré & small beer. We were recommended here by a Cambridge man of the name of Sedgewick a friend of Williams's [125] — We pay 212 francs a month servants included; & have for it an excellent room, a couple of breakfasts, a dinner & tea; & all (except the tea) is very good — There is likewise a Salon where there is a Soiree every Monday Evening     There are about a dozen people in the house; & there are some others who come to dinner     They are of all Nations. Medes Parthians & Elamites.[126] I am going to take a months dancing out of Coulon. You dance every other night & pay 30 francs a month. I think 15 lessons will do my job — I shall go to night under Sedgewick's wing — Nor shall I appear at the 2 next Soirees; — We went last night to the Opera, and saw the Comte Ory,[127] & a ballet the name of w^h I forget — They have a certain dancing damsel yclept Taglioni [128] who hath the most superb pair

[125] Thackeray was accompanied to Paris by William Williams (1804–1869) of Corpus Christi College, who had been engaged to tutor him. Williams took his B. A. degree (as seventh Senior Optime) in 1829 and his M. A. degree in 1834. He was associated with Thackeray in a comic periodical called *The Gownsman* (H. Astley Williams, *Notes and Queries*, Sixth Series, X, 1884, p. 419), and it was through him that Thackeray met FitzGerald in the autumn of 1829. In 1831 he became Curate of West Tilsted in Hampshire, and from 1833 till his death he was Vicar of St. Bartholomew's, Winchester.

[126] See *Acts*, 2, 9. Coulon belonged to a well-known family of dancers and taught dancing at the Opéra from 1808 to 1830. Thackeray relates in the character of Fitz-Boodle how these lessons came to be broken off: "In Paris, two Cambridge men and myself, who happened to be staying at a boarding-house together, agreed to go to Coulon, a little creature of four feet high with a pigtail. His room was hung round with glasses. He made us take off our coats, and dance each before a mirror. Once he was standing before us playing on his kit — the sight of the little master and the pupil was so supremely ridiculous, that I burst into a yell of laughter, which so offended the old man that he walked away abruptly and begged me not to repeat my visits." (*Works*, IV, 313)

[127] An opera by Rossini, made over in 1828 from *Il Viaggo a Reims* (1825), which had been written for the coronation of Charles X.

[128] Marie Taglioni (1804–1884), later Comtesse de Voisins, the most celebrated of ballet dancers at the Opéra between 1827 and 1847. Her famous ballets included *Dieu et la Bayadère*, *La Sylphide*, *La Fille du Danube*, and

of pins, & maketh the most superb use of them that ever I saw
dancer do before. Then there is Paul who will
leap you quite off the perpendicular & on the
horizontal & recover his feet with the greatest
dexterity: They are most inordinate card players here, & I am told play rather high —
I have just been enjoying the delights of
breakfast, and may proceed in my letter until Williams is ready to
give me his lecture. I saw Colonel de Sade the day after I wrote,
he asked myself & Williams to dine with him the day before yesterday — I was very much pleased with him he was very kind. Will
you take the trouble to dine with me? said he to Williams — He
seems a man who has read a great deal, and has recommended me
some new works on History & Moral Philosophy w^h he says are
excellent. I have had my hour with Williams whose teaching I
like very much it is as different to that of my late worthy tutor as
you may fill up the simile according to your own imagination —
After I have finished my letter I shall go read at the Bibliotheque
du Roi — As there are only seven hundred thousand volumes there
I may finish them easily before I get home again — I have seen
already some of the prints of w^h there are a most superb collection
of 5 thousand vols. The print-tables are however so full that there
is hardly a chance of getting a seat & room for your portfolio — I
have not been sight-seeing much — I took a walk almost round half
Paris the other day; returning from Notre Dame, w^h as I opine is
not so fine as Exeter Cathedral      The organ there only plays on
particular days; & the whole place hath an appearance of dirt and
decay w^h ill accord with an Englishman's idea of the great National
Temple — There are some very fine dresses locked up in cup-
boards, and some very greasy ones on the backs of the "Prates" [129]
Their dress is unpicturesque in the extreme — I cannot make it
look dirty as it should. They have got a huge piece of the true
Cross — w^h however is the only relic they have — The Robes &

---

*Flore et Zéphire.* Despite his burlesque of the last of these (*Works*, IX, xlv-
lxii), Thackeray had a real admiration for her.
[129] *Prêtres.*

pew cups &c used at the coronation of Napoleon are preserved
there — Portraits of him crowd the print shops — Likenesses of his Son & verses in praise of him are sold as
publicly as possible in the streets. You buy a pencil or
some such trifle and receive the book as a present. In his
portrait he is designated the Duc de Reichstadt.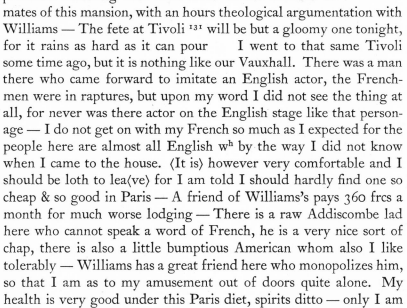

Sunday. I have heard a most execrable sermon from
the Bishop of Paris [130] to day, who, by the way, I did not
before know was in existence & have had a long foolish
profitless rambling talk with some of the amiable inmates of this mansion, with an hours theological argumentation with
Williams — The fete at Tivoli [131] will be but a gloomy one tonight,
for it rains as hard as it can pour      I went to that same Tivoli
some time ago, but it is nothing like our Vauxhall. There was a man
there who came forward to imitate an English actor, the Frenchmen were in raptures, but upon my word I did not see the thing at
all, for never was there actor on the English stage like that personage — I do not get on with my French so much as I expected for the
people here are almost all English w^h by the way I did not know
when I came to the house. ⟨It is⟩ however very comfortable and I
should be loth to lea⟨ve⟩ for I am told I should hardly find one so
cheap & so good in Paris — A friend of Williams's pays 360 frcs a
month for much worse lodging — There is a raw Addiscombe lad
here who cannot speak a word of French, he is a very nice sort of
chap, there is also a little bumptious American whom also I like
tolerably — Williams has a great friend here who monopolizes him,
so that I am as to my amusement out of doors quite alone. My
health is very good under this Paris diet, spirits ditto — only I am

[130] Presumably Michael Henry Luscombe (1776–1846), who in 1825 had
been consecrated to a continental bishopric by the bishops of the Scottish
episcopal church. He was also Chaplain of the British Embassy in Paris, and
in this capacity he officiated seven years later at Thackeray's marriage. See
below, No. 101.

[131] The *fêtes champêtres* at Tivoli, at this time the finest public garden in
Paris. They consisted, according to *Galignani's New Paris Guide* (1827),
p. 661, of "balls, concerts, conjuring, different experiments, aerostatic ascen-
sions, fire-works, and illuminations."

rather low & lonely sometimes.  I hear the Russians have demolished the Turks [132] of which I am sorry — Good night Dear Father
& Mother — Mary is asleep so she wont hear me if I say Goodnight to her —

I have been to see Mad[lle] Mars [133] in "Henri III et sa cour" a
drama w[h] as it is cannot be called a tragedy.  Her acting was most
extraordinary — I understood every word she said, and it was
curious to me to find that where my interest was very powerfully
excited I could comprehend the language so well     The costume
was as usual most scrupulously correct — The plot of the piece is a
good one — it relates to the assassination of the Comte S[t] Megrin
by the Duc de Guise, who entices S[t] Megrin to his house, by a note
from his wife with whom S[t] M is in love when he arrives the Duc
leaves him for a while with his wife, and then on coming to the
door finds it bolted — the bolt used is the arm of the Duchess, in
the meanwhile S[t] M. escapes at the window, but is there caught by
some of the Duc's followers & killed — The acting throughout was
most excellent —

The Algebra gets on very well, I am thinking of moving from
this house as there is no chance of learning French — I have heard
of a house in the Champs Elysees where for the same sum I shall
have the use of a cab: & a poney to ride on — a fine-library, & a
lesson in French every evening — I shall go there to day and see
how I like it — Williams wishes much to stay here but it is impossible to learn French here — This letter goes to England tomorrow by the Addiscombe hero who will take it in as short a time
as the mail he proceeds direct to Calais & thence by Steam-boat to
London

I must close my letter I find w[h] has been written at many different times — I have not heard from you at w[h] I wonder — & if you
take your meditated tour you are I suppose now about it — it is

[132] In the battle of Kulevcha on June 11.
[133] The great actress (1779–1847) of the Comédie Française, equally admired in classical and romantic drama.  Though she was fifty when Thackeray
saw her in Alexandre Dumas's melodrama, she did not retire from the stage
until 1841, her final rôle being that of Célimène in *Le Misanthrope*.  Thackeray appears to have seen her on July 23 (*Moniteur universel*).

now past eleven & M[r] Askell goeth at six to morrow — Let me hear soon from home, direct though as before Poste Restante for my abode is as yet unsettled here I am very comfortable but they speak no French & I might be as well in England. We are going to-morrow to see sights w[h] we have not done yet. A M[r] Butler a French-Irish Gent has got us one or two tickets for various places whose names I do not yet know — but I must close my paper & write myself Dear Father & Mother your affectionate Son. W. M. Thackeray.

The silk socks, & other silk goods are very dear. I gave five francs for a pair the other day after half an hour's bargaining. The bijouterie is cheap as I believe are most things w[h] are ornamental & not useful. The Champs Elysees are I hear very dangerous o' nights    There is a beautiful antique pistol of Italian workmanship on w[h] I have set my eye & w[h] I think I shall make my defender. I have only bought 5 prints since I have been here, four are very cheap & the fifth is a superb engraving of Sir R Strange — I cannot find Miss Sharp out by no means.

27.         TO MRS. CARMICHAEL-SMYTH
            6 AUGUST 1829

*Address:* M[rs] Carmichael Smyth. | Larkbeare House | Ottery S[t] Mary's | Devonshire | Angleterre. *Readdressed to:* Post Office | Weymouth. *Postmark:* FPO AU 10 1829. Hitherto unpublished.

54 Rue Neuve S[t] Augustin

Thrice have I been to the post-office inquiring for letters for M[r] Thackeray & thrice hath a negative been returned  as many more times has Williams inquired for me, & as many more inquiries have I made by a third person and now when they have come all three at one time after having sent a French commissionaire to search for them to find you have received no letter from me, when I dispatched one more than a fortnight ago! — I would have written again but recieving none from you, I naturally concluded you

were [134] on your tour and would wait till I heard from you — I
have left off the boarding house & have taken lodgings with Williams      The boarding house was an idle, dissipated ecarte-play-
ing boarding house all the people or almost all were English — I
got very thick there with a lady ycleped Twigg! Phœbus what a
name [135] — And Williams was if possible thicker than I — But I
found it would not do, for she was continually proposing parties of
pleasure to Versailles to S.<sup>t</sup> Cloud &c — To the former I went —
the latter however I refrained from. By moving to these lodgings
(w<sup>h</sup> we only did yesterday) & w<sup>h</sup> we have engaged positively for 1
month & most likely for two, we have escaped the fascinations of
the charming Twigg, and have or shall be enabled to read more
steadily. The rooms cost 200 Frcs a month 4 Pds each. We have
a salon, salle a manger, 2 bed rooms, & an antichamber, with a
kitchen — We are to engage a woman at 20 frcs a month to cook
for us, and as we have now seen the Restaurateurs &c. we shall be
glad to enjoy the comforts of a bifteck a l'anglaise, or a cotelette
de mouton au naturel — The Frenchmans cooking I do not like as
well as the Englishmans — Much however do I admire the wine.
A young man by the name of Butler, an Irish Catholic, who has
been educated here has been of the greatest possible service to us
in our lodgings for we were going to take lodgings of not half the
size & comfort for a larger price — The situation of these is most
excellent — close to the Boulevards, & a fine garden is before us,
into w<sup>h</sup> however we can only *look* — We went a party of four of us
to Frascatis [136] the other night — had I stopped at one time I
should have come away a winner of 200 Francs as it was I neither
one or lost — one of the party one 25 francs the other two lost 35 —
I should have lost most likely had I not in the hour of prosperity
lent the money I took with me to my friends — The interest in the
game Rouge et Noir is so powerful that I could not tear myself

---

[134] Thackeray wrote *where*.
[135] An echo of Byron's *English Bards and Scotch Reviewers* (ll. 399–400):
　　　Oh, Amos Cottle! — Phoebus! what a name
　　　To fill the speaking-trump of future fame! —
[136] A gaming house on the Rue de Richelieu, famous for its sumptuous *décor*
and aristocratic clientele.

away until I lost my last piece — I dreamed of it all night — & thought of nothing else for several days, but thank God I did not *return* The excitement has passed away now, but I hope I shall never be thrown in the way of the thing again, for I fear I could not resist — Of course I shall ⟨not⟩ go there again — I was not much affect⟨ed at⟩ losing but at winning — I am told that there w⟨ere some of⟩ the men of the table watching us the whole time, evidently expecting to make something by our party. There is however a game wʰ they say is infallible, it requires a capital of 75000 Francs wʰ I have not about me just now — Tell Wentworth Huyshe he is a man of no taste. I shall write to him as he desires — I intrusted my letter to a gentleman going to England. Rossini has lately produced a new opera wʰ has made the greatest noise — It is called William Tell.[137] The palace and gardens at Versailles are very splendid — We went there (a party of 5) the 1ˢᵗ Sunday in the month and had an execrable dinner wʰ cost not 75 Francs! Yesterday I had a much better one for two, than I had at Versailles for fifteen — I am greatly very greatly disappointed in the pictures here — I hardly see a tolerable one. The odious French style predominates, Even in Versailles where one might expect better things there are a number of pictures if not by David, at least in the manner of that paltry god of French adoration — The pictures are theatrical & a l'Anglaise but the theatres are natural — Mademoiselle Mars is most glorious, and Leontine Fay [138] at the Theatre de Madame the most delightful little creature I ever set eyes on; she has a pair of such lips! out of wʰ the French comes trilling out with a modulation & a beauty of wʰ I did not think it capable. The men have all that horrid twang wʰ I thought was only peculiar to tragedy.

I have begun this letter instantly after reading your three in order to save the post which goes out for England today. I must

[137] First performed on August 3.

[138] Mlle. Fay (b. 1811), later Mme. Volnys, had been on the stage since the age of five. In her earlier years she was billed as the "Petite Merveille," the French equivalent, one supposes, of "Infant Phenomenon." Apart from her considerable experience, her chief assets, as Thackeray indicates, were her beauty and her admirable voice.

therefore close my letter, & will have one ready for the post this day week — I want very much to exchange my watch for a new one, they are very cheap and very good — The ladies trinkets in the Palais Royal are the most enticing things as for taste that I ever saw — With a very few exceptions however they are ill finished, as is all the French furniture — It is like their own character plenty of varnish with but little *bottom* — Tell Aunt Becher I have bought her — But I will not say what it is for fear of diminishing that delightful suspense and agitation w^h a present of such extraordinary value and beauty must needs occasion — So I will leave you [to] guess whether it be a diamond necklace, or Cashmere Schall — I will however leave you as I said in suspense — Butler and I have long theological disputes — w^h I think do us both good — he has read a great deal relative to his own religion, of ⟨w^h⟩ however he sees the faults.

But I must conclude ⟨this⟩ epistle with remembrances to all at Larkbeare, with wishes for the prosperity of the farm and with love to the Farmer & his Wife, from their affectionate Son

W M. Thackeray —

I have given my direction — I believe the day of the month is the 6^th Thursday —

28.          TO MRS. CARMICHAEL-SMYTH
               20–28 AUGUST 1829

*Address:* M^rs Carmichael Smyth | Post Office. Weymouth. | Angleterre. *Re-addressed to:* Larkbeare House | Ottery S^t Mary. *Postmarks:* 28 AOUT 1829, FPO AU 31 1829. Hitherto unpublished.

I have just been seeing Perlet [139] at the Theatre de Madame — He acted an English milor — I can make nothing of him — His

---

[139] Adrien Perlet (1795–1850), a comic actor well-known in both Paris and London. The bill at the Théâtre de Madame on August 20 consisted of *Les Héritiers, Le Secrétaire, Rodolphe,* and *L'Artiste (Moniteur universel).*

English pronounciation of French was excellent his English was however very bad — He sang "With spirits gay I mount the box" — quoted Shakespeare, put his hands in his pockets and swaggered about the stage quite a l'Anglaise. My little Favorite Leontine Fay was as usual divine — I wonder at your objecting to the Theatre-going, for it gives me the best French lesson possible, and I am quite enough used to it not to feel the effects of it in the morning, especially as most of the Theatres are closed before 11 o'clock — I had a long reading of Algebra to day on my bed whither I retired sans chemises as a place of refuge from those little  — The Bibliotheque Portatif [140] is I think in fifty volumes — Bon soir —

Friday. I return home so sleepy generally that it seemeth more becoming & meet in me to hie to my bed than to sit down and expose my sleepiness on paper — I wrote in the first place Tuesday instead of Friday, and I do not know to what other little eccentricities my fancy may lead me I have been looking on for the last 2 hours at a game at Ecarté — Delightful & rational amusement. The money won goes to a fund wʰ we have for carriages excursions &c — I have not yet learned the game and stay as seldom as possible but I am obliged occasionally to stop for politeness sake — I don't know how it is that my love for Leontine Fay shᵈ go off but it is not so strong to day as usual. Williams is composing a Euclid in verse, and I am writing a dissertation on Shelley — I have engaged to do one for a periodical [141] wʰ is to appear at Cambridge next term not the Snob — My taste for Mathematics does not increase, my taste for old books and prints much I bought eight copies of heads from different masters the other day and gave for them — 2 francs — They are part of an album wʰ appears here called L'Album des Jeunes Artistes; the prints each of them 5 sous. I have bought

[140] It is impossible to say which of the several competing *bibliothèques portatives* Thackeray had in mind.

[141] *The Chimæra.* See above, No. 16.

likewise a picture for w.ʰ I was asked 7ˢ 6ᵈ in London for seven pence halfpenny here. I might have got it for 2/3 of the sum, but I am an admirer of coincidences — I am going to write to a M.ʳ Ori d'Hegenheim to give me French Lessons. Good night —

Saturday — Sunday. I have been to day to a village whose name I forget to see a ceremony very natural & very pretty. The young woman who has behaved herself the best of all in the village is crowned with flowers and receives 500 frcs. An old bishop attended. Behold the scene sketched with the hand of a Michael

Angelo. I am much disappointed in the Bishops Mitre. it is nothing but a pasteboard cap covered with tinsel and gilt paper. It does not beam with gems & gold as my fancy had pourtrayed — The priests are the ugliest dirtiest greasiest set of men I ever saw — They allow the hair to grow long & never (I believe clean it) — By the bye I had a most beautiful pair of ringlets tother day when my

face looked thus  now they are cut off & my hair is in the der-

niere mode thus  Adieu —

A chapter on Shirts.

Monday. I have got a pen with a set somewhat like unto thy pen dearest Mother and the 2 images of myself staring in on me; besides this I have got 3 new shirts w.ʰ I bought today for 5 francs each — For I did not tell you that I had had a misfortune when I first came to Paris the first morning of my arrival, a woman entered my apartment woke me & said something about linge & blanchisseuse — She took 2 chemises, a culotte & sundry pairs of stockings, as we removed to the Rue Rivoli ⟨that⟩ day I contented myself with desiring my linen to be ⟨sent⟩ after me, but all in vain — The fair maitresse d'hotel declares she received none, & miserable I could do ⟨noth⟩ing but storm, & buy new ones — My new shirts are of better quality than are my old ones. —

Wednesday. No journal yesterday, nor was there aught to record save the destruction of 3 mutton chops for dinner; nothing is there for me to say to day save that it raineth, & that I have had an interview with M. Ori who is to wait on me tomorrow at eight of the morn. He speaks English perfectly, also German & Italian I think I shall like him, for he seemeth a clever fellow his "fare" is 2 francs an hour. I subscribe to a circulating drawing Library where I may have plenty of things to copy for 6 frcs a month. I have been reading Devereux [142] but it is not so good as the dis-owned, altho' it is in the time of Swift & Bolingbroke. Addio —

Thursday. I have had my French Lesson but have not this in time for the post seeing that Williams gave me a spell of three hours in Mathematics. He is not at all niggardly of his time. Ecarté again this evening I am sick on't — I read a novel all the evening at the ecarté table. My Frenchman served young under Napoleon, he entered the army at 15 in 1812; as — Sergeant Major! but was promoted in the field of battle, & is a pleasant fellow enough, but dresses a la Snob —

I think you should let me off journalizing, for I cannot write anything connected taking it up as I do by bits & scraps — I want to go to the Luxembourg, but have no time. French Music is as

[142] Bulwer's *Devereux* and *The Disowned* appeared in 1829 and 1828 respectively.

dear as English and *I think* that neither of Rossini's last operas —
The Count Ori or William Tell are worth having; do decide
whether I shall buy Music or not — Tell Mary I am write about
usage the a is not broad.  Good night — I have left space for
tomorrow —

Friday — it rains as hard as it can pour.  No going out for me
today  My dear Father & Mother I hope you are well as I am at
this writing

No more at present from your affectionate Son W. M. Thackeray.


29.              TO MRS. CARMICHAEL-SMYTH
                      21 AUGUST 1829

*Address:* M^rs Carmichael Smyth. | Post Office | Weymouth. | Angleterre.
*Postmarks:* 21 AOUT 1829, FPO AU 24 1829.  Hitherto unpublished.

I have this moment read your letter, my dear Mother, w^h surprised me, and I confess hurt me, for I did not think I deserved
those strong terms of reproof in which it was couched — I mentioned that I had been to Frascati's — but for what went I?  to
gain?  No — It was a sight w^h I perhaps might never have another
opportunity of seeing, it was a curious chapter in the book of life,[143]
the perusal of w^h has done me the greatest good — it has taught
me not to trust so much in myself as before my pride or my ignorance would have led me to do; it has shewn me that I could not,
(as few could) resist the temptation of gambling, & it therefore has
taught me — to keep away from it — The same motive which
would have led me to a Theatre led me to Frascati's — I was
obliged if I went to stake my ten francs at the table instead of paying at the door — If I had not done so *I should never have arrived
at a piece of self knowledge, which I can conscientiously thank God
for giving me.*  I might have thought, as I did during the 1^st quarter
of an hour I was there, that it was a pleasant play, into which men
merely entered for amusement and gain — I should not have

[143] *Revelation,* 22, 19.

known that it was only for the *latter*. I might at another time [have] been induced to enter a gaming-house with more money than I had then in my pocket & *I should have as certainly staked it* — I have learnt the full extent of the evil. I have discovered my temperament & inclination with regard to it, and the necessity w$^h$ I did not then know of avoiding it — In what then am I so blameable? I went with *no* bad motive, no desire for gain. Mother, I came out with a knowledge of my own weakness of my own utter inability to resist a crime on w$^h$ I could before descant with all the knowledge of ignorance; I might have thanked God as the Pharisee did because I was "not such as the Publican" [144] — "I do not rush into destruction blindly & wilfully as this gamester, I do not hazard my family's welfare & my own, by throwing my money to the winds, or what is worse by seeking for gain in dishonest & ungodly wise — " I could not say this but I may say with the Publican, "Lord have mercy on me a Sinner" [145] — "Grant me strength to resist what Thou hast given me opportunity to see; it is not because I am weak, that Thou wilt desert me."

I will weary your patience no more my dear Mother by such a subject — Had it not been for the letter of this morning, you should have had a longer and a more amusing epistle than this, as it is I have no spirit to proceed, I will begin my journal for you to night, & will dispatch it this day week — Good bye till tonight my dearest Mother; & may God grant that you never again call me avaricious and mean when I am but curious, that you never again think because I before was ignorant that therefore I was good; or that because I am now aware of my own weakness I must be wicked —

Y$^r$ affectionate Son —

William M. Thackeray

[144] "The Pharisee stood and prayed thus with himself, God, I thank thee, that I am not as other men are, extortioners, unjust, adulterers, or even as this publican" (*St. Luke*, 18, 11).

[145] "And the publican, standing afar off, would not lift up so much as his eyes unto heaven, but smote upon his breast, saying, God be merciful to me a sinner" (*St. Luke*, 18, 13).

I said in my last letter I think, that I should go into one of the low gaming houses [146] — this of course unless I receive permission from you — I shall not now do.

30.          TO MRS. CARMICHAEL-SMYTH
                    2–4 SEPTEMBER 1829

*Address:* M^rs Carmichael Smyth. | Larkbeare House | near Ottery S.^t Mary's | Devonshire | Angleterre. *Postmarks:* 5 SEPT 1829, FPO SE 8 1829. Hitherto unpublished.

                                        Paris.

I was puzzling my unhappy brains over an ugly proposition ⟨in⟩ Hinds Trigonometry when your letter reached me (perhaps ⟨you⟩ will consider it praiseworthy in me that I did not read it till I had mastered my proposition) and now I have "taken up ⟨my⟩ pen" — to make comments thereon — There will be a long letter ⟨for⟩ you at Weymouth on Tuesday, but I fear it will not reach you quite so soon at Larkbeare. I do not admire Devereux as a ⟨whole⟩ so much as either of the other two novels of M.^r Bulwer's,[147] ⟨I⟩ think he has taken more pains about it than either, it is full ⟨of⟩ thoughts strong and deep, but he has strung his pearls on a poor & fragile thread, the story is I think the most misera⟨ble⟩ composition, I could write as good a one myself; I have been rather turning my thoughts to that kind of thing lately; as an Essay on Shelley is in progress for the Chimæra — There is an excellent motto (tho' a long one) in Devereux it is in the 3.^d v⟨olume⟩ at the end of a Book,[148] it is about Bezoni the Atheist. ⟨I shall⟩ write it very small; "I know that the intention of Bezoni was benevolence, & that the ⟨practice⟩ of his life was virtue, & while my reason tells me that my God will not punish the reluctant & invol⟨untary⟩ errors of one to whom all Gods creatures were so dear, my religion bids me hope that I shall

---

[146] Located for the most part in or near the Palais Royal. See *Galignani's New Paris Guide* (1827), pp. 178–181.

[147] *The Disowned* and either *Pelham* (1828) or *Falkland* (1827).

[148] The last lines of Book V, quoted almost exactly except for punctuation and capitalization.

meet him in that world where no error is, & where the great Spirit to whom all passions are unknown avenges the momentary doubt of his justice, by a proof of the infinity of his mercy" — There — it has not taken up much room and I think will express the character & I hope the fate of Shelley — You tell me to discontinue the acquaintance of Lady Twagg who is M$^{rs}$ Twigg. I am sure if you knew her you would not say so — When we first came to Paris, Williams grew very thick with her & I cautioned him against it, but now I have learnt her history (not from her own mouth) She married at 16 Col$^!$ Twigg who turned out a great brute to her & her sister. The Unfortunate M$^{rs}$ Twigg bore it all patiently until her sister came to live with her, who gave her the advice that Jerry Sneak [149] received from somebody, she tried & Colonel Twigg finding out whence the advice came swore her sister sh$^d$ leave his house she had no friends her parents are both dead, and M$^{rs}$ Twigg preferred living with her, so Col. T. brought them to Paris & left them there. Had I he⟨ard⟩ of this from her, I should not have been much inclined to like the p⟨erson who told it to me,⟩ but I have heard it from authority w$^h$ I cannot dou⟨bt for it was told to me⟩ by the most respectable p⟨erson . . .[150] th⟩at there was never a word breathed against her character; she never goes out with us without her sister, always receives us in the Public Salon of the boarding house — (once she invited us to tea in her own Salon) I never heard her speak a word w$^h$ was not perfectly lady-like, I receive from her plenty of good advice, w$^h$ as it comes from a very pretty mouth is the more pleasant, & yet luckless I — I am to cut her! I was talking with my friend Butler (who has asked me to go over to see him in Ireland) & he said, & I agreed, that if he had a sister he sh$^d$ be proud that she were such as M$^{rs}$ Twigg" — This last sentence is a very bad one — it contains 2 things w$^h$ may be construed into reasons for my liking M$^{rs}$ T; but I mean you to read it differently (I think I must have been asleep when I wrote this.)

[149] The henpecked husband of Samuel Foote's *Mayor of Garratt* (1763), who is urged by Bruin, his brother-in-law, to rebel against the domination of his shrewish wife.

[150] About five words are here concealed by a fold in the original.

Thursday. I find that the Post does not leave Paris to day, so that my letters have generally waited a day, now as there is no necessity for that, I shall send off my next letter tomorrow week. Yesterday was an idle day, except for French, my French Master & I set off after breakfast to see sights he is rather a snob in appearance But that is not of much consequence in Paris, inasmuch as a French Viscount de ma conoissance one of the most fashionable men in Paris is as bad — We went first to the Luxembourg, where we saw a number of bad pictures & a few good ones — The best one was a French frigate boarding an English one of twice its size & taking it — I did not think I had so much national conceit, but it hurt me & made me feel foolish. There was another very beautiful picture of the  Greek women of Scio looking on at the defeat of their husbands, fathers, uncles, aunts, sons, nephews cousins &c by the Turks [151] — I am disgusted with David, who stares you in the face at all the print shops — after leaving the Luxembourg, we went to the law court, & saw or heard an interesting trial, about the abduction of two pair of breeches Here is a "little French Lawyer" — I have twice asked at ⟨the⟩ P O for Miss Strange but in vain —

We then went to the mint, but could not get in we then went to the Palais des Arts but it was vacation time, we then went to the Corn Market, (Why they call it Halloblay [152] I don't know) and saw — several sacks of corn in a large room! we likewise viewed a couple of churches, & then adjourned to dinner, for w^h I paid, & w^h cost me 26 sous par tete! I w^d have given him a better repast, but he insisted on my going to this place — For all these sights I paid 10 sous so that my journey was not expensive — I am going at 1/2 past 2 to ride in the Bois de Boulogne so adieu —

[151] Delacroix's *Scènes des massacres de Scio*, first exhibited in the Salon of 1824.
[152] *Halles aux blés.*

Friday — We had a most wicked ride yesterday, galloping racing, leaping (positively) I had the pleasure of knocking over an unfortunate man     I had past him safe ⟨but when⟩ Butler holla'd to him he rushed up against my ⟨horse. My⟩ steed rapidly passed him by & as rapidly ⟨he⟩ sank prone on the ground They

charge 2 francs for most excellent steeds I am as stiff as poss: this morning but an hour much better for my ride, and likewise for Butlers dinner I was going to draw Monsieur le Vicomte de Nugent but I have expunged him — My sheet of paper is excessively large, so you must not think this a short letter — I think Williams is a little superficial in his Mathematical Knowledge, for now he can not explain himself so readily as he did in the beginning with the Algebra — But ⟨it is⟩ time for the post, so I must say good bye my dear ⟨Mother⟩ until next week — best love to all at Larkbeare, & ⟨no⟩ more at present from your affectionate Son

W. M. Thackeray —

31.     TO MRS. CARMICHAEL-SMYTH

10–13 SEPTEMBER 1829

*Address:* Mrs Carmichael Smyth. | Larkbeare House | Ottery St Marys | Devonshire. | Angleterre. *Postmark:* FPO SE 17 1829. Extracts published, *Memorials*, p. 346.

Thursday.

Your rebuke is not a just one, my dear Mother, as to my only half reading your letters, I have looked over the letter and you do not mention the day of your departure from Weymouth. I have but a short time to answer your letter for my French Master comes at 2 and stays for a couple of hours; I had begun my German lessons before your letter reached me with my French master whose mode of teaching I much like — I had a ride yesterday on a horse w^h lifted me two feet from the saddle at every step he took; he brought me home with my bowels in a sad state of perturbation, & my limbs as stiff as poss: To day I am rather worse as to my limbs but feel much better for the exercise — Will you lend me ten pounds to buy books with? I can get £20 worth for that sum here, and as I shall not return here again in a hurry I think I might take advantage of the opportunity. Perhaps you will send me over a brace of partridges, as you have so many. A man of my connoissance here killed 7 brace yesterday in the Bois de Boulogne. w^h by the way is a most delightful place, full of nice English looking lanes, where one may take one's 5 shillings worth of riding to ones heart's content — I am going to dine to day a long way off (in the Rue Grenelle by the Invalids) with two Cambridge men. There is a very pretty young girl at their boarding house who is going to be married to a gentleman comme ça — A fine figure for a lover, he just understands enough English to know that the 2 Cantabs quizz him, — but not enough to answer in return. he says he is a relation of Don Miguel's.[153] —

I have been reading Mathilde [154] by Madame Cottin with w^h I am much amused — I have enquired at Galignani's for M^r Lott [155] his name is not in the books. But my French Master is here & I must wait till tomorrows post to dispatch my letter.

— Saturday       I had to walk a mile and a half in the rain last night with nothing to keep it off but a sword-stick w^h is not so good as an Umbrella — It is quite a necessity in Paris of a night particularly in the large space between the Invalids & the town, where I learnt for my consolation that a man had been murdered two nights before. The Champs Elysees are as bad a mile of straight

[153] Dom Maria Evaristo Miguel, absolutist King of Portugal from 1828 to 1834.

[154] A popular novel of the Crusades published by Mme. Marie Risteau Cottin (1770–1807) in 1805.

[155] The original reads *for M^r Lott at Galignani's for M^r Lott.*

road, hedged on both sides by tall trees whence men may rush forth & bid you stand & deliver — If on a dark night some tree  should present itself to your view thus a little fancy might easily make it ⟨into⟩ a thief. — Did you know a M$^{rs}$ Goldie likewise a M$^{rs}$ Clarke who says she knows M$^{rs}$ Forrest very well. I have not met either of them, but Williams has made their acquaintance — Yesterday at dinner I got a ticket to see the Royal Palace [156] in the Palais Royal! — But it raineth at present in such wise, that I sadly fear my ticket will be to me of no avail — But tis an ill wind w$^h$ blows nobody good — Ducks & hackney-coachmen will rejoice in the rain — The hackney coach-men here are very indignant with certain vehicles called omni-buses w$^h$ can be drawn in less room than they can be described  In one of these you may be car-ried from one end of the town to the other for five sous. I am told that they are to be adopted in London. My French Master & I have long disputes about the battles

Sunday. My friends came half an hour before their time yester-day and so I was obliged to delay my letter another day, I have just received y$^r$ letter of the 21$^{st}$ of August in w$^h$ was conveyed your intimation about returning home. The Post Office have had the benefit of it; for it hath been broken open and I suppose read. I would rather it had been another letter or that it had come some time ago, for the coat is made seeing that I heard nothing against it from you. I was at the Duke of Orleans' palace yesterday, where I saw a number of large rooms and bad pictures: From what I read in your letter I think my best plan would be to go and ensconce myself in my rooms at Cambridge, instead of coming home for the fortnight     I shall be more willing to do so, as Williams will be there, he says he will give me an hour a day there. He talks of going to England on the 29$^{th}$ but he does not seem settled — In-

[156] In 1829 the residence of the Duc d'Orléans.

stead of his having much influence over me, it is quite the contrary, for I find him what is called a very good-natured fellow; who has wasted or dawdled away his time till the age of five & twenty, & will do the same I fear all his life  His mind is filled with vague literary projects w̲ḥ̲ he will never accomplish — In every thing but Mathematics he is deficient, there he certainly explains very well — I think the fortnight at Cambridge would do me much good for I have read but not *got up* what I have read, I fear my acquirements would not tell in the Examination Room      I will me thinks go out and take a walk, for it is a wondrous fair Sabbath morning — so no more at present from your affectionate Son.

W. M. Thackeray

Send Fawssett's Letter.

<br>

32.            TO MRS. CARMICHAEL-SMYTH
                    1 NOVEMBER 1829

*Address:* M̲ṛ̲ṣ̲ H. C. Smyth. | Larkbeare House | Ottery S̲ṭ̲ Mary | Devon. *Postmark:* CAMBRIDGE NO 1 1829, 2 NO 1829. Extracts published in *Memorials*, pp. 346–347.

Cambridge.

Your letter came a day too early, my dearest Mother as you would have recieved mine the day after the date of yours. I rebuke me with having no Journal but my days have passed in a very equable routine Mathematics & Classics, Classics & Mathematics We are reading Mechanics w̲ḥ̲ rather amuse me & would much more if in this our University simplicity were the fashion; as it is we have to wade & wander through darkness visible [157] — I did not tell you in my last that I transgressed in going to Covent Garden on my arrival in London, but as I had not to go into the open air, w̲ḥ̲ you thought would injure me, I think my sin was venial. By the "annexed plan" you will see that I could not be exposed to the

---

[157] *Paradise Lost*, I, 63.

caller air.[158] I saw Miss Fanny Kemble [159] &
was much delighted with her. We have had
a very animated debate on the advantage of
Potatoes to the human race; some wag has
asked whether the invention of parched pease
has been of advantage, w[h] is certainly as good a question as the
other.

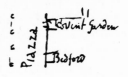

The weather is awfully cold here, I have been obliged to resort
to that vile of custom of putting my hands in my pockets. Williams has not yet paid me, he will in the course of a week I suppose      I've been reading Don Quixote since I came up it is almost
a new book to me. I have done myself the honor of calling
on Martin Thackeray the V. P of Kings he is not a very vice-
provostical looking fellow this is his costume
His coat is blue his — drab, & his gaiters yellow
leather — Somewhat like a footman out of livery.
I shall meet him to night I suppose at D[r] Thackerays where I am going after Chapel      Some
strange fatality seemed to attend me last week I
was positively late for Chapel five times & only
went three 8 being my broken N[o]; in consequence
I have recieved notice from that worthy man the
Dean that I must attend every morning & eve-

ning this week — Sunday Chapel is a great Lion — It is rather too
tedious for us who hear it so often. The anthems are rather long-
winded, & the chant of the psalms taketh up a long time. I have
been eating mock-turtle soup & mutton chop with Young to day;
w[h] he took by way of diet being laid up with a bad cold!  I am

[158] Scots for "fresh"; compare the opening lines of Burns's "The Holy
Fair":

>Upon a simmer Sunday morn,
>  When Nature's face is fair,
>I walked forth to view the corn,
>  An' snuff the caller air.

[159] See *Memoranda*. Thackeray saw Miss Kemble in *Romeo and Juliet* on
October 5. This was her only appearance during the interval between his
departure from Paris and arrival in Cambridge for the Michaelmas term, which
began in 1829 on October 10.

going to take a part I believe in a play; to be acted at a D$^r$ Jermyn's [160] at Swaffham a little distance from Cambridge. I am  to be the heroine! — My costume below. The little fellow is my lover & D$^r$ Faustus. We shall make a pretty pair. D$^r$ J has got scenes &c. My dress I shall make myself with the aid of your needle & thread, & some silver paper tucked to my white trowsers. My bed-maker is going to lend me a white gown. I must say good night for I have a letter to write to Carne. "Best wishes to the Cider — May there be 1000 hogsheads of it! Love to Father & Mary from your affectionate Son

W. M. Thackeray.

Sunday night —

33.        TO MRS. CARMICHAEL-SMYTH
              22 NOVEMBER 1829

*Address:* M$^{rs}$ Carmichael Smyth. | Larkbeare House | Ottery S$^t$ Mary. | Devon. *Postmarks:* CAMBRIDGE NO 22 1829, 23 NO 1829. Hitherto unpublished.

Cambridge. Monday [161] Night.

The weather is bitter cold inspite of wind in tempests ⟨&⟩ rain in torrents; these have had an uncomfortable effect on my eyes w$^h$ will prevent my writing a very long letter; I have therefore dis-continued my night reading. Do you know that I fear the Christmas Turkey must not smoke for me except at Cambridge. For I must read to take anything like a respectable degree. Dismiss your visions of wranglers, my dear Mother, if I am a Senior Optime [162] you should be very well content. These are however as

---

[160] Probably the Rev. George Bitton Jermyn of Trinity Hall, Cambridge, who had received an LL.D. degree in 1826.

[161] A mistake for Sunday, November 22, as the postmark shows.

[162] There are three classes of degrees with distinction in the Cambridge

unpleasant things to write of as they are to study. So we will no
more. My pumps were an inch too short, & the rain poured in
torrents so that I stayed at home instead of going to D$^r$ Thackeray's
Ball. Yesterday as I was walking home with a great tin box of oil
colors under my arm w$^h$ a man gave me, I met the charming
Mistress Pryme who invited me to a tea tomorrow. I belong to a
debating Club [163] now in our College only consisting of 7. There
are amongst them 3 1$^{st}$ Class Men, who are very nice fellows only
they smell a little of the shop. The Trinity boat has been most
ignominiously beaten by the Peter-House     Our freshmen this
year are not so many as the Johnians who are obliged to have 4
chapels & 2 dinners a day. I thank my Fortune daily I was not a
Johnian. It is the lowest, most childish, piggish punning place. I
am sitting in a mans rooms with a most excellent bottle of Claret
before me to w$^h$ I have paid sincere & frequent visits, I have however valorously broken the cork into the bottle, & there being no
corkscrew, must abstain from further potation. I was at a gay
dinner at Youngs yesterday. Good bye dear Mother I have a long
walk to take with my f⟨riends.⟩ I hope the storms wont visit the
estate. Love to father & Mary. Your affte Son —

W. M. Thackeray.

---

mathematical Tripos, those attained by the Wranglers, the Senior Optimes,
and the Junior Optimes.

[163] This club is described by Dr. William Hepworth Thompson (1810–
1866), Regius Professor of Greek from 1853 until 1866 and thereafter
Whewell's successor as Master of Trinity College, during the course of his
valuable recollections of Thackeray at Cambridge. Dr. Thompson writes that
it was in the Trinity College court "that I was first made aware of the name
of a tall thin large-eyed, full and ruddy-faced man with an eye-glass fixed *en
permanence* — the glass he has immortalized, — or ought to have done so —
for on consideration he supplied its place in his portrait of Titmarsh with a
*pair*. I did not know him personally until his second year, when a small literary
society was made up of him, John, now Archdeacon Allen, Henry, afterwards
Dean Alford, Robert — now Archdeacon Groome, and Young of Caius, with
another of whom I am not sure, and myself. We were seven — I don't know
that we ever agreed on a name. Alford proposed the 'Covey,' because we
'made such a noise when we got up' — to speak that is; but it was left for
further consideration. I think Thackeray's subject was 'Duelling,' on which
there was then much diversity of opinion. We did not see in him even the

34.            TO MRS. CARMICHAEL-SMYTH
                  16 JULY 1830

*Address:* M<sup>rs</sup> Carmichael Smyth. | Larkbeare House | Ottery S<sup>t</sup> Mary |
Devon. *Postmark:* JY 16 1830. Hitherto unpublished.

My dear Mother

   I have been twice to Whitehall to find M<sup>r</sup> Thornton & the Privy
Council Office, but I was unsuccessful in my search on both occa-

germ of those literary powers which under the stern influence of necessity he
afterwards developed. One does not see the wings in a chrysalis. He led a
somewhat lazy but pleasant and 'gentlemanlike' life in a set mixed of old
schoolfellows and such men as the two archdeacons named above; with them
and with my friend Edward Fitzgerald he no doubt had much literary talk,
but not on 'University Subjects.' He sat, I remember, opposite to me at the
'May Examination'; he was put in the fourth class. It was a class where clever
'non-reading men' were put, as in a limbo. But though careless of University
distinction, he had a vivid appreciation of English poetry, and chanted the
praises of the old English novelists, especially his model, Fielding. He had always a flow of humour, and pleasantry, and was made much of by his friends. At
supper-parties, though not talkative — rather observant — he enjoyed the hu-
mours of the hour, and sang one or two old songs with great applause. 'Old King
Cole' I well remember to have heard from him at the supper I gave to celebrate my election as Scholar. It made me laugh excessively — not from the
novelty of the song — but from the humour with which it was given. Thackeray . . . left us at the end of his second year, and for some time I saw him
no more. Our debating club fell to pieces when he went." (*Memorials*, pp.
347–348)
   Of the members of this debating club Thackeray was most intimate with
John Allen (see *Memoranda*). He saw little of Henry Alford (1810–1871),
Dean of Canterbury from 1857 to 1871, or of Robert Hindes Groome (1810–
1889), Archdeacon of Suffolk from 1869 to 1887, after he left college. The
seventh man, whose name escapes Dr. Thompson, was either Henry Nicholson
Burrows (1809–1859) or Charles Claydon Christie (b. 1810?), both of
Trinity College. In his diary Alford kept a record of the club's meetings
during 1829:
   "Nov. 9. — Met in Allen's rooms, and debated on whether Luxury is
necessarily an attendant on Civilisation.
   Nov. 13. — Met in Burrowes' rooms; debated on Painting and Sculpture.
   Nov. 20. — . . . At Christie's rooms debated about the Diffusion of Knowl-
edge . . .
   Dec. 11. — Last meeting of the Debating Society. Subject, Duelling."
(Mrs. Alford, *Life of Dean Alford*, London, 1874, pp. 49–50)
   The club was revived again after the Christmas holidays. For information

sions, & the dozen persons I asked to shew me where this mysterious office might be are as ignorant as myslf on the subject — The passport office, the Packet Office & the Bankers were all loyally shut yesterday,[1] so that it would have been impossible for me to get away tomorrow or rather tonight  Under these circumstances I thought my plan would be to stay here quietly, & get a German Master w^h I have done, & have just received your letter telling me to go down to Charlton.[2]  As I have 4 houses in London where a dinner is at my service, I really think that I cannot do better than stay.

M^rs Fawsett [3] has sent me some excellent letters for Dresden, & her sister M^rs Foster (who lives at Bedford & knows the D^r Thackeray [4] there) has sent me some more — to a General the Spanish & Italian Ministers, & to a gentleman [5] who will give me an introduction to the best literary society in the Place — I don't know how to account for all this attention to me  I suppose my friend Fawsett has been "soaping" me — By M^rs Fosters & Fawsett's recommendation I have taken a M^r Troppeneger for a Master, he comes to me this evening — & is a very well informed & clever man from what I hear of him — He too can give me excellent letters & recommendations most likely to some family such as you wish me to live with — I have not seen him yet, but from the high terms in w^h M^rs Foster & Fawsett speak of him I believe I could not find a better master.  Martin Thackeray is I believe an accepted lover of one of the Miss Fosters [6] w^h is the only way I can account for this

about its activities in 1830 and about the remaining months of Thackeray's brief career at Cambridge, see Appendix I.

[1] The funeral of George IV took place on Friday, July 15 (*Annual Register*, 1830, "Chronicle," p. 110).

[2] Where lived Colonel and Mrs. Forrest.

[3] Mother of Walter Barham Fawsett, Thackeray's friend at Charterhouse and Cambridge.

[4] Dr. Joseph Thackeray (1784–1832), *Genealogy* (39), was educated at Eton and King's College, Cambridge, where he received his M. D. degree in 1817. He was a very popular and successful physician in Bedford. See *Memorials*, pp. 145–161.

[5] Above *gentleman* Thackeray has written *nobleman*.

[6] Thackeray's surmise appears to have been unwarranted. See above, No. 13.

excess of cordiality to me — she has asked me to her house at Brickhill a handsome place near Bedford; & to her sons' in Baker Street so I suppose Martin & Fawsett have both been emblazoning my virtues in colours highly flattering & doubtless faithful —

Since I have been in town no theatres have been open — to day I dine with a School-fellow who is just going to be married — On Monday Kean takes his farewell of the stage, & performs an act in 5 of his best parts [7] — if you still think it better for me to go to Charlton, let me stay over Monday here; for this is the l⟨ast⟩ time I can see this little hero of the Sock & ⟨Buskin.⟩

— I have been employing my mornings in reading German & have got a book on something of the Hamiltonian plan — A weeks application will do me I think a great deal of benefit —

— Having made this agreement with M⁙ Troppeneger I can not I think retract, had I written to ask whether I should make it 3 days would have been wasted, so I did what I thought was for the best & what Father wished me at one time to do — I did not mention the number of lessons I should take of him — but some I think I ought to take — by Monday I shall have had 4 (one on Sunday) & can if you wish go to Charlton, but I think that my best plan will be to stay here  My lodging will cost me a guinea my breakfasts & waiter a guinea more.  My dinners nothing —

My companions were amusing enough, one of them had just come from South America, & had a good deal to say & to say well — The other had been in Spain with the Duke & was amusing enough, (w^h I percieve I told you before) — The night was cold & the day desperately hot  my face did much resemble in colour & heat a redhot poker or rather a warming pan.  I went to bed directly for I had no sleep — & woke in an hour as fresh as ever — Good by dearest Mother  Your affte Son.

[7] Act four of *Richard III*, act four of *The Merchant of Venice*, act five of *A New Way to Pay Old Debts*, act two of *Macbeth*, and act three of *Othello*. See the account of this performance in Harold Newcomb Hillebrand's *Edmund Kean* (New York, 1933), p. 312.

35.         TO MRS. CARMICHAEL-SMYTH
                    31 JULY 1830

*Address:* M<sup>rs</sup> Carmichael Smyth. | Larkbeare House | Ottery S<sup>t</sup> Mary's |
Devonshire | England. *Postmark:* FPO AU 5 1830. Published in part,
*Memorials*, p. 350.

Coblentz. July 31. 1830.

I had written a long letter to you, my dearest Mother, from
various places where I had stopped, but have with my usual carelessness lost it — it will I suppose fall into the hands of some German waiter who may instruct himself if he can with its contents.

After a passage of four & twenty hours we arrived at Rotterdam, not having had occasion on the way to part with any of the
precious meats w<sup>h</sup> you know I am such an adept at swallowing — I
saw Robert Frith, he has grown a great deal & has learnt to talk
English like a Dutchman. — The town of Rotterdam is the finest I
ever saw in point of comfort & cleanliness — the houses are magnificently well built and the people are — but you can read all
about the people & town in that entertaining book the Encyclopædia.
The next morning Tuesday at five I set off for Cologne, & we were
six and thirty hours on our voyage — There were no beds lots of
passengers who were strewed over the cabin on stools & sofas on
tables & under tables; I was out all the night, but managed to sleep
snugly on the top of some coals w<sup>h</sup> were placed on the deck — The
Rhine to Cologne is not as pretty as a Dutch Canal, there is nothing
to see on it, except here & there a town, & a little church almost
every hundred yards. These are the pre-
vailing fashions of churches — We had on
board almost all our London passengers —
who are in the most desperate hurry to get
on — We arrived at 3 at Cologne & many of
them were off again by five —
Cologne as the guide book saith had at
one time 365 churches and this the waiter & some gentlemen at the
table d'hote told me was exactly the no of days in the year. It had

likewise 11000 virgins who were destroyed by the Romans & whose unfortunate bones have been used to decorate a Church. The town is beastly — the Cathedral unfinished, the weather was hot beyond all bearing — & I was consequently in my own room a great part of the day employing myself between sleeping smoking reading, & eating raw herring & onions

Yesterday the beauties of the journey began, & I really think the Rhine is almost equal to the Thames. One or two views were of course magnificent — The ladies had got their Byrons to read when they arrived at "the castled crag of Drachenfels" [8] — here is something like unto it  There was a pretty little girl on board to whom I

talked the most delicious sentiment and quoted Shelley & Moore to her great edification & delight. I really did feel rather sentimental, & intended to have made some pathetic verses on her & the Rhine but she came from a boarding school at Boulogne, & that staggered my sentiment; & dinner was ordered & that entirely destroyed it — Last night we arrived here, tomorrow I go on to Francfort — A gentleman of the name of Balfour a fellow passenger is going with me presently to Ems about nine miles from Coblentz.

This is a beautiful place, magnificent old houses, old turrets old bridges &c — I have got one or two sketches: the Moselle & the Rhine here join; the grand fortress of Ehrenbreitstein looks over the town & here you must fill up the description from your imagination — There are some thousand of Prussian Soldiers in the town  I walked a mile with a regiment of them this morning at 5. (I went out to sketch) the band is the most beautiful I ever heard

[8] *Childe Harold's Pilgrimage*, canto III, lyric following stanza 55.

far super(ior to) the band of the horse Guards. The men are noble looking fellows in short blue jackets & black crop belts — I have met with some good figures among the people here and two who

were on board the steamer The boy with the pipe was exactly like Raphael & the man would have made a good study for a Buccaneer — We had on board 2 nobles with one of whom I have made acquaintance the Duc de Fitzjames the old Russian Admiral Tchelchagoff I have been writing with Seppia as I could get no ink. Good bye Dearest Mother till next week when I will write again.

I wish I could say something better than the stale & formal Remember me to all at home & believe me your affte Son

W. M. Thackeray.

36.      TO MRS. CARMICHAEL-SMYTH
?–12 AUGUST 1830

*Address:* Mʳˢ Carmichael Smyth. | Larkbeare House. | Ottery Sᵗ Mary's | Devonshire | England. *Postmarks:* BONN 12 8, FPO AU 20 1830. Hitherto unpublished.

Godesberg on the Rhine.

You will see by the direction of this letter that I am not where my last supposed I should be by this time. I am writing now from a village in the neighbourhood of the most beautiful part of the "Father of Rivers" — close to Drachenfels & its six sister Mountains; & not much farther from Nonnenwert. I was induced to come here by meeting at Frankfort a Cambridge acquaintance, a

German called Schulte [9] — He told me that if I would join his
party (w.h consists of M.r Baynon [10] a tutor of Jesus College Oxford,
& an undergraduate Trotter [11]) he would give me an hours reading
in German every day; & engage that I should live at as cheap a
rate as at any place in Germany. After we have stayed here for a
month he has asked me to stay the same time with him at his
Fathers in Westphalia; and I thought this would be the cheapest
and pleasantest plan I could pursue. He has given [12] me an introduction to a Gentleman at Dresden, with whom he stayed when
there — & he says that for me he thinks it would be an excellent
family to stay with.

The place where we are now staying is quiet, & cheap, and excessively beautiful. About three miles off is the town & University
of Bonn. We walked in a few days ago, & Schulte met one of his
old friends who took us to his room and gave us tea, & afterwards
took us to a commerz house where thirty or forty of the men were
assembled to drink smoke & sing — We were rather Lions &
treated most civilly — in fact the civility was rather overpowering
for with almost every one of these men we had to drink ein halbe —
half a tumbler of small sour wine — The men are raw dirty rough
looking cubs with little caps & long pipes — from half glasses some
bolder spirits proceeded to whole ones & there were half a dozen
men who pledged each other in four tumblers a piece. The men I
met were all of one club the Rhenanier (I wont answer for spelling) but in the University there are three more — The Prussians,
Westphalians and the Burschenschaft.[13] It is the pride of each of

[9] Franz Anton Schulte (b. 1805?) was the son of Catholic parents living
in Volkringhausen, Westphalia. He studied for a time at Göttingen and
matriculated in 1825 at Heidelberg. (Gustav Toepke, *Die Matrikel der
Universität Heidelberg*, 6 vols., Heidelberg, 1884–1916, V, 312) He was
never enrolled at Cambridge, but he did enter St. Alban Hall, Oxford, on
March 31, 1831. Thackeray later discovered to his cost that Schulte was as
dishonest as he was plausible.

[10] The Rev. David Beynon (b. 1793?), Tutor in Latin and Greek and
Lecturer at Jesus College, Oxford.

[11] Thomas Lowis Trotter (b. 1809?), who matriculated at Lincoln College,
Oxford, in 1828.

[12] Thackeray wrote *will* above *has given*.

[13] For an account of this liberal students' organization, see Heinrich von

these to insult the others, and thereby gain duels, of which they seem extraordinarily fond. On the night I was there, six or seven duels were got up; and are to be fought on Monday in an inn not far from this. Each Club has a president a vice & a sub who are chosen chiefly from their distinction in the duello — I became a great friend of the president of the Rhenaniers insomuch that he has invited us to a large party of the whole of the club (about 300) wʰ is to take place in a few days — he has got some duels on hand wʰ he has graciously asked us to come & see fought on Monday. The men's singing was I thought excellent, every man has to sing a verse in his turn, I piously & patriotically chanted out God save the King — In the course of the evening they all sung a hymn to the Rhine, upstanding and uncovered — On breaking up I found myself the only strictly sober man in the party although during the evening I had positively imbibed no less than six bottles of the wine — My potations cost me a dollar. 3 shillings — It was after the Port wine and Punch of Cambridge like so much milk and water or vinegar & water for it had an unpleasant effect on my internals; in fact the wine and the dinners have kept me &c &c

Monday. I have been to day to see the duels which took place

at the place before named — I will give you the best description I can    I have only a bad steel pen with which I can scarcely write

Treitschke's *Deutsche Geschichte im Neunzehnten Jahrhundert*, Theil II, chapter 7.

or draw. The men in hats are seconds whose business it is to strike up the swords of the combatants as soon as a blow is given by either party. They fight sometimes twelve & sometimes four and twenty rounds — but the instant a wound is given of the requisite depth breadth & length ⟨the ba⟩ttle is over & they kiss each other in ⟨the most⟩ friendly manner — In the dozen fig⟨hts I sa⟩w only one wound of any kind was given, & that was but a slight one — Schulte who was at Heidelberg and Gottingen speaks with contempt of these men — In those more enlightened universities men often fight with sabres & have no guard at all as here — his face is prettily picked out with scars w$^h$ he got in some of these contests — he is known here as an experienced master in the art of fence, so that if I have any quarrels I shall not hesitate in giving them to him to fight for me w$^h$ is quite etiquette. I have got to the end of my paper, & can only say God bless all at home; write to me Post Restante at Bonn, and the letters will reach me — Good bye dearest Mother

August 12.                          Your affectionate Son

                                        W. M. Thackeray.


37.            TO MRS. CARMICHAEL-SMYTH
                    15 AUGUST 1830

*Address:* M$^{rs}$ Carmichael Smyth. | Larkbeare House | Ottery S$^t$ Mary. | Devon.
*Postmark:* AU 23 1830. Hitherto unpublished.

                        Godesberg on the Rhine — Sunday.

One of our party is going to England tomorrow, so dearest Mother, I think I can do no harm if I send a few hasty lines home by him —

Since I wrote last, I have been doing little else but reading the German Grammar, a very praiseworthy but not a very pleasant employment — The students of Bonn their duels & their drinking bouts I have cut, for I think they are a wondrous stupid set of fellows — Yesterday morning (and this is by far the most extraordinary event w$^h$ has happened to me, Yesterday morning I say — I

went without my breakfast; & took a mighty long walk to Drachenfels; I was however exceedingly disappointed, for though the view
was of course more extended; yet as it only embraced long level
tracts of fields, I could have done very well without taking an hours
desperate walking up the hill, & another hours walk *to* the hill —
Not to mention tearing my boots, & running a nail into my heel. I
have been writing one of the most delightful letters to M^rs Foster
(the lady who gave me so many letters of introduction), quite a
model for style & elegance I made three copies of it —

That in w^h I have experienced the most serious disappointment
is the Wine — The much lauded Wine of the Rhine is to my indis-
criminating and barbarous J— something mighty similar to Epsom
Salts & Vinegar in taste & effect —

> Quid fles Asterie?  Horace [14]
> And then the F—s are sad Mother
> They bite me oh! so bad Mother
>     By day & night
>     The rascals bite
> I think they'll drive me mad Mother,
> I smoke twelve pipes a day Mother
> To drive the rogues away Mother
>     They don't care a — for
>     Your "flea-i-fuge" camphor
> What ever I do, they *will* stay Mother.
> And then my health don't thrive Mother
> I do nothing but scratch & grieve Mother
>     Unless post haste
>     I flee the place
> The wretches will flea me alive Mother.

The poetical effusion of sorrow in the last page is I am sorry to
say "founded on fact" — my left eye is at this writing a cruel
instance of the revengeful qualities of the race of fleas. I may as
well inform you that I have won your guinea, the Essay on
Miracles is in a high state of progression — I am thinking of trans-

[14] *Odes*, III, vii, 1.

lating Schlegel's Lectures on the Fine Arts [15] and offering it to the
Family Library — I believe he will be here to day & my friend
Schulte will introduce me to him — He was the grea⟨t friend⟩ of
Madame de Stael — and enjoys as high a reputation for talent &
learning as any man in Germany.

My sketchbook & I have almost parted company, for things

begin to lose their novelty but I should like to spend a few
thousand pounds on the castle of w$^h$ I have given you a sketch and
make a residence of it — Every old Castle and Hill, has its peculiar
legend & tradition I long to read German to understand them or
rather I long to understand German to read them.

Swarms of soldiers infest the country, there are going to be
reviews about 30 miles off, but I shall not budge to see them. They
have stuck up a poppinjay in the village, & tonight there are going
to be rustic sports such as you find in novels and Melodramas.
Good bye — "God bless Father & Mother & make me a good
boy" — It is an old prayer but a rare good one — Tell Mary that
the prevailing fashion for stockings here is sky blue, & the genteel
people wear a brass pot on their heads, & tie up their faces with a
linen handkerchief — Good bye dearest Mother  Yr affte Son

### W. M. Thackeray

[15] *Die Kunstlehre*, the first part of August Wilhelm von Schlegel's *Vorle-
sungen über schöne Litteratur und Kunst* (1801–1803). For the "Family
Library," see above, No. 25.

My letter has been but a short one, dearest Mother, but I am no adept in the ars scribendi — however I thought I would let you know that I was well in health save for wine w$^h$ doth occasionally afflict me & in good spirits save for fleas w$^h$ do incessantly torment me — But wine I need not drink, & fleas I must put up withal — shewing thereby an example of resignation & continence worthy to be imitated by all travellers —

38.          TO MRS. CARMICHAEL-SMYTH
              6-7 SEPTEMBER 1830 [16]

*Address:* M$^{rs}$ Carmichael Smyth. | Larkbeare House | Ottery S$^t$ Mary | Devon.
*Postmark:* OC 15 1830. Hitherto unpublished.

I am much obliged dearest Mother for all the long letters you have written me since I have been in Germany, for though I have not been lucky enough to receive any one of them, I conclude they are on the way and will reach me some day or other; You will see from the date of my letter that I am in Westphalia [17] on my road to Dresden, I shall go & stay for a few days with my friend Schulte's family, & then prepare myself for the delights of Dresden pictures & Dresden Society —

I think my stay at Godesberg was a profitable one, for I have now cleared most of the difficulties w$^h$ lay in my way, in learning German. From Godesberg we went to Cologne, & came on last Friday to this place. Cologne was in a rebellion, or a spectacle as here they call it — Elberfeld has shewn symtoms of a refractory nature, & so has Dusseldorf, but the steam-boats have been bringing down troops by thousands, with a prince of the blood at their head; & order is pretty well restored [18] — Cologne as I think I

---

[16] Though this letter was dispatched (as we learn below, No. 39) just three weeks before September 28, it did not reach England until eight days after Thackeray's letter of that date.

[17] Actually Thackeray was writing from Elberfeld in the Duchy of Berg, not far from the boundaries of Westphalia.

[18] The French Revolution of July 28 and 29 had widespread repercussions in northern Germany, resulting eventually in the abdication of the rulers of

told you is in size considerable, in aspect unpromising, & in smell odious. This is the prettiest town I have seen in Germany     it is comfortable & English-like, on our arrival here we had the greatest treat possible a dinner of roast beef, & a glass of port-wine — Elberfeld is I believe one of the richest towns in Prussia, they have here a theatre to w^h I am going to night. It will be the first I have entered since I left England.

Tuesday — Miss Schulte has broken her leg, & Frau Schulte is very unwell; so I have taken my place for Cassel, & shall depart this evening at 11. Here is a new & pleasant ballad called

The Legend of Drachenfels.
Famous I ween are the Rhines 7 Hills
    In song & ode & sonnet
I know of a legend old w^h tells
Of the best of the seven the Drachenfels
    And the Dragon who lived upon it.

Deep in the mountain his dwelling it stood
    And such was the terror w^h sat oer him
That baron & squire & yeoman good
Supplied him daily with prayers & food
    And did every thing else to flatter him.

Now the Dragon would eat of a singular dish
    And the people politely obeyed his
Orders right well, I only wish

---

Brunswick, Saxony, and Hesse-Cassel. See Treitschke's *Deutsche Geschichte im Neunzehnten Jahrhundert*, Theil IV, chapter 2.

I could say he eat of fowl or fish!
Alas — he eat *Maiden Ladies!*.

One by one did the Maidens fall
    Victims to his appetite
That he bolted them petticoats stays & all
And such was the monsters wondrous swall-
    low he only made one snap at it!

Now Maidens grew scarce, & the Dragon grew thin
    And the Dragons priests looked blank
Twas the only land, the World within
Where (merely exemption from eating to win)
    The Ladies loved Brevet Rank —

But what was the joy of the Cannibal beast
    This beast with the horrid digestion,
To find one day that a favorite priest
Had brought him a beautiful maid who professed
    The faith w^h was called the Christian! —

He gazed from his den at his prey, & saw
    There was something charming in her
And he opened wide his wondrous maw
And picked his teeth with his off forepaw
    As his way was before dinner.

⟨He viewe⟩d her above & he viewed her below
   And said, "I am happy to meet you,
"But we have not much time for talking now"
(Here he showed his teeth a horrible row)
   "For I just am going to eat you!"

But why doth he bow his conquered head
   As he grovelleth low before her
Why do his eyes late so fierce & red
Now wax as pale as the eyes of the dead
   As they wildly wander oer her! —

Little he recks for the sighs or the tears
   In her bright blue eyes w$^h$ swim
But the holy cross on her breast she wears
   The Cross hath conquered him.

He uttered a low & a chopfallen growl
   As he gazed on the holy sign
He gave her at parting a horrible scowl
And fifty miles round was heard his howl
   As he crawled into the Rhine! —

Merry I trow was the maiden grown
   To see the Dragon hobble hence
For so vast was the monster who from her had flown
That the tip of his tail was seen at Cologne
   While his head reached up to Coblenz.

Schlegels book w.ʰ I talked of translating is a spurious one. The Essay I shall *not* be able to send, for the friend who was to take it is obliged to return to England now — Such as it is it is nearly done, but it w.ᵈ be of no use to send up an Essay w.ʰ shewed no reading, & books have not been within my reach. Seriously I have been very industrious; & begin to like the Study more & more — Schulte is an excellent instructor — I have bought Schiller in 18 vol. bound for £1.1 [19] — it will amuse me in my long journey to Dresden. Good bye Dearest Mother, Love to father & Mary — Ever your affectionate Son W. M. Thackeray

Rebuke me not that I have said nothing of my course of life at Godesberg — Eating, sleeping & reading German formed the principal parts of it — By the time you receive this, I shall be settled I trust at Cologne with D.ʳ Brachmann or some comfortable family — Do write directly, for six weeks silence has made me rather uncomfortable, what would it have made you dear Mother, had I not written you a line for so long a time? — I shall leave Count Hompesch's letter here; but tho' this is not far from Dusseldorf, people do not seem to know him —

## 39.          TO MRS. CARMICHAEL-SMYTH
### 28 SEPTEMBER 1830

*Address*: M.ʳˢ Carmichael Smyth. | Larkbeare House | Ottery S.ᵗ Mary's | Devonshire | England. *Postmarks*: WEIMAR 29 SEP. 1830, OC. 7 1830. Published in part, *Chapters*, pp. 121–122; additions in *Biographical Introductions*, I, xviii–xxii.

Weimar [20] Tuesday. Sept.ʳ 29.[21]

My promises, dearest Mother, have been faithfully kept; and if you have received my letters as regularly as I have written them,

[19] No doubt the edition published in Stuttgart in 1827, a set of which with Thackeray's "juvenile autograph" was in his library when he died (*Catalogue of the Library of Charles Dickens . . . Catalogue of the Library of W. M. Thackeray*, ed. J. H. Stonehouse, London, 1935, p. 176).

[20] The Pumpernickel of *Vanity Fair* and the Kalbsbraten of *Fitz-Boodle's Confessions*. For an account of life there during 1830 and 1831, see Adelheid von Schorn, *Das nachklassische Weimar*, 2 vols. (Weimar, 1911–1912).

[21] A mistake for Tuesday, September 28.

you must have received every fortnight those gems epistolary poetical & graphical w^h I have punctually sent you; for this time I have delayed my letter a week in order to see, if I could have anything to answer in the letters I expected from England — This is the ninth or tenth week of my stay in Germany, & in all that time I have not been blessed with a single line from home! —

You see the direction to my letter, w^h will with your good leave be my direction while I remain in Germany    On arriving here I found an old Schoolfellow [22] who is staying with a German family here, & who said that the place was exactly suited for me; I made every inquiry & found he was in the right for without letters of introduction I have got into the best society of the place. There is an excellent German Master,[23] & a respectable family with whom I live, w^h I think were the three things you wished me to have while in Germany

[22] We learn from John Camden Hotten (*Thackeray*, p. 26) that Thackeray "was indebted in a considerable degree for the introductions he obtained to the best families in town" to William Garrow Lettsom, who was "attached to the suite of the English Minister at Weimar." It seems likely that Lettsom is the old schoolfellow whom Thackeray mentions, though there was no English Minister in Weimar at this time, and Lettsom's first recorded appointment in the diplomatic service was as Attaché at Berlin, August 5, 1831 (*Foreign Office List*, 1884).

[23] Dr. Friedrich August Wilhelm Weissenborn (d. 1852), who had lived in Weimar since 1823. He was the friend of Eckermann and the tutor of many young Englishmen, among them Dr. Norman MacLeod (1812–1872), Scottish divine, author, and chaplain to Queen Victoria, from whose letters or conversation the following portrait of Weissenborn was put together: "He was a cultivated scholar, and combined the strangest eccentricities of character and belief with the gentlest and most unselfish of natures. He was a confirmed valetudinarian. 'My side' had become a distinct personality to him, whose demands were discussed as if it were an exacting member of his household rather than a part of his body; yet Weimar would have lost half its charm but for old Weissenborn, with his weak side, his dog Waltina, his chameleon (fruitful source of many a theory on the 'Kosmos'), his collection of eggs, and innumerable oddities of mind and body. All the English who went to Weimar loved 'the Doctor:' and no father or brother could have taken a greater interest than he did in promoting their happiness and in directing their studies." (Donald MacLeod, *Memoir of Norman MacLeod*, 2 vols., New York, 1877, I, 46–47) Thackeray was coached through *Faust* by "good old Weissenborn" (*Works*, XII, 371), borrowed money from him, and corresponded with him for more than a year after leaving Weimar.

It seems the old Grand Duke [24] had a great love for English manners & English men, & tho' the present Duke is not quite so prepossessed in our favor yet he is happy to see all the Englishmen who come here, (& there are generally three or four residing) at his Court      I have accordingly had a pair of trowsers cut into breeches, & have had the honor of making my appearance in his august presence; and in order to become a complete courtier have taken a Master in the art of Waltzing & Gallopading — There is a capital library here w^h is open to me, & an excellent theatre w^h costs a shilling per night, & a charming petite societé w^h costs nothing.

Goethe the great lion of Weimar I have not yet seen, but his daughter in law [25] has promised to introduce me.

So much for Weimar w^h I think you will agree with me, is as good a place as I could possibly select for my stay in this country — The day after I wrote to you from Elberfeldt I went by diligence to Cassel, & a dull journey it was! I don't know whether the journey or its destination was the most interesting — at Cassel I was obliged to stay three days, there being no diligence, & any other conveyance was beyond my means. All the papers said there was a revolution there, during my stay, I saw nothing of it; the same was the case at Cologne so you may suppose that these German revolutions or "Spectacles" as they call them are no very dreadful things.

Everybody who goes to Cassel sees Wilhelmshöhe; which is I think far superior to Versailles, the water works are very refresh-

[24] Karl August (1757–1828), who was succeeded by Karl Friedrich (1783–1853).

[25] Frau August von Goethe (1786–1859), the former Ottilie von Pogwisch, had been separated for many years from her husband, who was a habitual drunkard. She sought consolation for her mismarriage in her polyglot literary salon and the attentions of a series of lovers. Young Englishmen met with her particular favor, as Thackeray humorously acknowledged by dedicating "To his Britannic Majesty's Consul in Weimar" a book of sketches that he gave to her (Walther Vulpius, "Thackeray in Weimar," *Century Magazine*, LIII. 1897, p. 921). Goethe, for whom she kept house, called her "Ein verrückter Engel" (Henry Crabb Robinson, *Diary, Reminiscences, and Correspondence*, ed. Thomas Sadler, 2 vols. in one, Boston, 1898, II, 110).

ing; there is a new Castle a l'antique with some tolerable pictures, a beautiful Chapel, & a delightful armory        I went in company with a German Student, & a Herr Professor, with whom I afterwards proceeded by diligence to Gotha by way of Eisenach, at Eisenach we staid two hours, I had time to see Luthers hiding place in the old castle of Worzburg, where while all the world were seeking him he was quietly lodged, translating the Bible & having occasional tiffs with the Author of Evil. They shew you a place in his study where in the height of his wrath he discharged an inkstand at the Devil, who had long tormented him in the shape of blue-bottle fly — In performing this pilgrimage to the Worzburg I lost my dinner & got thoroughly wet through, in this unhappy state I had to proceed to Gotha, under the racking pains of hunger & rheumatism, which I am sorry to say has been my constant companion since I left Elberfeld; I have had it [in] my shoulder & my face for some time I could not use my arms, & afterwards for a considerable period I could not use my teeth! —

I slept at Gotha & came on here, & here I trust will end my travels; for though the Society is small it is remarkably good, & tho' the court is absurdly ceremonious, I think it will rub off a little of the rust wh School & College have given me.

Now I am going to ask a very absurd favor; I want a cornetcy in Sir John Kennaways yeomanry! — the men here are all in some yeomanry uniform, & if hereafter I go to other courts in Germany or in any other part of Europe, something of this sort is necessary as a court-dress — It is true that here I can do without it, but in case of my going elsewhere I must have some dress or other, & a yeomanry dress is always a handsome & respectable one; as it is I have to air my legs in black breeches, & to sport a black coat, black waistcoat & Cock-hat; looking something like a cross between a footman & a Methodist parson.

I dont know whether the dress is expensive if so, of course I must give it ⟨up⟩.

I am making rapid progress in Gallopading & my natural grace & symmetry of person greatly contribute to my advancement in that Science.

Last night we had at the theatre a translation of Hernani, the tragedy by Victor Hugo which made so much noise in Paris; [26] I would recommend you to read it if possible — we have had 3 operas Medea,[27] & the Barber of Seville & Flauto Magico; Hummel [28] conducts the Orchestra her[e] is a picture w$^h$ is somewhat like him for Mary — The Orchestra is excellent but the Singers are not first rate.

I have got a book into w$^h$ I paste the play bills, & any costumes or groups or remarks w$^h$ strike me — I have fallen in love with the Princess of Weimar,[29] who is unluckily married to Prince Charles of Prussia; I must get over this unfortunate passion w$^h$ will otherwise I fear bring me to an untimely end.

There are several very charming young persons of the female sex here. Miss v. Spiegel [30] & ditto v. Pappenheim,[31] are the eve-

[26] For the epochal first performance of *Hernani* at the Théâtre Français on February 25, 1830, see Henry Lyonnet, Les *"Premières"* de Victor Hugo (Paris, 1930), pp. 16–40.

[27] *Medea in Corinto* (1813) by Johann Simon Mayr (1763–1845).

[28] Johann Nepomuk Hummell (1778–1837), piano virtuoso and composer, who had been in his youth the pupil of Mozart and Haydn and a fellow-student with Beethoven. He was court *Kapellmeister* at Weimar from 1820 till his death.

[29] Princess Maria of Weimar (1808–1877) had married Prince Friedrich Karl of Prussia in 1827.

[30] Melanie von Spiegel, later Frau von Seckendorf, was maid of honor and principal beauty at the court of Weimar, where her father, Baron von Spiegel, was Lord Marshal. Thackeray fell in love with her almost at first sight, and though his passion did not prove lasting, his memories of her remained vivid in later life. She is the Dorothea of *Fitz-Boodle's Confessions*, and Lady Ritchie (*Chapters*, p. 110) hints that Thackeray's wooing of her was abruptly terminated by the same mishap that befell Fitz-Boodle in courting Dorothea. After leaving Weimar Thackeray saw her once again, but, alas! how changed. Lady Ritchie (*Chapters*, pp. 117–118) describes the encounter, which occurred in Venice during the summer of 1853: "We were breakfasting at a long table where a fat lady also sat a little way off, with a pale fat little boy beside her. She was stout, she was dressed in light green, she was silent, she was eating an egg. The *sala* of the great marble hotel was shaded from the blaze of sunshine, but stray gleams shot across the dim hall, falling on the palms and the orange trees beyond the lady, who gravely shifted her place as the sunlight dazzled her. Our own meal was also spread, and my sister and I were only waiting for my father to begin. He came in presently, saying he had been looking at the guest-book in the outer hall, and he had seen a name

ning belles — As I have delayed my letter a week, I must write again next week — I will send you a couple of translations from Korner, w^h will I think amuse you; they ought were the⟨y⟩ anything like the original —

How do you like my new plan of folding letters; I have written them so that you may have a book full of them if you wish to keep them. Good bye dearest Mother, pray write now you know my direction for a certainty — There are no letters from you at Dresden for I have written twice to the post office; & there were none at Bo⟨nn—⟩ write to me bei Madame Melos at Wei⟨mar⟩ & I trust you will write soon — Love ⟨to⟩ Father; tell Mary I am thinking of having a fiddle Master — God bless you dearest Mother write soon to your affectionate Son.

W. M. Thackeray.

---

which had interested him very much. 'Frau von Z. Geboren von X. It must be Amalia! She must be *here* — in the hotel,' he said; and as he spoke he asked a waiter whether Madame von Z. was still in the hotel. 'I believe that is Madame von Z.,' said the waiter, pointing to the fat lady. The lady looked up and then went on with her egg, and my poor father turned away, saying in a low, overwhelmed voice, '*That* Amalia! That cannot be Amalia.' I could not understand his silence, his discomposure. 'Aren't you going to speak to her? Oh, please do go and speak to her!' we both cried. 'Do make sure if it is Amalia.' But he shook his head. 'I can't,' he said; 'I had rather not.' Amalia meanwhile having finished her egg, rose deliberately, put down her napkin and walked away, followed by her little boy." That Thackeray was loyal to his youthful impressions of Melanie is shown by another story. Dr. MacLeod, who four winters after Thackeray's visit had himself gone to Weimar and fallen in love with Melanie (Donald MacLeod, *Memoir of Norman MacLeod*, I, 48–49), told Lady Ritchie that "years and years afterwards, when [he and Thackeray] met again on the occasion of one of the lecturing tours in Scotland, he . . . and the rest of the notabilities were all assembled to receive the lecturer on the platform, and as my father came by carrying his papers and advancing to take his place at the reading-desk, he recognized Dr. MacLeod as he passed, and in the face of all the audience he bent forward and said gravely, without stopping one moment on his way, '*Ich liebe Amalia doch*,' and so went on to deliver his lecture." (*Chapters*, pp. 119–120) It may be said in passing that the identification of Amalia with Melanie is confirmed by a comparison of the original of this letter with the text given by Lady Ritchie in *Chapters*, p. 122; for "Miss v. Spiegel" Lady Ritchie reads "Miss Amalia von X."

[31] Jenny von Pappenheim (1811–1890) was the love-child of Diana von Pappenheim and Prince Jérôme Napoléon. She and her mother had come to

40.      TO MRS. CARMICHAEL-SMYTH
## 20 OCTOBER 1830

*Address:* M<sup>rs</sup> Carmichael Smyth. | Larkbeare House | Ottery S<sup>t</sup> Mary's |
Devonshire | England. *Postmarks:* WEIMAR 23 OCT. 1830, F NO 2 1830.
Published in part, *Memorials,* pp. 350–351.

Wednesday. October 20<sup>th</sup>

Thank God, dearest Mother, that I have once more seen the
old handwriting for w<sup>h</sup> I have been for three months looking in
vain — How my letters could not have reached you I know not, for
I h⟨ave⟩ put them all (except the last one, w<sup>h</sup> you got) into the
post with my own hand — So all the fruits of my pencil & my
muse are to waste their fragrance in the desert air! [32] — I sent you
several sketches, a long ballad about the Drachenfels, & certain
songs. However they will be no great loss to you — You ask me
to give you an account of the people with whom I am, the less I say
of them the better (that is of the Mistress of the house, for she
has been detected in cheating one Englishman & would have done

---

live in the tolerant society of Weimar after Diana's final separation from her
husband. In 1830 she was a maid of honor at Karl Friedrich's court and one
of the muses of Frau von Goethe's salon. Ottilia in *Fitz-Boodle's Confessions*
is drawn in part from Fräulein von Pappenheim, to whom Thackeray paid
court after he recovered from his infatuation with Melanie. Her recollections
of Thackeray are recorded in her memoirs (Lily Braun, *Im Schatten der
Titanen*, Stuttgart, 1910, p. 115): "Thackerays, *Vanity fair* rief mir wieder
lebhaft den liebenswürdigen Verfasser ins Gedächtnis zurück, der ein so
treuer Freund meines väterlichen Hauses war; sein treffender Humor, sein
weiches Herz sprechen sich in jedem seiner Werke aus. Er war hauptsächlich
in Weimar um sein eminentes Zeichentalent zu entwickeln. Während wir
um den Teetisch sassen und sprachen, zeichnete er die humoristischsten
Szenen. Sich selbst zeichnete er in einer Minute und fing immer beim Fuss
an, ohne die Feder abzusetzen, daneben pflegte er einen kleinen Gassenjungen
hinzustellen, der ihn verspottete, da er einen durch Boxen eingeschlagenen
Nasenknochen hatte. Sonst sah er gut aus, hatte schöne Augen, volles, lockiges
Haar und war ziemlich gross. Er gehörte zu den beliebtesten Engländern, die
sich in Weimar länger aufhielten, und deren gab es genug." Jenny married
Baron Werner von Gustedt in 1838 and retired to his estate in West Prussia.
For an account of her career, see Lily Braun's *Im Schatten der Titanen.*

[32] "And waste its sweetness on the desert air," Gray's "Elegy Written in a
Country Churchyard," l. 56.

the same by another y.ʳ humble Serv.ᵗ if she could; she asks 51 dollars, £8.12 a month for board & lodging, & wine I gave her ⟨this the⟩ first month, but at the end of it told her I should go into lodgings unless she gave me better rooms for 35 dollars without wine; she acceeded to this & I am now very comfortable as to lodgings, & very civil to my hostess; who I only see at dinner & supper. There are 2 other houses in the town where boarders are taken but they are dearer & not so good; so that I shall ⟨put⟩ up with the delinquencies of my hostess in consideration of her giving the best rooms & dinners in Weimar —

I saw for the first time old Goethe to day,[33] he treated me ver⟨y⟩ kindly & rather in a more distingué manner than he used the other Englishmen here. The old man gives ⟨occasionally⟩ a tea party to w.ʰ the English & some especial favorites in the town are invited; he sent me a summons this morning to come to him at 12, I sat with him for half an hour and took my leave on the arrival of the Gross Herzog w.ʰ being interpreted means the Grand Duke; as silly a piece of Royalty as a man may meet; His father was clever & popular, the present man is neither one ⟨nor⟩ the other, & in these troublesome times a man ought to be both to secure his throne. Every body talks French here so that I have had more practice for my French than my German. There is a court twice a week; tea & cards, the latter only for the elder part of the community; the gentlemen are obliged to stand from seven till half past nine when all the world at Weimar goes to bed. The theatre here is a remarkably good one, the boxes are laid out Gallery fashion without partitions so that you can go from one part to another & chuse your Society. The prettiest woman [34] I ever saw in my life is here & I have within the last two days fallen in love with her; I trust I shall continue so for I find the sensation novel & pleasing — her name is — but I wont say what her name is — but if ever she becomes M.ʳˢ Thackeray it will be well for her & myself. There is an English family here Sir Henry Vavasour [35] & Lady V. a Miss V a

---

[33] See below, No. 1118.     [34] Melanie von Spiegel.
[35] Second Baronet (1768–1838) of Spaldington in Yorkshire, travelling with his entire family. The "small V's" were girls.

Master Ditto, & 2 small V's whose sex I am unacquainted with —
I was obliged to give them up after the first visit; for Lady V
talked of nothing ⟨but Lords⟩ Ladies Maids & large estates in
Yorkshire, wʰ I thought seem⟨ed⟩ rather incompatible with two
pair of stairs, & two servants. The weather is what is called
himmlisch hübsch here that is to say warm enough to roast you in
the day, & cold enough to freeze you in the evening.

There are some pleasant people here Count & Countess Santi ³⁶
⟨with⟩ whom I have rather struck up an alliance — Madame de
Goethe very kind but withal a great bore; she cult⟨ivates every⟩
Englishman the other evening when I went to call on ⟨her I found⟩
her with three Byrons a Moore and a Shelley on ⟨her table.⟩
Every one of my letters of recommendation are I fear lost, I put
them together with sundry other things all my books & some
wearing apparel into a large chest, when I got to the diligence
office at Elberfeld I had a row with the Prussian (& saying Prussian
⟨is⟩ saying enough against anyone) who kept the office; ⟨because⟩ I
did not take off my hat to him — he said that my tru⟨nk could⟩ not
go with me by the diligence but that it should be s⟨ent⟩ after me
free of expense by the wagon; this is six weeks ago & where the
wagon the postmaster or the trunk is I am in utter ignorance, for I
have sent repeated letters to none of wʰ have I received answer —
The reason I did not go to Schulte's was that Madame Schulte was
very ill, & her daughter had broken her leg. God bless you dearest
Mother I will write to Father to morrow or the next day. ⟨Write⟩
me again soon. I am delighted with the Uniform wʰ arrived the
same day as your letter; only I dont think the pink rosettes look
well on the leather breeches, why the bawty ³⁷ should be picked
out sky blue I cannot concieve, however these are the only faults I
have to find with it. Good bye dearest Mother Your affectionate
Son ⟨W. M. Tha⟩ckeray.

Yours this moment read, Mary's letter the same day.

³⁶ Count Santi was Russian Chargé d'Affaires in Weimar from 1828 until
his death in 1841 (von Schorn, *Das nachklassische Weimar*, I, 152–153).
³⁷ ? Bow-tie ?

41.                    TO MISS WILKIE
                    29 OCTOBER 1830

*Address:* Miss Wilkie. Bookseller | 40 Charter House Square | London | England. *Postmarks:* WEIMAR 30 OCT 1830, FPO NO 11 1830. Hitherto unpublished.

> Weimar Germany.
> Friday. October 29. 1830.

Mʳ Thackeray would be much obliged to Miss Wilkie to procure for him the following articles.

6 Quires of ⟨the b⟩est Bath Paper gilt

Mordan's Pen (ivory) & 2 boxes of pens.

Frasers town & country Magazine for Aug. Sep. Oct. N⟨ov.⟩

The four last numbers of the Examiner & the Literary Gazette.

The Comic Annual, the Keepsake if published, & any 2 others of the best Annuals; wʰ Mʳ T will leave to Miss Wilkie's taste to select for him, if she will have the kindness to do s⟨o.⟩

Bombastes Furioso [38] wʰ may be got at Kenneths dramatic Repository Bow Street, the edition with Geo. Cruikshank's illustrations if published.

This parcel is to be sent directed to Dʳ Frohrib, Industrie⟨l⟩ Comptoir,[39] Weimar Germany, to Black & Young the foreign booksellers.


42.                    TO MRS. CARMICHAEL-SMYTH
                    17 NOVEMBER 1830

*Address:* Mʳˢ Carmichael Smyth. | Larkbeare House | Ottery Sᵗ Mary's | Devonshire | England. *Postmarks:* WEIMAR 17 NOV. 1830, FPO NO. 25 1830. Hitherto unpublished.

There are three letters now on their way to Larkbeare dearest Mother, which I suppose in the course of time you will receive —

---

[38] See above, No. 9.

[39] Dr. Weissenborn is described by Carl Schüddekopf (*Goethes Tod*, Leipzig, 1907, p. 181) as "Mitarbeiter am Bertuch-Froriep'schen Industrie-Comptoir."

What are the laws of the post I know not, your first letter I received ten, & your second twenty days after date.

At this present writing I am recovering from a fit of sore throat, which has for the last week deprived me of the power of speaking & almost of swallowing, forcing on me a temperance not at all agreeing with my habits or inclinations — The weather here is warm & fine, last year at this time, the ground had been two feet deep in snow for a month — The news here is that the King of the French has resigned, that William the fourth has been pelted by the populace, & the Duke of Wellington killed some say by the assassins steel, & others that he has been blown up a gas-pipe. There are some unpleasant rumours afloat about potatoes & mangel-wurzel, w$^h$ I will forbear to touch on.

The last time I wrote, I was, if you remember violently in love; I am still violently in love but it is with another person; [40] Tho' as there are only two young ladies at the Court of Weimar with whom one can fall in love, I don't know what I shall do at the end of another fortnight, about which time I expect again to be free.

I am disappointed in German. I begin now to be able to comprehend it a little, & must say that I have met with nothing which comes up to my expectation of the language. I have read Faust with w$^h$ of course I was delighted, but not to that degree I expected — some little pieces of various poets w$^h$ I think are all very very mediocre — I have read some French things of Victor Hugo's which I think you would like, they infinitely surpass all the horrors we have in England. Han d'Islande, Büg Jargal, & Le dernier Jour d'un condamné [41] — We have had his tragedy Hernani which made so much noise in Paris acted here — Hummel occasionally play[s] at court & at the theatre  The other evening he gave a concert for the benefit of certain children & widows — Beethovens Battle of Victoria was played; I never saw half a dozen men so excited as the English were, when Rule Britannia was played — I was amused with this celebrated piece of music first were heard

[40] Jenny von Pappenheim.
[41] Early romances by Hugo, published in 1823, 1826, and 1829 respectively.

the English drums & trumpets then French ditto then rule Britannia — then Malbrooke, then cannons & rattles representing guns, then Malbrooke sung small, & to conclude God save the King with Variations [42] — We were going to have had a play here, w^h is given up — The piece was written by myself & another, in a moment of sobriety we burnt it, & thus ended ⟨Will⟩iam Tell, w^h was the title thereof — It is needless to ⟨say⟩ that I was to have been the heroine.

Old Goethe's son is just dead; [43] he was from all accounts an excellent young man, always drunk post meridian his wife is not very disconsolate, but it will be a terrible blow to the old man; he died at Rome; I suppose he was the man that M^r & M^rs Phillips met in Switzerland — Remember me to all your neighbours dearest Mother; I am going courting now — Love to Father & Mary Your affectionate Son. — W. M. Thackeray.

I wish I had been at home to have administered a little correction to the hopeful Charles —

{I don't know what I have written dearest Mother, but I feel half tipsy with what I know not certainly not wine, as no drop of that has entered my mouth to day — whatever is the cause tipsiness is the effect,} excuse therefore my letter w^h is very rambling & unsatisfactory — Tell Mary I wonder I have not heard from her — I will write next to Grand Mamma — Good bye dearest Mother —

[42] In chapter 62 of *Vanity Fair* "Die Schlacht bei Vittoria" is performed in Pumpernickel with similar effect.

[43] August von Goethe died on October 27, 1830. His widow, who had long posed as a *femme incomprise*, wrote to a friend that she regretted the nature of her life with him rather than his death. "Du weisst es ja, ‚zu spät' ist das Losungswort meines Lebens gewesen; und so wird es auch hier sein." (*Aus Ottilie von Goethes Nachlass*, 2 vols., Weimar, 1912–1913, II, 291)

43.          TO MRS. CARMICHAEL-SMYTH
                    3 DECEMBER 1830

*Address:* Mʳˢ Carmichael Smyth. | Larkbeare House | Ottery Sᵗ Mary's |
Devonshire | England. *Postmarks:* WEIMAR 4 DEC. 1830, FPO DE. 13
1830. Published in part, *Memorials,* pp. 351–352.

                                        Friday December 3.

This is the only night in the week, dearest Mother, in wʰ there is
not a court or a play. & wisely is it ordained inasmuch as the Post
to England goeth out on this unoccupied night — Here is Christmas coming & I for the first time these ten years not at home to
participate in the turkey & ham — be it so — I must fast on kraut &
beef, while, you ye happy natives of England, luxuriate on mince
pies & lozenges plumpudding & cherry-brandy! — I firmly believe [44] (& as an experienced traveller my belief ought to be of some
weight) that my fatherland is the only place for being comfortable
in — there all the delights of life, here schnaps & stoves & rheumatism! — two months ago I was in love with two young ladies — but
the day dream hath passed away, & I am left here without a flame
(for as I said we have only stoves) & without a being who cares
twopence whether I stay or go — I tried an experiment the other
day, hinting that I was going to have £15000 a year, & the respect I
received was wonderful, but I have undeceived the natives, & am
treated sans respect & ceremony.

The old ladies here seem to be bent on marrying their daughters,
two have told me that they did not wish *much* money for their
Melanies or their Eugenies, but merely a competency — but I did
not speak on the hint [45] and as the respectable dowagers find they
can make nothing of me they almost cut me. You will think I am
talking scandal, but in this little place, as soon as an Englishman

[44] Thackeray wrote *I firmly belief.*
[45] Unlike Othello, after he has recounted his adventures to Desdemona:
                         She thank'd me,
          And bade me, if I had a friend that lov'd her,
          I should but teach him how to tell my story,
          And that would woo her. Upon this hint I spake.
(*Othello,* I, iii, 163–166)

arrives inquiries are made whether he is an eldest or only Son, and as all Englishmen are rich or supposed to be so, the round of mothers offer the round of daughters who are as you may suppose by this time rather stale.

I lament my trusty blue coat in England, it would be of amazing comfort to me here — We have had no snow yet, but the weather is awfully cold, so that a complete casing of flannel has been requisite — Old Goethe the Glory of Weimar & of Germany was very nearly carried off by the bursting a blood vessel — but the old man has recovered in an amazing manner, & now at 83 [46] writes as hard, & drinks as gaily as he did twenty years ago.

I have read a good deal of Goethe & Schiller, the latter is by far the favorite here — Goethe is by practice & profession a libertine, Schiller was on the contrary a man whose religion & morals were unexceptionable — It must have been a fine sight twenty years ago, this little court, with Goethe Schiller & Wieland & the old Grand Duke & Duchess to ornament it — The present Duke is I believe good natured, but he is imprudent & proud for he never will condescend to speak with any of his subjects who have not a von tacked to their names — He has got a big valet with whom he boxes occasionally, the valet as in duty bound, falls under the vigorous "coups" of his Königliche Hoheit; an officer told me that he saw him one day roaring on the ground, & the simple Grand Duke said, "Get up Fritz, have I hurt thee, here is a gulden to console thee" — The man must make a good thing of it if he does it with proper discretion —

Did not I tell you how cheap fur is here? You may have a pelisse for a guinea —

The more I see of it, the more I am sure that if I could in any way procure an attachéship, I could work my way in the profession — Most of the men are rich & idle: (I speak of the Berlin & Paris ones) & if a poor man ⟨would⟩ but be industrious — he would have a double spur & a ⟨double⟩ advantage — Of the four men at Berlin 2 have been in the guards & got tired, & now they are in the corps diplomatique and are tired — they say the profession is inter-

[46] Goethe was eighty-one at this time.

esting enough but the town is so dull — I have been taking a little recreation in the fields of Civil-law, & as I expected have not found the Pandects of Justinian much to my taste. I suppose however it must be — a clergyman I cannot be, nor a physician so I must drudge up poor & miserable the first part of my life, & just reach the pinnacle (or somewhere near it I trust, when my eyes will hardly be able to see the prospect I have been striving all my life to arrive at — These are the pleasures of the law — & to these I must I fear dedicate myself — As I have thought a great deal on the profession I *must* take; & the more I think of it the less I like it — However I believe it is the best among the positive professions & as such I must take it, for better or worse. I thought a little time ago the army would have done, but now I suppose there will be no war & no advancement. In this country, I could live & have a reasonable family upon the income I have that is if I can mend the expensive habits, wʰ that blessed University Cambridge has taught me — Don't suppose I lament not reading Mathematics, but I am sorry I ever was at the University — I do not regret my employment of time there, but of money — I am glad I have come here, for I am a good deal by myself, & read & think a little — and in learning German, I acquire a tangible money-getting advantage — This letter has been filled with I's, but they will interest my dear Mother, as they will shew her the state of mind & feelings of her affectionate son — W. M. Thackeray.

Best love for father, & "best wishes" for his farm — I have commenced a letter for Mary in the shape of a song of Goethe wʰ shall soon appear.

## 44. TO MRS. CARMICHAEL-SMYTH
### 31 DECEMBER 1830

*Address:* Mʳˢ Carmichael Smyth | Larkbeare House | Ottery Sᵗ Mary's | Devonshire | England. *Postmarks:* WEIMAR 1 JAN. 1831, FPO JA 10 1831. Hitherto unpublished.

Your letters always make me sorrowful, dearest Mother, for there seems some hidden cause of dissatisfaction, some distrust which you do not confess & cannot conceal & for which on looking into myself I can find no grounds or reason — {Idleness} not idleness irresolution & extravagance are charges w.ʰ have been long laid against me, & to which I know I am still but too open — but I can say that tho' still idle & extravagant I am not so much so as when in England, for here I have more inducement to industry & less temptation to expense.

You seem to take it so much to heart, that I gave up trying for Academical honors [47] — perhaps Mother I was too young to form opinions but I did form them — & these told me that there was little use in studying what could after a certain point be of no earthly use to me — they told me that subtle reasonings & deep meditations on angles & parallelograms might be much better employed on other subjects — that three years industrious waste of time might obtain for me mediocre honors w.ʰ I did not value at a straw, is it because I have unfortunately fallen into this state of thinking that you are so dissatisfied with me —

At school it was the same thing I never obtained anything like an honor there — I was not stupid — when I left school I had read as much of other subjects as any boy of my age — Do not lay it all to my wilful idleness — Mother mother would it not have been better to have consulted my inclinations & have fostered them than to have persevered in a system which was determined on long before the object of it had manifested any talents or desires for or against it — For ten years of my life I was at school, it was thought that this discipline of misery was necessary to improve & instruct me; with all the power I had I struggled against it — the system was persevered in — & the benefit of ten years schooling was a little Latin & a very little Greek — which a year at any other time would have given me — I know that the system you pursued you considered was the best — it might be that any other would have been attended with the same result — but I who was the object of

[47] Important factors in Thackeray's leaving Cambridge which he does not mention in the following paragraphs were his heavy losses at play and his fear that the temptation to gamble might prove too strong for him if he remained at the University. See Appendix IV.

it because now I am old enough to think & to act a little for myself am {called} *thought* idle & ungrateful — because I consider it unsuited to me, & do what I can to pursue a different one — Do not fancy me dearest Mother, angry or undutiful in writing what I have done — all my purpose in it is to beg & entreat you not to form wishes for my entering on pursuits wʰ if you thought as I do you wᵈ think it my duty to avoid — You will think me ungrateful, because I set myself so resolutely against what I know to be your wish, I am very young but if I have had any experience at all it has been in the sysem of education which you wish me to adopt — I wish to God that I could so alter or smother my feelings as to be able to adopt it — for then I should have at any rate the satisfaction of knowing that I acted according to yʳ wishes — but I can not smother them, I can not alter them — tho I have struggled long, much longer than you believe, Mother, to do so. In my reading & my pursuits here I have had a freedom which I never enjoyed in England — & I hope you will feel the benefit it has done me.

I will not alter or look again at a word I have written it may be badly written but it is strongly felt. It may give you some idea of the misery wʰ every letter I have had from home has given me — for they have all more or less spoken of the same subject — they have all told me that you are angry & discontented with me — & instead of looking forward with pleasure to the time of receiving your letter — I have been almost afraid to open them knowing the reproaches & the misery which not the words but the tenor of them conveys — Do not dearest Mother suppose anything ungrateful or undutiful in what I here have said — but I do trust you will feel more confidence in me — that you will not fancy that I can do nothing in life because I believe that study at the University is almost waste of time — that you will hope with me that I may be able to exert myself successfully or not as soon as age or circumstance may bring me to a worthier object & a nobler sphere.

The questions you wish answered I will to the best of my power the next time I write — There is no English Chaplain here — but the Germans are very good & I can now understand them pretty well — In the shape of writing I have translated several things of

Goethes a play of Kotzebues [48] — & am going to commence on a short history of Germany [49] which will instruct me both in history & German — When I first came here I did not go to Church very regularly as my attendance there was productive but of small profit — as I begin to comprehend the language of course I shall attend more regularly — The doctrine here is not near so strict as in England — many of the dogmas by w$^h$ we hold are here disregarded as allegories or parables — or I fear by most people as fictions altogether. They call our Religion in England too "objective" & not refined enough for their more mature understandings — But more of this another time, till then dearest Mother believe me in spite of what may be after all only a conceited rhapsody believe me dearest Mother your affectionate Son W. M. Thackeray

Dec 31.

[48] In the Morgan Library there is a fragmentary manuscript in Thackeray's hand with the following title page:

"The poor Poet — a drama in one act
from the German of
Augustus von Kotzebue.
as it was performed with unbounded
applause
at the Adelphi Theatre —

| | |
|---|---|
| Lawrence Simple | M$^r$ Matthews. |
| Edmond | M$^r$ Hemmings |
| Theresa | M$^{rs}$ Yates |
| M$^{rs}$ M$^c$Crab | M$^{rs}$ Daly." |

[49] The manuscript of Thackeray's incomplete translation of the *Kompendium der deutschen Reichsgeschichte* (third edition, 1819) of Konrad Mannert (1756–1834) is also preserved in the Morgan Library.

45.    TO MRS. CARMICHAEL-SMYTH
18 JANUARY 1831

*Address:* M^rs Carmichael Smyth. | Larkbere House | Ottery S^t Mary's |
Devonshire. | England. *Postmarks:* WEIMAR 19 JAN. 1831, FPO JA. 28
1831. Extracts published, *Biographical Introductions*, I, xxi-xxii.

I suppose dearest Mother that George [1] must have thought the
story of the caricature would raise me in your good opinion otherwise he would never have made it — I drew a caricature of M^r
Harte it is true, but as for publishing it it never once entered my
imagination — The said M^r Harte is a Jew, who wanted to persuade George to try for some borough, & pay all the expenses of it —
With the merit of having dissuaded him from this very hazardous
project I believe I must "gild my humble name."

I have left Madame Melos for I detected her in one or two
flagrant instances of cheating, & am now in lodgings at the Court
coopers in the Breiten Gasse — They are cheaper & much more
comfortable — for I am not interrupted in my reading, w^h I am
happy to say has been latterly pretty steady — It is a pleasant thing,
after a few months of pleasant study, to have all the thoughts of
great men & the beauties of great poets thus opened to one, & to
roam (chained as yet to a dictionary it is true) through regions of
w^h one has only heard, as of a Paradise to which only the elect are
admitted.

I went over to Erfurt the other day to see the Robbers,[2] a play
w^h is a little too patriotic & free for our court theatre; an actor of
this place accompanied me, & took me behind the scenes, thereby
revealing to me all the mysteries of a German theatre; he introduced me to Devrient [3] the Kean of Germany, who in several particulars resembles his illustrious brother of the sock or the buskin;

[1] Possibly George Carmichael-Smyth (1803–1890), the Major's youngest
brother, later a Major-General in the Bengal Army and the author of a *History
of the Reigning Family of Lahore* (1847).

[2] Schiller's *Die Räuber* (1781).

[3] Ludwig Devrient (1784–1832), the celebrated German Shakespearian
actor.

his great character is Franz Moor in the robbers, & I think I never
saw anything so terrible — Franz is a very wicked dog, who has
first induced his father to disinherit his elder brother Carl, & then
put that worthy & unsuspecting governor in an ancient tower to
starve! — Carl becomes captain of a band of robbers discovers his
father, burns his fraters castle of w.ʰ Franz was the master, & de-
livers himself into the hands of Justice. There is a prayer ⁴ w.ʰ

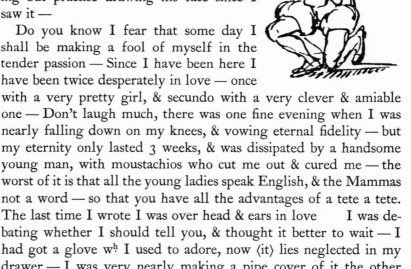

Franz makes while his castle is being attacked w.ʰ has the most awful effect that
can well be fancied — "I am no common
murderer mein Herr Gott" &c — that picture is as like the man as may well be w.ʰ is
saying a great deal, but I have done nothing but practise drawing his face since I
saw it —

Do you know I fear that some day I
shall be making a fool of myself in the
tender passion — Since I have been here I
have been twice desperately in love — once
with a very pretty girl, & secundo with a very clever & amiable
one — Don't laugh much, there was one fine evening when I was
nearly falling down on my knees, & vowing eternal fidelity — but
my eternity only lasted 3 weeks, & was dissipated by a handsome
young man, with moustachios who cut me out & cured me — the
worst of it is that all the young ladies speak English, & the Mammas
not a word — so that you have all the advantages of a tete a tete.
The last time I wrote I was over head & ears in love     I was debating whether I should tell you, & thought it better to wait — I
had got a glove w.ʰ I used to adore, now ⟨it⟩ lies neglected in my
drawer — I was very nearly making a pipe cover of it the other
day but I thought of the value at [which] I had once held it, & restored it to its obscurity — Now this bout is very well over, but
what I fear is that I may be popping the question some day, &
repenting very sincerely of it the day after. Here however I am
quite safe — for there is not a soul else to fall in love with —

⁴ In Act V, scene i.

I have nothing more to say, dearest Mother, but to wish you as good health & as mild weather as your son is enjoying here, I hope Miss Kennaway will not write any more letters in the name of Swing, unless she wishes a seven years trip to Botany bay or perhaps a life of religious seclusion on board the hulks — I admire Fathers new Seal very much — I should not at all wonder at soon having a beard, which I am sure Mary will be very happy to hear — God bless you dearest Mother, love to Father and all at Larkbeare

Your affectionate Son.

W. M. Thackeray.

Tuesday 18<sup>th</sup> January.

46.          TO MRS. CARMICHAEL-SMYTH<br>25 JANUARY 1831

*Address:* M<sup>rs</sup> Carmichael Smyth. | Larkbeare House | Ottery S<sup>t</sup> Mary's | Devonshire | England. *Postmarks:* WEIMAR, 26 JAN. 1831, FPO FE. 3 1831. Published in part, *Memorials*, pp. 353–354.

I did not, dearest Mother, complain of any particular expression or any particular letter, I only thought, that the tenor of all your letters was despondency & dissatisfaction — such was not your meaning I now know, but even had it been so — I know that *I should have deserved it* — That letter was an absurd & unkind effort on my part to put off the sense of my own unworthiness, by laying it on *you* — I have been idle extravagant & ungrateful, thwarting as it were by a regular system, all the plans your superior affection & experience had formed for me — This is the conduct w<sup>h</sup> the only child, who ought to have responded to the ceaseless & invariable kindness of two anxious parents by some thing like gratitude, something like industry, has been through the whole course of his life pursuing — But I am young yet, Mother, it is not too late, and trust one day to work for myself a name, & for you something like satisfaction & confidence in me. — The Bar I only gave up because I thought some thing better might be done for me, I know it is the only profession w<sup>h</sup> is at all suitable to me, & if I can count upon having tomorrow the feelings I have to day, I will fulfil as far as in me lies, the duties of it — I do not think of it with despondency, I look forward to it with gladness — not like the chimerical advantages resulting from triangles & parallelograms, but as a noble & tangible object; an honorable profession, & I trust in God a certain fame — I have been long eager to acquire this fame, and my method has been an original one, lying on my sofa, reading novels, & dreaming of it — but there is yet time and may God grant me the means of properly employing it! — A law degree, I can obtain, without a permanent residence at Cambridge, that is to say by residing there only a certain number of weeks in a year; that is to say if it is necessary to take a degree at all — this I could learn with more certainty in London than at the University — In 2 more months I shall have learnt German enough for practical purposes that is to say to be able to read with a Dictionary & a little trouble all that I wish — Shall I then return to England and begin on my profession? — I am nearly twenty years old at that age my Father had been for five years engaged in his [5] — I do believe Mother that it is not merely an appetite for novelty w^h prompts me but a desire to enter really a profession & to do my duty in it — I am fully aware how difficult and disagreeable my task must be for the first four years, but I have an end in view, & an independence to gain, and if I can steadily keep this before me I shall not I trust flinch from the pursuit of them.

The "row" in London is something like the caricature of M^r Harte — a romance founded on fact — We were walking in the Haymarket, & I was considerably ahead, carrying a dressing case w^h George had given me — and one of the party was insulted by some hackney coachmen  this was all the row in w^h I was ever concerned, there was some talk of fighting the hackney coachmen w^h however I did not second — had such an occurrence taken place of course I must have joined in it, but it is not an employment of w^h I am fond & I therefore kept away from it until I thought a combat was really about to commence when I came up — Nothing of the

[5] Richmond Thackeray entered the East India Company's Civil Service at the age of fifteen.

sort however happened — & in this lies the head and front of my offending [6] — I told one of the said impertinent jarveymen that I would call the police w<sup>h</sup> I believe stopped the disturbance —

God bless you dearest Mother — do not despair of me — I will go to the bar not a good mathematician, but a good lawyer — It is not fair that Mary should have the start of me in the marrying way — I hope to have yet the honour of gallopading at her hoch-zeit as they say at Berlin — Ask Father as a favour to me to get well again — I am but a poor hand at writing about affection & love but I hope you & he give me credit for feeling it — Grand Mamma's rout is over I suppose — It wont be long I hope before I appear at one of them in the fancy costume of a Gentleman of the court of Saxe Weimar-Eisenach &c. Good bye dearest Mother Your affte Son,

W. M. Thackeray.

25<sup>th</sup> January.

47.       TO MRS. CARMICHAEL-SMYTH
?-25 FEBRUARY 1831

*Address:* M<sup>rs</sup> Carmichael Smyth. | Larkbeare House | Ottery S<sup>t</sup> Mary's | Devon. | England. *Postmarks:* WEIMAR 26 FEB. 1831, FPO MR 8 1831. Published in part, *Memorials,* pp. 352–353; additions in *Biographical Introductions,* I, xxiii.

Men say that ———'s glancing eyes
    Wander too fond & free —
But in gazing thus on all the world
    They have a look for me!
As if the something something Sun
Was destined but to shine on one! [7]

The explanation

Blinded by the rays of her eyes I am giving myself extatically up to — (I cant finish this sentence) — You must fancy another

[6] *Othello,* I, iii, 80.
[7] There is a first draft of these lines in the Morgan Library Weimar notebook.

picture in w.ʰ the newcomer is standing between me & the Sun, & giving me leisure to see & be wise.

Here dearest Mother you have the beginning of a rapturous ode, on the innumerable beauties & perfections of a certain Mademoiselle de Pappenheim, with whom when I last wrote home I

fancied myself eternally in love — The fond & free wanderings of her eyes as noted above had been tolerated on my part, because I thought that they were directed oftener towards my unprepossessing physiognomy than to any other — & so they were for a week or more — but a gentleman [8] arrived who had been in the guards — is heir to ten thousand a year — has several waistcoats of the most magnificent pattern, & makes love speeches to admiration — he has therefore cut me out — as he will be cut out some day in his turn — Flirting is a word much in vogue — but I think jilting is the proper term in this my (unfortunate or fortunate as you please) desertion. In spite, therefore, of my efforts to the contrary I shall come home heart-whole at last. "Perish the man," says M. Benjamin Constant,

[8] Caledon George Du Pre (1803–1886), older son of James Du Pre, Wilton Park, Buckinghamshire. He served in the first Life Guards, was conservative M. P. for Buckinghamshire from 1839 to 1874, and in 1870 succeeded to an estate that thirteen years later was worth £10,500 annually (Bateman, *Great Landowners*, p. 145). He married in 1833 and had seven children. Thackeray neglects to mention among Du Pre's qualifications that he was a cousin of Du Pre Alexander (1777–1839), second Earl of Caledon.

who in the enjoyment of his first love — does not believe it will be his *last* [9] — My two first are over, I hope I may be yet allowed a few more before I have done —

I indited the first part of my letter a few days ago dearest Mother; & see that it concerns an "old flame of mine" as middle aged gentlemen say. The flame has gone out, & now I scarcely know what has become of even the cinders —

You will observe that I treated you to a a small type and a large sheet of paper, for I intended to pour out my whole heart to you — but now alas I have not any heart to pour out — I don't mean that I'm in love again, only that all the circumstances of my "attachment" are obliterated from my too fickle breast.

> This world is empty
> This heart is dead
> It's hopes & its wishes
> For ever are fled.[10]

as Schiller says; or rather as is said in an admirable translation of that great poet, by a rising young man of the name of Thackeray — Talking of Schiller — I am in possession of his handwriting and his veritable court-sword — & I do believe him to be after Shakspeare The Poet. I should like if I stay here until the spring to take a walk over the Hartz Mountains, & likewise if possible over the Saxon Swiss w^h is in the neighbourhood of Dresden. Some day when I have nothing better to do — I will return to Germany, & take a survey of the woods and country of it w^h are little known — I think with a sketch-book a note-book, & I fear still a Dictionary I could manage to concoct a book w^h would pay me for my trouble, & w^h would be a novelty in England. There are plenty of dry descriptions of public buildings, pictures views armories & so forth — but the People of Germany are not known in England, & the more I learn of them the more interesting they appear to me —

---

[9] "Malheur à l'homme qui, dans les premiers moments d'une liaison d'amour, ne croit pas que cette liaison doit être éternelle!" (*Adolphe*, chapter 3.)

[10] From Thekla's song in *Die Piccolomini*, Act III, scene vii:
Das Herz ist gestorben, die Welt ist leer,
Und weiter gibt sie dem Wunsche nichts mehr.

Customs, & costumes — and National Songs, stories &c with w^h the country abounds, & w^h I would be glad to learn, & the "British Public" also I think — I read yesterday in Galignanis' Messenger (the Paris English Paper) M^r Perceval's [11] speech for a General Fast — so much has it struck me that I think of setting aside a day for the purpose — it is a noble speech, I think, a relic of those glorious old Church and King times w^h are gone by I fear in my "Vaterland" — I have been reading Shakspeare in German, if I could ever do the same for Schiller in English I should be proud of have conferred a benefit on my country — Goethe is a noble poet, & as interesting an old man to speak to & look upon as I ever saw, but alas that I must say it — I believe he is little better than an old rogue — It was a character which I was very unwilling to give him, but it is the strict & uncomfortable truth — one would have thought that a genius so extraordinary as his would have been exempt from the little mean money-getting propensities to w^h it appears he is addicted — but I am at the end of my sheet. Love to all at home Dearest Mother Goodnight — ever y^r affte Son

W. M. Thackeray

Friday 25 Feb:

[11] Spencer Perceval (1795–1859), a son of the Prime Minister of the same name, was at this time M. P. for Newport on the Isle of Wight. A religious enthusiast affiliated with Irving's Catholic Apostolic Church, he interpreted the troublous times preceding the Reform Bill as a warning of God's displeasure with His people.

48.       TO ROBERT LANGSLOW
JUNE 1831

Hitherto unpublished. My text is taken from a transcript supplied by Mrs. Fuller.

Essex Court Temple,[12]

My dear Mr. Langslow,

It appears with regard to my engagement with Mr. Tapprell [13] some misunderstanding exists, which I am happy to be able to remedy.

I had asked a friend and country neighbour of mine Mr. Elliot the barrister, what course of reading he should recommend me to pursue and whether he could introduce me to a special pleader with whom I might read. This last question I asked him by letter the day I returned from Cambridge for I was sorry I had lost so much time and wished as much as possible to make up for my idleness. On the same evening (after I had sent the letter) you called on me and offered me assistance which I was most glad and grateful to accept. The next morning came a note from Elliott saying that he had spoken with Mr. Taprell with whom I might read either immediately or next term. Mr. Taprell recommended my beginning immediately, which I did.[14] You will now see, I am sure, that I was placed in circumstances which rendered it impossible for me to ask advice which otherwise I should so gladly have followed.

My only fault lay in not having consulted you before I com-

[12] Thackeray had chambers at 5 Essex Court from June 3, 1831, when he was admitted to the Middle Temple, until November, 1833 (John Hutchinson, *Catalogue of Notable Middle Templars*, London, 1902, p. 241). It will be recalled that the Temple figures in several of Thackeray's stories, most notably in *Pendennis* and "The Amours of Mr. Deuceace."

[13] William Taprell, a special pleader, whose chambers were at 1 Hare Court (*Law List*, 1831), was Thackeray's master for some months. G. P. Elliot had chambers at 2 Essex Court and went on the western circuit, Exeter and Devon sessions. He was a special pleader rather than a barrister. (*Law List*, 1832)

[14] Thackeray was admitted to the Temple during the Trinity term, which extended in 1831 from May 23 to June 13. He would otherwise have had to wait until November 2, when the Michaelmas term began.

menced reading, but I found myself in a manner committed to read with Mr. Taprell, and knowing myself to be so idle was glad to impose on myself a positive and necessary duty instead of one of a less binding nature, and as I now see the thing I do believe I was right.

Ever my dear Mr. Langslow,

Affectionately yours,

W. M. Thackeray.

I have heard from my uncle Frank whom I shall answer directly.

49.        TO EDWARD FITzGERALD [15]
18 JULY 1831

*Address:* Edward Fitzgerald Esq^re  Hitherto unpublished.  *Endorsed:* First Letter after our meeting in London in 1831.

Bridgewater July 18. 1831.

I must have a half hour's talk with you tonight, dear Fitzgerald, for I am quite alone & in no mood to pursue the very unpleasant task w^h I have taken on myself to perform — Have you been botanizing, or poetizing, or talking with your friend M^r Nursey [16] about Rembrandt & Elizabethan houses, or sailing on your river with your sister? — I dont know what should put me in so sentimental a mood, but do you know I have been for the last half-hour drinking tea, & thinking about you & your sister — you must find it very pleasant having a sister whom you can talk to & love as much as you will     I am staying here alone doing that stupid book [17] at the rate of about 3 pages a day, Schulte is here to be sure, but we

[15] See *Memoranda.*

[16] FitzGerald was living in a house owned by his father at Naseby. Among his neighbors was Perry Nursey of Little Bealings, an amateur artist and musician. The sister whom Thackeray mentions was probably Andalusia FitzGerald (d. 1879), later Mrs. De Soyres.

[17] Mannert's *Kompendium der deutschen Reichsgeschichte.* See above, No. 43.

THACKERAY IN 1831

*From a sketch by James Spedding*

have had 2 rows already, one about Matthew [18] who lives a little way from here & who has been to see me — he is improved in mind, & appearance for he does not look the rake he used — & has met with some very sad & trying experience since last I saw him — all that I hope for him is that he may get through every other difficulty as honorably as he has his late one.

I left London a very few days after you, for I felt very miserable & solitary there I used to go & walk in Regent Street but the place was a desert without your fashionable form      I tried the Divans,[19] & felt just as I used to do at School, on going into the "Strangers' Room" where I had last seen my parents so I did the wisest thing I could do paid my bill, & hastened home to an expecting family circle — Departing thence to Bridgewater I hied — German my object bold resolve my guide      I purpose here three days or more to stay — Whence to the Mansion of the Reverend J- Matthew's at Kilve near Bridgewater away Where if you wish to write to me you may, & this is all that I in rhyme can say —

Do write to me, old fellow, for a letter from you will do me good & make me happy — though I am tolerably happy at present, for I feel proud in thinking that my dinner only costs me eighteen pence & that in four days I have only drunk half a bottle of wine — The paper on w.ʰ I write cost me sixpence a quire & I have no doubt you will be a little angry with my economy that is if you read my letter — Now the answer I expect from you must be prompt & full the lines of it must be as close at least as these on this page, & the

---

[18] Henry Matthew (1807–1861), third son of the Rev. John Matthew of Kilve in Somerset, with whom Thackeray had been intimate during his second year at Cambridge and whom he later called "my idol of youth" (see below, No. 593). Though Matthew matriculated at Balliol College, Oxford, in 1825 and was enrolled at Sidney Sussex College, Cambridge, in 1830, he received a degree from neither university. In later life he was Rector of Eversholt in Bedfordshire. It may be surmised that he supplied some traits of George Brandon in *A Shabby Genteel Story*.

[19] The attractions of these smoking lounges are enthusiastically set forth in an advertisement for an "elegant DIVAN now open at 102, Strand" in *The Theatrical Observer* of July 19, 1830: "Here I find matchless cigars, exquisite coffee, profusion of magazines and newspapers, and elegant decorations render the establishment the very essence of comfort and fashion."

matter of it infinitely more amusing — Some fool has remarked in the Latin Grammar the blessed source of all my quotations that Gens humana novitatis avida est — at the present moment I most respectfully though decidedly deny the truth of the assertion as regards me — for lo!  I am surrounded by novelty & I regard it [not] — Balls routs & races I pass them by with scorn, & had rather receive a letter from you without a particle of news than any earthly blessing w$^h$ I can call to mind — but I have got a headache & am going to bed — God bless you

I am twenty years old to day, & I don't know why this birthday has awakened a number of solemn & unpleasant feelings, w$^h$ such an anniversary never raised before — But I was looking back yesterday, & I cannot find a single day in the course of my life which has been properly employed — I can only behold a melancholy succession of idleness & dissipation, which now leaves me without mental satisfaction, & I fear without proper repentance — I looked by chance at the opposite page after I wrote the word repentance, & do you know seeing that account of my dinners & wine drinking has quite gladdened me, & made me think there is some chance for me after all.  Of one thing I am determined that I never will practise the law, or at least will retire from it, before my business should occupy me too much — This perhaps is not very likely, & leaves me just in my old place in spite of what "I have determined" — Write to me very soon — how I do long for the time when we may roam through Regent Street, & drink fat chocolate as heretofore — And now I am come to a phrase, w$^h$ I find wondrous puzzling to construct properly — Believe me your — fill it up as you think old fellow — In the whole catalogue of yours truly sincerely affectionately &c — I can't find one half warm enough.

W. M. Thackeray —

Write to me at Budleigh Salterton Devon.

50.            TO FRAU VON GOETHE
26? AUGUST 1831

*Address:* A Madame | la Baronne O. de Goethe | Weimar en Saxe | Alle-
magne. *Postmark:* August 26, 1831. Partially published in translation by Dr.
Walther Vulpius, "Thackeray und Weimar," *Westermanns Monatshefte*,
CXXIX (1921), 590–592, who records the address. My text and the post-
mark are taken from a literal transcript by Professor Harold Strong Gulliver,
*Thackeray's Literary Apprenticeship* (Valdosta, 1934), pp. 28–29.

Larkbeare House Ottery St. Mary's Devonshire. I don't know,
dear Madame de Goethe, what excuse I have for troubling you
with a letter now, for I have no news to communicate, & if I felt
gratitude for your great kindness to me, I ought to have expressed
it long ago. Pray don't suppose that because I have been dilatory I
am ungrateful; & accept the only excuse I can make, that many
times when I wished to write, I have been very busy, & many more
times very lazy.

I arrived in England in time enough to be very ill myself, & to
find my father & mother in the same condition, as soon as I got well
I went to London & kept my first term at the Temple. When in
London I saw Naylor [20] once, Lettsom very often (he is going to
Berlin in DuPre's place as attache) Dupre I met in rather a characteristic situation for him, he was standing at the door of Howell &
James' (a famous ladies shop in London) watching a lady into her
carriage; we walked together and he told me he was desperately in
love! & at Almack's [21] that night would see the lady whomever she
might be. I hope somebody else recovered from it as easily as he

---

[20] Samuel Naylor (1809–1865), the translator in 1845 (1844) of Goethe's
*Reinecke Fuchs* (1794), had spent the previous winter in Germany, where he
was enrolled at the University of Göttingen. He was one of the young Englishmen with whom Ottilie von Goethe was in love, and Thackeray must have seen
him frequently in Weimar. That there was an imperfect sympathy between
the two young men is evident from a letter written by Naylor to Frau von
Goethe in 1833: "Thackeray I have heard of, and seen once or twice, but we
were never 'Du and Du' with each other, you know. His mind was low-born,
and his standard of wit coarse and unsuited to my habits." (L. A. Willoughby,
*Samuel Naylor and 'Reynard the Fox,'* London, 1914, p. 13)

[21] The famous Assembly Rooms in King Street, St. James's, where the most
fashionable balls in London were held. See Wheatley's *London*, I, 37–38.

has — Cockerel I met at Windsor (without Rattler) he was as frank & good-humoured as ever. Hodges too I fell on one day, either he deceived us or Hummel cheated him, for he played at none of his concerts. I thought I should like the theatre so much in London, but I fell asleep every night — how I long for the dear little Weimar Theatre where one could sit quiet & cozy in the parquet neither squeezed, smothered, or pelted. I have been hard at work (that is to say as far as lies in my nature) translating a German book — it is very stupid & uninteresting — but the Theatre is still my rage (don't think me conceited or say anything about it) I intend fully to try my hand at farce tragedy or comedy, wh/ I cannot yet say, all three perhaps.

Now I have said so much about myself (I suspect a great deal more interesting person to me than to you) I must ask about you & yours: Dear Madame de Goethe, (you must let me call you so, for you cannot prevent me from thinking so). You were but ill when I left you, I hope in the letter I am about to receive from you, (written in *German* language but English characters) that you will tell me that you are become quite well again & that your father is still likely to live long for Germany & you — Your children I need not ask of, they are of course well, I trust to be yet at Weimar before any one of them is an inch taller. Have you resumed the Chaos? [22] I hope so — will you send me some numbers in a parcel wh/ Dr. Weissenborn will make up for the slip of paper is for him; here are some little verses wh/ (if admissible) will I hope qualify me to receive the numbers.

## THE STARS

Now when mortal eyes do close
     Lo! their lids the stars are raising
And on us & our repose
     Those bright eyes of Heaven are gazing.

[22] This multilingual literary magazine, founded by Frau von Goethe and her friends in 1829, has been fully described by Lily von Kretschman in "Weimars Gesellschaft und das *Chaos,*" *Westermanns Monatshefte,* LXXI (1891), 235–264. If anything by Thackeray appeared in its pages while he was in Weimar, the contributions have not been identified. In the Goethe-Schiller Archives in

'Tis in vain, ye countless stars,
   That philosophers would see,
In yr/ glittering characters
   Fates & fortunes yet to be;

All ye tell us is, that while
   We do slumber & forget;
He who for our rest doth toil
   Remembereth & watcheth yet.[23]

By the bye I saw in Fraser's Magazine a song wh/ had originally appeared in your Chaos it began "Now yarely & soft my boys" — will you tell me who wrote it? [24] How is Miss Pappenheim? — I think a great deal about her, but am sorry to say have not been in love with her or anybody else for the last three months. Is Mrs. Rocheid recovered? has Parry [25] a son or a daughter? Among the presentations at Court some time ago I saw nearly at the bottom of the list "Captain Lawrence" — it was Unser! — of his fate or his acti⟨ons⟩ nothing more is known. I have to ask your pardon ⟨for⟩ that beggarly present I had the impudence to sen⟨d you⟩ but it was English paper & might I thought be useful. Will you do me a favour? whenever you want anything English, commission me, for now for the next thirty years I shall be in London 8 months of the 12. At the end of thirty years, I shall be most likely Lord Chancellor (at least my Mother believes so) & any one recommended by you for a *living* (church preferment) shall be sure to receive one. Were I to ask you to remember me to everybody who was kind to me at Weimar I must fill another sheet, so I will mention

---

Weimar, however, are preserved the manuscripts of two poems in Thackeray's hand which were presumably intended for *Das Chaos*. These have been printed by Dr. Walther Vulpius in *The Century Magazine*, LIII (April, 1897), 927.

[23] Published in the tenth number of the second volume of *Das Chaos*, which Professor H. S. Gulliver dates about October 27, 1831. In *Thackeray's Literary Apprenticeship* (pp. 32–33) the first draft of this poem is printed from the Morgan Library Weimar notebook.

[24] Thomas Carlyle.

[25] Patrick Parry, a popular Irishman living in Weimar who had helped to found *Das Chaos*.

no names at all.  Good bye Dear Madame de Goethe.  Believe me ever most sincerely & gratefully yours

W. M. Thackeray.

I shall be in London at the end of October, if you will be so good as to write to me, will you direct as above.

51.            TO  EDWARD  FɪᴛᴢGERALD
8–9 SEPTEMBER 1831

Published in part, *Biographical Introductions*, IX, xix-xx; facsimile of the first page in *W. M. Thackeray and Edward Fitzgerald*, ed. Clement Shorter (London, 1916), p. 15.

\*      \*      \*

— I have been thinking of a walking trip for us two next year — about this time say.  We will go like the German students in France or Germany wʰ shall it be?  I am really afraid of going to Italy on account of the fleas.  Really last year the whole pleasure of the Rhine was spoilt to me by those infernal animals — When we go to Italy together, we will I vote each take our own bed — how delightful an old caleche with one horse or two & a country servant! — We need not travel faster than we like — It is written, & then from Italy we will pass back through france into Spain  Fancy going to Spain the country of the THEED!  Black-eyed donñas (mark the ⁓) mules, robbers segars — We will have an antique vehicle with a pocket in front to hold our books 2 portmanteaux apiece (one for the bed which is indispensable — 3 brace of pistols each & a trusty Toledo to repel the attacks of the brigands, likewise a pair of seven-leagued boots to run away if necessary.  Fancy a "combat of eight" in some desolate Sierra        [drawing]

DRAWING IN THACKERAY'S LETTER OF 8 SEPTEMBER 1831

The carriage (of a peculiar construction) is in the back ground —
the mules are quietly gazing down the precipice the faithless postil-
lion (the miserable Pedro) has paid the price of his treachery — he
is lying in his top boots with his face cut in two by Captain Fitz-
Gerald — who is seen in the act of stamping out the wind of one
of the banditti while he is running another through the chin —
Hon the right hoff the pictur M[r] Thackeray is to be hobserved
(hafter the manner of a true Henglishman) he has fastened his
fistes hon the vizzens hof two of the robbers & his a squeadging out
hof their miserable souls — to the foreground in the left is a rude
cross! — Christians pray for the wretch who fell at that spot without having the good fortune like Mess[rs] F.G & T to save his life, or
most likely the bravery to defend it — By the bye I forgot this is a
holiday for loyal hearts till a fellow came to me for a subscription
to feast the poor on occasion of his majesty's coronation [26] — the
slave hath however departed with out his guerdon　　I told him —
that to comfort indigent honesty or to releive unmerited distress
my purse was always open, & alas my heart more ready than my
purse — but to encourage indiscriminate profusion or to foster unnecessary prodigality agreed as little with my principles as it did
with my means — & that therefore I never would sanction with
my support a measure w[h] my poverty shewed me was impossible &
my reason convinced me was impolitic — The man retired, struck
by opinions w[h] his good nature led him to deplore but w[h] his arguments could not controvert — (Repeated Cheering)

\*　　　\*　　　\*

God bless you — would that I could say it instead of writing it! —
but I ⟨. . .⟩ [27] having to use the words at all — I am quite loath to
go but I will I am cold & wan —

Friday — Really my first exertions of a morning & my last of an
evening are upon this letter, an't you penetrated overcome by such
friendship? — The consequence of coming to a little watering
p⟨lace⟩ is with me a profuse reading of novels — This morning in

[26] The Coronation of William IV on Thursday, September 8, 1831, is described in *The Annual Register* (1831), "Chronicle," 140–155.
[27] About four words have here been cut away.

bed I have been reading Destiny by the author of Marriage [28] very
clever indeed — Yesterday I read Harrington by Miss Edgeworth
likewise very good — To day I positively shall read & have a great
deal of chat with my bully Ned — my gossip — my writer of over-
tures my apostrophizer of primroses but this is humbug.

I am at this moment smoking one of the most fragrant segars in
the world I have been lying on my little sofa reading the last volume of Destiny w$^h$ is nearly as good as the first tinctured with a
leetle twaddle — A womans piety somehow does not suit me it is so
made up of exclamations — love — chastenings & so forth. Ask your
Aleesha to give you some of her verses & send them to me, they will
I sh$^d$ think be very rich — depend on it she has got lots — I shall
I think take to reading Young [29] when I come to London to make
my fortune it will be advantageous to quote from him I think —
the Rolliad is another book w$^h$ will tell with old gentlemen I think,
& Peter Pindar — these latter in their light sarcastic moments,
when they begin to talk politics after dinner — The poor Poles! I
fear it is all over with them, it makes me quite sick to read of the
Russians advancing, the Poles retreating, & the massacres at Warsaw [30] — it is very like the Siege of Jerusalem. What shameless
lies our government & France have been telling, about negociations
with Russia — & these d—d infernal Prussians breaking their promises of neutrality — If I were in the Army how I w$^d$ enjoy a campaign in Russia — merely to see their cursed conceit a little put
down — the scoundrels say they conquered Napoleon & not we —
I should rejoice to hear of 100000 French or so marching into
Berlin & kicking his Majesty Frederic William [31] off his throne his

[28] Susan Edmonstone Ferrier (1782–1854), who wrote *Marriage* (1818)
and *Destiny, or the Chief's Daughter* (1831); Maria Edgeworth (1767–
1849), whose *Harrington, a Tale* appeared in 1817.
[29] Edward Young (1683–1765), the author of *Night-Thoughts* (1742);
*Criticisms on the Rolliad, A Poem*, a series of Whig satires against William
Pitt and his supporters, published in *The Morning Herald* in 1784 and following years; John Wolcot (1738–1819), the Whig poet, whose assaults on
George III were written under the name of Peter Pindar.
[30] Thackeray probably has in mind the street riots that took place in Warsaw
on August 15 and 16. The city fell to the Russians on September 8.
[31] Frederick William III (1770–1840), who married Princess Louise of
Mecklenburg-Strelitz in 1793 and became King of Prussia in 1797.

theatres & his mistresses — People here fancy him a sentimental man always mourning for his Queen Louisa — he goes to three theatres every night & has every pretty actress at the three. From the statues I have seen of Louisa she must have been a delicious — for shame I wont go on in this way — I don't know why I wish for France to conquer Prussia, but there is something manly & straightforward & independent in the French — Pshaw! what a fool I am to talk politics, of w.ʰ I know nothing, I have but lately learnt the meaning of schedule A.³² What does the Duchess of Kent ³³ mean by refusing to come to the coronation? She will pay for it I think in her Regency — I am glad the last King of England is a good one really & truly I believe he will be the last      Brougham will be Lord Guardian or Lord Protector or something like — Who will be General in chief of the Armies of the British Republic? report says the Marquis of Makepeace: at all events who have greater claims to the office or greater talents & virtues to fulfil it! —

\*          \*          \*

52.          TO EDWARD FɪᴛᴢGERALD
29 SEPTEMBER 1831 ³⁴

Published in part, *Biographical Introductions*, IX, xxvii-xxviii; drawings reproduced in facsimile.

\*          \*          \*

Thursday — I have drawn so much this morning in the battle way that I begin actually to fancy myself a hero. I have done Napoleon in a dozen positions — Austrian soldiers — Prussian hussars, the Siege of Acre — a terrific combat between a Life Guards-

³² The list of boroughs that were to lose both members of parliament upon the passage of the Reform Bill.

³³ The former Princess Victoria Maria Louisa of Saxe-Coburg (1786–1861), mother of Queen Victoria.

³⁴ These fragments were written on Michaelmas day, Thursday, September 29, 1831.

man & a Cuirassier in w^h the latter is in the act of having his head
cut off, the blood is spirting from the wound in a most horrible &
edifying manner — My dear boy. This letter must go tonight & I
dont know what to say — What do you think I did last night — I
said my prayers for nearly half an hour & really went to sleep with
a sensation of comfort & ease that I have not felt for a long time —
I did not ask for anything except to have my doubts removed & my
strength of mind increased. There is another thing dear FitzGerald
that I will pray for — that you & I may be always as good friends
as we are now —

*        *        *

This is Michaelmas day & I should think from the look of y^r
brother in-law's house [35] you will have a goose happy you I feed
with my father alone — & we have got a corked bottle of wine to
finish that is the devil the bad wine goes so provokingly slow —
How I long for the sight of a dear green curtain again — after
going 3 times a week to the play for a year one misses it so, O the
delight of seeing the baize slowly ascending — the spangled shoes
w^h first appear then as it gradually Draws up legs stomachs heads
till finally it ends in all the glories of a party of "musqueteers"
drinking — a dance — an inn with an infinity of bells jingling or a
couple of gay dogs in cocked hats with pieces of silk dangling out

 of their pockets for hand-
kerchiefs — Yet another
month. & all this paradise
will be in my reach — really
London is to me only the
place where the Theatres
are — you seem determined
to go to Cambridge in spite
of all I can say but you'll come to London wont you from Cambridge — make flying visits of three or fours days & come to live
with me — now promise me this — & let me know fully your intentions in the next lett⟨er.⟩

[35] FitzGerald was living with his sister and her husband, Mary-Eleanor
(1805–1863) and John Kerrich (1798–1871), at their home, Geldestone
Hall, near Beccles, in Norfolk.

DRAWING IN THACKERAY'S LETTER OF 29 SEPTEMBER 1831

\*          \*          \*

on £700 a year one might marry — I dont like thinking of the
death of my parents for I find I calculate on it in a horrid way as
giving me a larger income certainly not more than as much again
as I have now — but how disgusting it is to catch oneself with such
thoughts! dear FitzGerald if ever you become a Xtian dont be
uncharitable towards your freethinking friends as you sh^d I fear
be — & explain to me all the steps by w^h you have arrived at the
belief —

Dont come to me for a whole fortnight but for two weeks — one
early in November tother betwixt it & December — How happy
you make me by telling me that you love me — I knew it before,
but I have it

\*          \*          \*


53.          TO EDWARD FɪᴛᴢGERALD
              2 OCTOBER 1831

Published in part, *Biographical Introductions*, IX, xvii-xviii, xxxiii.

Sunday. October 3.³⁶ 1831.

My last dirty epistle is still lying looking me in the face but I
begin another, & shall put into it some lines by Charles Lamb ³⁷
taken from your Every day Book —

| | |
|---|---|
| Here is Spensers February ³⁸ — copied from Hone & very pretty. | Margaret. What sports do you use in the forest? |
| | Simon. Not many some few as thus |
| | To see the sun to bed & to arise |
| [See drawings reproduced opposite page 162] | Like some hot amourist with glowing eyes |
| | Bursting the lazy bands of sleep that bound him; |

³⁶ A mistake for Sunday, October 2.
³⁷ From *John Woodvil. A Tragedy*, Act II, scene [ii].
³⁸ See *The Shepherd's Calendar*; Nathaniel Hone (1718–1784), R. A.,
was a miniature painter.

With all his fires & travelling glories round him;
Sometimes the moon on soft night-clouds to rest
Like Beauty nestling in a young Mans breast —
And all the winking stars, her handmaids, keep
Admiring silence while those lovers sleep,
Sometimes outstrecht in very idleness
Nought doing saying little thinking less
To view the leaves thin dancers upon air
Go eddying round, & small birds how they fare
When Mother Autumn fills their beaks with corn
Filched from the careless Amalthea's horn
And how the woods berries & worms provide
Without their pains when Earth has naught beside
To answer their small wants" —

And now as I am in the mood I shall drawn Cowpers summer
house for you from the same book       [drawing on opposite page]

*          *          *

The reason I liked & like Lᵈ Edward FitzGerald [39] so much was
from his likeness to you. I read the book just as if it had been your
history & then when I looked at the first page I saw your picture wʰ
increased the dear delusion — Would not you have been interested
in a book the hero of wʰ bore my name & boasted my handsome
physiognomy? — but your boasting about being better than Lᵈ E.
wont do — he was I think a very gallant honest warmhearted
fellow & for his ideas of morals let us not be too confident of our

[39] The Irish rebel (1763–1798); Thackeray had been reading Tom
Moore's *Life and Death of Lord Edward FitzGerald* (1831).

DRAWINGS IN THACKERAY'S LETTER OF 2 OCTOBER 1831

Drawing in Thackeray's Letter of 2 October 1831

own. I think the following picture represents properly the fate of philosophy — he looketh so steadily at the heavens that he heedeth

 not where he treadeth — What a quaint old picture Quarles [40] would have made of it! — I have been trying to find out what makes me fancy other people my inferiors — My Mother for instance — she can write much better letters & quite as good verses as I — why when one goes into company does one take care to consider everybody else a fool. Can a man judge of his own abilities? do you think that every fellow has the consciousness of having something superior within him with the nature of w[h] quality he is unacquainted though certain either from fancy or conceit of its existence. I see people do things far better than I can, & yet somehow my extreme good opinion of myself is by no means lowered — I never read Mason on self-knowledge [41] but it strikes me that if I had I should still be not much the wiser as to the motives origin or truth of such ideas of mental superiority as I entertain

\*   \*   \*

Walk up ladies & gentlemen & see what you shall see. it costs you nothing & nobody can see it twice — This exhibition tho' it's so cheap is quite the fashion — last year it was wisited by his M[y] K. George 4th & several of the nobility & gentry. This year it has been patronized by F. Marshal Diebitsch [42] & several thousand officers &

[40] Francis Quarles (1592–1644), the poet, whose *Emblems* were first published in 1635.

[41] *Self-Knowledge. A treatise, shewing the nature and benefit of that important science, and the way to attain it,* by the dissenting minister John Mason (1706–1763), first appeared in 1745 and had by 1811 reached an eighteenth edition.

[42] General Hans Karl Friedrich Anton von Diebitsch (b. 1785), commander of the Russian army which suppressed the Polish insurrection of 1830–1831, died either of cholera or by his own hand on June 10, 1831, not long after his bloody victories over the Poles at Crochow on February 25 and at Ostrolenka on May 26.

soldiers of the Russian & Polish army. Ladies & gentlemen now's
yᵉ time! a trumpet will sound at the end of the performance
afterwds it will be exhibited never no more.

\*        \*        \*

54.        FROM EDWARD FɪᴛᴢGERALD
5–9 OCTOBER 1831 [43]

*Address:* W. M. Thackeray Esq. | Larkbeare House | Ottery Sᵗ Mary | Devon.
*Postmark:* 10 OC 1831. Published in part, *Biographical Introductions*, IX,
xx–xxi.

My dear Thackeray, I have just come home from a walk of two
hours or so, and put my letter to you in the post. It rained so hard
in the morning that I could not get my early walk — so I lay in
bed; for I think there is no difference, in the matter of wholesome-
ness, between lying in bed, or sitting up; provided one does not
sleep, or have too much blanket. I gave you plenty of advice about
health in my last, I think. I shall come to London, with some of
my sisters, about the 20ᵗʰ of October — will you be there then?
Do, if you can. I had got over all doubts as to Christianity (that is
to say thoroughly disbelieved in it) except the Miracles — but I
think the evidence of them is to be doubted. But Paley is very
clever about them — it is a case made out as by a lawyer, and he
thoroughly answers Hume on the point of thinking any likeness
between Christ's miracles, and the Abbé Paris.[44] Religious people
are very angry with one for doubting: and say "You come to the
question determined to doubt, not to be convinced" Certainly we

[43] The postmark shows that this letter was mailed on Monday, October 10.
It was begun the previous Wednesday and finished on Sunday. FitzGerald's
date, evidently written at the time of posting, is a mistake for October 10.

[44] On this early instance of Fitzgerald's frequenting doctor, if not saint, see
Hume's *An Enquiry Concerning Human Understanding* (*Essays Moral, Political, and Literary, by David Hume*, 2 vols., ed. T. H. Green and T. H.
Grose, London, 1875, II, 101–103) and *A View of the Evidences of Christianity* (*Works*, 7 vols., London, 1825, IV, 6–8) by William Paley (1743–
1805). Sir Leslie Stephen summarizes the controversy in *English Thought in
the Eighteenth Century*, 2 vols. (London, 1881), I, 415.

do: having seen how many follow & have followed false religions, and having our reason utterly against many of the principal points of the Bible, we require the most perfect evidence of facts, before we can believe. If you can prove to me that one miracle took place, I will believe that he is a just God who damned us all because a woman eat an apple; & you can't expect greater complaisance [than] that, to be sure. You are wrong, my dear Thackeray, in fancying that Christ does not call himself God — every page of the Bible will shew you he did. There is one thing that goes some way with me: if Christ was not really God, he was either a fanatic, or an impostor: now his morals & advice are too consistent, and too simple & mild, for a fanatic: & an impostor, one fancies, would not have persevered in such a blameless life, nor held in his heart at once the blasphemous design of calling himself the son of God & a code of principles which the best & wisest of men never preached before. What do you say to this point? Think of it. I am in a quandary of doubts.

You are a genuine lover of the theatre. When we are in London we must go to the pit. Now, Thackeray, I lay you ten thousand pounds that you will be thoroughly disappointed when we come together — our letters have been so warm, that we shall expect each minute to contain a sentence like those in our letters. But in letters we are not always together: there are no blue devilish moments: one of us isn't kept waiting for the other: and above all in letters there is Expectation! I am thus foreboding because I have felt it — and put you on your guard very seriously about it, for the disappointment of such hopes has caused a flatness, then a disgust, and then a coldness betwixt many friends, I'm in mind. So think of meeting me not as I am in my letters (for they being written when in a good humour, and read when you have nothing better to do, make all seem alert and agreeable) but as you used to see me in London, Cambridge &c — If you come to think, you will see there is a great difference. Do not think I speak thus in a light hearted way about the tenacity of our friendship, but with a very serious heart anxious lest we should disappoint each other, and so lessen our love a little — I hate this subject & to the devil with it.

7 at night. I always come up to my room after dinner, at which we are not more than an hour: my sisters go into the drawing room, and I, as I drink no wine, come up here, and generally "spin a yarn" with you. Swift, Bolingbroke, and Pope were three very clever men — Pope I admire more and more for his sense. As to his poetry, I don't know of much. But still it is prose more beautifully and tastefully draped than any one has ever made it — and he has given even epigrams the appearance of poetry. I am angry with Hume for admiring the French so: and standing up so for polite manners to the ladies [45] — a practice which turns Nature topsy turvy. I have got the character of being rather a brute in society — can't help it; I am worth more, I believe, than any young lady that ever was made, so I am more inclined to tell them to open the door for me, than for me to get up and do it for them. This is a most horrid sentence, on second thoughts — for millions of girls have existed a million times more virtuous than I am; and I am ashamed of having said it. I ought to scratch out the sentence — but why should you not see that I can say a silly thing? (i.e. because I so often say wise ones — N.B. sic cogitat vanitas) I never do write poetry now: and am sure you will make a much better hymn to God save the Emperor than I could. Tis a noble air — I am elevated by my glass of port, & am looking round the table to see what I can be at. There is Byron — Hume — Helvetius — Diderot — Shakespeare. I have not read Shakespeare for a long time. I will tell you why. I found that *his manner* stuck so in my head that I was always trying to think in his way; I mean with his quaint words &c — this I don't wish. I don't think I've read him for a year. I expect a rich treat when I begin the old dear again. Your caricature of Death is a very good one indeed — don't exaggerate the faces, pray, but get them near to Nature — which will make it impressive — but excessive caricature will spoil it. I did not know that I had been so foreboding of Death in my last letter: I want to live long, and see every thing. I am glad you have taken to Cowper: some of his little poems are affecting far beyond anything in the English language: not heroic, but they make me cry.

[45] See, for example, Hume's *Essays* (*ed. cit.*) I, 158–159 and 193.

The Poplar field, is one of the best: & Alexander Selkirks Good Night — I am going to Hume — his Essays are the most clear I ever read.

Thursday morn. "Greece, for her wisdom famed for ages, and always quoted in our schools, could only boast of seven sages — think of the number of her fools!" This is a translation of a French epigram, a very tolerable one I think.

1/2 past one. What have I been doing the last hour? Behold these verses, they are the fruits, for they never came into my head before: but the wind was blowing hard at the windows & I some- how began to think of Will Thackeray: so the cockles of my heart were warmed, and up spouted the following: I have drunk a glass of port, & so sit down to transcribe them.

*1*

I cared not for life: for true friend I had none
I had heard 'twas a blessing not under the sun:
Some figures called friends, hollow, proud, or cold-hearted
Came to me like shadows — like shadows departed:
But a day came that turned all my sorrow to glee
When first I saw Willy, and Willy saw me!

*2*

The thought of my Willy is always a cheerer;
My wine has new flavour — the fire burns clearer:
The sun ever shines — I am pleased with all things —
And this crazy old world seems to go with new springs; —
And when we're together, (Oh! soon may it be!)
The world may go kissing of comets for me!

*3*

The chair that Will sat in, I sit in the best;
The tobacco is sweetest which Willy hath blest;
And I never found out that my wine tasted ill
When a tear would drop in it, for thinking of Will.

### 4

And now on my windows October blows chilly,
I laugh at blue devils, & think of my Willy:
I think, that our friendship will not drop away
Like the leaves from the trees, or our locks when they're grey:
I think that old age shall not freeze us, until
He creeps with Death's warrant to me and my Will.

### 5

If I get to fifty — may Willy get too:
And we'll laugh, thrill, at all that grim sixty can do;
Old age? — let him do of what poets complain,
We'll thank him for making us children again;
Let him make us grey, gouty, blind, toothless, or silly,
Still old Ned shall be Ned — and old Willy be Willy!

### 6

We may both get so old that our senses expire
And leave us to doze half-alive by the fire:
Age may chill the warm hearts which I think so divine,
But what warmth it has, Willy, shall ever be thine!
And if our speech goes, we must pass the long hours
When the Earth is laid bare with a Winter like our's,
Till Death finds us waiting him patiently still,
Willy looking at me, and I looking at Will!

There are my verses — I have polished them a little more, which has not done them any good. Take them, however, and may they tell no lies — I must go & get a walk — I am half blind with writing out these things.

5 o'clock. I have had a long walk, and have such such a composing vein to day that my head is in a swim of different thoughts. The metre of these verses has made me drunk; there is a rolling in it: or else this intoxication is a proof that I feel what I have said. I could do anything now — would you were here; I am just in the humour for a pipe. I desire you to make some lines to me as your Neddy. Wait your opportunity when a fit comes on you. Never

mind about their goodness: I dare say I shall think these bad to-morrow when I am cold.

7 at night. pp. (i.e. post port) My one glass is down — that descended upon a bed of boiled pork, which I had gorged before. Boiled leg of pork, parmesan cheese, & a glass of port, maketh a dinner for a prince. What shall I be at? I think I could versify enormously. I have more verses in my head about Willy: but you have enough, I think. Ye Gods! I am in a fit state of mind to sit with Willy in the Cynic Divan, or the Sultan's Divan! I believe I am mad today. What hath made me mad? A great October wind which whistles at my window when I am in doors and blows me along when out of doors — I think I could drive four-in-hand just now. Lord Edward's death [46] I have read — I think it dull very — I think he is a poor creature as to mind — he had the valour of a brute. He gave in to Revolutionary principles without thought, but through Irish impulse. I have a wondrous inclination for to sing — A glass or two more of Port would make me rate myself above 20 Lord Edwards. No Hume, no nothing reasonable have I read for I wish now that all morality was impulse, and all the system of the world too. I keep hurrying on my spirits, not letting them stop — hurra — hurra — the dead can ride [47] — i.e. those who are dead in heart. I don't pretend to have, like M$^{rs}$ Norton, a heart like a "withered nut that rattles in it's shell" but I see few people I care about, & so, oh Willy, be constant to me. Don't suppose I am drunk — only my one poor glass of port — but like the hare in March, I have my seasons. Perhaps tomorrow I shall be like a fellow after a debauch. In my walk to day I drew an old house near Beccles which I send. What a glorious tune the British Grenadiers [48] is — nothing goes so near to make me cry as that song. There is

[46] See above, No. 53.

[47] From Scott's "William and Helen," Stanza XLIX. Mrs. Caroline Norton gloomily asserts in a lyric on pp. 178–179 of *The Undying One and Other Poems* (1830):

My heart is like a withered nut,
Rattling within its hollow shell.

[48] Professor D. Nichol Smith reprints this anonymous song from the original broadside (1780) in *The Oxford Book of Eighteenth Century Verse* (Oxford, 1926), pp. 555–556.

great feeling in it. "When e'er they come to quarters in any country town, the lasses cry Huzza, lads, the Grenadiers are come: the
Grenadiers are come, my boys, their lovers hearts to cheer — then
hip, hurra, hurra boys, for the British Grenadier!" Capital stanza
that is, isn't it? & the time is noble. Oh Christianity, are you true,
and, if you are, must we give up liking the British Grenadiers!
Come to London — oh come, my dearest boy, & we'll yet have a
good meeting — My feeling of security is now so great that I
believe the great comet [49] will not touch us, but hit the cholera:
which, in it's turn, will fix on the comet, so as to purge it to death
in 24 hours!!!!

All we have to hope, in that case, is that the earth won't be the
Comet's for his purgings are assuredly fire. Good Night — I shall
be in London on the 20th or probably before. Come you up there,
and we will hunt for lodgings for three and be merry. Hurra!
hurra! hurra! God bless you, my dear Boy: may we never
part! 〰〰 Here is a flight of crows to the right of the
wish — a good omen.

Friday/ I think I made a fool of myself last night in my letter —
there is no affectation however for I was in tip top spirits. Today I
am also very well. Do you know anything of a Court of Love
which formerly was in Provence? It is mentioned in Hume's Essays.[50] I should like to know something of it: my head is already
at work cooking up some dramatic materials out of it. I am plan-
ning a play on it — I wonder where there is any account of it.
Howver, I suppose it was a court where lovers pleaded their causes
& their proposals & differences were judged. There are good materials for a play, and quite new.

7 at night. I Have been thinking of this plot all day

Saturd: Morning. Did not write much to you yesterday, certainly. Last night I was siezed all of a sudden with a tune I had
heard Fanny Kemble sing to — the fit remained on me all the
evening, and on coming up to bed I made some verses to it. I send

[49] Encke's comet, the reappearance of which was due on May 4, 1832.
[50] Hume's *Essays* (*ed. cit.*), II, 201.

you them and the tune, which you may get your Mammy to play
for you. It is a pretty tune — the words fol de rol. To day there is
a most extraordinary heat in the atmosphere — quite un*season-
able* — something seems brewing. We are all stupid. I will write
out the words to the tune.

*1*

Farewell to merry summertime — I hear the wintry gale
That bids me fill my pipe again, & tap the foaming ale.
The trees are dying fast without, & cheerless is the scene,
But tobacco leaves are sprouting, boys, and friendship's
evergreen!

2

In summer, Friendship wanders out along the sunny plain,
But she swears she never feels so strong as o'er the fire
again:
I hear the winds cry pipingly: — let's tackle to our cheer,
And drink a merry stirrup-cup to the departing year.

3

Old year full lusty hath thy youth, and summer manhood been,
Stretched out at ease beneath the sun, or in the forest green.
But now your pipe is cracked with age, & peevish you are grown,
While you chatter in the wood that you have starved to skin
and bones!

4

No matter, friends — kind Nature blows some good with ev'ry
gale:
And if October kills the year, he brews our nutbrown ale;
Then let's fill our glasses up, & drink his health with hearty
minds
In ale as yellow as his leaves, & stronger than his winds!

There you be — all done, no more fun. You can sing them an
you please — They are rather of the Williams order on a reperusal.
Sat night. Shall be glad to see you, my boy. This letter shall go

to post tomorrow. "Tomorrow to fresh Church & parsons new!" [51]
T'will be Sunday — Good Night.

Sunday. I shall send my letter. Shall I have one from you?
October 11. 1831

55.          TO EDWARD FITzGERALD
          16-23 NOVEMBER 1831

*Address:* Edward Fitz-Gerald Esq^re — | at M^rs Perry's, | Trumpington
Street | Cambridge. *Postmark:* NO 23 1831. Extracts published, *Biographical
Introductions,* III, xvi. *Endorsed:* First Letter after my dep: fro: London: in
Nov^r 1831.

Wednesday night. I am just come from the play where w^d you
believe it I was half crying — I dont think my room will ever
appear comfortable again — here are your things lying in the
exact place you left them — God bless you dear dear Fitzgerald —
I dont think you would have gone had you known how wretched it
makes me — I have not had such a cry since I was at school — I
am all alone now, dear boy one must follow your plan & steel
oneself against all such melancholy, but never mind pangs at
parting make pleasure at meeting — Good night — I shall go to
bed & think about you.

Friday — Have been with Wood into the country to a M^r
Matraven a good fellow but ostentatious & a snob —he treated us
royally & drove me to town in his gig on w^h he descanted largely
on the way — I am going to give him a feed here to day — very
humble — how I wish my dear boy could take tother end of the
table. Schulte has been here twice in my absence & threatens to
return — the Kembles [52] have called J. yesterday Henry to day —
he is a dear fellow & we talk about nothing but you & the theatres
the two things I like best in the world — w^h is a poor compliment
to you — are you happy at Cambridge? — My fingers are too cold
to write more — I shall read Undinchen [53] for an hour —

Saturday — am come to say good night to my boy & then to go

---

[51] An adaptation of the last line of *Lycidas:*
          Tomorrow to fresh Woods, and Pastures new.
[52] See *Memoranda.*
[53] *Undine* (1811) by Baron Friedrich de la Motte Fouqué (1777–1843).

to bed — have been out to a dinner have procured other invites, &
am returned sleepy & tired, but am awake enough to say God bless
you dear boy & to hope to see you again very very soon — if you
wont come here I will go to Cambridge — My letters here are
unlike the Larkbeare letters but I dont think I am fickle for all
that: H. Kemble is coming I hope to breakfast in the morning we
shall talk about you & be angry with you for leaving us. I think if
you knew all I felt you could not help being a little warm — it is
after all questionable whether roast beef is better hot or cold —
only when cold one requires a little something to flavour it. There
is a neat metaphor with which I shall conclude & most likely at the
end of the week send you this half finished — I have found Schulte
out in something like swindling — he asked me my Tailors name —
went to him & ordered 2 waistcoats & a coat telling him he was
going to Oxford — he told me positively that he had only ordered
two waistcoats — here are 2 fibs — of w$^h$ when I get my moneys I
shall inform him & request to have nothing further to do with
him — were I to say so now he w$^d$ not pay & as he goes away early
tomorrow I have thought fit to delay the communication until I
have my money in hand — Good night dear Yedward — have you
thought anything about me all day? — how I long for you while
you are callously eating & drinking chez sansum [54] & allen — dont
chump so — faugh — God bless you.

Sunday — I fear I must cut this sheet in half for I find so little
to say — have had the Kembles to breakfast John stayed with me
till five o'clock that is till three when we set forth on a walk — I
like him better, but he seems to me a very forced plant — in reading thinking & conversation beyond his natural growth. We went
round the Regents' Park & he had the talk to himself it was
agreable enough about his Spanish adventures & his friend General
Torigos's exploits [55] — he has asked me to his house — this will be
pleasant I should think in winter — M$^{rs}$ K is returned leaving her
daughter at Paris     Your shutters are opened & your chimnies

---

FitzGerald's copy of this romance, illustrated with a series of water-color
sketches by Thackeray, is now owned by Mr. Carlebach.

[54] John Sansum (b. 1810) matriculated at Trinity College, Cambridge, in
1828 and received his B. A. degree in 1832.

[55] John Kemble spent the winter of 1830–1831 in Gibraltar, whither he

smoking — this gave me another fit of blue devils — as also when Madame at the Rocher de Cancale [56] was surprized at my coming alone — Oh solitude where are the charms that sages have seen in thy face let them hug the old jade in their arms I'd give her a kick on her ace [57] — clever & unpremeditated — but th⟨is is⟩ the bitter sarcasm of despair, not the happy brilliancy of merry wit — I dont know why I've drawn this but now it is drawn it looks sad as is the designer The fact is when I am alone & thinking about you I get quite wretched — You may go & live at home if you like when you come to London & then there will be no too muchness, wʰ last time you were predisposed to feel though honestly I can say I did not myself. it is however comfortable to have you within six hours of me & I dont know why I dont come down — next Friday I should not wonder if I made my appearance — now for my tea, wʰ is all ready in a new tea pot     Good night boykin — God bless you Teddibus

Monday — have just got your letter shall be glad to see Sansum. Faithless Allen! — if ever one could have vouched for a man's constancy it would have been for his —

I am *coming* to you tomorrow [58] — Good bye —

had gone with Richard Chenevix Trench (1807–1886) to aid General Torrijos in his rebellion against Ferdinand VII of Spain. See Carlyle's account of the expedition in chapters 9, 10, and 13 of his *Life of John Sterling*.

[56] A famous Parisian restaurant on the Rue Montorgeuil, much frequented by Thackeray (see *Works*, VI, 155, and XIII, 592–595). He and FitzGerald had no doubt given the name to a favorite London haunt.

[57] Adapted from Cowper's "Verses Supposed to be Written by Alexander Selkirk":

> Oh, solitude! where are the charms
> That sages have seen in thy face?
> Better dwell in the midst of alarms,
> Than reign in this horrible place.

[58] Thackeray passed four days in Cambridge. See below, No. 57.

56.        TO MAJOR CARMICHAEL-SMYTH
8–10 DECEMBER 1831

*Address:* Major Carmichael Smyth | Larkbeare House | Ottery S? Mary |
Devon. *Postmark:* DE 10 1831. Extract published in *Biographical Introductions,* III, xviii.

My dear Father —

I am glad to say that I have been able to raise the 100 g? [59] My
Uncle Frank & M? Langslow consented to sell out stock for me to
that amount, otherwise I sh? have been in a sad predicament, for it
is considered here as a debt of honour, w? one is bound punctually
& immediately to pay. My Uncle Frank is I fear angry with me —
I wrote to him but he has not answered, he made me a communication through M? Langslow — however as he has done the needful
I will look over the indignation — Am going to dine in Montague
Place [60] to day to meet all the children. I dined there last Saturday
with a party — What do you think — M? Josiah Collis brought me
an offer from his father to lend me money! they are so civil to me
that they must want to get something from me — M?? Collis in her
elegant way called me a nasty wretch yesterday for smoking — The
Garrows [61] have cut me I think — disgusted I suppose by my asking
for the Marshalship — I find this work really very pleasant — one's
day is very agreeably occupied — there is a newspaper & a fire &
just enough to do — M? Taprell has plenty of business & I should
think w? be glad of another assistant whom I hope to provide for
him in my friend Kemble — with whom I am very thick — we
dont see each other more than twice a week, w? is I think an excellent preservative of friendship — Here was a piece of conceit w?
I am sure you will excuse me from scratching out — [62]

Saturday — on Thursday I caught a cold sitting here with wet
feet all day, but it has departed by my laying up yesterday — & I

[59] To pay a gambling debt. Francis Thackeray and Robert Langslow controlled Thackeray's funds until he was twenty-one.
[60] Where lived Dr. Turner and his family.
[61] Sir William Garrow and his family.
[62] Before this sentence Thackeray has overscored two lines. "From" should
read "for."

have bought a pair of clogs w.ʰ will keep my feet dry — have been
employed on a long pedigree case, & find myself very tolerably
amused — only it is very difficult to read dry law books & attend to
them — I sit at t⟨hem⟩ a good deal but proceed very slowly. I have
to lay out near 5 £ to day for these same ugly books. I am going to
give a gin & brandy party at my rooms to night — Colonel
Forrest told me you had ordered 3 doz. whiskey — but I shall have
very few days to drink it; for term begins again the 10.ᵗʰ January,[63]
& one must not be away, for then all the cases come tumbling in &
one gets more practice than ever, though there is enough now
Heaven knows. I cant come home for more than 12 days — I have
been talking with Taprell who recommends me strongly to stay in
town as he will have plenty of work for me      Good bye my dear
Father ever y.ʳ affte. Son W. M. Thackeray


57.        TO MRS. CARMICHAEL-SMYTH
               15–16 DECEMBER 1831

*Address:* M.ʳˢ Carmichael Smyth | Larkbeare House | Ottery S.ᵗ Mary | Devon.
*Postmark:* DE 16 1831. Published in part, *Memorials*, pp. 356–357; additions in *The New York Times Book Review*, December 5, 1926, p. 3.

I have written to Father dear Mother, & thought of course you
would have had the letter. I wrote to you just before I went
to Cambridge [64] where I staid four days feasting on my old
friends      I made my books a pretext for going there & found
them all safely stowed as was everything else belonging to me —
some day or other I shall keep another term — I was glad to find
the men so hearty & hospitable I could have staid there a month &
fed on each of my friends — Now here in London I occasionally
get a shy invitation to dinner on a pretty piece of paper. I suppose
in a year or two I shall be as ceremonious as the best of them — if
ever there was — I was going to say something against the law but

[63] The Hilary term at the Inns of Court extended in 1832 from January 11
to 31.
[64] This letter has not been preserved.

wont — I go pretty regularly to my pleaders & sit with him till
past five & sometimes 6      Then I come home & read & dine till
about 9 or past when I am glad enough to go out for an hour and
look at the world, as for the theatre I scarcely go more than once
[a] week, w.ʰ is moderate indeed for me — it has been lucky for
my purse that there has been a run of pieces at all the theatres, & I
think twice is generally enough to see the present run of things —
or anything at all — I find nothing so tedious as Shakspeare except perhaps some standard tragedies with Miss Fanny Kemble ⁶⁵ —
C Kemble has been very ill nearly given up his sons are great
chums of mine, & from the eldest I learn a great deal I am expecting a Cambridge man to breakfast but cannot treat him as I was
treated there — really the gormandizing quite astonished me I
used to be able to play my part pretty well but found myself quite
a delicate eater.

Friday  My Cambridge man did not come though I waited for
him till near one — in going to Chambers I met my old friend &
new acquaintance Curzon ⁶⁶ however he was much more cordial
than before & promised to come & see me the youth is in Parliament
but does not intend to spout — Yesterday I went with J. Kemble
to the Beggars Opera,⁶⁷ very good it is certainly the pleasantest
play (that is according to my thinking) in our language to see, &
in a few days come the Pantomimes ⁶⁸ huzza — I have kept my

⁶⁵ During the past two months Macready had appeared in *Richard III*, *Macbeth*, and *King John* at Drury Lane, and Miss Kemble was seen in *Henry
VIII* and *King John* at Covent Garden. She also played Belvidera in *Venice
Preserved*, Mrs. Beverley in Edward Moore's *The Gamester*, Bianca in Henry
Hart Milman's *Fazio*, and Mrs. Haller in Kotzebue's *The Stranger*. Thackeray's use of the last of these dramas in chapter 4 of *Pendennis* will be recalled.
⁶⁶ Robert Curzon (1810–1873), later (1870) fourteenth Baron Zouche,
entered Charterhouse in 1821. He matriculated in 1829 at Christ's Church
College, Oxford, which he left without taking a degree, and was returned to
parliament for Clitheroe in 1831. His travels in the East, the real work of his
life, began in 1833. They led to the writing of many books, the best known
of which is his *Visit to Monasteries in the Levant* (1849).
⁶⁷ John Braham (1773–1856), a famous tenor whom Thackeray never
tired of caricaturing (see below, Appendix II), sang the role of Macheath in
this performance at Covent Garden (*Theatrical Observer*, December 15).
⁶⁸ Elaborate extravaganzas, given the day after Christmas at the major

account pretty regularly & for term time very regularly for have begun a little Journal [69] w.ᵸ really prospers — I find it a great check on my expenditure to see those of the day before staring me in the face, as also a great incitement to my industry to see yester-day's idleness — but I am not very idle — have read the last of W. Scotts novels Castle Dangerous & thought it mighty poor one gets tired of long-winded descriptions of helmets & surcoats — the best of these stories that I have lately seen are the Romance of French history by Leitch Ritchie [70] — Luckily for me there is no getting novels at Ebers's [71] I have just finished a long winded Declaration about a mortgage & in half an hour shall go to my beefsteaks & porter — I have not called ever on M.ʳ Markham some men who know him say he is a great snob — Wood was to have given me a frank for this but it came with yesterdays date, so you must pay your postage dear Mother — on Christmas day I dine with my Uncle Frank. he & M.ʳˢ Thackeray called on me t'other day but I was not at home — God bless you dear Mother love to Father & Mary — ever y.ʳ aff.ᵗᵉ Son     W. M. Thackeray

This wonderful Monster is to be seen every day between 12 & 5 at M.ʳ Taprell's rooms in Hare Court Temple.

London theatres. Drury Lane offered in 1831 "a New Grand Christmas Comic Pantomime, with new Music, Scenery, Machinery, &c. entitled Harlequin & Little Tom Thumb; Or, the Seven League Boots!" In the cast were eight ogres with such horrendous names as Wolfstomach and Sheep-at-a-Mouthful. Covent Garden presented "a new Grand Comic Pantomime, called Hop o' my Thumb, & his Brothers; Or Harlequin & the Ogre," in which, as a counterpoise to the Drury Lane ogres, appeared "the Seven Young Ogresses." (*Theatrical Observer*, December 26) These details are worth remarking, for Thackeray retained his affection for the pantomimes through-out his life (see, for example, *Works*, VI, 570–573), and *The Rose and the Ring*, the best-loved of his own "Christmas entertainments," has close affilia-tions with the pantomimes.

[69] This has not been preserved.

[70] *The Romance of History: France* (1831), by Leitch Ritchie (1800?–1865).

[71] E. S. Ebers and Company, booksellers, 27 Old Bond Street.

DRAWINGS IN THACKERAY'S LETTER OF 15–16 DECEMBER 1831

58.                    TO JAMES FRASER[72]
                            1831?

*Address:* The Editor of Fraser's Magazine | Mͬ͢ Fraser Bookseller | Regent
Street.  Hitherto unpublished.

                                        5 Essex Court.  Temple.
    Dear Sir —
    I have ventured to send you a translation of Arndts "Feld
Marschale"[73] — It may perhaps be worthy of a vacant page in
your Magazine —
    I am, Dear Sir,
                    Your obdt Servͭ͢
                    W. M. Thacker⟨ay⟩
W. Fraser Esqͬͤ͢

    The Field Marshall from the German of Ernst Moritz Arndt

The squadrons are saluting, the merry trumpets blow.
Along the line the Marshal, is riding to & fro
His fiery steed full lightly, the aged warrior guides,
His sabre glitters brightly, he waves it as he rides —

O see!  how fierce & bright the warriors eyes do glow,
O see!  how snowy white, are the locks upon his brow,
He's old, but yet he will not his glorious post resign,
For age but makes him riper, like old & mellow wine.

And when the bad cause triumphed, & hope it was no more,
He raised his sword to Heaven, & bitterly he swore;
He swore, in scorn & anger, upon the blade so bright,
That he would teach the Frenchmen how Germans used to fight

    [72] Fraser was the proprietor of *Fraser's Magazine* — which was not, how-
ever, named for him — from its inception until his death in 1841.  Though
neither of the poems that follow was accepted by Fraser, much of Thackeray's
best periodical writing appeared in *Fraser's Magazine* between 1834 and 1853.
    [73] Thackeray's version of "Das Lied von Feldmarschall," which Arndt
(1769–1860) published in 1813, appeared at last in *The National Standard*,
May 11, 1833, p. 298, though not without alteration.

He kept his word, when loudly his country's warcry rung,
Then gaily to his saddle, the grey haired youth he sprung,
He kept his word full truly! & with an iron hand
Like chaff he swept the Frenchmen from his darling fatherland.

On the bloody field of Lützen, good service did he then
Upon the field were lying ten thousand slaughtered men,
And thousands more beside them, were fain to make retreat,
And carry to their master the news of their defeat —

At the Katzbach stream the Frenchmen learnt a goodly art from him
Albeit unused to water he taught them how to swim
Swim on Swim on or else go down in the deep & wide Ostsea
Where down whales throats Sir Sansculottes your resting place
    shall be —

At Wartbourg on the Elbe, a pretty chase he led them.
Their walls could not defend them, their ramparts never staid them,
Like hares the French were flying, from field to field they ran.
And loudly he was crying, his huzza, the brave old man!

He fought them & he conquered at Leipzig on the plain,
The Frenchmans luck there left him, & ne'er returned again;
And when the fight was over, & the victory was won,
And gained his Marshal's baton, for the deeds that he had done!

With brave hussars saluting, & trumpets blowing shrill,
Ride on, ride on Sir Marshall, our hearts are with the[e] still —
In father land or foreign, where'er your course may be,
Heaven prosper thee Sir Marshal — God fights for us & thee.

### An Evening Hymn.[74]

I ask not for riches, I look not for fame,
    Let soldiers & madmen go seek her;
But honesty needeth no Sir to his name,
    And a little's enough to buy liquor:

[74] This is one of Thackeray's rejected contributions to *Das Chaos*. Its text differs only slightly from that of the manuscript in the Goethe-Schiller Archives, first printed by Dr. Vulpius, *Century Magazine*, LIII, 927.

I rate him an ass, who despising his glass,
 For place or preferment will quarrel,
My creed I do hold with the Cynic of old,
 For he stuck all his life by his barrel.

When goblins & ghosts mid the children of men
 Were permitted by Satan to riot,
The parsons but threaten'd the Red Sea, & then
 The poor exorcised Devils were quiet.
Now all dæmons are rare, save the one that's called care
 But we've need of no priest to dismay him,
Right easy's the spell the dull spirit to quell,
 In the Red Sea of wine you should lay him,

Saint Peter in Heaven hath charge of the keys,
 (If his brother S! John's a truth-teller)
O were I an angel, how gladly I'd ease
 The old boy of the keys of the cellar!
Or if banished elsewhere, as a Sinner who neer,
 Has listened to prayer or to preacher,
Then may I be cursed with perpetual thirst,
 And to quench it an emptiless pitcher —

## 59.  TO MRS. CARMICHAEL-SMYTH
### 14–16 JANUARY 1832

*Address:* M^rs Carmichael Smyth. | Larkbeare House | Ottery S! Marys |
Devon. Published in part, *Memorials,* pp. 357–358.

5 Essex Court. Saturday — 14 Jan^ry

 The sun is shining for once in at my windows & the frost is biting
my fingers but I must have a little talk with my dear Mother before I go where I shall find no sun at all in M^r Taprells smoky
dingy back-shop, then I shall climb up my high stool & find "Instructions to draw Declaration" with a great thick volume of
Chitty [1] by the side of them & I begin to get quite au fait now at

 [1] Joseph Chitty (1776–1841) of the Middle Temple, author of many
legal treatises. See *Works,* II, 283.

finding the proper forms &c. This lawyers preparatory education is certainly one of the most cold blooded prejudiced pieces of invention that ever a man was slave to — I dont mean prejudiced but prejudice-making for a fellow sh$^d$ properly do & think of nothing else than L.A.W. Never mind. I begin to find out that people are much wiser than I am (w$^h$ is a rare piece of modesty in me) & that old heads do better than young ones that is in their generation for I am sure that a young mans ideas however absurd & rhapsodical they are though they mayn't smack so much of experience as those of these old cold calculating codgers contain a great deal more nature & virtue — I have been led to think so very much from seeing how my taste has altered & materialized these last 2 years I observed in unpacking my books how little I cared for most of those w$^h$ used to please me so much before, & how I separated the few historical books I had from the rest of the dross, w$^h$ after all is no dross —

 Because as for reading history merely to know facts I apprehend that such a knowledge would enable a man to shew off in society but w$^d$ do little else for him — Now there —

Dear Mother I drink your health in a cup of tea all these tremendous reflections have arisen from my having a new reading table & a volume of Robertson [2] by me *to be read* — I was trying to draw the view out of my windows between them hangs a picture of Napoleon, & under it is your Larkbeare — My chimney is ornamented with a whole lot of gim-cracks I 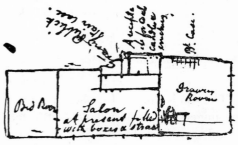 bought at Cambridge & my book-case crammed to the teeth so that really the room looks very comfortable  A man I knew in Germany

[2] William Robertson (1721–1793), the historian.

has just surprized me with a visit & Mʳ Taprell must mourn my absence for to day —

I have not been to the city for I got an ugly scratch on my thigh through my economy — for I had no light in my Salon & three or four nights ago I tumbled over a box set therein, wʰ box was covered with nails to the great detriment of my leg, & to the complete destruction of a pair of pantaloons — to day I di⟨ne with⟩ my Uncle Frank wʰ will cost me five shillings ⟨cab fare⟩ on Monday I will go to the city, but I think it wᵈ be better not to write to Mʳˢ Blechynden [3] until her letter arrives to us. I was very angry at Mʳˢ Hallidays [4] letter, but thought it better to say nothing about it; My Uncle Fᵏ seems to think her conduct most meritorious — he is very kind but asks me to dinner too often — three times a week — I met a pleasant party there last Monday — rather aristocratical — on Tuesday I feed at the Kembles' — Good bye dear Mother I have my best coat on & must hobble to Cadogan Place. Love to father & all besides —

W. M. Thackeray.

Sunday — I walked back half a mile because I had forgotten this letter, & then forgot it after all. I wish to heaven I could get over

[3] Richmond Thackeray's daughter by a native mistress. See *Memoranda,* Mrs. Carmichael-Smyth.

[4] The former Augusta Thackeray (1785–1849), *Genealogy* (54), Richmond Thackeray's sister. She and her sister Emily had gone out to Calcutta in 1802 to keep house for their brother Thomas. There she married Mr. Elliot, *Genealogy* (55), the Senior in Council, whom Mrs. Bayne (*Memorials,* p. 414) describes as "Richmond's dearest friend." After his death she married another intimate of Richmond's, Dr. Halliday (d. 1849), *Genealogy* (56). During these years she was the constant companion of Thackeray's mother, but the sisters-in-law eventually became estranged and were not reconciled until they met again late in their lives in Paris. In a letter to Miss Trimmer of January 23, 1844, William Ritchie contrasts Mrs. Halliday with Mrs. Langslow: "She has much of her sister's talent and wit (tho' not, I think, so delicate and happy) and is most kind-hearted and truly excellent, but with a great share of common sense, and a love of the world and society, which would make her shrink with horror from such a life as that preferred by her younger sister. Her manners are quite those of a lady of the old school, and a very fine old lady she is. Her excellent husband is the funniest

this foolish light headedness — to day I have been reading at home lying on the rug the best part of the evening — I find it is a fortnight since I wrote those last few lines do dear Mother pardon this — I did not think it had been a week ago till looking in my Journal this evening — This omission does not result from want of affection, but from the same unsteadiness & forgetfulness w$^h$ has cursed me all my life — I have kept a Journal now for six weeks [5] & begin to have hopes of amendment this is the only piece of resolution I ever atchieved — Good night dear Mother I am very very sorry for my neglect. I shall leave this bit for tomorrow.

Monday — I was again near too late & have only just time to say good bye dear Mother.


60.          TO FRAU VON GOETHE
              25 JANUARY 1832

*Hitherto unpublished. My text is taken from a transcript supplied by Mrs. Fuller.*

                                        5 Essex Court,
                                        Temple, London.
                                        Jan. 25th, 1832.

Dear Madame de Goethe,

   The bearer [6] of this letter comes recommended to your father-in-law by Mr. Carlyle. I hope I have not been too bold in promising him your good offices while he remains at Weimar.

---

old gent. you ever saw — eyes like saucers, and a nose like a rhinoceros, complexion like a carrot and a heart like a prince's. If, as I hope, you see them in England, you'll be amused at the contrast, and ask, as every one does, how could that fine old woman marry that little Doctor. Yet a happier old couple or more attached don't exist." (*Ritchies in India*, p. 130)

   [5] This journal has not been preserved.

   [6] Henry Reeve (1813–1895), who was educated at Norwich School and abroad, met Thackeray when he returned to England in 1831. Most of his mature life was devoted to letters, though he was successively Clerk of Appeal and Registrar to the Judicial Committee of the Privy Council. He wrote for *The Times* from 1840 to 1855 and edited *The Edinburgh Review* from the latter year until his death. A man of great social gifts, he was one of the best known London personalities of his day.

Six months ago I took the liberty of writing to you, and about three months since I sent one or two old books, which I am afraid may not have reached you. If you have received either the letter or the books, you will have learnt how very happy I should be to receive a line from you, if not, I can only repeat my thanks for your great kindness to me while I was in Germany, and my hope very soon to revisit it.

Ever my dear Madame de Goethe,

Yours most sincerely,

W. M. Thackeray

61.                    TO JOHN ALLEN
                    27 JANUARY 1832

*Address:* J. Allen Esq^re | 6 Upper Eaton St. | Pimlico. *Postmark:* 27 JA 1832. Hitherto unpublished.

Dear Johnny.

I could not come to you last night — it was too late — but I dine with my uncle tomorrow at 6 so I shall be in your neighbourhood or what say you to coming down here & then walking back together — send me a note by the tuppenny & say what you will do, if I am not in my own chambers I shall be at M^r Taprell's 1. Hare Court. Good bye till tomorrow aff^tly y^rs W. M. T.

Essex Court.

Friday —

62.                        DIARY
                2 APRIL–23 NOVEMBER 1832

Extracts published, *Biographical Introductions*, III, xix-xxviii and xxx.

Monday. April 2. 1832.

In the morning Kinderley & W^m Ri⟨tchie⟩ [7] called — he has grown a very fine boy afterwards I called at M^cDowell's & walked

[7] See *Memoranda.*

with him — called at Dicks & went to see Haydon's pictures [8] —
M[r] Haydon by dint of telling the world he is a great painter has
made them believe it — The Mock Election is very forced & bad —
Xenophon so so — & the rest of the pictures about as good as the
mock election. Was fool enough to buy some Venetian glasses for
a pound — Dined with Edwards & had a pleasant party enough —
went to see Father & Mother at Covent Garden.[9] The opera was
The Barber of Seville, w[h] my father pronounced very poor. Miss
Inverarity sang charmingly but has a mouth big enough to sing
two songs at once — Wilson had one of the freshest voices I ever
heard — It was meâ sententia a dozen times better than the opera
but not being Italian the ladies did not admire it so much. Here is
a long article for the 2[d] of April — Wrote some verses for Charlotte
Shakespear,[10] w[h] are not quite finished —

| | |
|---|---|
| Haydon — | 1 „ 6. |
| Glasses. | 1.0.0 |
| Theatre &c | 4.0 |
| Laundress | 7.0 |
| | 1 „ 12.6 |
| From former book. | 60 „ 10.6. |
| | 1 „ 12.6. |
| | £62 „ 3 „ 0. |

T. 3. Despatched my verses to Charlotte — dined at Woods,
was all day with Mother — went to the Adelphi [11] but found no
room, also to No 60 [12] where I lost 6/6.

Expences.                        6 „ 6.

[8] An exhibition of paintings by Benjamin Robert Haydon (1786–1846)
which was opened to the public on March 26 and had as its feature his recently
completed "Xenophon."

[9] Where the bill included Fanny Kemble in her own tragedy of *Francis the
First* and Rossini's *Barber of Seville* with Elizabeth Inverarity (1813–1846),
later Mrs. Martyn, as Rosina and Wilson as Fiorello (*Theatrical Observer*,
April 2).

[10] Miss Shakespear (d. 1849), *Genealogy* (86), was Thackeray's cousin.

[11] Where *His Highness the Prince*, a burletta of undetermined authorship,
had its first performance the previous night. Frederick Henry Yates (1797–
1842), father of Edmund Yates, appeared in the principal male rôle.

[12] A gambling "hell" at 60 Regent's Quadrant. See Appendix IV.

W. 4. Had a pleasant letter from Fitz-Gerald; Edwards and Caldwell breakfasted & ate 8 eggs between them besides meat. went to Mother & in the evening to Woods' leaving them at the Oratorio. Then to 60 *for the last time, so help me God* where I won back the exact sum I had lost the day before. read a novel called Stanly Buxton [13] by Galt; & went to bed at 10. Mʳ Dick tempted me very much by proposing a visit to Paris, but it won't do — I shᵈ fall in love with Charlotte before I got back. Was invited to a dance at Mazzinghi's but went not.

| Paid Stationer | 1 ⁿ 0 ⁿ 0. |
|---|---|
| Light Bore | 1 ⁿ 6. |

5 Th. Called with Father on Russell & Campbell, but found neither. Took a lesson in dancing, & dined in chambers with Caldwell played ecartè till four o'clock in the morning & lost eight pound 7 shillings — before I knew where I was, so much for reform. An excellent fellow by the name of Adamson won most of the money — a man called Forman * sung well but was very disagreable. Finished Stanly Buxton, very clever though rather dull — Mʳ Galt knows the world or seems to know it very well — but a man may write very wisely & be no Solomon.

| Willis for dancing | 1 ⁿ 1 ⁿ 0 |
|---|---|
| Lost at play | 8 ⁿ 10 ⁿ 0 |
| Expences | 1 ⁿ 6. |
| | 10 ⁿ 13.6. |

6 Friday — Woke well after my nights extravagance; & on sending to Lubbocks [14] for money received my cheque back again — wrote to mother on the subject — dined in Clarges Street & went with the Dicks to Cadogan Place,[15] where was a very merry pleasant party, wʰ broke up at 2 o'clock, was at Taprell's for the first time

* Since dead I believe at New Brunswick. see Court Journal 1ˢᵗ Septʳ. 1832. — [Thackeray's note.]

[13] *Stanley Buxton; or, The Schoolfellows* (1832) by John Galt (1779–1839).
[14] Sir J. W. Lubbock and Company of 11 Mansion House Street, who remained Thackeray's bankers during most of his life.
[15] Where lived Francis Thackeray.

these ten days, he having been out of town. The cholera has broken out at Paris & the Dicks have given up their trip.

| | |
|---|---|
| Cast & pictures. | 7 ″ 6. |
| Hackney Coach | 1.0 |
| Gloves | 1.6 |
| Paid ? | 4.6. |

7 Saturday — With mother most part of the day — & at Taprell's Father gave me £30 to last me three months —

| | |
|---|---|
| Boots | 1 ″ 12.0. |
| &cs | 2 ″ 0. |
| | ———— |
| | 2 ″ 8.6 |

8 Sunday — with Mother all the morning, & dined at Sir W. Garrows — a very pleasant evening — the old Gentleman was very communicative with his old-world stories — he shewed me his first fee book — £1800 made the first year — These golden days of the profession are gone by.

| | |
|---|---|
| Cab | 1 ″ 0 |

10 Tuesday.[16] Am just come from parting with Mother God bless her — dined with Banning who gave a handsome spread, the company was dull, & I fell asleep. Walked to the house of Lords & saw the Lords coming down to the second reading of the Bill [17] —

[16] A mistake for Monday, April 9.

[17] The agitation that attended the passage of the great Reform Bill is from time to time reflected in the earlier pages of this diary. By the spring of 1832 the only remaining obstacle to electoral reform was the Tory majority in the House of Lords. The Whig ministers got the Bill through its second reading in the upper chamber on April 14 by obtaining William IV's promise that he would make enough new Whig peers to outnumber the Tories if opposition continued. On May 7, however, the Whigs were defeated in an important matter of procedure, and when their leader, Lord Grey, asked the King to create fifty new peers, his request was refused. The Whig ministry resigned on May 9 but agreed to continue in office until a new government was formed. William turned in this crisis to the Duke of Wellington, the most intransigent opponent of reform among the Tories. Throughout England there was a growing determination to resist by force a Wellingtonian ministry, and it is fortunate that the Whig House of Commons was able to prevent the formation of a Tory cabinet. On May 15 the King had again to send for Lord Grey. Even then the tension was not relaxed, for Wellington refused to withdraw

The rascals hissed the Duke as he came down, in his old family state carriage, looking like a hero as he is — met John Allen [18] of Charterhouse he says there are a hundred & ten boys there — Left the men at Banning's drunk at half past eleven, a consummation, which I escaped by falling asleep for an hour in the middle of the drinking James Ritchie called, he has just been "whitewashed," & tells his story in a very different way, to what it has been told for him. Robert Smyth [19] called     I walked with him a little:

Segars                        2 „ 6

11 Tuesday.[20] Walked in the park with Gunning & settled about the new paper; [21] dined with Wood at the Hertford [22] a very splendid place & an excellent dinner called at Pattles [23] & Dupre's —

Expences                    11.

his opposition and the King would not agree to wholesale peer-making. Only on the afternoon of May 18, when preparations for revolt were almost complete, did William at length give Grey authority to create as many new peers as necessary. The Tories abandoned the fight; the third reading of the Bill was carried on June 4; and on June 7 it received the royal assent. See George Macaulay Trevelyan, *Lord Grey of the Reform Bill*, 2d ed. (London, 1929), Book III, chapters 4 and 5.

[18] John Allen (b. 1813) of Bath, who had entered Charterhouse in 1827.

[19] Robert Stewart Carmichael-Smyth, a younger brother of the Major's, later himself a Major of the Ninety-third Highlanders.

[20] A mistake for Tuesday, April 10.

[21] I have not identified this paper. Nothing came of Thackeray's plan to purchase it.

[22] According to the *London Directory* of 1837 there were taverns called the Hertford Arms at both Park Street, Grosvenor Square, and Grosvenor Street, Berkeley Square.

[23] James Pattle of the Bengal Civil Service, his wife, and their seven daughters. The first, Julia Margaret (1815–1879), married Charles Hay Camerson (1795–1880), Member of the Supreme Council of India from 1843 to 1848, in 1838. The second, Adeline (d. 1836), married Colin Mackenzie (1806–1881), later a Lieutenant-General in the Indian army, in 1832. The third, Sarah Monckton, married Henry Thoby Prinsep (1793–1878), a wealthy Indian merchant who was successively a director of the East India Company and a Director of Council of India after his return to England in 1843. The fourth married Dr. Jackson. The fifth married Henry Vincent Bayley (1815–1873), Judge of the Supreme Court of Calcutta from 1862 until his death. The sixth, Virginia (d. 1910), married Charles, third Earl Somers (1819–1883), and the last married John Warrender Dalyrymple.

W. Spoke to Goldshede about money for this paper, w.<sup>h</sup> he can't give me I think. had more talk with Gunnell; dined at Woods with him & M.<sup>c</sup> D. & on my way home dropped into the Strand Theatre where a Signor Benesontag alias Benson (as I heard in the pit) was ventriloquizing; M.<sup>r</sup> Rayners attempt at a monopolylogue was very unfortunate,[24] some twaddle about the reform bill was hissed as it deserved. Was not at Taprell's, & have not read a syllable of anything for 3 days. I must mend, or else I shall be poor idle & wicked most likely in a couple more years.

Was with a printseller [25] in G.<sup>t</sup> Newport Street who says he will share profits in caricatures with me., a handsome offer, all I have to do is to furnish the sketch —

| Expences | 2 |
| Theatre | 1 |

12 Thursday. Was at Taprells. wrote to Wood who promised to back my bill, called & sat with Gunnell sometime talking over the business — Went to Drury Lane & saw The Compact [26] a new piece by Planché, very good but very like Charles the 12.<sup>th</sup> Wallack looked & acted amazingly well as did Farren; H. Wallack acted a swindler & did it to the life, without I should think at all departing from his ordinary habits & conversation — Supped at the Bedford [27] with Matthew who is to breakfast with me. I have never known what adversity is or I should be able perhaps to understand his incomprehensible recklessness & quiet with things hanging over him, w.<sup>h</sup> if discovered might leave him a beggar & an outcast. I do not love him now as in old times & perhaps it is as lucky for me — for

[24] The principal attraction at the Strand was "Mr. Raynor, A Sketch exhibiting the Passions, Manners, Peculiarities, and Eccentricities of our Nature, entitled the WORLD AS IT RUNS; or, Fancy's Freaks" (*Theatrical Observer*, April 17).

[25] Henry Gibbs of 23 Great Newport Street.

[26] In which James William Wallack (1791?–1864) appeared as Juan Ravegos, Farren as the Archbishop of Granada, and Henry John Wallack (1790–1870) as Lope Mendez. *Charles XII* (1828) was also by James Robinson Planché (1796–1880).

[27] The Bedford Coffee House and Hotel in Covent Garden.

my pocket at any rate. Schulte has been seen at Bath, I wish I could catch him —

| | |
|---|---|
| John | 3 ″ 0. |
| Theatre | 3.6 |
| Luncheon | 6. |

13 Friday — Went to Gunnell but nothing was settled — Matthew breakfasted took some caricatures to Mr Gibbs who says he can dispose of them for me. 7 men dined the same party as on Friday with the addition of Matthew & a Mr Reid the Brewer — played ecartè & lost as usual — The party was very merry, Forman sang lots of songs.

| | |
|---|---|
| Lost | 2 ″ 13 ″ 0. |
| Luncheon | 1 ″ 0. |

14 Saturday — The second reading of the Bill in the Lords with a majority of nine — My newspaper scheme is done up, for want of funds. perhaps it has saved me a £100 perhaps I have lost a thousand by it — Unwell with a sore throat, & a stomach out of order. Caldwell & Mc D. dined off the remains of yesterday's feast. went to bed at 10, with a couple of pills in my internals

| | |
|---|---|
| Laundress | 2 ″ 9 ″ 6. |
| &cs. | 2 ″ 0 |

15 Sunday — at home in the morning doing my duty by the pills; in the afternoon went to Gunnells & thence to Montague Place [28] where I staid all the evening make pantomime tricks for John Henry.

16 Monday — Read law for about an hour went at 11 to the Somerset Coffee House to meet Dr Maginn; [29] whom I liked for

[28] Where lived Dr. Turner.

[29] William Maginn (1793–1842) was the son of a Cork pedagogue. He took his B. A. degree at Trinity College, Dublin, in 1811 and returned to Cork to teach in his father's school. When Dublin gave him an LL. D. degree in 1819, he had already begun to contribute to *Blackwood's Magazine* and *The Literary Gazette*, and four years later he came to London to try his fortune at journalism. He secured employment with several Tory periodicals and soon made himself known as one of the most learned, witty, and formidable writers of his day. In 1830 he was instrumental in founding *Fraser's Magazine*, where much of his best work appeared during the next decade.

his wit & good feeling — then to Montague Place to finish the pantomime trick — called at Kembles' Dupre's & Pattles' & dined at the Bedford. J Kemble & Pearson here till late in the evening talking metaphysics of w$^{\underline{h}}$ Pearson has read a good deal & Kemble amazingly little.

| Lunch & beggars | 6. |
| Segars & box | " 5.0 |

17 W. omitted to write this days journal out of pure idleness; went to Uncle Franks & found him ill in bed with a swelled face. bought a little wine at the Pantechnicon —

| Shirts | 3 " 9 " 0. |
| Segars | 9 " 0 |

18 Th: Ritchie breakfasted, in the afternoon went out & walked in the Park & elsewhere    Kemble & Wood dined here, I left them & went to bed at 3 o'clock — Walked in the Park with M$^{r}$ Dick & Kemble — & met the Duke looking like an old hero —

| Wine | 2 " 14 " 6. |

19 Th: H. Kemble breakfasted, we went to see the Rehearsal of the Easter Piece at C. G.[30] with Farley in his glory. Du Pre dined

---

Particularly after 1837, however, he drank to excess, and he died at last of consumption after a long sojourn in a debtors' prison had broken his health.

The fullest account of Maginn's place in Thackeray's literary development is to be found in Miriam M. H. Thrall's *Rebellious Fraser's* (New York, 1934), pp. 55–80. Though Dr. Thrall exaggerates the intimacy of Maginn's association with Thackeray, and though her list of "works probably attributable to Thackeray and Maginn in collaboration" (pp. 297–298) derives altogether from speculation, her thesis that Maginn strongly influenced the outlook and style of Thackeray's early work has much to recommend it.

It should be mentioned in passing that despite Dr. Thrall's arguments to the contrary (pp. 208–211), Maginn was certainly the original of Captain Shandon in *Pendennis*. The likeness may not be exact — Thackeray's portraits from life are never mere photographs — but it is none the less unmistakable.

[30] On Easter Monday there was performed at Covent Garden "a new grand melodramatic and operatic Chinese tale of enchantment, called THE TARTAR WITCH AND THE PEDLER BOY" (*Times*, April 23). See below, No. 64.

& asked me to Wilton for next week — Heard from Mother —
Mʳˢ Huyshe very ill.

Porter &c.                        3 ″ 0.

20 Fri, am just come from dissuading Mʳ Dick from going to
India — his brother Sʳ Robert ³¹ was there & a very consequential
selfish fellow I thought him — If ever by good fortune I should
rise to any situation wʰ may enable me to confer benefit, I will remember Dick's children — Poor fellow, I left him debating about
living cheap in Devonshire — called at Mʳ Protheroe's, Grant's, &
Forrests — Mʳˢ Forrest & I are very intimate now; she is very good
& kind, though these are qualities I begin to find out in women as
soon as I know them — I hope my ideas are all true. Poor old
Burke has had a third execution on her furniture & there is a
grand noise about it — Called & saw Grant, & made several betises,
wʰ seemed to amuse him. Wrote a piece of a letter to F. G.³²

Lunch —                          2 ″ 0.
Servant.                         2 ″ 0
John                             7 ″ 0
                              _____
                                 89 ″ 3 ″ 6.

21 Sat. Finished FG's letter went to Montague Place, & to
Burkes to get her from her lodgings, where was a terrible business;
it was only by swearing & threatening & bringing a witness that I
was able to get her out — however it was at last triumphantly
effected, though the old lady seemed to care infinitely more for her
crockery than for⟨. . .⟩ ³³

Laundress                        I ″ 5 ″ 0.
Books                            10 ″ 0.
Segars &c                        2 ″ 6.
Pictures                         I ″ 0.
                              _____
                                 I ″ 18 ″ 0.

³¹ General Sir Robert Dick, K. C. B., who fought in the Peninsular
Campaign and at Waterloo and died at Sobraon in 1846 (*Ritchies in India*,
p. 166).
³² Fragments of this letter are printed below, No. 64.
³³ A page has here been torn from the diary.

23 Monday. Wrote to Mother; went in the evening to see
Hunchback & the new Easter piece [34] — w^h latter was terribly dull.
Hunchback was good but not so good I think as it is represented, or
as the tragic productions of the author —

Eating &c.                              2 „ 6.

24 Tuesday — Breakfasted with Buller & went to Greenwich
Fair; in w^h however I was disappointed — a great deal of blackguardism, & very little fun. dined at Blakesleys [35] I like him very
much, he seems very amiable & I know he is very clever — met an
artist a M^r Macarton — who has asked me to come & see him. returned home & to bed at 2. ⟨. . .⟩ [36]

Boots                          I „ I „ O

[25 Wednesday.]
to Covent Garden to see Julius Caesar [37] — all the parts were admirably filled — Warde's Cassius was as good as Kembles Antony
w^h is giving it very high praise — Young I did not very much
admire — I sat for some time with M^rs Kemble & her daughters; &
then with the Dicks & the Shakespears. C Kemble had a most
splendid silver helmet & shield.

26 Th: All the morning with Buller [38] drinking ale & smoking;
went in the evening to the Strand Theatre,[39] & saw a clever thing

[34] The bill at Covent Garden on April 23 was made up of *The Tartar
Witch* and *The Hunchback*, a comedy by James Sheridan Knowles (1784–
1862), first presented on April 5, in which the author appeared with Fanny
Kemble (*Theatrical Observer*).

[35] Joseph Williams Blakesley (1808–1885), later (1872) Dean of Lincoln,
who had been Thackeray's contemporary at Trinity College, Cambridge. He
won the Chancellor's Medal and was twenty-first wrangler and third classic
in 1831, achievements which no doubt sufficiently attested his cleverness in
Thackeray's eyes.

[36] A page has here been torn from the diary.

[37] In this performance James Prescott Warde (1792–1846) played Cassius,
Charles Mayne Young (1777–1856) Brutus, and Charles Kemble Marc
Antony.

[38] See *Memoranda*, Charles Buller.

[39] "STRAND . . . THIS EVENING will be presented (3d time) a new
nautical drama, called THE LONG FINN; or, Picaroon's Prey. . . . After
which, an entirely new comedietta, called A FRIEND IN NEED. To con-

called the Long Finn — a great deal of good situation & dialogue
but very wild & incoherent. 〈. . .〉[40]

| Laundress | 5/. |
| Hosiery | 9. |
| Luncheon | 1 |
| Deduct | 1 " 3 " 6. |

[28 Saturday.]
went to Montague Place, & found them all dining before going to
Astleys [41] — whither we went in a party of ten, but the glory of
Astleys has departed  It was sadly dull.  Came home & sat drinking
gin-punch with Pearson till 1/2 / twelve

29 Sund — Breakfasted at Bullers & met his brother [42] a very
nice fellow very clever & very well read — Idled about all day till
dinner time when A Buller and Kinglake [43] dined with me at the
Bedford — At night went canvassing for "Percy & reform" — &
very successful we were — It was a silly prank [44] but has shown me
how easy it is to talk men over.  Found Kinderley tipsy with a
common beast of the town, & took him away from her, & home to
bed — much to the Lady's disgust & Kinderley's advantage — She

---

clude with a new mythological and musical extravaganza, entitled THE
JUDGMENT OF PARIS." (*Times*, April 25)

[40] A page has here been torn from the diary.

[41] Astley's Amphitheatre, Westminster Bridge Road, famous for its equestrian entertainments.

[42] See *Memoranda*, Arthur Buller.

[43] Alexander William Kinglake (1809–1891), the son of a banker and
solicitor at Taunton in Somerset. After some years at Eton, he matriculated at
Trinity College, Cambridge, in 1828 and took his B. A. and M. A. degrees in
1832 and 1836. About 1835 he made the tour described in his *Eothen, or
Traces of Travel Brought Home from the East* (1844). He was called to the
bar in 1837, having entered Lincoln's Inn five years before, but rarely practised. In 1854 he went out with the English army to the Crimea, where he
became friendly with Lord Raglan, and at Lady Raglan's request he two years
later began his masterly *Invasion of the Crimea* (1863–1887), the chief work
of his life. He was M. P. for Bridgewater from 1857 to 1868. Kinglake was
never married, but he was very popular in society. Thackeray saw him often
in later life at Mrs. Procter's, Mrs. Elliot's, the Miss Berrys', the Athenæum
Club, and the Travellers' Club.

[44] The joke apparently lay in associating Hugh Percy (1785–1847), third
Duke of Northumberland, a Tory magnate zealous against the Reform Bill,
with those who favored electoral redistribution.

threatens to set her bully on me.  Kemble asked us to an evening party but sent to put us off.  I wish to God, I could take advantage of my time & opportunities as C Buller has done — It is very well to possess talents but using them is better still — Kinglake is or says he is an Atheist, & tells everyone his opinions —

30. Monday.  Just as I had written my critique on Buller enter Martineau [45] who finds fault with him for the very things w^h I thought so creditable to him — he says he has *not* taken advantage of his opportunities — To be sure as to advancement & society & talent he has had greater than most men, not the least of them that Carlyle was his tutor — Went to chambers, dined in Hall, afterwards Kemble & Hallam sat here for an hour — read an article in Blackwood about A Tennyson abusing Hallam for his essay in the Englishman.[46]  Read the Monthly [47] w^h is cleverer than any of the others I think — & took a shilling's worth at the Strand Theatre to see The Judgement of Paris — a poor thing enough    Came home at 1/2 past ten with the intention of reading or writing & as usual fell asleep. — Was fool enough to order a seal w^h is to cost 3 guas.  Wrote various bad verses.

| Luncheon &c | 1 „ 0 |
| Theatre | 1 „ 0 |
| Cigar Divan | 1 „ 0. |

May. 1. Tuesday.  A miserable rainy May morning — went to Taprell's Littledale & Walker came to luncheon  Sat at home till 7 & went to see Macready in the Merchant of London [48] — a good play enough & admirably acted — The Easter piece was very pretty

[45] Arthur Martineau (1807–1872), who had matriculated at Trinity College, Cambridge, in 1825 and taken his B. A. and M. A. degrees in 1829 and 1832.  He was Vicar of Whitkirk, near Leeds, from 1838 to 1863 and Rector of St. Mildreds, Bread Street, with St. Margaret Moyses, in London, from 1864 until his death.

[46] In *Blackwood's Magazine* for May, 1832, pp. 721–741, "Christopher North" (Professor John Wilson) attacked Arthur Henry Hallam (1811–1833) for his fulsome praise of Tennyson in *The Englishman's Magazine* of July, 1830.

[47] *The New Monthly Magazine.*

[48] A drama by Thomas James Serle, first performed at Drury Lane on April 26 with Macready in the title role.

& had more pretensions to a play than the one at the other house. It is called the Magic Car. made a plot for a play w.ʰ would I think be a good one.

| Theatre | 3 ʼʼ 6. |
| Supper | 3 ʼʼ 0. |

Wed. . 2. D.ʳ Maginn called & took me to the Standard [49] shewing me the mysteries of printing & writing leading articles, with him all day till 4 — called on Goldshede — dined at the Sabloniere [50] broke my vow & one five pounds at play at 60 Quadrant — came home & sat writing against M.ʳˢ Norton & poetesses till near one when Martineau Birkbeck & Pearson came in —

| Crockery | 1 ʼʼ 8 ʼʼ 6 |
| John | 7 ʼʼ 0. |
| Dinner | 6 ʼʼ 6. |
| | 2 ʼʼ 2 ʼʼ 0. |

Deduct £5 won & 12/6 borrowed from G.

| | 96 ʼʼ 8 ʼʼ 6 |
| | 5 ʼʼ 13 ʼʼ 6 |
| | 90 ʼʼ 16 ʼʼ 0 |

Th. 3. At Taprells — dined here at Caldwell's expence with 2 sporting men M.ʳ Monro & M.ʳ Kay — the last an excellent fellow but poor went to Dobb's in the evening & played whist lost of course.

| Stockings | 6 |
| Lost at Whist — | 13 — |
| &cs | 1. |

F. 4. Idle all day & walked all the afternoon with Buller dined with D.ʳ Maginn at the Kean's head — a dull party of low literary men. M.ʳ Bailey [51] of the ⟨. . .⟩ [52]

| Custom House. | 1 ʼʼ 6 ʼʼ 6. |
| Dinner | 1 ʼʼ 0 ʼʼ 0. |

[49] A Tory evening paper, founded in 1827, with which Maginn was associated.           [50] The Sabloniere Hotel in Leicester Square.
[51] Frederick William Naylor ("Alphabet") Bayley (1808–1853), at this time editor of *The National Omnibus*. See below, No. 73.
[52] A page has here been torn from the diary.

[5 Saturday.]

| | |
|---|---|
| *Lost* | 2 ″ 7 ″ 0 |
| Dinner | 3.6. |

[6 Sunday.]

for a party at Kembles to w.ʰ I was invited — Read Eugene Aram but was much disappointed (as usual)    It is a very forced & absurd taste to elevate a murderer for money into a hero — The sentiments are very eloquent clap-trap.  There is no new character (except perhaps the Corporal) & no incident at all — Aram's confession [53] is disgusting, it would have been better, more romantick at least, to have made him actuated by revenge hatred jealousy or any passion except avarice, w.ʰ is at more variance with the character given him in the Novel, than w.ᵈ have been a hotter & (as we suppose) a nobler passion — The book is in fact humbug, when my novel is written it will be something better I trust — One must however allow Bulwer wit & industry I think unless his quotations were for his book & not from his memory. enough of Aram. Wrote yesterday to F. G. with a letter as from Herrick [54] — It might have been made pretty but was poor enough — How can a man know his own capabilities or his inferiority? — Not by reading — one acquires thoughts of others & gives one's self the credit of them. Bulwer has a high reputation for talent & yet I always find myself competing with him — This I suppose must be vanity — If it is truth why am I idle? — Here is enough conceit for to night —

| | |
|---|---|
| Dinner | 7 ″ 0 |
| | 5 ″ 4 ″ 0 |

[7] Monday — called at Kembles DuPres Dicks Uncle Franks & Allen's — Kemble read me some very beautiful verses of Tennysons. DuPre was just going from town & Allen had been gone 3 weeks. Dined at Wood's Hotel [55] & went to Matthews w.ʰ was dull enough

| | |
|---|---|
| Expences | 7. |

[53] In Book V, chapter 7.
[54] This letter has not been preserved.
[55] At 2 and 3 Arundel Street, Haymarket.

[8] T. Edwards came in in the morning & we went to the water colour wh took up most of the day till dinner time — when he Maginn Mr Banks [56] his friend, Buller & McDowell dined with me at the Bedford. went to 64 [57] & lost £10 — then returned to the Piazza [58] where I found Caldwell Kinderley & Paget & McD playing whist — fell asleep on the sofa & did not wake till it was light they were still playing — It is now ten o'clock & we have just come home after breakfast — I as fresh as a lark —

Expences 10 〃 13 〃 0.

May. 9. . W. The ministers the Reform Bill & the country gone to the Devil! [59] — went to the house of commons & got in with Curzon's order — It will be soon I suppose a house of delegates. Went to the exhibition [60] wh was very bad — dined at the Salopian,[61] very bad & infamously dear went to see Der Freyschütz [62] very good — Miss Schneider sung & acted very sweetly. the orchestra was admirable & the house crammed — nevertheless I went to sleep at the end of the second act, from the debauch of last night. Bought a big stick wherewithal to resist all parties in case of attack.

Expences 1 〃 10 〃 0

Th. May 10. Sate reading trials till one when Mr Dick called walked with him up Piccadilly & met Wm Ritchie just returned from Boulogne — Then to Forrests Mrs Forrest very kind & had taken the trouble to get a note for Mrs Tucker's party for me — but

[56] Percival Weldon Banks, (1806–1850) a crony of Maginn and a frequent contributor to *Fraser's Magazine* under the signatures, "Morgan Rattler" and "The Serjeant of the Law." In Maclise's drawing of "The Fraserians," which appeared in *Fraser's Magazine* for January, 1835, Thackeray is seated between Banks and John Churchill, another friend of Maginn.

[57] A gaming house in Regent's Quadrant.

[58] The Piazza Coffee House in the northeast corner of the Covent Garden Piazza.

[59] See above, April 10.

[60] Either of the Royal Academy or of the Water Colour Society.

[61] The Salopian Coffee House, 41 Charing Cross Road.

[62] Weber's *Der Freischütz* (1821) was given for the first time in England at the King's Theatre on May 9 (*Times*).

I did not go — sate at home reading instead or rather dawdling over trials & went to bed at eleven    Caldwell & I have made an agreement to get up every morning at nine — There is no row in London as I had expected.

| | |
|---|---|
| Dinner | 3 ″ 0 |
| Gloves | 3.6 |
| Cab. | 1 ″ 0. |

Fr. May 11. Idle all day dined with Maginn Grant & others at the Keans head — spielte und verlierte acht pfund.

Sat. 12. Woke with a headache from yesterday's excess walked about doing nothing but raising wind — dined at Montague Place & was introduced to Fraser of F's Magazine. — Thought him neither clever or good very different to hearty witty Maginn, who is a very loveable man I think — A large party at Forrests — they are very kind to me. Called on Wood.

Sun. 13. Breakfasted with Edwards sat all the morning with Dobbs & dined at Dicks — To day a Bishop has been pulled out of his pulpit — what may come to morrow perhaps a king may be pulled off his throne — This sounds very like clap-trap but I fear it will be true [63] —

Expences        2 ″ 6.

Monday 14. called on Buller walked with him to the Exhibition — then to D^r Maginn dined at Dicks — read — nothing as has been my custom the whole of this last month. I find I cannot read I have tried it at all hours & it fails — I don't know so much now as when I came to town & that God knows was little enough. I would make a vow to read 50 pages of law every day but it w^d be of no use. Heard from Fitz-Gerald — he is coming to town to see his sister married — what a short lived friendship ours has been; The charm of it wore off with him sooner than with me but I am afraid now we are little more than acquaintances, keeping up from old habits the form of friendship by letter —

Expences —        6 ″ 0.

[63] "Few contingent historical propositions," writes Trevelyan (*Lord Grey of the Reform Bill*, pp. 343–344), "are more certain than this, that if the

T. 15. All the morning with Wood in the evening with D<sup>r</sup> Maginn who dined with me — three bottles between us & a great deal of pleasant talk —

| | |
|---|---|
| Corkscrew | 2 ″ 6. |
| Porter | 8. |

W. 16. Maginn called — called on Heath [64] & at Montague Place where I dined & spent a pleasant evening. Read some of Montluc's commentaries [65] very entertaining — went to Edwards in the evening — heard from Mother ⟨. . .⟩ [66]

| | |
|---|---|
| Montluc | 3 ″ 0. |

[Thursday. 17.] des abends spielte ich, und bekommte fünf pfund. —

| | |
|---|---|
| Bacon — | 6. |
| Dinner | 3. |
| Cigar | 9 ″ 0 |
| &cs | 11 ″ 0. |

Fr. Again all day with Fitz-Gerald — went into the City & bought segars — dined at Dick's, & spent the evening at Edwards's — he is a good fellow & a kind though not very wise — Read some of Cavendish [67] w<sup>h</sup> is infamous, & some of the Radical very clever but dull. written I suppose in a hurry for money & not ⟨. . . Cam⟩bridge [68] days.

| | |
|---|---|
| Dinner | 4 ″ 0 |
| Letters | 2 ″ 0. |
| Lunch | 1 ″ 0. |
| | 1 ″ 16 ″ 0. |

Duke had taken office [between May 9 and 15] there would have been a rebellion."

[64] Charles Heath (1785–1848), the engraver, promoter of the popular early Victorian annuals.

[65] The *Commentaires* (1592), or memoirs, of Blaise de Lasseran-Massencome, Seigneur de Montluc (1501–1577).

[66] Ten lines have here been cut from the diary.

[67] *Cavendish; or, The Patrician at Sea* (1831) by William Johnson Neale (1812–1893); *The Radical: An Autobiography* (1832) by John Galt.

[68] Four lines have here been cut from the diary.

S. 18. One of the most disgraceful days I ever spent — playing from after breakfast till 4 o'clock at chicken hazard [69] with Caldwell & Kay; by good luck only a shilling was lost between all parties. dined with Heath at MacNivens & went with him to the Opera [70] — w.ʰ was very poor as was the ballet meâ sententia. behind the scenes I saw the rivals Brugnoti & Heberle — plastered with rouge & looking like she devils more than graceful women F. G. did not come. spielte und winnte eighteenpence.

|        |   6.    |
|--------|---------|
| Opera  | 8 „ 6.  |
| Dinner | 4 „ 0.  |

S. 20. Breakfasted with F. G. & sat here talking till 4 walked in the Temple Gardens for an hour, & dined at Dick's; talked about a country excursion & drunk punch at the Bedford. Read some New Arabian Nights [71] very wild & fanciful better I think than the old ones w.ʰ are too much frenchified.

| Dinner | 6 „ 0. |
|--------|--------|

M. 21. Fitz-Gerald here in the evening went to see Fidelio & Schroeder Devrient She acted & sung very nobly, but the opera nevertheless is dull went into Paget's [72] & found half a dozen men tipsy, w.ʰ fate however I did not experience —

| Opera  | 5 „ 0  |
|--------|--------|
| Book   | 2 „ 0. |
| Dinner | 6 „ 0  |

[69] Hazard, according to Serjeant [William] Ballantine (*Some Experiences of a Barrister's Life*, 2 vols., London, 1882, I, 52), was the principal game played in London gambling houses at this time. "There were two kinds," he explains: "French hazard, in which the players staked against the bank, and English, or chicken hazard, in which they played against each other, with a settled profit to the proprietors."

[70] Beethoven's *Fidelio* (1805) was given at the King's Theatre for the first time in England on May 18 (*Times*). This performance was also notable as the English début of the famous soprano Wilhelmine Schröder-Devrient (1804–1860). Among the dancers in the ballet was a Mlle. Herberle; her rival's name does not appear in *The Times*.

[71] The Rev. George Lamb's *New Arabian Nights Entertainments* (1826); earlier English versions derive from the French translation (1704) by Antoine Galland.

[72] Arthur Coyte Paget (1808–1833) entered Charterhouse in 1822 and

T. 22. Walked with Paget through the parks to Kensington Gardens where we strolled about & lay on the grass lunched at the Black Lion at Bayswater & dined with Paget — found half a dozen men comfortably settled in my rooms drinking, to w[h] 1/2 dozen were presently added as many more — at last got rid of them & went to bed at eleven.

| Allan Ramsay | 3.6. |
| Lunch &c. | 4 ″ 0. |

W. 23. All the morning at Bullers drawing caricatures — met M[rs] Austen [73] there a pretty pleasant woman. dined at Heaths & fell asleep soon after dinner, much to the company's amusement & my own. met Colonel Forrest who asked me to Charlton next week — Wrote a short letter to Mother.

| John | 3.0 |
| Soda | 1.6 |

Th 24. Again favored by Mess[rs] Cay & Co — went to see Black eyed Susan at Miss Inverarity's benefit [74] — read part of a novel called the Fair of Mayfair [75] a sensible book enough. after the play eat an enormous supper of lobster, for w[h] V. Caldwell payed.

| Expences | 10 ″ 0 |

Fr. 25. A hot day & an idle — dined at Kent's with a merry party meeting M[r] Clark [76] the author of 3 courses & a dessert.

---

served successively in 1823 and 1824 as Monitor and *præpositus* in Penny's House, where Thackeray was living. He matriculated at Caius College, Cambridge, in 1825 and received his B. A. and M. A. degrees in 1829 and 1833. He was called to the bar at the Inner Temple on November 16, 1832. In an album of Thackerayana in the Huntington Library A. J. Paget writes of him: "My brother was the . . . fellow pupil of the same conveyancer, with Mr. Thackeray. These sketches were for the most part, scribbled on any scrap of paper which my brother's table afforded, during the idle hours at chambers in Pump Court, Temple."

[73] The former Sarah Taylor, who in 1820 had married the eminent jurist John Austen (1790–1859). In later life Thackeray was on friendly terms with the Austens' daughter, Lady Lucy Duff-Gordon.

[74] Miss Inverarity appeared in the title rôle of Douglas Jerrold's *Black-Eyed Susan* (1829) for the first time this evening.

[75] By Mrs. Gore, published in 1832.

[76] William Clarke (1800–1838), a popular humorous writer, whose *Three Courses and a Dessert* appeared in 1830.

spielte und verlierte zehn pfünd — Schulte came here but I had not the pleasure of seeing him, he did not open my letter of abuse,[77] lucky for me, perhaps he will now pay me

| | |
|---|---|
| Dinner | 11 " 0. |
| Cloth | 7 " 0 |

Saturday — to Wednesday — Spending a pleasant time at Charlton where were Col! & Mrs Perter kind pleasant people — on Wednesday returned & went to the French Play & was much delighted with the acting of Madame Albert in Une Divorce[78]

spielte und verlierte funf pfund die mir Schulte bezahlt hat —

30 Th:[79] Called on Mr Mrs Nab out of town Mr Fraser not at home dined at Uncle Franks & brought home poor Selina[80] — They were all in a melancholy plight from the departure of the Dicks — God bless them for the worthiest couple I ever set eyes on — They left town to day after parting with their children in Cadogan Place The girls & Sir Robt went in a post chaise in the morning —

| | |
|---|---|
| Expences | 4/6 — |

Friday June 1st

Spent the morning with Ponsonby[81] came home read French

[77] This letter has not been preserved, but on the back of a page of sketches in the Paget Album there is the following fragmentary draft of a letter, which may have been intended for Schulte: "The day on which you promised to repay the money I lent you is past for some time. I see no sign of your fulfilling a promise so solemnly made on yr part, & so firmly believed on mine — It is useless to tell you how much inconvenience I have suffered through your neglect, because I supposed it . . ."

[78] The other attraction of the evening was Molière's *Le Bourgeois gentilhomme* (*Times*).

[79] A mistake for Thursday, May 31.

[80] Sarah Eliza Donnithorne ("Selina") Shakespear, *Genealogy* (90), who was left an orphan when her father died bringing her home from India in 1825.

[81] William Gledstanes Ponsonby, who matriculated at Trinity College, Cambridge, in 1826 and received his B. A. and M. A. degrees in 1830 and 1833. FitzGerald (*Letters and Literary Remains*, ed. Wright, III, 303) records a rumor that he was the original of Warrington in *Pendennis*. But see below, p. 206, note 88.

Memoirs & wrote a little; dined in chambers in the evening spielte
und verlierte ein pfund — went to Wood & sat with M⟨c⟩Dowell till
near one — Wrote to M⟨r⟩ Gibson about Matthew's business —
Schulte paid me £ 2 more on my entreaty, & wrote to me to say it
was nearly all he had — I dont know whether it is true or not —

Expences                              4 ″ 6.

S. 2. At home all day dawdling over Ponte's Mems [82] & putting
books into my new book case — went in the evening with Buller to
the Eagle Tavern [83] city road a precious place of rational entertainment. There was a concert, & a farcical Vaudeville superb grottoes
cottages & chinese lamps for the small sum of four pence. Went
home to Bullers & found that CB & I did not at all agree about
Tennyson — he is a clever fellow, *nevertheless*, & makes money by
magazine writing, in w⟨h⟩ I sh⟨d⟩ much desire to follow his example.
had a note from Curzon  he dines with me on Monday.

Bill for Umbrella (1830)    1 ″ 1 ″ 0
Porter &c                   1 ″ 0
Ham                         1 ″ 0
Expences                    5.6

Sunday 3. Drove in the Park with Heath & met M⟨rs⟩ Lettsom
who asked me to dinner went & in the evening to Kembles where
was a singing party —

Cabs                              2.16

M. 4. Breakfasted with Buller went about trying to dispose of
caricatures, & then read Magazines in the Kiosk — At 1/2 past 6
Buller & Curzon dined with me at the Bedford — Curzon is a noble
little fellow, as he was at school with all his old enthusiasm & no
humbug — When I supposed him grown cool it was I that was
conceited & not he — drank too much wine & went to Matthews:

[82] The *Memoirs* (first edition, 1823; enlarged second edition, 1830) of
Mozart's Italian librettist, Lorenzo da Ponte (1749–1838).
[83] Better known as the Grecian Saloon (John Hollingshead, *My Lifetime*,
2 vols., London, 1895, Vol. I, p. 25), an establishment in Hoxton which provided cheap amusement, in the form of burlesques, pantomimes, and melodrama, for the lower classes.

where I grew sick & sleepy so came home. Meeting Curzon again has made me very happy.

| | |
|---|---|
| Stock | 5. |
| Pens | 1 " 6 |
| Lunch | 1 " 0 |

T. 5. The day spent in seediness repentance & novel reading — dined in Hall      Edwards & Pearson came afterwards to my chambers & McDowell — read part of the Bravo,[84] wh I thought very poor — The Kings own very fair & Newton Forster [85] better still — I did nothing else all day except eat biscuits, a very excellent amusement & not so expensive as some others —

| | |
|---|---|
| Laundress | 1.6 |

W. 6. Was asked to Cadogan Place but did not go dined instead in Hall where was Grand day & grand feasting venison & goose. In the morning was at Ponsonbys & went to see the weathercock & Midas at the Strand Theatre [86] read Newton Forster & Edgeworths Tales [87] both very good.

| | |
|---|---|
| Soda | 5 " 0 |
| Theatre | 1 " 0 |
| Porter | " 6 |

Th. 7. Read Quentin Durward all the morning & was very much delighted with it; dined in Hall & went afterwards to Venable's [88] Rooms, who strikes me as being a mighty disagreeable fellow.

| | |
|---|---|
| Letter | 1 " 0 |

[84] By James Fenimore Cooper, published in 1831.
[85] Novels by Captain Marryat, published in 1830 and 1832.
[86] "STRAND . . . THIS EVENING will be performed (8th time) an entire new burletta, entitled DAMP BEDS. After which, THE WEATHERCOCK. To which will be added the burletta of MIDAS. To conclude with THE FOUR SISTERS." (*Times*, June 6)
[87] *Tales of Fashionable Life* (1809–1812) by Maria Edgeworth.
[88] George Stovin Venables (1810–1888), second son of Richard Venables, Archdeacon of Carmarthen, was at Charterhouse with Thackeray from 1822 until 1828, when he matriculated at Jesus College, Cambridge. He received his B. A. and M. A. degrees in 1832 and 1835 and became a Fellow and Tutor of his college. Called to the bar in 1836, he went on the Oxford

F. 8. All the day with the Bullers. dined there at 3, at 6 met a
certain Theresa [89] who came to call on him a very pretty disagreeable girl we saw her to the theatre, but being sane & sage I declined entering — came home with M^c Dowell & sat till half past
ten reading the travels of Misja Abou Taleb w^h amused me much —
then went to bed.

Saturday. 9. At home all day till hall time chiefly occupied in
writing & long letter to Fitz-Gerald — dined in Hall in the evening
went to Pearsons & M^cDowells — spielte und wie gewohnlich
verlierte. heard from M^r Gibson about his letter to Matthew

borrowed from Martineau. 10/

Sunday 10. Maginn with me all the morning — one of the
pleasantest I ever passed, he read Homer to me & made me admire
it, w^h I had never done before moreover he made [me] make a
vow to read some Homer every day w^h I dont know whether I
shall keep. his remarks on it were extraordinarily intelligent &
beautiful mingled with much learning a great deal of wit & no
ordinary poetical feeling — Perhaps I allow him this latter because
I found his sentiments agree with my own or rather mine with his.
Told him concerning Gunnells roguery but he was not angry
enough at it — called at Kembles & saw Miss Tot [90] who is a very

Circuit for a time and then devoted himself exclusively to parliamentary
practice. He was made a Q. C. in 1863. Meanwhile, he had come to be regarded as one of the most gifted of London's anonymous journalists. He
contributed an article or two a week to *The Saturday Review* for more than
twenty-five years after its founding in 1855, and the summary of events during
the past year in the December 31 issue of *The Times* was long from his hand.

Despite their early quarrel (see above, No. 7), Thackeray and Venables
were close friends. Morton McMichael, Jr. ("Thackeray's Visit," *Philadelphia
Press*, June 12, 1887) notes that Thackeray, in discussing *Pendennis* at a
dinner party in Philadelphia in 1856, "mentioned that Warrington, Pen's
good friend and mentor, was drawn from an old school chum of his, whose sad
story is finely indicated in the novel.

"He spoke with great affection of the man, and said that it was he who at
school had given him the broken nose, which suggested his adopting the nom
de plume of Michael Angelo Titmarsh."

[89] Charles Buller's mistress. See the account of her daughter, Theresa
Reviss, in *Memoranda*.

[90] See *Memoranda*, Adelaide Kemble.

nice girl, though no beauty — she is very clever & affectionate — Madame not visible — called at M̲ʳ̲ˢ̲ Pattles for the fourth time, equally invisible walked with Kemble in the Park, & met Curzon & appointed him for Monday — went to the Bedford & dined off turtle & cold beef — I wish the turtle had choked me — there is poor M̲ʳ̲ˢ̲ Blechynden starving in India, whilst I am gorging in this unconscionable way here. I must write to her.

Kemble & Johnstone sate drinking brandy & water here till near one — J Kemble told me of a play of F.G's of w̲ʰ̲ I had never heard & w̲ʰ̲ he must have been writing during our correspondence last year, this is not open of him. Kemble says it possesses very great beauties      I should like to judge for myself

Monday. 11. Curzon came in the morning & sat for a couple of hours      Then we went to see the Steam Gun & then to his house where I sat drawing till 6. dined at Woods & went to see the authorized version of Robert le Diable [91] — it was admirably played & sung & danced, but did not strike me as being anything super-excellent — The first drinking & gaming choruses were very pretty, & the resuscitation of the nuns very awful. The scenery was admirable — The nun scene the finest I ever saw on the stage. Heard from FitzGerald who sent me five pounds. Spielte und winnte fünf pfund —

| Paid Wood | 1 ʺ 7 ʺ 0. |
| Opera | 10.6. |
| Jarveys &c | 3 ʺ 0. |
| Gloves | 2 ʺ 0. |
| John | 6 ʺ 0 |
| Bacons Works | 1 ʺ 8 ʺ 0. |
| Lucretius | 2 ʺ 0 |
| Dinner | 3 ʺ 0. |
| Supper | 3 ʺ 0. |
| Cab | 2 ʺ 0 |

Tuesday 12. Received a note from Maginn w̲ʰ̲ called me to breakfast with him — was all day in search of Gunnell but in vain.

[91] Meyerbeer's *Robert le Diable* (1831), which was given for the first time in England at the King's Theatre on June 11. Adolphe Nourrit (1802–1839), the tenor for whom the title role was written, made his English début in this performance (*Times*).

In the evening to Maginn's again where was D^r Gifford,[92] a very learned & pleasant man.

Wednesday. Again all day in search of Gunnell, who however was not findable. went in the evening to Maginn & made him I fear a rash offer of lending him money.

| Dinner | 5 „ 0. |
| Glass &c | 8 „ 6 |
| Lucretius | 2 „ 0 |
| | 5 „ 1 „ 0. |
| Unaccounted | 13. 6. |

Thursday. Friday & Saturday no journal kept —

Spent          1 „ 0 „ 0

Sunday. breakfasted at home & spent the morning reading novels & writing hymns! — went to Maginn dined at the Barly-Mow & drank Sherry with him till ten — he then took me to a common brothel where I left him, very much disgusted & sickened to see a clever & good man disgrace himself in that way. His money matters press upon him I suppose & make him reckless — Thank God that idle & vicious as I am, I have no taste for scenes such as that of last night — There was an old bawd & a young whore both of them with child — The old woman seemed au reste a good natured beast enough with a countenance almost amiable — The young one was very repulsive in manner & face — Came home sickened & fell asleep instead of going to Kembles.

Dinner &c          5.6.

Monday 18. read the life of Marius in Plutarch breakfasted with M^r Macnabb & liked him very much a very quiet gentlemanly & kind man. Went about M's business — & then had a talk with Major [93] the bookseller who is quite a patriarch in his way a fat old fellow in black tights & gaiters, he has promised to let me have his books at trade price — tant mieux.

[92] Stanley Lees Giffard (1788–1858), LL. D., editor of *The Standard* from 1827 to 1845.

[93] John Major, whose shop was at 50 Fleet Street (*Pigot's Commercial Directory*, 1823–1824).

The Duke has been attacked in the streets — Bracy has just been
here he and some few policemen fought for him — Bracy walked
home with him — The Duke shook his hand & thanked him Bracy
says he has lived four & twenty years, but never felt so happy as to
day — Bravo Bracy — I did not think you such a trump before.
dined with Maginn Giffard & Score at the Barley Mow was very
much delighted with the goodness of Gifford —

Dinner                              5 ″

Tuesday — breakfasted with C Buller & met M$^r$ Templer [94] —
C Buller rec$^d$ a letter from Lyne,[95] his electioneering agent at
Liskeard begging him to come down immediately — he was too
unwell to go, but deputed Arthur & me with him! — at eight
o'clock we set off by the mail outside & after a dull cold, hot, damp
dusty uncomfortable ride of four & twenty hours arrived at
Plymouth

Cabinet Lawyer              8 ″ 0.
Fare                       2 ″ 14 ″ 0.
Expences                    1 ″ 6 ″ 0

Wednesday 20. We dined uncomfortably & then were glad
enough to go to bed — My sleep was pleasantly diversified by
bugs & lasted till seven.

Bill &c.                   15 ″ 0
                        _____
                         5 ″ 13 ″ 0

Thursday 21. When we crossed the water to Tor point & set off
to Liskeard by the mail here our first act was a blunder we went to
the wrong inn — this however was soon remedied, our trunks
were withdrawn & ourselves breakfasted at M$^r$ Lynes the Atty's —
a shrewd sensible snob of a fellow with whom we afterwards
dined — but the journey had so knocked me up that I had but a

[94] A country gentleman living in Teignmouth, Devon. He appears to have
been related to the Templers of Lindridge, Devon, a well known county
family.

[95] Benjamin Hart Lyne, an attorney and electioneering agent at Liskeard
(*Law List*, 1832).

weary a day of it — my face burning with the sun & the wind. Most of the day was occupied in composing an address for Charles Buller, the one he sent down being considered very unsatisfactory — Arthur's was fixed upon it was good but too wordy. Then we went to see two more attornies to con over the address & to drink tea. The address was finally delivered into the hands of the Printer; & at about half past 10 we set off in a pouring rain for Polvellan where we arrived at 12 & went gladly to bed —

Thursday 21.[96] Woke & forgot all my travelling troubles after a long sweet sleep. & found myself in a very charming house, in a pretty room & with a pleasant family — the servants all mistook me for Charles Buller this created a sentiment in my favour & I was very kindly received by Mr & Mrs Buller.[97] The day has passed pleasantly enough with a walk & a lunch & a ride & a dinner & a long talk afterwards about subjects of wʰ none of the talkers knew anything — I find here Sir John Lewis & two Miss Bullers, at dinner was a gentleman remarkable for nothing but his name — Captⁿ Toop Nicholas. The house is very pleasant, the master of it most kind & hearted & honest & the mistress a very charming woman, an ancient flame of my fathers — We rode to Morval, Mr Bullers,[98] & saw a nice plain Elizabethan house, & some noble

[96] Evidently an error for Friday, June 22.

[97] For Mr. and Mrs. Charles Buller, the parents of Charles and Arthur, see *Memoranda*. This was not Thackeray's first meeting with them, for Harriet Martineau was introduced to him at a dinner given by the Bullers in 1831. "Mrs. Buller did not excel in tact," writes Miss Martineau (*Autobiography*, 3 vols., ed. Maria Weston Chapman, Boston, 1877, II, 60), "and her party was singularly arranged at the dinner table. I was placed at the bottom of the table, at its square end, with an empty chair on the one hand, and Mr. Buller on the other, — he being so excessively deaf that no trumpet was of much use to him. There we sat with our trumpets, — an empty chair on the one hand, and on the other, Mr. J. S. Mill, whose singularly feeble voice cut us off from conversation in that direction. As if to make another pair, Mrs. Buller placed on either side of her a gentleman with a flattened nose, — Mr. Thackeray on her right, and her son Charles on the left. — . . . About Mr. Thackeray I had no clear notion in any way, except that he seemed cynical. . . ."

[98] John Buller (1771–1849) of Morval, the uncle of Thackeray's friends, a wealthy country gentleman who owned the Cornish seat of West Looe for which Charles Buller had been sitting since 1830. The Miss Bullers were no doubt his daughters.

woods the country in the immediate neighbourhood is very bold & fertile — & Polvellan itself as sweet a little snuggery as ever I saw.

Thursday 28. A pleasant week passed in idleness — dined on Tuesday at Morval, a fine house & an excellent Master. on Wed-

nesday rode with A. Buller for 12 hours canvassing & found much more intelligence and good feeling among the farmers than I had expected. There seems a class of farmers here unknown to our part of Devonshire — men with a tolerable education though not of a large property, like the Scotch farmers —

M^r Bullers house & park at Morval are very gentlemanly & English, & he himself as he sits at his table surrounded by his family portraits a fine specimen of a breed almost gone out now — The

country about here is very charming — well wooded & hilly —
The house where I am staying very pretty & all the present inmates
very agreeable — in fact I have spent a most pleasant week with
little reason to regret having left the Temple so suddenly.

My reading here has been chiefly of old French books collected
by the late proprietor Colonel Lemon — amusing enough certainly,
but not very instructive — Liaisons Dangereuses [99] — Paysan Perverti, Sopha, &c. he seems to have been an Epicurean in mind &
body! a sage remark — To day was occupied in reading Wilhelm
Meister,[100] and a wretched performance I thought it — without
principle & certainly without interest — at least the last volume —
Neither delicacy morality or philosophy as I thought, but not
being initiated have perhaps no business to judge of the latter — of
the two former most people are competent judges — If the mystick
statues scrolls & sphinxes &c — only typify the actual & bodily
part of the book why the mysticism is but a doting drivelling sentimentality not worth the pains of deciphering — It is a mean book I
think & have done with it — can a man with impure views of human
nature be a philosopher? What shall I say in ten years? — I perceive or think I perceive a great change in my character lately — I
have become much more worldly & far less open to enthusiasm —
not relishing poetry as I used or fancied I used — If I live to fifty I
dare say I shall be as cold-blooded & calculating as the worst of
them. but this is after the fashion of the German Prince so I will
have done twaddling & go to bed —

| | |
|---|---|
| Gloves | 2.6. |
| Ale &c | 1 „ 0 |

Friday 29. Spent in idling walking in a broiling sun before
dinner & sleeping after —
Saturday. Drove with Arthur Buller to Liskeard & dined with
M<sup>r</sup> Lyne — in the evening met the farmers & talked politics with

---

[99] *Les Liaisons dangereuses* (1782) by Choderlos de Laclos (1741–1803);
*Le Paysan perverti* (1775) by Restif de la Bretonne (1734–1806); *Le Sopha*
(1740) by Claude-Prosper Jolyot de Crébillon (1707–1777), called Crébillon
fils.
[100] No doubt *Wilhelm Meister's Apprenticeship and Travels*, Carlyle's translation (1824) of Goethe's novel.

them till 11 o'clock was much pleased with their manners & their sense —

Sunday. July 1. Wrote a bad song against Jope [101] & returned to dinner here at 3, have been much delighted with the goodness & humour of Jean Paul,[102] & much disappointed in an old favorite Hoffman — the extravagance of fancy, w$^h$ I used to admire so much now appears to me neither agreable nor extraordinary     The chief recommendation of the story I read (the Golden Pot translated by Carlyle) was the humour, w$^h$ for a German is very great — not so good however as Jean Paul's w$^h$ is very Rabelaisian — read Tiecks Trusty Eckhart. It is a very fine subject but might be made more of — The wandering minstrel from the Venus hill is very fine I think & would be a good character for a play made very wild but not ludicrous, a la Hoffmann.

Turnpike              1 „ 0
Goldsched's Rechnung die    CB. fur mich bezahlt hat — d

Monday July 2. It appears to me that a young man would command particularly attention in the house of Commons in the character of a {young & ardent} Tory — The higher his birth the better, for then his principles would not be so readily questioned, & his family distinctions would command a respect from the Adventurers who will be found I sh$^d$ think, in great numbers in succeeding Parliaments     He might shew himself conscious of his birth & yet despise it in others, & he would besides have greater advantages in speaking, from his principles, than y$^e$ advocates of reform. He could eternally descant on old times & old glories, when the people were contented as they were great & glorious under a system w$^h$ has

---

[101] Jope was electioneering agent for Edward Granville Eliot (1798–1877), styled Lord Eliot, later (1845) third Earl of St. Germans, a great Cornish magnate who had been Tory M. P. for Liskeard since 1824 and was Buller's opponent in this election.

[102] Thackeray had been reading Carlyle's *German Romance* (1827), the third volume of which is entirely devoted to translations from Johann Paul Friedrich Richter (1763–1825). "The Golden Pot" by E. T. A. Hoffmann (1776–1822) and "Trusty Eckhart" by Ludwig Tieck (1773–1853) are included in the second volume. Tieck's story tells how Eckhart is irresistibly attracted to the Venusberg by the magic piping of a wandering musician.

now well nigh raised them to rebellion — He c^d taunt them certainly not in a very Xtian spirit about their infidelity — & could enlist all the romance of the nation on his side — but then he could gain nothing but reputation, must be of a spotless life in fact a Tory knight with his country as his mistress (or rather his party) to whom he must prove his devotion not merely in attacking her enemies but in purifying himself [103] — Little Curzon has just the birth & fortune for this but not the genius. Trench from what I hear of him might perhaps answer — I'm not clear why I have been writing all this except that I have certain Parliamentary visions in my own head & am thinking of the best way of fulfilling them. Besides — during the whole of this day — I did nothing & so had nothing to write — w^h I have accordingly written.

I have made two or three unfortunate attempts at introducing opinions into this book — they are conceited, I think, & not amusing — it always seems as if I was writing for the world & not for myself.

Tuesday. July 3. Read part of Moores Sheridan [104] — all the literary part of his career. CBullers pamphlet on reform [105] with w^h I was very much pleased & an article of his in the New Monthly very spirited & witty. This is little for a day but more than I have read for a long time past — perhaps this kind of half intellectual reading might lead one to deeper study — The last four years of my life have witnessed but very little improvement in it — at 17 I was well informed at my age, but at 21 I know less than most men,

[103] This passage anticipates the tenets of Disraeli's "Young England" party, of which Thackeray was later to make good-natured fun. Curzon came to his mind because he was heir apparent to a Barony created in 1308 and to estates worth (in 1883) more than £6,000 a year (Bateman, *Great Landowners*, p. 494). Richard Chenevix Trench (1807–1886), who took his B. A. and M. A. degrees at Trinity College, Cambridge, in 1829 and 1833, amply justified Thackeray's confidence in his abilities. He was Professor of Divinity at King's College, Cambridge, from 1846 to 1858, Dean of Westminster from 1856 to 1863, and for the rest of his life Archbishop of Dublin.

[104] Thomas Moore's *Memoirs of the Right Honourable Richard Brinsley Sheridan* (1825).

[105] "On the Necessity of a Radical Reform" (1831). I have not identified Buller's article.

infinitely less than I ought to know. I wish to God I could settle myself into a little steady reading were it but for an hour a day. The early life of Sheridan is very interesting — his dreams about literary distinction his disappointments, & his final success. I think I could write a good comedy — I wish I had perseverance to try — Amen says my mother & so do I from the bottom of my heart —

Expences at Liskeard                    10

Newton Abbot.

Wednesday — July 4 — Left Polvellan at 12 for Plymouth, & from Plymouth came on hither [106] through the most beautiful country in the world — hills all covered with fine trees and lofty Dartmoor mountains, churches with high old towers & pretty cottages all snugly surrounded by noble trees & pleasant green fields, where the hay was lying just mown. Totnes seemed a quaint old town with a fine church a narrow street full of gable ends and a gate at the end thereof — looking (like Looe & all places hereabout, more like a foreign town than an English) But then the country was thoroughly & beautifully English — a happy quiet valley w$^h$ one w$^d$ have thought the jars & turmoils of the world never w$^d$ have reached — nevertheless, at Newton was a man selling seditious papers for a halfpenny, one of w$^h$ I was extravagant enough to purchase — it was a dull dialogue about the Union Coach & one Bill King —

Plymouth & Devonport are dingy squalid looking places, though the streets are broad and well paved & the houses large but in the part of the street through w$^h$ we came     I did not see a single good shop & but very few people — at Wheatley Hotel I eat at least 2 pounds of boiled beef & suffered for my beastly voracity all night. It is a better inn than the other where, in going to Polvellan I was almost sacrificed by the bugs. I felt very sorry to leave Polvellan though with the prospect of returning to it so soon for I have passed there a very happy fortnight & have made some very kind friends —

[106] To Teignmouth, by way of Totness and Newton.

| Coach hire | 13. |
| Pencil case & book | 10 |
| Segars | 3. |
| Coachman &c | 3 |

## Kingskerswell

Thursday — July 4 [107] — All day at Teignbridge idling & looking at the proceedings of the Cricket Club — came home in the
evening with M<sup>r</sup> Templer to his house here — & liked him & his
daughters & son who is just come from a voyage to China. There
were a great number of tigers [108] at the cricket club & Sir Lawrence
Polk who made himself a conspicuous ass.

Friday 5 — Walked to Sir John Lewis a mile & a half from
here, dinner at 8 and sat drinking till one very much amused with
the wit of M<sup>r</sup> Templer. Made a great fool of a governess who is
here & perhaps ditto of myself.

| Inn Bill | 6.6. |

Saturday 6,[109] Went to Heytor — part of the way with Henry
Templer behind me on horseback — M<sup>r</sup> Templer in his gig with
nine passengers following — The ride was pleasant & Heytor very
well worth seeing — The granite works there have as I am told
been Templer's ruin — The profits of the company are now better — London Bridge has been built of the Heytor granite & several
other public works — The country looked like ancient Britain wide
bleak looking hills with here & there a stone hut or a great rock —
There were 2 or three tors of very great beauty on the tops of
the hills, in all sorts of fantastical shapes — Was glad after a long
walk & a ride of 23 miles to get home. The party went off pleasantly enough with a scene or two from Miss Lewis Templer's governess — his oldest daughter is a very charming girl with whom I
would not mind falling in love.

| Expences | 5 ″ 0 |

[107] A mistake for Thursday, July 5, as the next date is a mistake for Friday,
July 6.
[108] "That man is a tiger," Major Pendennis remarks to Pen of Bloundell-
Bloundell (*Works*, II, 177), "mark my word — a low man."
[109] A mistake for Saturday, July 7.

Sunday. 8. After a merry day at Templers we set off in his cart to Newton, where we waited till 1/2 past 8 for the mail at about 1 we reached Plymouth.

| Segars | 1 | |
|---|---|---|
| Fare | 13. | |
| Coachman &c | 2 | |
| Bill at Newton | | 3/6 |
| at Kingskerswell | | 4 |

Monday 9. arrived by mail at 10 o'clock at Liskeard & found all the town in an uproar with flags processions & triumphal arches to celebrate C Bullers arrival. rode out to meet him & had the honour with some 1/2 dozen others to be dragged in with him. The gun was fired the people shouted & pulled us through all parts of the town. C Buller made a good speech enough then we adjourned to Mr Austen's where we lunched & then to submit again to be pulled about for the pleasure of his constituents — This business speaking pulling & luncheon lasted from 12 to 4 during wh time I was 3 times gratified by hearing my song about Jope [110] sung to a tune I suppose by some of the choristers — arrived at Polvellan at 6 & was glad to see it again for certainly they have been very kind —

| Fare | 6 |
|---|---|
| Coachman Guard &c | 2.6. |

Tuesday 10. Nothing happened to day — read Wallenstein in the morning dined at 2 rode with Mr Buller after dinner & got wet through drew pictures all the evening, & came to bed at eleven

. Wednesday 11. At Polvellan all day eating sleeping & dawdling; there arrived Mrs & Miss Hillier of the Caledonia, & Sir Wm Molesworth [111] who is standing for the county — the first 2

[110] See below, No. 67.

[111] Like his friend Charles Buller, Sir William Molesworth (1810–1855), eighth Baronet, was a Philosophical Radical. He represented East Cornwall in parliament from 1832 to 1837, Leeds from 1837 to 1841, and Southwark from 1845 till his death. Before his marriage in 1844 to the singer Andalusia Carstairs (d. 1888), who used the stage name of Grant, he lived a retired life, devoting much of his time to an edition (1839–1845) of the English and Latin works of Hobbes, but during the last ten years of his life he was a considerable figure in London society. He had a large estate at Pencarrow, and he

strike me as being fools, the last a sensible fellow enough. read
some of the robbers with C Buller & wrote to Father.

Trowsers.                            14.

Thursday 12. Set off with M$^{rs}$ Hillyar her daughter & Miss A.
Buller to Liskeard where we found young women in waggons singing hymns charity children banners &c all awaiting the arrival of
Sir W. Molesworth & C Buller who with M$^r$ & M$^{rs}$ Buller, were
dragged into the town by the infuriated populace The day had set
in fair & promised to smile on the 400 people who sat down to
dinner at one o clock, but the rain began & lasted during the whole
of dinner time — We adjourned to the town-Hall where the
members the attorneys & a farmer called Greig made speeches, this
latter was as fine an orator as ever I heard; came home at about
eight & spent a pleasant evening laughing with M$^{rs}$ Hillyar who
persisted in calling me by all names but my own, I in turn called
her Villiers Pilliers &c. she gave rather an affecting account of her
sons conversion to Catholicism — Sir W Molesworth went away.
he made a wretched speech as did everybody excepting CB &
Greig — M$^r$ Buller returned thanks he is a dear old fellow the most
good natured & amiable I ever saw.

Liskeard dinner            1 „ 0 „ 0.
  (not paid)

Friday 13. Heard from Mother & wrote to her — she is at M$^{rs}$
Shute's at Cowes. read some of Schillers Robbers with some young
ladies here. rambled about for an hour in the rain with C Buller.
& in the evening read Archenholz 7 years war.[112] drew a few caricatures, for the instruction & amusement of the amiable family. & this
was all that happened.

Arthur came back from Liskeard where there had been a tea-
drinking for the women & a second dance — M$^{rs}$ Hillyar talked a
great deal as usual. but somehow in rather an affecting manner,

---

left his widow 17,034 acres in Cornwall, Devon, and Huntingdonshire worth
£10,997 annually in 1883 (Bateman, *Great Landowners*, p. 313).
[112] *Geschichte des siebenjahrigen Krieges im Deutschland* (1793) by
Johann Wilhelm von Archenholtz (1743–1812).

she has it appears had more family misfortunes & gave us long accounts of Captain Hillyar's services & his bad luck —

Saturday 14. S. 15. Blank days chiefly occupied by M$^{rs}$ Hillyars voluminous conversation, w$^{h}$ is neither instructive or amusing —

M. T. W. 18. Spent 2 pleasantish days at Morval a nice old English house with an excellent specimen of a vieille cour gentleman for its master.

Here is the day for w$^{h}$ I have been panting so long,[113] w$^{h}$ now though it is come has not brought with it [114] any sensations peculiarly pleasant. but I am a man now & must deal with men —

Drew on Lubbock for £ 25

Thursday 19. Left dear little Polvellan & all the kind friends there & set off with Arthur for Plymouth — arrived at 12 & at one set off on the Steamer for Cowes — The passage was pleasant enough & the company soso  arrived at Cowes

| Passage &c | 1 ″ 5 |
|---|---|
| Gig | 14 |
| &c | 11. |
| Freight | 1 ″ 0 |
| Washing | 9 |
| Ann | 6 ″ 6. |
| Road | 2 ″ 6. |
| Debt pd Cowes | 5 ″ 0 |
| Serv$^{t}$ &c | 4 ″ 0 |
| Stationery | 7 ″ 6 |

Friday 20. where I found Mother & Mary. staid the day at M$^{rs}$ Shute's & came on to Shanklin on

Saturday 21. Found M$^{r}$ Hill [115] & his wife not a bit altered, & the only difference in their place a child of four years old who has sprung up since I was a little boy at Shanklin.

Sunday 22. Walked to Bonchurch a most charming walk — & heard a sensible sermon from M$^{r}$ Hill, saw a house belonging to a

[113] His twenty-first birthday.
[114] Thackeray wrote *without*.
[115] The Rev. Justly Hill (d. 1853), Rector of Shanklin and Bonchurch on the Isle of Wight and Archdeacon of Buckingham, who had married Jane-Helena Shute, a daughter of Samuel Shute by his first wife.

M.ʳ Lermon, fitted up after the Elizabethan stile — It is very pretty & perfect, but rather a cockney affair — Took some sketches about Bonchurch which is the beau ideal of an English village  Walked with M.ʳ Hill in the evening among some fields w.ʰ he has let out by 2 & 3 acres to different cottagers in Shanklin — the effect on these men has been extraordinary: poor desperate men are at once become sober rich & respectable. The fields were admirably cultivated, & we saw some of the tenants in them — with good coats & happy faces      I wish all landlords w.ᵈ adopt the same plan.

Monday 30 — After spending a pleasant week in the Island & 3 days with Aunt Becher at Fareham — I set out for Portsmouth where I passed the day

Expences          2 ‚‚ 0 ‚‚ 0

and on Tuesday 31. came in the Camilla Steam Packet to Havre was obliged to lie in a berth the whole of the way for fear of being sick — & was bitten to pieces by bugs — the passage was a very uncomfortable one of 14 hours & we did not land at Havre until 2 o'clock in the morning of

Wednesday August 1. — did not sleep well after my days work, at ten breakfasted at the table d'hote where were ten or a dozen people rather snobs than otherwise — however I talked my French very fast and found I could understand theirs; walked about the town after dinner, w.ʰ is dirty & picturesque — subscribed for a week to a library & reading room; dined at five with the same company supported by an additional influx of snobs — Read in the evening a Novel of P de Kocks called the Cocu [116] it is very clever & in spite of some descriptions w.ʰ might shock a squeamish English woman — it is very moral — there is however too much of it — In the night was as terrifick a thunder storm as I ever knew —

| | |
|---|---|
| (Bill at Inn. | 14.0.0 |
| Fare | 2 ‚‚ 2.0 |
| Boat | 2.0 |
| Expenses on board | 6./6) |
| | £  s |
| Commissionaire — &c | 4 ‚‚ 0. |

[116] *Le Cocu* and *Soeur Anne* were published in 1832 and 1825; *La Peau de Chagrin* in 1831.

| | |
|---|---|
| Beranger | 3.0 |
| Noel et Chapsal | 1.10 |
| Brace | " 15 |
| Library | 3.0. |
| Douane | 1 " 0 |

Thursday August 2. Spent a day much like the last — read Le Peau de Chagrin by Balzac, w[h] I liked very much — & Soeur Anne of P. de Kock's w[h] was better than Le Cocu — went to the Theatre & saw a pleasant little piece called Rabelais and part of an Opera La Neige [117] — These Frenchmen have certainly an admirable tact with their plays — so many good sayings & sharp epigrammatic points

| | |
|---|---|
| Collar & Coat | 10 " 0 |
| Slippers | 2 " 40 |
| Theatre | 3.0. |
| Gloves | 1 " 12. |

Friday Au. 3 — Encore des Romans — was however out a good deal making sketches in the morning, & in the evening walking for a couple of hours with an hotel acquaintance —

| | |
|---|---|
| Groseille | 1 " 5. |

Saturday 4 — Received a rowing letter from Lubbock enclosing a £30 note — & one from my Uncle Frank telling me of the death of his son.[118] went to the Theatre saw a pretty opera by Boieldieu — Les Voitures Versees [119] and a tolerably good farce. w[h] in English would do very well. Walked to Ingouville and made a sketch or two —

| | |
|---|---|
| Stock | 6. |
| Dictionary | 6. |
| Theatre | 3. |

Rouen

Sunday. Au 5. After some trouble procured my passport & at

[117] *La Neige, ou le nouvel Eigenhard* (1823), the music for which was written by Daniel Auber (1784–1871).

[118] Francis Talbot Thackeray, *Genealogy* (66), who was born on August 13, 1831, and died on July 19, 1832 (*Memorials*, p. 496).

[119] *Les Voitures versées* (1820), the music for which was written by François Adrien Boieldieu (1775–1834).

five in the afternoon set off by the Havre Steamer for Rouen. It
went nearly the whole way — What I could see of the country very
pretty ⟨. . .⟩ [120] but nothing ⟨. . .⟩ a fine old chateau ⟨. . .⟩ to the
⟨. . .⟩ I recollect ⟨. . .⟩ arrived here at 2 o'clock in the morning
⟨. . .⟩ got to bed at ⟨. . .⟩

| | |
|---|---|
| Bill & waiters | 50 ″ 0. |
| Passport &c | 6.0. |
| Bill on board | 21.0 |

Paris —

Sunday — August 12. After having from sheer idleness discontinued this my journal for a week, I have to begin it with rather a
prominent incident — on Friday morning I was the happy posses-
sor of a five pound note & a bag containing near five & twenty
pounds in five franc pieces — on coming home from the play at
10 1/2 — I find my secretaire broken open & my money gone. I
instantly set off to the Prefect of Police but he was not at home
then to Vidocq [121] who c^d give me no help then back again to the
Prefect who made many enquiries on Saturday but to no purpose,
so that I fear I shall never see my money again —

| | |
|---|---|
| Stolen. | 30 ″ 0 ″ 0 |

Monday 13. I write this on Tuesday and cannot for my life
recollect what good I did yesterday

| | £ |
|---|---|
| Expences | 10.0 |
| Map & print | 6.0 |

Tuesday. 14. Went with Gerrard [122] to S^t Cloud in a cuckoo, a
villainous conveyance, w^h goes at the rate of 2 miles an hour, the
park was pretty but the house [123] like a large lady's school — Then

---

[120] This and the following hiatuses are respectively of about three, four,
three, five, four, four, and four words.
[121] François Eugène Vidocq (1775–1857), the original of Balzac's Vautrin,
who had recently reëntered the Parisian police service. Thackeray may have
known the *Mémoires* published in 1828 under the name of this famous
detective.
[122] A young Madras captain, we learn below, No. 68.
[123] The Château de Gondy, a favorite resort both of Marie Antoinette and
of Napoleon. The royal manufactory of porcelain was situated at Sèvres.

we went to Sevres where I saw a great number of pretty tea cups & saucers, but the most interesting part of the exhibition the manufactory of the china is only to be seen by an order from the Minister — had a bad luncheon & no dinner. The weather a little cold ⟨. . .⟩ [124]

| Paper | 1 ″ 12. |
| Carriage to & from | 5 ″ 0 |
| Dinner | 2 ″ 0 |

W. Lay ⟨. . .⟩ [125] Monsieur ⟨. . .⟩otte w$^h$ is a poor thing after all. Then read a novel called rank & talent [126] w$^h$ is likewise poor went to the Varietes, and saw part of L'Enlevement & les Amours de Paris —

| Breakfast — | 5.0 |
| Chair | 8 ″ 0 |
| Theatre | 5 |

Th. 16. Subscribed to a place in the Palais Royal where is a very good collection of books a pleasant look out and quiet rooms to read in — read there The Revue des deux Mondes. w$^h$ appeared to have much cleverness, but to be full of the affectation of thought and style, w$^h$ French men nowadays mistake for genius the romances, the poetry the pictures seem to labour at a kind of eccentricity w$^h$ is the great fault & the only merit of the romantick school. The poets and dramatists of the old time had to combat agst the coldness of custom, & yet circumscribed in metre time and subject they occasionally produced true poetry    The gentlemen of the Ecole Romantique have thrown away all these prejudices, but still seem no wise better or more poetical than their rigid predecessors —

The passion[s] w$^h$ their ancestors discussed in perriwigs, are now in costumes more picturesque but still after all it is the coat that is changed & not the man — In the time of Voltaire the heroes of poetry and drama were fine gentlemen, in the days of Victor Hugo they bluster about in velvets and moustachios and gold

---

[124] Seven lines of the diary have here been torn away.
[125] This and the following hiatus are of about five and one words respectively.
[126] Published in 1829 by William Pitt Scargill (1787–1836).

chains, partly as in old times creating & partly following the prevailing fashion

I read to day a novel of Balzac's called the Peau de Chagrin,
w^h possesses many of the faults & the beauties of this school —
plenty of light & shade, good colouring and costume, but no character. &c, I will I think go through a course of modern French
reading and see if I can make an article for a review —

F. 17. S. 18. In the morning reading in the evening play w^h
after a little good luck had left me as I begun or nearly so —
There is a vow recorded in this book & God knows how it has been
kept. May Almighty God give me strength of mind to resist the
temptation of play, & to keep my vow that from this day I will
never again enter a gaming house —

Read 2^d Volume. Roi des Ribauds by Jacob [127] — very poor but
industrious — part of Hoffmann's Prinzessin Brambilla w^h I did
not admire — Victor Hugo Feuilles d'Automne very poetical
Cousins 1^st Lecture.

S. 19. I broke the vow I solemnly made yesterday — & thank
God lost the last halfpenny I possessed by doing so — At first I
had won back nearly all my losings & went away but the money lay
like fire in my pocket & I am thank heaven rid of it —

A dinner at the Trois Freres [128] was the cause of my lying — a
bottle of Beaune & 2 glasses of Malaga made my head hot & my
pocket finally empty —

| | |
|---|---|
| Dinner | 9 " 0. |
| Lost | 20.0 |
| Lemonade | 1.0 |
| M. lost at play | 65.0. |

W. 22. Read Cousins history of Philosophy — went to the
Louvre read at Galignanis & at the Palais Royal — am much
pleased with Cousin his style & his spirit — The excitement of
metaphysics must equal almost that of gambling at least I found

---

[127] A historical romance published in 1831 by Paul Lacroix (1806–1884),
under the pseudonym "Le Bibliophile Jacob." "Prinzessin Brambilla" by
Ernst Theodor Amadeus Hoffmann (1776–1822) appeared in 1821. *Les
Feuilles d'automne* was published in 1831.
[128] The Trois Frères Provençaux, a famous restaurant in the Palais Royal.

myself giving utterance to a great number of fine speeches & imag-
ining many wild theories w.ʰ I found it impossible to express on
paper. on Monday heard from Mother with the news of poor
Colonel Forrests death — on the 28.ᵗʰ of last month, from cholera —
he went with my father to Scotland was taken ill on board the
packet and died a few hours after his arrival at Dundee. had I
consented to have gone with my father to Scotland this valuable
man might have been spared to his family — What very trifling
events settle destinies & take away lives —

    T. Expences                    17.0.
    W. Expences                    2 ʺ 0.

Th — Douter c'est croire, car douter c'est penser, celui qui doute
croit il qu'il doute ou doute-t-il qu'il doute — S'il doute qu'il doute
Il detruit par cela meme son scepticisme — & s'il croit qu'il doute il
le detruit encore [129]

                                   £
    Expences                       45.

Sunday 26 — passed my time in different reading rooms — met
Lemann [130] who has grown more snobbish than ever — read various
newspapers & novels —

    Coat                           60.
    Breakfast                      4.
    Dinner                         4.
    Coffee &c                      2 —

W. 29 — Came home disgusted from the Porte S.ᵗ Martin after
seeing a new piece by Dumas called the fils de l'emigre [131] — I have
been able to think of nothing since —

Th. 30 To night I have seen a piece of a very different order
the Tartuffe — tolerably acted, and a pretty piece called Valerie
deliciously played by M.ˡˡᵉ Mars —

[129] I have been unable to find this passage in Victor Cousin's *Cours de l'histoire de la philosophie* (Paris, 1829), though the same argument is stated in
other words on p. 158 of the first volume of that work.
[130] Probably Michael Le Mann, who matriculated at Trinity College, Cambridge, in 1824, took his B. A. degree in 1829, and was in residence in 1830.
[131] Dumas never found it worth his while to publish this notorious *drame
brutal*, but some conception of its nature may be gained from a review in the
*Moniteur universel* of September 2.

F. 31 — Gerrard came to town from Choisy [132] & I went back with him & engaged a room for a month, at M. Au Roi's  It seems a comfortable place enough though the company is not what one would expect at Almack's — met here my old french master Ory [133] & was introduced to a pleasantish fellow by the name of Cook, who keeps a school in these parts —

September

Saturday — Went back to Paris for an hour w[h] I employed in packing & paying — & came back to Choisy at dinner time     The dinner was a tolerably good one, & the evening was passed pleasantly enough at Cooks drinking tea coffee & brandy, & smoking — Gerrard was too unwell to go. —

| Washing &c ⎫ | 20 ″ 0 ″ 0 |
| Guillaume ⎬ | |
| Jarveys ⎭ | |

Sunday. 2. Walked to Thiais where there is a fete, & played at billiards for the first time in my life —

Monday. 3 — Spent the day idling with Cook & Ory — dined with Cook who entertained us in the evening by reading verses, w[h] were very poor — he is however a nice fellow good natured & warm hearted — Gerrard went to Paris, to economize because he has a bed room there. — did not read a syllable of anything.

| Fete at Thias — | 1 ″ 10 |
| Wine | 2 ″ 0. |

T. 4 — Idle as yesterday — partook of a bottle of Champagne given by M[r] Kuhn, & drank tea at M[r] Bevan's [134] — I liked him & his family very much — he has a brother an Indian Captain — a most excellent simple hearted fellow — M[rs] Bevan is a very nice person who speaks what she thinks & thinks what a woman ought to — Napoleon's poet Laureat Lormian [135] was there. he is very

[132] Choisy-le-roi, a village seven and one-half miles south of Paris.
[133] Ori d'Hegenheim.
[134] Possibly the father of Thackeray's friends William and Samuel Bevan.
[135] Pierre Marie Baour-Lormian (1770–1854). The vogue of this popular poet of imperial days had waned, and he had become a sour old man, ill, nearly blind, and altogether out of sympathy with contemporary literature, who found congenial occupation in translating the Book of Job. It was no doubt

short sighted & called me a gros drole d'Anglais, the poor old gentle[man] was terribly frightened when he saw his betise — & would not speak to me afterwards.

Letters &c.                              2 „

W. 5 — Another day like the last — Jones [136] came down & lent me £10 w^h are very agreable to me at this time —

Washing —                              2 „ 16.
Tobacco —

Sunday 9 — Spent in reading Anastasius [137] — in dining, drinking tea at the Bevans, & on coming home dancing & playing ecarte a very religious & laudable Sunday. — have in these latter days been to Paris wo ich spielte, have read Notre Dame de Paris of w^h I think most highly as a work of genius, though it is not perhaps a fine novel. have read part of Pelham w^h I found rather dull & very impertinent. & have borrowed from Cooke Gibbon in one volume, with a weak wavering intention of reading it — Received a very welcome coat & trowsers from M^r Stechert [138] but found no letters at Paris — looked to day at a house in this place, w^h would answer excellently for 4 men who might by clubbing 200 a year together live like princes in this pretty village, & be in Paris in an hour was much pleased with the simplicity & kindness of Captain Bevan — find my ideas verging toward a novel. the plot is not yet conceived — but still I think something witty is coming — Amen —
In these days Clarke departed to England — went to Paris &

---

this encounter that led Thackeray in *The Newcomes* to attribute the following opinions to the Duc d'Ivry: "for the great sentiments, for the beautiful style give him M. de Lormian (although Bonapartist) or the Abbé de Lille. And for the new school! bah! these little Dumas, and Hugos, and Mussets, what is all that? 'M. de Lormian shall be immortal, monsieur,' he would say, 'when all these *freluquets* are forgotten.' " (*Works*, VIII, 325)

[136] Harry Longueville Jones (1806–1870), who took his B. A. and M. A. degrees at Magdalene College, Cambridge, in 1828 and 1832. For his subsequent history, see No. 542.

[137] *Anastasius; Or, Memoirs of a Modern Greek* (1819) by Thomas Hope (1770–1831). Hugo's novel was published in 1831, Bulwer's in 1828.

[138] Louis Stechert of 17 Argyle Street, Thackeray's London tailor.

lived at Jones's expence — dined with M$^r$ Bowes,[139] a good fellow. spielte und winnte 14 stücken gold — bezahlte zehn davon —

Tuesday. Sept$^r$ 17 — Went with Gerrard to Vincennes, & were rewarded for our trouble by finding that there was no admittance into the fortress — I had to pay the piper the ride was pretty through Maison & Charenton — read M$^{rs}$ Starke [140] — & some Gibbon w$^h$ I begin to find entertaining — in the evening read Gibbon & smoked in my own room. the company being dull below in the salon.

| | |
|---|---|
| Trip to Vincennes | 15. |
| Stock | 5 |

Wed. have just come from talking of debauchery & it's consequences — w$^h$ have made me long for a good wife, & a happy home — Jones came down —

Th. 20. read the 15$^{th}$ chapter of Gibbon played all the morning at "tonneaux" with Gerard & Jones for dinner & operas & perigord pies — heard from Mother a long letter telling me the money was sold out — unluckily perhaps for me.

| | |
|---|---|
| Lost | 2. |

F 21. Went to Paris in the morning saw Bowes & Wilkes who invited me to dinner on Tuesday. Spent money — dined at Cooks where I met M$^r$ & M$^{rs}$ Torre very nice persons — find myself growing loving on every pleasant married woman I see. —

| | | |
|---|---|---|
| Waistcoat | 22 | 25. — |
| Italian books | 36 | 30 |
| Coach | 3 | 20 |
| Stock | 6 | 5 |
| Lunch | 4 | |
| Gloves. | 3 — 74. | £ 75. since |
| Expences | 2 | July 14 — |

S. 22. Jones went all day at Cooks eating drinking smoking drawing —

[139] See *Memoranda*, John Bowes Bowes.
[140] No doubt *Information and Directions for Travelers on the Continent* by Mariana Starke (1762?–1838), a fifth edition of which was published in Paris during 1826.

S — 23 — Wrote to Weissenborn,[141] heard from Lubbock who sent me £120. danced in the evening 3 quadrilles — Miss Bautier came down, & M^me Bautier went away —

Th: — 27 — have been in Paris, but dont feel inclined to mention the expences or the occurrences of these days.

| | |
|---|---|
| Paid Jones | £ 10 „ |
| Weissenborn | £ 10 |
| Lent Gerrard | £ 10— |

F. 28 — Read Courier [142] & was very much pleased with him & his writings — called on the Torres whom I liked better than last time. perhaps because they invited me to dinner for tomorrow —

Sunday. 6 October.[143] Left Choisy and took up my quarters again at the Hotel Lillois — Cooke came up with me, we dined at Prevot and feasted magnificently for 6 francs.

| | |
|---|---|
| Paid M^rs Auroy. | 300 „ 0.0 |
| Expences | 24 „ 0 „ 0 |

M. 7.[144] dispatched a letter to Lubbock & a note to Ory, called on M^rs Impey Leman, & M^rs Wilks whom I found all at home. breakfasted in the Palais Royal & dined at Vefours went for a while to the Opera Comique but found it dull, spielte und fegelte [145] — read the Spectators workings of the House of Commons; a Canto or 2 of Wieland's Oberon.[146] & several newspapers — a very active day.

| | |
|---|---|
| Breakfast — | 1. |
| Dinner | 9 — |
| Cab. | 3. |
| Wieland | 4 |
| Subscription | 6. |
| Acc | 7. |

[141] I have not traced this letter.

[142] Paul Louis Courier [de Méré] (1772–1825), a set of whose works was in Thackeray's library when he died (*Catalogue*, ed. Stonehouse, p. 141).

[143] A mistake for Sunday, October 7.

[144] A mistake for Monday, October 8. Véfour's was a famous restaurant in the Palais Royal.

[145] An approximation of the preterite of *vögeln*, "to have intercourse," for which see Jacob and Wilhelm Grimm's *Deutsches Wörterbuch*, Volume XII, Part ii, p. 432.

[146] The narrative poem (1780) by Christoph Martin Wieland (1733–1813).

Wednesday. October — dined with Leman, met at his house 3 Spanish Counts, an Avocat, & a musician a pleasant party — afterwards went to M<sup>r</sup> Impey's where I saw M<sup>rs</sup> Pattle whom I liked very much — The company at M<sup>r</sup> I's was not the most refined in the world — called on Wilks & Bowes — heard from Lubbock — changed my quarters & got to my ancient apartments of No 5.

|  | £ |
|---|---|
| Wine | 30 |

Thursday — Took a cab & came down to Versailles, & thence to Petit Chesnay to Cay's — found his wife a kind & pleasant person; he returned himself at about 10.

| Cab &c. | 15. |
|---|---|
| Coach &c | 5. |

Saturday — Left Cay's after a pleasantish time, spent in seeing horses & dogs, came to Versailles to Madame de L'Etang's; where were M<sup>rs</sup> Pattle & M<sup>rs</sup> Beadle, here I passed a merry day, & at ten arrived again at my old quarters at Paris —

Tuesday 23 — Walked with Ory to Choisy & passed a pleasant day with Cook, returned on

W. 24: likewise on Foot; Cook accompanied us & slept here; however we made out the day but ill, & instead of going to the Louvre as we intended spent it reading & smoking.

Th. 25 — Had a nice letter from Mother — called on Bowes & M<sup>rs</sup> Ritchie whom much to my surprize I met lionizing yesterday in the Palais Royal — Went to the reading room, & read Old Moniteurs for a couple of hours; dined very humbly at home off soup & one cutlet; & went to the Theatre de Palais Royal — where I saw a tolerable piece La Fee aux Miettes [147] containing many lively couplets M. Jovial also good; & a new piece called La Sentinelle, w<sup>h</sup> I assisted in d—ing — it contained absolutely nothing, & the curtain went down before it's conclusion, thank Heaven.

| Changed a £20 note — |  |
|---|---|
| Bramahs Pensholder | 12. |
| Paper &c. | 3. |

[147] *La Fée aux miettes* was a "rêve en 2 tableaux" adapted from the short story of Charles Nodier (1780–1844). *La Sentinelle perdue* was hissed from the stage.

| Theatre | 5 |
| Schlegel | 18. |
| Dictionary | 7 — |
| Tennemann. | 7. |

Friday — 26. Took a French lesson, & read a little Schlegel; M<sup>r</sup> & M<sup>rs</sup> Ritchie called dined in the Palais Royal & spent a pleasant evening talking about Theatres with Bowes —

| Waistcoat | 35 — |
| Dinner | 5 |
| &cs — | 4 — |

Saturday 27 — Sent at last a letter [148] to Weissenborn with ten pounds; heard from Fitz-Gerald: took a short French lesson & treated Ory to a dinner & Franconi's [149] — The piece was very splendid Napoleon & all his army in excellent order & in great force; but I found 2 acts were enough; & left Ory to gaze on the glory of the French arms alone — Sievrac called early in the morning — read Fletchers Maid's Tragedy; but except for some few passages thought I confess not a fine play —

| Handkerchiefs | 28. — |
| Letters | 3 — |
| Franconi's &c | 10. |

Sunday 28. I have done little to day but pay money, dined very economically at Colberts & spent the evening with Bowes —

| Trowsers. | 35 |
| House bill | 47 ″ 0. |
| Wood &c. | 33 ″ 0 — |
| Dinner | 2 ″ 4 |

[148] Weissenborn apparently refers to this letter — which I have not traced — in a note of May 1, 1833, to another former pupil, identified by Schüddekopf (*Goethes Tod*, p. 181) as Charles Des Voeux: "I look into your last letter, and find to my utter contrition that you want to know little Thackeray's direction at Paris. If he have the organ of adhesiveness sufficiently developed for the occasion to keep him in the same house in the same city till now, he is still drawing both breath and caricatures at the Hôtel Lille, in Rue Richelieu. He wrote to me that he intended to stay at Paris for the winter. Now there's no knowing when that season ends, but I believe the other one has not begun yet. If you should write to him, remember me kindly to this old friend of ours. I remember now that I have given you the same direction already about the latter end of October last year." (Edward Dowden, "Goethe's Last Days," *Fortnightly Review*, LIV, 1890, pp. 338–339)

[149] Franconi's equestrian troupe, which performed military melodramas at the Cirque Olympique, Boulevard du Temple.

M. 29. Took a lesson, read Fletchers wit without money; called at M͏ʳ Ritchies & dined with him of woodcock pie, went to the Varietes,[150] & saw a very clever piece called Le dandy; more like genteel comedy than anything I have seen for a long time — There was a piece in w͏ʰ Arnal played, a poor thing called Les Cabinets Particuliers —

| | |
|---|---|
| Theatre | 5 |
| Window | 2. |
| &cs | 1. |

T. 30 — have done nothing all day. — took a very short lesson; read at the Palais Royal for an hour the (spurious) memoirs of Cardinal Dubois [151] — Dined at Colberts & passed the evening with Bowes — changed a £20 the last of six I had five weeks ago — read a little Schlegel, but was interrupted by Cay who took a bed —

| | |
|---|---|
| Dinner | 2 ″ 4 — |
| Cigars &c. | 1 ″ 10. |

W. 31 — Th. 1. F. 2. Sat 3. Went to Choisy and passed three pleasant idle days; W. drunk tea at M͏ʳ Torres & Friday at M͏ʳ Bevans: came home to day: & dined with Leman & his wife who received me very kindly — went to the Varietes, & saw charming Jenny Colon,[152] & Odry in the Marchands de Peaux des Lapins, a piece w͏ʰ w͏ᵈ suit Liston [153] I should think — heard rather a suspicious circumstance about my worthy instructor.

| | |
|---|---|
| Callot &c | 4. |
| Fare &c. | 3. |
| Theatre | 3. 1/2 |

[November] S. 4. Spent the morning with Lemann: read the

[150] Actually Thackeray went to the Théâtre du Vaudeville, where the bill included *Le Bal*, *Le Dandy*, *Un de plus*, and *Les Cabinets particuliers*. Etienne Arnal (1794–1872) appeared in the last of these.

[151] *Mémoires du Cardinal Dubois* (1815; re-edited, 1829).

[152] Marguérite ("Jenny") Colon (1808–1842) and Jacques Charles Odry (1781–1853). The other plays at the Theatre des Variétés were *Le Fils du savetier*, *Les Amours de Paris*, *L'Afficheur*, *Caligula*, and *La Dame au balcon* (*Moniteur universel*, October 29).

[153] John Liston (1776?–1846), a famous English comic actor whom Thackeray had often seen in London. Among his best rôles were Polonius, Slender, Bottom, Sir Andrew Aguecheek, Bob Acres, and Tony Lumpkin.

papers; & the Mems of a Page of the Imperial Court [154] — very entertaining passed the evening with Bowes, as usual drinking tea & talking about theatres — dined au Rosbif in the Rue Richelieu — brought home Woodstock to read —

| House bill & Serv.! | 53 " — |
| Dinner punch & segars! | 1 " 18. |

M. 5. read Quentin Durward in the morning & went for an hour to the Royal library; in the evening sat with Aunt Ritchie — read Chroniques de l'Oeil de Boeuf; [155] a scandalous but entertaining memoir of French History, under Louis XIV, XV, XVI — it however deserves to be burnt for its morals, & is not I suppose worthy a moment's credit —

| Dinner | 1 " 10. |
| Book — | 2.5. |
| Subscription | 8 " |

T. 6 All the morning at the Royal [library] looking at prints & cop⟨ies . . .⟩ [156] then at the read⟨. . .⟩ Colberts ⟨. . .⟩ din⟨. . .⟩

| Dinner | 2. — |
| Book | 6. |

[Wednesday. 7]

| Books — prints &c, | 32 |

I thought a pleasant fellow (perhaps because he was a Marquis) but whom everybody else thinks presuming & disagreable — he had a good natured English wife, who had exchanged her money for his title, taking the guineas stamp "a giving up the gowd for a that [157] — There were other characters whose names I dont know.

Th. 8. At the royal Library looked over engravings from

[154] *Mémoires et révélations d'un page à la cour impériale* (1830) by Emile Marc Hilaire (1796?–1887), called Marco de Saint-Hilaire.

[155] *Les Chroniques de l'Œil-de-Bœuf, des petits appartements de la cour et des salons de Paris sous les règnes de Louis XIV, Louis XV et Louis XVI* (1829–1833), a scandalous fabrication in eight volumes by G. Touchard-Lafosse (1780–1847).

[156] This and the following hiatuses are respectively of about three, five, seven, and seventy words.

[157] Adapted from Burns's "For a' that and a' that":

         The rank is but the guinea's stamp;
         The man's the gowd for a' that!

Leonardo da Vinci, Hollar, & Moreau. the latter very beautiful as
to execution & curious as to costume, (of 1770) — of Hollars famous etchings I confess I think but little; & for the engravings
from L. da Vinci there were not half a dozen good ones in the collection — read a little of Scotts life of Swift & dined with Bowes on a
turkey — News comes that the Duchess of Berry is taken.[158]

F. 9 — heard from Arthur Buller. Lemann called at 12 & took
me to see his fencing master Bertrand, then we went to an abattoir,
& assisted at the slaughter of certain sheep & oxen — the place is
admirably managed, & as clean as a drawing room — after the
abattoir drove with M.rs Lemann in the Champs Elysees; after the
drive dined & after the dinner went to the play Palais Royal & saw
a new piece — damned [159] — although it seemed to have plenty of
fun in it — saw La Fee aux Miettes, & a pleasant piece called Les
Maris et les Garçons — excellently acted by Philippe — There was
at the theatre a poor S.t Simonian who laughed very good naturedly
at the hits against his sect in the Fee aux Miettes — habe meine
schlechte Bucher verbrannte — Dank sey Gott — wrote some
verses for Bowes's Opera —

Sat 10 — A bad cold — went to the royal library & looked at
pictures — heard from Weissenborn — Cook came & dined. Went
to the Vaudeville & saw a play called Les jours gras de Charles
IX — admirably acted but poor except in situations w.h were very
good. to bed at 10 — trying to cure the cold.

| | |
|---|---|
| Theatre | 6 — |
| Eyeglass. | 5 |
| Washerwoman | 10 — |

S. 11. At home all the morning till 3 — Walked for an hour in
the Thuilleries & dined with Bowes — very uncomfortable with
the cold — heard from Uncle Frank —

| | |
|---|---|
| House bill &c. | 65. |
| &cs — | 2. |

[158] Marie, Duchesse de Berry (1797–1870), widow of the second son of
Charles X, had fled to England in 1830 when her father-in-law was deposed.
She returned to France during the insurrection of "La Vendée" and was cap-
tured in Nantes during November, 1832.

[159] *Un Antoine de plus* was hissed from the stage; Philippe appeared in
*Les Gens mariés et les garçons* (*Moniteur universel*, November 12).

M 12. Went to the Royal Library & looked at a few prints;
walked in the Thuilleries where I saw the King his Queen & umbrella,[160] dined at Lemanns & went with Madame to see Perrinet
Le Clerc [161] — a new piece at the Porte St Martin; by the same
author, & of exactly the same order as the piece at the Vaudeville —
The scenery & costumes were admirable — of the time of
Charles VI.

Theatre                                    7.

T. 13. At home all day — doing nothing. spent the evening
with Bowes, employing it as I had done the rest of the day. drew a
good deal. — & drank tisanne for the cough —

Dinner                                     2.5

W. 14 — Read a pleasant novel called La Laitiere de Montfer-
meil by Paul de Kock [162] — wrote to mother dined sumptuously at
Very's, & saw a piece about Voltaire,[163] & a couple of acts of a dull
tragedy called Mary Stuart at the Francais — drunk tea with the
Ritchies. & spent much more money than I have for many a day.

Print.                                     5.
Dinner                                     9.
Theatre                                    3.
Scissors                                   2.

Th. 15. heard from Fitz-Gerald & Mary: went to the Royal
Library: dined at Colberts & in the evening to the Palais Royal,
to see — Beranger, & Vert Vert — both of them clever & amusing

Theatre                                    4 —
Dinner                                     2.
Waistcoat-making                           8.

[160] Louis Philippe's famous umbrella was taken by the caricaturists of his
time as a symbol of the *bourgeois, juste milieu* character of the July Monarchy.
[161] *Perrinet-Leclerc; ou, Paris en 1418* was written by Auguste Anicet-
Bourgeois (1806–1871) and Joseph Simon (1803–1891), who used the pen-
name of Lockroy. It was first performed on November 3, 1832.
[162] Published in 1827.
[163] The bill at the Théâtre Français included *Voltaire et Mme. de Pompa-
dour* and *Marie Stuart*, Lebrun's adaptation of Schiller's tragedy (*Moniteur
universel*, November 16).

Fr 16 Wrote to Lubbock for £20. Went to Versailles, & spent a pleasant day with M⁻ˢ Pattle, slept at the H de Reservons

Bed &c                              3 —

S. 17 breakfasted with Cay at Chesnay, & returned with him & a Captain Wyatt to Paris — dined at Lemanns & went to the Italians — saw a poor opera of Bellini's Il Pirata [164] — then for a minute to Frascati's where I lost all I had —

Lost at play                        15.

Sunday. 18. Cay dined; spent the evening with Bowes, meeting an actor called Jones; who gave a melancholy account of his theatrical speculations, wʰ has cured me of some schemes I had formed of that nature —

House bills —                       56.
Dinner                              8. —

M. 19. Called on the Ritchies at their new lodgings in Place Vendome — went with Strachan to see the king pass to open the chamber: & heard the pistol wʰ was fired at his august head — spent the evening with Bowes — ✝ Wrote Fitz-Gerald, dined at Colberts —

Dinner &c.                          10.
Gloves                              3.

T. 20. At the library — looking at prints of the Revolution & copying them — dined with Wilks & spent a pleasant evening talking a great deal of nonsense to him & his pretty cousins —

Fr. 21. Read Tristan Le Voyageur,[165] & copied knights &c at the Royal library; dined with Lemann, & went to see Jane Shore [166] & Jeremy Diddle with the Wilks; with tickets wʰ Bowes gave me —

[164] Il Pirata (1827) by Vincenzo Bellini (1801–1835), performed at the Théâtre Italien.

[165] Tristan le voyageur; ou, la France au XIVᵉ siècle (1825–1826), a romance by Louis Antoine François de Marchangy (1782–1826).

[166] The arrival of an English troupe scheduled to perform at the Théâtre Italien is noted in the Moniteur universel of November 16. Thackeray saw Rowe's Jane Shore (1714) and Raising the Wind (1803), a farce by James Kenney (1780–1849), the chief character in which is Jeremy Diddler.

Th. 22. At the royal library, walked in the Thuilleries, & went with Bowes to the prem. rep. of Le Roi s'amuse [167] having the pleasure of paying ten francs for my place; the piece was not quite damned —

| | |
|---|---|
| Dinner | 7. |
| &c. | 1. |
| Theatre | 10. |

Friday 23. Determined on leaving Paris, took my place got my passport & paid my bills. went to the Th. Palais Royal & saw Napoleon at Brienne a pleasant piece nicely acted by Dejazet.[168]

| | |
|---|---|
| Dinner &c | 13. |
| Books | 25 |
| Gloves | 66. |
| Jeweller | 45. |
| Tailor | 160. |
| Lemann | 38. |
| Brush | 1. |

63.        TO EDWARD FITZGERALD
                APRIL? 1832

Hitherto unpublished.

*   *   *

Here am I on my high stool with an action ag^st Noah Thornley for debauching Martha Dewsnap whereby she became big & sick with child & whereby her father lost the services of her his daughter & servant so that you see Law is not altogether so dry a study as you w^d imagine it to be — This letter will be sent by a M^r Drury [169]

[167] The first performance of Hugo's drama, which is now remembered chiefly as the source of Verdi's *Rigoletto*, was also the last. It must have made a considerable impression on Thackeray, for in George Warrington's play of *Carpezan*, as described in *The Virginians* (*Works*, X, 537–538), there is a striking reminiscence of *Le Roi s'amuse*. The matter is discussed in my *Thackeray and France*, pp. 53–54.

[168] Pauline Virginie Déjazet (1797–1875), one of the most celebrated actresses of her time, had made her début at the age of five and was particularly skilful in playing masculine rôles.

[169] Henry Drury (1812–1863), later (1862) Archdeacon of Wiltshire, who

THACKERAY IN 1832

*From a sketch by Daniel Maclise*

Here is a scene at the Spotted dog a publick house near the
Strand where you pay tuppence to hear singing &— The faces
are not at all caricatured not even the eyebrows — The poor
devil to the right hof the picter sung a solo about
rosy Bacchus — the other two & a youth whose face I cannot
draw sung a glee the one eyed man base — Now you must give

DRAWING IN THACKERAY'S LETTER TO FITZGERALD OF APRIL? 1832

a friend of Martineau's, who goes to Cambridge at 3 o'clock by the Times — Martineau I like immensely & learn a good deal from him he is a very well read man & withal very modest as all well read men ought to be — On Tuesday I dined at Kembles, where there was a very splendid spread. C. Kemble is I think an excellent fellow & no humbug about him

\*        \*        \*

Here is a scene at the spotted dog [170] a publick house near the strand where you pay tuppence to hear singing &c — The faces are not at all caricatured not even the eyebrows — The poor devil to the right hof the picter sung a solo about rosy Bacchus — the other two & a youth whose face I cannot draw sung a glee the one eyed man base. Now you must give

\*        \*        \*

64.        TO EDWARD FITZGERALD
           20–21 APRIL 1832

Extracts published in *Biographical Introductions*, IX, xxxiv–xxxv.

\*        \*        \*

I am more idle than inconstant my dear Fi⟨tz⟩ for really I have not been in my chambers for h⟨alf an⟩ hour except at meals & in bed this last fortni⟨ght.⟩ Here is Good Friday,[171] & quiet & now or never ⟨I must⟩ write — Henry Kemble goes on Monday to joi⟨n his⟩ Reg.ᵗ in Ireland at Galway I believe but ⟨don't⟩ know where that is — He has been ordering new ⟨clothes⟩ every day this last month, & is said to look ⟨very⟩ handsome in his new uniform — John has bee⟨n to⟩ Paris & is returned with his sister Tot [172] or Po⟨l. Her⟩ real name I am not acquainted with; he ⟨says⟩ that the

was admitted to Caius College, Cambridge, in 1831 and took his B. A. degree in 1837.

[170] William Hillard was the proprietor of this tavern, located at 298 Strand (*Robson's London Directory*, 1837).

[171] Good Friday fell on April 20 in 1832.

[172] Adelaide Kemble.

Cholera has killed three times as ⟨many⟩ persons in Paris as are in the lists — h⟨earses⟩ are going about like omnibuses & dead car⟨ts in⟩ black because there are not enough of othe⟨r con⟩veyances to meet the "increasing demand⟨." It⟩ would not be a bad place to set up an On

\*     \*     \*

Henry & I went yesterday to Covent-Garden Theatre to see M<sup>r</sup> Farley rehearsing his new piece [173] — It was splendid beyond everything. There was a grand fight rehearsed in w<sup>h</sup> M<sup>rs</sup> Vining takes a principal part, & Eller the Harlequin; then there was an Ambush of Tartars who attacked an army of Chinese — The men

had got their swords darts banners &c, & their own clothes. At the end of the combat when the Chinese were slain, Farley in a fit of enthusiasm, cried out; "Now let every Tartar man, wave every Tartar banner, those who've got banners — " Really he seemed

[173] *The Tarter Witch, And the Pedler Boy* (see above, No. 62, April 19). Mrs. Vining appeared as Azim (Prince of Sensi), a Chinese; Eller as Kanghi, a Tartar. (*Theatrical Observer*, April 23)

quite like an artist or a poet, or a General who had just gained a
victory — Le sublime Didgar came in promiscuously & so did
Warde  Warde called him Diddlededum!  Fancy wit from Warde
applied to Didgar.  Then two dancers were abusing each other for
scandal — Really it was the most amusing scene ever I see.  We
went into the painting Room where the mystery was laid open to
us, by Grieve [174] — he showed us a number of models of scenes &
was devilish civil — lastly we visited the wardrobe & the Tailor
asked Henry to pay him a bill for Clothes

*     *     *

Expedition — I shall pause ⟨to drink to your⟩ good health my dear
old Teddibus — Saturday Martin⟨eau⟩ came in as I was a smoking
& writing ver⟨ses —⟩ care having left his heavy foot-marks there
⟨upon⟩ my fictitious & poetical forehead — Yesterday ⟨I made⟩ five
visits w.ʰ was a good thing, & dined at

*     *     *

65.             TO MRS. CARMICHAEL-SMYTH
                    23 MAY 1832

*Address:* M.ʳˢ Carmichael Smyth. | Larkbeare House | Ottery S.ᵗ Mary |
Devon. *Postmark:* MY 23 1832. Published in part, *Memorials*, p. 358.

Temple.
Wednesday.  May 22.

Here are hot weather & green trees again dear Mother, but the
sun wont shine into Taprells chambers & the high stools dont
blossom & bring forth buds.  Whenever I go out I hear nothing but
reform, & in chambers nothing but law neither of them very pleasant subjects.  O matutini rores auræque salubres! [175]  I do long so
for fresh air & fresh butter, I w.ᵈ say only it isn't romantic.  I wish
you would send me some pots of butter & jam, for here in this hot

---

[174] Thomas Grieve, an artist and member of the Garrick Club (Richard
Harris Barham, *The Garrick Club*, New York, 1896, p. 33), who had painted
the scenery.
[175] The first line of Cowper's "Votum" (1782).

Sweep-Steaks

A thorough bred one

Neck & Neck

A starting Post

weather the butter is like oil & jam is dear. FitzGerald has been to town for a few days his sister was going to be married but has got the measles instead so he is gone — The Forrests are gone to Charlton I wish I was there too for a week or so.

I have just seen Colonel Forrest in Lincolns' Inn fields, where I was walking rurally with Arthur Buller enjoying nature & smoking segars. I am to go down on Saturday & glad I shall be. Yesterday I took a long walk to Kensington Gardens & had a pleasant day & a pleasant nap on the green banks of the Serpentine — I wonder people don't frequent Kensington Gardens more they are far superior to any of the walks in Paris that are so much admired & talked of. Green peas & new potatoes are as I hear in a delightful state of forwardness & these are the delights of a London Spring. I am thinking of turning Parson & being a useful member of society & not a cringing blustering sneaking bullying lawyer. Yesterday on my return from my walk I was pleased to find four gentlemen drinking gin & water "cold without" not my guests but those of my opposite neighbour who has not got his sitting room furnished & so sends his company into my chambers — If my Uncle Frank had called & found men drinking gin at 4 o'clock in the day! Dear Mother the day is burning hot & I am so stupid that I must draw for you instead of writing here are some sporting caricatures wh I have been making.

It is better drawing stupid caricatures than writing more stupid nonsense. but a long walk I have had has made me very tired. Good bye dear Mother I will write again soon & make a longer letter.

W. M. T.

66.        TO MRS. CARMICHAEL-SMYTH
                    25 JUNE 1832

*Address:* M^rs Carmichael Smyth. | Budleigh Salterton | Devon. *Readdressed:* M^rs Charmicheal Smith | To the care of W. C. Smith Esq^e | No. 5 Furnivals Inn Holborn. *Postmark:* 7 JY 1832. Published in part, *Memorials*, pp. 358–359.

                    Polvellan. West Looe Cornwall.
                    Monday June 25. 1832.

Are you surprized dear Mother, at the direction? certainly not more prepared for it than I was myself — but you must know that on Tuesday last I went to breakfast with C Buller, & he received a letter from his constituents at Liskeard requesting him immediately to come down; he was too ill to come but instead deputed Arthur Buller & myself — so off we set that same night by the Mail arrived at Plymouth the next day & at Liskeard the day after; where we wrote addresses canvassed farmers & dined with attorneys        Then we came on here to M^r Bullers & here have I been very happy since last Friday except that just at this moment I am suffering under the effects of the outside journey having been divested of a considerable portion of the skin of my face, w^h is not at all favorable to my personal appearance — to remedy this I have this morning imbibed a black dose — w^h I have no doubt will in the course of the day restore me to my usual health & beauty.

I have been so occupied since Monday dear Mother that except at night I have had no time to myself now I am sleeping in a little cottage away from the house where there has been neither pen or ink until yesterday, & had there been both I should have had little to say except that I was very tired very happy & very well — These two last apply very well still but it is seven o'clock of a fine summer morning so I have no fatigue to complain of — On Wednesday I was riding for 12 hours canvassing rather a feat for me, & considering I had not been on horseback for eight months my stiffness yesterday was by no means surprizing — It was a very mad expedition but will bring me sooner to my dear Mother so I have no reason to regret its consequences — I have been lying awake this morning meditating the wise & proper manner I shall employ my vast fortune when I am of age — w.ʰ if I live so long will take place in 3 weeks — First I do not intend to quit my little chambers in the Temple, because £30 a year is better to pay than 90 the general price for good chambers — & the other 60 will do excellently well for poor M.ʳˢ Blechynden. Then I will take a regular monthly income w.ʰ I will never exceed. &c. The funds in Uncle Franks hands I cannot touch till M.ʳ Langslow sends a power of attorney from Malta. I am glad to find that it will be £4000 money & not stock as we had supposed. Just before I left town I saw M.ʳ Macnab & liked him very much — he has ⟨asked⟩ me down to Scotland some day or other I shall go — but when we are at Southampton we shall be near Havre & then dear Mother I will take that same little French trip we talked about — that is if you will spare me — I have come away with only a trunk full of things shall I be wanted at all in London? if so I could go up with Father, if not, come home to you and go with you to the Isle of Wight or stay quietly at home in snug little Salterton w.ʰ I think I sh.ᵈ like better than all.

God bless you, dear Mother, write directly & give your orders. Sir John Lewis is here & sends his love to Jim — he is a pleasant man I think: I have been to Morval a fine place belonging to Squire Buller who has been very civil to me as is every body here     M.ʳ C Buller is I think an excellent fellow. Young Charles comes down at the end of next week — if you want me sooner I will come if not I sh.ᵈ like to wait for the reform rejoicings w.ʰ are to take place on his arrival, particularly as I have had a great share in the canvassing. Goodbye again dearest Mother love to all ever y.ʳ affte Son.

67.　　　　　　TO EDWARD FɪᴛᴢGERALD
　　　　　　　5-7 JULY 1832 [176]

Published in part, *Biographical Introductions*, IX, xxi-xxiii.

　　　　　　　　　　　　　　　　Newton Abbot.

⟨. . .⟩ [177] I passed ⟨a⟩ v⟨ery⟩ pleasant fortnight at Polvellan,

*　　　*　　　*

Bullers place where I found plenty of amusement a beautiful
country & some kind friends — We canvassed for Charles very
assiduously & successfully pledging him to reforms in politicks &
religion of wʰ we knew nothing ourselves. but nevertheless the
farmers were highly impressed with our sagacity & eloquence.
Then we published addresses in the name of Charles Buller promising to lessen taxes & provide for the agricultural and commercial
interests, & deprecating that infamous traffic, wʰ at present legalizes
the misery of the West Indian slave — Then we wrote songs
awfully satirical songs here is a specimen.

　　　　　　　Alas for the tories
　　　If virtue & genius like Jopes should make slips
　　　What cause had the drivelling drunkard to own
　　　The dastardly deeds wʰ when sober he'd done
　　　And swear that no radical rascal should cope
　　　With the riches of Eliot the wisdom of Jope —

All this though I dare say you dont see it is very satirical & personal
Mʳ Jope was Lord Eliot's (the tory candidate's) canvasser & a very
shabby fellow who has done some rascally things when sober &
confessed them when drunk so now you see the point of it — It
goes on for several stanzas — in fact except — "The other day to
our town a captain of dragoons came down" &c I know nothing in
the language so severe.

　　Yesterday we left Polvellan ⟨. . .⟩ [178] & came to Plymouth then

[176] This letter was begun at Teignmouth on Thursday, July 5, and finished
at Newton Abbot on Sunday, July 8. The final pages are missing, however,
and the last words preserved were written on July 7.

[177] The first three lines of this letter are irrecoverably overscored.

[178] Three words are here irrecoverably overscored.

on to this place through the most beau⟨tiful co⟩untry I have ever seen — there is only one thing that equals it & that is the description I have given of it in my Journal. There were numbers of nice

old churches mostly of this shape & lots of green trees & green fields all girt round with the beautiful dartmoor hills — I dont think I ever took a drive of forty miles before without being tired — This morning I got up at 7 of the clock & walked about made a sketch out of the window w^h you shall see soon I hope, bought some stockings & am now about to eat some breakfast, though I am quite ill from devouring an immense quantity of boiled beef yesterday at Plymouth — My dear Teddikin will you come with me to Paris — in a month? — We will first take a walk in Normandy, & then go for a fortnight or so to Paris. I have a strange idea that I shall be in Italy before the autumn is over, & if my dear dear old Teddibus w^d but come with me we will be happy in a Paradise of pictures — what say you o my Teddibus — reco⟨llect I sh⟩all have money enough for us both ⟨of my⟩ own — nor am I half so extravagant as ⟨at⟩ Bonchurch & somewhere else — but I forget how it is ⟨spelled⟩ — the day before yesterday we went there on a picnic party and saw and eat a great deal —

The other day I read one of Irvings Orations,[179] w^h I think the

[179] *The Oracles of God, Four Orations* (London, 1823) by the Rev. Edward Irving (1792–1834), founder of the Irvingite or Holy Catholic Apostolic Church and friend of the Carlyles. The passage to which Thackeray refers is part of Irving's argument against religious controversy in the first oration (pp. 12–13): "The points of the faith we have been called on to defend, or which are reputable with our party, assume in our esteem an importance disproportionate to their importance in the Word, which we come to relish chiefly when it goes to sustain them, and the Bible is hunted for argu-

finest piece of eloquence I ever came across — it is a great pity he
has altered his opinions for there they seem very moderate & very
noble — I wish I could recollect a passage against Bible-commen-
taries — he says that if we need commentaries to sustain our faith
why do we object to pictures & statues to sustain our devotion —
"Therefore while the warm fancies of the Southerns have given
their Idolatry to the ideal forms of noble art, let us Northerns beware lest we give our Idolatry to the cold & coarse abstractions of
human intellect" — Ah said a parson to me when I shewed him this
but the Catholics don't sustain their devotion to God by pictures
they worship the pictures themselves — in fact said he the passage
is nonsense & the logic false — These fellows in the shovel-hats are
greater bigots than the Catholics — when you turn parson dear
Teddibus you wont refuse to see merit even in a Presbyterian —
O the 2 churches to morrow & the exhortation to the young communicants — ⟨fro⟩m a prosy long winded bigotted high-church
⟨parson⟩ who would not acknowledge the Bishop the other day
because he went to the Bible Society

We had grand fun at Liskeard they twice took the horses from
C Bullers carriage & dragged him in      Then there was a grand
reform festival, first we were met by a dozen banners & two dozen
young men in white trowsers who dragged in the popular Candidate — next came a waggon load of young ladies of all denomina-
tions of Xtians who from their seat w^h was all covered with laurels
chanted the heavens declare the Glory of God,[180] Sound the loud
timbrel & other godly and appropriate airs — Then the assembled
multitude was addressed by a Presbyterian Parson who vouched
for Charles Bullers sentiments moral & religious. Buller made a
very pretty impromptu speech himself addressed chiefly to six

ments and Texts of controversy which are treasured up for future service. . . .
If any helps are to be imposed for the understanding, or safe-guarding, or
sustaining of the word, why not the help of statues and pictures for my devotion? Therefore, while the warm fancies of the Southerns have given their
idolatry to the ideal forms of noble art — let us Northerns beware we give
not our idolatry to the cold and coarse abstractions of the human intellect."

[180] Psalm 19; "Sound the Loud Timbrel" in Thomas Moore's *Sacred Songs*
(1816).

hundred school-boys & girls who had come out to meet him — after all this was over 800 independent men sate down to dinner in the rain it is true, but the water w.<sup>h</sup> dribbled down their necks could not cool the warmth of their hearts or destroy the honest voracity of their appetites. Then came more speechifying & a tea drinking for the ladies was to have concluded the evening had not the unfortunate state of the weather caused the deferring of the tea drinking, & thus put a premature stop to the festive scene — ⟨. . .⟩ [181]

68.            TO MRS. CARMICHAEL-SMYTH
                    8 AUGUST 1832

*Address:* M.<sup>rs</sup> Carmichael Smyth — | at Miss Bechers. | Fareham. | Portsmouth | Hants. | Angleterre. *Readdressed:* M.<sup>rs</sup> Forrests | Sunbury | Middlesex. *Postmarks:* FPO AU 10 1832, 14 AU 1832. Published in part, *Memorials*, p. 360.

Hotel Lillois  Rue Richelieu.  Paris —
            Wednesday.  August 8

The tour is ended dear Mother, and instead of sight seeing in Normandy, here I am for a fortnight at least — I arrived last night from Rouen coming through some of the prettiest country I have seen in France with a great number of curious old buildings & Gothic churches, I think on my way back that I shall walk about forty miles of the journey, that is if the fleas will leave me alone. While I was at Havre I had no sleep by night or rest by day, & upon my word I believe they are the chief cause of my coming to Paris — Havre is a very fair specimen of a French town with a couple of fine streets and a hundred miserable dingy squalid allies, w.<sup>h</sup> however are the most picturesque things in the world — here is the view from my inn window at Havre — w.<sup>h</sup> is I think very picturesque & characteristic. At Rouen I had no time for sketches for I had scraped acquaintance with a young Madras Captain of the name of Gerrard with whom I went sight seeing, but as he did not seem much to admire the picturesque I did not ask him to wait for me.

---

[181] The remaining pages of this letter have not been preserved.

Houses w.ʰ I enquired about seem very nearly as dear as in England — My bill at Rouen for one day was a pound — Havre was rather cheaper but not much — Lubbock sent me some money in a rowing letter. My Uncle Frank says he has written to his broker in London to pay the dividends, but he did not know before that

he had been enabled to do so — he has just lost his son — The child was always sickly, and some time ago they seem to have made up their minds to losing it —

I had a pleasant drive yesterday from Rouen seated on the top of the diligence among the boxes & carpet bags, w.ʰ made comfortable sofas enough     Rouen is ninety miles & they make the journey in fourteen hours, w.ʰ is very fair — the estafette [182] does it in ten, of course  I went to the theatre directly and was very much amused — everything looks much more brilliant than when I was in Paris before; [183] and the tricolored flags look mighty clean & gay in comparison to the dirty napkins of the Bourbons, w.ʰ one used to see — The poor young Napoleon is gone — I read the other day in the Papers — "Hier S. M. a envoyé complimenter l'Ambassa-

[182] The courier.
[183] In April, 1830. See below, Appendix I.

deur de l'Autriche sur la mort du Duc de Reichstadt [184] — it is as
fine a text for a sermon as any in the Bible — This poor young man
dying as many say of poison, and this great big blundering block-
head of a Louis Philippe presenting his compliments on the occasion! O Genius, Glory, ambition what might you learn from this,
and what might I teach you only I am hungry & going to breakfast —

I have had my breakfast at the Cafe Colbert — bifteck aux
pommes de terres — poulet froid — dessert — et une demi bou-
teille du Vin Blanc — theres a breakfast for you! better than the
washy tea & the greasy muffins — and all for the moderate sum of
fifteen pence. It is a burning hot day. The cafes are crammed
with fellows drinking lemonade and I have got an attack of cholera
from that same—rather one of the symptoms—Galignani [185] wants
to do me out of seventy francs he declares that I went away three
years ago & forgot to return two novels from his library however
I intend to shew a great deal of firmness & resist the demand —
Now good bye dear Mother for it is post time,
and in spite of the heat I must go & seek out some
of my old friends — They have not got Napoleon
up in the Place Vendome as I had hoped. This is
the mode for the gentlemen here tell Mary —
Goodbye dear Mother ever y[r] affte. Son

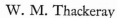

        W. M. Thackeray

[184] Napoleon François Joseph Charles Bonaparte (1811–1832), variously
known as Napoléon II and the Duc de Reichstadt, died on July 22.

[185] Galignani's English Book Shop, which had been founded in 1800, was
at this time managed by the original proprietor's sons, Jean-Antoine (1796–
1873) and Guillaume (1798–1882) Galignani.

69.                    TO EDWARD FitzGERALD
                      27–31 OCTOBER 1832 [186]

*Postmark:* 2 NOV. 1832. Published in part, *Biographical Introductions*, IX,
xxxix.

\*      \*      \*

I am just come home from Franconi's, where they are doing
Napoleon — the piece is as fine & tedious as the Covent Garden one
of last year — I could not sit it out — I saw however the battle of
Austerlitz, and must give the greatest credit to the troops on both
sides; the costumes were excellent, & the guns though they smoked
& flashed a good deal made very little noise — but there was no
charge of cavalry, no "combat of six" as at Astley's not even a
waggish suttler; — Dont you love the combats when the fellows

come on with their fighting swords — they are not up to it here —
The French love of clap-trap is amazing; Dessaix's dying speech
was almost encored; so were all Napoleon's remarks like Dieu
protege la France &c.

A propose of theatres there is to be an English one here this
winter with H. WALLACK for manager, he will of course do all
the genteel comedy parts, & be what they call Le Jeune Premier
here — This will be good fun — They have a piece here called
Louis Onze,[187] wʰ is capital — Ligier enacts Louis Onze his costume is above —

---

[186] This letter was begun on Saturday, October 27, when Thackeray went
to the Cirque Olympique (see above, No. 62, October 27), and finished the
following Wednesday.
[187] A tragedy by Casimir Delavigne (1793–1843), first presented on Feb-

\*    \*    \*

The Frenchmen are very anxious to know what a dandy means — a fellow asked me, & I pointed him out a rakish Englishman of the name of Clive,[188] who was in the orchestra — & with whom I was at school. — now Clive had on a marvellous dirty shirt, & looked drunk where as the man who acted the dandy had a splendid blue coat & black satin pantaloons — a novelty w$^h$ will I am sure be adopted by Wallack as soon as he comes

\*    \*    \*

considerable taste and liberality — Fancy my horror two ⟨days⟩ ago at seeing in the Palais Royal an aunt of mine [189] ⟨with⟩ 4 children & a nursery maid lionizing! — They are ⟨it⟩ appears coming to reside here—I have recommended Ver⟨sailles⟩ to them strongly. Good night dear Teddibus, I am going ⟨to⟩ compose myself to sleep over a German book of Schleg⟨el's⟩ w$^h$ I find excellent for that purpose — I am drinking your health in a glass of brandy & water "warm with⟨"⟩ of w$^h$ I send you a very faithful portrait —

Wednesday — The sun is so bright & the sky looks so mighty blue, that I think I shall stretch my long legs as far as Choisy. — I have a very bad excuse for not having finished my letter earlier, but this is the most unpleasant sheet of paper on w$^h$ ⟨I⟩ ever wrote, & really this is my sole excuse for not ha⟨ving⟩ dispatched my letter earlier — Since Monday, I have done nothing scarcely — that is to say I have read B⟨eau⟩mont & Fletcher w$^h$ I am sorry not to admire much, Schlegel's criticisms w$^h$ are very good; & the Mems of Cardinal Dubois a book excellently suited to the

\*    \*    \*

ruary 11, 1832, in which Pierre Ligier (1797–1872) scored a triumphant success.

[188] Theophilus Clive (b. 1808), who entered Charterhouse in 1821.

[189] Mrs. Ritchie.

70.      TO EDWARD FɪᴛᴢGERALD
          22 NOVEMBER 1832

*Postmark:* FPO NO 22 1832. Published in part, *Biographical Introductions,*
IX, xl.

\*   \*   \*

The English company begin here on Wednesday; yesterday I
was dining at Vefours in Company with H. Wallack the beauteous
Delhi! — he blazed in pins rings chains
all covered with diamonds, a white
stock a lilac satin waistcoat a blue coat
with buttons of brass & velvet collar —
a costume worthy of him & Theodore
Hooke —

Here is a copy of a beautiful scene in
a play called Perrinet Le Clerc, wʰ they
are now doing at the Porte Sᵗ M: it is of course full of horrors &
adulteries; but the scenery & costumes are charming; — The troops

come marching down the long black street in the middle of the
scene; then there is a row a man pitched into the river, & you
see old heads peeping out of the old windows

\*   \*   \*

young gentleman of small fortune; sought by my acquaintance, ⟨hon⟩oured by my tradesmen, & beloved by the poor, — so that mothers when they know me & my character shall prefer me to spendthrifts even tho' they are rich, & shall say to their daughters; better is economy with 500 a year than extravagance with five thousand —

So my dear Teddibus I request the pleasure of your company at dinner on the first Sunday of December; by w^h time I trust to be established in the Temple; & leading the life mentioned to you above —

\*　　\*　　\*

71.　　　　　TO GEORGE CRUIKSHANK
　　　　　　NOVEMBER 1832? [190]

*Address:* G. Cruikshank Esq^e | Amwell Street. | Pentonville. Hitherto unpublished.

Dear Cruikshank —

I have been to Paris for a couple of months or I should have thanked you earlier for your "Sketch Book" — I wish you w^d do me a favour, & eat a most sober mutton chop with me on Monday at 6.

Very truly yours.
W. M. Thackeray.

5 Essex Court.
　Temple — Friday —

[190] Cruikshank's *Scraps and Sketches* appeared in four parts between 1828 and 1832. Thackeray had chambers in Essex Court from the summer of 1831 to November, 1833. It seems likely that this note was written shortly after his return to London from Paris in November, 1832. Thackeray cannot be referring to Cruikshank's *My Sketch Book*, which was not issued till December 1, 1834.

## 72.    TO JAMES CARMICHAEL-SMYTH
### 29 NOVEMBER 1832 [191]

*Address:* J. Carmichael Smyth Esq^re | Larkbeare House | Ottery S^t Mary | Devon. *Readdressed:* To be forwarded directly | Sunbury. | Middlesex. *Postmarks:* NO 29 1832, LONDON DE. 3 1832. Hitherto unpublished.

Essex C^t —

Thursday 29.

Prepare your mind to undergo a great shock my dear Jimbo, & strengthen your understanding that you may bear the news I give you w^h when you have read aloud to the party in the drawing room will I fancy produce the following effect.

1^o Mother falls into a fit of hysterics, & Father rushes to assist her.

2. The lamp falls on the table in a shivering fit!

3. Mary who has been singing (in a quavering fit) stops in the middle of "Isle of Bea-u-u-ty, & falls off the musick stool

[191] Thackeray's cousin Jim had not yet set out for Larkbeare when this letter arrived. Mrs. Carmichael-Smyth consequently forwarded it to him, adding a note of her own on the third and last pages.

4. Jim no sooner comes to the words — I am in England, than he loses his senses & his balance at the same moment, & falls into the easy chair & into a convulsive fit —

5. JOHN entering promiscuously with the urn, drops it in sur- prize  The scalding restores Jim: Father & Mother go instantly to rest; but Mary lies on the floor senseless till the next morning when she is swept up by Martha; who has been herself lying in convulsions all night on the kitchen-dresser attended carefully by Betsy Cummins & the Prentice boy — Rachael has not been par-

ticularly affected only she is much thinner the next morning — Samuel rushes to Marthas aid with a bottle of brandy, but as he finds it dont do her much good — he thinks proper to finish it himself —

I left Paris on Saturday, was four & fourty hours in the Diligence coming 170 miles — four hours on the packet — such hours! w^h may be briefly described by this figure. — In a fort- night or less I hope to come home! but must first settle some affairs here; and this is all that I have to say for the present — so goodbye dear Jimbo. for ten days or so; when if you wish to pay me a compliment you may order Salterton Bells to be rung; never mind, tell Mother, about killing a fatted calf, because I've had enough veal in France — W. M. T.

------

My dearest Jim, your Uncle & I have tumbled out of our "hysterics" into a *quandary* about your journey, the countryman with his fox &c, was not more perplexed — As far as we know, there is no Exeter Coach that passes through Salisbury at any convenient hour; 3, or 4 AM: we believe to be the latest, & to get out of a warm bed at that hour for the outside of a Coach, would be worse than travelling all night, besides which, even if it could be arranged on that matter, there is a great objection to your sleeping on the road. Stage Coach travellers, are not the best attended to; & "not all the blood of all the" [192] Carmichaels would insure such a resting place for their illustrious representative as would be desirable, the additional difficulty too of a general election, would in all probability oblige you to put yourself into some dirty hole, where you would have more than one enemy to your rest to encounter — under these considerations

We wish that you should take an *inside* place of the

Devonport Mail & be at Haines to meet it
by *1/2 past 9* — if it be a fine night, put on

all your wraps, & mount outside, according to the directions in Mary's letter; but if it rains, make up your mind to a little of Roaldus's enjoyment,[193] rather than get a severe cold w.h may keep you prisoner at home, as you have been at Charlton — how very unlucky that the only day Coach should have stopped on the very Monday before you left Sandhurst — I should think that the poor

[192] An echo of Pope's *Essay on Man* (Epistle IV, ll. 215–216):
What can ennoble sots, or slaves, or cowards?
Alas! not all the blood of all the Howards.

[193] Roaldus, one assumes, must have been imprisoned in a dungeon at some time during his career. Thackeray, who was very proud of the fact that his grandmother was a Webb, writes of his relative General Webb in *Esmond:* "He came of a very ancient Wiltshire family, which he respected above all families in the world: he could prove a lineal descent from King Edward the First, and his first ancestor, Roaldus de Richmond, rode by William the Conqueror's side on Hastings field." (*Works*, VII, 221) See below, No. 1119.

knee would be spared much risk if y$^r$ Aunt Forrest [194] could put some kind of padding, not a paper cushion, inside of the pantaloon, in a manner that the *pant* wont be tightened thereby — And now my dear old Jim I hope we shall have no more writing but "sayings & doings" [195] & a merry Xmas with our dear *Roaldus,* whose return is quite an unexpected treat to me — of all things mind a good wrapper for your throat — I fear we must not look for Bob [196] as he is so much wanted, & Im sure poor Aunt Maria [197] requires all comfort     I think Bill's letter would give her a good laugh, he has not quite hit old John — Give our kind love to Aunt Forrest & the wee ones — & take care of yourself —

Ever yr most affec$^t$ aunt

73.     TO MRS. CARMICHAEL-SMYTH
2 MAY 1833 [1]

*Address:* M$^{rs}$ Carmichael Smyth. | 11 Porchester Terrace | Bayswater. Published in part, *Biographical Introductions,* III, xxxi.

I have been wanting very much to see you dearest Mother, but this paper [2] has kept me so busily at work, that I have really & truly had no time.

I have made a wood-cut for it of Louis Philippe [3] w$^h$ is pretty

---

[194] The former Georgiana Christina Carmichael-Smyth, younger sister of the Major, who had married Lieutenant-Colonel William Forrest in 1816.

[195] An allusion to Theodore Hook's *Sayings and Doings. A Series of Sketches from Life* (1824–1828).

[196] Robert Carmichael-Smyth.

[197] The former Maria Agnes Carmichael-Smyth (d. 1833), the Major's older sister, who had married Dr. Alexander Monro in 1800.

[1] A glimpse of Thackeray in the early months of 1833 is afforded by the "Reminiscences of Thackeray" which Major Frederick J. Goldsmith (b. 1819) contributed to *The Athenaeum* of April 11, 1891, pp. 474–475. Goldsmith writes that he first knew Thackeray, "when he, a young man of two or three and twenty, was looked upon by me, a boy of fourteen or fifteen, as a sort of good genius whose presence shed brightness over my out-of-school existence. He would sketch for me the very figures I delighted to contemplate, take me to the places I delighted to be taken to, and make himself the pleasantest of companions, although the difference of age was just a sufficient cause, in

good; but have only written nonsense in the shape of reviews — The paper comes out tomorrow afternoon & then I will come up to ⟨see⟩ you with a copy thereof⟨.⟩

I have been obliged to p⟨ut⟩ off the play, & everything else hav-

---

the estimation of most men, to bring about a directly opposite result. As an instance of his artistic tastes and capabilities, I remember walking with him one day when his thoughts were almost wholly engaged on the so-called 'African Roscius' — a Mr. Ida Aldridge, whom he had seen on the previous night in 'Othello.' He led me into a lithographer's (in or near Cornhill), drew from recollection the somewhat singular, but truthful figure with which his brain was haunted, and had, at once, several copies struck off for sale. At the sight of these, exposed afterwards in the shop windows, I felt a sort of boyish pride in the consciousness of having assisted, as it were, at their production. But I am not aware that any recreative pleasure experienced by me in after years can be compared to that which I derived from being treated by him to a *tête-à-tête* dinner in the City and then taken to the Adelphi Theatre, in those days a specially attractive resort to many men and women and *all* boys. It had a charming representative of domestic heroines in Mrs. Yates; a splendid Frenchman and 'part' actor in this lady's husband, the able manager; a pair of admirably contrasted and excellent *farceurs* in John Reeve and Buckstone; and a simply unrivalled 'villain' in Mr. O. Smith. All of these were to the fore on the night in question, when the performances consisted of the popular 'Victorine' [1831], and an adaptation of Fenimore Cooper's 'Bravo' [first played on February 11, 1833]. Much as I enjoyed the occasion from sheer boyish love of the theatre, I feel sure that my older and more experienced guide was almost equally amused and interested — my own appreciation of the treat throwing a certain weight into the scale."

[2] Thackeray had recently become proprietor of *The National Standard*, a literary journal edited by F. W. N. Bayley since its inception on January 1, 1833. It was announced in the issue of May 11 (p. 289) that the paper had changed hands and that Bayley had been dismissed. From that time until *The National Standard* ceased publication on February 1, 1834, Thackeray contributed to nearly every issue. At first he had Maginn as his co-worker, for the magazine which he is related by Mahony (Blanchard Jerrold, *The Final Reliques of Father Prout*, London, 1876, pp. 141–145) to have paid the Doctor £500 to edit can hardly have been other than *The National Standard*, but latterly he and his assistant Hume appear between them to have prepared the whole paper.

It may be surmised that Thackeray's account in *Lovel the Widower* of how Mr. Batchelor came to acquire the *Museum* derives from his own purchase of *The National Standard*. Certainly he is drawing on his memories of that paper when he writes: "I daresay I gave myself airs as editor of that confounded *Museum*, and proposed to educate the public taste, to diffuse morality and sound literature throughout the nation, and to pocket a liberal salary in return for my services. I daresay I printed my own sonnets, my own tragedy, my

ing actually done nothing except work this paper — I send a boy
with this, for I thought you might be glad to hear what my proceedings are; I was obliged to ask G. Templer to dine with me
to day as he leaves London immediately, & was very civil to me in
Devonshire — however, if you will have me, I wont go any where
on Friday ⟨or⟩ Sunday, even if the Duke of ⟨De⟩vonshire were to
ask me to dinner — God bless you dearest Mother　　I send you a
couple of Magazines w$^h$ I have received in my new capacity — love
to all —


74.　　　TO MRS. CARMICHAEL-SMYTH
　　　　　　　6 JULY 1833

*Address:* M$^{rs}$ Carmichael Smyth. | Larkbeare House | Ottery S$^t$ Marys Devon-
shire | England. *Postmarks:* 6 JUIL. 1833, FPO JY 8 1833. Extract pub-
lished, *Memorials*, p. 361; additions in *Biographical Introductions*, III, xxxi.

　　　　　　　　　Meurice's. Rue Rivoli.
　　　　　　　　　Saturday July 6.

　I have just found your letter dear Mother lying under a heap of
papers, where to guess from the date it must have been for the last
2 days; — however it was very welcome at last, for I had been expecting news from you for a week or more, & am glad that it was
so good when it came — I am here in my old quarters comfortable
enough except for the weather w$^h$ is burning hot, & for the bore of
packing up for a short visit to my friend Lemann's house at Brie;
where I shall be much ennuyeed I expect — there is however to be
a fete, & some other gaieties w$^h$ will relieve us a trifle — I have
likewise been for some days to Choisy Le Roi, & once to Versailles,

---

own verses (to a Being who shall be nameless, but whose conduct has caused a
faithful heart to bleed not a little). I daresay I wrote satirical articles, in which
I piqued myself upon the fineness of my wit, and criticisms, got up for the
nonce out of encyclopaedias and biographical dictionaries; so that I would be
actually astounded at my own knowledge. I daresay I made a gaby of myself
to the world. . . ." (*Works*, XII, 67–68)

　The only complete file of *The National Standard* of which I have knowledge is in the Harvard College Library.
　3 Printed in *The National Standard* of May 4, p. 275.

where I passed a pleasant day enough, & shall return some day next week I think — Here everything goes on as usual, & except that I have only once caught a sight of la belle Duvernay,[4] everything is gay & merry — I dont know how long I shall stay here, not long I think, but I hate settling long beforehand, & I dont much like the prospect of returning to town; but I must try & make this paper worth something, & I suppose, that to obtain that ⟨result my⟩ presence will be necessary on the other ⟨side⟩ of the water — It goes on very flourishingly as I hear, but I cant get subscribers for it here, the postage being so enormous that it quite overbalances the cheapness of the paper — It looks well however to have a Parisian correspondent; & I think that in a month more I may get together stuff enough for the next ten months [5] — I have been thinking very seriously of turning artist — I think I can draw better than do anything else & certainly like it better than any other occupation why shouldn't I? — It requires a three years apprenticeship however, w^h is not agreeable — but afterwards the way is clear & pleasant enough; & doubly so for an independent man who is not obliged to look to his brush for his livelihood; — an artist here has been counselling me very strongly to make the trial at least & here it can be done cheap, there are ateliers where one can work at a pound a month; & there are all other necessary means & appurtenances — An artist in this town is by far a more distinguished personage than a lawyer & a great deal more so than a clergyman — I went yesterday to call on one: [6] who received me

---

[4] Thackeray may have met Marie-Louise Duvernay (b. 1810) during the summer of 1829, when both were students of Coulon (see above, No. 26). She made her début as a dancer at the Opéra the following year and scored her first great success in 1833 as Miranda in *La Tentation* (1832), an opera-ballet by Jacques François Halévy (1799–1862). Retiring from the stage in 1840, she settled in London, where she married Stephens Lyne-Stephens (1801–1860), reputed to be the richest commoner in England. After his death she was known as Mrs. Duvernay-Stephens.

[5] The "Foreign Correspondence" that Thackeray wrote for *The National Standard* extends through only four issues (June 29 to July 20), but some of the translations that he published in subsequent numbers may have been made while he was in Paris.

[6] John Brine. See Appendix V.

quite en prince; he had an atelier twenty feet high, & fifty long, covered with all sorts of tapestry, old arms, china, carved chairs, & cabinets; he is a second rate man a little better than a drawing master, but I envy him his chairs & cabinets —

I have been a good deal with my aunt, she lives very much alone & is glad of someone to talk to of evenings; about all I have seen I refer you to the National Standard: to w^h I have written a great letter this morning, w^h must be my excuse for such a short one to you — God bless you dear Mother, give my Papa a thousand kisses for me & embrace Mary & James. every your affte Son.

### W. M. T.

M^rs Ritchie shewed me a long letter from Charlotte Shakespear full of her James"; ⁷ & one from M^rs Halliday, a most sour haughty & ill tempered epistle —

75.        TO MRS. CARMICHAEL-SMYTH
6 SEPTEMBER 1833

*Address:* M^rs Carmichael Smyth. | Larkbeare House | Ottery S^t Mary | Devon. *Postmark:* SE 6 1833. Published in part, *Biographical Introductions,* III, xxxii-xxxiv.

Garrick Club.⁸ September 6.

I am wanting very much to leave this dismal city dear Mother, but I must stay for some time longer, being occupied in writing puffing & other delightful employments for the N Standard — I have had an offer made for a partner, w^h I think I shall accept, but

⁷ James Crawford, *Genealogy* (87), of the Bengal Civil Service, whom Charlotte Shakespeare had recently married.

⁸ Thackeray had only recently joined this famous organization, which was founded in 1831 at 35 King Street. Since the avowed purpose of its charter members was to bring artists of all kinds, but particularly actors, into closer association with their patrons, its membership list was far more varied than those of older and more exclusive London clubs. Its liveliness and informality made it a favorite place of resort with Thackeray until his death, and in later years he was its best known member. See Percy Fitzgerald, *The Garrick Club* (London, 1904), pp. 54-71.

the business cannot be settled for a week or ten days — In the mean time I get on as well as I can, spending my mornings in S$^t$ Pauls Churchyard,[9] & my evenings in this Club, w$^h$ is a pleasant & cheap place of resort — We have thanks to me & some other individuals established a smoking room, another great comfort — I am writing on a fine frosty day, w$^h$, considering this is the heat of the Summer, or ought to be, is the more to be appreciated —

I find a great change between this & Paris, where one makes friends, & here though for the last three years I have lived, I have not positively a single female acquaintance — I shall go back to Paris I think, & marry somebody — There is another evil w$^h$ I complain of, that this system of newspaper writing spoils one for every other kind of writing; I am unwilling now more than ever, to write letters to my friends, & always find myself attempting to make a pert critical point, at the end of a sentence —

I have just had occasion to bid adieu to Regulus: he has been breaking bottles of wine, & abstracting liquor therefrom; & this after I had given him a coat a hat & a half crown to go to Bartholo-mew Fair — he lied stoutly, wept much, & contradicted himself more than once, so I have been obliged to give him his Congé, & am now clerkless. This is I think the only adventure w$^h$ has oc-curred to me, I have been talking of going out of town, but les affaires! — as for the theatres they are tedious beyond all bearing; & a solitary evening in Chambers is more dismal still — one has no resource but this Club; where however there is a tolerably good library of reviews, and a pleasant enough society — of artistes of all kinds, & gentlemen who drop their absurd English aristocratical notions. You see by this what I am thinking of. I wish we were all in a snug apartment in the Rue de Provence. Fitz-Gerald has been in town for a day or two, & I have plenty of he acquaintances, there are a number of litterateurs who frequent this Club, & the National Standard, is I am happy to say growing into repute — though I know it is poor stuff —

A friend of mine just come from the country says he shot ten

[9] *The National Standard* was published every Saturday morning by Thomas Hurst of 65 St. Paul's Churchyard.

brace on the 1ˢᵗ September, may Father have had as good sport; there are lots of partridges here for four shillings a pair.

Goodbye dear Mother, I hope the law business is blowing over, & the storm wʰ you must have heard, & wʰ is not yet lulled in London — I am going to make a play about the loss of the Amphi-trite ¹⁰ — God bless you, & all at Larkbeare  ever yʳ affte Son

W M Thackeray.

Here is a letter full of I's, dear Mother, but there is nothing to say: these are some of the characters of the Club ¹¹ — Smith is very like.

¹⁰ "We are prepared for a storm," Thackeray remarks in "Solitude in September" (*National Standard*, September 14, p. 157). "It shall not catch us as it caught the Amphitrite, unprepared." His projected drama was never written.

¹¹ John Poole (1786?–1872) was a well known dramatist who wrote *Paul Pry* (1825). James Smith (1775–1839) collaborated with his brother Horace in *Rejected Addresses* (1812). Don Telesforo de Trueba y Cozio (1805?–1835) was the author of a farce called *The Exquisites* and of various other works. He had come to England as a political exile and had considerable success in London society before he returned to Spain in 1834. Richard Barham (*The Garrick Club*, p. 24) describes him as "An excellent high-spirited fine Old Castilian, the very soul of honour and good-humoured to a fault." His portrait by Maclise appears in *Fraser's Magazine* for June, 1831, opposite p. 613.

76.          TO MRS. CARMICHAEL-SMYTH
                 22–30 OCTOBER 1833

*Address:* Mʳˢ Carmichael Smyth. | Larkbere House | Ottery Sᵗ Mary's |
Devon. | England. *Postmark:* FPO OC 31 1833. Published in part, *Memorials*, pp. 361–362; additions in *Biographical Introductions*, III, xxxiv.

                                        Monday 22. Monday 29.
   I spend all day now dear Mother at the Atelier & am very well
satisfied with the progress wʰ I make, I think that in a year were I
to work hard I might paint something worth looking at, but it
requires at least that time before one can gain any readiness with
the brush. The other men in the Atelier are merry fellows enough,
always singing, smoking, fencing, & painting very industriously
besides. Most of them have skill in painting but no hand for drawing — little Le Poittevin ¹² himself is a wonderful fellow — I
never knew so young a man paint so well & so rapidly & in so many
different lines. He has now gone to Brussels with a picture wʰ he
painted in eight days; wʰ would take most men as many months; I
want him to go to England for the exhibition of May. where if he
would choose a striking subject he would make I think a great
figure.
   The weather has set in very cold & rainy, I fortify myself with
bischoff and segars at the Atelier, & pass the evening generally with
my aunt or Mʳˢ Pattle — not going much to the theatres wʰ are not
very brilliant — I get tickets for the Italian Opera — where the
company is very good, & where there is a beautiful creature called
Grisi ¹³ — I saw my ancient flame Duvernay at the French Opera
the other day, & wondered how I could have ever been smitten —

   ¹² Edmond le Poittevin (1806–1870) had early and continued success as a
landscape painter. Since he began to exhibit in 1831, it is not surprising that
he should already have begun to attract students to his atelier. Thackeray
later studied with Lafond (see below, No. 81) and with Baron Gros (Eyre
Crowe, *Thackeray's Haunts and Homes*, pp. 9–12).
   ¹³ Giulia Grisi (1811–1869), the celebrated soprano, had made her Parisian
début on October 16, 1832, in Rossini's *Semiramide*. Thackeray saw her
many times in London and Paris during the next fifteen years.

Now this would be an awkward circumstance in marrying a wife, it will be better I think not to be in love with her at all — only to have a kind of respect, & esteem for the sharer of one's couch, & the payer of the baker's bills.

I dine to day with the Pattles & shall meet pretty Theodosia — I wish she had £ 11325 in the 3 per cts [14] — I would not hesitate above two minutes in popping that question w[h] was to decide the happiness of my future life — Goodbye. Must go to my work shop —

The artists with their wild ways & their poverty are the happiest fellows in the world — I wish you could see the scene every day in the Atelier     Yesterday we had a breakfast for five consisting of 5 sausages 3 loaves & a bottle of wine for 15 sous; there were no plates or knives accordingly the meat was carved by the fingers — afterwards pipes succeeded & then songs imitations of all the singers in Paris they are admirable musicians — & all this obstreperous gaiety grew out of the sum of three pence w[h] had been expended by each man [15] —

I have got no ink, dear Mother, & must write in bister — but what about? — I have nothing to say, have seen nothing, & done

[14] See Appendix IV.

[15] This picture of artist life is elaborated in *The Paris Sketch Book* (*Works*, V, 41–43).

little else but paint for the last week — however in that matter I have been very industrious, & shall make I daresay many thousands a year in a short time.

I admire your indignation about the old woman & the sack of beans [16] — It is translated from a very clever French story, w$^h$ is written in a sort of patois — I suppose I have not imitated it well — for I sent away the performance the day it was written, & one does not know good from bad then — I have sent nothing else, except a cheque, but the paper is very rapidly improving, & will form I have no doubt a property — in w$^h$ case it would be pleasant as an occupation and an income — I want now to settle (having first gone to Italy &c) to marry somebody with some money, & then to live in the little house in Albion Street. [17] going to Church regularly, rising early, & walking in the Park with M$^{rs}$ T. & the children — Then what interesting letters I could write you, about Billy's progress in cutting his teeth, & Tommy's improvement in spelling — as it is I have nothing earthly to talk about, except myself — & I am tired of filling my letters with I's — There are no new events here except a revolution — of tailors — 16000 angry journeymen are in arms — they insist that smoking should be allowed in the shop room or atelier as it is here called) and that the master-tailors should take off their hats on entering the same — in consequence no coats or inexpressibles can be made at Paris for weeks to come — it is a good specimen of French character — in w$^h$ there is always an absurd imitation at being chivalrous — a journeyman tailor or rather 16000 feel hurt that they are not received with the same respectful politeness w$^h$ is paid to a gentleman — & after all there is no reason why cutting coats sh$^d$ not be as good an occupation as cutting throats — for w$^h$ remark I beg to ask pardon of the present company — & here — dear Mother I am at the end of my sheet; the next letter will I hope be longer & more worth reading — I hear excellent accounts from Crittenden, tell P.A. a gentleman here has just had letters from the Partners who write in ex-

[16] "A Tale of Wonder," *National Standard*, October 12, pp. 228-229.

[17] The Carmichael-Smyths had bought or rented a house at 18 Albion Street in London. They moved there from Larkbeare in 1835.

DRAWING IN THACKERAY'S LETTER OF 22–30 OCTOBER 1833

THACKERAY IN 1834

*From a self-portrait*

cellent spirits and have been joined by M.<sup>r</sup> Mackellop with £130000 in Specie — God bless you dear Mother.

W. M. T.

Tuesday 30. I forgot my letter till too late yesterday — am going this morning to a grand Dejeuner d'Artistes where I am to meet all the celebrities of the town, & enjoy all the delicacies of the season — We have the finest weather in the world. After breakfast we go to S.<sup>t</sup> Denis. God bless you.


77.          TO MRS. CARMICHAEL-SMYTH
                   12 NOVEMBER 1833

*Address:* M.<sup>rs</sup> Carmichael Smyth. | Larkbeare House | Ottery S.<sup>t</sup> Mary | Devon.
*Postmark:* NO 12 1833. Hitherto unpublished.

Garrick Club. Tuesday.

You see from what address I write, dearest Mother, in the middle of a choking fog w.<sup>h</sup> almost prevents me from seeing what I put on paper.

The news of the dangerous illness of a friend & debtor of mine, brought me up to London post-haste. As it is I have not been able to see this man (Cay is his name) who is insensible, & who will not I fear pay five shillings in the pound — It is very hard on him & me, for I shall lose a hundred pounds by him — the poor fellow had a place of a thousand [a] year given him just before he was taken ill.

I arrived here yesterday morning, after leaving Paris at an hour's notice as usual, & repenting very much of my departure, w.<sup>h</sup> will not however, please heaven, be for a long time. I found my chambers [18] damp, my keys half an inch thick with rust, my Birchin Lane business [19] in a good condition, & my National Standard as usual —

[18] At 5 Essex Court, Middle Temple.
[19] A bill-discounting establishment with which Thackeray became associated shortly after his return from Paris in November, 1832. See Appendix III. It should be noted that when Barry Lyndon is enticed to London by the prospect

I intend to stop here, to sell my furniture, give up my chambers & my paper, by w.ʰ I shall have had the pleasure of losing £ 200 — It has increased in sale about 20 in the last 2 months — at this rate I shall be ruined before it succeeds.

After I have effected all these things, w.ʰ I shall do in ten days I trust — I shall come down to Lyme ²⁰ & see my old mother for a fortnight or so — that is if she will take me in — after my scurvy conduct last time — then I shall go back to Paris — I have made or fancied I have made so much progress in a month, that it would be a shame not to handle the brush with a little more perseverance — besides it is the only metier I ever liked —

I was very happy at Paris, & when I got here yesterday to my horrible chambers, felt inclined to weep — M.ʳˢ Beadle has had a child near dead — I made a vow to go to Church every Sunday for a year if it recovered — & I intend to keep it — God bless you dearest Mother — it is post time — love to all — ever y.ʳ affte Son.

W. M. T.

I was offered to go to Madrid for the Standard with £ 300 a year

78.        TO MRS. CARMICHAEL-SMYTH
               23 DECEMBER 1833

*Address:* M.ʳˢ Carmichael Smyth. | Lyme Regis | Dorsetshire. *Postmark:* DE 23 1833. Extract published, *Memorials,* p. 361; additions, *Biographical Introductions,* III, xxxiv-xxxv.

Monday. Decr 23.

The only fault I find with the N. Standard, dear Mother is that the end of the day, I am but ill disposed after writing & reading so much to read another syllable or to write another line, — It is true that to day I have a better excuse, having but a very few minutes to say, that I fear the Christmas pudding must be eaten without me; for my assistant Hume ²¹ has gone into the country & I am

---

of securing a loan, the offer is made by a "respectable firm in the city" with a "counting-house in Birchin Lane" (*Works,* IV, 263).

²⁰ Lyme Regis, near Ottery St. Mary in Devon.

²¹ See below, No. 241.

left here to do all the work; — Now I am anxious that the first
N⁰ for the year should be a particularly good one as I am going to
change the name to the Literary Standard, & increase the price to
three pence.²² With wʰ alterations I hope to do better —

I have been very comfortably installed in the new house ²³ for
ten days and like much my little study, & airy bed-room, I am sure
we shall be as merry here as possible; & I believe that I ought to
thank heaven for making me poor,²⁴ as it has made me much happier than I should have been with the money — however this is a
selfish wish for I must now palm myself on you & my father, just
at the time when I ought to be independent, & no burthen to you.

Thank Grandmamma for her very kind letter, but I am unluckily obliged to wait till the 6 of January, when all will be
settled, please God; but until then I think I shᵈ wait in London,
my departure would look awkward —

Thank you for sending the papers, but you should not have said
with the Editors compliments, but with the Proprietors, two distinct personages, — it is contrary I believe to etiquette for editors
to have anything to do with the commercial part of the paper —
the plan of abuse is I find successful, a man has so many good
natured friends that he is sure to be told of anything said or written
against him — & you will allow that all the abuse as yet has been
most conscientiously bestowed.

I am going to dine with Mʳˢ Barwick to day, who is very kind &
good natured — She has a son a pleasant fellow enough but with a
strange Israelitish look — My Christmas dinner is to be devoured
with Keane,²⁵ who has been amazingly civil     I wish that it might
be celebrated at Lyme; but we have only another month to wait,

---

²² With the issue of January 4, 1834, *The National Standard of Literature,
Science, Music, Theatricals, and the Fine Arts* became *The National Standard
and Literary Representative.* Its price was duly raised from twopence to
threepence.

²³ At 18 Albion Street.

²⁴ See Appendix IV.

²⁵ David Deady Keane (1810?–1870), whom Thackeray had known at
Trinity College, Cambridge, and perhaps in Germany, for Keane in 1831
received a Ph. D. degree from the University of Göttingen. He was at this
time a parliamentary reporter, but he was made a barrister of the Middle

when you will see how snug I am in the little back parlor —

I had a long letter from Mʳˢ Pattle ⟨. . . ⟩ ²⁶ who evidently desires to make a ⟨. . .⟩ — I wrote her back word that I was ⟨. . .⟩ see how she will bear the news — ⟨. . .⟩ up for I have a great deal to say ⟨. . .⟩ wʰ have occupied me this rainy morning — ⟨. . .⟩ interesting about England & America, & will ⟨. .⟩ ²⁷ much talking about, but demands reading ⟨. . .⟩ So God bless you dearest Mother and all wh⟨. . .⟩ you at Lyme, may the mince pies be as good as ⟨those⟩ of old days, & the turkey — but I take it that neither of our Christmas repasts will this year be a very merry one, & the fault is mine, but God bless you once more, I must go to work —

ever your affte Son.
W. M. T.

79.          TO MRS. CARMICHAEL-SMYTH
5 OCTOBER 1834

*Address:* Mʳˢ Carmichael Smyth. | Larkbere House | Ottery Sᵗ Marys | Devon. | Angleterre. *Postmarks:* 5 OCT. 1834, FPO OC 7 1834. Hitherto unpublished.

6 Rue Louis le Grand. —
Sunday —

A sad mistake has been made dearest Mother, with regard to the franking of a letter, wʰ I only discovered yesterday, after having given you as I fear several days of anxiety & distress — You will get with this a scrap in pencil wʰ I sent off, in my hurry, by a friend

Temple in 1835, had a creditable legal career, and became a Q. C. and bencher of his inn in 1864. See below, No. 246.

²⁶ This and the next five hiatuses are of about three words each.

²⁷ This and the next two hiatuses are of about a word each.

who was going to England, in w.<sup>h</sup> you will read, as here somewhat
more at large, how well & comfortable we all are —

The direction above is that of a boarding house where we have
been for the last fortnight, & where we shall stay until the 19<sup>th</sup> of
the month, when we go into very pretty furnished rooms in the
Rue de Provence. N.<sup>o</sup> 22; Grandmamma in the unlucky letter w.<sup>h</sup>
has been detained, has I think given a long account of the house &
its inmates, & of all the adventures & perils during our voyage
hither — She was terribly ill on the passage, as was the unappy
Miss Langford; w.<sup>h</sup> with other misfortunes such as the delay of our
baggage & the loss of her bag, made the commencement of our trip
somewhat cloudy & unauspicious.

— Our fortnight here has however passed very pleasantly with
the exception of a small scene arising from the delay of this letter;
several of the inhabitants of M<sup>me</sup> Durands' house can bear witness
to the extraordinary eloquence of the grandmother, & the dutiful
resignation of the grandson. But I am ready to bear any reproofs
of this kind, for (though it is somewhat late in the day to record
mes expériences in the character of G. M.) I see how very kind &
good she is — in fact though I have known her long, I don't think
I ever was intimate with her until now, nor did I before appreciate
the extreme warmth of heart, & the delicate benevolence w.<sup>h</sup> I think
I can now find out in her.

— This kind of writing is to be sure better fitted for "My Grandmother" a sentimental novel than for a letter to my Grandmother's
daughter; but if I did not praise, I should I think abuse; as I am at
this moment writhing under the stripes of her satire, & the public
expression of her wrath —

Under my guidance she has learnt to suck the eggs of French
conversation tolerably well — not so Arriet, who sits all day perus-
ing a book of dialogues w.<sup>h</sup> she reads aloud for the benefit of our
little Salon; trying the most extraordinary experiments on the r's
the en's & the u's — She is a snob of the first water, she puts rouge
on her cheeks, & sports little bits of sticking plaster on her countenance not to cover her pimples but to haggravate her beauty —

My Aunt Ritchie has been very kind & attentive, & a great

friendship is struck up between her & Grandmamma. She asks us to dinner every day, and is really a great comfort & consolation. I think that G M what with my Aunt, her boarding house friends, and one or two more acquaintances she has made will pass her time here more pleasantly than in England; although she talks ominously of leaving her bones in a foreign land, & declares that she is on the brink of ruin —

I have delivered your letter to M^rs Marriott, & heard her talk for two hours last Sunday: she is a foolish woman I think & talks most incessantly & conceitedly; however she was very kind, & begged me to call on her continually.

As for my studies, I have been working hard at the Louvre, & begin tomorrow at the Life Academy, w^h has not as yet been open: I have had no time to make original drawings, & I think it as well that I should not for some time to come — Studying these great old painters puts one sadly out of conceit with one's mean little efforts —

I have found a host of English acquaintances here & have been asked to innumerable dinners, w^h I have had little scruple in refusing seeing that G. M is very comfortable with some good natured ladies inmates of our boarding house —

— G. M offers to lend me the money to meet the neat wine bill, if W^m Smyth is with you, will you ask him if he has heard from Donovan; & whether he thinks it would be better to borrow, & wait for the chance of a sale, or at once to commit the whole to the hammer, if so, it sh^d be advertized at once, & knocked down without delay.[1] — God bless you now dearest Mother, and all with you at Larkbeare, write back directly for we are very anxious to hear as you may fancy. ever y^r affectionate Son.

W. M. T.

[1] These plans would appear to refer to a supply of wine which Thackeray laid in before losing his fortune and on which it was no longer possible for him to pay storage charges.

80.          TO EDWARD FɪᴛᴢGERALD
8 OCTOBER 1834

*Address:* Edward Fitz-Gerald esq$^{re}$ | Wherstead Lodge | Ipswich | Suffolk. | Angleterre. *Readdressed to:* Geldeston Hall | Beccles. *Postmarks:* 6 OCT. 1834, IPSWICH OC 10 1834. Hitherto unpublished.

Here is the third letter I have begun, dear Edward, in reply to that noble one w$^h$ I have just received from you — the two first were full of thanks, but I think I had better leave you to fancy these, finding it myself so difficult to describe them — What I like to think of better than your generosity or the cause of it, is the noble & brotherly love, w$^h$ I believe unites us together; my dear friend & brother, may God grant that no time or circumstance ever should diminish this love between us; it seems to me a thing w$^h$ one should cultivate & preserve as a virtue, as a kind of religion, of w$^h$ it seems to have usurped the place & I hope to exercise this power, — I might fill sheets with this kind of talk as I have done before; but I find when I look at what has been written that I have not expressed what I wanted — I wonder how sentimental writers manage to clothe fine thoughts in fine sentences — I suppose because they only act them — when they come to feel them they must be tongue-tied as I am. —

I am here in a boarding house with my Grandmother and a Miss Langford, who acts as the old lady's companion; this girl is very rich — she wears rouge & sticks little bits of sticking-plaster about her face by way of ornament, and drops all her h's — the people of the boarding house have settled that I am going to marry her — her miniature I send you, you can set it if you wish in a bracelet: There are some other characters in the boarding house — a little Doctor from Bath, who is about the size of Sir Geoffrey Hudson, and is always stroking his legs — a long Miss Brooke with grey hair & a ferronière, who looks as if she had committed a murder. I wish you were here to see them all, & to follow me on long walks to the Louvre — I am writing I know in a most rambling & unsatisfactory manner for I am obliged to keep up a conversation with me grandma —

I have copied at the Louvre two Titian portraits Leonardo's Charles VII. Interior by de Hoog, & woman playing on the harpsicalls by Terburg — They are all of them very bad, but I dont despair — to night I begin at the life academy; I will make the drawings you wish — I made two failures of the Sheriff, & the Gamekeeper otherwise you would have had them with the others — wh I fear you praise too much — at present I have on me a strange longing to paint Christ in the tomb with the 2 angels — a young man has sent an admirable painting from Rome on this subject, in the Eastlake [2] School, only broader & bolder. —

Yesterday at the Luxembourg I was astonished to see how bad everything was — there is not I think a single good picture among all the elite of modern French art — but then in return, the sketches in the novels, the penny magazines &c are full of talent — Delaroche's famous Jane Grey [3] is poor I think judging from the prints —

At the theatres there is plenty of good fun I [have] not yet seen the Juif errant, — or the Tempest [4] — though I have a strange longing to see Duvernay as Miranda — Therese looks most Madonna like & lovely, she has got a child after 4 years marriage — I don't think I am in love with her any more —

God bless you dear Edward —

wh means true to deth.

if you write (as you must) before the 19th October direct No 8 Rue Louis le Grand. after 22. Rue de Provence, where we have taken a very pretty little apartment —

This letter is I see as unfit to send as the others —

I will write again immediately.

[2] Charles Lock Eastlake (1793–1865), later (1850) knighted, of the Royal Academy.

[3] "Mort de Jane Grey" by Paul Delaroche (1797–1856).

[4] Thackeray is evidently referring to Halévy's *La Tentation*. See above, No. 74.

I am here in a boarding house with my Grandmother
and a Miss Langford. who acts as the old lady's
companion, this girl is very
rich - she wears rouge, & sticks
little bits of sticking plaister
about her face by way of orna-
ment, and drops all her h's - the people of the boarding house have settled that I am going to marry
her - her miniature I send you, you can set it if
you wish in a bracelet: There are
some other characters in the boarding
house - a little Doctor from Bath, who
is about the size of Sir Geoffrey
Hudson, who and is always stroking
his legs - a long miss Brooke with
grey hair & a ferroniere, who looks
as if she had committed a murder. I wish you were
here to see them all. & follow me to my walks at
the Louvre - I am writing I know in a most rambling
& unsatisfactory manner for I am obliged to keep
up a conversation with my Grandma. c

I have copied at the Louvre two Titian portraits
Leonardo's Charles VII. Interior by de Hoog, & a woman
playing on the harpsicalls by Terburg - They are
all of them very bad, but I dont despair - To night
I begin at the Life academy: I will make the drawing

A PAGE FROM THACKERAY'S LETTER OF 8 OCTOBER 1834

81.         DIARY

1–2 NOVEMBER 1834

Published in part, *Biographical Introductions*, III, xxxv.

Saturday 1 November —

All Saints' day was spent chiefly in talking theatricals with Bowes, & wandering through the town for exercise; dined with him in the evening; & went to Lafond's —

The conduct of the model, a pretty little woman, the men & the master of the establishment was about as disgusting as possible — The girl w$^d$ not pose but instead sung songs & cut capers; the men from sixty to sixteen seemed to be in habits of perfect familiarity with the model; and Lafond himself a venerable man with a riband of honor maintained a complete superiority by the extreme bathos of his blackguardism — au reste he is said to be an excellent man, & a good father of family — It is no wonder that the French are such poor painters with all this —

Returning in the evening to Bowes's I was amused & bored by an old Frenchman called Chateau Neuf,[5] who was mad about theatricals, & rested his fame on a piece of his, w$^h$ had been acted more than 50 years ago.

2. Breakfasted at Tortoni's in the morning with Casati,[6] off the well remembered fricassee de Poulet froide; & then passed to Tivoli, where we spent the morning in the godly amusement of pistol firing — called at Lemanns where Madame received me like a stranger, & occupied the rest of the day in flanerie on the Boulevard — Had a long talk with Jack Kemble who is impayable for blague but who has a big heart, & is a noble fellow —

A few domestic storms & scolds —

[5] Agricol de la Pierre de Chateauneuf, who was sixty-four years old at this time. Thackeray probably alludes to his *L'Amant timide, ou l'adroite soubrette*, a comedy published in 1803. (*Biographie nouvelle des contemporains*, Paris, 1827, IV, 355–356)

[6] A good friend to whose care Thackeray commended Brookfield when the latter visited Paris a few years later (*Lambert Catalogue*, p. 41).

82.              TO EDWARD FrrzGERALD
                    FEBRUARY 1835

Hitherto unpublished.

                    *       *       *

A new play by Alfred de Vigny called Chatterton is just out at
the Francais [1]      I have not seen it, but the plot seems very rich —
Chatterton kills himself because Lord Beckford (the Lord Mayor)
comes to him with several other Lords of his acquaintance, & offers
to make [him] his valley desham — He is lodging in a cabaret
kept by one Kitty & her husband — Kitty falls in love with the
poet & they pop off together — Talking of suicides a schoolfellow [2]

                    *       *       *

I am sure that in Germany ⟨. . .⟩ [3] yesterday at a M. Montalem-
bert's, I saw a lot of drawings & prints after Overbeck [4] & other
German masters, a Virgin copied from the original by S[t] Luke (&
it is so beautiful that I will take my oath she sat for it) and some
sculptures by two old Nuremberg monks, who have succeeded in
a most marvellous manner in restoring the fashions and feelings of
the pious middle age —

                    *       *       *


83.                  TO FRANK STONE [5]
                    17 APRIL 1835

Address: Frank Stone, Esqre., 84, Newman Street, Oxford Street. Postmark:
7, at Night, April 20, 1835. My text is taken from Lady Ritchie's From

    [1] The première of Chatterton took place at the Théâtre Français on Feb-
ruary 12, 1835.
    [2] Thackeray perhaps went on to relate the story told in "A Gambler's Death"
(Works, V, 98–106) of the suicide in Paris of a Charterhouse companion, a
story specifically stated to be, "for the chief part, a fact" (p. 105).
    [3] About six words are here cut away.
    [4] Johann Friedrich Overbeck (1789–1869), a leader of the German "pre-
Raphaelite" school of painting.
    [5] Frank Stone (1800–1859), later (1851) A. R. A., the son of a Man-

*Friend to Friend* (London, 1919), pp. 106–109, where the address and post-mark are also recorded.

Your letter was the first of the batch, my dear Stone, and was more welcome to me even than the hot-cross buns, which, on this day,[6] our religion ordains that we should devour. I have been a little spooney ever since the perusal of the letter, but my tears (and there were one or two upon my honour) were those of a pleasant content, when I thought of the half-dozen good fellows who felt so kindly for me. God bless all the boys and watch over the liquors they drink and the pictures they draw. As for myself — I am in a state of despair — I have got enough torn-up pictures to roast an ox by — the sun riseth upon my efforts and goeth down on my failures,[7] and I have become latterly so disgusted with myself and art and everything belonging to it, that for a month past I have been lying on sofas reading novels, and never touching a pencil.

In these six months, I have not done a thing worth looking at. O God, when will Thy light enable my fingers to work, and my colours to shine? — if in another six months, I can do no better, I will arise and go out and hang myself.

We have an exhibition here with 2500 pictures in it, of which about a dozen are very good, but there is nobody near Wilkie or Etty or Landseer; lots of history pieces or what they call here "école anecdotique" — little facts cut [out] of history and dressed in correct costumes; battles, murders and adulteries are the subjects preferred. Of costumes, I have amassed an awful collection, and this in truth is all I have done, except some infamous water-colour copies perpetrated at the Louvre when it was open. Now the old pictures are covered up until June by the performances of the modern men; there are lots of six-and-thirty feet canvases, but not a good one among them. Here is as good a portrait painter as

---

chester cotton-spinner, was already an accomplished painter when he came to London in 1831, though he had been given no formal instruction in art. By 1837 he was well known through the popular engravings made from his senti-mental genre water-colors. He was the close friend of Dickens as well as Thackeray.

[6] Good Friday, which fell on April 17 in 1835.

[7] See *Ecclesiastes*, 1, 5.

ever I saw, one Champmartin,[8] who has been abused by the Athenæum man.  No good water-colours this year, though I have seen
some by Roqueplan [9] (who is a little snob who condescended to do
me out of a five-franc piece) that are as fine as Reynolds', most noble
in point of colour, sentiment, force and so forth.

I wish you would tell me how you used to make that nice *grain*.
I have tried all ways in vain.  I had hoped to have gone into Germany for the summer, and on to Italy in autumn, but my governors
and the rest of our tribe are to come here in a month and I shall
not be sorry to stay, and have a little more copying at the Louvre.
Have you been asked to a tea-party by my Mamma? [10]  I wish you
would call there some day, for you are a great favourite, and if you
talk about the son of the house, you can't talk too much or stay too
long.  Mahony [11] gives me great accounts of you and Mac.[12]  O
happy men, you are on the high-road to fame and fortune — et moi,

[8] Charles Émile Callande de Champmartin (1797–1883) of whom the
critic for *The Athenæum* had written on April 4 (p. 265): "As to portraits,
Champmartin has a high name, which I leave to those who bestow it to vindi-
cate.  His portraits seem to me in the very worst style of catchpenny cleverness:
true, they display an adroitness resulting from practice; but sleight of hand
we know to be very compatible with charlatanism."

[9] Joseph Etienne Roqueplan (1802–1855), a pupil of Baron Gros, was at
this time known as a landscape and marine painter and later specialized as a
genre painter.

[10] The Carmichael-Smyths had given up Larkbeare and were living at 18
Albion Street in London.

[11] Francis Sylvester Mahony (1804–1866), who wrote under the *nom de
plume* of "Father Prout," was successively a Jesuit and a Catholic priest.  He
turned from the Church to letters in 1834, however, and the wit and learning
of the "Reliques of Father Prout," which appeared in *Fraser's Magazine* between 1834 and 1836, won him a considerable reputation.  Henceforth he
earned his living by writing for London periodicals, though after 1837 he was
rarely to be seen in that city.  He lived in Paris in a hotel on the Rue des
Moulins from 1848 till his death.  Mahony, who long remained one of the
most intimate of Thackeray's Bohemian friends, contributed the "Inaugura-
tive Ode" to the first number of *The Cornhill Magazine*.

[12] Daniel Maclise (1806–1870), the son of a Cork shoemaker, came to
London in 1827 and entered the Royal Academy schools the following year.
His vogue was established by the series of eighty portraits that he drew for
*Fraser's Magazine* between 1830 and 1838.  Thackeray does not appear in
this series, except in "The Fraserians" of January, 1835, but there are two

Portrait of That eminent Artist
done by himself an hour before
his suicide. — & dedicated to
his inconsolable Creditors

THACKERAY IN 1835
*From a self-portrait*

moi, pauvre jouet de la fortune, voyant jour par jour les espérances
du matin moquées par les horribles réalités du soir.  Je n'ai qu'à
lutter, à me resigner, à me consoler de mes propres malheurs dans
les succès de mes amis.  With this flare up in the French tongue for
the grammar of which I do not vouch, I must conclude my letter.

God bless you, my dear fellow.  I thank you very much for your
letter and for your feelings towards 1 who is most sincerely your
friend,

W. M. T.

84.            TO JOHN PAYNE COLLIER [13]
                 22 APRIL 1835

*Address:* J. P. Collyer Esq^re | Garrick Club | King Street Covent Garden.
Hitherto unpublished.

68 Grande Rue de Chaillot.<br>a Paris —        22 April.

Dear Sir —

I have only five minutes & this dirty scrap of paper to ask for
your aid & assistance in a matter pending between me & the Morning Chronicle — It appears that the Prop^rs intend to send a Correspondent to Constantinople — I have already applied for the
place, only as I can produce no proofs of my capability in the col-
umns of any newspaper, I am obliged to ask my friends to vouch
for the same —

Do you think that our conversations at the Garrick will allow

---

sketches of him by Maclise in the Garrick Club, one of which is reproduced
above, p. 185.  Maclise became an associate of the Royal Academy in 1835 and
a full member in 1840.  Though his contemporaries considered his paintings
of historical and literary subjects to have few rivals, he is remembered today
chiefly for his portraits and his frescoes.

[13] The Shakespearian scholar (1789–1883).  Collier had at this time been
connected with *The Morning Chronicle* for more than two decades, and he
did not leave its staff until 1847.  The career of literary fraud which he
initiated in his *History of English Dramatic Poetry* (1831) remained un-
suspected for many years.

you to speak a word or two in my favor, & will excuse the liberty I take in asking for your aid?

If so, perhaps you will mention me at head-quarters, a word from you will be, I am sure, all powerful and thus I shall be able to realize a favorite dream of mine, and to fill my sketch book to my heart's content.

Pray remember me to our old Garrick friends — I wish there were any such pleasant place here, or a few such good fellows as the refined Winston,[14] the elegant Moyes, the virtuous Darby to delight me with their social converse.

Ever my dear Sir.

Faithfully yours

W. M. Thackeray.

85.                    DIARY
              30 APRIL–11 JUNE 1835

Extracts published, *Biographical Introductions*, III, xxxv-xxxvi.

April 20.[15] 1835. —

Since writing the last page [16] — Lafond is dead — Kemble gone to England many months ago, Casati afraid to stir for fear of

---

[14] Without knowing anything of Winston or Moyes, I think it may be assumed that the former was not refined, nor the latter elegant. Barham (*Garrick Club*, pp. 22–23) writes of Tom or Elde Darby: "The brother-in-law of Lord Allen, with whom, however, he was at feud. It was a common remark in the Club that Darby could not be five minutes in the room without talking about at least as many lords, especially Lords Thanet and Lowther. He was much abused by the *Satirist* newspaper and taxed with having been a Government spy receiving douceurs from both parties. Darby was educated at the Charterhouse and was avowedly a man of profligate habits. Thackeray and Frederick White were in the habit of caricaturing him. He had lived long in France and in conversation frequently affected to have forgotten his English. A very mild, well-mannered man."

[15] A mistake for Sunday, April 19.

[16] Thackeray's diary entry for November 2, 1834. A letter from Henry Reeve to his mother of January 14, 1835, affords a glimpse of Thackeray during the intervening months: "Thackeray is flourishing, and after the opera we

bums [17] & I alone left to moralize on the instability of human affairs — I recollect my full determination to journalize every day and lo here is the issue thereof — it is one of the good intentions gone to pave what young ladies call *a certain place* — In these last five months I am puzzled to think what good I have done except a small, very small progress made in my profession — having read nothing but a few dull novels, & painted nothing worth looking at for a moment — On good Friday I got a number of letters from the boys in London — McClise, Cattermole,[18] Stone & the rest. it is pleasant to think that one could reckon upon half a dozen friends such as these good fellows are, they all write with an overflowing heart, seated at Lords drinking whiskey & water to my health. — Cattermole's letter is full of Walter Scottisms, wʰ come naturally from his lips, & quite without affectation, MacClise's full of Iricisms a little tipsy but very warm & kind, & Stone's in a round clerk-like hand very short but very hearty — I am sure this man would serve me in a pinch, though I know him the least of the 3 — They are the pleasantest letters I have had for a long time with mothers wʰ came the same day, telling me of her approaching visit — On Saturday I called on Crowe [19] about the Constantinople business — this will be a great lift for me if please God I can get it — and I shall see Abanah and Pharphar, & all the rivers of Israel [20] to boot — but I suppose it will be like my ten thousand other hopes. humbug —

21. Monday.[21] after an idle morning spent at Galignani's & at a Sale of armour, dined at my Aunts, where was my friend Strachan

took tea, and had a long talk of the doings of French artists. He complains of the impurity of their ideas, and of the jargon of a corrupt life which they so unwisely admit into their painting-rooms." (John Knox Laughton, *Memoirs of the Life and Correspondence of Henry Reeve*, 2 vols., London, 1898, I, 35)

[17] Bum-bailiffs.

[18] George Cattermole (1800–1868), a water-colorist who painted historical canvases in the romantic tradition. After his marriage in 1839 he settled at Clapham, where Thackeray occasionally visited his home.

[19] See *Memoranda*, Eyre Evans Crowe.

[20] "Are not Abana and Pharpar, rivers of Damascus, better than all the waters of Israel?" (*II Kings*, 5, 12)

[21] A mistake for Monday, April 20.

in a bran new suit of sables — he seemed to be very proud of his garments & sincerely sorry for the death of his friend — William R.[22] & I went after dinner to the Opera where there was much crowding for very little worth. After standing about for an hour at the door of the pit — I mounted to the amphitheatre where I heard the music of Moise to much greater advantage than in the regions below — Read in the night & this m^g^ M^c^Farlane's Constantinople [23] — a gentlemanly, pleasant well informed book, with no affectation & a great deal of amusement. —

The Bairactar & the three kings would make an excellent subject for a tragedy, & if I go Eastward — it will be a good occupation in the long evenings —

25. Have been tolerably occupied for these three days with a little drawing, w^h^ though very muddy is still I think the best I have done. — W^m^ Ritchie & his father went off on Wednesday in a bran new Diligence with 12 outsides in the English fashion, there was a world of people out to see the wonder & a concert of 2 'cornets a conducteur' — On Thursday tead at Miss Howards where was a big bullying Doctor, Verity by name, & good Col^l^ Rolles. Wednesday dined at Passmores, & was much pleased with his mother, & a little with his pretty forward sisters — Read half a volume of Thiers; [24] & a silly meagre pamphlet of L^d^ John Russell's hight the Establishment of the Turks in Europe.[25] sh^d^ read Von

[22] William Ritchie. The opera was Rossini's *Mosè in Egitto* (1818).

[23] *Constantinople in 1828; a Residence of Sixteen Months in the Turkish Capital and Provinces* (London, 1829) by Charles MacFarlane (d. 1858). The story in which Thackeray saw the subject for a tragedy is told in chapter 20. Sultan Selim is deposed from the Turkish throne by Mustapha, his cousin, and confined in the royal seraglio with Mahmood, Mustapha's younger brother, whose neglected education he busies himself with repairing. Meanwhile, Selim's devoted favorite, the bairactar, foments a revolution against Mustapha. The bairactar forces his way into the seraglio, only to find that Selim has been put to death. Mahmood becomes Sultan, imprisons Mustapha, and makes the bairactar his Grand Vizir. The bairactar does not long enjoy his new powers, however, for the Turks resent his rule, and he dies in a great fire set during a popular uprising. Mahmood has Mustapha put to death to prevent his restoration to the throne and alone remains alive of the three kings and the bairactar.

[24] *Histoire de la révolution française* (1823–1827) by Adolphe Thiers.

[25] *The Establishment of the Turks in Europe. An Historical Discourse*

Hammer on the same subject — I am rather disappointed too in
Thiers as far as I have gone. it seems somewhat weak after
Mignet.[26]

27-28. Drew a good deal though not very successfully & read
the 2nd volume of Thiers — The book improves very much on acquaintance — giving a very lively picture of those fearful times
and a very just character of the personages who figured in them —
The half page about Dumouriez [27] struck me as admirable for truth
& keen-sightedness — read a little play of Colin d'Harville's called
M de Crac [28] — It would be a good subject for an English Farce —
to be called "Gasconading" — Strachan gave a good specimen of
this quality on Sunday at my aunts —

— Copied my copy of La bonne mere for Miss G. —

30. have stopped at home a good deal in these latter days drawing in the morning, & dawdling over books of nights — Copied the
Bonnington for FitzGerald from whom I got a letter — made a
little drawing wh still shews a progress I think — read some more
Thiers and Wash. Irvings Tour on the Prairies [29] — a lively book
enough, but there is always something weak and ricketty in this
mans writings — He must polish his sentences to an amazing extent — to give them that air of jaunty pleasantness wh they all
have —

Dined at my Aunts this day, and met Martin Thack. and his
plain vulgar wife [30] — what an ass must a man be to espouse such a
little piece of insignificance merely for the sake of the money she
carries with her. — They were very fond however — Martin's
ambition seems to lie towards country-gentlemanship, & quorum-
ship — he has already a shallow look wh his Cheshire residence will
improve no doubt. —

---

(1828). Joseph, Freiherr von Hammer-Purgstall (1774–1856) published his
*Geschichte des Osmanischen Reiches* between 1827 and 1835.

[26] *Histoire de la révolution française* (1824) by François Auguste Mignet
(1796–1884).

[27] In the first edition, II, 65–66.

[28] *Monsieur de Crac dans son petit castel; ou, les Gascons* (1791) by Jean
François Collin d'Harleville (1755–1806).

[29] In the first volume (1835) of Irving's *Crayon Miscellany*.

[30] See above, No. 13.

[May] 4. The fête of the 1ˢᵗ was as dull as all days of pleasure are — fireworks, & concerts & people climbing up poles for watches — was obligated to give Miss Howard an arm for the whole day. for the other days — stayed at home & drew though to no purpose — except for one day when Brine ³¹ & I went to the Bibliotheque du Roi — & copied & admired Lucas von Leyden — a better man I think than Albert Durer mayhap as great a composer as Raphael himself

13. For the last 10 days I have seen or done nothing worth looking at — working mostly all day with a failure to console me in the evening — Drunk tea several times with Bowes. talking theatricals & escaping the stormy weather at home — Yesterday was such a row about a pair of boots, that I had like to have quitted the house, & shifted for myself in a garret a cellar in the streets or elsewhere. — Saw Crowe yesterday & drunk tea at his house at Batignolles, after walking with him through much mud to the top of Montmartre.

June 11. Tuesday the Louvre opened, and I made on that day & Wednesday a little copy of Watteau & of another picture —

It is very pleasant & calm to the eye to see the old pictures after the flaring gaudy exhibition wʰ shut up in January — I have been looking with much delight at the Paul Veroneses, and at some bits of the Rubenss. The Raphaels do not strike me more than they did before —

This our last day at Chaillot — and I am sorry to lose this most beautiful view — though I shall be happy enough in my little den in the Rue des Beaux Arts, where I intend to work hard & to lead a most pious sober & godly life: — .

³¹ See Appendix V.

86.     TO EDWARD FitzGERALD
MAY 1835

Published in part, *Biographical Introductions*, IX, xxxvi, xxxviii-xxxix; additions, including facsimile reproductions of the drawings, in *W. M. Thackeray and Edward Fitzgerald*, ed. Shorter, pp. 9-13.

Dear Edward — Your letter of this morning is a little too sensible but very welcome nevertheless, as every line must be w̲lcome from you — I am glad to hear of your happiness at Keswick [32] & feel not a little vain at Tennyson's message or wish — Write to me a good deal about Stratford on Avon when you go, you recollect that we had determined to make a Journey there together — I herewith send a very bad copy of a bad copy made by me of the Bonnington w̲ʰ I have managed to rob of all its grace & fantasticalness, & of its extraordinary delicacy of colour — the original is I think the finest water-colour drawing I ever saw in the world. Apropos of the shop — I have had a whole packet of very pleasant letters from the boys in London — one from M̲ᶜClise very mad & Irish, but very affectionate — on[e] from Cattermole full of Walter Scottisms — w̲ʰ are his natural manner of talk — with a long list of remembrances from Lewis [33] & the rest of the boys. — I was very much delighted with these honest kind-hearted letters, that enlightened my darkness here and made the scoldings of that day pass unheeded altogether.

Do you know that I have been applying to the Morning Chronicle for a correspondentship at Constantinople, & it is not improbable that I shall get this [w̲ʰ] will give me a handsome income for a year and fill my sketch book into the bargain — perhaps I might make a bargain with Chas Heath for a Picturesque Annual — I

---

[32] FitzGerald and Tennyson were visiting James Spedding in the Lake Country (Wright, *Life of Edward FitzGerald*, I, 126–127).

[33] John Frederick Lewis (1805–1876), the water-colorist, whose establishment in Cairo Thackeray visited in October, 1844, and described in chapter 15 of *Notes of a Journey from Cornhill to Grand Cairo* (*Works*, V, 725–729). He there recalls that Lewis in younger days was "the exquisite of the 'Europa' and the 'Trois Frères,' " and remembers "what a dandy he was, the faultlessness of his boots and cravats, the brilliancy of his waistcoats and kid gloves."

should be only obliged to write 3 letters a month, & should be sent into Eygp[t] & Syria to fish for news — it would be a grand piece of good luck I think — only it is too good luck for me. I have recovered from my idle fit and am making some drawings w$^h$ I like better than any I have done as yet. — thanks to burnt Sienna & the TOWEL. w$^h$ my dear Edward is next to God the greatest help to a painter in water colours. — I have seen those rough Lodges of Raphaele, & still do not believe — I am sure Flaxman is much finer for drawing feeling compo & so on. — I think I told you about a picture I had seen of the virgin by S$^t$ Luke — I am quite sure it is like her, it is remarkable for a very curious development of the organ of Veneration, & is a simple head like that of X$^t$ on the Cloth.

Not having wherewithal to fill this large sheet of paper I have drawn you a view of a little street close by, w$^h$ strikes me as very quiet & characteristic of this dear old country of France. — what is more there are actual nuns in this village, w$^h$ though within the barrier is altogether countryfied — I have drawn you one of them has she not a Hollar-like look? — likewise on the right of the picter you behold an old dwarf who sits at our door in the Sun, of w$^h$ thank God there is plenty — & to whom I intend someday to give a half-penny. I read the other day a review of Tennyson's poems in the 'Voleur' — I was glad to see that his name had penetrated so far; & he will be pleased to know that they call him, Jeune enthousiaste de l'ecole gracieuse de Thomas Moore — This week I have read a lot of books — 3 vols of Thiers's Revolution, M$^c$Farlane's Constantinople — and Wash. Irving's new book — all 3 are very amusing I think & Thiers awful — what surprizes me in this book is that there is no blague, no humbug about patrie reconnoissance & the rest of it of w$^h$ he is so liberal in the Chamber — Louis Seize — Danton — Mirabeau — & Dumouriez are the heroes up to this time & most admirably drawn they are — I think I should have turned spouter at the Union had I seen this book in our Cambridge days.

DRAWINGS IN THACKERAY'S LETTER TO FITZGERALD OF MAY 1835

Next week begins the kings Fete & fun of all kinds, 3 days afterwards the prisoners of Lyons are to be tried, & not long after I
hope to be on my way by Venice to Constantino: —

I am obliged to put up my packet: & so God bless you dear
Edward

Yours ever. Affectionately

W. M. T. —

87.            TO MRS. CARMICHAEL-SMYTH
                   18–23 JULY 1835 [34]

*Address:* M^rs Carmichael Smyth. | 18 Albion Street. | Hyde Park Terrace |
London. *Postmarks:* PARIS 23 JUIL. 1835, 10 JY 25 1835. Hitherto unpublished.

I don't know dearest Mother why you have deprived me of my
usual birthday privilege whether it is because you intend to come
so soon to Paris that a letter would be unnecessary; or whether you
wish to punish me for my own remissness w^h I confess & deplore —
if it is for the first reason I can only say that G. M & I have been
looking out every day for I don't know how many months, and if
for the last that my hand is at work from morning till night, and
that I have got a strange antipathy for letter-writing — au reste
you know very well that I don't think about you the less, because I
don't write, for a man does not forget his best friend & his greatest
consolation, when he is alone, and neither very well nor very
cheerful. — not after a bitter & fruitless day's work, such as is
every day's work now, or a scene with a certain old lady, you may
suppose that I think about home and the dear Mother who would
sympathize with my failures and hasten, I think, my successes, and
would not hurt me with bad words, such as with a wonderful eloquence and ingenuity are rung into my ears by G. M.

Still it hurt me very much to be obliged to leave her,[35] as I have

---

[34] This letter was begun on Thackeray's birthday, Saturday, July 18, and
finished the following Thursday.

[35] Thackeray had moved to 1 Rue des Beaux Arts on June 11 (see above,
No. 85).

done, and to reject the stipend w$^h$ she made me for a while — but I
am sure I was right in quitting her, and giving up the pitiful
money — however I made the separation as smooth as possible —
did not hurt her feelings and I believe we are better friends now
than when we were together — She comes to see me very often —
and I walk stoutly up three times a week to be scolded — now that
we are parted nobody can be more anxious than she about my health
& so on — she has employed every kind of entreaty to get me
back — but I have stood firm — I dont think

— but I wont talk any more about this business, for it has vexed
me a good deal & you more I fear.

I have likewise been laid up with a little spirt of sore throat &
fever; w$^h$ is over long since, leaving the inconvenience only of a
Doctors bill, likewise you heard how I fell from a horse at Mont-
morency [36] — another Doctor's bill — I asked G. M six times for
the money to pay it and really could not find it in my heart to ask
her again.

— Luckily Frank [37] sent me £25 but it was well nigh swallowed
up and I must by hook or crook get 10 more w$^h$ will last me till

[36] This mishap, which occurred during a picnic excursion to the woods of
Montmorenci, is described by Thomas Adolphus Trollope (1810–1892), the
brother of Anthony: "Thackeray, then an unknown young man, with whom I
that day became acquainted for the first time, was one of our party. Some
half-dozen of us — the boys of the party — thinking that a day at Montmorenci could not be passed *selon les prescriptions* without a cavalcade on the
famous donkeys, selected a number of them, and proceeded to urge the strongly
conservative animals probably into places, and certainly into paces, for which
their life-long training had in no wise prepared them. A variety of struggles
between man and beast ensued with divers vicissitudes of victory, till at last
Thackeray's donkey, which certainly must have been a plucky and vigorous
beast, succeeded in tossing his rider clean over his long ears, and as ill luck
would have it, depositing him on a heap of newly broken stones. The fall was
really a severe one, and at first it was feared that our picnic would have a truly
tragic conclusion. But it was soon ascertained that no serious mischief had
been done, beyond that, the mark of which the victim of the accident bore on
his face to his dying day." (*What I Remember*, 3 vols., London, 1887–1889,
I, 288–289). Trollope was mistaken in attributing Thackeray's broken nose
to this accident (see above, No. 7), though it is of course possible that in the
fall his nose was broken a second time.

[37] Francis Thackeray.

September when comes his neat Div.$^{d}$ of 25 — I must begin on the poor little capital that's flat — the deuce is in it if I can't make my own livelihood in a couple of years — I have at this moment a good offer — a publisher here will give me a good deal to do — for I have been highly recommended to him, but he wants views of cities w.$^{h}$ are out of my line. I have made five drawings of one place here in Paris, and have cut them up one after another for they were too bad to shew him, these repeated disappointments make me ready to hang myself. in fact I am as thoroughly disheartened as a man need be — for I can do nothing — and yet I know I have got the stuff to make as good a painter as the very best of them, but I wont brag or grumble any more — you shall have this scrap of a letter as it is — only do do dear Father & Mother, set out on your journey, & bring a little consolation to your uncomfortable & affectionate Son.

W. M. T.

1 Rue des Beaux Arts.

    Faubourg S.$^{t}$ Germain.

    Thursday I think — I wish you would send a note & ask Fitz-Gerald to dine — he you know is my crony next to you — and you needn't mind the expense for he only eats potatoes & drinks water.

God bless you.

## 88.     FROM EDWARD FitzGERALD
29 JULY 1835

*Address:* Monsieur Thackeray | 1. Rue des Beaux Arts | Faub:$^{g}$ S.$^{t}$ Germain | à Paris. *Postmarks:* IPSWICH JY 29 1835, ANGLETERRE PAR CALAIS 1 AOUT 1835. Published in part, *Biographical Introductions*, IX, xlii-xliii.

Wherstead. July 1835.

Dear Thackeray,

    I was very glad to get your letter [38] last night: for I assure you that I have long been wishing to write to you — But in the letter

---

[38] This letter has not been preserved.

which I received in Cumberland you seemed to be not very fixed in your abode, especially as your Governor was just coming over: and in your packet which had the drawing in it, and which I only got a month ago, you gave no address: but, so far from it, talked of going to Constantinople. What has become of those Eastern plans? For my part, I am glad you stay at Paris, and work at your Art. But you tell me that my letters are rather too sensible: and I know well what that means. So I will write in a looser way. Marry then, I have got up at seven o'clock this fine morning to answer your letter: and I am sitting in no other clothes but that ancient red dressing gown, and inditing of this letter upon that capacious but now battered rosewood desk which you must know by this time — But, by the Lord, I feel I am going hugely sensible — and then again I think that I am a greater fool than ever — These opinions succeed by turns, one naturally drawing on the other. We are going to leave this place,[39] as my Father is determined to inhabit an empty house of his about 14 miles off: & we are very sorry to leave this really beautiful place. The other house has no great merit. So there is nothing now but packing up sofas, and pictures, and so on. I rather think that I shall be hanging about this part of the world all the winter: for my two sisters are about to inhabit this new house alone, and I cannot but wish to add my company to them now and then — I suppose that I shall occasionally trip up to London, and so forth, to see the ancient Johnny [40] and others. He, poor fellow, has been alarmed about his wife's health: for she has had a cough all the year, and could not get rid of it. I never heard of so much consumption as there is this year — I suppose from the long protracted winter — What has been ailing you? You, who defied all these weaknesses? I wish your shabby scrap of a note had been longer to tell me more about yourself — But you were ever a lazy dog in pen matters: except in that immortal summer of foolscap,[41] which I do not forget: but, having got all your

[39] Wherstead Lodge, which the FitzGeralds gave up at this time for Boulge Hall (Wright, *Life of Edward FitzGerald*, I, 129).
[40] John Allen.
[41] 1831.

letters of that time, bring back to myself very really — after thinking what I could tell you about other people, and the world at large,
I find that myself is the readiest object to enlarge upon. So, you
must hear about me to the end of the chapter, I believe — I made a
pleasant stay in Cumberland, and then staid a month at Warwick,
where I was very happy, being out all day, and wandering about to
Stratford upon Avon, Kenilworth, and such places — It is a seedy
thing to attempt to tell you about these things: am I not on the
brink of talking about "the immortal Swan of Avon?" [42] I am —
and prudence bids me retire from the danger — And now, my dear
Boy, do you be very sensible, and tell me one thing — think of it in
your bed, and over your cigar, and for a whole week, and then send
me word directly — shall I marry? — I vow to the Lord that I
am upon the brink of saying "Miss —— do you think you could
marry me?" to a plain, sensible, girl,[43] without a farthing! There
now you have it — The pro's and con's are innumerable, and not to
be consulted: for I have at last come to a conclusion in morals, which
is this: that to certain persons of a doubting temper, and who search
after much perfection, it is better to do a thing slap dash at once,
and then conform themselves to it — I have always been very un-
manly in my strivings to get things all compact and in good train —
But to the question again — An't I in a bad way? Do you not see
that I am far gone? I should be as poor as a rat, and live in a
windy tenement in these parts, giving tea to acquaintances — I
should lose all my bachelor trips to London and Cambridge, I
should no more, oh never more! — have the merry chance of
rattling over to see thee, old Will, in Paris, or at Constantinople, at
my will — I should be tied down — these are to be thought of: but
then I get a settled home, a good companion, and the other usual
pro's that desperate people talk of — Now write me word quickly:
lest the deed be done! To be sure, there is one thing: I think it is
extremely probable that the girl wouldn't have me: for her parents

[42] "Sweet Swan of Avon!" (Ben Jonson, prefatory verses to the 1623
Shakespeare folio).

[43] No doubt Elizabeth Charlesworth (1812?–1899), daughter of the Rev.
John Charlesworth, Rector of Flowton, near Ipswich, in Suffolk. See below,
No. 894.

are very strict in religion, and look upon me as something of a Pagan — When I think of it, I know what your decision will be — NO! — How you would hate to stay with me & my spouse, dining off a mutton chop, and a draught of sour, thin, beer, in a clay-cold country — You would despair — you would forsake me — if I know anything of myself, no wife would ever turn me against you: besides, I think no person that I should like would be apt to dislike you: for I must have a woman of some humour lurking about her somewhere: humour half hidden under modesty — But enough of these things — my paper is done, & I must wash myself, & dress for breakfast — this letter is written with dirty fingers, and incomptis capillis — My dear boy, God bless thee a thousand times over! When are we to see thee? How long are you going to be at Paris? What have you been doing? The drawing you sent me was very pretty — So you don't like Raphael? Well, I am his inveterate admirer; and say, with as little affectation as I can, that his worst seraph fills my head more than all Rubens and Paul Veronese together — "the mind, the mind, Master Shallow!" [44] — You think this cant, I dare say: but I say it truly, indeed — Raphael's are the only pictures that cannot be described: no one can get words to describe their perfection — next to him, I retreat to the Gothic imagination, and love the mysteries of old chairs, Sir Roger's [45] &c. — in which thou, my dear boy, art and shalt be a Raphael — To depict the true old English gentleman, is as great a work as to depict a Saint John — and I think in my heart I would rather have the former than the latter — There are plenty of pictures in London — some good Water colours by Seuri [46] — Spanish things — two or three very vulgar portraits by Wilkie, at the Exhibition: and a big one of Columbus, half good, & half bad — There is always a spice of vulgarity about Wilkie — There is an Eastlake, but I missed it.

[44] If an allusion be intended, it is not to Shakespeare's Justice Shallow.

[45] In a letter of 1834 to John Allen FitzGerald wrote: "Don't you think it would make a nice book to publish all the papers about Sir Roger de Coverley alone, with illustrations by Thackeray?" (*Letters and Literary Remains*, I, 30). The drawings are again referred to in Thackeray's letter to FitzGerald of October 7, 1836.

[46] No doubt the French painter Gabriel Bernard Seurre (1795–1867).

Etty has boats full of naked backs as usual: but what they mean, I didn't stop to enquire — He has one picture, however, of the Bridge of Sighs in Venice which is sublime: though I believe nobody saw it, or thought about it but myself — The Exhibition was a good one, on the whole, I think — Mr Hunt [47] filled the Water Colour with boys looking into lanterns &c &c So now I come back to end where I began upon my first side — This brings things round very mystically — And so, farewell, and be a good boy: & let me hear from you soon — You may as well direct to me at the new place, which is Boulge Hall, Woodbridge, Suffolk —

I am as heartily as ever yrs most affectionately,

E. FitzGerald.

89.       TO WILLIAM RITCHIE
SEPTEMBER 1835

My text is taken from *Family Letters*, ed. Mrs. Warre-Cornish, pp. 16–20.

Paris, Sept., 1835.

My dear William, — The thing is impossible — I am tied to my Mama's tail, and must maintain myself in this position for some weeks longer. We are going I believe to Strasburg, whence it is my intent to voyage viâ Munich to across [*sic*] the Tyrol into Italy.[48] Besides this I am arrived at such a pitch of sentimentality (for a girl [49] without a penny in the world) that my whole seyn, etre, or being, is bouleversé or capsized — I sleep not neither do I eat, only smoke a little and build castles in the clouds; thinking all

---

[47] William Henry Hunt (1790–1864), a humorous painter whose work Thackeray greatly admired.

[48] Thackeray did not make this trip.

[49] See *Memoranda*, The Shawes. Henry Reeve (Laughton, *Memoirs*, I, 59) wrote to his mother on January 16, 1836: "I have seen a good deal of Thackeray this last week. That excellent and facetious being is at the present moment editing an English paper here, in opposition to Galignani's. But what is more ominous, he has fallen in love, and talks of being married in less than twenty years. What is there so affecting as matrimony! I dined yesterday with his object, who is a nice, simple, girlish girl; a niece of that old Colonel Shawe whom one always meets at the Sterlings." Nothing is known of the newspaper to which Reeve refers.

day of the propriety of a sixième, boiled beef and soup for dinner, and the possession of the gal of my art. This must account for my neglect of Jane,[50] which has been shameful, the fact is that I have been so busy of evenings uttering the tenderest sentiments in the most appropriate language, that I have never had the heart to disturb her among her virgin companions — God knows how it will end, I will, if I can, bolt before I have committed myself for better for worser. But I don't think that I shall have the power. My mama has given me a five franc piece to amuse myself with, and stop away for a day, but like the foolish fascinated moth I flickers round the candle of my love.

I suppose you go up in October [51] — I would write you some very delightful moral sentiments on the occasion only you see I am in such a state of mental exhaustion that it is impossible to form connected sentences, much more to pour into your astonished ear the sound of sonorous moralities which are likely to have an influence on your heart — only, my dear fellow, in the name of the Saints, of your mother, of your amiable family, and the unfortunate cousin who writes this — keep yrself out of DEBT — and to do this you must avoid the dinner parties and the rowing (boating) men — however, you will see John Kemble who (particularly when he is drunk) will give you the finest advice on these and other moral and religious points.

I look forward with a good deal of pleasure to my trip. I am sure it would do you much more good to come with me, than you can get from all the universities in Christendom. I purpose going from Munich to Venice by what I hear is the most magnificent road in the world — then from Venice if I can effect the thing, I will pass over for a week or so into Turkey, just to be able to say in a book that I have been there — after which I will go to Rome, Naples, Florence, and if possible pay a visit to dear Mrs. Langslow, who considering all things will I am sure be charmed to see me — then I will go to England book in hand, I will get three hundred guineas for my book — then I will exhibit at the Water Colour Society, and sell my ten drawings forthwith, then I will mar . . .

[50] See *Memoranda*, Jane Ritchie.
[51] To Trinity College, Cambridge.

ISABELLA SHAWE ABOUT 1835
*From a sketch by Thackeray*

You recollect the picture of Jeannette and her *pot-au-lait* on the Boulevards, as likewise the milk pail of Alnaschar in the A. Nights,[52] if you don't, Tony will tell you. Give my love to him, and aunt and everybody. I am going to write to Frank [53] (for whom I have bought a plan of the battle of Wynendael) so I need not impart to you any of the affectionate remarks, which I intend making to him. God bless you my dear William, I will write to you sometimes on my travels, and when I am settled my wife will always be happy to see you at tea.

Your loving Cousin,
W. M. Thackeray.

90.          TO EDWARD FITzGERALD
OCTOBER 1835

*Address:* Edward FitzGerald esq^re | Boulge Hall | Woodbridge | Suffolk. *Re-addressed to:* Geldeston Hall | Beccles. *Postmark:* OC. 7 1835. Hitherto unpublished.

\*          \*          \*

I have been making German translations for this new paper [54] here are two [55] the best I think though they have been cut out by that Jackass the Editor.

[52] In the years after he lost his fortune the story of Alnaschar and his tray of glass (the equivalent of Jeannette's milk pail) became for Thackeray a symbol of his own history. Alnaschar buys with a hundred pieces of silver inherited from his father a stock of glassware, which he displays for sale before him on a large tray. While he awaits his first customer, he dreams of the prosperity that lies ahead of him. His fantasy reaches its culmination when he thrusts from him with his foot the Grand Vizier's daughter, whom he has married and who is humbly offering him a glass of wine. A loud crash jolts him back to reality. He has kicked his tray to the ground, and the glass in which he has invested his patrimony lies shattered before him. ("The Barber's Fifth Brother," *The Arabian Nights' Entertainments*)

[53] Francis Thackeray, the antiquarian of the family, was greatly interested in Wynandael, the most notable battle fought by his kinsman General Webb. (See below, No. 1119.)

[54] I cannot identify this paper. Thackeray's connection with it appears to have been transient.

[55] These translations, of "Der König auf dem Turme" by Johann Ludwig Uhland (1787–1862) and a poem by Friedrich, Baron de la Motte Fouqué (1777–1843) are printed in *Works*, XIII, 128–129.

The King on the Tower. —
The cold grey hills they bind me around
The darksome vallies lie sleeping below,
But the winds as they pass over all yon ground
Bring me never a sound of woe.

O for all I have suffered & striven
Care has embittered my cup & my feast
But here is the night, & the dark blue Heaven
And my soul shall be at rest.

Ye golden legends writ in the skies
I turn towards you with longing soul
And list to the awful harmonies
Of the burning spheres as onward they roll.

My limbs are weary, my sight nigh gone
My sword it hangeth upon the wall.
-Right have I spoken & right have I done
When shall I rest me once for all?

O blessed rest! o royal night
Wherefore seemeth the time so long
Till I see yon stars in their fullest light
And hear their loudest song. — Uhland.

### To a very old 'oman

#### 1

And you were once a maiden fair
A blushing virgin warm & young
With spotless brow that knew no care
And myrtles wreathed in golden hair
Upon a bridegrooms arm you hung.

#### 2

The golden locks are silvered now
The blushing cheeck is pale & wan,
The spring may bloom the autumn glow,

All's one — in chimney corner, thou
Sitst shivering on.

### 3

A moment & thou sink'st to rest
To wake perhaps an angel blest
In the bright presence of the Lord,
O weary is life's path to all,
Hard is the strife & light the fall,
But wondrous the reward!

La Motte Fouqué.

*   *   *

Is not this little sheet of paper honestly filled? — It looks almost like old times; I wish you would begin sending me good long letters as before I will riposter with others, for I get up very early of mornings now when I can't draw somehow, but feel only inclined to epancher mon coeur either to my mamma my Isabinda, or my Friend!

I declare before God, that the view of Paris from my window is magnificent, there is a thundering rack of majestic clouds

*   *   *

91.        TO JOHN MITCHELL [1]
10 MARCH 1836

*Address:* To | John Mitchell Esq.[re] | Librarian &c — | Old Bond Street. *Postmark:* 10 MR 1836. Hitherto unpublished.

Sir.

I am sorry that I cannot understand from y.[r] note, what is the drawing wanted to complete the set of Flore et Zephyr [2] —

Perhaps you will have the kindness to send me a few lines, & let

---

[1] Mitchell (1806–1874) was a theatrical and musical agent who transacted his business at a bookshop in Old Bond St. He later managed Thackeray's first series of lectures in London.

[2] A series of lithographed caricatures, which constitute Thackeray's first separate publication.

me know, what is wanted, and I will send you back the necessary drawing without delay.

I am Sir,

Your obedient Serv.<sup>t</sup>

W. M. Thackeray

4 Rue du Chemin de Versailles.
    Pelouse de Chaillot
    Friday. March 11, 1835.[3] —
I do not know whether you propose to publish any letter-press with the drawing, will you allow me to see it, before its appearance.


92.                 TO ISABELLA SHAWE
                    10 APRIL 1836

*Address:* Mademoiselle Shawe — | 4 Rue du Chemin de Versailles | Pelouse de Chaillot | a Paris. *Postmarks:* CALAIS 10 AVRIL 1836, 11 AVRIL 1836. Hitherto unpublished.

Hotel Quillacq.                Calais, Sunday. 10 o'clock

I am arrived safe dear Puss, as you will see by the above lithography, after a dismal journey of 40 hours spent in the Rotonde, with a society of two actors who are going to join the French company at London; & a drunken one eyed woman with a sickly child of eleven months. The two actors were very kind merry young people, disposed to take things as gaily as they might; and the little infant amused us by its innocent prattle; and by the continual exercise of — a certain quality in w.<sup>h</sup> my Puss is sadly deficient. Fancy this undeviating odour for forty hours to a sentimental young man like me, occupied with sweet thoughts about my little woman, and being obliged continually to hold my nose, at the moment when I was desirous of wiping my eyes.

— Does it not seem like a dream? I can hardly fancy yet that we have parted, for I had you with me always in my sleep w.<sup>h</sup> was a comfort; and I am sure I did not cease to think of you while wak-

[3] A comprehensive error for which it is difficult to account. As the postmark shows, this note was written on March 10, 1836.

ing; I saw the moon shining in the night, and do you know it made me happy to think that it was shining on the dear little house in the Pelouse. I have now only ten minutes to write to you for the post departs at half past 10, and I have nothing but these sentimentalities to utter, but still you will be glad to have a few lines, I think, and know that I am well & *hungry.* that the day is quite calm & bright; & that we shall have God willing, a quick & pleasant passage over the water at 3. So that by the time you get this, I shall be most likely at home, and shall know my fate about the Brussels business [4] — If the paper should succeed & I have determined in

[4] Thackeray had been offered the post of Brussels correspondent on a projected newspaper in which Major Carmichael-Smyth was interested. "The time was believed to be remarkably opportune for the new journal," writes Hotten. (*Thackeray*, pp. 72–73); "the old oppressive newspaper stamp being about to be repealed, and a penny stamp, giving the privilege of a free transition through the post, about to be substituted. The project was to form a small joint-stock company, to be called the Metropolitan Newspaper Company, with a capital of 60,000*l.*, in shares of 10*l.* each. The Major, as chief proprietor, became chairman of the new company; Laman Blanchard was appointed editor, Douglas Jerrold a dramatic critic, and Thackeray the Paris correspondent. An old and respectable, though decayed journal, entitled the *Public Ledger,* was purchased by the company; and on the 15th of September, the first day of the new stamp duty, the newspaper was started, with the title of the *Constitutional and Public Ledger.* The politics of the paper were ultra-liberal. Its programme was entire freedom of the press, extension of popular suffrage, vote by ballot, shortening of duration of parliaments, equality of civil rights and religious liberty, &c. A number of the most eminent of the advanced party, including Mr. Grote, Sir William Molesworth, Mr. Joseph Hume, and Colonel Thompson, publicly advertised their intention to support the new journal, and to promote its circulation." Thackeray's Paris letters signed "T. T.," which appeared in *The Constitutional* between September 19, 1836, and February 18, 1837, are reprinted in *Mr. Thackeray's Writings in "The National Standard," and "Constitutional,"* ed. W. T. Spencer (London, 1899). For his subsequent services to the paper, see below, No. 109.

Thackeray later drew on his memories of *The Constitutional* in describing Philip's activities as Paris correspondent of *The Pall Mall Gazette.* "It was wonderful," Thackeray writes (*Works,* XI, 322), "what secrets of politics [Philip] learned and transmitted to his own paper. He pursued French statesmen of those days with prodigious eloquence and vigour. At the expense of that old King he was wonderfully witty and sarcastical. He reviewed the affairs of Europe, settled the destinies of Russia, denounced the Spanish marriages, disposed of the Pope, and advocated the Liberal cause in France with an untiring eloquence."

my wise mind that it shall, there is no earthly reason why we should not marry in a few months, and in a few years have children to emulate the charming offspring of my friend the drunken one-eyed cook.

I found here a whole parcel of letters w.ʰ had been lying for me for 3 years, they related chiefly to my being "ruined" in 1833, and have given me no very pleasant recollections as you may suppose — but I never should have found my little woman had it not been for the loss of my money, so I think I have reason to be thankful.

I don't know how to make excuses or arrangements concerning the vast heap of rubbish w.ʰ I have left at Chaillot — Now it is that, as my better half you are called upon to exercise your discretion in the proper selection of a box, & in the disposition of the articles to be inserted; — I shall give you Carte Blanche, and have furnished you with an occupation, w.ʰ as it will demand a considerable portion of your time, will likewise call forth the brightest faculties of your understanding.

And now God bless you, dearest little Wife, take care of your health, and let me see you happy & fat & smiling at the end of the few weeks when please God we shall meet again. Give my love to y.ʳ Mother,[5] and Tommy — and imprint a k⟨iss on the⟩ cheek of Clark — God bless you again.

y.ʳˢ<br>W. M. T.

Write directly, and four or five times a week.

93.                    TO ISABELLA SHAWE
                       14 APRIL 1836

*Address:* Miss Shawe. | 4 Rue du Chemin de Versailles | Pelouse de Chaillot | Paris. *Postmark:* 14 AP 1836. Hitherto unpublished.

18 Albion Street. Hyde Park.<br>Thursday 14 April.

My dear Trot, I passed the ocean in safety, and have been in Mothers arms ever since Monday night at nine o'clock. We had a

---

[5] See *Memoranda*, Mrs. Shawe. Both Tommy and Clark were girls, boarding-house friends of Isabella.

very pleasant passage from Calais, & I fell in love with a pretty French girl with whom I talked the whole way — you may fancy what were my feelings on again revisiting my country, and how much ale I drank to welcome my return — I am at this moment under the effects of some — finding myself stupid & I am ashamed to say somewhat sleepy under the baneful effect of the essence of Malt & hops. Everybody is very well here, my Father grown quite young under the Homœopathic system,[6] and my Grand Mother fully determined on revisiting Paris. I have not yet been with your Uncle,[7] but I shall see him tomorrow probably, or at least once before he comes here to dinner next Tuesday.

The Newspaper affair goes on very well, all the Shares were taken and many more applied for, yesterday was a grand dinner [at] the Sollicitor's M<sup>r</sup> Nokes,[8] and I was introduced to the directors, and the Editors of the new journal. The head man [9] is a very clever fellow I think, and I have no doubt that the Paper must flourish — But it is agreed that I am to be the Paris Correspondent, and not to go to Brussels, and they will give me three or four hundred a year — Think upon this dear Puss, et puis! — My father says I could not do better than to marry, my mother says the same. I need not say that I agree with the opinion of my parents — so, dearest, make the little shifts ready, and the pretty night caps; and we will in a few few months, go & hear Bishop Luscombe read, and be married, and have children, & be happy ever after, as they are in the Story books — Does this news please you as it does me? Are you ready and willing to give up your home, & your bedfellow, and your kind mother, to share the fate of a sulky grey headed old

[6] The Carmichael-Smyths were for many years convinced advocates of homeopathy.

[7] Colonel Arthur Shaw.

[8] John Nokes, attorney, of 13 Charles Street (*Law List*, 1836).

[9] Samuel Laman Blanchard (1804–1845), a journalist and poet, who before associating himself with *The Constitutional* had edited *The True Sun* from 1832 to 1836. From 1841 until his suicide in 1845, two months after the death of his wife, he was connected with *The Examiner*. Thackeray wrote an affectionate article about his old editor in *Fraser's Magazine* of March, 1846 (*Works*, XIII, 465–479), à propos of Bulwer-Lytton's collection of Blanchard's essays called *Sketches from Life* (1846).

fellow with a small income, & a broken nose? — Dear little woman, think a great deal on this now, for it seems to me that up to the present time (& considering the small chance of our union you were wise) you have avoided any thoughts as to the change of your condition, & the change of sentiments & of duties, w^h your marriage with me must entail —

— At this point dear Puss, I fell asleep last night, and on reading over what I wrote it seems to me that the matter and style fully shew to what a pitch of dullness I had arrived. — but I did not sleep much in the night, for I was awake thinking of this lucky change in my affairs, and of the chance it gives me of speedily returning to you — In a very few more weeks I shall be with you, and in a few months joined to you never please God to separate from you. Is it not a great blessing for me, who had a week ago only a doubtful future, a precarious profession, and a long and trying probation, to see competence & reputation so near me as they now seem to be.

I have been telling my Mother of your ills and your thinness, and she earnestly begs that you will go to one of the Homœopaths in Paris, and explain to him the whole state of your case. *Now I ask it as an especial favor that you should do this* — for the system if it be true will cure you, and if false can do you no possible harm, for the hundredth part of a grain of medicine is all w^h they will give you to take.

I hear a sad account of John Stirling,[10] he spits blood they say

---

[10] Despite the gravity of his pulmonary complaint, John Sterling (b. 1806) did not die until 1844. He and Thackeray seem never to have been intimate, though both were Trinity men, and Thackeray was "always a close friend of the Sterling house" (Carlyle, *Life of John Sterling*, Part III, chapter 3). Each had the other's good will, however, and Sterling was among the first of Thackeray's contemporaries to recognize his true stature as a writer. "I got hold of the two first Numbers of the *Hoggarty Diamond*," Sterling wrote to his mother on December 11, 1841; "and read them with extreme delight. What is there better in Fielding or Goldsmith? The man is a true genius; and, with quiet and comfort, might produce masterpieces that would last as long as any we have, and delight millions of unborn readers. There is more truth and nature in one of these papers than in all ————'s novels together."

and must go very soon, but I will see the Colonel to day I hope, and hear more. I am going on a series of visits, and dear old Mother is making as much of me as possible — Mary wrote fifty invitations yesterday for a grand tea party and hop in honor of my arrival. She fancies that all the world is eager to see me. I have seen Fitz-Gerald who has promised to come to Paris and see *us.* I was very glad to see my old friend again. My father's conduct to me in this Paper business has been very noble, he was offered a very handsome remuneration for his services as Director (£200 a year) — but he refused, all he wanted was he said that I should be employed on the Journal. God bless him for a good fellow as he is.

Here you have the whole of my budget of news, and I am as you may suppose longing for a sight of your little hand writing. I think tomorrow's bag, somehow, will have in it a letter for me. Be very happy dearest, and grow well and fat, and hope for the day when we shall meet again, and for the long long days w^h please God we shall pass together. Every body here sends you their love, I feel very happy to see them all so fond of you, and to know how much more they will love you, when they know you more, God bless you, dear woman, give a kiss to your dear Mother & to Jane [11] for me, and ask either of them to give you a thousand for my part. I am off now with Mother avisiting. — W. M. T.

94.                    TO ISABELLA SHAWE
                       18 APRIL 1836

*Address:* Miss Shawe. | 4 Rue du Chemin de Versailles | Pelouse de Chaillot | Paris. Hitherto unpublished.

My dear little Puss. I grudge sadly the loss of time w^h must ensue in the sending of our packets by the vile Ambassadors bag, but I suppose the coppers must be regarded and the little delay submitted to — Here is Monday, & you wont receive my letter until Friday. — Friday w^h will bring me another little letter from you, somewhat more copious I trust than the half-sheet of last

[11] See *Memoranda,* Jane Shawe.

week — but never mind, dearest, it was very welcome, it told me
that you loved me, and prayed for me, & wanted me back again, as
please God, I soon shall be. See what great news I bring you, it is
arranged that I am to come back to Paris & have £450 a year! Our
Paper begins on the 23ᵈ of next month, and I must of course be
back some days before, in order to prepare matters — but I am to
go a long journey first I believe, though I have but a very short
time to perform it — To Hamburgh, The Hague, & Brussels in
order to look about in those cities and to establish correspondencies
for the Constitutional long life to it — So look about at the furniture shops, & think seriously of the wedding clothes — I have
ordered my blue coat; & intend to sport it tomorrow to astonish
your uncle who dines with us. — I went to see him the other day, &
liked the old gentleman very much, he was exceedingly kind, &
cordial; while there old Mʳ Stirling ¹² came in who likewise shook
me by the fist, & proposed that I should go & dine with him at
Knightsbridge that day. — but I have made a vow not to dine away
from home, except on business, and so was obliged to decline — I
was very sorry to refuse, for he spoke most affectionately of you &
I longed to see somebody who knew you & loved you — To be sure
they all do here, and it gratifies me very much as you may fancy.
Everybody seems to receive me with open arms, nothing but hand
shakings & invitations to dinner. I have seen all my painter friends,
who are the merriest most hospitable devils imaginable, and have
made calls right & left, on Wednesday I am going to the Bullers
who have a very fine house in Westminster. Nobody has quizzed
me about my coming marriage for wʰ I am thankful. I took some
Homœopathic (from two Greek word[s] ὅμοιος & παθεια) last
night for my cough, & really it did me much good. have you been

---

¹² Edward Sterling (1773–1847), an Irish journalist who had been staff-
writer for *The Times* since 1812. His personality and the hospitality that he
and his wife dispensed at their home in Knightsbridge are described in Carlyle's *Life of John Sterling*, Part III, chapter 5. Colonel Shawe was one of his
oldest friends. After the Thackerays came to London in 1837, Sterling made
them welcome at Knightsbridge and got Thackeray employment as book reviewer for *The Times*. When Sterling withdrew from *The Times* in 1840,
Thackeray's connection with the paper appears also to have terminated.

to the man as I asked? Mary was cured of exactly the same disease, by the most trifling doses imaginable. —

You see that to punish you for your sins, I only send you a half-sheet of paper, but I will write by the next bag or perhaps before if the fit comes upon me. Pop the enclosed for Tackeray into the twopenny after having politely sealed it, the other is for Mamma concerning the arrangements with Madamasel. Give my love to Miss Clarke and do not tell Poop that I forgot her letter for four days. I must shut up now for I am going to make a speech to the board of Directors, about gratitude, pride, future exertions & so forth; my appointment was confirmed on Saturday and I am obliged to say something polite. My father is turned a great Orator, and we have politics here from morning till night — And now shall I tell you, how I think of you of mornings, and dream of you of nights, how happy I am at this prospect of independence, and of marriage — w.h must very soon take place now dearest, for there is little use that I can see in delay — You must make up your mind to the change, dear Woman, and I do believe though I say it that shouldn't, you will have as good a husband as ever little Woman had. Ask your dear Mother to bestow 10000000 kisses on you and place them to the account of your obedient Servant. W. M. T.

I forgot everybodys love w.h is sent hereby.

95.    TO ISABELLA SHAWE
        21–25 APRIL 1836 [13]

Hitherto unpublished.

Monday 25 April.

My dear Puss I am going to scold for here is a week passed and I have no letter from you. You who have nothing to do from morning till night except to please yourself and spouse. What have you

[13] This letter was begun on Thursday, April 21, the day after Thackeray dined with the Bullers; it was finished the following Monday.

done in all this long week, have you been getting up early and taking little glasses of salts and healthifying yourself against a coming event? Your old Uncle dined with us on Tuesday, and a dear old gentleman he is, of course as you may suppose I was very kind to him, and really he seems so good so honest, & so fond of you, that he has quite won my heart — He told me that M<sup>rs</sup> Stirling was prepared for the visit with w<sup>h</sup> I threatened her, and w<sup>h</sup> I certainly shall pay her, for she thinks & speaks so kindly of you, that I feel quite grateful to her — Why should I want everybody to love you? — from vanity I suppose, and because I hope that a little of this good opinion will come to me by reflection.

— Yesterday I dined at the Bullers, and was very glad to see these kind friends of mine once more, one of their old servants with whom I condescendingly shook hands, said it was like one of the family coming back again, and really the way in w<sup>h</sup> they receive me would make one suppose that my name was Buller & not Tackeray as it is. Charles is to join us in our new paper scheme, and to write leading articles for us — but I very much fear that my new blue coat will not so soon be put into requisition as I hoped; for the Paper is not nearly so advanced as we had expected. It is true that I am appointed Paris correspondent with the salary about w<sup>h</sup> I bragged when I wrote last — but there is very little money actually subscribed for the Paper, although there are thousands of nominal subscribers, — but never mind, I will not be cast down and please God before long my little wife will be mine, mine till Death do us part. My old friend, FitzGerald is sitting by my side, and we have been talking about old books & pictures and you, and smoking segars to my hearts content — This visit to London will have been profitable to me in one sense at least if in no other, for it is well to renew one's old friendships and acquaintances, and I have met with much cordiality & kindness from people who did not as I thought care a straw about me. I have not been to my old haunt, The Garrick Club, because of the coppers, for I should instantly be obliged to pay my years subscription of half a dozen guineas — more than it is worth, although the Club has got a fine new gallery of pictures in my absence, and is about to give a grand

MR BOZ    MR TINTO    Mr MAC.    Mr PROUT.

*Drawn by W. M. Thackeray*
*at St James's Square 1838*

DICKENS, THACKERAY, MACLISE, AND MAHONY IN 1836

*From a sketch by Thackeray*

Shakspeare dinner at w^h I should like very much to assist.[14] I have invited myself to breakfast one morning with the Colonel, and shall go on Saturday most likely; my facetious friend Reeve dines with us to day, & the Priest Mahoney has rendered me a visit — He is the greatest scandal monger in Europe, and has spread the news of my approaching marriage among all the people — I am glad of it, for it spares me trouble, and them surprize. I don't know what to tell you or to talk about except the people I have seen, and dread that this big sheet of paper & these close lines will not much amuse you.

— Friday — Your Sunday letter dear Puss has just reached me, and very happy I was to receive it — but what in God's name have I been saying to hurt you (for I see you are hurt) and your Mother? — What a scoundrel should I be were I to endeavour to weaken such a tie as exists between you two — The separation to w^h I alluded did not go farther than the bedroom — If I recollect rightly this was the chief object of my thoughts at the moment, and I opined that you would be unwilling to quit your bedfellow, and your present comfortable home for another with me. If you are my wife you must sleep in my bed and live in my house — voila tout — I have no latent plans — no desire for excluding you from those whom I sh^d think very meanly of you, were you to neglect.

— Amen — But I am charmed to hear dear Woman, that you are so well and so merry — I won't say that I am content with a half sheet once a week, but you will write more easily as you grow more used to it, & before long I shall have a couple of half sheets twice a week I hope. I have been all day at a Committee of our Newspaper, and things look much better than I had expected — We have really got a very good sum of money, and with a very little more shall be able to carry our undertaking gallantly forward. My mother is canvassing for shareholders & has written to the Colonel, so I suppose you will have a copy of the Question and a copy of the answer, by the same post. — See what straits you put

[14] It appears that Thackeray was unable to resist these attractions, for William Charles Macready (*Diaries*, 2 vols., ed. William Toynbee, New York, 1912, I, 299) met him in the Garrick Club on April 26.

me to — all y$^r$ letters come to me a week old, and you will not receive this for seven mortal days — I left my little Puss this day fortnight at this time — and I think I have dreamed of her for fourteen nights, and thought of her during every hour of my waking —

— If you had looked in my room hanging upon the glass you would have seen the chain — I took it off just before I went — and envied it that it was to be round my dear child's neck when I was to be so far away from her. — I am much obliged to Lady Coote for her kindness, and will wait upon her duly & thank her at my return. And so you are to go to Brussels — I grieve, but can say nothing, only some fine morning I must come & fetch you to a snug apartment in Paris with a spare bedroom, w$^h$ please God your Mother will occupy often & long.

— Sunday. You should follow my example in letter writing — and give me a few lines every day, and you will see a half sheet grow speedily into a sheet, & what is more you will give me no cause to grumble. Yesterday I was at M$^{rs}$ Bullers who had been to see the Stirlings — M$^{rs}$ S was in very low spirits about her son, whose illness is unfortunately confirmed, he is to leave this country speedily, and reside for some time at Rome — M$^{rs}$ Buller says that nothing can exceed the affectionate manner in w$^h$ M$^{rs}$ Stirling speaks of you — And Reeve has brought me the same report. Why don't you write to her Pussy? — It is a great blessing to have such good friends, and a great folly to lose them for the sake of a little indolence. —

I can't think what I wrote in my letter w$^h$ has vexed you — to be sure I was very sleepy (from ale drinking) while I wrote the first part, & have forgotten almost entirely its contents — besides this prospect of marriage made me grave & moral and of course prone to sermonize — I am glad that you look at the thing more cheerfully — Suppose you were to commence some of your duties at once & say "I am sure that my husband can not be too well pleased at my putting off writing to him to the last day, and then tearing a sheet of paper in half in order to make my letter as small as possible — I am sure that he thinks of me daily & hourly, that he feels hurt at any conduct of mine w$^h$ may bear an appearance of neglect, and elated by the smallest & most trivial mark of my affection — Could I not manage to sacrifice a little of my idleness, to devote to him ten minutes in the day, and to favor him with a whole sheet of paper?" — There is a pretty little speech for you to make — Read it again, dear little woman, and see whether you who have mastered the mysteries of stocking mending, who have penetrated the depths of the Rule of Three, who have attained the very acmè of pickling, and arrived at the perfectability of pie crust, have not some other little conjugal duties to perform, one of w$^h$ (& not the most easy) is the duty of affection.

— There — I tried to swallow my disgust, but it would come out — and now I have had my scold, I feel somewhat easier — You must take all these scoldings, you know, as compliments — for I should not scold if I did not care for you. Have you been to hear Bob Lovatt to day? — We have had but 2 rainy days since my arrival and unluckily both of them have been Sabbaths — so that I have been unable to hear my mothers favorite preacher M$^r$ Boone.[15]

— I dread thinking to what a length this letter will arrive, if I have a few more such rainy days to pass at home. For as I sit here alone I grow thoughtful & querulous, and discontented because I can not have what I most want — you — your little red-polled ghost pursues me everywhere, the phantoms of some of your songs are always in my ears — but melancholy & pale as ghosts should be; and of mornings I wake very early and toss about in my bed & think of you — in fact now that the little excitement of seeing my parents has worn off, I am as miserable as a young gentleman need be — our parting thank God will not be for long,[16] for really I can

[15] James Shergold Boone, a former Charterhouse master. He had become minister of St. John's Church, Paddington, in 1832, where he was a successful Evangelical preacher until his death in 1859.

[16] Thackeray's hope that the parting "will not be for long" may be a reflection of his disappointment in not securing the assignment to illustrate *The Pickwick Papers*. Some time before Thackeray returned to Paris, he made the acquaintance of Dickens. Robert Seymour, the original illustrator of *The Pickwick Papers*, had committed suicide earlier in April, and Dickens was

not bear it — I don't know what conjurations you have used, dear Pussy, but I can't live without you that's flat — and I have grown to such a pitch of jealousy, that I was actually quite angry at your Mother's telling me that you were so well & happy — I was in a rage that you were not miserable like myself — Did you ever read anything more sentimental than this in Sir Charles Grandison or the sorrows of Werter? and yet it is not exaggerated in the least.

Monday. I am going to put up this dingy epistle dear Puss and carry it to your Uncle's — I shall not read it, for I know I was in a very bad humour yesterday, which my little Trot must pardon, as she will have many other such fits of spleen to bear & to forgive. Tell yᵣ Mother that she who thinks so kindly of me, must not think so ill of me — as to suppose that I could have any desire to separate you and her — I am very sorry to hear of her illness — and wish she wᵈ try these Homœopaths who are working miracles.

God bless you, dearest — if you will send me seven double letters every week I will most willingly pay the postman. My Mother and all here send their warmest love to you, and their kindest re-membrances to your Mother & Tommy. Goodbye. W. M T.

---

looking about for another artist. Thackeray later recalled "walking up to his chambers in Furnival's Inn with two or three drawings in my hand, which strange to say, he did not find suitable" (Speech at the Royal Academy Dinner, May, 1858; reprinted in Lewis Melville's *William Makepeace Thackeray*, 2 vols., London, 1910, II, 115).

96.              TO WILLIAM JERDAN [17]
                  22 APRIL 1836

*Address:* W. Jerdan Esq^re | &c &c | Literary Gazette. Hitherto unpublished.

18 Albion Street
Hyde Park Terrace
Friday. Apr. 22.

My dear Jerdan.

Will you give me a little puff for the accompanying caricatures? [18] — As to their merits, being a modest man I am dumb; but
that is no reason why my friends sh^d be silent — Besides this is my
first appearance before the public, and I trust that my wages and
my character will improve, by the judicious praise w^h I hope to
receive from you.

I wish I could come to the Garrick but I am here for ten days
only, and I think I had better keep the six guineas. ever yours

W. M. Thackeray.

[17] Jerdan (1782–1869) was editor of *The Literary Gazette* from 1817 to
1850, a fellow-member of the Garrick Club, and a good friend to Thackeray
in his apprentice days.

[18] An appreciative half-column is devoted to *Flore et Zéphyr* in *The Literary Gazette* of April 30 (pp. 282–283).

97.                    TO JOHN MITCHELL
                        22 APRIL 1836

Hitherto unpublished.  My text is taken from a transcript supplied by Mrs.
Fuller.
                        To John Mitchell,
                            33, Old Bond Street.
Dear Sir,
    Enclosed are three puff-provokers which I should be obliged
to you to send with copies of Flore and Zéphyr.  Could you despatch
one to Dr. Maginn to-day?
                        Yours obediently,
                        W. M. Thackeray.

18 Albion Street,
Hyde Park Terrace.
Friday April 22nd, 1836.


98.                    TO ISABELLA SHAWE
                        2 July 1836

*Address:* Miss Shawe. | 10 Rue de Ponthieu. | Fbg S! Honoré.  *Postmark:*
JUILLET 2 1836.  Hitherto unpublished.
                        Saturday Morng.
    How have you passed the night dear Pussy?  not so badly as I
did, I hope, with my tormentors the bugs — I don't know that I
have anything special to say, only to warn you that I shall expect a
little note from you every morning now we are away from one
another.
    You see you will have a capital excuse for rising early now, for
you may occupy yourself for an hour before breakfast in writing to
me your doings of the day before — I am in the middle of a great
bowl of raspberries and cream, and wishing for my little gour-
mande to share it with me: and if you wont eat raspberries with
me this year, I hope at any rate that you will eat peaches (they

come in the middle of August I believe) — So look out and be ready dear Puss to marry me soon, for I am determined to do it, whether the Constitutional sh$^d$ come out or not.

I think it most likely that some accident has knocked up the paper, for it was to have appeared on the 5$^{th}$ of this month, and I have had no notice; all that we must do in event of the non-success of the paper, is to take a little place here or in London and trust to Providence and our pictures — I am sure to succeed if I have you with me, and we have plenty of money until the day of success shall arrive —

I dont mean to give up seeing you altogether,[19] but will call with your Mother's permission, once or twice a week, and see how your health is and your little crop grows, but don't for this make an excuse for not writing to me, or else I shall grow as angry and as uncomfortable as I was the other day about the unlucky getting up business — God bless you dearest, salute Tommy with a kiss, and ask her to give you half a hundred and place them to the account of your most obedient Servant.

W. M. Thackeray.

15 *bis* Rue Neuve S$^t$ Augustin.


99.                TO ISABELLA SHAWE
                    3 JULY 1836

*Address:* Miss Shawe | 10 Rue de Ponthieu | Fbg. S$^t$ Honoré. *Postmark:* JUILLET 3 1836. Hitherto unpublished.

Sunday. July 3.

I intend that my letter to you, dearest Puss, shall stand me in lieu of morning prayers, for I am sure that the half hour w$^h$ I pass every morning in thinking about my dear little wife, brings me as

---

[19] Thackeray tells the story of Mrs. Shawe's attempt to break off his engagement to her daughter in chapters 24 to 28 of *Philip*. The attendant circumstances are no doubt rather different in the novel, but the situation in which Mrs. Baynes, Charlotte, and Philip find themselves is essentially the same, and their portraits are drawn from Thackeray's memories of Mrs. Shawe, of Isabella, and of himself as a young man.

many good thoughts and good feelings as though I were to sing through the Litany — In the first place I have been thinking how much good this (not unlooked for) separation may bring to us both; it makes me love you a great deal better than before, for I feel your value the more now I have lost you, as it were: it will put the intimacy w.ʰ ought to exist between your Mother & me upon its proper footing; for I think that when we are not too intimate or familiar we shall be much better friends; and finally it will make my little Trot conquer two lazinesses that beset her, not writing letters, and lying abed — for I still insist, and most anxiously look out for your little daily letter.

Now I want you to tell me everything in these letters, everything w.ʰ you feel and w.ʰ you do — Do not think about turning the periods for they will come of themselves, or of making points of wit (a sin into w.ʰ you seemed inclined to fall in our last letter-writing days) — for these only cramp your style and your heart too. When you used to be alone with Janey, I used to hear your little tongue, babbling away as gaily and as quickly, as I hope your pen will now for me; and for myself, do you know I feel more pleasure in writing to you, and telling you my whole heart, than I should in five-hundred kisses; I don't know how it happened that we were never left alone; but I never could tell you all that I felt about you, when we had always two lookers on, and I am sure though you may not perhaps be yourself aware of it, that your own heart has never as yet had fair play, and that where your words are questioned rudely, and your feelings scarcely permitted to shew themselves, there is no wonder that a certain habit of coldness & indecision should have sprung up. —

I think I know of a better plan, dearest, than has hitherto been pursued, to cure these evils, and for this you must have recourse to me, you must love me with a most awful affection, confide in me all your hopes and your wishes your thoughts and your feelings; for I want you to be not a thoughtless and frivolous girl, but a wise and affectionate woman, as you will be, dearest Puss, if you will but *love* enough. God bless you, dearest Wife. This being Sunday is a Sermon day.

I am going to M^rs Crowe to day, & to my Aunt tomorrow so I don't know when I shall see you.

100.                    TO ISABELLA SHAWE
                            5 JULY 1836

*Address:* Miss Shawe ——. Hitherto unpublished.

                                    Tuesday. 5 July.

Dearest Pussy I shall write you only a very few lines, for I am in a bad humour with a bad headache, & propose to cure it by coming to see you this evening.

When I said you were frivolous I meant no harm, all women are so I think from their education, and I want my wife to be better than all women; and then comes the definition of the word, a woman who occupies herself all day with her house and servants is frivolous, ditto she who does nothing but poonah-painting and piano forté, also the woman, who piddles about prayer-meetings, and teaches Sunday schools; into w^h 3 classes, I think, the race of women are divided. but I want my Puss to be a little paragon, and so it is that I am always belabouring her with advice;

Yesterday I gave a genteel supper party, having purchased a patty w^h stunk upon being cut up, a bottle of brandy, and two of the inestimable Seltzer-water, Stevens [20] with his tremendous voice, and the windows wide open through the whole neighbourhood, might have been heard singing 'King Death,'[21] at the place de la Bourse — and I painted a portrait, very like let me tell you, for the porter knew it, and the porter's little girl fell into extacies at the resemblance — And here you have all my doings; I have left off eating almost but dthrinckh in a most extraordinary manner; having demolished three cups of tea, while writing this and the letter in w^h it comes enclosed.

[20] Little is known of Augustus Stevens, a Parisian dentist who was one of Thackeray's oldest friends in the English colony of that city. He is the "brave AUGUSTUS" of "The Ballad of Bouillabaisse" (*Works*, XIII, 63).

[21] By "Barry Cornwall" (Bryan Waller Procter).

— In order to save appearances I despatched this by a porter, I must and will write to you and hear from you every day, and will let no squeamishness as to servants prevent me. If you were a decided little woman you w$^{\underline{d}}$ make a point of giving your letters to me to Augustine to put in the post, and let her & the porteresses tell what stories they may.

God bless you dearest Wife.

101.                    TO ISABELLA SHAWE
                        JULY 1836 [22]

Hitherto unpublished.

My love for you is greater than I thought, for it has withstood this terrible three days trial. I have tried to leave you, & you will hardly credit me that I felt obliged to return — for I do not be-

[22] Thackeray's estrangement from Isabella and the writing of this letter followed shortly after July 6. As he himself came later to realize, her attempt to withdraw from their engagement was an expression of her mother's feelings rather than of her own. Only a few days intervened between quarrel and reconciliation, for their marriage took place on August 20. The ceremony is recorded in the following entry from the "Register Book of Marriages in the House of the British Ambassador in Paris": "William Makepeace Thackeray of the Parish of St. John Paddington in the County of Middlesex Bachelor and Isabella [Gethin Creagh] Shawe of the Parish of Donerail in the County of Cork Spinster and a Minor were married in this House with the consent of her Mother Isabella G. Shawe this twentieth day of August in the year one thousand eight hundred and thirty-six. By me, H. M. Luscombe, Bishop and Chaplain. This marriage was solemnised between us W. M. Thackeray, I. G. [C.] Shawe. In the presence of V. Spencer, I. G. Shawe, Senior, J. W. Lemaire." (Herman Merivale and Frank T. Marzials, *Life of W. M. Thackeray*, London, 1891, pp. 107–108)

The only information we have concerning the honeymoon of Thackeray and his wife is recorded by Mrs. Warre-Cornish, who writes that in the autumn of 1836 "he brought 'the diminutive part of me,' — as he wrote accepting his aunt's — Mrs. Ritchie's — invitation to stay with her and her husband at their country-house at 'les Thermes,' now a part of Paris. Mrs. Thackeray's carefully trained voice and charm in singing was long remembered by all who heard her at 'les Thermes' or in Paris, where the young couple lived through a winter in the Rue Saint-Augustin." (*Some Family Letters*, p. 20) This visit cannot have lasted long, for Thackeray's first letter to *The Constitutional* is dated "Paris, Sept. 17."

ISABELLA SHAWE IN 1836
*From a sketch by Thackeray*

lieve in spite of all this heartlessness on your part, that you ever can be other than my wife — You may recollect, that after our second quarrel, we made a kind of vow that, happen what would — you & I were bound together & married before God, & that I told you but a few nights since, that I had prayed to Him to give me aid in quelling any improper desires w<sup>h</sup> might create your disgust or lessen me in y<sup>r</sup> esteem.

If you feel that after our three months' marriage for I can call it no less, you are sick of me & my love, *tell me so with your own lips* — you have not spared me, God knows, through all this business & I see no reason why I should be called on to be polite, merely to spare you the bore of an interview.

There was no reason why you sh<sup>d</sup> have been offended at my asking you so repeatedly 'if you loved me' — you did not answer 'yes' once in ten times, & as you see there was after all some cause for the question.

But I will not venture upon being satirical although I assure I could {cut a great figure} do so with great eclat in the present instance — I will only state to you the question as honestly as I can. —

You have written to all y<sup>r</sup> relations, & declared to them that you had no doubt as to your feelings for me — has my conduct since these letters been such as w<sup>d</sup> change your love? — you are bound in honor to answer me, for you owe me justice at least if nothing more. You have committed yourself in the world's eyes; if this marriage do not take place.

— Should anything occur to your Mother w<sup>h</sup> God forbid, where will you & your sister live? — with your Aunt Mary? — Or will you return to the man who loves you still, better than you deserve, Isabella — for if I have given needlessly vent to my feelings you don't know how often I have smothered them; if I have hurt you by my warmth, have you never wounded me by y<sup>r</sup> coldness? — And w<sup>h</sup> was the most praiseworthy sentiment of the two? mine when I gave up to you everything — soul & body — or yours when you remembered that there was one thing stronger than love in the world & that — Decorum? —

However, take me or leave me — I never can love you as I have; although you fancy that my love for you was not *'pure'* enough — it was a love of w͏ͪ any woman in the world should have been proud, & w͏ͪ I never can give to any other — but still dearest, I love you; forgive me my trespasses as I here remit you yours, and you will restore happiness to your family, & to one whose misery you never can feel or know, please God. —

W. M. T.

102.          TO MRS. CARMICHAEL-SMYTH
                    SEPTEMBER? 1836 [23]

Extract published in *Thackeray and his Daughter,* p. 3.

Tuesday night.

Dearest Mother I dont know what strange disinclination for writing has got hold of me, but when the day's work is done, I can hardly muster courage to take a pen, and even for my regular labour I have of late given it over to my clerk — to whom I dictate while striding majestically up and down the room.

I am sorry to tell you we are the laziest people in all Paris, my wife has fairly beaten me, and we never breakfast before eleven o'clock. I am ashamed and angry every morning of my life, but do what I will scold or laugh she won't get up, & I am only too glad of an excuse to lie in bed — fancy that out of the 24 hours we spend at least eleven in bed — the consequence is I am grown so fat that you will hardly know me when you see me again, and what is worse my whole day is over in five hours; I tell you this to unburden my mind for it makes me disgusted with myself, to think I waste my time so dreadfully.

You see I am in a bad humour, w͏ͪ has been gained by a long letter from Sheehan [24] w͏ͪ you will read in the Con this morning; —

---

[23] This letter appears to have been written not long after Thackeray's first dispatch to *The Constitutional* of September 17.

[24] John Sheehan (1812–1882) was the son of an Irish hotel keeper. Though called to the Dublin bar in 1835, he chose journalism rather than the law as

there is some infernal treason going on at Madrid, of w.<sup>h</sup> it is impossible to get the secret — The Queen & Don Carlos have got some private arrangement; — and I take upon myself to grow ill-humoured because of it.

We have been passing the evening with the Bullers, drinking tea and talking scandal & politics; and have had a visit from M.<sup>rs</sup> Fagan to day, a very pretty young woman who seems disposed to be very civil — Yesterday we entertained a select party, a M.<sup>r</sup> Jones a relation of Col.<sup>l</sup> Shawes, and his son M.<sup>r</sup> David Jones. My Mother in law who was present talked as big as S.<sup>t</sup> Paul's: she is a singular old deevil, and has become quite civil of late. I don't know why I dislike her so much. My little Puss bating the laziness is the best little wife in the world; I never knew a purer mind or a better temper, or a warmer heart (for me & mine) or a — but I won't bother you with further particulars.

If Costello [25] has no translator under him I think he does his work very well, for there is a column or more of foreign intelligence besides what I send — I don't wonder that he has no time to write leading articles (and they are quite as well out, for he has not the wit) for the arrangement the very reading of the papers must take him a great deal of time. With me, it is not what I shall send, but what I shall not send, that takes time; — I am very glad I have not been about for rumours, I am sure they only mislead; — You see I always come back to the Shop. P.A's last speaks rather gloomily of it amen. I am sorry for him, and his risk and loss for my sake — Dearest Mother here is a short scrawl written at midnight, write to us plenty of long letters, though I repay them so badly, but they make me happy for the rest of the day. I am sure I

his profession. He served as Madrid correspondent of *The Constitutional* until 1837, when he replaced Thackeray as the paper's Paris correspondent. After *The Constitutional* ceased publication, he became parliamentary reporter to *The Morning Herald*, and in later life he contributed to many magazines and newspapers. We learn below (No. 736) that he figures in *Pendennis*.

[25] Dudley Costello (1803–1865), another Irish recruit to Grub Street. After several years in the army he came to London in 1833 as a free-lance writer. His engagement with *The Constitutional* was followed by posts as foreign correspondent of *The Morning Herald* and *The Daily News*.

love you better since I was married than before, perhaps it is because being so happy, I am grown a little more *good*. God bless
you dearest Mother. I am as well as possible and Isabella as well
as can be expected. —

W. M. T.

103.          TO EDWARD FɪᴛᴢGERALD
               7 OCTOBER 1836

*Address:* Edward Fitz-Gerald Esq.ʳᵉ | Naseby | near Welford | Northampton-
shire | to be forwarded. *Postmark:* 10 OC 1836. Published in *Unpublished
Letters by W. M. Thackeray*, ed. Clement Shorter (London, 1916), pp. 7–10.

15 bis Rue Neuve Sᵗ Augustin —

Friday 7. August.[26]

My dear Edward. Your two letters arrived a day after each
other, the first coming last in the order of Scripture.[27] — As for the
money, you have made me so used to these kinds of obligations, that
I dont say a word more, but I feel very much your kind and affectionate letter, and long to have you with me.

As for the little wife it does not change one in the least it is only
a new quality that one discovers in ones'self, a new happiness if
you will, for my dear old friend, any thing so happy, so quiet, so
calm you can't fancy; at this moment I am smoking a segar (wʰ my
little woman has got for me) in the very drawing room — the state
apartment of the race of Tackeray! I intend with your money to
buy chairs and tables, to decorate this chamber, for as yet I have
only hired them; and I have got your portrait and further more as
the comble of sentiment I shall make Mʳˢ Tack write to you on this
very sheet of paper.

I am sorry to say that I like the newspaper-work very much, it
is a continual excitement, and I fancy I do it very well, that is very
sarcastically, and though as we agreed about literature, sarcasm
does no good either to reader or writer, I think in politics where all

[26] A mistake for October, as the postmark shows.
[27] *St. Mark,* 10, 31.

are rogues to deal with (y.r hble Serv.t among them) a man cannot sneer and scorn too much, and bring the profession into disrepute — but the poor picture-painting is altogether neglected; and for this neglect I can give you no better illustration, than to tell you that it seems like quitting a beautiful innocent wife (like M.rs T. for instance) to take up with a tawdry brazen whore.

But you don't know how happy it is (to return to the marriage business) to sit at home of evenings, and pass pleasant long nights lolling on sofas smoking & making merry: dear Edward do come and see me, it w.d do your heart good to see how happy I am.

See here is a fine picture of a clock w.h decorates the room where I am sitting, and is moreover my property — underneath it is a piano, & on the piano is a little straw bonnet, and altogether it is the comfortablest little picture w.h can be conceived it has taken me half an hour to draw for I have been painting the clock up so dexterously.

— I had a very handsome commission of £50 to make some etchings, but I have tried & made such miserable work that I must give them up I find. It is a sad disappointment, for I had hoped to have done much in that line. I am surprized you have not got the Sir Rogers — Two English Artists, a M.r Elmore [28] and a M.r Johnson [29] took charge of them, one of them he who was to deliver them lives close to Portland Place, his father is a Doctor Elmore, and in the

[28] Alfred Elmore (1815–1881), who undertook to deliver Thackeray's sketches of Sir Roger de Coverley, was studying at this time in a Paris atelier and at the Louvre. His father, Dr. John Richard Elmore, lived at 9 New Cavendish Street (*Royal Blue Book*, 1846).

[29] Probably John Johnson (1801–1878).

C. Guide you will find the address. Warwick Street I think —
Cavendish Street M$^{rs}$ Thackeray says with her compliments —

I have become a woful bad scribe since I have begun to sell my
pen at so much a line, and so you must not expect as many letters
as of old, but if you will take the Constitutional you may have the
pleasure of hearing of me every day or if you will but trip across to
Paris (and who can do it more easily or has promised it more often?)
my wife will give [you] the best of vegetables and the warmest of
welcomes — I have got a snug little room called majestically Le
Cabinet de Monsieur where I smoke all day and enlighten the
Lon⟨don . . .⟩ [30] about ⟨. . .⟩ [31]

104.        TO JOHN MITCHELL KEMBLE
                13 DECEMBER 1836

My text is taken from catalogue 183 of Bernard Halliday (November, 1934).

15 bis Rue Neuve St. Augustin,
                                                        Paris
                        Dec. 13, 1836.

My dear Kemble.

I write from the most interested motives, Mr. Beaumont [32] is
about to bring forth an Evening paper I hear; and you must be
aware how much he will need a Paris Correspondent. Pray give
me your vote and interest, should the worthy Member for Northumberland persist in his intention.

I suppose you know how I exercise the same office for a Radical
morning paper, the "Constitutional" — who in fact, has not heard
of T. T.? But I have plenty of time for another similar duty and
plenty of employment for the additional weekly-guineas it might
bring — My dear fellow, do your best for me for our friendship is

[30] About five words have here been torn away.
[31] The final lines of this letter have been torn away.
[32] Thomas Wentworth Beaumont (1792–1848) was a wealthy Philosophical
Radical who helped to found *The Westminster Review*. Nothing came of his
plans for an evening paper. He represented Northumberland in parliament
from 1830 to 1837.

old, our life is short, and our fortune uncertain: also as you know, I am a married man (and you can understand my situation), and have an alarming prospect before me of many additions to the race of Roaldus de Richmond.[33] You also are probably in a similar state — wife, children coming, and nothing in three per cents. Why do we take wives? why do we make children? Thou knowest as well as I, Beowulf,[34] *we must be hammering at the head of the spear.*

Seriously (or as Joe Hume [35] says seriatim) do your best for me: if you encourage me perhaps I will send an article for the review [36] (we want lightness to my thinking) so that you see this note is, as all letters from married men should be, entirely about my own pocket and interest, which I want you to support.

I have nothing to tell you, except that I am grown strangely fat, and am the happiest man in the neighbourhood; I have a good wife, good dinners, plenty of work, and good pay — Can a man want more?

I suppose I may offer my kindest regards to Mrs. Kemble, as, having seen a letter and lock of her hair, I may be considered as an old acquaintance. Remember me too to all the rest of your family, father, mother, and sister, they were very good to me as you know.

Can I do anything here for you? M. Leon Faucher [37] spoke to me of you the other night; he is a dull prig I think, but very good at his specialite. Goodbye my dear Kemble.

Ever yours,

W. M. Thackeray.

[33] See above, No. 72.

[34] See *Memoranda*, The Kembles.

[35] Thackeray's gibe at the diction of Joseph Hume (1777–1855), the Nabob and politician, appears to have been amply justified. It is said of his parliamentary career in the *Dictionary of National Biography* that "He spoke longer and oftener and probably worse than any other private member."

[36] *The British and Foreign Review.*

[37] Faucher (1803–1854) was a journalist and politician of some repute whom Thackeray seems to have met at the home of Eyre Evans Crowe (Sir Joseph Crowe, *Reminiscences*, p. 83). His specialty appears to have been the financial aspects of political economy.

Write to me if you have got anything good to give me in the review, or if you have not and are disposed to write, or what style of article you want.

105.    TO WILLIAM HARRISON AINSWORTH [1]
JANUARY 1837

Hitherto unpublished.

Dear Ainsworth, I'll do everything what's possible to heighten the charms of your immortal book the admirable Crichton; [2] and with this noble purpose this little scrap I write on, to say I'll do you drawings such as never man had sight on; and neat vignettes w^h all the world will surely take delight on; and though I have but half a month I'll do em all in spite on; Could Dan MacClise, who's near to me a minnow to a Triton; For father Prout swears out and out in talent I'm a Titan; and you and he do seem to me Harmodius and Aristogeiton; [3] but now as with such puzzling rhymes it is too hard to fight on; I recommend thee o my friend this paper for to sh— on.

### W. M. T.

If you seriously choose to have the drawings write to me, and give me a few subjex, here is one I send, where you will see Catherine's tower, & the old Hotel de Soisson — pulled down these 100 years.

[1] Thackeray was grateful for the kindness shown him at the very beginning of his career by Ainsworth (1805–1882), who had already established himself as one of the most popular of contemporary romancers, and for ten years he was a good friend of the older writer. But Thackeray's great success with *Vanity Fair* came at a time when Ainsworth's vogue was fading and caused a coolness between the two men that was never altogether overcome.

[2] *Crichton* was published without illustrations not long before March 4, 1837, when it was reviewed in *The Athenæum*. The third edition, with illustrations by "Phiz" (Hablôt K. Browne), appeared in 1849.

[3] Harmodius and Aristogeiton, the tyrannicides.

This is the cypher of Henry & Catharine.[4]

106.                TO JOHN MACRONE [5]
                    JANUARY 1837

*Address:* John Macrone Esq.[re] | S.[t] James's Square. *Postmark:* JA 19 1837. Facsimile of first page published by A. M. Broadley, *Chats on Autographs* (New York, 1910), p. 222.

My dear Macrone,

Mahony has just brought me y.[r] letter — I will send you half a dozen drawings [6] by Wednesdays Post, (w.[h] will cost you money) — I tried them on the Copper, but what I did was so bad, that I felt mortified at my failure, and did not care to write to you about it — besides I was rather disgusted at not getting a line from you.

You must send me vol 1 as well as Vol 111. your friend Reynolds you recollect had the 1.[st] Vol, and I have never been able to get it back — I wish you joy that you were out of the reach of that gentleman.

Mahony was wrong in saying I had finished all the drawings, he found three finished & a parcel of Sketches; but they will take no time to finish. This week I have painted a large picture of *Dando* [7] by w.[h] I hope to procure immortality, & two smaller draw-

_____

[4] Henri III and Catherine de Medici, who figure in Ainsworth's romance.
[5] A minor London publisher under whose imprint *The Paris Sketch Book* appeared in 1840.                    [6] For Ainsworth's *Crichton.*
[7] "Dando . . . was an oyster eater. . . . He used to go into oyster-shops,

ings — besides writing those famous letters to the Constitutional, w^h the two people who read that Paper declare *unparallelled* (how do you spell it?)

If you will have the sketches, send me the book in no time, I will not keep you waiting, for I work better than I did 4 months ago, and as quick as a house on fire. How are MacClise's Frontis-piecesseses? [8] Give Ainsworth a shake of the hand he has praised me so much that I must love him ever after, although neither he nor you write me a word. Upon my soul and honour you shall have 6 drawings by Wednesdays post. Ever yours respectfully. W. M. Thackeray.

Will you give me £ 50 20 now for the 1^st Edition of a book in 2 Wollums. with 20 drawings. entitled Rambles & Sketches in old and new Paris by I have not

---

without a farthing of money, and stand at the counter eating natives, until the man who opened them grew pale, cast down his knife, staggered backward, struck his white forehead with his open hand, and cried, 'You are Dando!!!' He has been known to eat twenty dozen at one sitting, and would have eaten forty, if the truth had not flashed upon the shopkeeper. For these offences he was constantly committed to the House of Correction. During his last imprisonment he was taken ill, got worse and worse, and at last began knocking violent double knocks at Death's door. The doctor stood beside his bed, with his fingers on his pulse. 'He is going,' says the doctor. 'I see it in his eye. There is only one thing that would keep life in him for another hour, and that is — oysters.' They were immediately brought. Dando swallowed eight, and feebly took a ninth. He held it in his mouth and looked round the bed strangely. 'Not a bad one, is it?' says the doctor. The patient shook his head, rubbed his trembling hand upon his stomach, bolted the oyster, and fell back — dead. They buried him in the prison-yard, and paved his grave with oyster-shells." (*Letters of Charles Dickens*, ed. Dexter, I, 470) Thackeray's first magazine story, "The Professor," written for *Bentley's Miscellany* of September, 1837, concerns this strange personage.

[8] The "Gallery of Illustrious Literary Characters" that appeared in *Fraser's Magazine* between 1830 and 1838.

of course written a word of it, that's why I offer it so cheap. but I want to be made to write, and to bind myself by a contract or fine.

Think now about the advantages of this offer (I mean the one in the fiddle case) — I want something to do — & w^d be right glad to do this.

107.           TO FRANK STONE
             20 JANUARY 1837

My text is taken from Lady Ritchie, *From Friend to Friend*, pp. 109–111.

         15 bis, Rue Neuve St. Augustin, Paris,
             20 January, 1837.

My dear Stone, — I have sent some drawings to London, which I want to be submitted to your Committee,[9] and for which I hope you will act as the God-Father or Patron. I fear very much that my skill in the art is not sufficiently great to entitle me to a place in your Society, but I will work hard and, please God, improve. Perhaps also the waggish line which I have adopted in the drawings may render them acceptable for variety's sake. There is no man, I think, except Hunt who amuses himself with such subjects. I hope you and Cattermole will say a good word for an old friend and here I leave the business; confiding in friendship; trusting in Heaven; and pretty indifferent about failure, because I don't think I deserve success as yet.

I have sent the drawings to my Mother in Albion Street; will you, like a bold fellow, take them under your charge and present them on the first Wednesday in February before the astonished Board? I wish I had had more time to work, but the newspaper takes up most part of my time, and carries off a great deal of my enthusiasm. Mahony, who brings me news of the boys, says that you are all flourishing, and rich — Maclise with a fine house in Fitzroy Square, and Cattermole in possession of Windsor Castle, I think.

[9] The Committee of the Water Colour Society.

Cannot you manage a trip here? Only twenty-five shillings and I promise you dinners, breakfastses and every delicate attention on Mrs. T's part and mine. Lewis was here, and very much to my disappointment, I never knew of it until his departure. My letter is very incoherent, and yet I am sober, but the fact is three women are chattering at my elbow and I can scarcely write or think.

Goodbye, my dear Stone, here is a very short letter, all about my own interests, but I have to write so hard for money, that I can't write for love. Send me a line about the lads and yourself, and salute them all for the sake of your old friend,

W. M. Thackeray.

108.            FROM EDWARD FITzGERALD
                    5 APRIL 1837 [10]

*Address:* W. M. Thackeray Esq^re | 18 Albion Street — | Hyde Park | London. *Postmark:* 5 AP 1837. Hitherto unpublished.

My dear Thackeray, I send you the Beranger's [11] complete: except the end of the stanza about the demoiselles in the Roi d'Yvetot — If it is wrong pray set it right, or send me a translation of the words, for I cannot construe them. Your wife can, I am sure — I found also the Souvenirs du Peuple, and the Convoi de David: which I send — Do not feel bound to use them because I have sent them: indeed I think the Roi d'Yvetot is the only perfect one: the rest have much of the French sentiment about them —

---

[10] Thackeray and his wife appear to have moved from Paris to the Carmichael-Smyths' home at 18 Albion Street early in March (see below, No. 115). Thackeray's last Parisian letter for *The Constitutional* is dated February 15.

[11] It is not known what use Thackeray intended to make of FitzGerald's translations of Béranger's "Le Roi d'Yvetôt," "L'Ange gardien," "Le Convoi de David," "Le Grenier," and "Les Souvenirs du peuple." Three years later he printed his friend's "Roi d'Yvetôt" and "The Garret" in *The Paris Sketch Book*, in both cases after extensive revision, and these two translations have hitherto been regarded as his own work. The three remaining translations are here published for the first time.

You and I know each other too well to need any ceremony about such matters as these: use them if you choose — If they are printed, the chorus, or refrain should always be printed at full length after each verse: for it is a necessary part of the composition, and should not be merely thought of, but absolutely read — I will send your Roi d'Yvetot,[12] if you wish: it is a paraphrase, and a very proper pendant to your Roger Bontemps — If you have some minutes to spare write: & give me the sense of the stanza I ask about — yrs ever, E FG. Boulge Hall, Woodbridge.

P.S. Your Roi d'Yvetot has far more spirit than mine, but is not so literal — You have made a beautiful drawing too, which I should like you to see: but I know you would lose it if I sent it to you — Pray do remember me most kindly to M⁙ Thackeray: for you cannot think how well I remember the very ⟨likeness⟩ of her —

> There was a King of Yvetôt
>    Of whom Renown hath little said:
> He let all thoughts of glory go,
>    And dawdled half his life abed —
> And as every night came round
> By Tessy with a nightcap crowned
>    Slept very sound —
> Sing ha, ha, ha, and he, he, he
> That's the sort of King for me.

> 2

> And every day it came to pass
>    Four meals beneath his belt he stowed:
> And step by step upon an ass
>    Over his dominions rode.
> And whenever he did stir
> What think you was his escort, Sir?
>    Why, an old cur —

[12] "The King of Brentford," first published in *Fraser's Magazine*, May, 1834, and reprinted in an altered form in *The Paris Sketch Book* as a companion piece to "Jolly Jack," Thackeray's version of Béranger's "Roger Bontemps."

Sing ha, ha, ha, and he, he, he,
That's the sort of King for me.

### 3

His charges ran to no excess
   Save from a somewhat lively thirst:
But he that would his people bless
   Odds fish! — must whet his whistle first
So for himself a pot he drew
From every barrel opened new,
      As Caesar's due:
Sing ha, ha, ha, and he, he, he,
That's the sort of King for me —

### 4

Firmly in all the ladies' hearts
   Was this sagacious prince installed:
And with strict justice on their parts,
   'The father of his people' called —
No other soldiers did he raise
But such as might at targets blaze
      On holidays.[13]
Sing ha, ha, ha, and he, he, he,
That's the sort of King for me.

### 5

Neither by force, nor false pretense,
   He sought to make his kingdom great:
And made, oh princes learn from hence,
   'Live and let live' his rule of state.
T'was only when he came to die
That the people, who stood by,

---

[13] These lines, concerning his translation of which FitzGerald was doubtful, run in the original:

      D'ailleurs, il ne levait de ban
      Que pour tirer, quatre fois l'an,
         Au blanc.

Were known to cry:
Sing ha, ha, ha, and he, he, he,
That's the sort of King for me —

The portrait of this best of Kings
    Still does the duty of a sign,
And o'er a village tavern swings
    Famed in that country for it's wine —
The people in their Sunday trim
Filling their glasses to the brim
      Look up to him:
Singing ha, ha, ha, & he, he, he,
Thats the King, the King for me —

------

### The Guardian Angel.

A beggar drawing near his end
    Saw his good angel at the door:
And said to him — 'Now my good friend,
    Trouble yourself for me no more.
Good angels bring one little joy;
But never mind — good bye, my boy.

#### 2

Am I what people call God's heir,
    Born on a strawheap in a loft?'
'Yes,' said the angel, 'I took care
    That the straw was fresh & soft.
      Good angels —

#### 3

What had I left me, but a face
    And tongue, of brass, to take folks in with?
'What!' said the angel — 'Of my grace
    An old friar's wallet to begin with' —
      Good angels —

4

Then 'listing, to the wars I went,
　　And lost a leg e're I got out —
'Well, said the angel, be content,
　　That leg would soon have had the gout' —
　　　　Good angels —


5

Then with a pocket I made free,
　　And the law got me by the ears —
'Yes, said the Angel, t'was through me
　　You only were in gaol three years —
　　　　Good angels —


6

Then I must needs make Love my game,
　　And from the chase retreated sore
'Yes, said the Angel, but through shame,
　　I always left you at the door."
　　　　Good angels —


7

Next a wife I took in tow,
　　And never was a worse miscarriage:
'Yes, said the Angel, but you know
　　We angels never meddle with marriage.'
　　　　Good angels &c.


8

Is this the peaceful end that ought
　　To crown a life of pain and toil? —
'Yes, said the angel, 'and I've brought
　　A priest with rag and holy oil."
　　　　Good angels &c.

### 9

Shall I then to hell go pat,
  Or fly away to happier spots? —
'Why, said the angel, as to that,
  You may — or may not — let's draw lots' —
    Good angels.

### 10

So this poor soul with faltering tongue
  Made the folks merry round his bed:
He sneezed — the Angel as he sprung
  Upward for Heaven 'God bless you' said —
Good Angels bring us little joy:
But never mind — good bye, my boy.

---

The Funeral March of David.

'Hold back! — you go no further here' —
  They heard the frontier sentry call
Who the dead painter on his bier
  Were bearing to his native Gaul.
'Soldier,' they answered in their gloom,
  Does France proscribe his memory too?
And you deny his ashes room
  Who left eternal fame to you?'

### Chorus

Exiled, unfriended and forlorn
  He pined beneath a despot's eye:
Thrice happy those who live and die
  In the dear land where they were born —

### 2

'Hold back — you cannot pass, I say' —
  The soldier still in fury cries.
'Soldier, as even in death he lay
  Toward France he turned his dying eyes —

For her alone and all in all
   He wrought in exile and in woe:
And made from many a palace wall
   The genius of her people glow —
      Chorus —


3

'No, no — hold back — you cannot pass' —
   The soldier, somewhat touched, returned —
'The man that drew Leonidas
   With equal love of freedom burned —
With him began the bright array
   Of conquest and of art, when France
Spurning the bonds of Kings away
   Rose like a giant from her trance —
      Chorus —


4

'No, no — I cannot let you on —'
   More gently said the soldier then —
'Soldier, t'was he that could alone
   Portray the greatest of great men.
While Homer raised his soul above,
   And round the imperial eagle flew,
He seemed elect to picture Love,
   But t'was Prometheus whom he drew —
      Chorus —


5

'No, no — you cannot pass the walls'
   The soldier said in accent mild —
'Soldier, at last the hero falls,
   And the great painter is exiled —
Death reaches him in foreign lands,
   Death — a sad and bitter one —
Oh France, hold forth a mother's hands
   To the great ashes of thy son —
      Chorus.

### 6

'No, no — I dare not yield to you' —
 The soldier all in tears replied —
'Well, let us turn — Sweet France, adieu
 Land of our birth, our love, our pride!
Quenched is the glory from whose birth
 The blaze of Roman art decayed —
We go to beg six feet of earth
 Where these great ashes may be laid —
  Chorus &c


### The Garret.

With pensive eyes the garret I review
 Where in my youth I weathered it so long:
With a wild mistress, a staunch friend or two,
 And a light heart that bubbled into song.
Making a mock of life, and all it's cares,
 Rich in the glory of my rising sun,
Lightly I bounded up four pair of stairs
 In the brave days when I was 21.

### 2

It is a garret — let him know't who will:
 There stood my bed — how hard it was & small:
My table there: and I decipher still
 A half made couplet charcoaled on the wall.
Ye joys, that Time hath swept with him away,
 Rise up — ye royal dreams of love & fun:
For you my watch I pawned how many a day
 In the brave days when I was 21.

### 3

And thou, my little Nelly, first of all —
 Fresh, & fresh drest as daisies, in she flies:
Her little hands already pin the shawl
 Across the narrow window curtain wise —

Along the bed she spreads her flowing gown
    For coverlet, where coverlet was none —
I have heard since who paid for many a gown
    In the brave days when I was 21.


### 4

One noble evening, when my friends and I
    Tarried in full chorus round the little board,
A shout of triumph mounted up thus high,
    And the deep cannon through the city roared:
We rise: we join in the triumphant strain:
    "Napoleon conquers!  Austerlitz is won!
"Tyrants shall never tread us down again!" —
    Oh the brave days when I was 21 —


### 5

⟨Let us be⟩ gone — the place is sad and strange —
    How far, far, back these happy times appear!
All that I have to live I'd gladly change
    For one such month as I have wasted here.
To dwell in one long dream of love and power
    *Quaffing of
    {By founts of} hopes that never would outrun
And concentrate life's essence in an hour
    Give me the days when I was 21.

---

His glory in the land shall grow,
    The people's household talk, and song:
The humble cottage hearth ere long
    No legend but of him shall know.
Thither the country folk shall meet
    And to some aged Grandam say
'Some tale of bygone times repeat
    'To while the winter night away.

*Which of these is best? —

'Though his ambition wrought us ill
The people glory in him still,
        Yes, love him still:
Tell us about him, Grandmother,
        Tell us a tale of him' —


2

'Children, I saw him passing here
  With a train of monarchs — oh!
  Many, many, years ago —
It was in my bridal year.
He came on foot, and, trampling o'er
  The very hillock where I sat
A grey riding coat he wore,
  And little military hat.
I shook with fright to stand so near,
But quoth he, Good day, my dear,
        Good day, my dear!" —
"And he spoke to you, Grandmother,
        He spoke to you here" —


3

"After that I went by chance
  To Paris, and I saw him pass
In procession to High Mass
  Followed by the Court of France.
Every one was glad and gay:
  They gazed upon their king with pride:
Saying, 'What a glorious day.
  'Heaven is always on his side' —
A sweet smile was on his face
For God have given him of his grace
        A little boy:" —
"Oh what a day that, Grandmother,
        What a day of joy!" —

### 4

"But when ill luck came to the land,
   And her army overthrown,
We seemed to keep the field alone,
And fight the battle singlehand —
One night, just as this night might be,
   I heard a rapping at the door:
I open it — Good God, t'is he,
   Followed by only three or four —
Down sat he in this very chair
'Poor France! what wars, what wars,' quoth he,
       'The country tear" —
"And so he sat there, Grandmother,
       In that very chair!" —

### 5

"I'm hungry" quoth he — I apace
   Brown bread and wine before him set:
   He dried his garments dripping wet,
And dozed before the fire a space —
He saw me crying, when he woke:
   'Cheer up, quoth he — 'I hasten, dame
To rescue Paris from the yoke,
   And to avenge my country's shame.'
He went: and I have sacred kept
The glass he drank from e're he slept,
       And ever will — "
"And still you have it, Grandmother
       And you have it still."

### 6

T'is here — well after a long while
   The lion heart was hunted down:
   He, whom a Pope was brought to crown,
Died heartbroke on a barren isle —
Long time we said, 'It cannot be:

    Wait but a little: he will come
Like thunderstorms across the sea,
    And scare the boasting stranger home.
We waited, waited, till hope fled:
We said despairing, He is dead —
    And all was true: — "
"Well, God be with you, Grandmother,
    His blessing be with you."

109.        TO THE DIRECTORS OF THE
              *CONSTITUTIONAL*
              29 APRIL 1837

Published by Mr. Wilson, *Boston Evening Transcript*, July 31, 1920.

Constitutional Office
162 Fleet Street Saturday
April 29$^{th}$ 1837 —

Gentlemen

At the last general meeting, you were good enough to confide to me temporarily, the post of Managing Director, vacated by the retirement of M$^r$ Stevens —

I presumed at the time, that there would have been money enough to carry on the paper for a few weeks, while the negociations were pending which were to secure success —

Of this I have not the slightest doubt, the persons engaged with me in the management of the paper share the opinion, for they are working at almost nominal salaries, in confident hopes of better days. But I am sorry to say our funds are totally inadequate to meet the present expenses — the sums due can only be slowly collected — while a heavy & regular account is to be discharged every week. The paper would long since have stopped, had not these deficiencies been met as they occurred, by one of the Directors the only one who has remained at his post, & whose extraordinary exertions & sacrifices, have maintained the Constitutional hitherto — Major Smyth — It would be folly on the part of that gentleman, to continue to meet alone, the risk & cost of an establishment in which you are as much interested as he — such sacrifises could only injure & could little benefit the paper —

Without a sum of at least a thousand pounds, I am sure it is perfectly useless, that the Constitutional should proceed — should you be inclined to advance such a sum, I do most confidently believe, that in three months the paper would be at a paying point; & in a year, would yield a very large dividend — Without it — you may as well close the doors of your office, & pay the liabilities which will fall upon you.

Let me beg you to remember, *that you will have a larger sum to pay if the paper should drop, than if it should continue* — that you are severally liable, for the present debts of the company, that the paper must fall, if you do not come forward in its aid, & that it is certain of success if you do —

I have been anxious to bring the matter to a crisis, for I am sure that in the present uncertainty, no good can be done with the Constitutional — It may linger on, but will never prosper or it may die of exhaustion some Saturday night, because [of] the persons who had advanced thousands to maintain it —

I can only say for my own part, that I will gladly contribute towards the necessary supply, & will take a loan note from the Company for £100, if the rest of the Shareholders are willing to complete the sum — without it — it is impossible to continue the paper — [14]

I am gentlemen

Y^r ob^dt Serv^t

W. M. Thackeray.

[14] *The Constitutional* lingered on till July 1. The farewell address in the issue of that date, explaining why the paper proved a failure, is reprinted in *Mr. Thackeray's Writings in "The National Standard," and "Constitutional,"* ed. Spencer, pp. 293–297.

110.                   TO JOHN RITCHIE
                        30 APRIL 1837

*Address:* A. Monsieur Ritchie | Rue des Thernes. | aux Thernes | pres Paris.
*Postmark:* PARIS 5 MAI 1837. Published in part in *Ritchies in India,* pp.
27–28; the whole letter by Mr. Wilson, *Boston Transcript,* July 31, 1920.

My dear Mʳ Ritchie. The above letter [15] is written in my public
capacity — you will see that it gives a gloomy picture of affairs
here — the fact is our paper [16] is well-nigh ruined for want of a
few pounds. We have before us the best prospects in the world —
a thousand coffee-shop men have sworn to take in a number of the
Constitutional, our circulation since my administration has been
slowly but daily increasing, and all our fine prospects are likely to
fall to the ground, because our shareholders hold back, and because we want such a mean sum as a thousand pound — why Shallow could lend it to Falstaff from his own private purse! [17] Shall I
put yʳ name down for a loan note? — I have succeeded in getting
3 already besides my own.

I have also to beg for 10£ the amount of your instalments. Since
our arrival in London, I have been so busy as not to have a moment
for writing, and saying that we have not forgotten our friends at
Thernes; my wife has not much to do, to be sure, but she is very
lazy — we are looking out for a little Thackeray in a month.[18]
William has been to see us; and your friends the Jaffrays have
been very kind, giving us good dinners at their house in Eaton
Square. My lady Rodd [19] was good enough to say that, she re-

[15] Thackeray's letter of April 29.
[16] Thackeray wrote *our will paper.*
[17] See *II Henry IV,* Act V, scene v.
[18] Anne Isabella Thackeray was born on June 9.
[19] The former Jane Rennell (1777–1863), *Genealogy* (16), daughter of
the famous geographer, Major James Rennell (1742–1830), *Genealogy* (8).
Miss Rennell in 1809 married Captain John Tremayne Rodd (d. 1838),
*Genealogy* (17), who later became a Vice Admiral and a K. C. B. Both in
her father's home and her own she saw excellent society, for Major Rennell's
accomplishments gave him the *entrée* to the London world, and Sir John Rodd
was a favorite with the "Sailor King," William IV. Mrs. Bayne (*Memorials,*
p. 258) observes: "Accustomed to them from an early age, Lady Rodd was a

gretted exceedingly that I could not come to dinner *when asked last
year* — She does not seem at all disposed to repeat the experiment.
The Provost's daughter [20] came suddenly to see us, and invited us
to a grand repast — These are the only gaieties of w[h] I have been
guilty since we came to London — for most of my hours are spent
in Fleet Street, in the cause of the Constitutional. With love to
my Aunt, and cousins believe me my dear M[r] Ritchie most truly
yours W. M. T.

18 Albion S[t]

Sunday. 30 April.

III.                TO JOHN MACRONE
                    26 JULY 1837

*Address:* John Macrone Esq[re] — | 3. S[t] James's Square.  Hitherto unpublished.

Halbion S[t] Igh Park.
Wednesday. 26 July.

My dear Mac.

I have read through Maceroni's [21] first 4 sheets as per order.
— by twisting and turning, by suppressing 20 pages or near, and
rewriting some part of the remainder I think we can make something of it — There seems to be *stuff* in the book, and I think that
if the adventures in the rest of the volume are so interesting as you
describe them to be, we might make a fierce, strange, interesting
book — wild and Robinson-Crusoe like: but you should have Maceroni's assent; and give me only his adventures, d—— his language,
and his reflections moral religious and scientifick.

The book must be rewritten, and will cause a world of trouble.

---

woman who received and expected attentions; and she always had an influence
in our family which was not possessed by any other person."

[20] Mary Ann Thackeray.

[21] Colonel Francis Maceroni (1788–1846), whose manuscript Macrone
published as *Memoirs of the Life and Adventures of Colonel Maceroni* in
1838. The revision that Thackeray proposed does not seem to have been
carried out. Maceroni's language remains pompous and awkward, and his
adventures are sadly diluted with "reflections moral religious and scientifick."

— The Colonel must give you carte-blanche about alterations, and not disown the book when published. We may make a hero of him, by these means; if after the works publication he blusters or denies it, the sale would be seriously injured. Get a paper from him (even though it cost you a few pounds) allowing all emendations, and by the blessing of Heaven, Maceroni shall live a thousand years — that is if his adventures are such as you state them —

I have a notion that I could make a very fine book of it: and some hundred pounds too, — for you will give me a share in the plunder.

Yrs undoubtedly<br>W. M. T.

You will perceive that it will be necessary to make the Editor and the Biographer friends — I must be acquainted with the man's *idiosyncracy* to use a short word.

112.       FROM EDWARD FɪᴛᴢGERALD
1 SEPTEMBER 1837

*Address:* W. M. Thackeray, Esqre. | 18. Albion Street. | Hyde Park. London.
*Postmarks:* LOWESTOFT, SP 1 1837. Hitherto unpublished.

Dear Thackeray,

I am glad you are in full employment again: indeed, I don't think you need ever fear of being without it — I have been here ever since I last wrote: but shall soon leave the place, which is a very pleasant place, to my thinking — I am very glad to hear you say you have been drawing: is Dando a good subject? — He certainly was a great man: having that inward magnanimity that independence of fortune and money, so much admired by Ben Jonson in Lord Bacon, and by Lamb in Elliston.[22] I trust he was

---

[22] Lamb illustrates the "essential *greatness*" of Robert William Elliston, the actor, by citing Ben Jonson's words about Sir Francis Bacon: "But I have, and do reverence him for the *greatness*, that was only proper to himself; in that he seemed to me ever one of the *greatest* men, that had been in many ages. In his adversity I ever prayed that heaven would give him strength; for *greatness* he could not want." ("Ellistoniana," *The Last Essays of Elia*)

not crazy: I mean, that I should be very disappointed if his impish-
ness was not the result of deep conviction — His name is a good
illustration of sir name's going by contraries — Dando a semper
recipiendo — but 'recipiendo' is too mild a word —

Sir Frizzle Pumpkin [23] seemed to me a painful joke: perhaps it
was meant to be so. I do not mean that it was a heavy joke: but
that it was more sad than merry. The *Hints* to Authors was very
laughable indeed — The writer must be a humourist, as you describe
him. Pray have you seen anything of the Kembles? — Jacky is
going on swimmingly with his Review,[24] I hear: it certainly is a
very cheap one, and as it is supported by Beaumont is independent
of the private politics of booksellers — My friend Donne [25] is
writing articles in it: and I believe they are good ones. you can tell
me nothing of the Tennysons, I suppose: I wish you could. As to
my going to see you in London, it is not impossible: I should like
to be with you there some days: but I must hear how family plans
are settled first. My Father and Mother are going to Paris for a
month, like your's —

How very stupidly I write, to be sure: you must not think me
tired of you on this account: but I cannot write to anybody now;
except to Browne [26] of Bedford, who tells me how many pike he

---

[23] Both *The Adventures of Sir Frizzle Pumpkin* (1836) and "Hints to
Authors" (*Blackwood's Magazine*, October, 1835; February, March, and May,
1836) were written by the Rev. James White (1803–1862), at this time
Vicar of Loxley in Warwickshire. When his wife, the former Rosa Hill, inherited a considerable property from her father, White gave up his living and
retired to Bonchurch on the Isle of Wight. He was on friendly terms with
Dickens as well as Thackeray.

[24] *The British and Foreign Review.*

[25] The Rev. William Bodham Donne (1807–1882), a direct descendant of
John Donne, attended Bury St. Edmunds Grammar School with FitzGerald
and John Mitchell Kemble. He passed his life in lettered retirement, being an
esteemed contributor to *The Edinburgh Review*, *The Quarterly Review*, and
*Fraser's Magazine*, as well as to *The British and Foreign Review*. In 1857 he
succeeded Kemble as Examiner of Plays in the Lord Chamberlain's office and
held that post until his death.

[26] William Kenworthy Browne (1816?–1859), the son of an alderman
and one-time Mayor of Bedford, had been one of FitzGerald's closest friends
since 1832. Thackeray does not appear to have liked this harmless country
gentleman, whom he "would call . . . 'Little Browne'," writes FitzGerald

has caught, and how many foxes he has killed, and so on. For now you are married, I dare not write nonsense, and what Mrs Butler calls 'potter', to you: I don't try not to do it: but I instinctively do not do it — Elegant language — I have just written to the said Browne a long and circumstantial account of my proposing to a young lady: I think he must be taken in: and I look forward with pleasure to the letter of congratulation that he will write — You don't know what a good boy he is: I suppose there are more such than I am aware of: I fancy that the better virtues and character-istics of Englishmen have slipped away from the aristocracy, and settled among the trading classes apart from London, who are yet unspoiled — Is this humbug? — As to Carlyle's book [27] I looked into it, but I did not desire to read it — I do not admire the Ger-man school of English. What a mistake to suppose that when you write of troublous times & scenes, you must write in that abrupt hur-ried manner, as if you were carried away by what you have to de-scribe: a writer should feel himself master of his subject, — I rub out something that you would hate.[28] We have lost Summer, I fear: what cold days: When shall we go to Rome together, Thack-eray? — I think I should like to spend this winter there: but it can-not be — Rome ought to be seen: though you would abuse the Fresco's famously, to be sure. Spedding [29] is still in London, and

---

(*Letters and Literary Remains*, ed. Wright, IV, 289), "which I told him he was not justified in doing."

[27] *The French Revolution*, which Thackeray reviewed in *The Times* on August 3. Carlyle remarked of his notice: "The writer is one Thackeray, a half-monstrous Cornish giant, kind of painter, Cambridge man, and Paris newspaper correspondent, who is now writing for his life in London. I have seen him at the Bullers' and at Sterling's. His article is rather like him, and I suppose calculated to do the book good." (*Letters of Thomas Carlyle to his Youngest Sister*, ed. Charles Townsend Copeland, Boston, 1899, p. 86).

[28] Before this sentence FitzGerald has overscored half a line.

[29] James Spedding (1808–1881) matriculated at Trinity College, Cam-bridge, in 1827 and received his B.A. degree in 1831. Having an independent income, he followed no profession, though he was employed in the Colonial Office between 1835 and 1841. He devoted the greater part of his life to the study of Bacon, publishing his *Works* with Robert Leslie Ellis and D. D. Heath between 1857 and 1859 and his *Life and Letters* between 1861 and 1874. For many years he made his home in bachelor chambers at Lincoln's

to be heard of at the Club in S$^t$ James' Square. If you and Mrs T— are alone in Albion Street, do ask him to come and see you. I shall come and stay with you if I can positively: in the middle of next week I go to Boulge with my sisters. With kind remembrances to your lady believe me ever yrs

E. F. G.

113.                TO JAMES FRASER
                OCTOBER 1837

Hitherto unpublished.

18 Albion Street
Sunday.

Dear Fraser.

Here is a paper on Skelton [30] — I expect you will pay handsomely for it; for it is good fun.

---

Inn Fields, though latterly he lived with relatives at Westbourne Terrace. Despite his bent for scholarship, he found much time for sport and society.

Spedding met Thackeray at Cambridge and was long his intimate friend, as an album of Thackerayana that he kept abundantly testifies. Several of the drawings in this album, which is now owned by Mr. E. Arthur Ball, are reproduced above; see No. 22, No. 48, and Appendix IV. His sobriety of manner and devotion to learning made him the subject of a good deal of amiable chaff on the part of Thackeray and of FitzGerald, an even closer friend. On January 16, 1841, for example, we find FitzGerald (*Letters and Literary Remains*, ed. Wright, I, 91) writing to Frederick Tennyson about a portrait of Spedding given him by Samuel Laurence: "not swords, nor cannon, nor all the Bulls of Bashan butting at it, could, I feel sure, discompose that venerable forehead. No wonder that no hair can grow at such an altitude: no wonder his view of Bacon's virtue is so rareified that the common consciences of men cannot endure it. Thackeray and I occasionally amuse ourselves with the idea of Spedding's forehead: we find it somehow or other in all things, just peering out of all things: you see it in a milestone, Thackeray says. He also draws the forehead rising with a sober light over Mont Blanc, and reflected in the lake of Geneva. We have great laughing over this. The forehead is at present in Pembrokeshire, I believe: or Glamorganshire: or Monmouthshire: it is hard to say which. It has gone to spend its Christmas there."

[30] John Henry Skelton's *My Book; or, The Anatomy of Conduct* (1837) is the subject of "Fashnable Fax and Polite Annygoats," the first of the Yellow-plush Papers, which was published in *Fraser's Magazine* for November, 1837.

If you don't like it, or can't put it in this month, please send it me back: I can place it advantageously elsewhere.

I think I could make half a dozen stories by the same author, if you incline. —

Very truly yours

W. M. Thackeray.

114.          TO EDWARD FɪᴛzGERALD
19 FEBRUARY 1838

*Address:* ⟨Edward⟩ Fitz-Gerald Esqʳᵉ — | ⟨Bo⟩ulge Hall | Woodbridge | Suffolk. *Postmark:* FE 19 1838. Hitherto unpublished.

\*          \*          \*

I took her to see Werner ¹ — it was a perfect roar on her part and very complimentary to Macready. What a grand collection of clap-trap that play is! — but there is no soul in all those fine words, and grand sentences; like old fashioned damask gowns all flowers and finery, and so stiff that they stand up by themselves, you fancy at a little distance there is somebody inside the gown — I will put this you may depend upon it into my next Magazine paper — it is the devil of that trade that one is always thinking of making good things. I began a Journal

\*          \*          \*

115.          TO MRS. THACKERAY
3 MARCH 1838

*Address:* Mʳˢ Thackeray | 13 Great Coram Street. | Brunswick Square | London | Angleterre. *Postmarks:* BOULOGNE 5 MARS 1838, LONDON 6 MAR. 1838. Hitherto unpublished.

Hotel d'Angleterre. Balong.² Saturday evening

My dearest Trot, at this presn momint the stormy and bagnifisnt Otion is about ten miles of. It is ate o'clock, and we have all had

¹ The tragedy (1822) by Lord Byron, of which Macready had given a command performance before the Queen on November 17, 1837.

² The first paragraph of this letter is written in the English peculiar to

our brexfastes, and are preparing for our lunches. I've had tea, brednbutter, and coal-bile-biff, but I couldn eat much, because my heart was full a thinking of my Toaby, and lickwise my stummick w.ʰ (besides brexfast) has two doz: hoysters in it eat last night after parting from you. From home I went to the G.³ where I found seffral chaps, and we kep it up quite joly till 2, when I came on bord. — it was almost a shame to be mery, when my wiff was sad as I thought, a layin awake in bed and thinkin of her habsint Alonzer — but, its better in these suckinstansies to be joly than sad, and so I did. +

I found that it was necessary to leave off writing if I wished to avoid womiting, and accordingly at + stopped and lay down and read the Casquet for the next two or three hours — We arrived here at a quarter before 4, a very pleasant easy passage of only 10 1/2 hours, and here I am at the old quarters — seated at that very sofa where I recollect my dear little Toby a year ago. I can see the little place where she used to sit, and the spot occupied by the 'dancing Quaker' of an American.

There was a fine blue sky when we arrived here, although it had been pouring all day in England, and Mʳˢ Foube the landlady makes affectionate enquiries after you, the same barber who shaved me last year, has just now performed the same operation — nothing is changed except that Toby is absent, and Alonzo is desolate. I am writing nonsense you see, for the post goes off at 9 in the morning tomorrow, and I have nothing to say about to day — nothing, except that I dozed all day and thought of Mʳˢ T. that I am here and shall stay here a day or so, writing Yellowplush, and concocting a Fraser paper with Maginn if I see him, and that I shall be very glad to come back again to my dear little wife whom God bless and make comfortable as well as Miss T. and Mʳˢ S. and all others whom we care for. Why have I written you such nonsense? — I hardly fancy that I am away from you — Goodbye dearest Wife your affectionate

Makepeace

---

Yellowplush. Thackeray was engaged upon the literary footman's "Foring Parts," which appeared in *Fraser's Magazine* for April.
³ The Garrick Club.

MRS. THACKERAY ABOUT 1838

*From a sketch by Thackeray*

116.            TO JAMES FRASER
                5 MARCH 1838

Published in *The Charleston News* during 1886. My text is taken from *The Pall Mall Budget*, January 20, 1887.

                    Boulogne, Monday, February.[4]

My dear Fraser, — I have seen the doctor, who has given me his commands about the hundredth number.[5] I shall send him my share from Paris in a day or two, and hope I shall do a good deal in the diligence to-morrow. He reiterates his determination to write monthly for you, and to deliver over the proceeds to me. Will you, therefore, have the goodness to give the bearer a check (in my wife's name) for the amount of his contributions for the two last months.[6] Mrs. Thackeray will give you a receipt for the same. You have already Maginn's authority.

Now comes another, and not a very pleasant point, on which I must speak. I hereby give notice that I shall strike for wages.

You pay more to others, I find, than to me; and so I intend to make some fresh conditions about Yellowplush. I shall write no more of that gentleman's remarks except at the rate of twelve guineas a sheet,[7] and with a drawing for each number in which his story appears — the drawing two guineas.

Pray do not be angry at this decision on my part; it is simply a bargain, which it is my duty to make. Bad as he is, Mr. Yellowplush is the most popular contributor to your magazine, and ought to be paid accordingly: if he does not deserve more than the monthly nurse or the Blue Friars,[8] I am a Dutchman.

[4] A mistake for March, as the next letter shows.
[5] The April number of *Fraser's Magazine*.
[6] We learn from Thackeray's account book for 1838 (see Appendix VI) that he received £25 from Fraser on April 16. Since he contributed only a five page story and a single illustration to the April number of *Fraser's Magazine*, most of this sum must have been paid from Maginn's balance.
[7] There were sixteen magazine pages to a sheet.
[8] Two other long series in *Fraser's Magazine*, the former by Mrs. Harriet Downing, the latter by George Wightwick (Thrall, *Rebellious Fraser's*, pp. 276–277).

I have been at work upon his adventures to-day, and will send them to you or not as you like, but in common regard for myself I won't work under prices.

Well, I dare say you will be very indignant, and swear I am the most mercenary of individuals. Not so. But I am a better workman than most in your crew and deserve a better price.

You must not, I repeat, be angry, or because we differ as trades-men break off our connection as friends. Believe me that, whether I write for you or not, I always shall be glad of your friendship and anxious to have your good opinion.

I am ever, my dear Fraser (independent of £ s.d.), very truly yours,

W. M. Thackeray.

Write me a line at Meurice's,⁹ Rue de Rivoli. I can send off Y. P. twenty-four hours after I get yours, drawings and all.

117.                  TO MRS. THACKERAY
                      5 MARCH 1838

*Address:* Mʳˢ Thackeray. | 13 Great Coram Street | Brunswick Square. *Post-mark:* MR 7 1838. Hitherto unpublished.

My dearest Toby-kins  A waiter from this Inn goes to London tomorrow, & is to be the bearer of this twopenny.  Please fold up and seal the letter to Fraser,¹⁰ and send John with it, *with your compliments to wait for an answer,* he had better be there about 1— You will see I have determined to strike for wages, a hazard-ous experiment perhaps but a right one, he pays more to others and why not to me, who am not his cleverest, but certainly his most popular man.

Saturday after writing that stupid letter to you, I went to bed very tired and slept till half past twelve on Sunday morning, a very little while after getting up I dined with Maginn, having

⁹ *The Pall Mall Budget* reads *Maurice's.*
¹⁰ Of March 5.

first had a walk of two or 3 miles about this dull town upper and lower. We were pretty merry and very sober; to day I have seen him again to arrange matters about a Fraser paper [11] w^h will be very bad, and since then have been dining and writing Yellow-plush — but I don't intend M^r Fraser to have it, until I have more from him —

The 2 days here have passed away certainly but in a very strange stupid way — it is very dismal to come to a lonesome room, and have no Toby to come and disturb me; but never mind, it is all for the best; there is no great hardship to be sure in being away from home for 3 weeks on a very pleasant trip, but I feel as if I had left one of my legs in Coram Street, and get on very lamely without it — all this serves to show one how closely a wife gets about the heart, and how ill one can do without her. Comment m'est il arrivé de detester tant la solitude?

I am amused with the bustle and scandal of this little town, & heard yesterday stories about the Doctors, the Clergymen, the married & unmarried women of this place w^h w^d take a dozen pages to fill. Little Maginn likes it very much, he has done very well poor fellow in coming here for he is repandu in the small parties, and has society w^h he never had before. M^rs M. looks really very well & swears you are charming w^h perhaps makes me forget her snobbishness. Madame Foube to whom I had taken a great liking, I now find to be a humbug. She said to day at dinner in one of the loudest whispers I ever heard, that I spoke French almost better than a Frenchman — that is my opinion of the case.

I go tomorrow at 9 by a new coach called the Heagle: we are to be in Paris in 22 hours — say 28, and there is a contrivance in the coach for keeping the feet warm, an excellent notion. I shall send a line by Friday's bag till when God bless my dearest little wife, and ditto for mother, and little Toby. Write a word by post and direct to Meurice's — Rue de Rivoli

Is not this an affecting letter to Fraser? — I must do it; and au reste if I am cut out of Magazine work altogether, I can, please

[11] Nothing seems to have come of this collaboration.

God, get better employment w$^h$ will gain me a little durable reputation. Good bye dear Wife. W. M. T.

On 2$^{nd}$ thoughts I send by post — send *immediately* to F. Maginn may change his mind, and there is no harm in getting 20
pound    You had better write a note enclosing it with y$^r$ compts.

Ask Fraser to send *immediat.* a list of all the portraits in his Mag.
to me at Paris.


118.                    TO MRS. THACKERAY
                        11–14 MARCH 1838

*Address cut away. Postmark:* 14 MARS 1838. Published in part, *Biographical Introductions*, III, xl-xli.

Sunday 11 March.

My dearest Dobbs. I have only 2 words to say to night, being
very sleepy and tired, though I dont know with what. Last night
the Crowes took me to a swarry, after w$^h$ as I had eaten no dinner
and was monstrous hungry, I went to the Café Anglais & ate a
wing of cold fowl. There I found 2 old Charterhouse friends, &
there I sate until 3 o'clock, so did not get up till 12, & wrote all day
in my room till 6 when I went to dine with Thackeray — it is a
great pity that his wife is no better than she should be. She is a
kind ladylike pretty woman, with a very charming manner w$^h$
only can belong to a good woman. Yesterday I dined at M. A's,[12]
who far from being uncomfortable was as gracious as possible; we
were very happy for we talked all night of my dearest wife, till I
longed to be home, and with her. It is almost a blessing that I
came away, for I see now more strongly than ever, how much I
love her, and how my whole heart & bowels go with her. Here
have we been nearly 2 years married & not a single unhappy day.
Oh I do bless God for all this great happiness w$^h$ He has given us.
It is so great that I almost tremble for the future, except that I
humbly hope (for what man is certain about his own weakness and
wickedness) our love is strong enough to stand any pressure from

[12] Mrs. Shawe's.

without, and as it is a gift greater than any fortune, is likewise one superior to poverty or sickness or any other worldly evil with w^h Providence may visit us. Let us pray, as I trust there is no harm, that none of these may come upon us, as the best and wisest man in the world prayed that he might not be led into temptation.[13] My dear dear wife may God preserve you to me & me to you.

— I have been sitting for ten minutes pen in hand thinking about this last sentence, & not being able to write more on the same subject — I think happiness is as good as prayers, and I feel in my heart a kind of overflowing thanksgiving, w^h is quite too great to describe in writing — This kind of happiness is like a fine picture — you only see a little bit of it, when you are close to the canvass, — go a little distance & then you see how beautiful it is. God bless my dearest wife, & mother, & little Tomkins — I dont know whether I shall have done much good by coming away except to be so awfully glad to come back.

Monday. too tired tonight to say anything except good night — dined at O'Donnell's [14] Stupid. away early, reading newspapers & as sleepy as if it were 3 o'clock though its only 11.

Tuesday. My dearest Snobs, I don't know what I have done these 2 days except to eat good dinners — and to grow so tired of a night as scarcely to be able to write you a line — Yesterday I did none of my business, nor to day though I waited 2 hours at the chamber of deputies to get in. I was to pay 8 francs for my place, & luckily grew so disgusted with the delay that I went away — a quarter of an hour after M. Montalivet [15] who was to speak pretended to faint & the séance terminated abruptly. To day has been remarkable for visits of all kinds M^rs & Miss Shawe. M^rs Butler. M^r Ritchie and others of the haut ton. I brexfasted with the Crowes and dined with the Times Correspondent — a kind, but very dull man. Au café de Paris. The dinner w^h every Englishman orders,

[13] *St. Matthew*, 6, 13.

[14] Almost nothing is known of this obscure journalist, who was one of Thackeray's most intimate friends during the late eighteen-thirties and early eighteen-forties. But see below, No. 266.

[15] Comte Marthe Camille Bachasson de Montalivet (1801–1880), the French statesman.

sole, beef, roast partridge, champagne & so on. Afterwards we went home to his sister, who is a tolerably agreeable woman, and going to be cut for the cancer directly     She is very poor, & has been paying visits to Hahnemann [16] for 2 months who promised to cure her, she paid him 2 pounds a visit, and is only worse than ever. As for doing anything it is impossible. tomorrow, Thursday to y$^r$ Mamma, and Saturday I am obliged to dine out — or rather I won't refuse, and the good of one's coming here is lost. I shant have done a single line when I come back, & spent 25 pounds — never mind — the holiday will do no harm for ooooooooooooooooooooooooooooooo-oooooooooooooooooh! how I long to be back with my Toby. I was up very early yesterday finishing a very bad drawing for Fraser.[17] — I almost hope he won't insert it — to day I have done o — I wish I had brought my Toby after all. I have been looking for father & have written him a letter, but no PA. he will come I suppose tomorrow — God bless my dearest wife, and mother & Miss Tacklety, I will write no more nonsense for tonight.

Wednesday. Your second long letter is just come dear Toby, and I write this before breakfast to tell you all that has happened since midnight when I wrote the last half sheet — I am in a funk for I have been communing with myself this morning and find on looking to my purse that my expences have been quite marvellous — only 14 left out of the 28 sovereigns with w$^h$ I set out. To be sure I have bought a pound's worth of gim-cracks, & thirty shilling's worth of books, and as much of boots — but since my arrival I have not written a line, I have scarcely seen a thing — so completely am I hampered by my friends. To day however I must & will begin and shall shut up this letter, bolt my breakfast, rush to the omnibus, and see Pere la Chaise, and a number of curiosities before the day is over and dinner time come — nasty dinner how it treads on the heels of breakfast, and the day is spent in vain guttling and gorging — The man who was to have taken me to Thiers was ill yesterday, tomorrow however we go to a couple of

[16] Samuel Christian Friedrich Hahnemann (1775–1843), a well-known homeopathic physician who had a large and wealthy clientele in Paris.
[17] Published in *Fraser's Magazine* for April, p. 404.

great parties — you would have laughed tother day to have seen me preparing for one and gravely mending my breeches. *

I have read to day matter enough to make two good stories, and think I can see my way into the next Yellowplush. We must work like tigers when we get home & no mistake — breakfast at 8 walk at 2 with M$^{rs}$ Thack: no club, and a light dinner. Here goes to write you a cheque, I am very near run dry I fear.

How shall I fill this page? — I think by M$^r$ O Reilly's hackney coach adventure — He had been to a theatre on the Boulevard and was coming home with a lady — it was midnight — no lamps in the Boulevard — no hackney coaches — and pouring cats and dogs — At last a man came to him and asked if he wanted a coach? — Yes says the cheerful correspondent of the Times, and in he jumped, he & his fair lady — Well 2 men got on the box, & when after half an hour O Reilly ventured to open one of the windows, he found they were driving Heaven knows where! — tearing madly down solitary streets or rather between walls — the more he cried out the more the men would not stop, and he pulled out a penknife (w$^h$ he always carries about because his corns plague him) and folding his arm round the waist of M$^{rs}$ O R, determined to sell his life at a considerable expense. At this instant, o bonheur! — providence sent a man into that very street, w$^h$ before or since was never known to echo with a mortal footstep — Swift as lightning, the young correspondent bust open the door of the coach, and bidding the lady follow sprung out — they landed in safety, down came one of the ruffians from the box O'Reilly with gigantick force seized his arm uplifted no doubt to murder the gentleman of the press. He held him writhing in his iron grip until the stranger arrived — whom seeing tother chap on the box instantly flogged his horses, and galloped away in the darkness & solitude. The poor wretch who was the companion of his guilt, now sunk on his knees, when the stranger looking at him fixedly and fiercely, drew from beneath his cloak a ⟨. . .⟩

That is all. God bless you dearest Wife.

119.      •      TO MRS. THACKERAY
15–17 MARCH 1838

Hitherto unpublished.

Thursday.

My dearest Toby. Since yesterday I don't think any wonderful
events have taken place: I dined with Jones whom you don't know,
and went in the evening to see a new play [18] at the Français, chock
full of sentiment, but tolerably entertaining; to day I have done a
little towards the book — two or 3 hours that is to say, at the
Bibliotheque du Roi: then I had a talk with M.r Galignani, and
have engaged for the next 3 or 4 days, or most probably so long as
I stay, to do a little work for his paper, in the room of a poor fellow
by the name of Battier, who is now lying at the point of death, with
a wife and 4 children & not a penny in the world. he is correspondent to the Morning Advertiser, & I have promised to write his
letter for him, as well as to do his Galignani work [19] — the whole
may occupy 4 hours every day, but 2 of these must be from 8 to 10
in the morning, w.h hours are usually spent by me in bed — This
work will at least pay my bill as long as I am here, and can do me
no great harm. I did a bit of it tonight after coming from your
mothers where I dined — very gracious — M.rs Jupp of the party,
& Jane was going with her to a concert. After the dinner, the
Galignani, & the dressing I went with Crowe's friend M.r Cerclet [20]
to a swarry at the Minister of Commerciseses. That great man in a
very affable manner said that it was rainy weather, after w.h I left
him, & was carried to M.r Dupin's, the President of the Cham. of
Deputies: a man in spectacles with a large tin star, who talked

[18] *Isabelle ou deux jours d'expérience* (1838) by Mme. Virginie Ancelot
(d. 1875).

[19] There is no means of distinguishing the work Thackeray did for
*Galignani's Messenger* between March 15 and early April, since his task was
to prepare digests of material from other journals. I have not seen a file of
*The Morning Advertiser*.

[20] Antoine Cerclet (1796–1849), publicist; André Dupin (1783–1865),
President of the Chamber of Deputies from 1832 to 1840.

about Lord Brougham for 1/2 a minute, when we parted delighted with one another. I could just as well have fancied these places before going but it is well to have seen — a hall, a crowd of lackies, an antechamber; a great groom of the chambers who shouts out your name, about a hundred gentlemen in black coats, and a dozen ladies — voila tout, but it will spin into 6 pages or so, & looks well in a book. Your mother is looking better, and Janey I left in the arms of her coiffeur: she is amazingly improved, I think, and to all appearance she & the old lady are very good friends. I saw the picture of little Toby, & the sketch of you w[h] was like you then, though not much now — your figure having dowdified somewhat. How I wished to be back with the originals! Never mind — if nothing comes of this absence there will be this good that I value my home a thousand times more than ever — though this I have had already the honor to remark. Last night a dreadful accident befel me — I slept in a bed that had never been made having gone out with the key & never returned all day. God bless you dearest of my wives — I am really not so partial to any 1 of them as to you. I have not dreamt of you once c'est drôle.

Dear Wifey — nothing more to say to day, excep that I got up at 7 as I will please the pigs tomorrow morning, though now it is 1 o'clock. I wrote for M[r] Galignani some very splendid articles morning and evening, and passed the day in eating an enormous breakfast, making a drawing and dining at Crowe's — after w[h] came work at Galignani's again, and a tea party at Darley's.[21] Miss Hamerton [22] Brine's sister in law as was to be was there, a little plain oldish woman, but charming for Irish simplicity and good humour — Is not this a pretty way to see Paris? — Highho, I wish I had you at my tail — perhaps you w[d] egg me on, & we sh[d] go see sights together — I have had a kind invitation from M. Cerclet to vittle with him tomorrow, & am to meet deputies, littérateurs, and all sorts of remarkable people, a ce qu'il dit —

[21] William Darley, an Irish painter whom Thackeray saw frequently at the Crowes' apartment in Paris (Sir Joseph Crowe, *Reminiscences*, pp. 17–18).

[22] Either Bess or Maria Hamerton, two elderly spinsters who made their home in Paris. They were close friends of Mrs. Carmichael-Smyth.

— What a strange business is politics! I begin to find myself
all of a sudden furiously interested about M. Thiers and Count
Molé [23] — whom I saw last night by the way as perhaps I told you
in the other page — the political game is either easier or more interesting than that played in England, certainly the actors are more
amusing. I have been looking out for P. A. but no signs of him.
Since that I have been smoking a segar, and heard all sorts of nice
stories from a man here in the Coffee room — they are very dirty
being all about water-closets, but very good fun; & I think I shall
stick them in to my book in some way or other. Is not this pretty
stuff to write about? How I do look forward to all-fools day, O
blessed first of April, when I shall, please God, see my dear wife
again; without whom I can neither work, nor even be merry when
I am idle — perhaps my dear little woman is writing to me at this
moment! God bless her, and my mother, and my little baby and
all. I shall go to bed now and think about you for a few minutes,
when perhaps I may fall sound asleep, and wake quite ready for
tomorrow morning's work — at least it pays my daily expenses if
it does no more. I salute you with a kiss.

Saturday. The dinner at Cerclet's has just come off, and I have
met half a dozen bellysprees. It was very good fun to hear these
men jabbering politics; — Crowe who was one of the party talked
better ⟨. . . ⟩ [24] Some of the lads were celebra⟨ting . . .⟩ University & a great friend of the ⟨. . .⟩ each other at the end of the
⟨. . .⟩ cleverly; having a fine dict⟨. . .⟩ liberty of the Press —
That say ⟨. . .⟩ wondered, for if the liberty ⟨. . .⟩ cries Mᴿ Rossi
when I vent⟨. . .⟩ were so *very* free, why they ⟨. . .⟩ noses — Sir,
says he, we do a⟨. . .⟩ a demi-mots — So devilish ⟨. . .⟩ *names!* —
and then he went ⟨. . .⟩ [25]

[23] Comte Louis Mathieu Molé (1781–1855), a well known politician.
[24] This and the following hiatuses are of about ten words each.
[25] The rest of the letter has been cut away.

120.       TO MRS. THACKERAY
20–25 MARCH 1838

*Address:* M<sup>rs</sup> Thackeray. | 13 Great Coram Street | Brunswick Square | London. | Angleterre. *Postmarks:* 25 MARS 1838, LONDON 27 MAR 1838. Extracts published in *Biographical Introductions,* III, xli-xlii.

Tuesday. March 20.

My dearest woman — Your letter of Friday I have only got now — your mother put it in the post yesterday, and it has been all this while travelling hither — to be sure I went out at 8 and it is now near midnight. I have been at work all day, and at play; 3 times to Galignani's — to the salon again to see the pictures, and to the theatre des Variétés where Odry was superbe. Tomorrow I am going to be very busy making a narticle for the Times,[26] & here are my doings present & to come     I am very sorry to hear of PA's going [27] — it will cost him £ 800 and make mother miserable — he had much better keep the 800 if he has got them, than throw them away upon such an uncertainty. Why be so anxious about repairing losses? — He can live at Boulogne for 200 a year, and his income is that, I suppose — still. As for us please God we shall struggle on, but we must let a part of the house, or the whole, and have one man and so on — There is a chance of 350 [or] 400 a year for me here if I like it — poor Battier is dying, & his place is worth as much; but then I throw away a very good position in London, where I can make as much, and a little fame into the bargain — I feel uncomfortable at the notion of all these chops and changes; and sorry to think of father meditating a move — all our present ills have come upon us by attempting to force fortune, and this is but another speculation — if it were to fail — if he, not a very young man, were to find the climate disagree with him — what has he to do? — to come back poorer than ever, or to stay & not live long enough for money-earning — Let us have none of it. Try and see if you can let the house, or at any rate

---

[26] "The Exhibition at Paris," which appeared in *The Times* on April 5.

[27] Major Carmichael-Smyth planned to return to India to recoup his fortune, much as does Colonel Newcome in chapter 26 of *The Newcomes.*

decrease the establishment. My game as far as I see it is to stick to the Times — I don't know quite what I am writing about, being all of a ferment with this ugly news, — if my veto goes for anything PA will not leave the country on a speculation — and so God bless my dearest wifey & all at home, and the little Toby of all, who may be there for what we know. —

Wensdy My dearest Puss — I have got out of bed & am sitting in my shemee just on purpose to say good night to you. I have been writing all day. There came a letter from FitzGerald, & 1 from my G-Mother which has been 48 hours on the road it is trop fort. Good night, & kiss babby for me.

Thursday. I have just come from seeing Marion Delorme [28] a tragedy of Victor Hugo, and am so disgusted and sick with the horrid piece that I have hardly heart to write. The last act ends with an execution, & you are kept waiting a long hour listening to the agonies of parting lovers, & grim speculations about head-chopping, dead-bodies, coffins & what not — Bah! I am as sick as if I had taken an emetic. I have been writing all day, & finished and dispatched an article for the Times. My next visit will be to the Spanish pictures, the next to Versailles & on Monday week, please God, I will be home with my dearest little woman — not having done a great deal it is true, but somewhat — and having learnt the good of home if nothing else. poor Battier is a little better, & there are some hopes for him. Fancy him dying and his wife and 4 children without a penny! — I dined at Crowe's — he is always doing some benevolent action, and has got a new friend to be kind to — a Doctor Wright. Living at Saint Germain, having a family and gaining 48 pounds a year by teaching. This nasty play has made me lugubrious — otherwise I don't know why I entertain you with such dismal tales. O'Donnell gave me and Darley a dinner yesterday at Terre's,[29] where the waiter asked me for Madame. I felt a kind of pleasure in seeing even his ugly face. O Toby Toby what a thing is sentiment! — The carriages are all tearing about the streets, this is mi-careme, and there are a dozen

[28] First performed in 1831.
[29] Terré's Tavern, celebrated in "The Ballad of Bouillabaisse."

masked balls — I don't like going alone, specially as I must be up & at work at 8 in the morning — I get 15 francs a day from Galignani while I stop; there is not much trouble except to go there 3 times every day. God bless my dearest wife.

Saturday. I wrote nothing yesterday preferring to go to bed and have the luxury of reading your letter at ease. I was all day at the Spanish Gallery, then chez ta mere where I dined, having first broken my promise & paid a visit to my Grandmother. To day I have been to Versailles, and afterwards to the Opera with a stall w^h M^r Galignani gave me. It was a benefit, and all sorts of oddities from all sorts of theatres were played, everything intolerably tedious except an act from a very old opera — Orpheus by Gluck, w^h was neither more nor less than sublime — Dupré [30] is the most delightful tenor I ever heard with a simplicity and beauty of voice and method quite delicious — as good as Rubini without his faults — singing his notes steadily, with no tricks or catches or quavers — and such music! — like very fine Mozart, so exquisitely tender and simple and melodious that by all the Gods, I never heard anything like it. The Versailles Gallery is a humbug — a hundred gilded rooms, with looking glasses and carved ceilings, and two thousand bad pictures to ornament them. There is not 1 in the whole collection, that I would care to see again.[31] You see I have got a little settled, just as I am going away; please God I shall be at home on Monday week — o quel bonheur; I don't think I will ever leave you again my dear little woman. Poor Jane began to talk about you, and burst out crying, in a kind of agony. I am glad to find she loves you so much poor thing: and I made her give me a kiss to bring to you. Part of her grief is love for you, part is exquisite wretchedness I do believe — She has no one to love or to speak to: and your mothers solicitude only makes matters worse. We must have her to England that's flat: I got 1/2 a moment to tell her so alone — if he could but manage the old lady! — I am

[30] Gilbert-Louis Duprez (1806–1896) and Giovanni Battista Rubini (1795–1854) were among the most famous tenors of their time.

[31] "Meditations at Versailles" in *The Paris Sketch Book* was inspired by this visit.

wretched myself to think of the profound wretchedness of this poor little girl. for so it must be. Let us see what can be done to comfort her, and give her a little something to pour her heart into: for it is dammed up as it were, & must take all sorts of unnatural channels to give itself vent. Your Ma & I are on the best terms possible, & have not had the shadow of a row. God bless my wife, I shall keep this little scrap for tomorrow.

Sunday. A glorious warm day after snow frost & rain yesterday — As soon as my work is over I am going to Choisy le Roi, where I shall pass the night — A very few days more and I shall be at home with my dear little Toby. I was going to say I w$^d$ not write any more, but I will, it is a comfort to me to talk to you for a minute everyday. Dont be alarmed about Janey, she is very well, but profoundly bored — perhaps your Mother's excessive attention to her only makes her more unhappy. My G. M. in despair has gone into a boarding house till 1 May. Nobody sent her a line or said what was a doing — God bless you —


121.                    TO JAMES FRASER
                        APRIL 1838 [32]

Hitherto unpublished.

Dear Fraser

I have been in town since Tuesday, but have been so busy as not to be able to come down to you. Here is a Yellowplush,[33] rather long but the whole must go in, for the story (w$^h$ wants another part to complete it) w$^d$ be spoiled by being split into 3. I say nothing — but I should not be surprised if you sent me a fifty pound note for it — I think it by far the best of the Yellowplush bunch — the last is infamous I will send the picture in a day or two, but hope to call

[32] Written shortly after Thackeray's return to London, which seems to have taken place on Tuesday, April 3.

[33] The first part of "Mr. Deuceace at Paris," published in *Fraser's Magazine* for May. The story's concluding installments, for it was split into three after all, appeared in June and July.

before then. The fact is after bullying you about money matters I am rather ashamed to show my face. How goes it with you? Well I hope.

Very truly yrs

W. M. Thackeray

122.            TO  GEORGE  WRIGHT
                  23  MAY  1838

Hitherto unpublished. *Endorsed:* Thackeray W^m | 13 G^t Coram S^t | May 23 | 38.

13 Great Coram Street.

Wednesday. 23 May.

My dear Sir

My terms were twenty *guineas* for the 24 pages [34] — such rich men as you and M^r Tilt must not rob me of my shillings — Twenty guineas, and of course no bills.

I shall see M^r Cruikshank in the course of the week, and will talk over matters with him. The plan is the most difficult matter of all.

Truly yours

W. M. Thackeray

G. Wright Esq^re

[34] Of "Stubbs's Calendar; or, The Fatal Boots," which appeared with illustrations by Cruikshank in *The Comic Almanack for 1839*. This volume was published by Charles Tilt (1797–1861), a very successful book and print dealer, who had offices at 86 Fleet Street. Wright was evidently one of his associates. See Henry Vizetelly's *Glances Back through Seventy Years*, 2 vols. (London, 1893), I, 104–105 and 108–110.

123.                    TO MRS. SHAWE
                        12 JULY 1838

*Address:* M*rs* Shawe. | 2 Avenue Marbœuf. | Champs Elysées | a Paris. *Post-marks:* LONDON 12 JUL 1838, CALAIS 14 JUIL. 1838. Hitherto un-published.

13 Great Coram Street Brunswick Sq*e*
Thursday. 12. July. 1838.

My dear M*rs* Shawe.

We had intended to keep profoundly secret an event w*h* has just occurred. M*rs* Thack after walking to Piccadilly on Monday, and eating a tolerable dinner requested me to fetch a medical gentle-man w*h* I did, and on my return had the pleasure to find another Miss Thackeray [35] arrived in my family, and her mother just as unconcerned as if nothing had happened. the child is hideous of course, but when I left home in the morning I left Isabella per-fectly happy, giving her a nice milk breakfast: and as cool and as comfortable as any woman possibly could be. I sent in the pride of my heart the announcement of her delivery to some of the papers the day after the event occurred; but on returning home it was resolved that the advertisement should be withdrawn, and that neither you nor my mother sh*d* be written to, until 3 or 4 days were over and all anxiety at an end. Fancy my disgust at finding that, after all, the announcement had got into an evening paper, on Tuesday: though the Editor had promised me solemnly to with-draw it. I only learned the news ten minutes ago, and hope in heaven you may not have seen it, for you might be anxious about dear Isabella's condition, and think there were some painful reasons for our withholding the news. No such things thank God! She produces children with a remarkable facility. She is as happy and as comfortable as any woman can be.

We have got a new nurse a very good one, and a most excellent, watchful, tender nurse in Mary: [36] who is about her, and keeps

[35] Jane Thackeray, *Genealogy* (102).
[36] Mary Graham.

the house for me, and performs all the kind offices for her and the baby á merveille. We have been [none] the worse I assure you for being alone: th⟨e last⟩ time there were too many cooks to our ⟨broth,⟩ all excellent ones: but I make a vow that for the 15 next confinements there shall not be more than *one*. I am now going home to write to my mother and my grandmother and M⟨rs⟩ Sterling and the Colonel 37 and M⟨rs⟩ Buller, and to carry to Isabella a nice copy of the Pickwick Papers w⟨h⟩ my friend FitzGerald has just given me for her.

Miss Thackeray on seeing her new sister wanted to poke one of her eyes out and said teedle deedle, w⟨h⟩ is considered very clever. The Doctor in attendance is no less a person than Sir Charles Herbert 38 the very pink of accoucheurs.

I find everything perfectly as well on coming home as I left; there is no symptom to occasion the least anxiety, she is perfectly well without any fever, and sound asleep: so sound that I don't like to wake her: but I think I may send you her love without.

Yours in the greatest possible haste

W M T.

## 124. TO GEORGE WRIGHT
### JULY 1838

My text is taken from an undated George D. Smith catalogue.

July

Dear Sir,

You need be under no alarm about the other months, as soon as I have finished my Fraser Paper 39 which will take me a week, I shall go to work again on the Almanac.

Yours ever

W. M. T.

37 Colonel Shawe.
38 Sir Charles Lyon Herbert (d. 1855), M. D.
39 "Mr. Yellowplush's Ajew," *Fraser's Magazine*, August, pp. 195–200.

125.   FROM MRS. THACKERAY TO MRS. SHAWE
23 JULY 1838

*Address:* M<sup>rs</sup> Shawe. | 2 Avenue Marbœuf | Champs Elysées | a Paris. *Post-marks:* LONDON 27 JUL 1838, ANGLETERRE PAR CALAIS 29 JUIL. 1838. Hitherto unpublished.

July 23<sup>rd</sup>

My dearest Mam — Tomorrow being post day and fearing William will not have time to write as I know there is somebody coming this evening to talk upon some business, I will write you a few lines myself. We are perfectly well that is the babe & self, indeed to tell you the truth, I have been so for the last fortnight lying in bed, Doctor, Nurse &c. have been all a farce, but after the bad business we made of it last time I was determined to submit to black dose, castor oil pills, or any other abomination that was ordered the fruits of which, or rather Gods good will I have not had a particle of fever and *I nurse* the dear little No 2 most comfortably and she thrives every hour thank God — Great fat deedle deedle, is extremely fond of her sister, but shows her affection in rather a rough manner, she would willingly poke out little 2's eyes or pull her out of ones arms by her long robes, all out of pure love, she hushes her to sleep and exclaims, oh! oh! in a very patronising manner. She held out her fat arms that the small babe might be put in but that was an experiment we were not willing to try, I am happy to say she promises fair to walk alone in a short time she can already go a short distance. Would Janey like to be Godmama to the little one? as I purpose calling her Jane. Before I was confined I had bought her a book which I intended W Ritchie to have taken for her birthday the 2 July — I have also got those lives for you I told you of so long ago. I must look out for another opportunity to send them.

Janey's book are the memories of Oberlin, a good old pastor of the Alps.[40] W's friend FitzGerald made me a present of a hand-

---

[40] *Memoirs of John Frederic Oberlin, Pastor of Waldbach* (1830), a compilation which had considerable popularity among pious readers in England and America.

some book to amuse me while in my room; it was very attentive of him I must now say dear Mama that I wish more than ever that the misunderstanding between you and M. G.[41] was cleared off — she has been to me every thing the most affectionate sister could have been, not sparing herself any trouble, that nothing should retard my recovering speedily and making such arrangements as tended to every ones comfort      I wish she could herself speak

with you to convince you she never entertained such ideas as you supposed she did but for a very short space of time, when W convinced her she laboured under a strange mistake.[42]

Tell Jane how charmed her sister is with her continued letters — it is very affectionate of her to write so often.

Isabella is obliged to give her baby a dinner: and I to go down to mine: she bids me shut up and say goodbye.

W. M. T.

126.      TO GEORGE WRIGHT
4 SEPTEMBER 1838

Hitherto unpublished.

Sep 4/38

Dear Sir

I send you Nos 4. 5. 6.[43] — No 3 I have in my head — and likewise No 7      I hope to fix on No 8 in the course of the day: and will send the four subjects immediately to Mᵣ Cruikshank.

Yrs in great haste
W. M. T.

[41] Mary Graham.
[42] The remainder of the letter is in Thackeray's hand.
[43] Of "Stubbs's Calendar."

127. TO ?GEORGE WRIGHT
4 SEPTEMBER 1838

Hitherto unpublished.

Sept$^r$ 4/38

My dear Sir

I have just sent to M$^r$ Cruikshank the subjects for the four next illustrations: and shall have the text of them for you in the course of the week. Will you send me the 10. .10 we talked of by the bearer: for I may consider the half as fairly done I should think. I have a little child lying sadly ill in my house: if please God she recovers: the other 4, subjects at least, and I hope writing too, will be in your hands next week.

I am very truly yours
W. M. Thackeray.

I enclose you the letter to Cruikshank for your satisfaction — if you know his address please dispatch it: if not perhaps you will let a boy carry it to his house whither he told me to forward his letters.

128. TO GEORGE CRUIKSHANK
4 SEPTEMBER 1838 [44]

Hitherto unpublished.

My dear Cruikshank —

In May. Ensign Tims is sitting with the Miss Crotty whom you have before drawn, her father and his own father and mother and the Doctor at tea. The Old Shoemaker whom Tims swindled out of the boots in March makes his appearance: he is Miss Crotty's uncle and by way of a marriage present pulls out the boots in Tim's face — Tim disgusted. the Shoemaker triumphant. Miss Crotty and the rest of the company horrified — the latter turns him off.

June. Ensign Dobble and Lieutenant Tims have been making love to 2 butcher's daughters. The father comes home drunk and

[44] The four subjects for Stubbs's Calendar" described in this letter are those that Thackeray promises to send immediately to Cruikshank in his note of September 4 to Wright.

they fly for refuge to the yard — the moon is shining upon a couple of ghastly carcasses in the slaughter house. Tims is seen in a corner with his sword drawn defending himself against a great bull-dog. Dobble in an agony of fear is on his knees close by the butcher's block. The butcher drunk stands over him with an immense cleaver, and vows that he will have his head off. The parlour door may be opened, and some people observed coming in —

July. Captain Waters the brother of the pretty girl whom Tims rejected for Miss Crotty, meets M.ʳ Tims in a coffee-room at Portsmouth — 2 parties are seen one of military & tother of naval men. Waters a big burly fellow holds Tims by the nose between the 2,

and explains the manner in w.ʰ his sister has been treated. Make about 4 men of each party sitting at a bow window near the sea. ships & so forth. Waiter grinning.

August. He is married at last to a widow with immense property. In a few days the Coach brings down to him half a dozen children of whom he knew nothing. In a month more while they are all at breakfast a strange gentleman appears who arrests M.ʳ Tims for £2000's worth of debts, contracted by his late wife.

Make her a Jewish looking woman; and the bailiff another. The children likewise with a Hebrew look. Make Tims a very military looking man in an immense braided frock coat: the children round him & their Mother he starting from the bum.

I cannot very well keep up the 5 years distance between each adventure and shall alter the little preface at the beginning of January so as to suit it to what comes after

Yrs ever W. M. Thackeray.

129.          FROM EDWARD FitzGERALD
29 NOVEMBER 1838

*Address:* W. M. Thackeray Esqre. | 13. Gͭ Coram Sͭ | Russell Square | London. *Postmarks:* IPSWICH NO 30 1838, 1 DE 1838. Published in part, *Biographical Introductions,* IV, xiv-xvi.

Dear Thackeray,

Thank you for your last letter, as also for the former one accompanying a very beautiful drawing, which I take pleasure in looking at — I am very glad you are engaged in a way of life that you like: that is a good thing indeed, which most people miss — It would seem that I ought to be able & willing to write plenty of letters as I have nothing in the world to do: but it is all I can do now to manage one. When you see Spedding pray remember to tell him that I did write him a letter, which I put into the fire because it was pert: and got nearly through another lately which I abandoned because it was all about nothing — He has so much to do, that one has no right to expect any letter from him: but give him my hearty love — all this you will forget, you rascal —

I will exalt your name as a politician forever if you will contrive to persuade me that we have nothing to fear from the domineering Russia — It is not the present fuss made about her that makes me tremble, but I have always been afraid that she was the Power kept in pickle to overwhelm Europe just as men were beginning to settle into a better state than the World has yet seen — If she were out of the question we should [do] very well —

THE

# LIBRARY

OF

# USELESS KNOWLEDGE

BY

ATHANASIUS GASKER, ESQ. F.R.S. &c. &c.

LONDON
WILLIAM PICKERING
MDCCCXXXVII

C. WHITTINGHAM          PRICE FIVE SHILLINGS          TOOKS COURT CHANCERY LANE

THE COVER OF EDWARD WILLIAM CLARKE'S
"LIBRARY OF USELESS KNOWLEDGE"

There is but one
Whose being we do fear. & under her
Our Genius is rebuked, as it is said
Marc Antony's was by Caesar — [45]

Another illustrious Author [46] says "Joy to the Jews, & Russia pays the expense &c" [47] — but this is in the way of Revelations, & there-

[45] *Macbeth*, III, i, 54–57.

[46] During 1837 there was published in London Part I of *The Library of Useless Knowledge* "by Athanasius Gasker, Esq. F. R. S. &c. &c.," a pamphlet of fifty-two pages devoted entirely to an "Auto-Biographical Sketch of the Editor." This curious production, of which no further portions appeared, was written by Edward William Clarke, who took his B. A. degree at Jesus College, Cambridge, in 1829, and later became Rector of Yeldham in Essex. He was the son of Edward Daniel Clarke (1769–1822), traveller, antiquary, and Professor of Mineralogy at Cambridge, and certain aspects of his father's history and character are reflected in his account of Athanasius Gasker. Neither FitzGerald nor Thackeray seems to have known Clarke, but both had been interested in his strange personality by William Williams, with whom he had been intimate while at Cambridge, and to FitzGerald's zeal we owe the only fragment of Clarke's writing, apart from *The Library of Useless Knowledge*, that has been preserved, a prologue which he wrote for private theatricals at Cambridge. (*Letters and Literary Remains*, ed. Wright, IV, 112; and I, 92–93.)

The reputation of *The Library of Useless Knowledge* never extended beyond the circle of Cambridge men to which Thackeray belonged, and today Athanasius Gasker is altogether forgotten. Yet his memoirs are not altogether unworthy of a place in the literary tradition that includes *The Tale of a Tub*, *Tristram Shandy*, and *Sartor Resartus*, though more extravagant and obscure than any of these. Athanasius dwells on three episodes in his eventful career: his attempt to draw attention to his writings by attacking the Lord Mayor of London (pp. 4–10); his dispersal of a secret meeting of the higher English clergy convoked to censure his *Tenebræ; or, The Invisible Visible*, a work in six folio volumes (pp. 12–30); and his abortive lecture at Pedaster House on *The Sexes of Facts, or the Economy of Discussion*, one of his later publications (pp. 32–47). On this framework is erected an astonishing structure of broad farce, parody, subtle humor, and burlesque erudition. But as FitzGerald points out (*Letters and Literary Remains*, ed. Wright, I, 136–137), it is Clarke's inimitable peculiarities of style that give him his place as a humorist. "I suppose this would be the most untranslateable book in the world," Fitz-Gerald writes. "I never shall forget how I laughed when I first read it."

The only copy of *The Library of Useless Knowledge* that I have seen is in the Library of Congress.

[47] *Library of Useless Knowledge*, p. 49.

fore inexplicable — I study Clarke's book more & more, & see something new every time. Do you know anything of a 2ⁿᵈ part — The last delicate touch that I became aware of was when, after the catastrophe at Pedaster House, Mrs Gurley carries off Athanasius in *her gig*, which was waiting for her at the door — [48] You will herewith draw Mrs Gurley's gig — Thank you for your desire that I should come on a visit to you in London. I have been within an ace of coming up: but I do not think I shall now. Your accounts of Jack [49] are very fine — I have been staying two days with Donne who contributes to his Review, & is a very delightful fellow. If you ask Jack about him I dare say he will inform you in a whisper that he is one of the most distinguished Generals alive — My sisters and brother in law broke out into just praises of your Yellowplush the other day, not knowing who had written it: so I had the satisfaction of insinuating with an air of indifference that I knew the Author well — They are also not quite certain but that I wrote it myself: so that I gain every way — I see poor old Macready toiling away at the Tempest 3 times a week: the papers talk of there being full houses: but I conclude that that is undoubtedly a lie. Miss Horton [50] must be a pretty Ariel: there is some knavishness in the expression of her face which must be suitable — Now farewell dear Thackeray & make my duty to my Lady, & believe me ever yrs

E. Fitzgerald —

P.S. If you happen to go to Edmonton, or to meet Mrs Gurley in her gig between that place & London, do not forget to give her my Compᵗˢ

"Here one of the Bishops was sick, & was obliged to be taken out: — I did *not hear what became of him* — " [51]
Who can write like that! —

Thursday. November 29 —

[48] The same, p. 47.
[49] John Kemble.
[50] Priscilla Horton (1818–1895), later Mrs. German Reed.
[51] *Library of Useless Knowledge*, p. 22.

130.            TO THOMAS BARNES? ⁵²
                29 NOVEMBER 1838

My text is taken from a facsimile in *Centenary Biographical Introductions*, VI, opposite p. xviii. *Endorsed* (by Thackeray): February 1858. Found in an old portfolio.

                              13 Great Coram Sᵗ
                              29 November 1838

My dear Sir:

I beg to send you my account with the Times ⁵³ for November & remain

                Your very faithful Servᵗ
                W. M. Thackeray.

The Times to W M Thackeray.

| Novʳ | | | |
|---|---|---|---|
| 2 | Annuals | 2 1/4 | |
| 8 | Steam in the Pacific | 3/4 | |
| 12 | Henry V. | 3 1/4 | |
| 16 | Fraser | 2 1/4. | |
| 27 | Krasinski | 1 1/2. | |

                    10.   0.

                £21 .. 0 .. 0

⁵² Barnes (1785–1841) was editor of *The Times* from 1817 to 1841.

⁵³ The full titles of the articles listed below are: "The Annuals," "Steam Navigation in the Pacific," "Tyler's Life of Henry V," "Fraser's Winter Journey to Persia," and "Count Valerian Krasinski's History of the Reformation in Poland." The first, third, and fourth are printed in *Centenary Works*, XXV, 125–160.

131.          TO BRYAN WALLER PROCTER? [54]
                 29 DECEMBER 1838 [55]

Hitherto unpublished.

13 Great Coram Street
Saturday Dec.ʳ 29.

My dear Sir.

The Russell Institution [56] is open to anyone who chooses to pay a yearly subscription of 3 guineas: but the library is very meagre, though large: it is good for English history, law, topography & so on: has not fifty French books & no others: but I have a catalogue at my house and if you ever wander in such a direction it is at your service. Brunswick Square ought to be respectable being only accessible to the gig-keepers.

We are as well and merry as you can wish us: we invariably have a repast of mutton chops at 6, and if you will favor us with a visit I will ask Spedding and we will have a great pipe-smoking

I am concerned to see in the Morning Chronicle that Lady Morgan's [57] eyes are so weak that her ladyship is obliged to forego all literary occupation.

Ever yours

W. M. Thackeray

[54] See *Memoranda*. There appears to have been some private joke between Thackeray and the Procters about Lady Morgan's eyes. Thackeray recurs to the topic in a letter to Mrs. Procter written early in 1839.

[55] During the years Thackeray lived in Great Coram Street December 29 fell on a Saturday only in 1838.

[56] A subscription library in Russell Square. It was housed in a building originally intended for assemblies and balls (Henry B. Wheatley [and Peter Cunningham], *London, Past and Present*, 3 vols., London, 1891, III, 191), and Thackeray later noted its "melancholy appearance of faded greatness" (*Works*, V, 339).

[57] The former Sydney Owenson (1783?–1859), who had married Sir Charles Morgan in 1812. She was the author of a number of mediocre novels and had in later years a considerable position in London society. As is pointed out above (*Memoranda*, Theresa Reviss), Professor Stevenson has found certain parallels between her career and that of Becky Sharp.

132.                    TO MRS. PROCTER [1]
                       JANUARY 1839? [2]

Hitherto unpublished. My text is taken from a transcript given Lady Ritchie
by George Murray Smith.

My dear Mrs Procter,

   I have found a part of the fatal boots and have the honour to
lay them at your feet.

                        [*sketch*]
         EXPLANATION OF THE HALLEGORY.

as is shewn in the annexed historical picture (the pen was
so good for this work that I could not refrain)     The
elegant young man represents the 2dy Postman. The
pages tipify, the 22 duodecimos. The beef-eater the satisfaction of the author, who has so often served you in that
capacity. Her Majesty on the Throne is —— (a lady whose
*hair* has been most passionately admired by the celebrated
author of the Lives of Eminent Statesmen[3]). She looks
somewhat stern at the audacious offer of the postman who
is supposed with the utmost humility to ask pardon for his
venturing into her presence, with such a load.

           Vivat Regina. No money returned.
           Children in arms NOT admitted.

   I stop the pens to ask if you have seen an attack on Mrs Jameson [4]
in the Times this morning. I am the author of course: as of the
article on Procter — in this last one against poor Mrs J. I think I

---

   [1] See *Memoranda*.
   [2] This letter was almost certainly written early in 1839. "Stubbs's Calendar;
or, The Fatal Boots" appeared in *The Comic Almanack for 1839*, which was
placed on sale shortly before the Christmas holidays in 1838, and Thackeray's
concern at the state of Lady Morgan's eyes continues the joke begun in his
letter of December 29, 1838.
   [3] John Forster, who published *Lives of the Statesmen of the Commonwealth*
between 1836 and 1839 as part of Dr. Lardner's *Cabinet Cyclopaedia*. See
*Memoranda*.
   [4] Anna Brownell Jameson (1794–1860), a poetess and miscellaneous writer
of some repute, had recently published *Winter Studies and Summer Sketches in*

have been as disgustingly offensive vulgar and impertinent and cowardly as I ever was in my life. I really don't think I ever matched it.

I had very nearly found out the name of the panegyrist of Ben Johnson last night — it is a young Scotch reporter of the paper, and a very silly unfortunate fellow as my informant gives me to understand.

What do you think of my having dined at Power's [5] on Sunday where Forster was, who did not say a single rude thing during the whole evening! Lady Morgan's eyes are still I regret to say in such a state as to preclude [6] the possibility of her Ladyship's engaging in any literary avocation.

I am always, dear Mrs Procter,<br>Faithfully yours,<br>W. M. Thackeray.

P. S. I think I may ask pardon here for writing all the above nonsense and so much of it. I have been thus long precisely because I have got some very pressing work to do, and should have been employed about anything else.

133.          TO JOHN MITCHELL KEMBLE
          MARCH 1839?

*Address:* J. M. Kemble Esq[re] Hitherto unpublished.

Dear Johann.

I send the 1st part of the Article [7] — It was unluckily begun in the middle and I could not get it before. On Tuesday or Wed you

---

*Canada,* and Procter had just brought out an edition of *The Works of Ben Jonson, with a Memoir.* Thackeray was later instrumental in securing a pension for Mrs. Jameson. See below, No. 786.

  [5] William Grattan Tyrone Power (1797–1841), an Irish comic actor.

  [6] The transcript reads *produce.*

  [7] Probably Thackeray's long notice of the "Speeches of Henry, Lord Brougham," which was published in *The British and Foreign Review* of April, 1839. But the reference may be to another article, which has not been identified.

shall have the rest 15 pages or so — the present I take to be about 25.

Yours till Deth

W. M. T.

Not a single soul except my wife, knows what I have been doing. —

134.     TO MRS. CARMICHAEL-SMYTH
MARCH 1839

*Address:* M*ʳˢ* Carmichael Smyth. Published in part, *Thackeray and his Daughter*, pp. 5–6.

My dearest Mother. The India Bill, wʰ had 3 months to run, I sent to Lubbock's to get accepted, for it would have required 2 visits on my part to the City and is better done by them — Young Price was to carry sundry letters and the map of India and was to set off the week before last — we have been so careless as never to ask whether he *has* set off but I will send tomorrow and learn particulars. Isabella will tell you how we have been gadding to Gravesend, and how dear little Pussy enjoyed the trip: it was delightful & the wind and the sunshine have made me pleasantly tipsy as it were, for I am not used to them in London wʰ generates sluggishness of body and often mind too — I wish I could afford more frequent trips one to Paris above all for profit as well as for pleasure but it is not unprobable that something may turn up to keep me in London for the whole of the summer or at least within reach of it —

What shall I say to you about our little darling who is gone? [8] — I don't feel sorrow for her, and think of her only as something charming that for a season we were allowed to enjoy: when Anny was very ill dying as I almost thought, it seemed to me wrong to pray for her life, for specific requests to God are impertinencies I think, and all we should ask from him is to learn how to acquiesce

[8] Jane Thackeray died on March 14, when she was little more than eight months old. Memories of her death inspired the last paragraphs of chapter 12 of *The Great Hoggarty Diamond*.

and now I would be almost sorry — no that is not true — but I would not ask to have the dear little Jane back again and subject her to the degradation of life and pain. O God watch over us too, and as we may think that Your Great heart yearns towards the innocent charms of these little infants, let us try and think that it will have tenderness for us likewise who have been innocent once, and have, in the midst of corruption, some remembrances of good still. Sometimes I fancy that at the judgement time the little one would come out and put away the sword of the angry angel I think her love for us and her beautiful purity would melt the Devil himself — Nonsense, you know what I mean. We have sent to Heaven a little angel who came from us & loved us and God will understand her language & visit us mildly — Why write you this mad stuff dearest Mother? — God bless you and all besides        I shall write G. M: and thank her for her money & use it too —

Your affte W M T

135.        TO GEORGE CRUIKSHANK<br>MAY? 1839

*Address:* George Cruikshank Esq$^{re}$ — | Amwell Street | Pentonville. Published in part by Mrs. Anne Lyon Haight, "Charles Dickens Trys to Remain Anonymous," *Colophon*, New Series, IV (1939), 45.

My dear Cruikshank

Enclosed is a programme [9] w$^h$ Wright & I concocted — Tilt had a plan too of his own but it is impracticable — You may take any liberties of course, & when you have done the first 4 plates I will make the writing.

I wanted to tell you of an event w$^h$ need not much alarm you — I heard Dickens sing 'Lord Bateman', and went home straight and made a series of drawings to it: w$^h$ are now in part on the copper: & sold to a publisher. Only 2 days ago I heard that you were occu-

[9] For "Barber Cox and the Cutting of his Comb," a story written by Thackeray and illustrated by Cruikshank, which appeared in the *Comic Almanack for 1840.*

pied ⟨with⟩ the same subject.¹⁰ I'm not such a fool as to suppose that
my plates can hurt yours: but warning is fair between friends and I
hope thro' death and eternity we shall always be such

Yours ever

W M T.

136.            FROM MRS. THACKERAY TO
               MRS. CARMICHAEL-SMYTH
                    15 MAY 1839

*Address:* Mʳˢ Carmichael Smyth. Hitherto unpublished.

May 15ᵗʰ
13 Gt Coram St
Brunswick Sqᵉ

My dearest Mother. You will be wondering at our not writing. I
had prepared a packet to send by William Ritchie as well as the song
for Mary & a Mag for you but by some unlucky mischance William
could not recollect the number of W R's abode so I must send by
Robert Smyth who in a promiscuous manner gave me to understand if I sent anything to him it would eventually reach Paris. We
have just received your letter of the 12ᵗʰ Mama might just as well
have written herself to say when we might expect her. Certainly
she has strange ideas of things, for if all the world were too proud
to ask slight favors or accept them, what a nice world it would [be]
and it is merely rather a proof of an ungenerous spirit to like to

¹⁰ *The Loving Ballad of Lord Bateman* was published with Cruikshank's
illustrations shortly before June 15 (*Spectator*, 1839, p. 568). There now
seems no reason to doubt that this version of a story long familiar in ballad
lore came, as the "Warning to the Public" in Cruikshank's edition states, from
the repertory of a public singer who performed on Saturday nights outside a
wine-vaults in Battle-bridge. Dickens (*Letters*, ed. Dexter, I, 216) supplied
the burlesque editorial apparatus and made minor alterations in the text, but
Thackeray, to whom for many years the authorship of the ballad has been
ascribed, had no hand in it. His drawings were first published by Lady
Ritchie in 1892 ("Lord Bateman: A Ballad," *Harper's Magazine*, LXXXVI,
124–129), after having lain *perdus* in the drawer of an old table for half a
century. The originals are now in the Morgan Library.

lay others under obligations to you but to consider it too great a tax
for oneself, cherishing a spirit of pride incompatible with the de-
nomination of Christian however as S: Paul says "Judge not for in
that thou judgest another thou condemnest thyself.¹¹ Though I do
[not] think *we* have this fault I am sure we have many others as or
more blameable seeing that it has pleased God to make us more
clearsighted in some things.  Now as I fancy my *practice* will avail
me more than preaching for some time to come I will turn to other
matters.  My dear Mother we see *no* necessity *under* the *sun* why
you should tear your dear heart and make us unhappy by thinking
of India Besides there was a report that Charley Buller was to be a
cabinet minister and if so there might [be] a chance of getting
something for you or for us.  It would be better for you because I
doubt if William would like any regular work half so much as
what he is doing now.  And when we are in a straight Pa has always
something to pull out of his purse, but I fear it would not be so if
the tables were turned though I assure you I keep my account very
right and W complains how little money he is allowed to spend and
how M⁽ʳˢ⁾ T. will ask how!  We met Charles Buller at M⁽ʳ⁾ Carlyles
yesterday he laughed & joked about it but of course neither said
yea or nay.  They say to gain the support of the Rads they must
give some of them office  I am almost afraid to talk politics in a
letter but as this goes by hand I confess we were rather disappointed
as there was an insurrection ¹² that it was not a good one.  But this
is very foolish to say, we rejoice to think you are living in the
Avenue St Marie and do not pray be too venturesome into the heart
of Paris     John Kemble has payed us the money ¹³ which, W.
will replace immediately     We were so thankful to Pa for such
prompt assistance I had spent my last £ I think we should be foolish
not to take in M⁽ʳ⁾ Waller.¹⁴ he is perfectly gentlemanlike and quiet

¹¹ *Romans*, 2, 1.
¹² There is an account of this Parisian *émeute* in *The Times* of May 15.
The Thackerays and the Carmichael-Smyths were fervent republicans who
would have welcomed the fall of the July Monarchy.
¹³ For Thackeray's article in the April *British and Foreign Review*.
¹⁴ Procter's younger brother, the former Nicholas Procter, who had in 1816
changed his name to Waller in consideration of being made the heir of Bryan

and it would be a great anxiety off one's mind to know one was living rent free  Any who could despise us for being honest would not be worth retaining in one's friendship and M^r and M^rs Procter use all their influence to induce their brother to come where he would have the luck of such nice host & hostess.  He has not yet made up his mind.  Should he not come we have no fear for the future      I must say good bye

I must put up this for being in a hurry. — J. Kemble has just paid and I restore with thanks £ 30.[15]


137.          TO MRS. CARMICHAEL-SMYTH
                        16? MAY 1839

Hitherto unpublished.

My dearest Mammy.  M^rs Shawe and Jane are up-stairs, and we have passed a very amicable evening together and I can't do better than send you a half sheet to wind up the evening.  Jacky Kemble has just paid me 34£ and so I can send back 30 with a great deal of thanks: not because I wouldn't keep such a sum, but because I don't want it and it is much better with Pa than with me.  Fancy my in-genuity in carrying Isabella's letter to the J. U. Service Club [16] for Bob with a heap of others, and leaving it there unsealed with the money in it, for 4 hours, and finding it afterwards quite safe — to go I hope tomorrow by the Captain and the young Barrowknight. Don't think ab^t India for a minute or two I do believe that Chas Buller is going to be a Cabinet Minister, and then who knows what may happen.  Pa may get an Island of Barataria [17] with me for secretary but let us wait for this or give up the scheme altogether for I am sure at our time of life India would be unhealthy, and why

Waller, the wealthy great-uncle for whom Procter was named (Armour, *Barry Cornwall*, pp. 42–43).

[15] This final paragraph is in Thackeray's hand.

[16] The Junior United Service Club at 11 Charles Street.  Bob was Captain Robert Carmichael-Smyth.

[17] See *Don Quixote*, Part II, chapters 44 to 53.

not stay at home in Paris or Boulogne that is, where your little will keep you as well & happy as you can be anywhere else. I think quite different from you that the proceeding of the Queen [18] has been the most disgustingly unconstitutional insolent and arbitrary of any that ever was known. Don't talk about the spirit of a woman — the Queen has no business to be a woman. She is a machine worked by ministers, and a set of Whig chambermaids about a dull, obstinate, vain, silly creature like this little Vick are enough to pull down the institutions of the whole country. The rascally, lying, pettifogging Whigs were beaten — never mind by whom — but deservedly beaten and they came back — how? upon the shoulders of the maids of honour. Fye psha, pooh, nonsense, for shame, humbug: I am furious at the cant w$^h$ makes a saint out of the self willed vulgar little mind, w$^h$ has no right for the sake of her little partialities to stop the march of parties in England or to put an end to the fair strife and tug w$^h$ has been the welfare of our country as I think. All this (only better expressed) I wrote to the Chronicle, but the Chronicle wdnt have it and I must try something else     Isabella is against the Chron: & so indeed am I, but I have never rejected it; and am now only waiting to know what they want.

In the meantime I have got a world of business to do: and must set to this very minute. So farewell. Our lodger has made up his mind to come in at the beginning of the next quarter — I don't much relish it: but needs must — God bless you dearest Mother and all at the Havynew     your affectionate

WMT.
I T.
A. I. T.

Who has got the loveliest frock in the world.

[18] In the so-called "Bedchamber Crisis." Queen Victoria's favorite, Lord Melbourne, had resigned as Prime Minister on May 8. The Queen asked Sir Robert Peel to form a ministry but obstinately refused to remove certain of her ladies-in-waiting who were Whig in sympathy. Peel would not act in the face of this opposition, and the Queen was enabled to recall Melbourne. His reconstructed ministry remained in office for more than two years. See Sir

138.　　　　　　　　TO HENRY COLE [19]
　　　　　　　　　　　　JUNE 1839

My text is taken from Cole's *Fifty Years of Public Work* (London, 1884), II, 143.

Dear Sir, I shall be glad to do a single drawing, series, or what you will for *money*, but I think the one you sent me would not be effective enough for the Circular: [20] the figures are too many for so small a sized block, and the meaning mysterious — the river to be a river should occupy a deuce of a space. [*Sketch*] Even this fills up your length almost. What do you think of a howling group with this motto, 'GIVE US OUR DAILY BREAD;' the words are startling. Of course I will do the proposed design if you wish it.

139.　　　　　　　　TO HENRY COLE
　　　　　　　　　　　　JUNE 1839

Hitherto unpublished.

My dear Sir,

　I sh[d] have been delighted to attend your swarry, but must write all night after eight. The block shall be sent you tomorrow without

---

Sidney Lee, *Queen Victoria* (new and rev. ed., London, 1904), pp. 96–103. The unwillingness of the Whig *Morning Chronicle* to accept Thackeray's article is understandable.

　[19] Cole (1808–1882), afterwards (1875) K. C. B., was at this time an assistant keeper in the Record Office, but he had many outside interests. He was the associate of Charles Buller and other liberal politicians, and he had considerable talent as a water-colorist, engraver, and fashioner of *objets d'art*. He was later the most active member of the executive committee for the Great Exhibition of 1851, and from that year until 1873 he served as Secretary of the School of Design in South Kensington. In 1833 he had married Marian Bond, who gave him three sons and five daughters. From 1839 onwards Cole and his family were among Thackeray's intimates.

　[20] The supporters of free trade had established the Anti-Corn-Law League in October, 1838. Their leader Richard Cobden, wishing to secure an illustrator for *The Anti-Corn-Law Circular*, turned for advice to Cole, who was thus enabled to send Thackeray a sketch, the subject of which was suggested by Cobden, showing "Poles offering bread on one side of a stream, and people starving on the other; a demon in the center preventing the exchange" (*Fifty Years of Public Work*, 2 vols., London, 1884, II, 143).

fail at Whitehall. Schönberg [21] sends me a proof of a little vignette w<sup>h</sup> I enclose.

Yours ever

W M T.


140.                    TO HENRY COLE
                    21? JUNE 1839 [22]

*Address:* Henry Cole Esq<sup>re</sup> | Record Office. Whitehall. Published in Cole's *Fifty Years of Public Work,* II, 146.

My dear Sir

I am very sorry to tell you of my misfortunes — I have made 3 etchings on the Schönberg plan of the Anglo-Polish Allegory: and they have all failed — that is the inventor Schönberg considers they are not fit for his process: that is, I fear the process will not succeed *quite* yet.

I shall however do the drawing tomorrow on a wood-block, and will send it you sans faute: unless I hear from you that you are not inclined to deal with a person who has caused so much delay.[23]

Yours ever

W M Thackeray

[21] The inventor of a new process of engraving, which Thackeray had been persuaded to use for his Corn Law designs.

[22] Cole wrote to Cobden on June 22, shortly after the receipt of this letter, to explain why the engraving of the Anglo-Polish allegory had been delayed. Some conception of Thackeray's professional position at this time may be gained from his friend's account of his qualifications. "The artist is a genius," Cole writes (John Morley, *The Life of Richard Cobden,* 2 vols., London, 1881, I, 214–215), "both with his pencil and his pen. His vocation is literary. He is full of humour and feeling. . . . Thackeray is the writer of an article in the last number of the *Westminster Review,* on French caricatures, and many other things. For some time he managed the *Constitutional* newspaper. He is a college friend of Charles Buller." Writing to Cobden, Cole could hardly elaborate on Thackeray's literary connections, the most important of which were with the Tory *Times* and *Fraser's Magazine.*

[23] The two designs by Thackeray that at length appeared in *The Anti-Corn-Law Circular* are reproduced in Cole's *Fifty Years of Public Life,* II, 145.

141.                     TO JAMES FRASER
                           1 JULY 1839

My text is taken from a facsimile in Adrian Joline's *Rambles in Autograph Land* (New York, 1913), p. 195.

13 Gt. Coram S<sup>t</sup> 1 July.

Dear Fraser

Do make up my account now directly — if you owe me so much the better  I am hard up and want money, if you don't, so much the better too, for you that is: and I shall know where I am.

Semipiternally yours<br>W. M. Thackeray.

Impromptu

In case you owe send what you owe<br>In case you don't dont send you know.


142.              FROM MRS. THACKERAY TO
                  MRS. CARMICHAEL-SMYTH
                        3 JULY 1839

*Address:* M<sup>rs</sup> Carmichael Smyth | No 4 Avenue St Marie | Fau<sup>bg</sup> du Roule | a Paris. Hitherto unpublished.

July 3<sup>rd</sup><br>13 Gt Coram St.

My dear Mother.  William received your letter yesterday, and I am preparing this to go with a budget by one of Lady Macleod's manifold brothers.  You fancy us in a nice little cottage at Addlestone a few miles from Windsor no doubt  Annie frisking with young lambs and chirping with birdlings, but no such good luck a letter from *M<sup>rs</sup> J. Kemble* undid all that *magnanimous* John had promised, not that to say the truth we put much faith in his "Spanish Style"  Though they did not find it convenient to lend us the cottage they very generously offered to secure *lodgings in the* *village* for which we were to pay 15 a week. of course we declined the happiness of going there. So William told you how we talked all one day about going to Paris, well, I would not say anything about it because I thought it would tantalize you. He seems to think if he could be secure of parliament not dissolving he *ought* to go, the people *want* his book have *almost* agreed to pay his journey, he would carry an article for the British and Forr'n (as M^rs Crowe says) to do and at present there is very little to do here, of *course* we should go too. that article on Lord Brougham was William's It was very much talked of at the Reform Club.

Stone is doing a Portrait of W.[24] they say it is excellent so I hope he intends to do whats handsome by me and give it to me. Who do you think came to see us today M^rs Polly M^rs Smith of Pennsylvania! We like her very much for your sake, but I confess I should not have been prepossessed by her physiognomy however it is pleasing. She says all the world you knew by some extraordinary chance are to be congregated in the Isle of Wight and she should be so happy if you could transplant yourself there. "The brow" [25] came to see us last night. Fitz who never heard of him before exclaimed, "How handsome he is, what a beautiful brow" this is a fact. People here are "chaumed" with him, and he talks as if he were possessed with fifty thousand tongues. All in the world half the people in the world require is a little excitement to make them happy. I am half cross with Fitz and his tail (M^r Morton [26] forms part of it) They seem as if they could not breathe without William, and thats all very well but they forget they have 300 or 400 a year to take life easy upon, and though we may have *double* that yet it must be earned. I must say that I believe Fitz would give W. his last shill^g and often thinks of what he can do that is obliging to me. I believe he has as much to suffer in other respects as any one. One sister mad and the second that he dearly loves dying of a complaint of the lungs. Then he has to grieve over the

[24] Presumably the portrait reproduced in *Thackeray in the United States* (I, 81), which is, however, dated 1836 by General Wilson.

[25] Not Spedding, who was an intimate friend of FitzGerald, despite No. 112.

[26] See *Memoranda*, Saville Morton.

selfishness and utter heartlessness of his Mother,[27] who does not
seem to care if her children live or die  I wish I was rich sometimes
but if with riches comes such a love of the world as to make one
forgetful of the ties of nature may I ever remain as I am.  Totty
and I were picking daisies and clover in the gardens in Brunswick
Sqe when she had got a handfull she said she must "carry them
home and put [them] in a glass of water" so there they are and
the sweetest nosegay that has adorned our table this year.  Henry [28]
is here and left Mama & Jane well and in good spirits.  He and
Uncle dined with me today.  W. is gone to Greenwich to write
something in peace and quiet pray answer quickly all I asked for
Miss G C. as she asks me whether you have answered without
ceasing.  Fancy M[rs] Macquillavray is going to be married directly
but Miss Fraser desired I would say nothing about it so I have told
you.  She leaves *every* child behind and returns to India the 1st of
August.  The man they say is quite a treasure and I am sure his
affection must be most disinterested.  I wish Annie Fraser married,
I like her so very much I wonder the man did not prefer her to her
sister.  Love to Pa would he like a pair of worked worsted slippers
for next winter?  I have got a large piece of work in hand  I have
accomplished a peony in a bush of green leaves.  Would it be a
good spec to send it to my grandmama in Ireland?  as a pillow
or stool for her drawing room  I wish my Uncle Arthur would
make our little queen daisy his heiress.  But this [is] all vanity saith
the preacher.[29]  I went to the Foundling and heard the Messiah.
I never shall be able to tell what I felt.  It seemed to give one an
idea of what music in Heaven must be.  The only thing to interrupt
the lofty tone it gave to one's thoughts was the Duke of Cambridge's [30] head continually bobbing when the music went slow it
went slow, when the music went fast it went fast so fast that I do
not understand now how he stopped it.  it is constructed on a spring

---

[27] The former Mary Frances FitzGerald (d. 1855), a very talented and
imperious lady, descended from the FitzGeralds of Kildare and wealthy in
her own right, whose devotion to society left her little time for her children.

[28] See *Memoranda*, Henry Shawe.

[29] *Ecclesiastes*, 1, 2.

[30] H. R. H. Prince Adolphus, first Duke of Cambridge (1774–1850).

wire I suppose.  Now good night pray write to us pretty often        I
will try and send you Catherine        Love to PA GM and Mary
and as much as possible to yourself

Ever my dear Mother y<sup>r</sup> aff<sup>t</sup> I T.

Who would like very much you for to see

143.                    TO GEORGE WRIGHT
                          15 JULY 1839

*Address:* G. Wright Esq<sup>re</sup> | Mess<sup>rs</sup> Whitehead & Co | 76 Fleet Street.  *En-
dorsed:* rec<sup>d</sup> July 15/39 address Galignani's.  Hitherto unpublished.

13 GC. Street

My dear Sir

If you receive this time enough please to send me my M.S.[31]
immediately        I am going to Paris for a month & shall stop on
the way 2 days at Boulogne sur mer (letters post paid, *Poste
restante*) where I would finish the 4 first papers according to your
wish.  I will send 4 more from Paris before the 15 of next month,
upon my sacred honour as a nobleman.  I set off tomorrow morning
at 10 exactly up to w<sup>h</sup> time I can receive the MSS. at my house.

Yrs ever

W M T.

144.                TO MRS. CARMICHAEL-SMYTH
                        19 NOVEMBER 1839

*Address:* M<sup>rs</sup> Carmichael Smyth | 4 Avenue Sainte Marie. | Faubourg du
Roule. | Paris.  *Postmarks:* LONDON 19 NOV. 1839, 21 NOV. 39 CALAIS.
Hitherto unpublished.

My dearest Mammy.  If you are wise in paper you will recognize
this 1/2 sheet and where it comes from.  It is part of 'Parents in
India or embarking for India' and here by God's blessing we are
all in Coram Street after a dismal coach-trip, a pleasant passage

---

[31] An outline of "Barber Cox and the Cutting of his Comb."

and nobody sick. Missy is at this moment looking at your picture, in expectation of certain mutton-chops for w$^h$ she is very eager. She did not sleep two hours in the coach-night, and kept us all wide awake like a dear girl, plumping from one person's knees to another and roaring at intervals. On board the steamer as we had to occupy berths in the great cabin, where there lay on the floors, on sofas, tables &c some sixty or seventy other ladies and gentleman, Miss Thackeray was good enough to begin howling at 2 o'clock in the midst of a profound silence, and to continue that exercise until her father and nurse had left their berths and carried her on deck, where she enjoyed the moonlight much. Returning in about an hour to the cabin, she recommenced the amusement of howling, and greatly delighted everybody: for though most people wanted to sleep, they infinitely preferred the contemplation of that dear little babe, to any such vulgar délassement.

I can hear a great clinking & clanking in the next room w$^h$ shews that the mutton-chop discussion has commenced. Missy is as well and brisk as possible, her mother ditto, and I as always better for the sea-trip.

We had M$^{rs}$ Beadle on board with the 2 Pattle girls,[32] who are prettier than their sisters: all the others, 4, are married and multiplying vastly M$^{rs}$ B says: and she adds that M$^{rs}$ P. is adored by her sons-in-law. There's a wonder for you!

This is a very fine day for London indeed, and I can see quite across the back yard where there is a dirty clothes'-line hanging that can be distinguished as clearly as possible. Isabella declares herself satisfied with the piano: and I feel almost as if we hadn't been out of the house, making a vast number of plans as usual, and sporting that grave thoughtful countenance w$^h$ strikes one so on entering London, it always comes upon me at Greenwich, and lasts until I get to Paris. You must not go for to alarm yourself about my infinite struggles hardships & labours every one of them do good — and a man's mind would get flaccid and inert if he were always to have others caring for him, and providing his meat & drink.

The Allens refuse John and I am heartily glad of it: the old

[32] Theodosia and Virginia Pattle.

man has had some inkling of the transaction I think for he looks vastly glum: I'm sure however that we shall be able to keep him, and a coach and four too, for I am more and more convinced of the infinite elasticity of my purse. Look how it shrunk up when I did not want it in Paris: dear Paris, dear Mother, dear damp room stinking of segars, dear organs grinding all day: the place remains in my eyes dressed up in perpetual sunshine: and wears a bright holiday look. This has a tough work-day appearance — and so much the better — look how every body is pushing forward and looking onward, and anxiously struggling — amen by God's help we will push on too: have we not long legs (I mean of mind and body) and why should we lag behind? Go on, in God's name, and try to be honest — why sermonize however? — only that such thoughts always make their appearance on the Custom House stairs and since I'm here there are no adventures worth recording.

Goodchild sends her love, I left her abruptly at the Custom-House without even an adieu: she found out the names of most of the people on board, and became very intimate with many of them. The stench from the ladies' cabin when the door of that repository was occasionally opened, would have charmed any amateur: what could the black hole in Calcutta have been, I wonder? — even in the diligence and the Steamer there were dangers of squeezery and suffocation: and I feel a great deal sorer than I can describe politely to you.

The ladies have come from their mutual chops & pronounce them excellent: much tenderer than in France and Miss Thackeray having wiped her paws in the tails of my coat proceeds to write as follows God bless my Granny [33] this is written by Mʳ & Miss T together

[33] This sentence is written in a round, uncertain hand. Lady Ritchie retained surprisingly vivid recollections of these early days. "Almost the first time I can remember my parents," she writes (*Biographical Introductions*, IV, xiii-xiv), "was at home in Great Coram Street on one occasion, when my mother took me upon her back, as she had a way of doing, and after hesitating for a moment at the door, carried me into a little ground-floor room, where some one sat bending over a desk. This some one lifted up his head and looked round at the people leaning over his chair. He seemed pleased, smiled at us, but remonstrated. Nowadays I know by experience that authors don't get on

Dearest Mother, we all send our loves and kisses to you — and affectionate remembrances, for all round about Pauline's [34] dinner-table I wish I were back to the tough Paris chops again, tender as the London ones are. God bless you all  W M T.


145.          TO MRS. CARMICHAEL-SMYTH
              1–2 DECEMBER 1839

*Address:* M^rs Carmichael-Smyth. | 4 Avenue S^te Marie | Faubourg du Roule | Paris. *Postmark:* Decembre 6 1839. Extract published in Lady Ritchie's *Chapters from Some Unwritten Memoirs*, p. 135; additions in *Thackeray and his Daughter*, pp. 7–9.

Sunday. Monday. December 1. 2.

My dearest Mammy. Isabella seems to have written an enor-mous letter to Mary, and I suppose in all those pages and crosses has given you the whole news from Great Coram Street, w^h amounts exactly to o. We have had a succession of pleasant yellow fogs: one to day so bad that we can hardly see. We have led a tolerably

---

best, as a rule, when they are interrupted in their work — not even by their own particular families — but at that time it was all wondering, as I looked over my mother's shoulder. Another impression remains to me of some place near Russell Square, of a fine morning, of music sounding, of escaping from my nurse and finding myself dancing in the street to the music along with some other children. Some one walking by came and lifted me up bodily onto his shoulder, and carried me away from the charming organ to my home, which was close by. As we went along, this stranger, as usual, became my father, whom I had not recognized at first. Old John, in his funny knee-breeches, used to open the door of that early home in Coram Street. I think the knee-breeches were yellow plush: it was probably the livery of the Car-michael-Smyths, for Old John had come up from Devonshire and Larkbeare, where he had faithfully served them all. I loved Old John. He used to teach me to sip porter out of a pint pot, and to take my part when I was naughty; I can hear him still calling for Missy's chop, and announcing the important fact that she was crying for her dinner. I had a fine time of it. My mother used to give me chocolates, and play prettier dance tunes even than organs in the street outside. . . . The drawing-room windows opened to a balcony; on the other side of the room, my mother, with pretty shining hair, used to sit at her piano."

[34] The Carmichael-Smyths' faithful French maid, who remained with them for many years.

sober and regular life, always up before nine breakfast over by ten books books books all day until night when to my great consolation FitzGerald has been here to smoke a segar and keep me company until one or so. Otherwise like affectionate people M^rs Thack and I fall asleep straightway after dinner — and no bad amusement either. I find the beef and mutton lies plaguy heavy on the stomach, and causes this propensity to dozing. I can't drink either Port or Sherry and long for a little wholesome claret to enable me to perform the gradations of functions.

We have seen nothing and no one: I once to the play where I was very much bored by Bulwer's new piece: [35] and yesterday, after working here from ten o'clock until 10 with 1/2 an hour's dinner fancy that, I indulged in a smoking match until 2 w^h did the greatest possible good. This is interesting news, isn't it?

Well, what else is there? M^rs Brody [36] has gone to visit her relatives at Wapping — from six o'clock until ten last night Miss Thackeray roared incessantly in a hearty furious fit of passion w^h w^d have done your heart good to hear. I don't know what it was that appeased her but at the expiration of these four hours the yowling stopped and Miss began to prattle as quietly and gaily as if nothing had happened. What are the mysteries of children? how are they moved I wonder? — I have made Missy lots of pictures, and really am growing quite a domestic character. Kemble's child [37] can sing twelve tunes but is as ugly as sin in revenge. However we must n't brag: for every body who comes into the house remarks Missy's squint that strange to say has grown quite imperceptible to me.

The little child is perpetually prattling about you all: and walks in the Shondileasy, with Ganny and Aunty and Polie [38] just as if she were in France instead of here. There is a grand power of imagination about these little creatures, and a creative fancy and belief that is very curious to watch: it fades away in the light of

[35] *The Sea Captain*, first performed at the Haymarket on October 31 with Macready (*Diaries*, ed. Toynbee, II, 29) as Norman.
[36] Jessie Brodie. See below, No. 177.
[37] Gertrude Kemble (1837–1882), later Lady Santley.
[38] Mrs. Carmichael-Smyth, Mrs. Ritchie, and Mary Graham.

common day: [39] I am sure that the horrid matter-of-fact child-rearers Miss Edgeworth and the like, with their cursed twopenny-halfpenny realities do away with the child's most beautiful privilege. I am determined that Anny shall have a very extensive and instructive store of learning in Tom Thumbs, Jack-the-Giant-Killers &c what use is there in the paltry store of small facts that are stowed into these poor little creatures' brains?

I have just turned off a thundering article against Bulwer: [40] and yesterday had the misfortune to read the Comic Almanack — anything worse or more paltry cannot well be imagined — it is as bad, very nearly, as the prints w^h illustrate it: and these are odious. Cruikshank I suppose is tired of the thing and bends all his energies to the illustrations of Jack Shepherd [41] &c — I have not read this latter romance but one or two extracts are good: it is acted at *four* theatres, and they say that at the Cobourg people are waiting about the lobbies, selling *Shepherd-bags* — a bag containing a few pick-locks that is, a screw driver, and iron lever, one or two young gentlemen have already confessed how much they were indebted to Jack Sheppard who gave them ideas of pocket-picking and thieving w^h they never would have had but for the play. Such facts must greatly delight an author who aims at popularity.

Since writing the above I have been out to take what they call fresh air here: and am come home half choked with the fog: the darkness visible of Great Queen Street was the most ghastly thing I have seen for a long time. O for smiling Paris and sunshine! if I can make some decent engagement with a bookseller I will pack off my traps, let the house again, and come somewhere at a decent distance from my dear old mother.

I have been reading a power of old newspapers and reviews concerning Napoleon,[42] and very curious the abuse is of that char-

[39] Wordsworth, "Ode. Intimations of Immortality from Recollections of Early Childhood," l. 76.

[40] "Epistles to the Literati. No. XIII," a Yellowplush paper concerning *The Sea Captain*, which appeared in *Fraser's Magazine* for January, 1840.

[41] Ainsworth's "Newgate novel," the most popular specimen of a genre Thackeray was at this time attacking in *Catherine*.

[42] For the essay "Napoleon and his System" in *The Paris Sketch Book*. "I

acter. old Southey is one of the chief mud-flingers and it is good
to read the Quarterly Review that settles he was 'no gentleman'.
What are the Tories about any such truculent Inquisitionism as the
Times preaches now, such wilful lying and injustice never was —
the Times is angry with the Queen for not having said anything
about the Protestant Religion in her marriage-declaration [43] w^h
was very modestly nay piously worded. The swindling blas-
phemer! it is frightful this dragging of God into the question, &
hideous Pharisaical assumption of superior piety.

I wish you could get Carlyle's Miscellaneous Criticisms,[44] now
just published in America. I have read a little in the book, a nobler
one does not live in our language I am sure, and one that will have
such an effect on our ways of thought and prejudices. Criticism has
been a party matter with us till now, and literature a poor political
lackey — please God we shall begin ere long to love art for art's
sake. It is Carlyle who has worked more than any other to give it
it's independence.

Here are 3 pages of nothing as I promised: we propose to get up
at eight tomorrow and are at this very minute in the act of going to
bed. God bless my dearest Mother. Missy particularly told me to
send her love, & had proposed to write too but is now snoring.
Love to all

W M T.

---

thought at one time," Thackeray wrote many years later (*Works*, VII, 681),
"of making a collection of the lies which the French had written against us,
and we had published against them during the war: it would be a strange
memorial of popular falsehood."

[43] Printed in *The Times* of November 25, together with the first of several
hostile leaders.

[44] *Critical and Miscellaneous Essays*, published in four volumes in Boston
in 1838 and in London in 1839.

146.   TO MRS. CARMICHAEL-SMYTH
16–20 DECEMBER 1839

*Address:* M<sup>rs</sup> Carmichael Smyth. | 4. Avenue S<sup>te</sup> Marie | Faub<sup>g</sup> du Roule | Paris. *Postmarks:* LONDON 20 DEC 1839, ANGLETERRE 22 DEC. CALAIS. Hitherto unpublished.

December the something

My dearest Mammy  This must be a half sheet for the house does not contain one entire one, and I am writing on 'An officer of experience has infallible cure for the &c.' [45]  Your letter only arrived last night: it went to Colonel Shawe at Bognor who left us for Paris 10 days ago, poor old man, and talks of being with you very soon.  The third Cavalry are ordered back to Bengal so there is a chance for your Italian trip.  I am up to my ears in business writing and yet very little done.  This horrid book will be finished in 6 weeks please God, and now for the 1<sup>st</sup> time I begin to fancy that it will be tolerably pleasant.  Then I shall try a republication of the comic stories,[46] and by dint of puffing, hope to do something with them then I shall try something in a new way, then I shall marry the Grand Viziers daughter, and giving her a kick &c [47] — O this London is a grand place for scheming, and rare fun for a man with broad shoulders who can push through the crowd — In the meantime I am poor like all schemers, and shall be obliged to use the £ 21 due at January over w<sup>h</sup> Pa has given me the control — for we have plenty of bills to pay: and I am disappointed of my great fifty pound article that was to have been my standby — there has been no time to write it.

Your advice regarding Brody & the country girl at 6 £ would be a poor economy saving us 8 £ a year and giving us a bad serv<sup>t</sup> instead of a good one: besides in June Brody will have plenty to do for M<sup>rs</sup> Thack's arrondissement increases daily — She, I, Pussy have got colds mine just going away.  Little Pussy is delightful &

[45] Another page from the book mentioned above, No. 144.
[46] *Comic Tales and Sketches* "by Michael Angelo Titmarsh" did not appear until 1841.
[47] See above, No. 89.

that's the fact, her voice drives all cares out of one's head — if one had any — not that I have it seems to me often quite wrong to be happy when according to Cocher, I should be perfectly cast down at my gloomy condition & poverty. As for letting the 1st floor I consider we are bound to G. M. I don't want her to leave you but if she comes to England as is likely, it would be much better for her & us that she should come here.

We are having the house painted outside as per lease and there is at this minute such an infernal clattering scouring tramping door-banging that I dont know what I write. Missy's little voice I can hear carolling in the parlor. Isabella comes to pay me a visit every 1/2 minute or so, and I'm not as angry as I ought to be. Yesterday we had 4 to dinner — Collier of the M. Chronicle who has puft me, Jacky Kemble and his wife: they are really good souls, and Frank Stone who complains of his bad luck in the way of portraiture. We smoked segars in the drawing room.

— This was written 3 days since: when I was fairly obliged to leave off on account of the din and riot. Yesterday we had a dinner at the Procters who are amazingly kind & hospitable — I told them of your news, how Lady Bulwer panted to have her children back again and everybody roared and cried fudge. The woman is known for her horrid selfishness about the children — used publicly to declare that she loved her dogs much better — and told Mrs — whom we knew that seriously her daughter was the most unlikeable, ill-tempered, wicked child possible — The best thing Bullwig could do would be to send her the children, if he wanted to vex her he could not take better means.[48]

You will have the old Colonel by this time — no more letters free alas. so tell Miss Polly to warn her friends not to send her such whacking letters — t'other day came a packet from Escot wh the Colonel refused & we sent by Lady Macleod, that must have

[48] Bulwer and his wife had separated in April, 1836. Louisa Devey's Life of Rosina, Lady Lytton (1887), admittedly a vindication of its subject, affords the only detailed account of their subsequent relations. Though Miss Devey insists that it caused Lady Bulwer great anguish to be deprived of her children, as she was in 1838, there is reason to believe that Thackeray's view of the case is substantially correct.

had two or three skirts in it, some volumes of sermons, flannel, baby linen &c &c — There are 2 or 3 more letters in the house likewise for Miss Gra[ha]m. If she chooses to pay 5 or 6 shillings she may have them. We paid I don't know how much for a letter to Mʳˢ Nixon: and I don't know how much more for one from Helen: all waiting opportunities to be dispatched. Is it not disgusting that they won't diminish the foreign postage? — mean & tantalizing. (the door bell has rung 7 times in 1/4 hour, poor John!) — (poor me it was a dun)

John Allen has got a place under Govᵗ £ 600 a year: an Education-inspectorship.⁴⁹ Fancy the Tories his friends being in a rage at his accepting it and accusing him of ratting, treason & what not. I think Govᵗ has done very well in appointing such a man — I wish I saw more of him, his virtue is I am sure catching.

Here is just come in a hare and a brace of pheasants from Fitz-Gerald's brother in law Kerrich another virtuous man — So good, sober and religious such a fine English squire — if I had 3000 a year I think I'd be so too — 1 pheasant goes to Miss Fraser, 1 I think I'll send to Jas Fraser Bookseller, and the hare to the Revᵈ Doctor Turner who asked us to dinner for Xmas day — there is no knowing the good Malmsey from the bad — I'll send her 4 bottles of the mal here & some to Aunt Becher. Alexander's ⁵⁰ cruise is almost over — he has been with his wife however 7/8ᵗʰˢ of the time.

There is a long letter from Goody ⁵¹ somewhere in the house but I can't read it that's positive — her first note gave me such trouble that I made a vow agsᵗ all others. She is at Newcastle or some such place: and I hope she'll stay — one couldn't say no to her application for she is a worthy woman, and we are poor: but I'm sure I shᵈ have gone mad with her clack. —

Fonblanque ⁵² promised to dine here t'other day — but refused

⁴⁹ See *Memoranda*.
⁵⁰ A half-pay Captain in the Royal Navy with whom the Carmichael-Smyths were friendly.
⁵¹ The Miss Goodchild mentioned above (No. 144), evidently one of the many forlorn derelicts befriended by Mrs. Carmichael-Smyth.
⁵² Albany Fonblanque (1793–1872), one of the most brilliant of Victorian

when he heard of John Kemble's coming — F is a very kind &
gentlemanlike individual — you know about that vacant place on
the Examiner he said he had written to M^rs Fonblanque to ask her
to sound my wife & see if I w^d take it — it w^d be great labor & no
pay but if I had the courage to keep it for 3 years I should have a
good smattering of politics, and might so hope to maintain myself
in a comfortable dishonesty for the rest of my days. We dine with
the Stirlings Xmas day & I with M^r Power comedian Xmas eve —
last week we all vittled at the Harris's, who were delighted with
Anny — the little wretch went through all her tricks, & danced
and sang and giggled just as she used to do before admiring Gran-
nies. She is a noble little thing, and a perpetual source of pleasure
to me thats the fact: may God keep her to us, and we do our duty
by her & ourselves. That was a dismal present to leave for you
when we came away: but it seemed to me some great treasure that I
was sharing with you.

You'll be glad to hear that for the moment I am quite well. I
was very bad for ab^t 10 days & then all of a sudden & I cant tell
how quite recovered — what a pity I had not taken some of Jaber's
medicine — when I sh^d perhaps, have been converted to Homœopathy at once — I wanted Procter to try it: his eldest child ⁵³ has
the most frightful bleedings vomits basins of blood &c. I w^d not
mind in such a case calling Quin ⁵⁴ — what do you think of the

---

journalists. He was the son of John de Grenier Fonblanque, a well known
jurist, but though he studied law as a young man, he was already supporting
himself by newspaper writing before he was twenty. After contributing to
*The Morning Chronicle, The Times, The Westminster Review*, and *The
Atlas*, he in 1826 began his long connection with *The Examiner*. He was
editor of that magazine from 1830 to 1847 and proprietor from sometime
after 1830 until 1860. During the early years of his editorship he made *The
Examiner* the recognized organ of the Philosophical Radicals. When this
party disintegrated, Fonblanque's journalistic services became less useful, and
he accepted a post in the statistical department of the Board of Trade. A man
of handsome presence and elegant manner, he was much seen in society. He
and Thackeray were for the most part firm friends, though Fonblanque occasionally sided with Forster, his associate on *The Examiner*, in the latter's
quarrels with Thackeray.

⁵³ See *Memoranda*, Adelaide Anne Procter.

⁵⁴ Frederick Hervey Foster Quin (1799–1878), M.D., the first homeo-

Norrington case & Doctor Epps [55] — do you recollect any thing of a person lying for 10 days in the same way immoveable? Epps however has been badly treated. It appears the woman *did* get 2 doses of castor oil unknown to him & so was relieved temporarily.

Dearest Mammy I think you have heard all that I have to communicate and I must write something that shall fill my empty pockets, how the money goes to be sure! there is a novel remark for you, how it comes in too I thank God, or will w^h is better it is very profitable to keep only 2 or 5 pounds in the house, & so have no extravagancies or temptations to spend. The sky looks blue overhead I shall mount my clodhoppers for a walk, and then and then come in and do a ferocious quantity of business.

Friday. We have just been on the point of calling for candles so dark was it at breakfast. and I open the letter to say that I am going to separate from my wife, being bound on a trip to Leatherhead to the Bullers, I shall stop tomorrow probably, and hope to profit by the fresh breezes — Do you know I have many serious thoughts of a country life — not too far from the British Museum that is — and have a very warm partiality for gardens. With this God bless my dearest Mammy and all at Paris.

W M T.

Dear Gzanny. I send you note for G.P. you write me? Gzanny mus write for you. Will you write note to me? I send a kiss for Gzanny.

Missy.[56]

A letter just came for you from Aunt B She [is] quite well.

---

pathic physician to practice in England. He was long prominent in the London world and a member of the inner circle at Gore House.

[55] Mrs. Norrington died under the ministrations of Dr. Epps, who was treating her on the homeopathic system. At the inquest that ensued, the coroner was a certain Mr. Payne, an acknowledged enemy of homeopathy. His jury returned the verdict that Mrs. Norrington's death was "accelerated by improper treatment." (*Spectator*, December 14, p. 1177.)

[56] This postscript is written by Thackeray, but the signature is apparently Annie's.

147.            TO MRS. CARMICHAEL-SMYTH
                23–31 DECEMBER 1839

*Address:* M<sup>rs</sup> Carmichael Smyth. | Avenue S<sup>te</sup> Marie | Faubg. du Roule | Paris.
*Postmarks:* LONDON 31 DEC. 1839, 2 JANV. 40 CALAIS. Extract published in *Biographical Introductions*, I, xxiv.

My dearest Mammy. I found your melancholy letter about
poor Madame Vaudricourt on returning from Leatherhead to day:
what a dismal blow for the survivors poor things — as for the person dying I don't think one need pity them & am not sure on the
contrary that I don't envy them. It is surely the best way, if one
might choose, to go off at once thus, without dismal delays and
partings from relatives and fierce bodily pains. Along with your
letter was one from poor Salt — all but a dead man, he writes that
he is in bed with consumption w<sup>h</sup> the Doctors pronounce incurable.
Fancy such a death-bed as that, my God, cold, want, wretchedness,
starvation, indifference — all these to bear along with the death-
pang that is common to rich and poor. I feel ashamed of my own
comfort and happiness in thinking of this dreadful groveling
misery — it seems like a reflection upon God who has bestowed his
gifts so partially. Look at these unequal lots in the fortunes of
men, and see how completely circumstance (of personal disposition
or outward fortune) masters all — and one begins to think of Vice
and Virtue as here practised, with profound scorn or else with
bitter humiliation and debasement; — you orthodox people say
there is no Virtue among men, and too that there is no Vice: Both
are Lies as far as the world is concerned — which is which? a
hideous phantasmagorial jumble it seems, & not a reality. One has
however the conviction or hope that a state of things may be when
there shall reign an Abstract Good — I mean that the whole Uni-
verse may go to shivers & that still Good must remain, serene and
eternal, and superior to all conditions of matter — whereas with
matter Evil dies too. Lust and Hunger make evil, but these die
with the body. There is to be sure the horrible Hell Fire, w<sup>h</sup>
declares Pain to be eternal and obliges God thus perpetually to
sanction Evil: just fancy it — we who know how intolerable a

minute's pain of body or a single stroke of sorrow is, we who, the worst of us, have *some* good in us fancy a scream of agony through eternal ages, and an ever present sorrow to be our ultimate boon from God or the ultimate condition of any single brother man! Judas Iscariot came into the world with diseases from his mother, and phrenological bumps — who shall visit the sins of his carcass upon his immortal soul? — By all w<sup>h</sup> I want to argue that Good is of necessity Eternal, independent of matter & existing in spite of it — that evil is material only — and that that future state w<sup>h</sup> we all look for when our bodies are dead (as for the resurrection of the body that can't be — our bodies crawl away into worms, or bud into daisys & buttercups, or explode into Gas all w<sup>h</sup> again undergo modifications) — our bodies then being dead, our souls if they live cannot but be happy.

To w<sup>h</sup> you will say: that a person holding such notions may murder, thieve slander and commit every possible crime — and so he may. But are you and I prevented from committing murder from fear of Hell? not a whit. A child leaves the bread & butter for fear of a whipping, but that *is* certain and the child's intelligence only half-formed our plan surely is or should be, not to keep from doing wrong for fear of punishment but to try & do right out of love of Good. I hope the latter part of the fable of Lazarus & Dives was intended for children — persons that is who had but indistinct notions of morals — there is nothing moral to me in the notion of Dive's howling in flames, and begging for dear pity's sake for a drink of water w<sup>h</sup> the other cannot give him.[57] Punishment with us among each other in the world is very well — or rather very ill — a poor war between wrong and us: for we have no means of keeping Wrong in order but by belabouring and bullying it — But this is a bad imperfect means: as are all systems of Terror & Revenge. They do not prove themselves. One act of violence is not right because it has been preceded by another. For instance suppose a man is making faces at me & I give him a box on the ear; or suppose I am mistaken & fancy that the man is making faces at me and so give him the box — in either case the

[57] *St. Luke*, 16, 24.

box is bad, philosophically & religiously we have no right to re-
taliate but we are obliged to make such bargains & compromises for
peace & quietness' sake. However all this has been beautifully said
by our Saviour two thousand years ago — the question then comes
why should God exercise reprisals? reprisals w$^h$ are morally wrong
and unphilosophical? — it can't be — but the God believed in by
all rude nations, the Jews as much as any other, has been material —
Hell-fire is material, the concession & the bargain of the Atonement
material, Heaven, harps, angels fluttering to & fro &c material
&c &c &c

What can have been the occasion of the above rhapsody I don't
know — it was written a week ago, and since then Anny has had
the paper & I have trampled it under foot, & now I can't conceive
what has been the cause of the tirade. My compassion for Salt I
think but since a week my compassion has diminished, for would
you believe it? the monster and his family are starving and have
the impertinence to send to us every second day the impolite
rogues, what do they mean by plaguing gentlemen thus? I thought
myself a very fine fellow tother day (Friday) when I gave him a
shoulder of mutton minus 3 slices, a loaf & a bottle of wine & a
brase of shillings — but now am most cruelly plagued by the poor
wretch's importunity — and begin gravely to say 'We cant be
always giving' Heav⟨ens⟩ what a lie! If I fancy a bottle of wine
or a dinner at the Garrick I can always find a reason why it sh$^d$ be
not only pardonable but necessary — & so the world wags.[58]

I am writing under the influence of four grains of diabolical
calomel. We were to have gone to Carlyle's tonight, but 4 good
dinners last week were too much for my poor dear insides and I
was compelled last night to dosify. What horrid poison to be
sure — what a fine night of fever did it give me, and a sweet
morrow of — never mind what. I am writing this in the — no I
an't.

Tuesday. You will see by the firmness of my hand and the calm-
ness of my style that I am to day restored to perfect health by the
aid of the poison of yesterday: and after a dinner mild but agree-

[58] *As You Like It*, II, vii, 23.

able have just received your letter, dearest Mammy — You were quite right to be alarmed as usual; Isabella has grown so round that we all agree that she will be worse before she is better and poor dear Missy with a dreadful fall the other day: for w^h Brody was obliged to give her medicine. After taking it — it's effect was instantaneous the poor little patient said with an intelligence beyond her years 'Mamma Brody give Missy bread and butter, make Missy's bottom quite well.' and well it was & has been ever since. What do you and Father say to this? The child fell, hurt herself, roared, and was instantly cured by an inward application of bread and butter. Apropos her pimples disappeared on the day of her landing and have been absent ever since — here she comes prattling down stairs, Isabella who has written you an immense letter asked her if she had any message to Granny, & was ordered by her to say 'My Granny God bless you.'

You must pay the whole hog for this letter dismal as it is, for it is too late for us to post it. There is to be penny postage you see in 10 days, but no penny postage for us — we shall be obliged to pay one and eightpence as usual Isn't it provoking? Do not be alarmed at the handsome way in w^h I have complimented the Catholic Church — I don't think I shall turn to it. But remember that it was *the* church for 13 hundred years, and that it produced, Saints and Sages, who is to doubt; are we to cry fy at such a respectable old family, because we happen to have been born out of it. Besides if I recollect it was only in alluding to the wishs of certain young ladies that I spoke, saying that Miss Wiggins the Protestant could not quite blow down this vast institution by her miserable twopenny trumpeting, whereas Miss Tomkins the Catholic could not upset tremendous Luther by writing a silly book against him'. It seems to me sheer impertinence on both sides: for not in this way, nor by such people are mighty questions to be argued. I've not to tell you for the first time that I distrust ladies arguments (excuse the imperence) but I think they are much too tender loving prejudiced people to argue with

And now God bless you in the new 10 years that are about to begin. I think they will be more lucky for us than the last 10:

though God knows I have had luck enough for my latter share: and you have only a right to complain because it is the fashion to say that people are unfortunate who have lost their money. Dearest Mammy we know better than that, and so God bless all we love and make us sober humble cheerful whatever luck betide us. With w.ʰ farewell till next year. W M T.

31 Dec.ʳ 1839


148.        TO JOHN MITCHELL KEMBLE
                     JANUARY? 1840 [1]

*Address:* J. M. Kemble Esq.ʳᵉ | &c &c &c.  Hitherto unpublished.

My dear John,

I have now 1/2 done one of the most amusing spicy articles on Willis [2] that ever was seen. Will you have it & pay for it when you get it for I am dunned by a dreadful tailor — the only dun I have in the world. The art will run 15 pages.

But what must be done is an article on SOCIALIST & CHART-

---

[1] This note was written early in 1840, some months before the publication of *The Paris Sketch Book.*

[2] Thackeray's acquaintance with the American man-of-letters Nathaniel P. Willis (1806–1867) had begun in the summer of 1839. On July 26 Willis wrote from London to his associate Dr. T. O. Porter that he had secured a new contributor for their avowedly piratical journal *The Corsair.* "Who do you think?" he inquires. "The author of 'Yellowplush' and 'Major Gahagan.' I have mentioned it in my jottings, that our readers may know all about it. He has gone to Paris, and will write letters from there, and afterwards from London, for a guinea a *close column* of the 'Corsair' — cheaper than I ever did anything in my life. I will see that he is paid for a while to see how you like him. For myself, I think him the very best periodical writer alive. He is a royal, daring, fine creature too." (Henry A. Beers, *Nathaniel Parker Willis,* Boston, 1885, p. 254.) The first of Thackeray's eight letters to *The Corsair* is dated "Hotel Mirabeau, July 25, 1839," the last "Paris, October, 1839." These papers, some of which appeared in *The Paris Sketch Book,* were collected in 1870 by John Camden Hotten under the title *The Students' Quarter, or Paris Five- and Thirty-Years Since.* Thackeray later drew upon his memories of *The Corsair* in chapters 31, 33, and 34 of *Philip,* in which the hero writes a series of weekly letters for a New York paper called *The Gazette of the Upper Ten Thousand.*

IST PUBLICATIONS.³ Owen, O'Connor &c. With this I will make a grand row if you will let me: shouting for household suffrage & a citizen-guard as our only safeguard.

Say Done & you shall have Willis on the 15ᵗʰ ⁴ & the Socialists on the 30ᵗʰ That infernal article on French fashionable novels ⁵ is done *now* but too late, for I must print it all in my book.

Yrs ever

W M T.

149.                  TO JAMES FRASER
                      14 JANUARY 1840

Hitherto unpublished. My text is taken from a transcript supplied by Mrs. Fuller.

14th. Jan., 1840.

My dear Fraser,

I send the conclusion of Catherine, thank Heaven it's over, and a paper by J. Hamilton Reynolds, which he wants to have published this month and who would be a capital aid to your magazine.⁶ My sending it, is the more meritorious because his paper

---

³ This essay, which would have been a companion piece to Thackeray's "Half a Crown's Worth of Cheap Knowledge" (*Fraser's Magazine*, March, 1838), does not appear to have been written. Such a subject could hardly have been treated without reference to the Socialist Robert Owen (1771–1858) and the Chartist leader Feargus O'Connor (1794–1855).

⁴ Thackeray's half-completed article was accepted neither by Kemble nor by Alexander Blackwood, to whom it was subsequently offered. Thackeray at last found a place for his material in *Fraser's Magazine* during 1841 (see below, No. 203). In after years he wrote two more articles about Willis, an account of his *Dashes at Life* for *The Edinburgh Review* (October, 1845; see below, No. 312) and "On an American Traveller," *Punch*, June 29, 1850, pp. 7–8.

⁵ "On Some French Fashionable Novels," which was duly published in *The Paris Sketch Book*.

⁶ Fraser does not seem to have accepted this essay by John Hamilton Reynolds (1796–1852), the poet and friend of Keats. At least there is nothing in the February number of *Fraser's Magazine*, in which the conclusion of *Catherine* appeared, that would have anticipated Thackeray's projected "Town of London in a Drama."

(I have seen only a page or two of it) knocks up my project of "The Town of London in a Drama".

I have a confused notion of having made myself very disagreeable the other day. I fancy your wine, that wonderful beer, and above all the imperial whiskey had a deliterious effect upon my politeness. Pray pardon me.

Yellowplush has been so well received, (I looked for abuse in the Spectator and found extraordinary praise) that I think we might have one or two more papers by him.[7]

Yours ever,

W. M. T.

Will you give me by bearer the number containing the Titmarsh critique on Mr. Lemon [8] — last December I think — and if you are the gentleman I take you for, you will look out all the ms. of Catherine, and all of Yellowplush and present them to

W. M. T.

[7] "The gem of the [January] number is a letter from the illustrious flunky Charles Yellowplush to his brother littérateur the 'Honrabble Barnet' Sir E. L. Bulwer, on the 'Sea Capting' and the 'preface to the fourth edition!' As a piece of criticism it is sound and searching; and the playful, yet cutting ridicule, is so adroitly applied that one would think MAGINN himself had donned the masquerade livery of Yellowplush." (*Spectator*, January 4, p. 17.) Despite these kind words, Yellowplush made no further appearances in *Fraser's Magazine*.

[8] I have not been able to identify this article. Thackeray's description cannot possibly apply to either of his contributions to *Fraser's Magazine* for December, 1839, "On the French School of Painting" and "The Great Cossack Epic of Demetrius Rigmarolovicz."

150.                         TO ?
                    15 JANUARY 1840

Hitherto unpublished.

                        13 Great Coram S$^t$ 15 Jan. 1840.
                        Russell Sq$^{re}$

Sir

I am engaged to furnish letters for a Continental Newspaper —
the most influential perhaps, of any published abroad,[9] and sh$^d$ be
very glad to ask your advise with regard to the tone that these forth-
coming letters sh$^d$ take. It may possibly be useful to Gov$^t$ to have
such a mouth piece, and remembering your kindness on former
occasions (when I had the honor to be fetcher-&-carrier of vast
state-secrets for the Globe) [10] I have ventured to ask permission
again to wait on you sometimes.

I have carte-blanche as to praise or abuse of all measures persons
or parties. The Editors of the paper do not know (& indeed no
person in London does know) who their correspondent may be,
and as it is my wish to convince them that he is one of the most
important personages in this empire, I need not say that I am interested in maintaining a most profound and solemn secrecy.

If it sh$^d$ not be worth your while to give me an occasional audience or aid will you be so kind as to consider this note as private: it

[9] There is nothing to identify this paper or to show how long Thackeray's
connection with it lasted.

[10] Thackeray may have become associated with *The Globe*, a Whig evening
paper that was "the recognised channel for ministerial communications, especially favoured by Lord John Russell" (H. R. Fox Bourne, *English Newspapers*, 2 vols., London, 1887, II, 95), through Charles Buller, who was one of
its editorial writers. We learn from John W. Irvine ("A Study for Colonel
Newcome," *Nineteenth Century*, XXXIV, 1893, pp. 593–594) that on one
occasion in the last years of his life Thackeray was shown the Charterhouse
Green Book, "so that he might con over the names of his school contemporaries.
When he came to his own name, what should he find recorded after 'Trin.
Coll. Camb.' in the column assigned to subsequent careers? No author of
*Vanity Fair*, *Pendennis*, &c., but simply 'Sub-editor of the *Globe*'! At this,
Thackeray professed the greatest indignation. 'Besides, I never was sub-editor
of the *Globe*,' he cried, 'I wrote for the *Globe*, but I never was sub-editor.' I
need hardly say that the faulty record was erased, and a worthier was entered
in its place."

has been written with the laudable wish of serving myself & not the Gov.ᵗ but the latter might occasionally be served by the aid of a ten-thousand copy newspaper. I am Sir

Your very faithful Serv.ᵗ

W M Thackeray

151.        TO MRS. CARMICHAEL-SMYTH
              18 JANUARY 1840

*Address:* M.ʳˢ Carmichael Smyth. | Avenue S.ᵗᵉ Marie | Fbg du Roule | Paris. *Postmarks:* LONDON 18 JAN 1840; 20 JANV. 40 CALAIS. Extracts printed in *Biographical Introductions,* IV, xxiv, xxvii-xxviii.

19 Jan.ʸ 1840.

My dearest Mammy. This great boon of the penny-postage [11] has brought only bad luck to me for the Foreign Bags are abolished for all private letters & Lettsom who was here the other day says that he and all his brethren are denied the privilege as well. We are getting on as usual. I always behind hand & floundering in my business and having something particularly pressing to do just at that moment when I am writing to you. At this moment Madame you may console yourself by knowing that I ought to be at some other work, w.ʰ is boiling and bubbling up in my brains in spite of me — I am very much alarmed about the state of the country — not alarmed that is, for what can I lose? but quite certain that a certain part of us are going to the deuce and that a tremendous revolution is preparing. There will be no end to it when it comes, and you will have barricading again at Paris, and there will be similar work all through Europe. The orthodox say it will be the battle of Armageddon [12] after w.ʰ the Millennium. There are a million and a half of chartists armed banded & corresponding closely with one another — their plan is not to meet in large bodies at all but their officers meet, and their officers' officers and these have corresponding delegates who direct the operations: had it not

[11] Established on January 10.
[12] *Revelation,* 16, 16.

been for a rainy night and the cowardice of that scoundrel Frost [13] we might have been now the British Republic for what I know and Queen Victoria in her uncle's dominions of Hanover. What have we got to resist these fellows? — ten thousand men in the 3 kingdoms who might be swallowed up body and bone before this great devouring monster of Chartism. Ten thousand stand of arms were seized upon in the city the other day — this seems all gôbe-moucherie doesn't it? And yet I do believe it to be all true I have had it from very good authority indeed — and thank God that the Chartists have not a man at their head who might set the kingdom in a blaze. With their views about property and robbery in fact of course a revolution effected by them could not last long: and the fit would soon be over: but the deuce is that one must take it and bear it and be in a fever for a couple of years until a deal of blood-letting had brought the disease down.

Our dear little woman is wonderfully well thank God and improves daily having I think a fine frankness and generosity of character. She has the best nurse in the world — fancy the poor woman giving away two pounds of her wages the other day to a poor Scotchwoman to bury her father-in-law with — a very silly gift for the man ought to have been buried by the Parish who begin to demur now on account of this very sum of money. It appears to be a great superstition among the Scotch however to bury their dead respectably and at their own charges — people are known to starve and die and yet to have a little stock of shillings to bury themselves withal: w^h provision they will not touch — no not to save their lives. FitzGerald is in London the sight of him always makes me happy and idle too I am sorry to say: but he is off again on Monday to wait on his sick sisters at Hastings. You must not be too angry

---

[13] On the morning of November 4, 1839, John Frost (d. 1877) led a large body of armed Chartists in an attack on Newport. Other bands of workers that were to have participated in the uprising were prevented from joining him by a heavy rain, and his untrained mob was easily dispersed by soldiers stationed in a Newport hotel. Twenty-two Chartists were shot, and Frost himself was captured and condemned to be hanged. His sentence was later commuted to transportation for life. See chapter 7 of David Williams's *John Frost* (Cardiff, 1939).

with Isabella for in your situation you have not experienced the rage w^h the receipt of an unpaid letter puts us into. By paying 1^d people would prevent us from paying 2^d and this 2^d sticks in our throats more than any other sum. What a strange meanness! I feel it myself and stamp and fume as if ruin were at hand. I am writing this at the British Museum waiting until my books come. I have finished Catherine and now am casting about for some other subject: it is not generally liked and I think people are quite right. A new Yellowplush addressed to Bulwer has made a great noise and has hit the Baronet pretty smartly. it is very good natured however: but you won't like that either: and it is better that ladies should not relish such grotesque humour: Rabelais, Fielding & so forth (apart the indecencies) are not good reading for women, & only for a small race of men — I don't mean to compare myself to one or the other mind — but the style of humour is the same. There is a story called Ten thousand a year [14] in Blackwood that all the world attributes to me, but it is not mine — only better: it is capital fun: of a good scornful kind. Here come my books & so adieu for an hour or 2.

Will you present my humble compliments to M^rs Butler and tell her that the wages of M^r Goldsworthy have just fallen due. and that that gentleman having an extra claim of £ 4 agst me for board wages I presented him with a sum of 7.18 remaining exactly 5£ in his debt. I w^d have paid all but for a very good reason having such a heap of bills to discharge at Xmas that my purse was bled most cruelly. He is a very honest old fellow and would not charge me for his lodging at all.

We met Lady Rodd tother day in the Park; fancy the woman sending to us the next day an immense black card with 'Lady Rodd & family return thanks &c' a year & a half after Rodd's demise! — The Ritchies have got a very pretty house in Albany Street over-looking Regent's Park, and came to us (the younger 1's) one night when M^rs Buller did us the honor to dine. The poor old soul saw Missy and wondered that we did not give her medicine *twice a*

---

[14] By Samuel Warren (1807–1877), published in *Blackwood's Magazine* from October, 1839, to August, 1841.

*week*: pray God, she may never want it. She has a charming place at Leatherhead, and that little girl [15] whom she has adopted so strangely — she is ruining her and killing her with physic — it was really melancholy to see the airs and selfishness of the child.

Isabella goes tonight to the play [16] with the Kembles; M<sup>rs</sup> K wrote to her the other day enjoining her to appear in *mourning* — in mourning O ye gods for the Landgravine of Hesse Homburg! What a world of humbug it is — Tuesday I have promised to go to Tennyson's out of town near Epping: in a month have a notion of paying a visit to Lettsom at Ramsgate & altogether have a most earnest longing after fresh air. I have written the kindest of letters to Frank Thack: & M<sup>r</sup> Langslow and am glad to be reconciled with the former. M<sup>rs</sup> Dick is going they say to lose a seventh child by water in the brain. We have been on a sweet trip to Clapham to see my friend Cattermole who has married a charming little wife and has a beautiful place, and on another to Chelsea to see Carlyle and M<sup>rs</sup> C — pleasanter more high-minded people I don't know. If you were here and could be intimate with John Allen my how you would respect him — the man is just a perfect Saint nor more nor less: & not the least dogmatical or presumptuous: but working striving yearning, day & night in the most intense efforts to gain Christian perfection — and yet this world would not be so good a world as it is were all men like him: it would be but a timid ascetic place in w<sup>h</sup> many of the finest faculties of the soul would not dare to exercise themselves — no man however can escape from his influence w<sup>h</sup> is perfectly magnetic.

Dearest Mammy I have no more to say — yes, we have invited Jane Shawe to come and her mother has accepted not for herself but her daughter — this however *is* all and so God bless you and all at the Havenue, and may we have a merry meeting in the Summer somewhere: and don't be too eager for my letters and I promise you not to be so remiss as I have been: and will always

---

[15] Theresa Reviss. See *Memoranda*.
[16] *The Clandestine Marriage* (1766) by David Garrick and George Colman the elder (1732–1794) was the principal attraction at Covent Garden on January 18 (*Times*).

love you, about 10000000000 times less than you love me, but as much as ever I can. I have eaten many bumbums as Missy calls them, and the little thing prattles ceaselessly about her Granny. God bless both of you.

— I hear from M<sup>r</sup> Salt about 4 times a week, the poor wretch is most profuse in his expressions of gratitude.

152.  FROM MRS. THACKERAY TO MRS. SHAWE
24 JANUARY 1840

*Address:* M<sup>rs</sup> Shawe | Doneraile | Co Cork | Ireland. *Postmarks:* 25 JA 1840, JA 26 1840. Hitherto unpublished.

Janry 24.
13 Gt Coram St
Brunswick Sqr.

My dearest Mam. We have been cross writing for I have sometimes received a letter from you the very day I sent one. I fear from the strain of your last you are not very willing Jane should come to London  I assure you it was in no way a proposition of hers, wholely a plan of William's by which he thought as you have often wished my companionship for her it would second your views as well as be a beneficial change for her spirits and mind altogether. It is very difficult for me to advise or say more than I have already done concerning the point you have so much at heart, but still there are so many things that even two or three years better acquaintance with men & manners have taught me to look at in less austere a light than I might have done at Jane's age, that I think had I the happiness of having her with me I might in conversations combat ideas and notions of perhaps *ideal perfection* which do not exist in this tainted world. Your kind invitation is wholly impossible of acceptance in the first place were not the difficulties of travelling with one *live* child and one *embryo* so great I could not think of carrying a *confinement* (now that I know what that is) to your house. In the second place we are *slaves* to certain "suckers of men's brains" you will say "I am sure they cannot get much in that

way out of *you* M^rs^ T." to which I answer there is nothing to be
got of *them* unless we remain steadily here in this Babylon and my
half is miserable if he is away from me three days. What would
he do if I left him at such a time as my confinement? He was invited to go into the country the other day an hour before he was to
set off a great gust of wind blew down the gable of ours & our
neighbour's house this was a pleasant little incident to the tune of
5 or 6 pounds we shall have to pay for rebuilding it. he then proposed remaining at home for fear the roof should tumble down on
us, when I represented to him that supposing it did he could not
prevent it by breaking his engagement. accordingly his portmanteau was carried to the coach office and he departed, we were all in
bed and almost asleep when a thundering rap aroused us and
Monsieur made his reappearance along with his portmanteau, unable to bear the apprehension of the roof falling in, he was to have
visited the Dicks at Stansteadbury & his Uncle Francis Thackeray
Rector of Brockbourne. The Ritchies being here brings us more in
contact with the Thackeray part of the family, we were at a large
dinner party there two days since where we met a complete assembly of Uncles & cousins unknown to *me* before    I was taken by
some friends to the Glocester box at Covent Garden. I had the
*felicity* of sitting opposite the Duchess of Kent and could not but
pity 3 *gentlemen* who like *footmen* and "like 3 jolly tinkers stood
all in ⟨a ro⟩w" the whole time. I saw Emily Forest's marriage in
the paper "Sure such a pair for constancy ne'er were seen" I never
can think of him without also calling to mind a pair of "Leather
Breeches" there used to be some story about "in the days when he
came courting" I would rather marry Jane than all the others in a
bundle but still I am heartily glad poor Emmy got the man of her
heart. M^rs^ Ritchies house is now continually invaded by a set of
young sucking barristers that look more like shop boys escaped
from behind the counter than the sons of gentlemen. Johnny is
*grand* he sports a starched white neckcloth and a very smart waistcoat and looks as if he dare not put his chin in an easy posture for
fear of crumpling the former M^r^ Ritchie always asks after my
*Mam—mee* and sister, as they do all Emily grows sweetly pretty

and is very fond of Anny who now salutes her Papa with "What a funny fellow you are Papa," she is delighted to be employed in carrying messages and knows every letter in the alphabet except E & F Her eye gets worse I think and I really must take some active measures with it I fear the sight is weak as she will turn her head in the manner of a canary bird it is a thousand pities such a noble looking child as it is. It is striking 1 o'cl. so good night or good morn⁰ I will write to Jane in a day or two.

153.        TO JAMES ROBINSON PLANCHÉ ¹⁷
                        FEBRUARY 1840

Published in facsimile by Planché, *Recollections and Reflections* (London, 1872), II, opposite p. 40.

My dear Planché

My wife is mad to see the sight at Covent Garden on Friday,¹⁸ can you get me a ticket to go behind the scenes? —

                                        Ever yrs
13 Great Coram Sᵗ                    W M Thackeray
Brunswick Sqʳᵉ

¹⁷ Planché (1796–1880), the dramatist, writes in his *Recollections and Reflections* (2 vols., London, 1874, I, 170–171): "My acquaintance with Thackeray commenced some time before he joined 'The Garrick,' and while I was the guest of his cousin, Captain Thomas James Thackeray, in the Rue du Faubourg St. Honoré, during one of my many visits to Paris. He was at that time a slim young man, rather taciturn, and not displaying any particular love or talent for literature. Drawing appeared to be his favourite amusement; and he often sat by my side while I was reading or writing, covering any scrap of paper lying about with the most spirited sketches and amusing carica-tures. . . . A member of 'The Garrick,' who was specially unpopular with the majority of the members. was literally *drawn* out of the club by Thackeray. His figure, being very peculiar, was sketched in pen and ink by his implacable persecutor. On every pad on the writing-tables, or whatever paper he could venture to appropriate, he represented him in the most ridiculous and deroga-tory situation that could be imagined, always with his back towards you: but unmistakable. His victim, it must be admitted, bore this desecration of his 'lively effigies' with great equanimity for a considerable period; but at length, one very strong — perhaps too strong — example of the artist's graphic and satirical abilities, combined with the conviction that he was generally objection-able, induced him to retire from the club."

¹⁸ Queen Victoria and Prince Albert paid a state visit to Covent Garden on

My dear Planché

My wife is mad to see the sight at
Covent Garden on Friday, can you get
me a ticket to go behind the scenes? —

Ever yrs

W M Thackeray.

Friday, February 14, 1840, to see *The Fortunate Isles*, a masque written by
Planché in honor of their marriage. Thackeray's request for tickets was granted
by Charles Mathews, manager of Covent Garden, in exchange for a drawing
similar to that above. (*Recollections and Reflections*, II, 40.)

154.            TO MRS. CARMICHAEL-SMYTH
                11–15 FEBRUARY 1840

*Address:* M⁽ʳˢ⁾ Carmichael Smyth. | Avenue S⁽ᵗᵉ⁾ Marie | Faubourg du Roule |
Paris. *Postmarks:* LONDON 15 FEB 1840, 17 FEVR. 40 CALAIS. Extracts published in *Biographical Introductions,* IV, xix, xxvi.

My dearest Mammy. I am beginning the old tricks 15 Feb. again:
but am in truth very busy, with a dozen irons in the fire, so that one
must keep running incessantly from one to another and losing a
great deal of time too. We have a fine morning after the Queen's
rainy wedding day,[19] w⁽ʰ⁾ however finished with a beautiful moonlight night, that set the illuminations off to great advantage. Isabella & I went out to see at eleven o'clock, after the maidens had
been out before us, and had the pleasure of sitting in one of about
ten thousand cabs that were abroad to see the foolery — it was
nothing to compare with the Champs-Elysées last year; nor should
I have gone, but that Isabella had her heart fixed on the sight (a
bull) and she does not put me to much pains or expense in the way
of amusements. Little James White made his appearance yesterday looking very fat and chirping, though he has met with severe
disappointment in his building-speculations in consequence of the
monstrous bad faith of a certain Countess who made him, upon
honour only, pull down a house he had built, build up another, and
refused both at last. This has thrown him sadly back. He says of
the Shutes that Squire Hollingworth whom they all believed to
be a man of money has not a single maravedi they live at Seven-
oaks with Matilda. Emily & the mother dwell together at Cowes,
and Isabella here at Pimlico.[20] The Archdeacon's [21] lies, White
says, are grown more monstrous than ever: and this is all the
gossip I know concerning them.

We had a basket of game sent us last week, and instantly issued
cards for a dinner-party, but received by Heaven's grace six re-

[19] February 10.
[20] See above, No. 15.
[21] The Venerable Archdeacon Justly Hill (1781–1853), Mrs. Shute's
brother-in-law. See above, No. 62.

fusals, & so sent 1/2 the game to the Allens, and gobbled up the rest to our own private cheeks. We asked the Dicks, M^rs Dick is charming, I think, with a most delightful voice, eyes, and manner — not clever, but fresh and vivacious: we are to go down to see them some day Missy & all — they have a fine place, I am told, and I shall be glad of a sniff of fresh air. Old Frank was at the Ritchies' some time ago: a moody discontented man, talking much of his cares and his poverty and his heavy duties. he has a good wife and children of whom he seems very fond, a good house & five hundred a year. What are men sighing after? By way of contrast comes a noble letter from Aunt Becher (with a couple of hams by the way) I can hardly fancy anything finer than the old lady's letters: how they put to shame us grumbling he-philosophers. I have been for two months she says *by my own fire-side*, meaning poor thing that she has been ill with cold: but is quite well now, 'saw her friends' twice last week, & is for ever so many parties this week.

Poor old John has been ailing since the above: and your letter come not in very good spirits I think: Isabella has had a letter w^h tells how her Grandmother is on the point of death: M^rs Shawe having been up with her for 7 days without going to bed — the old lady's complaint is diarrhœa and she is going without the slightest pain — I have had all sorts of plans in contemplation since I wrote: one of a weekly paper to be written entirely by me. it is only this minute broken off: on a question of money — for I can't afford to tear myself to pieces for 6 guineas a week. To day too I have seen Blackwood a civil man, with plenty of room for me in his Magazine: [22] there is no lack of such work, but the deuce is the wear &

[22] It was to the Rev. James White that Thackeray owed his introduction to Robert Blackwood (d. 1852), who with his brother Alexander (1806–1845) was at this time managing *Blackwood's Magazine*. "By the by," White wrote to Blackwood, "there is a friend of mine that I promised to introduce to you. He is the cleverest of all the London writers, I think — his name is Thackeray; a gentleman, a Cambridge man. I told him he had better not waste his time with the inferior magazines when he writes the best things (he is the Yellow Plush of 'Fraser' and the Major Gahagan of the 'New Monthly'), but go at once to you. He is shy, I suppose, for he said he wished you would *invite* him to contribute. If you will let me know whether you wish to hear from him I

tear of it: and the wear and tear of London — there has not been five minute's cessation of knocks & bell-ringing this blessed day: and between times my wife comes in with the prettiest excuses in the world. I must go to the garrets that's positive or O for a lodge in some vast wilderness [23] — the Jack Straw at Hampstead for instance, where I could write and not be half wild with waps and wings as at this present-ramping as poor old John says, who has an attack of lumbago, and is a sad coward in pain. No wonder poor old man. When he and I made up accounts, after my absence he told me M$^r$ Allen had given him three pounds w$^h$ he placed against six weeks board wages. was it not fine of the old fellow? — and was it not fine of Brodie to give two pounds out of her wages to a poor countrywoman: and was it not fine of Fitz: on whom I had been obliged to spunge — yesterday I sent him some of the money back: and received a letter in return as follows 'What the devil do you mean?' — my 10£ note was enclosed in the letter — Don't be frightened however about me I have lots coming in.

The stair carpet is in an elegant state of raggery and I have made a bargain with a carpet-man, who is to give me another, for a poem concerning him — there's for you. When GM comes it is my porpus to put her into the back drawing room: for I like to sleep next the nursery & it would be inconvenient to remove that a story higher with all the water-fetchings, coal-scuttlings &c. The two maids do the work very well but uncomfortably of course, and John calls down blessings upon them from his bed for their activity towards him. The poor are very good to the poor.

I am not going to write for the B & F.[24] Jacky Kemble gives himself such airs that he may go to the deuce his own way. Hydrencephalus shall be sent by the very first hand. I could not find it when M$^{rs}$ Matheson went. Clements has sent a receipt; and Salt

will communicate your reply; or if you wish to see him, he lives No. 13 Great Coram Street, Russell Square. He is also literary reviewer in the 'Times'." (Mrs. Oliphant, *William Blackwood and His Sons*, 2 vols., Edinburgh and London, 1897–1898, II, 196) For the issue of Thackeray's conversation with Blackwood, see below, No. 166.

[23] Cowper, *The Task*, II, 1.
[24] *The British and Foreign Review*.

a letter for W C Smythe Esquire w^h shall be forwarded anon. The books are at D^r Thompson's. What am I to do about Lovett? [25] It is a very hard case upon a worthy man in ill health — not a hard case upon a man in good health who if he fights against Governments as Lovett has done must expect retaliation. I am sure if the Chartists were in, and men opposed them as they do the present ruling class the Chartists would be quite right in screwing down their enemies for preservation's sake. But this is a point on w^h we shan't agree.

Tell O'Donnell that on the receipt of his letter I sent the warmest letter to Gifford,[26] & have had no answer; if the place is still vacant bid him write to Rob^t Blackwood who spoke very highly of him, and says that he knows all the Standard people well — he goes to Edinburgh tomorrow.

White stopped with us one day — and was very much pleased with FitzGerald and Tennyson — poor Allen is in trouble a boy dying in his house, with a mother staying there distracted: and here you have the sum & substance of all our troubles. Mine are very small, or (d— the bell there it is again) (My wife has been in twice) order and early rising would cure most of them, and I pray for these. I have just paid my only dun the 24£ tailor, thanks to G.M.: & don't owe 30 in the world — being owed £100 — so don't be anxious about me dear Mammy but wait. One good hit and I am made; all my works will then sell 50 per cent higher, and, please God, enable me to save for the little ones. The Judges stand [up] for me: Carlyle says Catherine is wonderful, and many more laud it highly, b⟨ut it is⟩ a disgusting subject & no mistake. I wish I had taken a pleasanter one & am ⟨now⟩ and have been for a fortnight in the pains of labor: horrible they are: and dreadfully cross to my poor little wife in consequence. She had much better let me go away on these occasions but she won't. Leigh Hunt has produced a charming play [27] and my lady is going with the Kembles

[25] William Lovett (1800–1877), drafter of the "People's Charter," had been imprisoned in Warwick jail for seditious libel. His health was permanently impaired by the treatment that he received there.
[26] Stanley Lees Giffard. See above, No. 62, June 12.
[27] *A Legend of Florence.*

in their private box: Fitz is to come too, and I intend to stop at home & work. Meanwhile I must go out for air, and will close this cantankerous ill-humoured rambling piece of dullness: and post the same. Admire the new seal: what absurd Jackassery induced me to buy it? We are all wondrous well in health, & my dear little Missy as gay as a lark God bless her: and you dearest Mother and all round your fire. Mine is out of course, and I am shuddering perhaps this is the cause of the ill-humour: not another have I thank God.

W M T.

155.                    TO MRS. PROCTER
                    16 FEBRUARY 1840

Hitherto unpublished. My text is taken from a transcript given to Lady Ritchie by George Murray Smith.

                                        13, Great Coram Street,
                                        17 February, 1840.[28]
My dear Mrs. Procter,
    On receiving the famous valentine I determined to send back the most witty graceful gallant reply that ever was written; and have been sitting almost ever since at my desk brooding for hours and hours upon this wonderful piece of wit.

[Sketch]

    Well, here is Sunday night and not one single piece of fun has been conjured up, nor any 'miracle' instead of it.[29] All I can say is that the buttons are beautiful and that I shall be proud to wear them, but beautiful as they are (my soul, Madam, being above buttons) I hope you will allow me to take higher ground and value

[28] Evidently a mistake for Sunday, February 16, 1840.
[29] An echo of Edward Young's impromptu epigram, written with the diamond pencil of Lord Stanhope (later Lord Chesterfield):

        Accept a miracle instead of wit;
        See two dull lines, with Stanhope's pencil writ. —
                (Joseph Spence, *Anecdotes*, London, 1820, p. 378)

the present not so much for itself as on account of the quarter from which it came.

Your faithful subject,

Orson.[30]

*[Sketch representing "Orson going to Court, after having been conquered, enslaved and finally polished and presented to the world by Valentine."]*

156.        TO MRS. CARMICHAEL-SMYTH
3 MARCH 1840

*Address:* M[rs] Carmichael Smyth. | 4 Avenue S[te] Marie | Faub[g] du Roule | Paris. *Postmarks:* LONDON 3 MAR 1840, 5 MARS 40 CALAIS. Extract published in *Biographical Introductions,* IV, xxix. I have followed a transcript supplied by Mrs. Fuller as far as the break in the text; the closing fragment is taken from the original owned by Mrs. Fuller.

My dearest Mammy. The last letter I wrote, never man was in worse humour with a jangling of bells and an opening and shutting of doors in the house that was enough to drive one mad. This commences if you please under better auspices before breakfast, the sky above being of a most beautiful blue and I snug in the back parlour, having no taste of the cutting east wind.

I have been for a week with Lettsom to Ramsgate, where we should have been very happy but for this latter incommodity of wind. It was so bitterly cold as to render walking absolutely out of the question and I was obliged for the most part to content myself by looking out of window upon one of the most beautiful little

[30] Fitz-Boodle's compliment to Mary M'Alister goes some way towards supplying Thackeray's missing sketch: "She called me Orson, and I was happy enough on the 14th February, in the year 18— (it's of no consequence), to send her such a pretty little copy of verses about Orson and Valentine, in which the rude habits of the savage man were shown to be overcome by the polished graces of his kind and brilliant conqueror, that she was fairly overcome" (*Works,* IV, 286). Thackeray probably knew this story through a ballad in Thomas Percy's *Reliques of Ancient English Poetry* (1765), where Valentine and Orson are, of course, brothers, not lovers.

prospects in the world, Pegwell Bay, which lies before Sir William Garrow's cottage.

Here comes a certain little person toddling in who says, "Papa, breakfast's ready." The fact is my dear little Pussy has grown to be more delightful than ever. She is wonderfully well: and talks quite plainly, and has a thousand charming ways. John Allen sent her the other day a great book of scripture prints, those from Mant's Bible,[31] but a great scene took place when she came to Abraham sacrificing Isaac: she cried and screamed and said, "No, he should not kill poor little boy," and tried to pull Isaac off the altar. Truly out of the mouths of babes and sucklings [32] comes wisdom. I don't like to show her these pictures, for they are almost all of them painful, and relating to some scene of death or punishment

Arthur Shawe [33] is here, a merry pleasant gentlemanlike fellow without a particle of the brogue: his stories about his mother are rich: the old lady is stark mad and so seems to be the best of the family. They are all hated in the county to a wonderful degree, vulgar, stingy, extravagant, bad landlords, bad neighbours and the juice knows what.

Tell Grandmamma or any charitable person, that I am in a scrape, two friends of mine Martin Thackeray and Sir Henry Webb, have put my name up at the Reform Club: [34] now I gave them no sort of authority but certainly said I would like to belong to that Club, never contemplating it however, not having twenty guineas to spare. Now that the deed is done however, I shall not withdraw for the Club will bring me into cohesion with Liberal men, and keep me out of temptation to write for Tory papers, of which the pay and the number is by far the greatest. The entrance is twenty guineas.

I have had a reconciliation with the Times: [35] old Barnes is

---

[31] *The Holy Bible*, "prepared and arranged by the Rev. George D'Oyly, B. D., and the Rev. Richard Mant, D. D." (1817), which contains many plates, chiefly after old masters.

[32] *Psalms*, 8, 2.                    [33] Isabella's older brother.

[34] With the Garrick and the Athenæum one of Thackeray's three favorite clubs. It is described as the Polyanthus Club in *Works*, VI, 627-638.

[35] A review by Thackeray entitled "Krasinski's Sketch of the Reformation,

excessively kind and the delay has been my fault. I am working for them a little now and hope to get a sweet little sum of money ready by the dear 25th. Bless the Quarter days, how they come round, and the darling taxes, and the charming servants wages. Don't be frightened I have £21.0.0. in my pocket and am owed £30 more: besides the book [36] whenever that is ready, half of Vol. I. is at the printers.

\* \* \*

to evacuate the premises, but John cannot go out in this cold weather, and she makes herself very useful on messages. I quite agree with you about the charms of independence, and at the end of the lease here shall certainly sink into something less magnificent than this present mansion in Coram Street — in the meantime I am not at all frightened about matters here, for I owe scarcely twenty pounds, am rising in the world, and don't see any cause to be uneasy.

On second thoughts don't trouble my G. M. about the R. Club. The old lady said she wd give 100 a year from the 1st of January, but there is no need to recall her promise, and let her leave it or keep it as she likes; sure enough she is a generous old lady to us, and it is a shame to press her too hard.

You see O'Brien and Ayre are let off.[37] I am Radical enough to be heartily sorry for the former's escape; a swindling incendiary he seems to me that will do more harm to the advance of real Liberty, than the Tories can do. It was these rascals and bigots, that broke up the fair Commencement of the republic in France, and brought about the necessity of that tyrant Napoleon. I am charmed to see that Thiers has beaten old Louis Philippe at last.[38] A couple of

---

etc." published on March 5 was his first contribution to *The Times* in many months.

[36] *The Paris Sketch Book.*

[37] The Chartist leaders James Ayre and James Bronterre O'Brien (1805–1864) were tried for sedition at the Newcastle Assizes on February 29 and acquitted.

[38] "The French Ministerial crisis terminated much sooner than was generally expected. It is said that the King, being convinced that no Ministry could get through the session of the Chambers with THIERS in opposition, resolved to

letters are just come to hand for you, 1 from Aunt B. tother from Lady Smyth.[39] And so God bless my dearest Mammy, and all round her chimbley corner.

157.          FROM MRS. THACKERAY TO
              MRS. CARMICHAEL-SMYTH
              11 MARCH 1840

*Address:* M^rs Carmichael Smyth | No 4 Avenue St Marie | Faub^g du Roule | a Paris. *Postmarks:* LONDON 12 MAR 1840, 14 MARS 40 CALAIS. Hitherto unpublished.

                                        March 11^th
                                    13 Gt Coram St.

My dearest Mother. This is the first evening for an age I have had to myself and for a long chat with you. The books were sent to the Club and I hope by this time you have received them. I went into at least 6 book sellers shops to get the number of heads of the people containing "fashionable Authoress" [40] without success ours having been lost and we do not know the man's address to get it back. We have had just as beautiful weather here as you in Paris so I have been going about with Arthur every day almost after Anny's dinner, William and I set off per Kent road to Watford yesterday, a pretty little village where we bought a penny roll and sitting on a bench, eat it we had very little money and so we could not afford to dine we returned by Harrow always managing to be too late or too early for the train  It was a bright day and Harrow Hill looked most beautiful as did the handsome school house so charmingly placed on the side of the Hill. I think one day sufficed to shew us we could not live in the country. There was a kind of

---

make terms with that clever person, and support his efforts to form a Cabinet." (*Spectator*, March 7, p. 217)

[39] Lady Harriet Carmichael-Smyth (d. 1870), wife of Major-General Sir James Carmichael-Smyth.

[40] One of Thackeray's contributions to the second series of *The Heads of the People*, a sequence of drawings by Kenny Meadows with accompanying text by various hands.

JANE SHAWE

*From a sketch by Thackeray*

small bustle going on amongst the Town's people it being market day which was quite at variance with the calm tranquillity of the air. We saw very few houses to be let only gentlemen's residences with ground attached to be sold or let on lease. I had in a letter to my Mother advised her to fix upon some place *near* London thinking she would find it pleasanter for the sake of salubrity as well as cheapness but I think she is rather off her purpose of coming I went to see one or two places and M⁵ Nasmyth was so kind as to come with me they asked 20£ a month in a boarding house & exorbitant prices every where for apartments. In Doneraile she has a very nicely furnished house for 40£ a year. and everything proportionately cheap I wrote her from the first that we expected G M. and therefore there has been no question of her coming to us. I have not heard when M⁵ Parker is going to Paris but I suppose the time draws near, If G M has really any thoughts of coming to us she will surely decide by M⁵ P's return. We hardly like to press this point because she might regret afterwards having left you, to do *us* a great benefit she might do what would be most irksome to herself. I should feel no scruple about my Mother because we should be conferring equal benefits, but then could we manage so as to be perfectly seperate except at breakfast & dinner? W says at this present he would much rather *let* the rooms to a stranger    John's worthy wife carried her point and purposes bringing herself, her two daughters, & her mangle to Town What do you think I'd better do Mam? Why go back to Devonshire, by all means said I her son wrote her word that if she did not come up directly she would not see John alive and that the old boy had a deal of money but that he would not *tell* where it was. She has made some engagement with a lady, whom she says was "particularly pleased with her appareance" on the strength of which she departed to fetch her goods & chattel up from Devon. I said all I could to keep her away, and John was too much afraid of her to say anything    As she is to keep this lady's house during the summer months and that she called to learn all about her will you write me word whether she is sober honest and cleanly I know she is. Now I am sure you are dying to hear about Annie, It would make you laugh to hear the tone in which she says "I be Mama and you be little girl" and then I am to be nurse and the Mama and we drive in a coach to the Regents Park and there get out and walk with our babies the little tongue running on at any rate you please and this game of the babbies lasts for hours  Then we have a "yeading" of little books, and you know how she will listen to the same thing over & over & over again.  Her great delight is to hear the history of Dame Hubbard & her dog amplified long conversations between the two must be invented W. was drawing little Red Riding Hood but he was obliged to substitute a dog for the wolf for Annie got very angry at the notion of Wolf eating up grandmama, with which true version M[rs] Dowling who was here would annoy her. Did I ever tell you I took her into church one Sunday when I had been walking with her and she would not leave me, she sat quiet for a long time but at last got up on the seat and pointing at the Clergyman who was preaching said very loud "Mama what's that man saying" M[rs] Nasmyth begged when I wrote to let Mary know that *all* Jeremy Taylors sermons were published at six shillings that neither Hooker's or Tillotsons are published in any cheap classics or edition the lowest price being 18 S — She says every time I see her she will write herself but has some constant interruption.  Missy is to let her know whether she shall send the 6 s. book.  We are to dine tomorrow at Martin Thackeray's bad luck to him, he went and without leave posted up W.'s name at the Reform and as ill luck would have it they have not given him a single black ball at which M[r] Martin is highly elated and I wish he would pay for the mischief he has done William's *present* determination is not to enter the Club for 4 months by which time he will be able to work up the money.  G P. is *too* kind and so W feels.  My Mother is to give me some part of my allowance to defray the expenses of my approaching business M[rs] Allen says it always costs her 20£ but I think this must be a little stretch, 3 guineas to a nurse 5£ to an accoucheur and 3 more for washing, I shall have M[r] Powell a man in great practice and whose charges are very moderate indeed.  I am as well as possible and the only thing I suffer from are violent cramps that make me dance out of my sleep and frighten poor W. who imagines sometimes he must set out for the Dᴙ Did you hear Mᴙ Chave preach at Marboeuf? he married a charming girl I knew in Paris Albinia Bowden niece of Mʳˢ Valpy's. He is not ⟨a man⟩ to be liked  I am going to take GMother to see Scotts & W. ⟨. . .⟩ ⁴¹

There is a prodigious correspondence carried on between Mᴙ Somerville ⁴² and Arthur.  Of course there is very little mention of Jane he once said if *Arthur's Sister* really cared for him she would not object to live in Doneraile or in the country with him  I suppose him to be a kind hearted peacefully disposed man but not sufficiently "flush" to keep pace with Miss Jane's notions.  Will you tell G P. that they have sent to say a gentleman has offered 10£ for his picture of "Dead game" at the Pantheon they want an answer *immediately*.  I wish I could peep in at your soirée.  Write us a description and what a treat to hear Mʳˢ Friar sing old Ballads I shall carry this to the Post for once in a way.  There were two vulgar women called with Lady Macleod a Mʳˢ Angelo who said she knew you and her Sister.  The Harrisons called but I was out Love to Mary and all  Ever yʳ afft.  I T —

We continue *good children* in getting up of mornings now that it is not bitter cold.  Your ham tastes ⟨very⟩ sweet we kept the last until ⟨it⟩ was quite *dry*


## 158.  FROM MRS. THACKERAY TO JANE SHAWE
### 20 MARCH 1840

*Address:* Miss Shawe | Doneraile | Co Cork Ireland. *Postmarks:* 21 MR 1840, MR 23 40. Published in part, *Thackeray and his Daughter*, p. 5.

March 20ᵗʰ
13 Gt Corman St
Brunswick Sqʳᵉ

My dearest Jane  Arthur has used up all my nice paper, so I shall use up all papers one of which I now devote to your service.

---

⁴¹ One word is here obscured by a fold in the letter.
⁴² "Dennis Haggarty's Wife" (*Works*, IV, 497–514), the most merciless of

When A. first came we used to go about a great deal in the day I accompanying him by way of shewing him his way, (that is leading him out of it,) he soon discovered his organ of locality was better developed than mine, so now I leave him to shift for himself. We went at first and called on every body we knew, *except* the Duke of Wellington, the Queen, Prince Albert and a few of that "clique" whom *we* thought *we might* dispense with. The Sterlings gave us a dinner and a dreadful dull one it was I half expect they were offended at William's not going, and so we have neither heard or seen anything of them since. M^rs Anthony [43] is going to join her husband in Canada. She is as disagreeable a piece of puffed up pride as might be met in a days walk, all because her Grandfather was General Baird, her Aunt Lady Doneraile and her Uncle the Bishop of Killaloe    I am sure she adds neither honor or glory to the race & so I have "finit" with her as Annie says. But I pray you do not let this last paragraph get into the "Neraile Chronicle" for I ought not to say any thing. that would hurt dear old M^rs Sterling, who has always been so kind to me. Arthur is very much liked by some of W.'s best friends there is a mutual liking between him & Fitzgerald who has now left Town I am sorry to say. Also W Ritchie and M^rs Ritchie does nothing but tell me he is "handsome witty & gentlemanlike" I do not repeat this to him. Last night he went with them to a ball, and I take it very kindly of them thinking of him when there is amusement in the way, Where do you think he and *William* and *Arthur Buller* and 1/2 dozen others went to the other day? Do not scream! To a boxing match! and I had only ordered a leg of mutton for dinner, and in they all poured at 6 o'clock. not the boxers but the gentlemen. "I gave them no encouragement my dear said W. but they *would* come" at which there was a hearty laugh as if they thought it a very good joke.

---

Thackeray's shorter stories, appears to have been suggested to him by Somerville's persistent wooing of Jane Shawe, though Jane, unlike Jemima Gam in that tale, did not marry her suitor. Mrs. Gam is Thackeray's earliest portrait of his mother-in-law.

[43] The former Charlotte Baird (d. 1863), daughter of Major-General Joseph Baird, who had married Antony Coningham Sterling (1805–1871), K. C. B. (1860), the brother of John Sterling.

Nothing suffered but the leg of mutton and I could not help thinking W. & A. had ⟨been⟩ engaging in pugilistic exercise they ate like famished wolves. Uncle Shawe has ⟨been⟩ staying at Cannes with Lord Brougham he has now returned to Nice He writes to Arthur in good spirits apparently and with a steady hand. I fear his money matters are in a sad state. I send Mʳ Shawes last letter to me. I can't think why he makes such a fuss about their paper as thick. I am sure I have never sent a letter that I have not paid 5ᶠʳ for in France 1/2 a crown, 5ˢ and *once* 7ˢ through John's stupidity The next I send him shall be on *Silver* paper. About James Norcott not only to *one* but to two widdows might the good folks in his country marry him He is in the predicament of the ass between two bundles of hay one widdow is ugly has an aversion to the letter H. except in *himproper* places the other is handsome but has six children they are both rich I hear Arthur might have tried his chances with the pretty "vidder" but 6 was "ung poo trop fort Tell Mama not to bother herself about the family vault if my Uncle Arthur makes the pleasant proposal again I should politely beg him to put himself in first. Ask Mam if she has still got a pair of opal earrings I used to wear and I should be much obliged if she would let me have them I have none I can wear in the day but a french pair which are made of brass No mortal can get Mʳˢ Butler to say when she is coming, or what she is going to do. I suspect she would like us to write a *pressing* invitation but then when she grew tired of us she would say she only came because *we wished* it and I think it is better she should be guided by her own impulse. It would be unpleasant if when the Smyths were in Italy she discovered she would rather have gone with them Mʳˢ Smyth says she is breaking fast with all her oddities she has been a generous old body and will not have to reproach herself with spending her money lavishly or selfishly. I have never yet got as far as Kensington I should think Mʳˢ Parkers house must be a mere shell divided into 4 rooms I will go & see it some summer day It seems to me madness her *going to Paris* to fetch a quarter or 1/2 year's money spending 5£ on the journey but I suppose she knows her own business best. I wish you would give me a list of the prettiest airs in the Sonnambula,[44] or any that you sing from ⟨. . .⟩ [45] that one that every one admires so much "Ah non giunge uman pensiero" I only like Be⟨llini's⟩ solemn and plaintive melodies  Do you sing "Come per me sereno" and "Ah! non credea mirati

"Si presto estinto fiore

both out of Sonnambula    Do you recollect Albinia Bowden? She married a M͏ͬ Chave a clergyman one of the highly evangelical. The Ritchies don't admire him at all    They think he has no consideration for his wife of whom they are very fond    When she was very large he wanted to drag her up to Paris when the Ritchies interposed and begged he would allow ⟨her⟩ to remain quietly with them; at ⟨the bi⟩rth she was delivered of a dead chi⟨ld.⟩ — Charity ought to begin at home.

Now what will you give me in return for this long letter? Another    In the meantime give my kind regards to M͏ͬ S m v l l [46] or compliments if you think the former is too familiar    Indeed he's a beautiful preacher says James North and as nice a fellow as you would see anywhere. Well it is pleasant to have everyone's good word    Now God bless you my Janey — Arthurs love to you and both our loves to Mama    W. gets up early works hard all day and then I let him gad of an eveng.

159.        TO MRS. CARMICHAEL-SMYTH
                    MARCH 1840

Extract published in *Biographical Introductions*, IV, xix.

My dearest Mammy  Your letter with compliments has just come to hand; it is very ingenious in you to find such beauties in

[44] Bellini's *La Sonnambula* (1831). Isabella selects three arias sung by Amina, one of the great soprano rôles of the day: "Come per me sereno" (Act I), "Ah! non credea mirati" (Act III, scene iii), and "Ah! non giunge uman pensiero" (Act III, scene iii).
[45] This word is indecipherable.
[46] Somerville. See above, No. 157.

Catherine w.ʰ was a mistake all through — it was not made disgusting enough that is the fact, and the triumph of it would have been to make readers so horribly horrified as to cause them to give up or rather throw up the book and all of it's kind, whereas you see the author had a sneaking kindness for his heroine, and did not like to make her utterly worthless. The B.R.C is stolen from the French: ⁴⁷ I don't see why you should not care a fig for ordinary people, w.ʰ is what (elegant expression!) I wanted to paint: it is just concluded and when this unfortunate book is done as 1 vol & 3/4 are I hope to get to something stabler and better, and not fritter away time as now.

Tell G. M with my love, that if she intends coming to England we shall be very glad indeed ⟨to⟩ receive her, and that she will do me a greater benefit than she is aware of in keeping out some people whom I must invite unless she comes. The back Drawing-room can be made very comfortable for her, and she would be very useful at that period when parturient M.ʳˢ Thackeray shall be stretched on the straw. If she don't come I must ask M.ʳˢ Shawe and if I ask M.ʳˢ Shawe, storms, whirlwinds, cataracts, tornadoes will be the result. I think Isabella is never so well as when she is in her present condition she is fat, rosy, healthy thank God, and gets up too pretty well in the morning as does your humble serv.ᵗ before eight o'clock. I have been out to day breakfasting with the Bullers, a huge repast of sausages, muffins, eggs, and what not, w.ʰ has given me a huge appetite for dinner, w.ʰ is to consist of roast mutton, w.ʰ is to be ready in half an hour, w.ʰ I am whiling away in this rational manner.

There is a talk of old Charles Kemble being knighted! — think

⁴⁷ "The Bedford-Row Conspiracy," which appeared in *The New Monthly Magazine* from January to April, is "stolen" from a *nouvelle* by Charles de Bernard (1804–1850) called *Le Pied d'argile.* Thackeray follows his French source quite closely and makes few changes beyond those occasioned by transposing the locale of the tale from France to England. He adds a good deal — the election dinner in his first chapter is altogether new — , and he modifies a few details that might seem risqué to English readers, but the machinery of his plot is the same, and his characters are the English twin-brothers and sisters of their French originals.

how great Jackey will be under the circumstances: he has some rare anecdotes about the Queen and Prince Albert the last on undoubted authority is as follows. His Royal Highness the Prince being at Goldsmith's Hall drunk too much wine, so much that on returning home it was thought proper to get a private bed for him. But the Queen would not hear of this — and what was the consequence? — I am sorry to say His Royal Highness was ill all over her Majesty. Disgusting effects of drunkenness! On the morning after the marriage he & she were walking on Windsor slopes at 8 o'clock, he actually smoking a cigar! — This is a fact, and I wonder the Tories have not taken hold of it, as a sign of the horrible immorality of the Court. The bigotry and wicked lies of that abominable old Times do really make one — as the Prince was after the Goldsmith's dinner. It is abusing the Irish to day *for not getting drunk.* We had Edward Gibbon Wakefield [48] at breakfast this morning — a rogue if ever there was one. I am sure by his face and the sound of his voice.

Arthur Shawe is still with us a good humoured rattling lazy lad — we can't get him up until 12; and Isabella says she can understand now that you ought to have been very angry though you never showed it, at our laziness at Paris. What the juice have Tom Thackeray [49] & Lawson been about? — they are both gentlemen and I can't conceive what could bring them to meddle with

[48] Wakefield (1796–1862) was in 1840 an influential colonial statesman, yet there were episodes in his earlier career that warranted Thackeray's estimate of his character. He had made a successful runaway marriage in 1816. When he tried to repeat his coup ten years later, however, he had less luck. The ceremony by which he was united to a wealthy schoolgirl whom he had abducted was invalidated by act of parliament, and he was sentenced to three years in prison. Realizing, no doubt, that his opportunities in the future would be found outside of England, he began in confinement the studies that formed the basis for his later work on colonial policy.

[49] Thomas James Thackeray (1796–1877), *Genealogy* (43), was educated at Eton and St. John's College, Cambridge, where he took an M.B. degree in 1820. He inherited a competency and followed no profession, passing nearly the whole of his mature life in Paris. Mrs. Bayne (*Memorials*, p. 85) writes that "He was a most agreeable man of the world, and had a fair share of good looks." He was the author of *The Soldier's Manual of Rifle Firing* and of a French play, often erroneously attributed to Thackeray, called *L'Abbaye de Penmarque* (1840). He also wrote the libretto for John Barnett's opera, *The*

such dirty work — I believe still it is some lie or stratagem of that mad she-devil or she-dog (excuse manners) Lady Bulwer. To think of her getting 50 £ from a poor publisher who has apologized 3 times to her! [50] — it is too monstrous this woman the foulest wickedest libeller in England herself. Here's the P soup.

Tell PA with my compliments that we have had fried bread with it the water-pease is very good, and I have no doubt will work wonders nay it has, Lettsom who is in Paris knew some of the Professors of the Science in Germany. I shall send a line to him & beg him to call on you. 'Might I have done if he chose' is dreadful grammar & no mistake but what matter? the world does not care whether it be bad grammar [or] good.

Miss Thackeray and her mother are at this moment dragging carts round the room, and yelling Taytoes in a way that precludes all possibility of grammar: Miss T remarks that the taytoes are very dear at a penny a bushel, and that she will only give five franks — I believe that on this matter the daughter knows very nearly as much as the mother, who has a noble want of the organ of number. The Child is the same, for though she knows all her letters, we can not get her to count two.

Will you please to get an accompanying parcel conveyed to Crowe one of whose gamins will carry it to Lachevardiere: and when the Lawsoman trial comes on, send me a paper — the Tribunaux if possible. Miss Callaghan shall have the money — it seems to me that money is spent the very instant it comes into the house: but we get on very comfortably with none.

"Tell Granny that I will send over my love. Here's a letter, it's my Anny's pens. Tell Granny that I am giving tea to my donkey: and there was a fly in Donkey's tea: and I dont know what else." You will know from whom this comes, and I shall close my letter with it. When did I write last? — I don't like to think but I write write all day on this very paper. God bless my dearest Mammy, and all round your fireside. W M T.

---

*Mountain Sylph* (1834). Thackeray had been friendly with him at least as early as 1832 (see above, No. 153).

[50] A libellous paragraph concerning the conduct of Lady Bulwer at a ball

160.          TO MRS. CARMICHAEL-SMYTH
                      APRIL 1840

*Address:* M^rs Carmichael Smyth. | 4 Avenue S^te Marie | Faubourg du Roule. |
Paris. *Postmarks:* illegible. Extracts published in *Biographical Introductions,*
IV, xviii-xix, xxv; additions in *Thackeray and his Daughter,* pp. 11–13.

My dearest Mammy. Look at the stamp and you will see to
what a pitch of enjoyment I have been elevated.[51] I came down
here solely to have the pleasure of dating my letter from Whitehall, and of knowing the day of the month, w^h is before me on a
great card that these luxurious reformers alter with the day. Missy
& I begun a letter to you yesterday her's was. "Granny, Here is a
letter. I wish my love some day to her. I been Zoologilan gardens,
see eflums, and camels leopards, and monkeys and ostriches, &
every thing." — this is all Miss Thackeray's letter: thank God she
is very well this bright weather, as is her Mamma who is grown to
a decent size and who will want consolation earlier than June as I
fancy. Why won't my dearest Mammy come over for a month or
so? She would be a great comfort to us, and who knows but we
might at the end of the time take her back to Boulogne & there
pass a summer month or two? Lettsom told me that you talked of
coming and surely it is wrong not to come from the mere dread of

given by Lady Aylmer in Paris appeared in the *Court Journal* of October 19.
Lady Bulwer brought suit against the editor and was awarded fifty pounds
damages and costs. If Miss Devey (*Life of Lady Lytton,* chapter 11) is to be
believed, this journalistic attack was one episode among many in Bulwer's
campaign to discredit his wife and deprive her of her place in society. There
is no question, in any event, that Lawson and his clerk, Thomas Thackeray,
were acting as Bulwer's agents when they endeavored to recover by bribery
the letters that he had written to Lady Bulwer. Charges were brought against
the two men, and their trial, which excited lively interest both in London
and in Paris, began on March 27. It was abruptly terminated in April, when
Bulwer, as was his right by law, forbade his wife to bring suit. (Devey, *Life
of Lady Lytton,* chapters 12 and 13)

[51] Thackeray is writing from Gwydyr House, Whitehall, the home of the
Reform Club until its removal to Pall Mall (*The London Clubs,* London,
1853, p. 51).

parting — a wise old lady of forty seven ought to be more philosophical.

My book has not got on much since I wrote last nor indeed have
I done much, but I am in a ceaseless whirl and whizz from morning
to night, now with the book, now with the drawings, now with
articles for Times, Fraser, here and there: and though it's such a
long time since I did write, indeed & indeed I've nothing to say,
the days pass away to me like half-hours, or rather like no time at
all, clean forgotten as soon as spent; one being exactly like the
other and passed in a kind of delirium. The chief news is that the
hot weather has brought the bugs: and these do lead me a pretty
life sureloi: poor Isabella wakes too with my tossing and jumping
out of bed, and cursing and swearing: I do believe this is the greatest annoyance I have. Arthur Shawe killed *fifteen* in his bed last
night and to day the whole house stinks with a compound of
camphor & turpentine, that we are applying to the bedding and
floor.

This was begun on Sunday: since when your long letter has just
come in: and Colonel Shawe's remonstrance about Arthur: of a
certy my Mammy when she has determined on a point is mighty
resolute — the poor lad does not cost us ten shillings a week that's
a fact. We never drink wine now, and never have since he made
his appearance: a bottle of gin serves us for a week nearly: and he
is happy and contented. We give no dinner-parties: the only person
I have had in the house is an honest fellow who w^d have been
puzzled to get a dinner elsewhere: & economy is the order of the
day. Let the poor lad alone until G M. comes when there will be
an excellent excuse for sending him about his business His Mother
writes yesterday that Jane has refused her Somerville for *the
eighth time*: they are going to leave Ireland or Doneraile now &
thank heaven the arrangement with G M. precludes the possibility
of my offering them a gête. I read your article about Jack Sheppard, and such is the difference of taste, thought it poor stuff: quite
below the mark, & inferior to the remarks on the same subject
with w^h Catherine was concluded, & w^h are to my notion — but
never mind what. I have just done a huge article on G. Cruik-

shank for the L. & W.[52] w.ʰ I will send you when it appears. And furthermore am bringing out on my own account a weekly paper called the Foolscap Library. I think it will take: and the profits of it are so enormous if successful that I dont like to share them with a bookseller: there is no reason why I should not make a big lump of money by it.

The new Boz [53] is dull but somehow gives one a very pleasing impression of the man: a noble tender-hearted creature, who sympathizes with all the human race. You will see in the Cruikshank article, some remarks against myself: [54] I fail by sneering too much: but I think Foolscap will succeed it begins with the adventures of Dionysius Diddler [55] all in pictures like M. Vieuxbois — quite fabulous: but a good likeness of Lardner & Bulwer introduced. I have read the whole of the latter's procès and feel much pity for him: his wife is the most graceless, drunken, lying, debauched &c possible, and if you could see his letter & the documents in support of it you would say so.

And now pray dearest Mammy, spite of lame foot think of our back-drawing room, and how useful you would be. I'm afraid of GM. and the nurses rowing. When the confinement comes I shall certainly apply to M.ʳˢ Shawe. She has no business to be ordering fallals & leave her daughter without her allowance.

John if you please has got a new coat & weskit, and is as deaf as a stone. I borrowed 20£ to get into the Reform*: a man to whom I lent 30 once, sent to offer me this: it was very kind and I was glad to be under the compliment to him. I don't know that I shan't have to borrow from PA. for the Foolscap: — the thing is a fortune: but wants ab.ᵗ £30 to start it: however I have some, and shan't want yet. 1000 gives 8£ profit Why shouldn't I sell 5000,

[52] "George Cruikshank's Works," *London and Westminster Review*, June, 1840.

[53] The first (April) number of *Master Humphrey's Clock*.

[54] See *Works*, XIII, 291–292.

[55] See *Works*, XIII, 651–669. Thackeray also satirized Dr. Dionysius Lardner (1793–1859), the scientist and miscellaneous writer who edited *The Cabinet Cyclopaedia* (1829–1846), in "Mr. Yellowplush's Ajew" (*Works*, III, 339–340).

10000 copies? they will pay me 40 or 80 a week: 80 a week is 4000 a year of w.ʰ I would put by 3 at the very least &c &c: see Alnaschar in the Arabian Nights. And so God bless my dearest Mammy: and all at number 4: how bright it must look now. My dear old Paris! W. M. T.

\* There was no use in keeping this awful circumstance from you you'd have found it out. My other debts dont amount to 20 more.

161.      FROM MRS. THACKERAY TO
MRS. CARMICHAEL-SMYTH
30 APRIL 1840

*Address:* Mʳˢ C Smyth | No 4 Avenue Sᵗ Marie | Fauᵇᵍ du Roule. Published in part, *Thackeray and his Daughter*, pp. 10–11.

April 30ᵗʰ

My dearest Mother. We were right sorry to hear of your accident, for sometimes a sprain becomes a tedious job though you make light of it, and indeed if you have the same *deleeshus* weather we have here it must be very annoying, but I think this is being Job's comforter. You must have a ⟨. . .⟩ ⁵⁶ for a couple of hours a day that the ankle should take its ease until quite well and that you should rejoice in air that is so necessary for the rest of your phisique, and if John relieves you quickly we will shower such a power of thanks on his little person as — will do him no harm: bless him

We followed your advice about "mein bruder" and I think it was certainly for every body's benefit, he will now make more active efforts to get sent ⟨to⟩ India, his stay here was altogether unforseen when he first came and it was to avoid what I thought a most foolish expedition to Nice or Germany to meet my Uncle (which project the old gentleman seemed to listen to) that I first offered him an asylum here. I hope he Arthur feels as thankful to William as I do for his kindness and patience. Now I will tell you

⁵⁶ This word is indecipherable.

something queerish, my Mother and Jane on the 6th of May leave Doneraile for where? Mount Madford Exeter! there has been a negotiation between her and Miss Dowell and as my mother says in very figurative language "The birds of the air have nests & foxes have holes but she has not where to lay her head [57] she will try how Exeter will do she is to be boarded and lodged for 130£ a year for the two!! is this to be done think you? There has been the 8th or 9th eclaircissement between Jane and the Parson and my Mother seems to say *Jane* is *now floored* at the idea of his having after great patience bid her farewell for ever but I cannot understand the story. I have never heard from the first but that she refused him, but if the girl took chocolate and appeared otherwise satisfied to be in his company there is no doubt it was unkind & highly injudicious to say the least of it, and I hope she will take warning for the future.

"Here is Miss Annie, say I am very fond of writing and I have a great many play toys in my basket and I send my love to Granny, and I have been to the zoololican Gardens tomorrow." Did William tell you how she declared the rhinoceros's skin was tied on and that it was not smooth like her own. We were at an evening party at the Allens, after exhausting the small store of songs I know, they requested to have "Nix my dolly Palls fake away" [58] a queer thing to sing to grave J Allen but I do think it will be queerer still when he takes his *music lessons* he and his wife are both going to learn to sing having discovered a professor who teaches people totally devoid of ear. A brother of his and his intended gave me a ticket and took me to hear the Messiah at ⟨Ex⟩eter Hall very kind, and I could not imagine how 2 so ugly could be so much in love with each other. I suppose Clementina is gone by this time     They have asked us twice in the eveng and always are anxious to hear of you, if anything exists it is a kind of

---

[57] *St. Matthew*, 8, 20; *St. Luke*, 9, 58.

[58] ". . . at the time of 'Jack Sheppard,' . . . that admirable comedian Paul Bedford sang a song with a refrain of 'Nix my dolly pals, fake away,' which was the popular air of the barrel-organ and the ballad-singer for the next season" (Lord Lamington, *In the Days of the Dandies*, London, 1906, pp. 148–149).

awkwardness Mary Scott feels after the Baugh accusations. But I assure you she seems anxious it should be righted. William is full of his Dionisius.[59] I want him to run no risks and be content to 1/2 profits, for it has yet to be proved that there will be profits. He says I am a *coward*, but I think we are properly balanced. The Engravers spoil his designs in the most *cruel* manner   They are something in the style of M. Vieuxbois, and he proposes bringing out 12 for sixpence. I do not like to send you any until they are properly got up. It is a kind of pastime for W. for you know it gives him no trouble to *sketch* —

I wish Polly were here to take advantage of tickets for German opera which W. has been promised Fidelio & der Freischut[z] and all the rest of them, I must make mine over to somebody because I do not feel much at my ease towards evening. We have had a great "chasse aux punaises" every bed was taken into the garden well scoured and stuff rubbed in  W. has had *one* night's rest since. The beginning of your letter was rather mysterious but nous avons nos idées la dessous, we received in an *indirect* way an odd communication which was answered with *all* caution but we thought it best to say nothing about it as we signified we should *not* stir in the affair suggested therein  I hope I have not mistified you. Now I think I have nothing more to say. The nurse I have hired can give me but 3 weeks, and I trust I shall be getting well by that time because it will be pleasanter to get rid of a frowsy fat woman out of the room at that time of year. She is *well* recommended by M[rs] Allen and I am to pay her at the rate of 3 guineas a month. Arthur will decamp next week he says he is the *only* officer who has not joined, and he hopes to be on board ship the 1st week in June. He goes to Chatham meanwhile —

Thank you for the letter to William  Since the hot weather the man is greatly better but I fear the child is scarcely in a state to be carried to Finbury Square  Her's is not rheumatic gout but a swelling of the belly, and a wasting of the body — a complaint which has no *name* that I can learn. When G M fixes the day of her journey will you have the kindness to send me a line. I am

---

[59] See above, No. 160.

looking out for M^rs Parker [60] who will I hope bring me a good account of y^r foot and every body  Best love and always your afft I T

Annie & I set seeds in the garden. She kept running out every 3 minutes to see if they had grown up.

162.          TO MRS. CARMICHAEL-SMYTH
                      MAY 1840 [61]

*Address:* M^rs Carmichael Smyth | 4 Avenue S^te Marie | Faubourg du Roule. Extracts published, *Biographical Introductions,* IV, xxi-xxii, xxvi.

My dearest Mammy M^rs Parker has brought us full accounts of you all and very sorry we are to hear how you are a cripple sighing for the fresh air w^h must be beautifully fresh in dear old Paris just now. Our fine weather is on the point of breaking up I think, and am confidently informed that the farmers want rain. All of our race are very well, thank God, that is were at 12 o'clock this morning when I left home upon most important business connected with the Foolscap library w^h after 3 weeks botheration I fear is going to nothing — not from any fault of mine I believe but from the blundering of printers &c w^h is not worth writing about      I have been rejoicing in the Exhibitions this week w^h always set me in a fever for a certain number of days, and set me buying painting-boxes and thinking that I have missed my vocation. This M^rs Parker is an excellent hearty creature, and I like to listen to her talk. As for that booby Long, I think it is a pity that you did not let PA speak to him, for in the first place the man is such a cowardly creature that he would never think of resentment, and fifthly and to conclude, if he did, a pere de famille, an old soldier of 60 years of age has quite a right to govern his own family, and to give hints to persons intruding upon it. What a cowardly beast it must be to

---

[60] One of Mrs. Carmichael-Smyth's Parisian friends.

[61] This letter was written during the first week in May, when the exhibitions of the Royal Academy and the Water Colour Society are opened to the public.

write you that letter. I'm very glad (fireeater as I am by nature and afraid of nothing but a dentist) that the scenes did not take place in London: I'm sure I should have made an expectoratoon of his eye — w$^h$ is better as it is.

Arthur Shawe of whom you seem all of you so fond is going for real good and all on the 13$^{th}$ and this news is true because he has orders to join at Chatham on the 14$^{th}$ w$^h$ metropolis he will leave on the 5$^{th}$ of June for Bengal and China. He is a lazy good-humoured ignorant youth perfectly at ease with himself as perhaps you may have remarked young gentlemen of his age are, and a great hand with the ladies. He left a love at Dublin about whom he discoursed to his sister very tenderly when he first came, but the lovely Waddell has quite put the Dublin beauty's nose out of joint, and M$^r$ Shawe has been paying her mamma and aunt frequent visits to tea. Those good-natured people are always happy to have him or anybody. The other day with a great deal of elegant wit, Arthur knocked at the door and said to the servant, 'Pray tell the ladies that an impertinent young gentleman is below who begs they will give him a cup of tea! To w$^h$ the servant replied, 'Please Sir the ladies are all out — I don't know why I tell you this silly story, but it made me laugh more than any I have heard for a long time. Here is a man shouting out We shall have this Lord William Russell murder [62] a nuisance and so it is the stupid town talks about nothing else, and the stupid Times and Standard are lecturing the town upon the remissness of the police and the Whigs of course. As a measure of defense I intend to murder old John and rob him of his money. I take it the master is poorer than the man; but don't be too anxious about us — We have spent £ 200 since Xmas: w$^h$ is not much although a great deal, but with wages 2 houserents & &cs we can't do it much under. I think you are inclined to be hard upon — but never mind what.

M$^{rs}$ Shawe who had made agreements with M$^{rs}$ Powell, & long

[62] Lord William Russell (1767–1840), brother of the fifth and sixth Dukes of Bedford, was found dead on the morning of May 6. His valet, François Benjamin Courvoisier, was placed on trial for his murder on June 18 and hanged on July 6.

life to them both, to go and live at Exeter, has given up that scheme and is now going to take up her quarters near a town called Cork in Ireland. Jane does not seem to know what to do or rather her mother for her: the girl seems to have an liking [63] for the gentleman she has refused 8 times, and Mamma is always hovering about him. I wish we could have the poor girl with us but this cannot be without her nightmare of her Mother. G.M's room shall be elegantly arranged for her when she comes: how I wish my dear Mammy could or would come too, and hail the appearance of her new grandchild.

I have lots of work on hand. so much that I am half distracted with it and do little: but am going to do wonders directly. "Doctor Johnson," says M$^{rs}$ Thrale, "please to read these manuscripts, I have several others when you have done these, for Doctor I have plenty of irons in the fire" — to w$^h$ the Doctor replied Madam you had better put these *along with your other irons* [64] — a good fate for the works of most of us. Dickens is sadly flat, with his Old Clock: [65] but still sells 50000.

Poor Frank Bacon, who cut me I think I told you, being much too fine after his marriage to know such humble persons as self and wife, is in a rapid decline, cannot walk across the room, and coughs for hours together. His poor wife is just on the point of confinement. I don't like to think of her, or of where mine w$^d$ be, should God please to remove me. pray heaven that I may live to leave something behind for her and the little ones. Thank God I am very well: never better in certain points. I mean those w$^h$ are accustomed to trouble me. So the Hygeist in spite of his pills has gone the way of all flesh. M$^{rs}$ Parker has a good story of your tea-party, and the 4 distingués gentlemen who intoxicated the ladies. :if I had taken little Jake's medicine, you would have complimented him on the cure. Here is the rain rushing down in such a torrent that I shall be an hour before I get home being at this present at the Garrick

[63] Thackeray wrote *inkling*.
[64] In William Roberts, *Memoirs of the Life and Correspondence of Hannah More*, 2 vols. (London, 1834), I, 200, this story is related of Dr. Johnson and a certain Mrs. Brooke, who had written a tragedy called *The Siege of Sinope*.
[65] The second number of *Master Humphrey's Clock*.

after working indeed till very late tonight. Three o'clock dinners are the ticket, I had one for a shilling to day, and lots of work afterwards, at home I have been trying night-work lately, but always tumble to sleep at nine o'clock, always eating too much. I was engaged to the Bullers who wanted our whole race, but Madam is too large, and I too busy. It w^d be a great pleasure to see Annie tumbling about in real grass: she is a noble little girl that's the truth, and is not made too much of: by w^h I don't mean to insinuate odious comparisons. God bless you, dearest Mother and all with you. Here is a letter about nothing at all, but nothing as usual is everything I have to say.

Your letter just come. I have been thinking of the very matter you propose, & shall most probably wait till the book is done. What a noble fellow Osborne is! — it makes somebody else blush at his selfishness.

163. TO MRS. PROCTER
22 MAY 1840

Extract published in *Biographical Introductions*, IV, xxvii. My text is taken from a transcript given Lady Ritchie by George Murray Smith.

Leamington,
Friday, 23 May,[66] 1840.

My dear Mrs Procter,

You have just seen the last of Carlyle's lectures [67] and are fealed with a tender peaty for the human race, pray forgive me for my trespasses, for the fact is that I am at this minute at Leamington — a hundred miles away from a good dinner that I know will be ready at six o'clock on Sunday. If you could but see how wonderful the country is — the country of Shakespeare — *the old homes of England* [68] standing pleasantly in smiling cowslipped lawns whence

[66] A mistake for Friday, May 22.

[67] *Lectures on Heroes, Hero-Worship, and the Heroic in History*, delivered from May 5 to 22, 1840.

[68] The description that follows may be regarded as a burlesque variation on Mrs. Hemans's "The Homes of England."

spring lofty elms through, or rather I should say amidst, which breezes whisper melodious, the birds singing ravishing concerts, the sheep browsing here and there and waddling among the fresh pastures like walking door mats, the tender lambs trotting about on thick legs, the cows, bullocks or kine looking solemnly with large eyes from betwixt their crooked horns, the lusty rustics sauntering round about whistling, [*sketch*] the fat yeomanry cavalry swaggering through the green lanes, — [*sketch*] I am sure you would excuse me for asking permission to pass a few days in this paradise of a place. How I wish for Leigh Hunt or any friend who really loves the country!

Truly yours, dear Mrs Procter,

W. M. Thackeray.

164.          TO MRS. CARMICHAEL-SMYTH
              1 JUNE 1840

*Address:* M^rs Carmichael Smyth. | 4 Avenue St^e Marie | Faubourg du Roule | Paris. *Postmarks:* JU 1 1840, 3 JUIN 40 CALAIS. Hitherto unpublished.

My dearest Mammy. The two small patients are getting on very well: and very much against my will (for I have grown to hate letter-paper as somebody does holy-water) I sit down to inform you of this circumstance. I think we have been all the better for quiet in the house: and find that the professional nurse does the business quite satisfactorily. It is M^rs Allen's woman, a quiet cheap body. The horrible book is at last done — all but the last page: this page has taken me 3 days I have such an unnatural slowness upon me. And think of my pleasure with 7/6 in my pocket when I sent to Cunningham for the £ 50 to find that I was not to have it until the book was *published* w^h mayn't be for months. What was I to do? to curse to stamp to rage to meditate pawning my watch but blessed be fate. Celestial Fraser owes me £ 20 or near it and so I shall perhaps be all the better for the delay of the 50 being obliged to make a dreadful scuffle of work all next month instead of idling. The time at Warwick was delightful, only not quite easy in mind enough, for I was always afraid of Isabellas being confined in my absence: and the dear little woman is so good and uncomplaining that I can't bear to think of any neglect — any positive neglect I mean — as for jollifying after a day's work I cant help that, and sh$^d$ be good for nothing without it.

Arthur Shawe sets off on Tuesday, and I will if I can write to M$^{rs}$ Halliday, and Marian Irving [69] about him. Charlotte [70] we met at M$^{rs}$ Ritchies as I suppose Isabella told you, a charming amiable simple creature with just enough sense to be agreeable why is it that one does not like women to be too smart? — jealousy I suppose: a pretty selfish race we are truly. and Lady Morgan has shown how cruelly the ladies are kept down.[71]

Indeed and indeed my dearest Mammy I can't write — I have got no ideas. This paper has been before me for an hour and I sit stupidly pondering. With it goes a letter for Tom Thackeray w$^h$ has been owing 2 months at least. Don't be angry with me or frightened. I am well in health, fat in body, easy in mind tolerably well to do in purse: but so intolerably stupid that I had better at once shut up this letter, and pack it off to M$^r$ Bidwell. Never mind that but God bless my dearest Mother and all with her. Missy is delightful she is very kind to me, and comes to see me in bed. the little baby is very like the dear little one we lost — strangely like in voice. Brodie has made the mother some new night-caps w$^h$ vastly become her, with flies to the ears much prettier than Mary's charity caps. I am inclined to think it is the bugs that make me so dull. Up stairs & down stairs & in my lady's chamber [72] equally buggy. J'ai — in the back drawing room that is I sleep there being at this writing at the Reform Club — hang them they are at work as bad as ever. No signs however of them in the day, no remedies

[69] The former Marianne Shakespear, *Genealogy* (88), who in 1835 had married Major Irvine (d. 1849), *Genealogy* (89). Her husband, later Colonel Irvine, C.B., was a distinguished officer in the Bengal Engineers. After he returned to England late in his life, he served as Director of Works to the Board of Admiralty. See *Memorials*, p. 317.

[70] See *Memoranda*, Charlotte Ritchie.

[71] In her novel, *Woman and her Master* (1840).

[72] From the nursery rime, "Goosey, goosey, gander."

available but in the night weeping, tossing, groaning, cursing, and a great deal of expectoration upon the bumps that rise here and there — You can't get at some of the places. the beasts how I hate them.

My dearest Mammy  The immortal Paris Sketch Book is this instant concluded: after unheard of throes and pangs of labour, w$^h$ have been going on at intervals ever since the last desperate section of this letter was written.

My dear Granny I have a number of play-toys, and have pleasure pleasure's happy. Little Sister only but sucks and sleeps and it cries out wa wa wa. I send Granny my loves, my loving loves. I'll come over & spend the day with her. I would be most happy to come. I can't spare my love because I'm going to send it to somebody, I'm going to send it to ⟨sister⟩ but Ive got 2 loves, and send the old one to Granny. — With ⟨these⟩ declarations on Missy's part I had better close this letter dearest Mother  Your's has just come to hand, and G. M's maid must as you say take up her abode with the cook: for I occupy the other spare bed in the back drawing room. I am not surprized that Marriott sh$^d$ commence his attack,[73] — won't it be better for you all to take a trip quietly to Brussels or Nice on the road to Italy? — at least to have some legal advice as to Marriott's power to annoy you. His creditors are the people I suppose who press for the firm is bankrupt. God bless you — all quite well.

### W M T.

[73] Though Major Carmichael-Smyth's chief motive for moving from London to Paris in 1838 was to take advantage of the inexpensiveness of life in the French capital, it cannot be denied that he left behind him financial obligations which might have proved troublesome had he remained in England. One Hickman, a creditor of *The Constitutional*, had claims against both the Major and Thackeray as stockholders of that short-lived paper, and his threats of legal action gave Thackeray considerable uneasiness until the later months of 1843, when a settlement appears to have been effected. The Major was also indebted to a railroad — which went bankrupt in 1845 and ceased to trouble him — and a gas company. Thackeray compounded with the latter for five shillings in the pound on July 18, 1848, and was able to write to his mother that at last "dear old GP is no longer a Robin Hood."

165.     FROM MRS. THACKERAY TO
MRS. CARMICHAEL-SMYTH
28–29 JUNE? 1840

*Address:* Mrs Carmich[ae]l Smyth | No 4 Avenue St. Marie | F<sup>bg</sup> du Roule.
Hitherto unpublished.

My dearest Ma, M<sup>rs</sup> Parker is here and says she will send this
tomorrow, after I had written to you last week came your letters,
with the news of good Col Charles,[74] and though we grieved for
all your grief yet being the complaint that cured me of much, we
cannot but think & hope it will so act for G P's brother with Gods
good will. Mary's last letter was in more cheerful spirits so I hope
she keeps up "the Elders" The trunk is in preparation, G M seems
to be making a gathering of nice things and I hope this time nothing will be omitted and I have only 3 nights caps for Polly and a
collar for Granny. Your gal sits in a small chair with her work box
before her, and her little dollies all displayed, where's your sister
says the D<sup>r</sup> and the babe in the cradle is instantly produced. The
real babe [75] flourishes beautifully. I could wish it had been stouter.
but all stout children are not strong for M<sup>rs</sup> Allen's are so, and one
cannot put a foot to the ground though 2 years of age. We have
not fixed the childs name Charlotte Ritchie & GM will be Godmama's and I think we must make Merrick [76] Godpapa he considers it a *great* compliment

29<sup>th</sup> We have just received yr letter and I hope G M is telling
you M<sup>rs</sup> Angelos good news her husband in a letter dated 12<sup>th</sup>
April says Col Smyth was in perfect health She is a nice lively
woman and recollects you all perfectly. Have you heard of the
Boulogne project je ne m'en mêle pas parceque je ne sais comment
cela arrangerait tout le monde. The book will very very soon be
out, I am sure if it does not make a great noise, it will be owing to
the stupidity of people in general. Fancy W.'s friend Dowling

---

[74] See *Memoranda*, Colonel Charles Carmichael.
[75] Harriet Marian Thackeray, who was born on May 28.
[76] Isabella's brother-in-law.

getting a place in Canada of 1000 a year!!! W. tells him to have a look out for us we may all emigrate yet fo⟨r anything⟩ we know. My Ma did give a favora⟨ble⟩ reply to my application for the renewal of my "fortin" but I shall not receive it till 14ᵗʰ July when Cox & Greenwood pay her pension. In your next will you kindly tell me what the "Burmese Prize Fund" means because they tell my mother that my fathers share has been paid over to that same & she cannot get it

I do not know what William is doing just now I see long sheets coming from Fraser ⁷⁷     Miss Annie says I must teach her to write and she will teach her Sister by & by  Love to all. there is 1/2 a sheet just arrived for W.  We have seen Darley.  We cannot regret Mʳˢ V D her race was run.

La GM n'a pas voulu me laisser mettre *Le Col* dans la malle mais je l'enverrai plus tard.

The Alexander business is going on right.


166.        TO ALEXANDER BLACKWOOD
29 JUNE 1840

My text is taken from Mrs. Oliphant's *William Blackwood and his Sons*, II, 240–241.

13 Great Coram Street, Brunswick Square,
29ᵗʰ January ⁷⁸ 1840.

Some years back you used to have pleasant papers in 'Blackwood' called "The world we live in." ⁷⁹  I should be glad to do something of a like nature if you are disposed to accept my contributions.  No politics, as much fun and satire as I can muster, literary lath[er] and criticism of a spicy nature, and general gossip.  I belong to a couple of clubs in this village, and can get together plenty

⁷⁷ Proofs of "A Pictorial Rhapsody" and the first part of "A Shabby Genteel Story," both of which appeared in *Fraser's Magazine* for June.

⁷⁸ A mistake for June, as the reference to Courvoisier's hanging "next month" shows. See above, No. 162, n. 62.

⁷⁹ A series of sixteen essays which appeared in *Blackwood's Magazine* between November, 1836, and April, 1838.

of rambling stuff. For instance, for next month Courvoisieur's
hanging (I'll go on purpose), strictures on C. Phillips's [80] speech,
the London Library, Tom Carlyle and the 'Times,' Bunn's new
book, of which great fun may be made, and an account of Willis
that may be racy enough. If the project smiles upon you, as the
French say, please write me word. I can't afford to begin and send
MSS. in advance, for if you shouldn't approve the design my labour
would be wasted, as the article would be written for your special
readers, and no good next month.[81]

167.        TO RICHARD MONCKTON MILNES [82]
              2 JULY 1840

My text is taken from Reid's *Life of Milnes*, I, 426.

Coram Street, June [83] 2nd.

My Dear Milnes, — I shall be very glad to make one at the
hanging, and shall expect you here. Yours ever,

W. M. T.

168.        TO RICHARD MONCKTON MILNES
              5 JULY 1840

My text is taken from Reid's *Life of Milnes*, I, 427.

My dear Milnes, — You must not think me inhospitable in refusing to sit up. I must go to bed, that's the fact, or I never shall
be able to attend to the work of to-morrow properly. If you like

[80] Probably Charles Phillips (1787?–1859), the barrister. Carlyle was instrumental in founding the London Library, which opened its doors in May,
1841. *The Stage; both before and behind the Curtain* (1840) by Alfred
Bunn (1796–1860), the theatrical manager, had recently been published.
[81] We learn from Mrs. Oliphant (*William Blackwood and His Sons*, II,
165–166) that the "bundle of prose and verse mingled" which Thackeray
sent to Blackwood was returned. "The sketches were not in those days considered good enough for the Magazine."
[82] See *Memoranda*, Lord Houghton.
[83] A mistake for July. See above, No. 162, n. 62.

to come here and have a sofa, it is at your service; but I most strongly recommend sleep as a preparative to the day's pleasures.

Yours ever, W. M. Thackeray.

169.          TO MRS. CARMICHAEL-SMYTH
6?–18 JULY 1840 [84]

*Address:* M^rs Carmichael Smyth | Avenue S^te Marie. | Faubourg du Roule | Paris. *Postmarks:* 18 JY 1840, 20 JUIL. 40 CALAIS. Hitherto unpublished.

My dearest Mammy. Your melancholy letters reached us yesterday, and I can heartily sympathize with your anxiety for that noble fellow so ill & so far away. His case does indeed seem a very dangerous one, but dont you think that you all since you have become converts to the new faith are somewhat too hard upon the old one, and are inclined when a invalid is following the common doctors, to be too easily alarmed about him? Pray God you are in this case, and that your patient will be restored to you safe. Poor old John has been long afflicted with the same complaint w^h is wearing him down & putting him to much pain and w^h will kill him they say unless he will submit to an operation I don't know what to counsel about this, for the old man is very timid, and if any fatal consequences were to result it would be a sad thing for us to think over.

His wish that his friends here should pray for him is very affecting I think — there are some people so good that I would not dare to pray for them: nor have we any right to pray for specific objects at all or interferences with the Almighty plan, all that we sh^d ask for, as I fancy, is strength to do our duty and to act in obedience or resignation to the Divine Will. A man can't recommend himself to God too often I suppose, or call to mind that he is walking under Gods Providence — this however is no doubt what prayers mean and such an exercise cannot fail to be humbling & yet inexpressibly

[84] It seems likely that Thackeray began this letter after witnessing Courvoisier's hanging, an experience that profoundly depressed him. The letter was finished on his birthday.

consolatory to a man — Good God when shall we have strength to do the duty w.<sup>h</sup> we see, and learn to resist temptations & suffer afflictions? I am frightened at my own indolence as I think of it and of all the evil w.<sup>h</sup> it has fathered. How is one to learn to shake it off, and to do one's duty? For this it is fair to pray, for every man is as it were master of his own fate so let him struggle to the utmost to alter and amend it. — I don't know why I am putting all this into a letter, and always beginning talking of myself, when another's misfortunes or danger are spoken of — How much more generous and compassionate women are than men     I am sure that you & Mary feel more warmly Charles Smyth's case than he does himself

My dearest Mamma this letter was begun days ago, and being then in a particularly dismal mood I could not finish it. I have now only a few minutes to wish you a good day, knowing that you will be on the look out for a letter by this post, in commemoration of the immortal 18 July. I send you an Examiner by w.<sup>h</sup> you will perceive that Forster though he has tried to praise Titmarsh, does not care for it much: and abuses the drawings.[85] the Times is very good natured to it yesterday, but in small print, w.<sup>h</sup> is a great differ-ence in the Publisher's view. I wonder if the pictures are very bad? Morton and FitzGerald say they are, but I am always pleased with my most unsuccessful productions.

I have been to see Courvoisier hanged & am miserable ever since I can't do my work and yet work must be done for the poor babbies' sake. It is most curious the effect his death has had on me, and I am trying to work it off in a paper on the subject.[86] meanwhile it weighs upon the mind, like cold plum pudding on the stomach, & as soon as I begin to write, I get melancholy.

How can I get you over the book? I shall get a copy & dedicate it properly to you, the printed dedication is to Monsieur Aretz the tailor, and pretty queer I think.

[85] Forster's four column review of *The Paris Sketch Book* appeared in *The Examiner* of July 19, pp. 451–452. *The Times* gave the book a third of a column of small type on July 17.

[86] "Going to See a Man Hanged," published in *Fraser's Magazine* for August.

Isabella thank God is a great deal better and has had scarcely any physic — the babbies flourishing as I am — G. M talks of coming to pay you a visit. She has been very comfortable here, & in the course of her whole visit has not heard or used a rough word. She stands 2 bottles of Champagne to day in compliment to your son & Morton & O'Donnel are to dine with me —

My dearest Mother I shall shut up this meagre scrap & pray God to bless you and my father & Polly. Your affte  W M T.

Dont fancy that anything is the matter because the letter is gloomy — I have had blue devils for a fortnight owing to that hanging, & shall be well as soon as the article is off.

170.                    TO MRS. PROCTER
                        7 JULY 1840

Extract published in *Biographical Introductions*, IV, xxii. My text is taken from a transcript given to Lady Ritchie by George Murray Smith.

                              Great Coram Street,
                              Tuesday, July 7th 1840.
My dear Mrs Procter,

I shall be very glad indeed to dine on Wednesday. My friend Morton and I called one evening about a fortnight since: but you were engaged in giving one of those many feasts for which your house is famous, and we were obliged very disconsolately to walk away.

The greatest poet in the House of Commons [87] came here yesterday morning at half past three, and we drove together in his famous fly (which had been sitting up all night) to Newgate to see Courvoisier killed. It was a horrible sight indeed, and I can't help mentioning it for the poor wretch's face will keep itself before my eyes, and the scene mixes itself up with all my occupations. Notes, however small, are not even exempt from it: and I expect to be

[87] Milnes, who was at this time M.P. for Pontefract, had just published his fourth volume of verse, *Poetry for the People, and Other Poems* (*Athenaeum*, July 11).

very agreeable and lively tomorrow with long full particular descriptions of it.

Most truly yours, dear Mrs Procter,

W. M. T.

171. TO JAMES WILSON [88]

12 JULY 1840

*Written inside the cover of a copy of* The Paris Sketch Book. *My text is taken from a transcript supplied by Mr. A. H. Driver.*

13 G Coram St
Bloomsbury Sq
12 July. 1840

My Dear Wilson,

I don't ask you to treat this book according to its merits for I know very well that in a Government newspaper gentlemen do not take impartial views of things: but I do solemnly and pathetically adjure you to give poor Titmarsh a puff, for surely no man ever wanted one more than he.

Truly yrs dear Wilson

W. M. Thackeray

172. TO JOHN FORSTER

12 JULY 1840

*Hitherto unpublished. My text is taken from a transcript supplied by Mrs. Fuller.*

13, Great Coram Street.
July 12, 1840.

Herewith comes a book that has been a long time in labor and about which both author and publisher are very doubtful. Can you

[88] Wilson (1805–1860) was at this time editor of *The Anti-Corn-Law Circular* (Sir Henry Cole, *Fifty Years of Public Work*, I, 57, note) and after 1843 of *The Economist*. His daughter married Walter Bagehot.

say a word or two concerning it? Some of the papers are I believe not bad, and a good notice from you would help poor Mrs. Macrone hugely.

If you write, can you do so directly? The season is very late.

173.          TO BRYAN WALLER PROCTER
                    JULY 1840

Hitherto unpublished. My text is taken from a transcript given Lady Ritchie by George Murray Smith.

Sir,

I have to acknowledge the receipt of a dozen bottles of Bordeaux wine from yourself, and of a small packet of sweet cakes from your lady.

The wine is not of the first growth but I do not for that reason propose to send it back. I am not proud, although author of the most popular work that has appeared in the present day.

As a friend of yours, a gentleman by the name of Chorley quarrels with the book in question on account of its 'lack of gentility'.[89] I have determined to curb in future that laissez-aller which appears to have offended him and to write only in the genteel style.

Accept then my impressed compliments for your wine and with them the assurance of my distinguished consideration.

Baron de Titmarsh,<br>Great Coram Street,<br>Grosvenor Square.

[*sketch*]

This is particularly genteel. T. O.

On the other side, I could not, writing in the genteel manner, express my feelings more strongly. My dear Procter, it was very

---

[89] Chorley argues that Thackeray is more at home when he describes Parisian caricatures or "A Gambler's Death," than when he deals with French fashionable novels; "for the world of 'musk, amber, and Japan,' Mr. Titmarsh is something too free and easy" (*Athenaeum*, July 25, p. 589).

good of you to think of such a present, and my wife and I enjoy it I assure you heartily. Chorley's is a capital notice I think, and the sly reproach for ungentility a compliment. I'm afraid Forster is right about the badness of the drawings; everyone agrees with him but the Spectator [90] and the author.

[*sketch*]

174.     TO HENRY FOTHERGILL CHORLEY [91]
18 JULY 1840

My text is taken from Henry G. Hewlett's *Henry Fothergill Chorley* (London, 1873), 2 vols., I, 122–123.

13, Great Coram Street,
Brunswick Sq.,
18th. July, 1840.

My dear Chorley,

Name anything you wish as a proof of my gratitude, and I will do it for you. Never was such a good-natured puff as that in the "Athenaeum" of "Titmarsh".[92]

My best respects to Washington.[93] I called at the Privy Council to see him t'other day; but they told me that Guizot had just stepped out.

Your faithful and obliged,
Michael Angelo T.

[90] It is asserted in the *Spectator* (July 18, p. 689) that Thackeray's illustrations are "masterly, and distinguished by grotesque drollery, of a caustic kind, that is shown to advantage in hitting off the expression of villains and their dupes."

[91] Chorley (1808–1872), who joined the staff of *The Athenaeum* in 1833, served as chief literary and music critic of that magazine for more than thirty years. Thackeray had been introduced to him by their common friend Mrs. Procter.

[92] Chorley's four-column review of *The Paris Sketch Book* was published in *The Athenaeum* of July 25.

[93] Henry Reeve, whose translation of Guizot's *Washington* had just been published (*Literary Gazette*, July 11, p. 455). He and Chorley shared a house in London at this time.

175.          TO MRS. CARMICHAEL-SMYTH
                    30 JULY 1840

*Address:* M^{rs} Carmichael Smyth | 4 Avenue S^{te} Marie | Faubourg du Roule | Paris. *Postmark:* 31 JY 1840. Published in part, *Biographical Introductions,* IV, xxix.

July 30. 1840.

Why I have not written to my dearest Mammy is indeed hard to say — not from excessive occupation certainly for I've done nothing these 10 days except pass 3 very pleasantly in the midst of the rain at Leatherhead. I think Durham's death [94] is a piece of good fortune for Chas Buller, who has been weighed down by the corpse as it were of that man. What the Times say of him is very just I think, as far as the appreciation of character goes — not so as to the Canada failure, the rascally Whigs & Tories swamped that between them when is the day to come when those 2 humbugs are to disappear from among us? Don't be astonished. I'm not a Chartist, only a republican. I would like to see all men equal, and this bloated aristocracy blasted to the wings of all the winds.[95] It has been good & useful up to the present time — nay for a little time longer perhaps — just up to the minute when the great lion shall shake his mane, and scatter all these absurd insects out of it. What stuff to write to be sure. But I see how in every point of morals the aristocracy is cursing the country — O for a few enlightened republicans men to say their say honestly, and dare to do and say the truth. We are living in wonderful times, Madam, and who knows may see great things done: but no physical force — the bigotry of that & of the present Chartist leaders is greater than the bigotry we suffer under. — Well this is a way indeed of filling a letter to one's Mamma.

[94] John George Lambton (1792–1840), first Earl of Durham, died at Cowes on July 28. His obituary notice appeared in *The Times* on July 29 and 30. Buller had been Chief Secretary to Lord Durham while the latter was High Commissioner and Governor-in-Chief for Canada in 1838 and 1839.

[95] *Psalms,* 104, 3.

I must tell you about the carriage: that I forgot, and ought to have spoken of a month ago. It is bad news. The carriage owes £ 25 and won't fetch anything — not 10, not 5 in fact nothing: for there is no demand for carriages of this make, new sorts have sprung up pilentums & such like, and the machine was at first a fancy machine &c. There are 4 sales a year, shall Marks sell? that is if he can. Persons might possibly buy, by hearing of a wonderful cheap carriage in the Papers.

My dearest Mammy I want to send you the book, about w$^h$ you have no business to speak in such terms. It has been very much puffed — eight or nine good puffs at least, and is selling very well about 400 have been got off already. Enough to pay all the expenses of authorship printing &c. and to leave 500£ profit to the publisher if the rest are sold. Longman [96] the great publisher and Chapman & Hall [97] Dickens's publishers with whom I have opened negociations seem to be very willing to enter into treaty with me: & I hope that something good will come out of it all — something better than that odious magazine-work w$^h$ w$^d$ kill any writer in 6 years. What do you think of Titmarsh in Ireland that is my next plan — I could make a good thing of it I think; and get 300£ for my 3 months work instead of 120 w$^h$ the Magazines w$^d$ pay me. We shall see whether any of the Publishers can be brought to pay. I make fine Alnaschar visions [98] on the subject: but they all begin with 150£ in them. With 150 I write a book worth 300 pay 150 off, have 150 to go on with while writing another book worth 400 — and so at the end of the year there I am ready to begin a new work and with 400 in my pocket — all this is quite feasible reasonable possible probable — and if I can catch Longman or Chapman will I hope come to pass! Fancy having 500 ye Gods what a treasure! Let us pray for this consummation. I will break from the Magazines that's flat. I sent to Fraser for money tother day whom I

[96] Thomas Norton Longman (1771–1842), proprietor of *The Edinburgh Review*.

[97] Edward Chapman (1804–1880) and William Hall, whose famous publishing house was founded in 1830. Besides Dickens's books, they issued those of Carlyle, the Brownings, and Anthony Trollope.

[98] See above, No. 89.

never overdrew 10£ & whose best man I am — he refused me &
not because I had overdrawn my account, but because he had not
had time to make it up, & thought I might have overdrawn it.
There's a pretty liberal fellow for you. perhaps Grantley Berkely
was not so very wrong in beating him.[99] Such pens ink and paper
I've on hand: that's why I write generally at the Reform Club:
and not here in the drawing room with G M opposite reading
Humphrey's Clock & much puzzled, and Isabella on the sofa. She
is all but well thank God, & the baby a dear little fat flourishing
podge of flesh as one says. Another blot. Missy I have just left
lying on her stomach. It is inordinately hot: we are all in the most
melting condition possible; and all well. I think I have a touch of
the gout really & truly, for 3 months there has been a regular
ceaseless pain in my great to, not sewere but steady & he looks red,
this is the beginning of gout all my friends inform me, & I suppose
that 1 day or other I must look for the completion of it.

I went to Dorking from Leatherhead & saw my pretty Charlotte
Crawford. There is nothing about her but simplicity: & I like this
milk-&-water in women — perhaps too much, undervaluing your
ladyship's heads, and caring only for the heart part of the business.

Have taken a fine advantage of one of the blots, & shall clap my
seal on the space it occupies. Thus it is in human life that we make
our failings as serviceable to us as our virtues can be. I have been
reading Allan Ramsay's Poems, the Banantyne Controversy [100] w.h
proves Scott to be a rogue — and a noble article in the British Critic
on Pauperism w.h has affected me extraordinarily, likewise some
French novels — noble occupation for grey headed fathers of
families, how happy are those who read to instruct themselves —
yes, besides I have read Ranke's "History of the Popes (in the way

[99] In retaliation for a savage review by Maginn in *Fraser's Magazine* of his
historical romance, *Berkeley Castle*, Grantley Berkeley (1800–1881) had in
1836 horsewhipped Fraser.

[100] The exchange of pamphlets concerning Scott's financial transactions between Lockhart and A. Ballantyne in 1838 and 1839; "Pauperism and Alms-
giving," *British Critic and Quarterly Theological Review*, July, 1840, pp.
195–257.

of business) [101] with much pleasure. It is a great book, and may be read with profit by some persons who wonder how other persons can talk about the "beautiful Roman Catholic church in whose bosom repose so many saints & sages" Saints & sages do sleep there, and everywhere under God's sun; I think & hope God bless my dearest Mammy & Good night. Dont fancy I want money — I have lots.

176.     FROM MRS. THACKERAY TO
         MRS. CARMICHAEL-SMYTH
         4 AUGUST 1840

*Address:* M[rs] Carmichael Smyth | No 4 Avenue St Marie | Fau[bg] du Roule. | Paris. *Postmark:* 4 AU 1840. Hitherto unpublished. *Endorsed* (by Lady Ritchie): Dear Dear Sad letter AR.

My dear Mother I have not had a pouring forth to you for a length of time "cos why" my body has been unhealthy and *consequently* my spirits low. I am *really* quite a different being and have a kind of wish that every body should feel happy. Well let me tell you about *"The Book"* My dearest M A must we not be thankful that it has more than answered *all our fullest* anticipations, we have been sorry not to have been able to send it sooner it is now "in chimin" There have been reviews in half a dozen papers all so favorable I have not seen them but M[r] Cunningham the publisher has promised to let me have them and I will then write extracts for you The woman Benand might as well have taken them but she wouldn't so I couldn't help it. In the midst of all this the dear lamb has been christened "Harriet Marian" so she can be called Polly and Harry and Harriet Charlotte Ritchie and her maiden train came to church the lassies behaved like queens for Annie came with us and the sobriety of the little puss was admirable as to the little sweet one she is just like —— but if every care, I confess to

[101] Reviewed by Thackeray in *The Times* on June 10, August 11, and August 18.

you I feel myself excited my strenght is not great and my head
flies away with me as if it were a balloon. This is *mere* weakness
and a walk will set me right but in case there should be incoherences
in my letter you will know what to attribute it to. William too I
fear is a little agog for he thought he should like to see the Belgian
pictures and so nothing would serve him but to put himself into a
steam boat and set off to Antwerp.[102] He says he will make a series
of articles for Blackwood that it was necessary for his health and
that he is sure that Titmarsh in Belgium will take as Titmarsh in
Paris. I tried to persuade him not to go but it seems as if I was
always to damp him, and that I am to go a round of old saws such
as "It is the tortoise and not the hare wins the race" mais enfin il ne
m'écoute pas and I must e'en let him make his fortune his own
way. I do mind my own business as much as possible but one cannot but be interested. He is to be back on the 15th he has plenty
of grist as have we so it is not that makes one uneasy. I try to think
my fears imaginary and exaggerated and that I am a coward by
nature, but when people do not raise their expectations to too high
a pitch they cannot be disappointed. His address is Poste Restante
Brussels. To look at *all sides* of the question the *best* parts of the
Paris book were written last year under the *exitement of travelling*.
as soon as you have accounts and we can't admit of misgivings we
shall hope to hear the young ones are quite well.

G M is quite well I have settled that affair with M^rs Parker. I
had not been told she came to dine on that day she has been here
since, mais c'est une femme *sans tête* she makes the most *injudicious
repetitions*. Let us be frank but let us not say things that hurt the
feelings of others.[103]

I believe I am a goose for having written all this but you won't
know what to think if you do not hear from me.

I T.

[102] Thackeray appears to have left London on August 1. He returned on
August 16.
[103] See below, No. 179.

177.        TO MRS. CARMICHAEL-SMYTH
                20–21 AUGUST 1840

*Address:* M^rs Carmichael Smyth. | Avenue S^te Marie | Faubourg du Roule.
Paris. *Postmarks:* MARGATE AU 21 1840, 23 AOUT 40 CALAIS. Extract
published, *Biographical Introductions,* IV, xxx.

> 1 Bridge Terrace
> Margate. August 20. 21.

My dearest Mammy. It seems to me that now is the first time
since many weeks that I have had the time to write to you: for
while on the Belgian trip, all I did was for money & with sight-
seeing and sketching and having good dinners and sleeping on
benches of afternoons and writing between times the day was completely spent. Indeed it was a delightful trip, pleasure & sunshine
the whole way — & more absence of care than I have enjoyed for
many a long day — not that I am very careful. But it seemed a
sin to be unhappy in that wonderful blue sky, and so I was as
virtuous as possible I mean as jovial. When I came back having
spent 14£ I sold my mss. to Chapman & Hall for 70 — that is a
little book on Belgium & the Rhine to come out as a guide-book
next year.[104] I have made an agreement with them for Ireland.
£100 down, £100 on publication £100 more by degrees up to 1200
copies the end of the edition. Indeed my luck stands me wonderfully in stead: for I was beginning to have a scuffle for money.
G.M. like a trump advanced 25 part of w^h enabled me to make the
Belgian tour, the rest remaining with M^rs Thack. in my absence.
    That young woman I am sorry to tell you I found in such an
extraordinary state of languor and depression when I came home
that old Powell counselled me to bring her immediately to the sea
side, and here we are arrived this very night. She has got the
better of her first complaint but this was succeeded by excessive
lowness of spirits that came on in my absence: [105] nor did G.M &

---

[104] This book was never published, nor does Thackeray appear to have used
his travel notes in any other way.
[105] See Appendix VII.

she as I fancy get on very merrily together. I have had a sad battle to fight since Sunday when I came home: but this is our marriage day & thank God the fresh air & the sunshine & the little excitement of travel have done wonders for her, & she has gone to bed tired and happy. Don't allude to it at all, or only to say that you are charmed to hear she has got round. Indeed the air & bustle acted on her like a charm. There can be nothing the matter with her (but indigestion), for she has plenty of milk, and the infant is as fat & smiling as babe can be. It is always at her, & this pulls her down of course very much. We have got a charming green little lodging here, but very dear 2 1/2 guineas a week, every body else asked 3 or 4 for rooms not so good. All our windows look to the sea, if you call this sea. A queer little sitting-room with a glass door that walks straight into the street and two neat smart bed rooms 1 on the top of the other. We dined at the Inn, and sent Missy & Brody [106] & the baby on before. Missy I found lying on her stomach, a great deal more than half asleep. She said to Brodie 'I have come a long long way, but I wish to kiss Papa & Mamma before I go to bed.' God bless her. She is a noble little girl. Your big heart would have thumped to see her toddling about the deck, embracing in her fine innocent warmth every little child about her. I find myself growing much more sentimental as I grow older. This world is not near such a bad one as some of your orthodox pretend. We are not desperately wicked but good & loving many of us: our arms reach up to heaven, though the Devil to be sure is tugging at our heels. My dearest old Mammy I think of you often & always indeed I do: and know I shall never go to Hell for if I went you in Heaven w^d be miserable, & there you know people must be happy. I told G M. to send you a puff out of the Glasgow Argus the biggest & strongest of all. M^rs Procter

---

[106] "We had a friend," Lady Ritchie (*Biographical Introductions*, V, xiii) writes of the autumn and winter of 1840; "a faithful and loving-hearted Scotch nurse, called Jessie Brodie, who rather than quit my father in his troubles at that time, broke off her own marriage, so she told me shyly, long years after. She helped my father to nurse my mother at first, then [later, in Paris,] he left her in charge of the nursery, and removed from his grandmother's in order to be nearer to doctors."

sent me a letter from her mother [107] t'other day almost as strong: it was good of her to send it, though I know really how much this sort of flummery is worth. In spite of the puffs they have only sold 500: but this is many more than I expected. Where I have been bad is about the drawings. i paper the Spectator that I have no connexion with, and is seriously the only paper that understands matters of art (I swear I always said so before) says that Titmarsh is the best designer going: by Jove he is right, tho I can't get anybody to think so.

How delightfully quiet this night is! The ripple of the water is most melodious, the gas lamps round the little bay look as if they were sticking flaming swords into it. What is it that sets one's spirits chirping so, on getting out from London? poor old Gran is there alone she would not come with us, & has got a crotchet that Isabella dislikes her — indeed she doesn't, but old Gran is a sad pestering old body for all that. She is very kind ⟨to us.⟩

I see the people walking about in slippers and get the most strange recollections of this place from the old time when we were here. I remember a dingy little bed-room where you used to come and wake me of mornings. I remember running for the steamer and Pa giving me 10/ — I remember going with Col. Forrest that night to see the two Gentlemen of Verona why the deuce should these things remain so clear? I have forgotten a number more important.

We have been out to walk on the sands Missy famous. Baby ditto. My wife better in health but very low. For the last 4 days I have not been able to write one line in consequence of her. I must work now double time. God bless my dearest Mother, and I hope I shall have a more cheerful letter to write the next time I do so. I shall take Isabella to Ramsgate & see if M⟨rs⟩ Lettsom will invite us. To crown my joys I am bitten to pieces by bugs. Sweet home indeed!

We have the lodgings for a week.

[107] The third Mrs. Basil Montagu, formerly Mrs. Thomas Skepper.

178.          TO MRS. CARMICHAEL-SMYTH
          ? AUGUST–1 SEPTEMBER 1840

*Address:* M^rs Carmichael Smyth. | Avenue S^te Marie | Faubourg du Roule Paris. *Postmarks:* MARGATE SE 1 1840, 3 SEPT 40 CALAIS. Hitherto unpublished.

1 Bridge Terrace. Margate.
Tuesday. 1 September I think.

My dearest Mammy. As the Poet observes, you have got hold of the wrong end of the stick about Catholicism — those obnoxious remarks [108] w^h have been setting my dear old Mammy in such a fidget being written by M^rs Sand, and not by Titmarsh who is only answerable for the omission of the inverted commas w^h w^d have made them over to their right owner. Concerning Judaism, I believe it is pretty generally allowed that the doctrine of a future state did not obtain among the Jews till they learned it in the Babylonish captivity. Except that passage in Job,[109] w^h has nothing to do with the matter, being applied by J to his own bodily condition find another in the O.T. — one that says expressly there is a Heaven for the good & something else for us wicked ones. Such a doctrine of such importance ought to be taught by something more than implication, & should not be left to honest persons to decide whether it is so or no. Who were the Sadducees who denied the resurrection? Your book does not prove it as clearly as you say. As for Catholicism you may have your fling at it: but I am sure that the Xtian church has existed in it in all ages — it would be an insult to God to say it had not. Recollect who you are a woman with intense organs of love & respect born in Church-of-Englandism — do you think you would not have had the same love for Catholicism if you had been bred to it? Indeed you would, as I fancy, in any other creed. God forbid you should not: a woman reasons with her heart that you do Madame for all you fancy that you are unprejudiced, & I should like to show you how the assertion that

[108] See *Works*, V, 198.
[109] Apparently *Job*, 19, 25–27.

every word of the Bible from Genesis to Malachi proves Jewish belief in the immortality of the Soul cant be supported, and the argument about Moses Montefiore [110] is beside the question. But by Jupiter-Ammon, as I go through the world it seems to me that I am the single person in it, who am always right. People will not look dispassionately, but never mind God's sun shines over us all Jews, Heathen Turks, Methodists Catholics, Church-of-England men, but this is an old story that I have often told. It seems to me blasphemy to say that out of a certain sect there is no salvation, Heaven forbid say you: well then one sect is as good as another, and as men have different eyes noses and we sh^d be monstrously bigotted if we were to say that such and such a hook or such and such a swivel shd be damned — in like manner let us accord the same charity to men's minds w^h are all different & must all worship God their own way. Indeed it is something noble I think to think even of this difference: that God has a responding face for every one of these myriad intelligences, and a sympathy with all. Why then be anxious that those we love should cast their religious thoughts precisely in our mould? This is the meaning of that article ab^t M^rs Sand; — let people leave others alone in religious matters; that's all I argue.

I am or fancy I am growing more serious upon these matters — especially now that my poor little woman is so low. Indeed it is a hard matter to resist catching the infection for I am always with her: nor can I get much work done with the pitiful looks always fixed on me — and I am so unused to living alone keeping back perforce a great fund of animal spirits that want to break out in the shape of argument or jollification that the bottling of them in is annoying to me. Without my favorite talk about pictures or books I am good for nothing — yes for a little to be a nurse, and I pray God many times a day to keep me stiff to my duty — The 2 duties are very hard however — to work & to act as nurse too, but they get lighter daily 1^st from habit, and next because M^rs Thack is improving though slowly indeed — for of mornings especially her

[110] Sir Moses Haim Montefiore (1784-1885), later (1846) first Baronet, the stockbroker and philanthropist.

spirits are curiously low, she is so absent then that I don't like to trust her. It is all stomach I believe I was such a fool as to take only 1 sitting room, and rue that silly piece of economy heartily. as for Miss Thackeray she as you may fancy does not disturb me the least — never asks questions, never tumbles down & hurts her nose, never begins to roar: but she is the life & soul of the house with her tantrums —

This next part of the letter is addressed to my dear Miss Graham as she is the only Capitalist of our family. Chapman & Hall before they give me the £ 100 want the security of some solvent person that their money should be reimbursed in case of my death or non-fulfilment of my contract. I asked G. M, but the old lady refused in a fright, fancying I wanted her money &c. — Now if Mary will write me a letter saying My dear William I have ——— in the funds, and I shall be happy to be your security with Messrs Chapman & Hall, in any manner they like: and if this letter is sufficient without any further documents I promise hereby to honour their draft for 100£ in case of your death, or on receiving proof of the nonfulfilment of the contract "Messrs C. & H may refer to Messrs Lubbock & Co as to my respectability — " Such a document as this I say will get me 100£ in a jiffy, and please God Mary's money will not be wanted & I shan't die until the book is completed. As soon as I see myself decently in the way of making money & have had my stricture [111] cured I will insure my life.

We have I trust escaped from a pretty kettle of fish. Mrs Shawe who had not heard from her daughter for a month, threatened unless she were answered by return of Post to set off from Ireland and come to see her. The best of it is that her letter was delayed a couple of days in London before it was sent hither, and I am not yet certain that we shan't see her in one of the steamers — if so there will be scenes, and more nervousness on poor Isabella's part: who ⟨is⟩ low still, but has no flights such as she had during my absence, & on m⟨y⟩ arrival. G. M. is angry with her for not answering when spoken [to] — the ⟨poor⟩ thing did not do this from sulkiness but from sheer absence & depression. You & Polly must

[111] See Appendix XXVIII.

not in the future be so open in your talk to M^rs Parker, M^rs P. repeated to Isabella just before her confinement every word you said, about her faults not doing her duty & so on, & in the course of her depression the poor thing had worked up these charges so as to fancy herself a perfect demon of wickedness — God abandoned & the juice knows what: so that all the good of your reproof was that she became perfectly miserable, & did her duty less than ever.[112] It was an unlucky time to lecture her that's all: when she is better talk away and amen. — This is of course a secret.

Dearest Mammy this is stupid stuff & has taken several days writing. God knows I have enough on my brains just now if I do it properly. Thank God I thrive under it though, and have managed to do about £ 20 worth of work for the Times this fortnight,[113] and am now deep in a Shabby Genteel Story for Fraser.[114] I have not sent you the former numbers, because I want them to refer to. God bless you. We are all prospering. Missy as brown as a berry. Mamma well, & I just on the point of setting out to a little quiet Inn two miles off, where I have quiet, & a tea-garden to myself, as for writing here except when the folks are in bed it is impossible.

P.S. Dont you go for to take any of M^rs Shawe's freaks & come off out of pity for me. I sh^d be glad to see my dear Mammy but she w^d do more harm than good here

Direct to London

[112] See above, No. 162.

[113] Thackeray's article on "Fielding's Works" appeared in *The Times* of September 2.

[114] The concluding installment, chapters 7 to 9, published in *Fraser's Magazine* for October.

179.                  TO CHAPMAN AND HALL
                        8 SEPTEMBER 1840

Hitherto unpublished.

                              13 Great Coram S$^t$ Brunswick Sq$^{re}$
                              8 September. 1840.

Gentlemen

    I propose to publish a couple of volumes called Titmarsh in
Ireland, of the size and somewhat of the nature of my Paris Book,
and I shall be glad to make arrangements with you for the purchase of the book upon the following terms.

    £ 120 to be paid on hand
        50 on the delivery of the MSS.
        40 on the sale of the 1$^{st}$ 250.
        35 2$^{nd}$ ........................... 250. 500
        35 3$^{rd}$ ........................... 250. 750.
        35 4$^{th}$ ........................... 250. 1000
        35 5$^{th}$ ........................... 250. 1250. —

Half-profits in a second edition if it sh$^d$ be called for.
After this the copyright is mine. the Plates will be not less than
12 besides vignettes wood-cuts &c., and will be executed by myself.
Unless illness or any domestic calamity sh$^d$ intervene I propose to
deliver the work to you before the 31 December.

                              very faithfully yours
                              W M Thackeray.[115]

[115] After Thackeray's signature appears the following document, written in
another hand: "Memorandum of an agreement entered into between William
Thackeray Esq$^e$ of 13 Great Coram Street Brunswick Square on the one part
and Edward Chapman & William Hall, publishers on the other part.
    The said William Thackeray agrees to write a work to be called Titmarsh in
Ireland to consist of two volumes of the size & somewhat of the nature of the
Paris Sketch Book — & the said Edward Chapman & William Hall agree to
purchase the copyright thereof on the conditions following —
    W$^m$ Thackeray engages to write the work, and deliver it into the hands of
Chapman & Hall by the 31$^{st}$ December & to execute the plates both designs &
etchings for the same

180.        TO MRS. RITCHIE
### 10 SEPTEMBER 1840

Hitherto unpublished.

10 September. 1840.

My dear Aunt.

We found Charlotte's kind note on our return from Margate, where the sea-air seemed to do my dear little invalid a great deal of good. We have been in London only 3 days, and now she is just as bad as ever she has been — there is something in the air of this dismal Coram Street that seems to give us all the blue-devils.

This being the case, we are all going off in a body to M$^{rs}$ Shawe at Cork: there I shall leave the little part of the family and go wandering about as best I may. I send back the prescription with many thanks, when I could make my wife take the medicine it seemed I think to revive her: but she has a vast aversion to all Doc-

---

Chapman & Hall engage to pay for an unlimited right and interest in the sale of an impression of fifteen hundred copies as follows. —

£120 to be paid down this day
   50 on the delivery of the MSS.
   40 on the sale of the first 250 copies
   35 "   "   "   "   "  second 250 "
   35 "   "   "   "   "  third 250 "
   35 "   "   "   "   "  fourth 250 "
   35 "   "   "   "   "  fifth 250   "
   35 "   "   "   "   "  sixth 250   "

£350                1500

And in case of a Second Edition being required, half the profits of the same to be divided between the said William Thackeray & Edward Chapman & William Hall.

That subject to these conditions M$^{r}$ Thackeray will assign to Chapman & Hall the entire copyright of the first & second editions of the work entitled Titmarsh in Ireland, when called upon so to do —

London 8$^{th}$ September 1840

W. M. Thackeray.<br>Edward Chapman<br>William Hall."

It will be noted that the sum to be realized by Thackeray on an edition of 1,500 copies is actually £385 rather than £350.

tor's stuff. Also I return, with my humblest compliments to Miss Jane her book of Versailles that I thought I had restored months ago — but we are very careless about things from w^h we have had all the good we can get.

Old John will garrison the house; — we intend to make an absurd kind of attempt at letting it. Good bye my dear Aunt I hope I shall be able to send you better news from Potatoland.

Ever yours affectionately.

W M Thackeray

181.          TO MRS. SHAWE
10 SEPTEMBER 1840

Hitherto unpublished.

My dear M^rs Shawe.

From your letter I gather that you will scarce have room for us in your little cottage, but I think to see her Mother & sister will do my poor Isabella a great deal of good — so I have brought her from Margate, made my arrangements with the booksellers here, and shall come off by the Jupiter (or its companion) steamer on Saturday we shall be with you by Tuesday: [116] and please God your care & the Cork air will set our poor little woman to rights again — Do what he will a man is but a bad nurse, and you & Jane must look to the little woman and get her back to spirits again. There is nothing but lowness the matter with her as I've told you: but this came on as bad as ever almost, directly we reached London.

Will you look out for a bed for me, and I think one for Missy & Brodie: we shall all be with you please God on Tuesday: and I write in the greatest hurry: having 20 more letters to send.

Affectionately yrs

W M T.

[116] There was at this time a steamer plying weekly between London and Cork. The passage from London to Dublin required seventy hours; that from London to Cork cannot have taken many less. (James Fraser, *Handbook for Travellers in Ireland*, London, 1844, p. 1) Thackeray and his family embarked on September 12 and reached Cork on September 15.

182.        TO MRS. CARMICHAEL-SMYTH
10 SEPTEMBER 1840

*Address:* M^rs Carmichael Smyth | Avenue S^te Marie | Faubg du Roule | Paris.
*Postmarks:* 10 SE 1840, 12 SEPT. 40 CALAIS.  Hitherto unpublished.

My dearest Mammy. Your letter arrived this morning, and
dear Polly's voucher, of w^h there is however no need. I have made
my arrangements with C & H, who have given me £120 down, &
with this I shall be able to clear off some small scores, and carry the
whole case to boot. A boat leaves London every Saturday: 3 days
on the voyage, but it will do Isabella good I think, and so please
God we shall all be at Cork on Tuesday. Cook goes. John remains
behind to take care of the house, & let it if possible — a difficulty
this dull season. When the book is done dearest Mammy we may
talk about Italy or what you will: I tried C & H very hard to take
an Italian book now but they would not. So we must wait.

Poor Isabella's lowness of spirits came back directly on returning
to London: I think it would drive me mad to be much longer alone
with it, and I am sure female companionship w^d be the best thing
for her. I was thinking of writing to you, and sending my wife &
bab[e]s to Boulogne but she will be well with her mother, while
she is unwell — a bull: but I mean there will be no scenes and
quarrels. A couple of months please God will set her up somewhat,
and will suffice or nearly so for my Irish tour. The children are in
famous health: and so am I only my rogue of a wife makes me
melancholy. God bless you all, & thank my dear Po⟨lly⟩ for her
letter — I'm going to send the *plate-chest* to C & H's [117] — a kind
of genteel pawn, but they seem manly straight forward people: &
liberal rather than otherwise. We were not 3 weeks at Margate, &
it cost £ 32 — O Titmarsh Titmarsh why did you marry? — why
for better or for worse. Let us pray God to enable us to bear
either. I have lots of letters to write, & am just as dismal as possible.

[117] Thackeray did not recover his plate chest from Chapman and Hall until
after he moved to Young Street in 1846. See below, No. 1604.

God bless all: the next letter please God will be from the beautiful city called Cork. I trust your India mail has brought you good news.

183.          TO MRS. CARMICHAEL-SMYTH
                    17 SEPTEMBER 1840

*Address:* A M. | Monsieur de Vaudricourt | 4 Avenue S<sup>te</sup> Marie. Faubg du Roule | Paris. | M de V. est prié d'expedier cette lettre à M. le Major Smyth. *Postmarks:* CORK SE 17 1840, 23 SEPT. 40 CALAIS. Hitherto unpublished.

Grattan's Hill. Lower Glanmire Road. Cork.
17 September 1840.

My dearest Mother. We arrived here on Tuesday after a long horrible journey of three days and four nights that I can't think of now without shuddering. My dear wife's melancholy augmented to absolute insanity during the voyage, and I had to watch her for 3 nights (when she was positively making attempts to destroy herself,) [118] and brought her here quite demented. She is better — a little better — just now, and the Doctor a very eminent & experienced man of these parts gives me the strongest hopes of her, and narrates 500 instances of similar maladies w<sup>h</sup> he has cured. M<sup>rs</sup> Shawe says that she was herself affected with melancholy when she nursed, and a lady has just this minute left her who was mad herself & tried to destroy herself in the same way. Jane & her mother have done my poor patient a great deal of good, We have lodgings next door, the children with their Grandmother sometimes, sometimes with an old Irish nurse here who tends a number of brats of the house, fine rosy respectable children. I write this by my dear little woman's bedside, who won't permit me to leave her, but I bear up very well. Indeed & upon my honour I find myself rather relieved than otherwise now that the matter has come to a point, I can see what I never did till now that she has been deranged for

---

[118] Though there is some conflict in Thackeray's testimony on the point, it appears that Isabella first tried to kill herself on Sunday, September 13, and renewed her attempts at suicide the following night.

several weeks past. On the day I went to Belgium she began to
laugh as I went away, — she has been in this mood more or less
since her confinement. Every single medical man I have met has
told the same story. They say she must be treated with calmers,
restoratives, plenty of food & quiet & very little diet — the dear
baby thrives on the bottle as well as ever.

What my plans will be, of course I can't say — they will depend
upon the recovery of the dear little woman. I am not the least cast
down, or uncomfortable in mind or body. — This seems a sort of
heartlessness in me, but when a matter has come to a head I feel
little more anxiety concerning it — and what do you think I'm
about at this minute? busy making a play w.ʰ Charles Mathews
promises to give particular attention to for Covent Garden. This I
can do as I want no books for the purpose — as for Chapman &
Hall they must wait. God bless all.          · W M T.


184.          TO MRS. CARMICHAEL-SMYTH
              19–20 SEPTEMBER 1840

*Address:* A. Monsieur M. de Vaudricourt. | 4 Avenue S.ᵗᵉ Marie. Faub.ᵍ du
Roule | Paris. | pour Madame Smyth. *Postmarks:* CORK SE 20 1840, 25
SEPT. 40 CALAIS. Hitherto unpublished.

at M.ʳˢ Mahony's. Grattan's-Hill Cork.
Saturday 18 ¹¹⁹ September

My dearest Mammy. Your letter reached me safely here yesterday with Miss Hamerton's kind enclosures — please God I shall be
able to profit by them. Thank Heaven my little woman is prospering, and is, not quite restored again, but astonishingly better, as
well as she was at Margate certainly for now I see more clearly
than I did then — much better than she has been since our horrible
steam-boat journey. I longed to send her to you: but you were on
the move, & it seemed cruel to interrupt your promised journey of
pleasure. The Doctor says Isabellas progress is extraordinary, & I
have just left her upstairs with Jane, who is excellent in her atten-

¹¹⁹ A mistake for Saturday, September 19.

tions to her, and who is reading to her verses from the Psalms, w.^h the other is repeating with perfect good sense and in that pretty touching voice, you know of. She could no more have done this 3 days ago than fly. Yonder is Anny with her stout voice roaring above those of 1/2 a dozen good-natured dirty little companions that she has found in the children of the worthy mistress of the lodging-house. Little baby is purring & smiling the dearest creature ever seen, but what grieves me is that poor Brodie, sickening yesterday, is now on her bed with headache pains in her limbs & fever. Pray God it be nothing serious. I never saw anything more beautiful than that woman's attention to the children on board the steamer. She was sick almost every 1/4 of an hour, but up again immediately staggering after the little ones feeding one & fondling another. Indeed a woman's heart is the most beautiful thing that God has created and I feel I can't tell you what respect for her.

M.^rs Shawe, as usual brags bustles bothers prates incessantly of her great merits & sacrifices, but is good in the main — one must not judge too hardly a woman who is really & truly demented. Jane is excellent, & has done more good to her sister than Mother or husband. Poor Ben Creagh an uncle of Isabella was absolutely blubbering as he shook hands with me, and tears seem always at the command of these good-natured simple people. I was affected yesterday by hearing that Caroline Spencer [120] came to visit the Shawes, & hearing of Isabella's case, the 3 knelt down, and Caroline S. prayed for three-quarters-of-an-hour. It was a sweet prayer says M.^rs Shawe, awestricken at the eloquence of Caroline. Whatever it was it was a good and kind one: and indeed a warm heart is better than all the heads in the world. Jane has sense talent and feeling — poor thing poor thing that she sh.^d be condemned to live ceaselessly with such a woman, or such a whirlwind.

We have just had a scene — fancy that — in the midst of all this trouble she can't keep her monstrous tongue quiet. Don't *you* however come forward. It would only make matters worse.

Sunday. The Doctor, a very benevolent old gentleman has just been with my wife, and pronounces her still better. What we shall

[120] A member of the Parisian English colony, visiting in Ireland.

have to contend with after her return to health will be the most difficult malady of all — the profound abattement and disgust of life under w.<sup>h</sup> she labors. She does not care in the least for me or her children as yet: and if not most carefully watched would I am confident make another attempt on her life. This day week was the last — O blessed God that prevented the committing of the crime, and saved her as he did.

When she is better, dearest Mother you must come to my aid as I am sure you will, and help in the hard task of guarding her body, and healing her soul. The place here is wonderfully peaceful and bright: the church bells are ringing, and in the midst of all this trouble I can't help feeling a kind of happiness & tranquillity. Brodie thank God is much better, Missy slept with her Grandmother last night — of course roaring the whole time, and I leave you to fancy M.<sup>rs</sup> Shawe's account of the transaction, & of the agonies endured by her blessed Jane — Jane is cordially jealous of you all, but I don't dislike that she sh.<sup>d</sup> take her Mother's part. We go pretty smoothly to day, and shall probably not have another row till Tuesday —

God bless my dearest Mother: and all round your table wherever that may be — I wish you would all of you take a trip to Bruges it is within 16 hours of London, the prettiest calmest place in the world: but all these matters must be arranged a long while hence.

W M T.

185.    TO MRS. CARMICHAEL-SMYTH
21–23 SEPTEMBER 1840

*Address:* Madame Smyth | chez M. de Vadricourt. 4 Avenue S.<sup>te</sup> Marie | Faubourg du Roule. Paris. *Postmarks:* SE 24 1840, 26 SE 1840. Hitherto unpublished.

Monday 22? [121]

My dearest Mammy. Our poor patient has to day made such a wonderful progress towards convalescence, that my heart is full of

[121] Actually Monday, September 21.

gratitude towards Almighty God, and I must sit down and be happy awhile with you. She has been laughing and talking affectionately and simply (with some little wanderings of very small account,) and she has been weeping a good deal & deploring her faults and feeling her errors, and she has had our darling Anny with her who looked up and prayed God to bless her dear Mamma, — it is the first day since the horrible day when her malady broke out, that she has seemed to care for her children, and I cannot but feel that her recovery is near at hand. Thank God for it a thousand times. Oh my dearest old Mother, that I had you here to fling my arms round your neck, and have some one to whom I could tell my happiness, and who would share it. — There is only poor Brodie of whom I can make a friend: and indeed her steadfastness and affection for the little ones deserves the best feelings I can give her. The poor thing has been very unwell, but never flinched for a minute, and without her I don't know what would have become of us all. When my little woman gets well — as she will please God. It must be your task to *keep* her so: to put her mind into healthful train and make her able to perform the duties w^h she will be called on to fulfil. We have both of us avoided them as yet, and not met them honestly as we should. I must learn to love home more, and do my duty at the fire side as well as in my writing-room: and I do see how out of all this dreadful trial profit will come to us, if it shall please God to let us have the chance. Make me more humble, O God, & less selfish: and give me strength to resist the small temptations of life that I may be fitted for the greater trials.

Tuesday. To day's progress is not so great as yesterday's as how should it [be] but thank God my little woman is perfectly sensible (except twice in the day after long conversations) and though very melancholy none the worse for that for it is a *moral* melancholy as it were: and she is deploring her own unworthiness &c. The old Doctor who at his 5^th fee said he sh^d be glad for the future to visit me every other time as a friend, is very skillful and tender I think and has been putting the young woman's stomach right by some of those abominations w^h you don't like to hear of. I attribute her illness very much to her extraordinary indolence and apathy in

MRS. SHAWE

*From a sketch by Thackeray*

MRS. SHAWE

*From a caricature by Thackeray*

this matter of medicine. Tears prayers threats I used to use in vain
with her: but the cloud was upon her then, though I did not know
it, and we must pray God to put her mind clear.

But for this you must come to my help. I don't like to tell you
of the conduct of Mʳˢ Shawe: so unmotherly has it been. As far as
bringing her daughter tea and dinner & sitting by her bedside she
is well enough: but she has a spare room in her house and refused
to receive her on account of her nerves (she has been very ill that's
certain) & those of her darling Jane. She abused me for bringing
her away from London, said her daughter had been denied to her
in time of health to be thrown on her in sickness, and so on. She
tried to pump out from Brodie whether I had been ill-treating her
or not, and I scarcely get a meal at her home but I am obliged to
swallow an insult with it. — but why talk of it? the woman is mad,
more desperately self-deceived than any I ever knew — I am
obliged to take all of her conduct in silence, for if I said a word, and
this is the damnable ⟨advantage of the⟩ ¹²² woman: she would bring
the war into my own terri⟨tory by taking revenge⟩ upon my poor
wife, withdraw herself & Jane from her ⟨and so you see I⟩ am at
her mercy. Every time I see the woman I pray God ⟨for poor
Isabella's⟩ sake to keep me out of a quarrel. What a fool I was to
⟨believe that such a⟩ woman would behave decently, and give a
shelter ⟨to her daughter. I⟩ declare to God when she refused, and
talked about ⟨her nerves, God forgive⟩ her; responsibility; and her
darling Jane, I was quite ⟨sick at heart, and⟩ yet this woman humbugs herself, and has I am pe⟨rsuaded no thought⟩ at this minute
but that she is performing her duty ⟨in the most perfect &⟩ admirable way! It would do you good to hear Brodie ⟨express her scorn
&⟩ hatred of her.

So you see that as soon as we can move her with saf⟨ety, we
must. The Doctor⟩ says a sea-voyage will soon be calculated to do
h⟨er not the least⟩ harm, you must dear Mother & Father devise
some ⟨means of caring for⟩ her, and I must retrace my steps, and

¹²² A third part of the second sheet of this letter has crumbled away. I have
tried to fill the gap thus left in the text, but it should be kept in mind that my
restoration is altogether conjectural.

come back ⟨to Ireland, for out⟩ of the £120 given by Chapman & Hall, I have only £⟨. . . remaining, my⟩ servant's wages & other expences having swallowed ⟨the rest & all the sums⟩ that were due to me. The book must be done some⟨time soon, that is⟩ clear, now if I can but venture to separate mysel⟨f from poor Isabella⟩ now is the time of my fortune. But for these sad ev⟨ents, I was a made⟩ man — You must all lay your heads together and thin⟨k how to pull us⟩ from the mire: — and thank God I can trust in you⟨r help. Write to me as⟩ soon as you can, but not a word to Mʳˢ Shawe — a ⟨. . .⟩ [123]

Wednesday. I was on duty yesterday and could find no time to take my le⟨tter to the post. I can't give⟩ you any account of a decided advance to day — except this. My wife is quite ⟨sane, but very melancholy⟩ low, & ennuyée. I cannot interest her with reading talking or children⟨. She appears to have no⟩ affection for them, but seems devoured by gloom, thinks she has entailed ⟨all kinds of misfortune on⟩ me, and that she was never fit to be a wife. The old story, & alas partly the ⟨truth. One of her forms⟩ of wandering is to fancy when people go out of the room that they will never c⟨ome back — more hopelessness⟩ and want of trust in God than mania. As soon as ever I can I will move her ⟨from here, for the house is⟩ in a filthy state, & it is only now for 3 months that her tongue begins to grow f⟨luent. . . .⟩ [124]

⟨. . .⟩ [125] into her former state. Here is the little baby come in to ⟨kiss me good night — ⟩ what a smiling charming little wench it is. God bless ⟨you all. Put your⟩ heads together & think what may be done.

W M T.

---

[123] From one to three words are missing here.
[124] From one to five words are missing here.
[125] Two or three words are missing here.

186.          TO MRS. CARMICHAEL-SMYTH
                 30 SEPTEMBER 1840

*Address:* M$^{rs}$ Carmichael Smyth | Avenue S$^{te}$ Marie | Faubourg du Roule |
Paris. *Postmarks:* CORK SE 30 1840, 5 OCT. 40 CALAIS. Hitherto unpublished.

I wish you could see the stately drawing room in w$^h$ ⟨. . .⟩ [126]
Irish order of architecture. Two of the blinds wont go: a ⟨. . .⟩
There is no paper to the walls but in revenge a grand ⟨. . .⟩ piece
that cost £20, and horrid pictures of the house p⟨. . .⟩ a chair that
is shoved against it to keep out the wind ⟨. . .⟩ the finest cracks
though quite new. There is no poker ⟨. . .⟩ well, and my supply of
coals is brought me on a ⟨. . .⟩ of an old saucepan. I wish you could
see Paggy the ⟨. . .⟩ Isabella says like a hearth-broom — it is the
exact sim⟨. . .⟩ blowsy children with an old nurse with whom Anny
p⟨. . .⟩ young woman has already got a decided brogue.

In this manner have we been going on. Isabella is well with the
children now thank God, and begins to be touched by natural
beauty: of w$^h$ there is an astonishing deal in the neighbourhood, the
rides about (we have been out the last 4 days) are charming, and I
long to have a sketch book & put down some of the scenes I see —
in a little time perhaps this will be feasible but not yet. No scenery
could be more wild, tender, gay, solemn, romantic & trimly-culti-
vated than we have seen to day: wonderful rocks, gardens, pastures
rivers, waterfalls, & buildings that might keep a man painting for
years in the circuit of a couple of miles. It is ten o'clock dearest
Mother, and as I was awake at 3, then at ⟨work a⟩nd pretty well
employed until now, I shall say God bless you and all at ⟨home⟩:
and grant that my little wife amends as she has done these 2 day⟨s.⟩
⟨. . .⟩ [127] till now, writing at her bedside. The little baby is just
come home from being vaccinated — it is the dearest, smilingest
little thing never out of humour     Anny was with her, and in a

---

[126] About four words are missing in this and each of the nine following
hiatuses.
[127] Six lines have here been torn away.

great passion at the idea that any one was going to put little Sissy to pain

Shall I buy PA some shirts here? beautiful ones with linen fronts very fine & well made for five shillings a piece — such cost 9/ in London, and 15 in Paris.

How glad I sh$^d$ be to make the Italian trip — if this woman w$^d$ but get better and if Matthews w$^d$ but accept my play, I have done near 3 acts of the 5, I would fling myself at the Irish book and get it off my hands and be as happy as a king in Spring: with money in my pockets too. God bless you dear⟨est⟩ Mother

W M T.

30 September

187.          TO MRS. CARMICHAEL-SMYTH
             4–5 OCTOBER 1840

*Address:* M$^{rs}$ Carmichael Smyth. | 4 Avenue S$^{te}$ Marie | Faubourg du Roule | Paris. *Postmarks:* CORK OC 6 1840, 12 OC. 40 CALAIS. Hitherto un-published.

My dearest Mammy. Your dear kind letter was of great comfort to me, for though I knew very well that you would sell your smock if need were to help me in my want, yet it is pleasant to have the testimony of it, & I have been half tempted to fling it in M$^{rs}$ Shawe's face, and say there Madam you who prate about self-sacrifices, you bragging old humbug see the way in w$^h$ my mother welcomes your daughter, & think how you have received her yourself. But the woman is mad that is the fact or so monstrously unreasonable that it is in vain to talk reason to her, she never speaks but to brag and to lie, and doesn't know truth from falsehood.

Alas I can't tell you that my dear woman is better — better she is in bodily health certainly, sleeping, eating, digesting better, and better she was in mind for 3 days past, but to day she has been clouded & rambling again. However when I look back to her worst days 3 weeks ago and her worst day this week, I see confidently the progress she has made and gratefully thank God for it.

Dearest Mother you don't know what she did this day 3 weeks: but as M$^{rs}$ Shawe has told it to Miss Carry Spencer, & Miss Spencer to her sister and all the gossips at Paris you must hear it. On this Sabbath day, on board the boat, the poor thing flung herself into the water (from the water-closet) & was twenty minutes floating in the sea, before the ship's boat even *saw* her. O my God what a dream it is! I hardly believe it now I write. She was found floating on her back, paddling with her hands, and had never sunk at all. This it was that told me her condition     I see now she had been ill for weeks before, and yet I was obstinately blind to her state, and Powell & the surgeons must tell me that there was not the slightest reason to call a physician, that nothing was the matter with her, that change of air w^d cure her & so on. O God what a mercy this was! I hardly remember the thing now — so sudden was it: it did not shock me at the time either. I don't know why: but it is better you should know it from me, than from any of M^rs Spencer's gossips who might suddenly pour it out upon you at Paris.

In the next night she made fresh attempts at destruction and the first week here was always attempting to quit the bed: You may fancy what rest I had. I had a riband round her waist, & to my waist, and this always woke me if she moved. But lately she has made no sort of similar attempt, and only yesterday spoke of it in terms of the greatest remorse and sorrow, nor will she I do believe fall again into the same frightful mania. But she has for the present the greatest dread of steamers, & I fear for some time to come putting her to the risk of a voyage. There is a little boat to Cove 7 miles off. When she is better I may practice her on that: and then I must get her to Dublin, from Dublin to Liverpool by night with a dose of opium from L to London, from London to Dover, & so on. It will cost me £ 40 to bring them all that way: nor dare I separate her from the children: for though she does not care for them when near, she is wretched if away from them indeed & indeed I hardly see my way at all just now. We must ⟨wait⟩ until she is ⟨muc⟩h better before we venture on a move.

Monday 5. We are a little better this morning as is always the case on a sunny day. I have been for a little walk into Cork. Dan O'Connell is coming in in state, a great occasion but I dare not allow myself to go from home for so long a time as 3 hours. My wife won't sit still, wont employ herself, wont do anything that she is asked & vice versâ. Mong Jew what a time of it, from four o'clock till nine this morning — as soon as ever I was asleep my lady woke me. She had had a decent slumber herself from eight until four, & when awake herself will give me no rest. Never mind as Anny says when she breaks the tumblers, the discipline is good for one's disposition if not very improving to the mind, and my health thank God is famous. The country round about is delicious: how I wish I had the time to draw some of it! : but my work now that the woman is better is just ten times more harassing than before. Poor Pa must look out for a draw some day or other.

I have nearly done the 4ᵗʰ act of my play — it is by no means a masterpiece but has some good lively stuff in it I think. Three acts are already with the C. Garden people: how I shall jump if it be accepted, but that is too much luck!

I write this day to old John concerning the house, putting it into the hands of Messʳˢ Pearsall & Jorden from whom I got it. I could entertain you with some more troubles if I liked, but for this time you have enough.

I have been reading the Court Martial of poor Captain Reynolds, and that scoundrel Lord Cardigan.[128] When are we to get rid of this insolent scum of lords altogether? — such a republican as I am

---

[128] Richard Anthony Reynolds (b. 1807), who had been Thackeray's schoolfellow at Charterhouse, was senior captain in the Eleventh Hussars, the regiment of James Thomas Brudenell (1797–1868), seventh Earl of Cardigan. On August 25 Lord Cardigan gave a large dinner at his home, during the course of which he let fall an observation prejudicial to Reynolds's character. Reynolds remonstrated with his superior in two letters, the second written after he had been directed not to address Lord Cardigan except on official business. This offence led to his court-martial early in October. During the trial he was permitted to offer no extenuating evidence, though it was obvious that his insubordination had been provoked by Lord Cardigan's arbitrary and tyrannical exercise of power. Later in the month he was found guilty and cashiered. (*Spectator*, 1840, pp. 919, 942–943, and 1020) Meanwhile, Lord Cardigan had on September 12 wounded Reynolds's friend Captain Harvey Tuckett in a duel. He was tried before the House of Lords on February 16, 1841, for firing a pistol with intent to murder, but found not guilty. For a brief account of the character and career of this notorious Victorian rake, see G. E. C.'s *Complete Peerage*, ed. Gibbs and others, III, 16–17.

becoming! but not in your way — What I want is strong government and social equality. This is stuff to write.

I wish you could see Missy in the bath, such a picture of health
and beauty, and our dear dear little Harriet, that I love more than
the last even — the sweetest tempered little thing God ever made
surely. The mother notices them but seldom. God bless you dearest Mother and all in Paris: how I wish the sea did not divide us!
but pray God it won't long. Farewell: I'm in famous health &
condition.

188.              TO MRS. SHAWE
                  11 OCTOBER 1840

*Address:* M^rs Shawe. | Grattan's Hill. | Lower Glanmire Road. | Cork. *Post-
marks:* BRISTOL OC 11 1840, CORK OC 14 1840. Hitherto unpublished.

                  14 Hope Square Clifton. Sunday.
Dear M^rs Shawe.

After a very calm but tedious passage we reached this at 6 this
morning, & my dear little wife is I think better for the change —
better in health & in mind. Pray God she may continue so.

I have determined on staying here for a week unless she should
get worse: & have written you a long letter of 9 pages w^h I shall
keep by me for a week before I send or burn it [129] it is a very free
one: but I shall be able to know at the week's end whether you are
as much in fault as I think you, or whether I have been in a passion, or whether I have any business to lecture you. All points for
calm consideration.

You said I think there was money for Isabella at the agents, in
that case had you not better make the order payable to me, as it is
probable our poor patient won't be able or willing to sign her name.
I need not beg you also, seeing how I am situated to use your best
endeavours to get the arrears of her allowance paid up.

                              Truly yours
                              W M Thackeray.
I have been begging Isabella to write a word here but in vain.

[129] This letter has not been preserved.

189.          TO MRS. CARMICHAEL-SMYTH
                    11 OCTOBER 1840

*Address:* M^rs Carmichael Smyth | Avenue S^te Marie. | Faubourg du Roule |
Paris. *Postmark:* 16 OCT. 40 CALAIS. Hitherto unpublished.

14 Hope Square. Clifton. Sunday.

My dearest Mother. That woman at Cork became so odious to
me, (I have written her a letter of 9 pages, w^h composition occupied
me on board the steamer) — that on Friday morning lying in bed
awake with my poor Isabella really worse than she had been for
some time, worried by the howling of Anny, by the paw-pawing of
her mother, & the discomforts of the place — that I say lying
awake for 4 hours I said to myself why am I to stay longer here? —
and this bright thought having occurred to me, I instantly felt myself happier, got up, walked to the Doctor who advised me to go
by all means, and so came off at 2 o'clock by the Queen Steamer,
giving M^rs Shawe no hint of my departure until 1: when she was
advising me to put Isabella into a mad-house. We had a very calm
passage though a tedious one reaching this place just 1/2 an hour
too late for the tide, & so being obliged to lie outside all night, w^h
spared some expenses ⟨. . .⟩ ¹³⁰ only save me another night in my
boots. My wife is decidedly ⟨. . .⟩ ¹³¹ though the better is very
bad indeed: but still I can't he⟨lp . . .⟩ if judiciously treated. All
that I had by going to Cork is as fol⟨lows:⟩

| Passage & extra expences &c | 15£ |
|---|---|
| Doctor, Nurse & Apothecary. | 20£ |
| Lodging bills, & Cars to drive &c. | 10£. |
| Personal expences, & other charges. | 4£. |
| Passage from Cork to Bristol &c | 9£. |
| | 58£. |

---

¹³⁰ Two words are missing here.
¹³¹ This and the following hiatus are of about five words each.

I have 20£ left within a few shillings: and could be ⟨. . .⟩ [132] in my pocket on Tuesday: but this air is very fresh & balmy ⟨. . .⟩ very oppressive. If my wife grows no worse I shall keep her he⟨re . . .⟩ my dear Mother can come to me. Do come dearest Mother: ⟨. . .⟩ give me some money — somehow or the other.

We will then see what is to be done. whether I shall come ⟨. . .⟩ a second series of the Sketch-Book: wʰ I could easily sell I presume: or wheth⟨er my wife⟩ shall go into some asylum near London, making over the children to you — ⟨Or what⟩ else. There will I do believe be no war. Brodie is going to leave me soon, she is to be married to a man very well to do in the world: but she won't go until something can be done with the children & their poor mother.

There are the people at Church singing hymns — it was this day 4 weeks that Almighty God was so wonderfully gracious to me. Indeed I have a thankful spirit to him, & see good in the midst of all this misfortune: — it seems almost wrong to be happy — and yet I am. Dont come if you are unwell: but certainly otherwise. The expence will be not much greater: for I must have a whole coach to travel in here, a rotonde in France & so on. I doubt about the Havre & Rouen boats, because they are public, & may not have private cabins.[133] Farewell: and God bless all.    W M T.

---

[132] This and the following hiatuses are of about five words each.

[133] It did not prove feasible for Mrs. Carmichael-Smyth to come to London, and Thackeray had consequently to take his family to Paris. Lady Ritchie (*Biographical Introductions*, IV, xxx-xxxi) has left an account of the last part of their trip: "After my mother's illness the little household in Coram Street was broken up, and we all went abroad. I can remember my father punishing me as we travelled to Paris all night in the creaking diligence. I wanted to get out and walk, and they wouldn't let me, and I cried on and on. There was a man in a cap I didn't like, with his nose against the window. He frowned at me when I looked at him. My father was in the corner of the diligence oppo-site to me and the nurse and the baby, and he struck a match, and lit up a little lantern, which he held up to amuse me. But I only cried the louder. Then he said gravely, 'If you go on crying, you will wake the baby, and I shall put out the candle;' so I went on crying, and I woke the baby, who began to cry too; then the man in the corner scolded again, and my father blew out the lantern, and suddenly all was dark. I could not believe it, never before had I been so severely punished. 'Light it, light it,' I screamed. 'No,' said

I have written to M^r Ritchie, a long & what you will call a cowardly letter, the upshot of w^h is that I intend to make him pay me all he owes me — I can't be squeamish any longer. I have said that I shall put the matter into Hicks's [134] hands, & shall write to you for accounts &c.


190.              TO JAMES FRASER
                  3 DECEMBER 1840

Hitherto unpublished.

                    4 Avenue S^te Marie.
                 Faubourg Du Roule. Dec^r 3. 1840.
Dear F.

I left purposely the Shabby Genteel Story in such a state that it might be continued in the Magazine or not as you and I liked best. Would you like it to be continued? [135] In that case I should like to write the whole story off, and of course be paid for it on delivering over the MSS. Some 4 sheets I think would complete the affair. Please let me know whether I shall proceed with it, for though I can't afford to begin any new articles at your prices this one had better be gone through with if you think fit.

I shall probably publish the whole tale w^h has a very moral ending in a volume with illustrations.

---

my father's voice in the dark, 'I told you I should put the light out if you cried.' All the time the man in the corner kept on moaning and complaining, and the diligence jogged on, and I suppose I went to sleep on my father's knee at last. I remember hearing him long afterwards speak of that dreadful night, and of the angry Frenchman, who kept saying, 'J'ai la fièvre, mon Dieu. J'ai la fièvre.' The next thing I remember is arriving quite cheerful at Paris, and my grandmother and my grandfather coming down the curling stairs to meet us in the early morning and opening their arms to us all."

[134] Leonard Hicks, of Hicks and Marris, 5 Gray's Inn Square (*Post Office London Directory*, 1847). A few years later the name of his firm had been changed to Leonard Hicks and Son (*Watkins's London Directory*, 1855). He was Thackeray's solicitor for nearly two decades.

[135] Thackeray did not begin *Philip*, the sequel to *A Shabby Genteel Story*, until twenty years later.

I have got a very decent price from Cunningham for a republication of my comic miscellanies, and shall take care this time to say that some of them come from Fraser's Magazine. I thought you would have managed to give Titmarsh a puff.

Will you please to address the enclosed to Maginn?

truly yours<br>W M Thackeray

191.            TO GEORGE CRUIKSHANK
                      1840? [136]

*Address:* Geo Cruikshank Esq^re | Myddleton Terrace | Pentonville. Hitherto unpublished.

George Cruikshank Esq^e

Dear G. C. Although the accompanying papers are rejected by Blackwood who sends them to you herewith, let me caution you agst any such folly as imitating his example. They will suit your book [137] to admiration.

I was in such a cursed hurry of business during the 4 days I was in town as to know that an interview with you was no good. Indeed it wasn't my fault that I broke my promise to you.

Yrs ever dear Cruikshank<br>W M Thackeray

[136] This and the following note appear to have been written not long after June 29, 1840, when Thackeray arranged to send Alexander Blackwood a selection of manuscript. See the letter of that date.

[137] Possibly a reference to the *Comic Almanack* of 1840, illustrated by Cruikshank.

192.            TO  GEORGE  CRUIKSHANK
1840

Hitherto unpublished.

13 G.$^{t}$ Coram S.$^{t}$
Sunday

Dear Cruikshank

Please to send me back my M S. as soon as possible

Yrs

W  M  Thackeray.

# APPENDICES

# APPENDIX I

## PASSAGES CONCERNING THACKERAY IN JOHN ALLEN'S DIARY FOR 1830–1831.

Extracts published in Grier's *John Allen*, p. 29. Original in the Library of Trinity College, Cambridge.

### 1830

January 31: Thackeray came in sat talking with him, & went with him to St Mary's to hear Evans preach against Systems of Morality [1] returning met Young who asked us both to wine with him, after Hall Thackeray sat a little with me then went to Young's where we met Ebden,[2] Bayford,[3] Crawford,[4] Harman, Mazzinghi, Baker & Carne

February 1: went to Thackeray's & walked with him to Roe's ye Fitz-william . . . Thackeray & Young came in & we supped together after supper we played 2 rubbers Cards in which I lost sixpence —

2: called on Thackeray & went with him to Mazzinghi — after we had stayed there some time we set out for Hall but turned back & determined to dine at Mazzinghi's — Morris [5] also (of Christ's) dined with us — over wine Carne came in, took coffee — went with Thackeray to his rooms & stayed there till Sansum came in — Then went to Hailstone & Alford's — very bad sore throat — at Thackeray's rooms I wrote a note to Fitzgerald.

3: Thackeray came in, we had some serious conversation when I affected him to tears he went away with a determination tomorrow to lead a new life, Prayed for him Fitzgerald & myself afterwards in tears

4: went to morning chapel, called Thackeray. *prayed* . . . went with Thackeray to Young's —

5: had a letter from Fitzgerald saying he was reconciled to his mother

---

[1] See *A Course of Sermons Preached Before the University of Cambridge* (1830) by Robert Wilson Evans (1789–1866), Fellow and Tutor of Trinity College, and later (1856–1865) Archdeacon of Westmorland.

[2] John Watts Ebden of Trinity Hall, B. A., 1832, M. A., 1835.

[3] Allen knew two brothers named Bayford, both of whom were residing at Trinity Hall in 1830: James Heseltine Bayford (1805?–1871), LL. B., 1828; and Augustus Frederick Bayford (1809–1874), LL. B., 1830, LL. D., 1839.

[4] William Conolly Crawford, B. A., 1832, M. A., 1835; and James Woolley Harman (1808?–1854), B. A., 1831, M. A., 1835; both of Caius College.

[5] Laurence Stuart Morris (1810?–1885) of Trinity College, B. A., 1832, M. A., 1835.

thank God for it . . . went with Thackeray & Young to Alford's
rooms where the debate was Whether y$^e$ Elizabethan age merited being
called y$^e$ golden age of English literature — made a very silly attempt at
speaking —

6: went to Thackerays & took coffee there — where I met Sansum
sat up late there

7: went to call on Thackeray, found him in bed. waited & took coffee
with him afterwards he recommended me to apply for y$^e$ u$^d$ mastership of
St. Peter's Pimlico — went to ask Peacock about it — he said he would
give me capital testimonials but thought it scarcely good enough for
me — wrote home about it [6] . . . Thackeray came up — expressed
some doubts of X$^t$ being = with God, read over St Matthew together &
he was convinced thank God for it

8: dined after Chapel with Thackeray where I met Crohone,[7] Sansum
& Young — during wine Hailstone came in sat there latish

10: I went to Thackeray's rooms where I found Sansum & Matthew
of Syndney . . . after supper . . . went to Thackeray's Thackeray
gone to bed Sansum & Matthew gone.

11: went to Thackeray's where I found Sansum who played chess
with me Matthew came & took Thackeray out walking

12: called on Thackeray . . . the Society met at my rooms, where
the debate was whether the capabilities of a country affected its political
state made a tolerable speech — Christie did not speak, Thackeray did
not come — . . . went to Thackeray's found that he had had a silly
quarrel with Evans [8] but that all was then made up —

13: at 1/2 past 5 went to dine with Sansum where I met Thackeray
Evans Broking [9] Matthew & Heaviside — Thackeray got a little
elated — .

14: found a letter from James thoroughly disapproving of the school
at Pimlico . . . Sat with Thackeray till Chapel time Sansum was
there

15: Thackeray had asked me to dinner but I did not go

16: Sitting in my rooms Thackeray came up

18: sat with Carne late when Thackeray came in

[6] For the present Allen's parents persuaded him to decline this position, which
was worth £200 annually, but he held it for a short time after taking his degree in
January, 1832 (Grier, *John Allen*, pp. 27–29).

[7] Probably George Birmingham Crohon (b. 1810?) of Trinity College, who
matriculated in 1829 but did not graduate.

[8] Probably Thomas Evans (b. 1806?) of Trinity College, who matriculated
in 1828 but did not graduate.

[9] Arthur Brooking (1810–1890) of Trinity College, B. A., 1833, M. A.,
1836; James William Lucas Heaviside of Sidney Sussex College, B. A., 1830,
M. A., 1833.

20: at 5 went to dine with Thackeray, where I met Dickinson [10] Hailstone Hind — went away at 9 to read

23: gave my umbrella to Thackeray for his alarum clock . . . went to Young's to return his Encyclopaedia, found supper going on there, stayed, & met Thackeray Harman Haines [11] Mazzinghi Heskith Ebden & Grome —

24: went about 9 to Thackerays where I found Heaviside Baker, Carne Mazzinghi, Bayford, Matthew Bayford supped there

26: went to Hall, Burrows sulky ∴ Thackeray cut yᵉ debate &c. wanted me to open very angry &c. . . . went to Christie's to debate on Lord Strafford's character Hailstone at Law's,[12] Burrows & Thackeray at Mazzinghi's poor debate —

28: at 10 went to Carne's to breakfast where I met 2 Lushingtons,[13] Young, Mazzinghi, Thackeray Baker Hailstone, G. Allen,[14] Leigh of Corpus: Ley of Trinity Dickinson Heyworth

March 2: learnt from Peacock that Williams had been admitted [15] Decʳ 29 —

3: Thackeray came in — Carne came in afterwards & sat talking till late

6: called on Thackeray . . . went to evening chapel — afterwards Mazzinghi came & took tea. Young came up, afterwards Sansum, made bishop tea & made Thackeray an apple pie bed, went to enjoy joke [16] &c.

[10] Probably Henry Strahan Dickinson (b. 1810?) of Trinity College, B. A., 1832, M. A., 1835.
[11] Probably William Clark Haines (1807–1864) of Caius College, B. A., 1833, later (1854 and 1857) Premier of Victoria; Wickham Mayer Hesketh of Trinity Hall, B. A., 1831, M. A., 1835.
[12] Probably William Law (b. 1801?) of Trinity College, B. A., 1826, Fellow, 1827, M. A., 1839.
[13] Edmund Law Lushington (1811–1893) of Trinity College, B. A., 1832, M. A., 1835, married Tennyson's sister and was Professor of Greek at the University of Glasgow from 1838 to 1875. His brother Henry Lushington (1812–1855), B. A., 1834, M. A., 1837, was Chief Secretary to the Governor of Malta from 1847 to 1855. Both had been at Charterhouse with Thackeray.
[14] George John Allen (1810–1883) of Trinity College, B. A., 1833, M. A., 1836, later (1843–1857) Master of Dulwich College; Edward Morris Leigh, B. A., 1832, M. A., 1835.
[15] To holy orders.
[16] This was by no means the only joke played on Thackeray by his friends. "I remember once being at Allen's rather late one night with other friends," Mazzinghi wrote to Grier (*John Allen*, p. 38), "and on leaving we said we would give Thackeray a turn; and finding he had retired to rest, but had left his 'oak unsported', we entered and made all kinds of unearthly noises as a charivari to him. He called out, and we replied in feigned voices, mine being a falsetto. Whereupon he threw open his door, and we could mark in the obscurity a gigantic figure advancing wrapped in white towards us, but having in his hand, it turned out, a

7: Up at Morning Chapel sat at Thackeray's rooms for an hour

9: read . . . some of Bolingbroke's letter on Abp Tillotson's Sermon,[17] in order that I might convince Thackeray, he assumes the point & by that assumption proves it.

10: called on Sansum where Heaviside, Thackeray & Broking came in successively

12: our Society met at Thackeray's rooms — Hailestone spoke most wretchedly

18: Heathcote [18] called on me also Thackeray walked out with the latter in Trinity Walks & had a long & interesting conversation with him about Bolingbroke &c — Poor dear fellow!

19: after Evening Chapel went to y^e Society at Thompson's rooms, Burrows & Thackeray absent . . . Debate about the Utility of University System

21: I read Paley's Evidences till 11. returning home turned in at Thackerays & there found Sansum & Carne

26: Society met at Youngs, Debate — Comparison between the talent of Nap. Buonaparte & O Cromwell — Burrows resigned, adjourned Society till October —

28: Thackeray came up & took breakfast with me, Lloyd also came up

29: borrowed Thackeray's pistol

30: turned into Young's where found Larken [19] Thackeray came in went with him to chapel — afterwards ate a beefsteak with him, Harris by went with them to Sansum's where we met Bailey & had coffee —

31: wrote a line to Fitzgerald gave it to Thackeray [20] & found there Sansum & Harris —

---

powerful missile in the contents of his water-jug, which he threw in our direction, harmlessly, I think; at all events, no one of us ever, that I know admitted having been reached. Thackeray, indeed, chuckled rather over his revenge, and next day inquired which of us had spoken in the thin voice, for, he said, him he had well dowsed. I had personal reasons for knowing the contrary. I mention this anecdote because I thought that Allen had been one of the charivari party, but on reminding the Archdeacon at Prees of the occurrence fifteen years ago, he at once disavowed all solidarity in, and even all memory of the affair, and that somewhat indignantly."

[17] "A Letter Occasioned by One of Archbishop Tillotson's Sermons," first published in Bolingbroke's *Works*, ed. David Mallet (1754).

[18] Probably John Edensor Heathcote (b. 1811?) of Trinity College, B. A., 1833, M. A., 1836.

[19] William Pochin Larken of Jesus College, B. A., 1826, M. A., 1830.

[20] Thackeray was about to depart on a surreptitious visit to Paris, where Fitz-Gerald was living with his aunt, Miss Purcell. "I remember as a boy," he writes in *The Roundabout Papers* (*Works*, XII, 393–394), "at the 'Ship' at Dover (*imperante Carolo Decimo*), when, my place to London being paid, I had but 12s. left after a certain little Paris excursion (about which my benighted parents never knew anything), ordering for dinner a whiting, a beef-steak, and a glass of negus, and the bill was, dinner 7s., glass of negus 2s., waiter 6d., and only half-a-crown

April 22: Thackeray came up to me in y$^e$ evening

   23: went to Evening Chapel brought Thackeray Alford & Thompson to take coffee with me — walked about to Roe's & to Corpus with Thackeray . . . Thackeray gave a letter & seals from FitzGerald after Hall.

   24: Thackeray came up — went to Thompson's to supper Christie Burrows Hailstone Warren [21] Thackeray Alford & Gibbs & Martin of Queens there

   28: called on Thackeray, Sansum, Cookesley & Mayhew [22] there

   30: after Hall walked about with Thompson called with him on Thackeray — Hinde of Corpus there — staid there then Sansum & Harris came in

May 4: after evening chapel walked to Bridges with Sansum & then with him had coffee at Thackerays . . . sat reading Peveril of Peak there.

   5: Thackeray & Young came in

   7: Up at morning chapel then walked about with Thackeray in the walks &c — till 1/2 past

   11: went to Thackerays where I stayed till late —

   13: wrote to Fitzgerald got Thackeray's £5

   29: called on Thackeray

June 2: called on Thackeray

   4: got up on Bath mail . . . travelled down

## 1831

June 6: I called on FitzGerald 39 Portland Place went with him to the National Gallery & to Somerset House very tired with pictures — after dinner went with William [23] to see Matthews & Yates very stupid but

---

left, as I was a sinner, for the guard and coachman on the way to London! And I *was* a sinner. I had gone without leave. What a long, dreary, guilty forty hours' journey it was from Paris to Calais, I remember! . . . I met my college tutor only yesterday. We were travelling, and stopped at the same hotel. He had the very next room to mine. After he had gone into his apartment, having shaken me quite kindly by the hand, I felt inclined to knock at his door and say, 'Doctor Bentley, I beg your pardon, but do you remember, when I was going down at the Easter vacation in 1830, you asked me where I was going to spend my vacation? And I said, With my friend Slingsby, in Huntingdonshire. Well, sir, I grieve to have to confess that I told you a fib. I had got £20 and was going for a lark to Paris, where my friend Edwards was staying.'"

[21] Probably Charles Warren (b. 1808?) of Trinity College, B. A., 1831, M. A., 1834; Joseph Gibbs, B. A., 1832, M. A., 1835; Robert Martin, B. A., 1832, M. A., 1835.

[22] William Mayhew (b. 1808?) of Trinity College, B. A., 1836, M. A., 1854.

[23] William Allen, one of John's older brothers.

in my way there I by chance hit on Thackeray to my excessive delight.

7: At 10 took FitzGerald with me to breakfast with Thackeray at the Bedford

9: saw Thackeray & FitzGerald at the Bedford —

10: I called at the Bedford on Thackeray & FitzGerald but they not there

# APPENDIX II

## THE FITZGERALD ALBUM.

In the Berg Collection of the New York Public Library there is a large scrapbook on the first page of which FitzGerald has written: "This volume of W. M. Thackeray's Drawings, Fragments of Letters &c from the year 1829 till 1850 bequeathed to Annie Thackeray, his Daughter, by his Friend Edward FitzGerald. Woodbridge. December 25/1864." It has proved possible to place some of the fragmentary letters that FitzGerald includes, in their proper niches among the rest of Thackeray's correspondence, but many of the briefer excerpts defy dating. These are accordingly brought together below under topical headings. The captions under the drawings, many of which have been reproduced before in *Biographical Introductions*, IX, are for the most part FitzGerald's.

### I. WEIMAR (1830–1831).

[Drawing 1]

[Drawing 2]

[Drawing 3]

*Devrient. Shylock.*

[Drawings 4–8]

*Drawn on a Weimar Playbill. 1831.*

*Rosa*            *Junker Kaspar*
*Nebel*              *Schelle*

### II. LARKBEARE (1831).

[Drawings 9–13]

*W. M. T. Larkbeare. 1831.*

[Drawings 14–19]

*Cottage at B. Salterton*     *The Governor*     *W. M. T.'s Study.*
                            *Larkbeare*

about General Whitelock [1] — I don't hate him for being such a coward — but he was the greatest tyrant possible, he actually tried at the horse-guards to establish corporal punishment for subaltern officers! — A good-natured coward one can pardon but a bullying wretch like this has I think neither pity or pardon —

---

[1] Lieutenant-General John Whitelocke (1757–1833), who was cashiered in 1808 for his incompetent management of the British campaign to recapture Buenos Ayres and spent the rest of his life in retirement.

[Drawing 21]
*General Whitelock (at Sidmouth)*

I have lost M$^r$ Elton who was my chef d'oeuvre    This is a faint representation of him not near so like him as the first I did — In one hand he holds a dirtyish white handkerchief in the other a blue cap with a band of gold the admiration of all the young gentlemen of Sidmouth — I wish I could give due effect to his immense gold chain, but that is unfortunately impossible.

[Drawing 20]
*Elton: M. C. of Sidmouth.*

*Visions of W. M. T's Correspondent —*

I have drawn my house w$^h$ looks very pretty I think, if one could have one or two quaint old flower beds — & a lawn in front & behind it would I think make a nice place.  Here is a feeble representation of y$^r$ blue-frock coat, w$^h$ may heaven preserve — The young person with whom I intended falling in love this vacation — is I grieve to say

[Drawing 22]
*1$^{st}$ In his celebrated Coat.  1831 —*

[Drawing 23]
*2$^{nd}$ In a Weimar Court Dress.*

[Drawing 24]
*3$^{rd}$ In After-Life.*

about to finish a segar — My Mother is well, & my Father I think likes the place — We are going to build a house here, there is one partly built of w$^h$ I give you the elevation as at present & my alteration —

[Drawing 25]

Ask M$^r$ Nursey to draw you a rough plan & elevation for a small house with 4 sitting rooms (one with a bed room adjoining for me) & bed rooms &c to match — that is if you can ask such a think of a professional man — No Don't —

## III.  LONDON (1831–1832).

1 Hare Court.  Temple.
W. Taprell's Esq$^{re}$
Saturday.

[Drawing 26]

Here I am sitting on a high stool in a special pleaders office writing a letter to my dear old [Fitz.]

[Drawings 27–28]

DRAWINGS FROM THE FITZGERALD ALBUM

DRAWINGS FROM THE FITZGERALD ALBUM

DRAWINGS FROM THE FITZGERALD ALBUM

DRAWINGS FROM THE FITZGERALD ALBUM

DRAWINGS FROM THE FITZGERALD ALBUM

DRAWINGS FROM THE FitzGerald Album

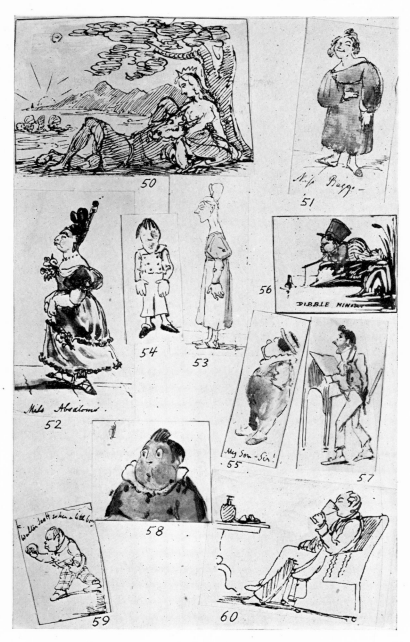

DRAWINGS FROM THE FITZGERALD ALBUM

[Drawing 29]

I have been writing a "Bachanalian" Song admirably calculated for this
fellow to sing at Offley's — it is at present in a very promising state as to
ideas; should I put it into rhymes I will send it we will go to these places
in November — The picture as to Costume & cut is exactly like a young
debutant I met at the cider cellar ² only it is impossible properly to paint
nankeens, they have when well washed a beggarly look quite beyond my
powers — I have got into a way of using vermillion & mixing all my
colours with it — I must give it up — by the bye I congratulate you on
your improvement in writing —

[Drawing 30]                              [Drawing 31]
                    *Leigh Hunt*

fancy Leontius on his balcony at Peckham-Rye or Hoxton doffing his
bonnet to some literary friend — I cant make him as dirty as I w^d
wish —

Song as sung by Madame Vestris with tremendous applause! —

> 'Tis pleasant to glide at even-tide
>     The moonlit waves along
> And pause to hear the Gondolier
>     Chant forth his evening song —
>         Hark oh hark!
>         Oer the waters dark
> Heavily tolls the bell of S^t Mark!
>         Listen oh listen
>         From church & tower
> The bells they chime the midnight hour!

[Drawing 32]

> Our gondoliers have no idears
>     Of singing such sweet ditties
> They spit & stare & slang & swear
>     In this most vast of cities
>         Hark oh hark
>         From wharfs & walls
> Heavily chimeth the bell of S^t Pauls!
>         Listen oh listen
>         The waterman's song
> Dieth away in that deep ding dong! —

[Drawings 33–34]
                    *Braham. Sir Huon.*

---

² See below, No. 515.

[Drawing 35]

*Phillips, and a great Chorister — "Robert the Devil"*

[Drawing 36]

[Drawing 37]

*Vedy!*

[Drawing 38]

*Tom Cooke*

[Drawing 39]

*C. Kemble. Henry VIII.*

[Drawing 40]

*Beggar's Opera.*

[Drawing 41]

*M.ʳ Power*

[Drawings 42–44]

## IV.  PARIS (1832 and 1835).

& relief to the good — There is a large trim garden with waterfalls, & delightful square avenues — & there is besides a pavillion, wʰ is for sale, & wʰ I have had an incomprehensible longing that you should buy — this is close to the palace looks over the gardens, & is represented here —

[Drawing 45]

I believe it [is] this house wʰ induces me to write to you such a dull descriptive letter. — On the right of the picter is a clipped row of trees, & for the rest you see the beautiful garden & the towers of the palace — had I £500 I should long to possess this — as for you I wish you could alienate a part of your patrimony & purchase it — we would fit it up in the old style, & live in it after the manner of Orestes and Pylades —

[Drawing 46]

I am writing just now for a friend the Paris bulletin of a daily paper: he has a clerk a respectable grave man of fifty five, an immense fool. I wish you could hear our conversations.

Curzon has told me, apropos of Castles, that there is a Chateau in Normandy, with an excellent garden a wilderness & some land to let furnished for 16 a year shall we 2 take it & be nothing to the world for a year? —

[Drawing 47]

I have not made my chateau that paradise w$^h$ might have been expected from my taste. ⟨. . .⟩ ³ Good bye now dear FitzGerald. Write me a letter soon, for the warm weather is coming & I am growing roman-tick — God bless you

[Drawing 48]
*Nourrit, in "Robert le Diable"* —

[Drawing 49]

## V.  MISCELLANEOUS (chiefly 1831).

[Drawing 50]

I have been reading Midsummernights dream, God bless it — did you ever sit on a promontory & hear a Mermaid on a dolphins back uttering such dulcet & harmonious notes that the rude sea grew civil at her breath And certain stars shot madly from their spheres to hear the sea maids musick? ⁴ — Or do you ever go in hill in dale forest or mead by paved fountain or by rushy brook or on the beached margent of the sea dancing your ringlets to the whistling [wind?] ⁵

[Drawings 51–53]

Miss Absaloms one of the pupils at the finishing school — I trust her appearance will explain her acquirements character fortune &c — I think her one of my masterpieces — I have one or two more but will not send them till you can get them for nothing —

[Drawings 54–59]
*Selections from a Boys' School.*

Now I have been making myself a glass of punch & here is your health God bless you my dear old boy & may you & I drink many glasses of punch together

[Drawing 60]

There I have written such a letter, as you never yet wrote take example by it, & send me such another      But I must to my work so God bless you dear FitzGerald ever your affectionate friend —

W. M. Thackeray

³ FitzGerald has here irrecoverably overscored three lines.
⁴ *A Midsummer Night's Dream*, II, i, 149–154.
⁵ The same, II, i, 83–86.

# APPENDIX III

## ACCOUNT BOOK FOR 1833

The few pages that follow are almost the only record of Thackeray's connection in 1833 with a bill-discounting firm in Birchin Lane. Though he must have derived much of his knowledge of the shadier aspects of London life from this venture, he avoided all reference to it in later years. Indeed, when an acquaintance of his youth maliciously alluded to his experience in "note-shaving" during the course of an article for *Fraser's Magazine*, Thackeray secured his dismissal from that periodical. See below, No. 246.

---

| | | | | | |
|---|---|---|---|---|---|
| January | 25 | Self on Adamson £300 due 28 January 1833. interest pble 25 Jany | | 7 | 10 |
| | | Maginn's bond [1] £250 interest pble 25 June 25 January | | 11 | 5 |
| | 31 | Hall on Meyer 3 mo. £40 „ 0 „ 0 17 January due 20 April | } 62 10 10 0 | | |
| | | Summers on Horth 28 Jan^y 27.14.9 due 1 May | | | |
| February | 1 | M^r Fred. Braithwaite [2] 103. G^t Russell S^t lost at play | 668 | | |
| | | Paid notes Smith Holmes | 400 | | |
| | | Half of Adamsons bill | 150 | | |
| | | rest in notes | 118 | | |
| | 2 | Bought bill for 99.10 Bronatte on Hatchett 4 mo. dated 22 January | } 105 10 6 | | |
| | | Gwynne on Hill £13.2.6  2 mo. dated 26 December | | | |
| | | Bought Belgian Stock at 79 1/4 | 2000 | | |
| | | Sold 1323 3 1/2 11 — Consols | | | |
| | 5 | Bought. dated 31 Jan^y | | | |
| | | 1 ^mo Forbes on Lisle 25. | | 24 | 0 |
| | | 3 ^mo Rainger on Watts 30 | | | |
| | | dated 28^th January — | | 27 | 10 |
| | | Paid Phillips rent | 28 | | |
| | | Pin arabs | 1 | 0 | |
| | 6 | Bought bill £48.12.0.  2 mo dated 10^th Jan^y | 45 | 0 | 0 |
| | | 6 ^mo Curzon £400.0.0 | 320 | | |
| | 8 | Yewens on Champneys 3 ^mos (to be renewed till 12 June) 10 Dec^r | 125 | | |
| | | Yewens 3 mos 6 Feb. | 25 | | |
| | | 2 ^mos to be renewed to 12 June | 100 | | |
| | 9 | sold 400 Belgian bonds 83/1/4 — with comm^n 332.10 | 283 | | |
| | | bought — Chard on Maddox 3^mo 5 Feb. | 22 | | |
| | | Smith on Herbert 2 ^mos. 2 Feb. | 25 | 15 | |
| | | Jukes on Sharp 2 m^os 1 Feb. | 20 | 0 | |
| | | | 317 | 15 | |

[1] Thackeray lent Maginn £500 in all. See below, p. 508.

[2] Frederick Braithwaite, surveyor, 103 Great Russell Street (*Robson's London Directory*, 1837).

| | | | £ | s | d |
|---|---|---|---|---|---|
| | 15 | bought Thorpe on Thorpe. 3 $\frac{m}{}$o £80.0.0 | 71 | 0 | 0 |
| | | dated 25 J$\underline{y}$ sold 200 B. B.$^{nds}$ 83. | 165 | 15 | 0 |
| | | Bought White on White 3 $\frac{m}{}$o (29 Dec$^r$ 32) £100 | 92 | 10 | 0 |
| | | | 163 | 10 | 0 |
| | 21 | Rec$^d$ Hall on Meyer | 40 | 0 | 0 |
| | | Bought 10 doz. Wine | 19 | 0 | 0 |
| | | Rec$^d$ | 11 | | |
| | | Owing from Goldsmid | 10 | | |
| | 27 | Sold 1000 Belgian Bonds | 851 | 5 | 0 |
| | | paid into G. & Co — | 850 | 0 | 0 |
| March | 1 | Gwynne on Hill | 13 | 2 | 6 |
| | | protested ! — | | | |
| | | Forbes on Lisle p$^d$ | 25 | | |
| | 4 | Forbes on Lisle — due 25.0.0 paid 2 March | | | |
| | 13 | Hutchison on Dennis due — | 48 | 12 | 0 |
| | | Yewens on Champneys to be renewed to 12 June | 125 | 0 | 0 |
| April | 2 | White on White d. | 100 | 0 | 9 |
| | 4 | Jukes on Sharp due paid | 20 | | |
| | | sold 500 Cons — | 438 | 15 | 0 |
| | 4 | P$^d$ Joy | 350 | | |
| | | Self | 4 | 15 | 0 |
| | | Surplus in G's hands | 84 | 0 | 0 |
| | | Jukes on Sh$^p$ p$^d$ | 20 | 0 | |
| | | Paid into G's — | 104 | 0 | 0 |
| | 5 | Smith on Herbert. | 25 | 15 | 0 |
| | 10 | Yewens on Champneys to be renewed to 10 June 100 | | | |
| | 27 | Thorpe on Thorpe (d) | 80 | 0 | 0 |
| May | 1 | Bill for 27 14.9. due | | | |
| | | Divds due. | | | |
| | | Rainger on Watts due — 30 | | | |
| | 8 | Chard on Maddox due | 22 | 0 | 0 |
| | 9 | due Yewens on Champney | 25 | 0 | 0 |
| | 25 | Bronatte on Hatchett due | 99 | 10 | 0 |
| | | Interest on M's Bond. | 11 | 10 | |
| August | 8 | Hughes on Curzon due. 6 $\frac{m}{}$o £400 | 320 | | |
| | 23 | unveiling Mosaic | | | |
| December | 5 | Stephen | | | |
| | 8 | Stephen | | | |

# APPENDIX IV

## HOW THACKERAY LOST HIS PATRIMONY

Four years before he died Richmond Thackeray was rewarded for his devotion to the affairs of the East India Company by an appointment as Collector for the District surrounding Calcutta, one of the most lucrative posts in the Bengal Service. He was thus enabled to provide amply for his wife and to leave his son nearly £20,000. This modest fortune was entrusted to the care of Richmond Thackeray's uncle Peter Moore [1] — an Indian magnate who died in poverty at Dieppe in 1828 —, of Francis Thackeray, and of Robert Langslow, until Thackeray should reach his majority.

But Thackeray did not wait until he was twenty-one to begin to dissipate his inheritance. In the summer of 1829 he visited Frascati's famous *salon* in Paris and was seized by a passion for play which he did not shake off until four years later when he had no money left with which to wager. On his return to Cambridge he continued to gamble, though without significant loss until just before he left the University the following June. Then, writes Mrs. Fuller (who learned of the episode from Lady Ritchie), "two card sharpers, finding out that he would inherit money on coming of age, marked him as suitable prey, took lodgings opposite to Trinity, made his acquaintance, and invited him to their rooms to dinner and écarté. At first he was allowed to win and the stakes were raised, then luck changed and he lost and lost and lost. The sharpers, satisfied with their gains, quickly took their departure." Sir Theodore Martin relates the sequel of this story. He and Thackeray

> were walking one afternoon through the playrooms at Spa . . . and stopped at the Rouge et Noir table to look on. Thackeray touched his elbow, and asked him to look at a tall man, in a seedy brown frock-coat, at the other end of the table. The man's appearance was that of a broken-down gentleman, who had still the remains of a certain distinction of manner. They walked away, and Thackeray said, "That was the original of my Deuceace; I have not seen him since the day he drove me down in his cabriolet to my broker's in the City, where I sold out my patrimony and handed it over to him." Thackeray then added that this man and another had, in the early days, . . . eased him not literally of his patrimony, but of a round fifteen hundred pounds.[2]

---

[1] There is an account of his career in Hunter's *The Thackerays in India*, pp. 100–110.

[2] Merivale and Marzials, *Thackeray*, pp. 235–236.

"SHARPERS"

*From a sketch by Thackeray*

The heavy price that he had been made to pay for an evening's entertainment seems to have sobered Thackeray for a time. In any event we hear nothing further of gaming in the letters written from Germany during the winter of 1831–1832. When he was exposed to the temptations of London during the following autumn, however, he found that the gambling virus was still in his blood. In the metropolis during William IV's reign, writes Serjeant Ballantine,

> gambling-houses of every degree were publicly open in many of the West End streets and squares, and although at this period they were not interfered with by the police or other authorities, they were illegal, and liable to indictment, and there was a nest of scoundrels who lived upon them. . . . Leicester Square, the Quadrant, Bennett Street, Bury Street, and Duke Street were full of them. No concealment was affected. They were open to all comers, who were at some of them ushered in by powdered footmen. . . . I believe that in most of these hells the chances of gain were assisted by flagrant trickery. At some of the principal — those, for instance, in Bennett Street — the decorations of the rooms were very elegant. Perfect quiet and decorum were observed by the players, who were generally of the better class.

In these establishments, Serjeant Ballantine continues, hazard was the favorite game, but roulette, which afforded the best opportunities for cheating, was found in all the lower houses.

> I need not recapitulate the way in which unwary people were inveigled into these places. A class of gentry called 'bonnets' were actively engaged in this employment: but when it was thought that a good thing was on, the proprietor would say out loud, 'We may as well be quiet: put up the bars.' The intended victim supposed this to mean that other people should be shut out, but the accomplice took it as a direction to manipulate the table by raising, which was done by machinery, an almost imperceptible obstruction before any number which would have secured to the player a large stake.[3]

Thackeray's diary for 1832 reveals that he haunted the "hells" of the West End and took a hand in many private games of hazard with men of his own age and social position. In one of the latter engagements he lost £668.[4]

All together Thackeray can hardly have gambled away less than £3,000, but in view of the insight that he gained into the darker side of human nature and the underworld of European capitals, his experience was not dearly bought. Its immediate reflection is to be found in such stories as "Dimond Cut Dimond" in *The Yellowplush Papers* and "A

[3] *Some Experiences of a Barrister's Life,* pp. 43 and 51–53.
[4] See above, Appendix III.

Gambler's Death" and "Captain Rook and Mr. Pigeon" in *The Paris Sketch Book*, and it appears less directly in "A Warning to Travellers" in *The Paris Sketch Book*, in "Foring Parts" and "Mr. Deuceace at Paris" in *The Yellowplush Papers*, and in many pages of Thackeray's novels.

Not by gambling alone, however, did Thackeray show the spirit of an heir. His living expenses between 1829 and 1833 must have exceeded £3,000; he lent Dr. Maginn £500; and he spent considerable sums both on *The National Standard* and on his bill-discounting business. Even so the greater part of his fortune was still intact when ominous rumors reached England in the latter part of 1833 concerning the Indian bank in which his money and much of Major Carmichael-Smyth's was invested.[5] The rumors were soon confirmed, and most of what remained of Thackeray's fortune (£11,325, it would appear from his letter of October 22, 1833) was swept away. Once again he made artistic capital of costly experience, for this failure later supplied him with the episode of the Bundelcund Bank in chapters 62 to 64 and 69 and 70 of *The Newcomes*.

So it happened that in December, 1833, sixteen months after he came into his inheritance, Thackeray wrote that he was ruined. And in July, 1835, we learn that on the "poor little capital" remaining to him he received a quarterly dividend of only £25.

[5] "The collapse of the banking houses in Calcutta, with their failure for seventeen millions sterling between 1830 and 1834, involved in one gigantic ruin the military and civilian families of Bengal" (Hunter, *Thackerays in India*, p. 57).

# APPENDIX V

## "THE COUNT'S" ADVENTURES

If Thackeray's years as an art student did not enable him to paint a single successful picture, they at least served to develop his inimitable gift for caricature. Those who judge his artistic talent solely by the illustrations to his books, where his line has become grossly distorted in being transferred from sketch to wood or steel, hardly realize the excellence to which he attains in his early comic drawings. Since recent processes allow modern craftsmen to reproduce an artist's sketches with perfect fidelity, it has seemed desirable to include in this edition, as a sample of Thackeray's work at its best, facsimiles of *"The Count's" Adventures*, one of the liveliest of his sequences of caricatures.

These drawings, which are here published for the first time, have an interesting history. Among Thackeray's friends in Paris during the years before his marriage was an eccentric Scotch artist named John Grant Brine. Brine's quarters were a sort of warehouse for "painter's properties, in the shape of costumes, armour, carved chests, plate, and glassware," we learn from Sir Joseph Crowe, who continues:

I recollect being in his rooms at a party on a winter's evening. He was doing the honours to several ladies grouped round a spider table at which my mother dispensed tea and confectionery. Over the table hung a Venetian glass lamp. At one side of the chimney-piece close by, a tray displayed some rare crystal ware; in a corner stood a piece of costly armour. The fire burnt low in the grate, and the servant was called to replenish it. Some one observed that she put a piece of carved oak into the grate, and Brine rose, cup in hand, to the rescue. But his shoulder unawares struck the hanging lamp, which canted, pouring a streak of oil into a lady's dress. She in her fright rose and dropped the contents of her teacup into the coat skirts of a gentleman near her. He in his flurry knocked down the armour. The panoply fell with a crash on the crystal tray. There was a pretty general average of breakage and loss. But it was wonderful with what equanimity Brine bore the disaster and consoled his friends for their alarm. Shortly after these events Brine shut up his painting-room and went to Madrid, where I believe he succeeded in painting a few portraits without achieving more than 'a success of esteem.'

Thackeray . . . was unmercifully humorous and funny on the subject of his alleged adventures in the Spanish capital. He gave him the nickname of 'The Count' and made a legend out of his travels which he was brought, in the most amusing way, to illustrate in our house. Being a constant visitor of ours he had a seat always ready for him on Saturdays at our table, would come into the drawing-room about an hour before dinner, and hardly have time to sit down when we children surrounded him and begged for a drawing. For my sisters he drew a coalheaver running open-mouthed after a little girl; for us all he did something, and then he bethought him of the adventures of Brine. . . .

When Brine returned to us and saw the legend of the Count in sketch and text, he was delighted with it, acknowledged Thackeray's skill in reproducing his face and figure in such varied attitudes and positions, and — to show that he also could seize a likeness — drew a full length of Thackeray, with his flattened nose and a square glass in his eye, looking out upon the world with the humorous twinkle which brightened his features when he meant some friendly mischief. Soon after that Brine went to London, and, leaving pictorial art, gave himself up wholly to illustration, getting an engagement on the 'Illustrated News', which proved sufficient to keep him alive till, at last, poor fellow, he fell into a decline and died of consumption.[1]

Crowe's account of Brine's character and accoutrements reminds one unmistakably of the absurd young artist Andrew or Andrea (as he prefers to call himself) Fitch, who has an important rôle in Thackeray's *Shabby Genteel Story*. We are introduced to Fitch, a "youth of poetic temperament, loving solitude," in the second chapter of that tale, when he comes to the seaside resort of Margate in the dead of winter to take lodgings with the Ganns.

Andrea was here then, in the loneliness that he loved, — a fantastic youth, who lived but for his art; to whom the world was like the Coburg Theatre, and he in a magnificent costume acting a principal part. His art, and his beard and whiskers, were the darlings of his heart. His long pale hair fell over a high polished brow, which looked wonderfully thoughtful; and yet no man was more guiltless of thinking. He was always putting himself into attitudes; he never spoke the truth; and was so entirely affected and absurd, as to be quite honest at last: for it is my belief that the man did not know truth from falsehood any longer and was when he was alone, when he was in company, nay, when he was unconscious and sound asleep snoring in bed, one complete lump of affectation. When his apartments on the second floor were arranged according to his fancy, they made a tremendous show. He had a large Gothic chest, in which he put his wardrobe (namely, two velvet waistcoats, four varied satin under ditto, two pairs braided trousers, two shirts, half-a-dozen false collars, and a couple of pairs of dreadfully dilapidated Blucher boots). He had some pieces of armour; some China jugs and Venetian glasses; some bits of old damask rags, to drape his doors and windows: and a rickety lay figure, in a Spanish hat and cloak, over which slung a long Toledo rapier, and a guitar, with a riband of dirty sky-blue.[2]

[1] *Reminiscences*, pp. 18–21.
[2] *Works*, XI, 22.

This is Brine, certainly, and these are the trappings that Crowe describes, enriched by the spoils of the Madrid expedition. Though Thackeray has not lost his liking for his friend, he no longer regards him with the amiable and forgiving affection of actual life. In his early stories, at least, Thackeray is a merciless realist, who does not suffer fools gladly, and he has, furthermore, to draw Andrea's character in terms that harmonize with the prevailing mood of the sordid drama on the fringe of respectable Victorian society to which the poor artist furnishes rather bitter comic relief. Andrea falls in love with Caroline, the persecuted slavey of the Gann household, and makes a spectacle of himself by his sighs and piteous looks. He reads Byron and paces his chamber all night long composing poetry. But Caroline is in love with a clever and unscrupulous young aristocrat, who for no very creditable reasons has taken refuge in Margate under an assumed name. Unable to cope with his rival's adroit manoeuvres, Andrea at last challenges him to a duel. He conducts himself bravely, for he feels that his romantic dreams are coming true. Is he not venturing his life for the woman he loves? After the exchange of shots, however, it is revealed that there were no bullets in the pistols. His spirit broken by this rude shock, Andrea abandons his pretensions to Caroline, and allows himself to be carried off by Mrs. Carrickfergus, a fat widow who has pursued him to Margate. An account of the Fitch-Carrickfergus nuptials, taken from *Galignani's Messenger*, forms the huddled conclusion of *A Shabby Genteel Story*. The two are married at the British Embassy in Paris by Bishop Luscombe, just as Thackeray and his wife had been, and the bridegroom is attended by his friend Michael Angelo Titmarsh. An unobtrusive pathos is latent in these lines, for when Thackeray wrote them, he had begun to realize that his wife was insane.

*"The Count's" Adventures* were drawn five years earlier during the happiest period of Thackeray's life. They are altogether light-hearted, and their hero is a sort of nineteenth century Don Quixote, who lives in a fantastic cloud-cuckoo land. Yet his character is that of Brine and Andrea Fitch; only the setting and the mood are changed. It should be noted that these sketches do not form a complete series. They are taken from the original album in the Widener Collection of the Harvard College Library, from which three pages have been removed, one after the sixth drawing and two after the seventh.

# "THE COUNT'S" ADVENTURES

*From sketches by Thackeray*

The Count heads a charge of the British Legion
N.B. The Legion is not visible, having bolted.

Sitting on a barrel of Gunpowder Cabrera calls upon him to abjure his religion
His Excellency says that he (his Excellency) will see him damned first —

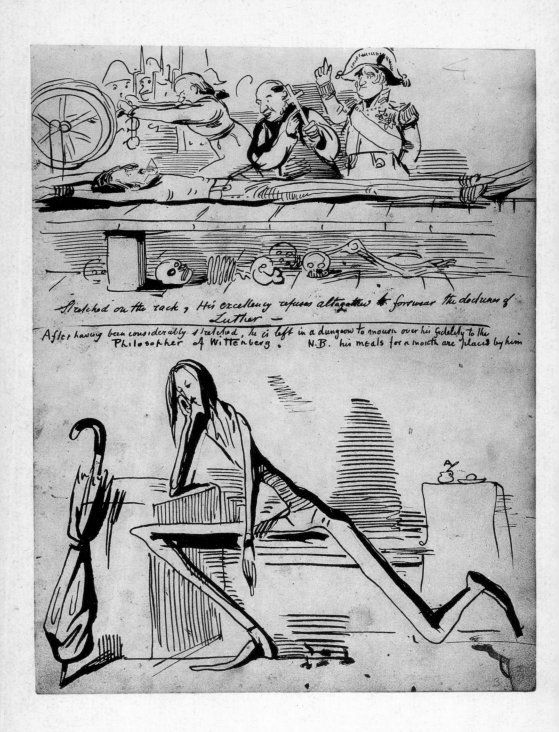

Stretched on the rack, His excellency refuses altogether to forswear the doctrines of
Luther —

After having been considerably stretched, he is left in a dungeon to mourn over his fidelity to the
Philosopher of Wittenberg.    N.B. his meals for a month are placed by him

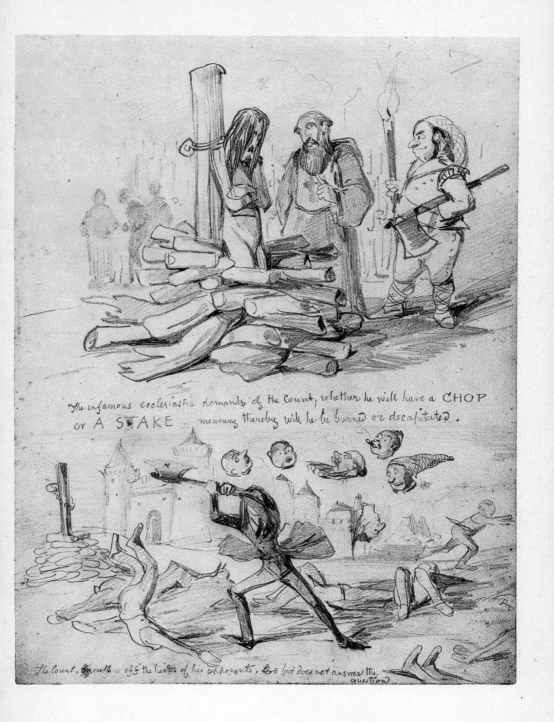

The infamous ecclesiastic demands of the Count, whether he will have a CHOP or A STAKE . meaning thereby will he be burned or decapitated .

The Count, executes off the heads of his opponents, & but does not answer the question

Another view of the same

Such is the Ingratitude of Princes

So the Count proposes Marriage
to the Queen of all the Land
Passing in her handsome carriage
Driving has her two in hand. —

The Count dreams of the Queen

And coming to his rendezvous discovers that she is
only the Cat housemaid.

Don Rafael Inarote, Don Sancho de Panca, don Guzman d'Alfaracha, don Juan Alvarez de Mendez y Cali, lovers of the fair Ximena await the count's on his way from an assignation with her.

Wonderful effects of the Count's Serenade.

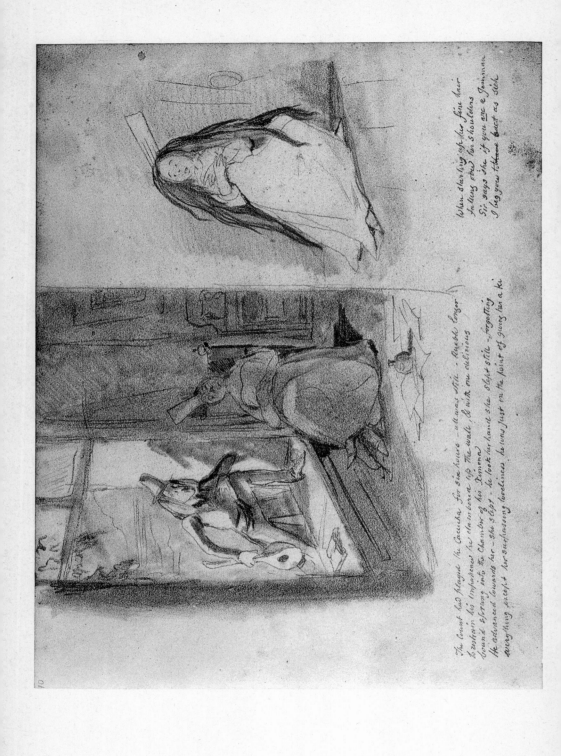

The Count had plagued the Cenci for six hours – always still – Angelo longer & restrain his impatience he clambers up the wall, & with one delirious bound & strong into the Chamber of his Diamond. He looks towards her – she slept still – forgetting He advanced towards her – she slept. He look'd on her she slept still – forgetting everything except her overflowing loveliness, he sung just on the point of giving her a ki

When starting up her fine hair fa ling cried her shoulders Sir says she if you are a Jemima I beg your tithune beat as stek

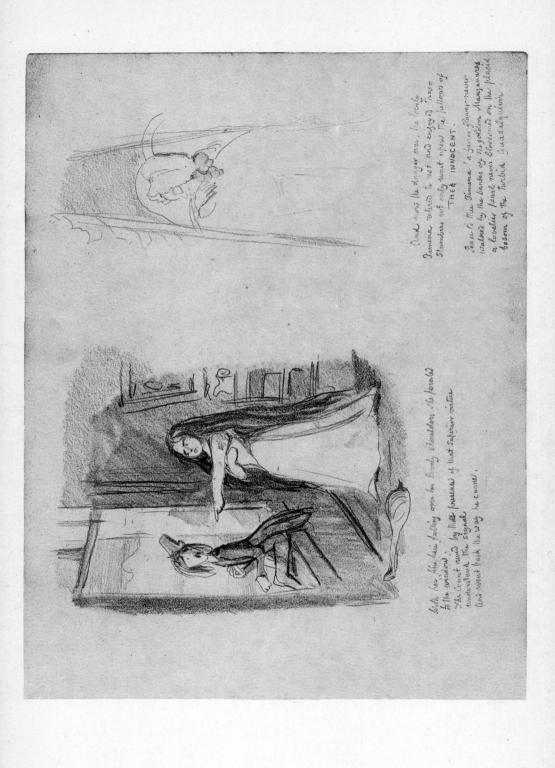

Artist [making?] a portrait of [the] Boatswain, & the Guard [Washington?] by some visitor

Having joined the Syrian
expedition he makes
a sketch of the
Mountain

To his astonish
ment while
sketching, the
Mountain rises

APPENDIX VI

# ACCOUNT BOOK FOR 1838

Extracts published in Johnson's *Early Writings of William Makepeace Thackeray*, pp. 43–45 and 52–56. Original owned by Mrs. Fuller.

Receipts and disbursements, 1838

Cheques drawn

|        |    |               | £  | s  | d |
|--------|----|---------------|----|----|---|
| Dec    | 28 | Rivington     | 8  | 15 | 0 |
|        | 30 | Self          | 10 | 0  | 0 |
| Jan    | 9  | Ruddell       | 5  | 5  | 0 |
|        |    | Winston       | 11 | 6  | 0 |
|        | 15 | Self          | 10 | 0  | 0 |
|        | 23 | Mother        | 10 | 0  | 0 |
|        | 31 | Self          | 10 | 0  | 0 |
| Feb    | 5  | Mother        | 10 | 0  | 0 |
|        | 8  | Self          | 5  | 0  | 0 |
|        | 14 | Poor's Rates  | 3  | 4  | 0 |
|        | 20 | Drawing Acad  | 5  | 0  | 0 |
|        | 18 | Self          | 5  | 0  | 0 |
|        | 21 | Do            | 10 | 0  | 0 |
| Mr     | 1  | Do            | 10 | 0  | 0 |
|        |    | Mrs Thack     | 10 | 0  | 0 |
|        |    | Aretz [1]     | 7  | 10 | 0 |
|        |    | Mother        | 15 | 0  | 0 |
|        |    | Courtenay     | 10 | 0  | 0 |
|        |    | Mother        | 10 | 0  | 0 |
|        |    | Self          | 5  | 0  | 0 |
|        |    | Mother        | 10 | 0  | 0 |
|        |    | Self          | 20 | 0  | 0 |
|        |    | Self          | 5  | 0  | 0 |
|        |    | Mother        | 15 | 0  | 0 |

Received

|             |    |    |   |    |                    |
|-------------|----|----|---|----|--------------------|
|             | 74 | 17 | 0 | 20 | December. paid to Lubb. |
| Addison [2] | 20 | 0  | 0 | 24 | —                  |
| J Delane [3]| 22 | 1  | 0 | 1  | Jan. (Lub)         |
| Colburn     | 9  | 0  | 0 | 3  | Jan. } Lub.        |
| Fraser      | 20 | 0  | 0 | 4  | Jan } Lub.         |
| Delane      | 13 | 0  | 6 | 2  | Feb. } Lub.        |
| Colburn     | 7  | 0  | 0 | 15 | Feb } Lub.         |
| Fraser      | 20 | 0  | 0 | 1  | March. Cash        |
| Daly        | 11 | 0  | 0 | 25 | March Cash         |

[1] See the Dedicatory Letter to *The Paris Sketch Book*.

[2] Thackeray contributed eighteen colored plates to *Journey to Damascus and Palmyra* (1838) by Charles Greenstreet Addison (d. 1866).

[3] This and the following entries record Thackeray's receipts from magazine and newspaper articles. Delane was editor of *The Times*, and Colburn was proprietor of *The New Monthly Magazine*. I have not been able to discover what periodicals employed Daly and Swinton.

| | | | | |
|---|---|---|---|---|
| Galignani | 8 | 0 | 0 | 28 March Cash. |
| Swinney | 9 | 9 | 0 | ——— Cash |
| Isabella | 13 | 0 | 0 | ——— Cash |
| Colburn | 4 | 0 | 0 | 10 April Cash |
| Fraser | 25 | 0 | 0 | 16      Lub. |
| Fraser | 20 | 0 | 0 | 5 May Lub. |
| Times | 14 | 0 | 0 | |

| | | | | |
|---|---|---|---|---|
| Dec. 27 | Paid by cheque | | | |
| | Mr Rivington rent 1/2 quarter } | 8 | 15 | 0 |
| | Lamp and candles | | 18 | 6 |
| | Watchstand | | 3 | .0 |
| | Garrick | | 1 | 6 |
| 29 | Theatre | | 10 | 0 |
| | Coach and Fees | | 5 | 0 |
| | Garrick | | 3 | 6 |
| 30 | Gown for M A. | 8 | 15 | 0 |
| | Presents for Jane & Mrs Shawe & Punchladle | 2 | 2 | 0 |
| | Paid Washerwoman | | 7 | 0 |
| 31 | Johns Xmas box | 1 | 0 | 0 |
| | Garrick | | 1 | 0 |
| 3 | Sundries | | 5 | 0 |
| | Mrs Shutes Servt | | 10 | 0 |
| | Hackney coach | | 5 | 0 |
| | Isabella | 1 | 0 | 0 |
| 7 | Sundries  Coach hire &c | 1 | 10 | 0 |
| 9 | Club Subscription | 6 | 6 | 0 |
| | Bootmakers bill | 1 | 5 | 0 |
| 10 | Sundries | | 15 | |
| 15 | ——— | 2 | 0 | 0 |
| | Isabella | 4 | 0 | 0 |
| 22 | Isabella | 2 | 0 | 0 |
| | Sundries | 1 | 10 | 0 |
| | | 43 | 5 | 5 |

| | | | | |
|---|---|---|---|---|
| Spent in a month | 53 | 5 | 6 | |
| deduct | 8 | 15 | 0 | gown |
| | 8 | 15 | 0 | rent |
| | 3 | 0 | 0 | Mrs Shawe |
| | 6 | 6 | 0 | Garrick |
| | 26 | 16 | 0 | Leaving 33  0  0 monthly expenses |

Sent to the Times my acct for 10 1/2 cols.                    13
                                                                                7
                                                                                6  Earnings

                                                                                26

24 pages in Fraser
Yellowplush.[4]  Trollope

[4] To *Fraser's Magazine* of January, 1838, Thackeray contributed "The Yellow-plush Correspondence. No. II. Miss Shum's Husband," an illustration, and reviews of Mrs. Trollope's *Vicar of Wrexhill*, Bulwer's *Ernest Maltravers*, and Miss Landon's *Ethel Churchill*.

Bulwer — Landon and a design
Received from the Times   22  10  0  (L)
wrote Marlborough [5] — 2
wrote Love [6] on Wednesday night, after dining at the Shutes
Called at Colburns & received  9  0  0
Wrote a little Etiquette [7] and read Life of George IV. Went to Englefield green, stopping Friday & returning Saturday. Saw the Windsor pictures — Some magnificent Vandykes and Rubens — specially a battle-piece or Portrait — Bernard of Weimar with the king of Hungary — most gorgeous in colour, conception and effect, The Lawrences in the Waterloo chamber struck me as sadly dauby after the noble Rubens — careless, chalky, & feeble. The rooms are very fine fine to a pitch of meanness.
On the 6. 2 cols 1/5 in the T. on Duchess of Marlborough
       Received £20 from Fraser.
  11   2 cols 1/2 Lady C. Bury [8] Wrote Holt.[9]

        Vidi in remotis carmina rupibus
        Bacchum docentem, credite Posteri,
        Nymphasque discentis et aures
        Capripedum Satyrorum acutas.[10]
                DANDO [11]
        Der König in Thule.

  31 January. Holt in the Times 1 1/2. Wrote on Penny Newspapers for Frazer.[12]
   1 Feb. Yellowplush [13] III Frazer Gahagan [14] — New Monthly
  23 Mother for house                                10   0   0
  31 Sundries                                         2  10   0

[5] A review of *The Duchess of Marlborough's Private Correspondence* for *The Times* of January 6.

[6] A review of Lady Charlotte Bury's *Eros and Anteros; or, Love* for *The Times* of January 11.

[7] Walter Hamilton (*Notes and Queries*, Ninth Series, II, 1898, pp. 267–268) offers the following explanation of this entry: "In the thirties Messrs. Longmans had published a pretty little handbook (12mo.) entitled 'Hints on Etiquette and the Usages of Society, with a Glance at Bad Habits'; motto, 'Manners make the man.' This had a large sale; my copy, dated 1837, is of the fourteenth edition. It is not illustrated. The popularity of this work naturally gave rise to a parody, and early in 1838 Charles Tilt, of Fleet Street, issued a little book, similar in size and binding, entitled 'More Hints on Etiquette, for the Use of Society at Large, and Young Gentlemen in Particular. With Cuts by George Cruikshank.'" Hamilton suggests that this burlesque may possibly be by Thackeray, though he has seen it attributed to Dickens.

[8] Thackeray reviewed Lady Charlotte Bury's *Diary Relative to George IV and Queen Caroline* as well as her *Eros and Anteros* in *The Times* of January 11.

[9] A review of *The Memoirs of Holt, the Irish Rebel* in *The Times* of January 31.

[10] Horace, *Odes*, II, xix, 1–4. Compare *Works*, XII, 202.

[11] See above, No. 106.

[12] "Half-a-Crown's Worth of Cheap Knowledge," *Fraser's Magazine*, February.

[13] "The Yellowplush Correspondence. No. III. The Amours of Mr. Deuceace — Dimond cut Dimond," *Fraser's Magazine*, February.

[14] "Some Passages in the Life of Major Gahagan," *New Monthly Magazine*, February.

|  |  | £ | s | d |
|---|---|---|---|---|
|  | Bookbinder on acc.̣ | 1 | 0 | 0 |
| 1 | Isabella | 4 | 0 | 0 |
| 3 | Carpenter bill | 1 | 15 | 0 |
| 5 | Mother for house | 10 | 0 | 0 |
| 8 | Money spent | 3 | 5 | 0 |
| 9 | Isabella | 1 | 0 | 0 |
| 14 | Poor Rate | 3 | 4 | 0 |
|  | Isabella | 1 | 0 | 0 |
| 16 | Beach in advance | 1 | 0 | 0 |
| 20 | Sundries | 2 | 0 | 0 |
|  | Drawing acc.̣ | 5 | 5 | 0 |
|  | Dinner | 1 | 1 | 0 |
|  | Mother | 1 | 0 | 0 |
|  | Sundries | 1 | 14 | 0 |
| Trip to Paris Tailors bill &c. | Mother | 10 | 0 | 0 |
|  | Isabella | 5 | 0 | 0 |
|  | Isabella | 10 | 0 | 0 |
|  | Aretz | 10 | 10 | 0 |
|  | Self | 35 | 0 | 0 |

Wrote for Fraser on the Penny Press and Yellowplush No IV [15]
Feb. 1. For Colburn Gahagan II.[16]
Yellowplush in April [17]
Letter from Paris [18]
Southey Times 16 April [19] —

En voyant ces lieux on j'ai passé ma premiere enfance, en comparant l'état paisible on j'etois autrefois, a l'agitation et aux terreurs que j'éprouve aujourdhui, je me suis dit bien des fois 'j'ai cherché dans plusieurs combats a rencontrer la mort, je ne puis plus la redouter elle sera un bienfait pour moi — *mais Je voudrais revoir une seule fois Joséphine.*

---

The Épaves were people of colour in the Mauritius who not being able to give any account of themselves were seized and sold by [the] government.

Donalieu was a mulatto in this case — he lives in the neighbourhood of the country lodge belonging to M. de la Rebeliere — Rebelieres wife and ward fall in love with him — The husband discovers his wife's love: vows vengeance, has Donalieu seized imprisoned & brought to the market — He turns out to be a slave belonging to Mad.ᶫᶫᵉ de Kerborn

[15] "The Yellowplush Correspondence. No. IV. Skimmings from 'The Diary of George IV,' " *Fraser's Magazine*, March.

[16] "Historical Recollections. By Major Gahagan," *New Monthly Magazine*, March.

[17] No doubt "The Yellowplush Correspondence. No. V. Mr. Deuceace at Paris," which appeared in *Fraser's Magazine* for May, and would have been written in April.

[18] I have not identified this article.

[19] A review of *The Poetical Works of Dr. Southey* in *The Times* of April 17.

who reclaims him — Rebeliere produces the Code Noir w[h] condemns D. to be flogged for insult to a free white. Mad[lle] de K. says she will marry him: and thus the flogging is saved.

---

Mad[lle] Louise very rich ennuyeé going to the eaux is robbed by a band. One of them a very handsome young brigand pays some attention to her — she finds herself over head & ears in love with him (on one occasion saves his life) — She goes to Paris. The brigand follows her, he has inherited a fortune & grown respectable. He stares at her nightly at the theatre and when she goes to the country, gains admission to her house. She finds him dreadfully vulgar is cured of her love: & virtue is rewarded in the shape of a young man who has long been sighing in vain for Mad[lle] Louise — Valdepeyras.

---

A woman is disappointed of her lover by the power that another woman has over him. The lover dies, the woman's endeavours to revenge herself over her rival.

### Ernest's Story.

Louise is the daughter of the Suisse of the Duchess de — : being very *gentille* she is brought up along with the Duchess's daughter — the Duchess's son the Count falls in love with Louise & Louise with him. He is very unprincipled and extravagant: he borrows money from the Jews: threatened with arrest he steals jewels from his mother and wants Louise to run away with him. One of the jewels is found in Louise's room (find a pretext). She is accused but will not give up the name of the criminal. (This must end in the best way it can.)

Diane de Chivri is born blind She has a father & 3 brothers She lives with her G. M. an old Carlist: It is the time of the Berri rebellion in La Vendée: the old lady hears that a gentleman is asking for shelter: she believes it to be Leonard Aston a celebrated Vendean — it is the V. de Furieres who is running away for debt: but takes the name of Aston.

To avoid suspicion he is sheltered in Diane's pavillion. One night the soldiers come. Diane has no way of saving him but by putting him by her bed. He ravishes her: she dares not cry out for fear of the soldiers: she loves him.

Diane tells the news to the G. M. The old lady calls the father & the 2 eldest brothers and tells her story: they set out to murder Aston. He fights and kills the 2 brothers.

Perplexity, éclaircissement, Aston marries Diane: and kills Furieres — F. Soulié [20]

[20] See Soulié's *Six mois de correspondance: Diane et Louise* (1839), which was dramatized later in 1839 as *Diane de Chivri.*

# APPENDIX VII

## THE PSYCHIATRIC CASE HISTORY OF ISABELLA SHAWE THACKERAY

The data from which this psychiatric case history is assembled are to be found in the letters from Thackeray to Isabella Shawe, a few letters written by her, many letters from Thackeray to his mother, and some others. These are listed below.[1] With the patient buried 2,000 miles away in 1893 and the action taking place one hundred years ago, an accurate evaluation is, of course, impossible. Yet the description of her symptoms in the letters and the story of the development of the illness supply one with enough facts to make reasonable a tentative diagnosis.

Before her marriage, Isabella Shawe seems to have been a happy, bright girl with a quick mind and ability to turn a phrase aptly. Thackeray usually spoke of her as the "dear little woman" and once as "red-poll," so one pictures a small lady with red hair, fine manners, and much restraint in love relations. When they were engaged Thackeray seems to have been impetuous at one time and frightened her. Although they apparently could discuss being bedfellows and having children, it seems that passion shocked her. Such a reaction is to be looked on as normal in an age when girls were poorly educated and well protected. Moreover, she appears to have lived a life of ease, in a small way, lying in bed late and idling her time away under the guidance of a resentful, widowed mother to whom keeping up the appearance of gentility was all-important.

She was married at the age of eighteen, and her four years with Thackeray before her illness seem to have been happy ones, although she bore three children and had many responsibilities. The first child was born within a year (June 1837). The birth was relatively easy and she seems to have met the situation normally. The child, Anne, was healthy and caused only the usual amount of trouble. In the late autumn she was pregnant again and Jane was born in July 1838. The next months were difficult and the baby died in March 1839. There is nothing to indicate that the mother showed any unusual signs of emotional disturbance throughout this trying period. In October or Novem-

[1] Letters of Thackeray to his Mother: 1840: Jan. 19, Feb. 15, May 27, July 18, Aug. 21, Sept. 1, Sept. 12, Sept. 17, Sept. 20, Sept. 24, Sept. 26, Sept. 30, Oct. 1 (?), Oct. 6; 1841: Feb. 27, April 15; 1842: June 30, Sept. 30; 1844: June 1. Letter of Isabella Shawe Thackeray to her mother-in-law, Aug. 4, 1840. Letter of Thackeray to Edward FitzGerald, Jan. 14, 1841.

ber she was pregnant again and went through this in good spirits and without untoward symptoms. The child, Harriet, was born on May 27, 1840. There were no especial obstetrical difficulties mentioned, and for a few weeks all appears to have gone well.

The first hint of mental illness is found in a letter from Thackeray to his mother in which he says on July 18, 1840: "Isabella is better." Isabella says in a letter to her mother-in-law August 4: "I feel myself excited, my strength is not great and my head flies away with me as if it were a balloon. This is mere weakness and a walk will set me right but in case there should be incoherence in my letter you will know what to attribute it to." (There is no incoherence in the letter.) Later is another significant remark: "I try to think my fears imaginary and exaggerated and that I am a coward by nature." By August 21, it is obvious that she is depressed and is described by Thackeray as "very low. For the last four days I have not been able to write a line in consequence of her." She remained "low in spirits" with "fretful looks" especially in the mornings and seemed so "absent" at that time that Thackeray did not "like to trust her." She often had feelings of guilt and "worked up these charges so as to fancy herself a perfect demon of wickedness." There was a short improvement early in September, but when the family started for London on September 12 to sail for Ireland her depression deepened. On the thirteenth, when at sea off the Isle of Wight, she went to the water closet of the boat and climbed out the window, dropping into the sea. She was in the water for twenty minutes before she was found "floating on her back, paddling with her hands." "The next night she made fresh attempts at destruction." On the seventeenth they arrived at Cork and boarded near her mother's house. The experience of the voyage augmented her "melancholy" to "absolute insanity" and she landed "quite demented." During the next two weeks her mood varied, described as "low and ennuyee," lacking in "interest and devoured by gloom," "clouded and rambling." At times the feelings of unworthiness come up and she says she was "never fit to be a wife," but she made no more suicidal attempts. She "won't sit still, won't employ herself, won't do anything she is asked and vice versa."

After this the psychosis seemed to become chronic, and three months later, in writing to Edward FitzGerald on January 14, 1841, Thackeray says: "At first she was violent, then she was indifferent, now she is melancholy and silent and we are glad of it. She bemoans her condition and that is a great step to cure. She knows everybody and recollects things but in a stunned confused sort of way. She kissed me at first very warmly and with tears in her eyes, then she went away from me, as if she felt she was unworthy of having such a God of a husband."

During the next year she was in a state of "indifference, silence and sluggishness" with variation up and down, sometimes showing slight interest in her children, at other times apathy. Various treatments were tried in England and on the continent. A month's strenuous hydrotherapy at Boppart on the Rhine made her "extraordinarily better," but the improvement was short-lived. At last Thackeray put her in a mental hospital at Chaillot where she was "perfectly happy, obedient and reasonable" (March 1843). During the next year, however, she seems to have become less reasonable and to have had strange ideas or trains of thought, "if you can call it a train." In 1846 Thackeray says: "The poor little woman gets no better and plays the nastiest pranks more frequently than ever." In 1848 he remarks: "She cares for none of us now." In this state she lived on under a nurse in England until 1893, fifty-three years in psychosis!

In discussing the cause of this mental breakdown the fact that the patient's mother had periods of depression after her children were born is probably important. Although mild depressions are common enough during the nursing period, there is abundant evidence that Mrs. Shawe was unstable and difficult. So if blame is to be placed, it may well begin with putting it on the egg, with stressful environment as secondary. Life before her marriage was not easy for Isabella Shawe, and the year of engagement to Thackeray had stormy passages with the mother, who wished to break up the match, and with the lover as mentioned above. Then the four years of marriage, though happy, brought heavy physical burdens — three pregnancies in quick succession. Added to this were all the adjustments to marriage and the grief over losing a child. There is no evidence that Thackeray himself was a cause of trouble; in fact, he seems to have made a positive contribution towards happiness.

The diagnosis is schizophrenia, of a type that often begins with depression and ideas of unworthiness a few weeks after childbirth.[2] Some of these patients get well spontaneously in a few months and the diagnosis of a "post-puerperal depression" is made. Others seem to drift into a permanent state of apathy and live the rest of their lives in an unreal world of fantasy, with gradual mental deterioration. Such was the fate of Mrs. Thackeray.

STANLEY COBB, M.D.

[2] E. A. Strecker and F. G. Ebaugh, "Psychoses Occurring during Puerperium," *Archives of Neurology and Psychiatry*, vol. 14, page 239 (1926).

# INDEX OF CORRESPONDENTS

## IN VOLUME I